HANDBOOK ON SEXUAL ABUSE
OF CHILDREN:
ASSESSMENT AND TREATMENT ISSUES

Lenore E. A. Walker, Ed.D., A.B.P.P., is a licensed psychologist and President of Walker & Associates, a Denver-based consulting firm providing psychological services, mostly in the area of psychotherapy, forensic evaluations, and expert witness testimony, to victims of violence. She is also the founder and Director of the Domestic Violence Institute, which conducts research in this area.

Dr. Walker has worked both in private practice and on the faculty of Rutgers Medical School, Colorado Women's College, and the University of Denver. She received her doctoral degree from Rutgers, the State University of New Jersey, in 1972, her master's degree in psychology from City College of City University of New York in 1967, and her bachelor's degree in psychology from Hunter College of the City University of New York in 1962. In 1979 she earned the Diplomate in Clinical Psychology from the American Board of Professional Psychology and in 1986 was inducted into the National Academy of Practice in Psychology as a Distinguished Fellow. She was honored by being inducted into the Hunter College Alumni Hall of Fame in 1986. In 1987 she received the coveted American Psychological Association Board of Professional Affairs Distinguished Contribution to the Profession in the Public Interest Award.

Dr. Walker has written extensively in the area of domestic violence and women's mental health policy. She has published several books, including *The Battered Woman* (1979), *The Battered Woman Syndrome* (1984), *Women and Mental Health Policy* (1984), *Handbook of Feminist Therapy* (1985) with Lynne Rosewater, and *The Male Batterer* (1986) with Daniel Sonkin and Del Martin and has several more forthcoming, including one that details her experiences as an expert witness in homicide cases.

Handbook on Sexual Abuse of Children

Assessment and Treatment Issues

Lenore E. Auerbach Walker

Ed.D., A.B.P.P.

Editor

SPRINGER PUBLISHING COMPANY
New York

Springer Publishing Company, Inc.
536 Broadway
New York, NY 10012

89 90 91 92 / 5 4 3 2

LIBRARY OF CONGRESS
Library of Congress Cataloging-in-Publication Data
Handbook on sexual abuse of children: assessment and treatment issues
　　Lenore E. Auerbach Walker, editor.
　　p.　　cm.
　　Includes bibliographies and index.
　　ISBN O-8261-5300-3
　　1. Child molesting—United States—Handbooks, manuals, etc.
2. Sexually abused children—Rehabilitation—United States—Handbooks, manuals, etc.　I. Walker, Lenore E. [DNLM: 1. Child Abuse, Sexual—psychology. 2. Child Abuse, Sexual—United States—legislation. 3. Psychotherapy. WA 320 H2365]
HQ72.U53H345 1988
362.7'044—dc19
DNLM/DLC
for Library of Congress   87-35648
                                                                              CIP

Printed in the United States of America

Contents

Introduction   *ix*

Acknowledgments   *xxi*

Contributors   *xxiii*

PART I   Overview

1 The Effects of Childhood Sexual Abuse: A Review
  of the Issues and Evidence   3
Shirley Joseph Asher, Ph.D.

2 The Incidence and Prevalence of Intrafamilial and
  Extrafamilial Sexual Abuse of Female Children   19
Diana E. H. Russell, Ph.D.

3 The Psychoanalytic Legacy: From Whence We Come   37
Hannah Lerman, Ph.D.

PART II   Impact on the Child

4 Assessing the Long-Term Impact of Child Sexual Abuse:
  A Review and Conceptualization   55
David Finkelhor, Ph.D. and Angela Browne, Ph.D.

5 The Impact of Sexual Abuse on Children: Empirical
  Findings   72
Jon R. Conte, Ph.D. and Lucy Berliner, MSW

6 Correlates of Incest Reported by Adolescent Girls
  in Treatment for Substance Abuse   94
Glenace E. Edwall, Ph.D. and Norman G. Hoffman, Ph.D.

Forensic and Mental Health Assessment

n as Witnesses: What Do They Remember?   109
. *Goodman, Ph.D. and Vicki S. Helgeson, Ph.D.*

8 Legal Issues in Child Sexual Abuse: Criminal Cases
   and Neglect and Dependency Cases   137
   Gregory F. Long, J.D.

9 Incest Investigation and Treatment Planning by Child
   Protective Services   152
   Cassie C. Spencer, MSW and Margaret A. Nicholson, MSW

10 New Techniques for Assessment and Evaluation
   of Child Sexual Abuse Victims: Using Anatomically
   "Correct" Dolls and Videotape Procedures   175
   Lenore E. A. Walker, Ed.D.

11 Assessment–Intervention Interface Using the Theme
   Creation Test for Youths   198
   Barbara R. Slater, Ph.D.

12 Guidelines for Assessing Sex Offenders   216
   Kevin McGovern, Ph.D. and James Peters, J.D.

PART IV   Treatment Approaches

13 Play Therapy with Children Who Have Experienced
   Sexual Assault   249
   Lenore E. A. Walker, Ed.D. and Mary Ann Bolkovatz, M.S.

14 Retrospective Incest Therapy for Women   270
   Christine A. Courtois, Ph.D. and Judith E. Sprei, Ph.D.

15 Nonoffending Mothers: A New Conceptualization   309
   Lorna A. Cammaert, Ph.D.

16 A Family Systems Approach to Treatment   326
   Spencer Friedman, Ph.D.

17 A Developing Behavioral Treatment Model:
   One Therapist's Perspective Within a Community's
   Evolving Response   350
   Lee C. Handy, Ph.D.

18 Assessment and Treatment of Sex Offenders
    in a Community Setting   365
Steven C. Wolf, M.Ed., Jon R. Conte, Ph.D.,
and Mary Engel-Meinig, MSW

PART V   Prevention

19 "Taking Care of Me": Preventing Child Sexual Abuse
    in the Hispanic Community   387
Barrie Levy, M.S.W., LCSW

Epilogue

Retrospective Incest for Men: A Personal History   405
Carl E. K. Johnson, J.D.

Index   *429*

Introduction

The need for a compilation of the most up-to-date information on child sexual abuse became apparent while I was serving on a special joint committee of the Colorado Women Psychologists (CWP) and Colorado Women's Bar Association (CWBA) that met monthly from 1982 through 1984. It was decided there that our state was not doing an adequate job in either legally protecting or psychologically helping children who have been sexually abused. As women professionals, we felt we had something more to offer our professions in order to change this sorry state of affairs. Discussions within each of the small groups that made up the dinner table revealed both familiarity with the inadequacies in each of our respective professions and great ideas for ways to respond more effectively to the child victim.

A joint meeting of both associations was held in early 1982 to address issues of mutual concern in our professional work with children who had been sexually abused. Each organization appointed four members to a special joint committee, a historic first. We met once a month for 2 years and it became apparent that although we all were experienced in working with child sexual abuse victims, we were at different places in our understanding of the rapidly expanding underlying knowledge base.

At first we xeroxed articles so that each of us could become equally familiar with the existing legal and psychological literature. Much of what we read is reported in this book. We also shared stories about cases, recognizing there was nowhere else to go to get the necessary feedback to work in this difficult area and still keep to the confidentiality necessary to protect our clients. We were dismayed by the woman-blaming attitudes of existing training programs. So we also served as a peer support group while learning the common features each of us experienced with the "system's" own process. We defined the "system" as all of the social services, medical, legal, and mental health components.

Our early plans were ambitious. We wanted to change everyone's attitudes and behavior toward these children, to make them more child-centered. We wanted the victims to be reempowered so they would become survivors. We searched the country for effective model programs. In this book, you will read about many that we found. Later on we became more specific and outlined a more practical goal. But first we tried to understand what was being done well by the system and what needed immediate change. We also defined our terms more precisely, using *incest* to designate sexual behavior of fathers and fatherlike figures toward children in their families. Rarely are women incest offenders predatory in the same way as are men. All other cases were designated as child sexual abuse, molestation, or assault—used interchangeably.

We ourselves represented various parts of the system of which we were so critical. Our group included a juvenile judge, a prosecuting attorney, an attorney who served as a guardian ad litem or children's attorney, and one who had a private mediation service. We also had three psychologists in private practice and one who worked for a mental health organization. Several had teaching experience and one worked within the minority community. Two worked with children in psychotherapy and one specialized in preventive mental health services, while all provided services to adults who had formerly been abused. Our group had representation from the minority community and all eight of us had significant stature within our respective professions. One member had extensive legislative experience in her background, which helped us understand the new state laws passed during our own term. Eventually, we added more members, including several social workers who had direct knowledge of the social services system and of the volunteer guardian ad litem system popular in our community. Then, as we became more focused on economic impact, we invited representatives of other women's professional organizations including certified public accountants and economists. Denver is rich with women's professional organizations, and all were pleased to work together on our exciting project.

At that time, we recognized that no one but the victim and sometimes the family actually understood the economic disaster a sexual assault on a child produced. There were developmental disturbances that were costly to remediate, school failures, psychological trauma, and loss of achievement motivation, all of which had never really been measured in terms of actual and potential financial damage. In addition, the state outlays an enormous sum of money to provide social service caseworkers who can sometimes become part of the problem instead of the solution. Legal expenses such as court costs, prosecutors, children's attorneys, and, occasionally, court-appointed defense attorneys' fees, medical and psychological experts' costs, and long-term psychotherapy fees need to be figured into the equation as direct costs. We know that the greatest increase in child-protection team cases are those involving sexual abuse of children—here in Colorado as well as in the rest of the nation and in Canada. As Spencer and Nicholson point out in Chapter 9 of this volume, few additional budgetary resources have been allocated. A few civil lawsuits designed to recover actual and punitive costs for damages have been won by women claimaints against their former sex offenders. But, actually, the greatest cost is born by you and me and the rest of society.

Recognizing that if the perpetrator were forced to bear the economic burden of his misdeeds he might be more likely to cease his sexual misconduct, in 1984, the start of our third year together, we began an ambitious project to measure the cost of child sexual abuse to its various victims individually and to the state collectively. While we were collecting the data, we were subjected to the political whims of a new administration in the state psychological association's women psychologists' affiliate, which eventually forced us to terminate our efforts. Perhaps we were treading too close to the male power system, which includes women who do not support feminist issues. Maybe we were early victims of the current backlash formed by those who believe they have been unjustly accused and judged. Or perhaps we really did gather too much community support ourselves and usurped the power of the association, as we were accused of doing. Whatever the reason, the committee never finished the economic analysis and chose to stop functioning formally in June 1984.

This book is a result of our 2-year project. We found out much of the information presented in these 20 chapters the hard way, piece by piece. We located those whom we identified as the most outstanding experts in their particular field and wrote to them for unpublished as well as recently published articles. What we learned stunned us. There is an enormous amount of empirical data on child sexual assault coming from research programs, but these data rarely get integrated into the application of law, social work, medicine, or psychology. The "system" has a life of its own that resists change.

Even techniques proven effective are difficult to get communities to implement. One such example involves the advances in the physiological measurement of sexual arousal patterns that can be utilized in a variety of ways for assessment and treatment of pedophiles and incest fathers. The equipment and trained professionals were not available then in Colorado, as in almost all but a small number of states. Today there is only one small program operational.

Another problem is the persistance of the outdated notion that the incest mother always knows and thus must be treated as a co-offender. The data presented here support the feminist position that most daughters successfully protect mothers from knowing about the incest for a variety of reasons, even though they unreasonably blame their mothers for not guessing their terrible secrets. The most important support in helping a victim heal is from the nonoffending mother, as reported by Conte and Berliner in Chapter 5 of this book, as well as by others. In Chapter 15, Cammaert discusses the perpetuation of the myth of the colluding mother by mother-blaming social services workers, psychologists, psychiatrists, and medical personnel, which further robs the child of her ability to heal. Juvenile courts pressing dependency and neglect charges against the mother for failure to protect the child may also unwittingly be destroying the child's resources to heal. Continued use of poorly performed polygraph examinations or of inadequate psychological test batteries to rule out a man's possible pedophilia are inappropriate when studies such as those of McGovern and Peters (Chapter 12) and of Wolfe, Conte and Engel-Meinig (Chapter 18) demonstrate less fallible methodology.

We also found it difficult for concerned professional advocates to successfully introduce legislation that could benefit the child sexual abuse victim. For all our society's stated concern about children, our legislators only seem to pay attention to issues that impact directly on the constituents who can vote for them. Because of several high-publicity cases in Colorado in which judges gave lenient sentences to proven child molesters, a statewide community action group called Society's League Against Molestation (SLAM) was formed. They persuaded the politicians to introduce the legislation so desperately needed, and our joint committee supported them. Greg Long in Chapter 8 outlines how the new legislation works in Colorado as well as similar laws nationally. Basically, it provides for the evidentiary introduction of statements a child makes to others that would otherwise not be admissable under the hearsay rules. This includes statements made to professionals who can testify in lieu of the child, if it is determined that testifying may psychologically or medically harm the child. Videotaped depositions as discussed by Walker in Chapter 10 are also allowable to substitute for the child. While use of "anatomically correct" dolls has come under serious criticism, it is still an excellent assessment tool if utilized appropriately. These are certainly improvements, but in practice unless testimony is given that independently corroborates that the abuse has occurred, the child will have to testify or the case will not be taken forward. Psychological evidence, which according to the latest research data presented here in Asher (Chapter 1), Finkelhor and Browne (Chapter 4), and Conte and Berliner (Chapter 5) is as valid and reliable as is physical evidence, is still not always seen as sufficient to meet the legal tests. Obviously such evidence cannot be used alone to prove innocence or guilt; rather, it can help determine whether or not the child has been sexually abused.

I have tried to bring together the latest information presented by knowledgeable authors so that all who work in this area will have the data readily available. Part I presents an overview of the issues and evidence about the longstanding history of childhood sexual abuse. Psychologist Shirley Asher (Chapter 1) clearly demonstrates that power and control issues predominate when adults exploit children sexually. Arguments still float to the surface every now and then that under some circumstances children who have sex with adults will not be harmed, but Asher's review of the literature demonstrates that children *never* benefit from such misuse. Asher also places child sexual abuse on the continuum of violence against women; she sees it as one more way for men to dominate those who are less powerful, usually women and girl children. She calls for the dramatic changes in our society demanded by feminists to stop the oppression of women and children by men who do not suffer any negative consequences for their hurtful behavior. These changes include an end to discrimination by men against women, along with an end to all forms of violence against women and children.

In Chapter 2, Diana Russell puts child sexual assault into perspective by delineating its incidence and prevalence rates. In her epidemiological research, she found that over one third of the women randomly selected to be interviewed had been sexually abused as children; most were assaulted when they were under the age of 14 by fathers and by other family members. Russell, too, puts child sexual abuse on the continuum of men's abuse against women. Her definitions of abuse and her carefully developed interview techniques are responsible for piercing the silence of many women who try to bury these painful memories. She suggests that others have not obtained her more accurate prevalence and incidence rates because of their inability to encourage women to remember and talk about their abuse. The newer research on battered women supports Russell's analysis and calls for better interviewing techniques. So does the new retrospective incest therapy discussed by Courtois and Sprei (Chapter 14), which reveals the high percentage of women who seek psychotherapy where they later uncover memories of childhood sexual abuse. These high incidence and prevalence rates gathered retrospectively support the high rate of child sexual abuse cases coming to light now, despite the backlash that tries to suggest that these cases did not occur because they cannot be legally proven.

Hannah Lerman (Chapter 3) tells us why we have had so little firsthand information about incest and child sexual abuse. The legacy from Freud taught us not to believe children's or even adults' self-reports about such abuse. Lerman presents the evidence that it was Freud's inability to deal with his own personal issues that caused him to reject his earlier "seduction hypothesis" and—instead of focusing on the male offender—turn his psychoanalytic constructs against the victim. The psychoanalysts believed that child victims fantasized such sexual contact in order to fulfill their deepest sexual Oedipal longings. The victims' emotional distress was viewed as being caused by the conflicting sexual feelings aroused by fantasy, and most traditional analysts did not give up this mostly erroneous belief until the data were right in front of them. Some still will not accept the truth about men's maltreatment of girl and boy children.

In Part II, we move directly to the data that document the negative impact of sexual abuse on the child. David Finkelhor and Angela Browne in Chapter 4 present their comprehensive review of the literature delineating the long-term impact and then provide a conceptual model in which to understand it. Their grouping of reported symptoms under the four major traumagenic categories provides a useful organization schema for both treatment and assessment of legal damage. The traumagenic dynamics include (1) *trauma-tic sexualization,* which is the process by which the child's sexuality is distorted and rendered dysfunctional; (2) *stigmatization,* which refers to the sense of guilt and shame that damages the child's self-image following abuse; (3) *betrayal,* which occurs specifically when children are harmed by those whom they have trusted; and (4) *powerlessness,* which describes the child's loss of control and belief in her or his personal efficacy. Their unique comparisons with both empirically and clinically based data demonstrate that the skeptics who suggest that the child's harm from sexually assaultive experiences is greatly exaggerated are clearly wrong. These findings need to be integrated into treatment programs, as Walker and Bolkovatz (Chapter 13) and Courtois and Sprei (Chapter 14) begin to do.

Conte and Berliner (Chapter 5) provide the data from one of the first major outcome studies. They measured the psychological impact of sexual abuse on the children seen at the Harborview Medical Center Sexual Assault Treatment Program, one of the earliest and best-known programs in this country. These findings confirm many of our commonsense expectations and give us new directions to explore. Their statistics confirm that most children are sexually abused by family members, usually fathers or fatherlike figures, or by ac-quaintances. Only a small number are molested by strangers. Children who heal the fastest and most completely are those who do not report the abuse to the social service or legal system. This certainly supports the CWP-CWBA Joint Committee's consternation with the "system" and also causes us to wonder how best to restore its child protection mandate. They also demonstrate the clinical importance for professionals of dropping their women-blaming stance and changing their attitude to one of support for the mothers so they can provide support to their children. Support from a nonoffending mother and from other siblings were the top two factors that promoted healing in the children seen at the clinic. Conte and Berliner's data also call into question the typical social services practice of removing children from their homes to provide physical safety. Perhaps more consideration should be given to alternative options such as having a caseworker move into the home during the crisis period or even filing court orders to remove the offending parent while simultaneously providing crisis intervention services to the rest of the family. The new domestic violence prevention laws make this option easier now.

The impact of sexual abuse on adolescents has been approached from a different perspective in Glenace Edwall and Norman Hoffman's (Chapter 6) analysis of teenage girls in a substance abuse treatment program. They found significant differences between those girls who were sexually abused and those who were not. For example, among the sexually abused girls there were significantly more suicide attempts, their self-concept was poorer, and they had more difficulties with the legal system. Not surprisingly, there was also a correlation with physical abuse of themselves and with sexual and physical abuse of other family members. Their findings strongly suggest that when teenage girls are in trouble for other matters, their sexual abuse history should be carefully investigated. Chemical dependency is one way that abuse victims may find some relief from their intense pain.

Part III builds upon the first two parts and delineates various new assessments. The question of credibility of a child's report is frequently debated as more child sexual abuse is uncovered. In Chapter 7, Gail Goodman and Vicki Helgeson review the social psychology literature on children's memory and find that children are at least as reliable as adults and sometimes even more so. Young children under the age of 5 are better able to retrieve their memory when given props and some concrete information. Sometimes this can be construed as putting suggestions into the child's mind. The fine line between gathering the necessary data for legal situations while also gathering sufficient information to formulate a treatment plan can cause confusion. Goodman and Helgeson provide excellent suggestions for enhancing the child as a witness, and their work should put to rest those skeptics who do not believe that young children know what they are talking about. Their work also demonstrates the ways in which very young children can be manipulated by adults to repeat suggestions of behavior that did not occur. Goodman's empirical study of the impact of trauma on children's memory is quite relevant here. She finds that memory actually becomes sharper as the child focuses in on the traumatic situation. These are important data for expert witnesses to use in order to validate children's statements.

Greg Long (Chapter 8) continues with a discussion of the legal process in criminal and juvenile proceedings. Long, a district attorney in the Colorado Rocky Mountains and former president of the Colorado District Attorney's Association, has had firsthand experience in prosecuting both types of cases. Following Long's methods should reduce the numbers of cases where poorly prepared prosecutors go forward, only to damage the credibility of the whole judicial process. Even with the new laws, admissability of expert witnesses and hearsay testimony is still problematic, and the matter of protection of the child may be pitted against the legal objectives of winning a defense or prosecution. Confidence in the expert witness can guide attorneys so that they do not unnecessarily risk further psychological damage to a child. More psychologists and mental health professionals than ever before are being called to appear as expert witnesses. Long provides a discussion of their role. Therapists also need to become familiar with the process in their own jurisdiction, which is probably similar to Long's accounts. This will help them provide support for the child client as she or he goes through the legal system, as well as help them to prepare for being called as an expert witness.

In Chapter 9 Cassie Spencer and Margaret Nicholson discuss the ideal child protective services integrated response to a child sexual abuse call. Every state has mandatory and voluntary abuse report laws. A coordinated approach with a collaborative police detective and social services interview can minimize the numerous interviews most children are subjected to. Adherence to the suggested guidelines can also minimize the alarming number of unfounded accusations made in poorly investigated cases. Spencer and Nicholson provide much of the initial and revitalizing training for social service workers in the six-state region of which Colorado is a part. They have developed an effective intake and evaluation format as well as appropriate psychotherapy goals. Their practical considerations make this chapter useful to anyone who finds herself or himself having to make a decision based on such an interview. In many cases, lawsuits are dismissed because the mental health worker who performed the intake, either purposefully or without thinking, contaminated the child's responses by not recognizing the difficulties presented by suggestibility and by asking leading questions. A lack of information about children's development at a particular age and the child's strict adherence to discipline may also cause problems. Examples of good interviews and relevant questions to ask are provided.

Walker's chapter on assessment techniques that use anatomically "correct" dolls and videotape equipment (Chapter 10) gives practical suggestions for clinicians who will be interviewing children. A description of an evaluation with appropriate sequences specified is provided to assist both the first-time evaluator as well as the more experienced colleague. Especially helpful are tips about interviewing very young preverbal children. Interpretations of young children's responses to the evaluation are also presented here. Communication of findings and ethical issues in protecting raw data are also discussed.

Use of a newly developed projective technique to assess children is discussed by Barbara Slater in Chapter 11. Slater's results should satisfy critics demanding experimental evidence that sexually abused children do relate differently to naked and clothed dolls than do those not sexually abused. Her comparisons with a control group who were diagnosed as emotionally disturbed demonstrate the differences in children with similar symptoms caused by dissimilar etiology. In an attempt to standardize this new assessment device so that it is useful for both children and adolescents, Slater has collected empirical data revealing how the children really feel about the abuse. Most need to be able to express their rage but are still too young to begin to feel power and control over their own lives. It is not surprising that among a population of special education children there would be those who have been sexually abused. School psychologists' routine assessments need to be more sensitive in identifying them. Interference with schoolwork, cognitive functioning, and working up to one's intellectual capacity can be related to the sexual abuse, as Slater demonstrates. She also explores the use of a storytelling technique together with the test figures as a way to help children retell the abuse story to facilitate healing. She presents a new technique that has much promise.

The last chapter in this part deals with assessment of the sex offender. Psychologist Kevin McGovern and District Attorney Jim Peters come together in Chapter 12 to write of their highly successful assessment protocol and guidelines currently used in Portland, Oregon and Vancouver, Washington, and quickly catching on elsewhere. They explain what each psychological test measures and how to choose whether or not it is included as part of a particular battery of tests. They also discuss the penile plethysmography examination, not only explaining its limitations but also discussing how difficult it is for offenders to control their physiological sexual arousal even when verbal lies or distortions are commonplace. Although it cannot prove that a man committed a particular act, information obtained from it can be used in conjunction with other observable behavior to corroborate the findings for the child. Their appendix with copies of their assessment guidelines should prove quite popular, especially as more cases are uncovered.

Part IV of the book explores the various therapeutic or treatment options. The authors in this section present the most timely intervention options, each based on theoretical or empirical underpinnings. In these chapters therapy with children and adult women who were previously victimized and therapy with mothers of sexually abused children have some similar themes. They both take into account the situational realities of a society that does not behave in ways that reinforce the value of its women and children.

Each group appears to have experienced further trauma by our child protection and legal services. Each is made to feel like the guilty party. Therapy that places the child's healing within the context of her or his family system and of the community is powerful. Yet its process should be kept from lessening the responsibility of the offender, a common mistake when those untrained or without a feminist political consciousness apply systems theory to treatment of family violence. Finally, to complete the intervention modalities, therapy procedures with the offender are presented by those who developed a model at one of the finest offender programs available in the nation.

Chapter 13 by Lenore Walker and Mary Ann Bolkovatz describes a feminist approach to play therapy, particularly with very young children. The process of therapy is described and applications to the sexually abused child are outlined. Particularly interesting is the attention paid to the roles of repetition (called ritual) and spirituality in play therapy. Goals are outlined and specific techniques are discussed. Many have been adapted from Walker's earlier writings on intervention with battered women and adult sexual abuse victims.

In Chapter 14 Christine Courtois and Judy Sprei provide an excellent presentation of the retrospective incest therapy they have been facilitating. Women therapists have noted that often clients who come in with other presenting problems soon begin to tell of childhood sexual abuse incidents, and they begin to remember long-forgotten incidents that are still influencing their behavior. Even more common, now that the secret is out publicly, are the women who seek therapy to put these childhood experiences behind them. The program Courtois and Sprei describe is the latest application of therapy to help these women heal.

Lorna Cammaert (Chapter 15) expands our empirical understanding of the role of nonoffending mothers and sets forth an applied-intervention program that ought to replace the older, less valid women-blaming models. The incest victim often displays great anger toward the mother for not protecting her and not recognizing the clues she is certain she has put forth. Yet that is an unrealistic expectation in many situations; the mother, either because of her own abuse or her own insensitivity to the daughter's perhaps less explicit cues, could not have been expected to know what was really happening. Previous medical and social work models took this clinical information along with mothers' expressed feelings of guilt to mean that they really did know but had unconscious motivation not to act. This erroneous assumption often occurred side-by-side with another myth, that the incestuous father was not getting enough sex from his essentially "frigid" wife and so he turned to his daughter, with the mother's tacit permission. As Wolf, Conte, and Engel-Meinig's (Chapter 18), Handy's (Chapter 17), and McGovern and Peters' (Chapter 12) empirical data show, incestuous fathers tend to be obsessed with sex and are especially aroused by children no matter what their wife's performance. Friedman argues that there is a subset of incest fathers who are expressing affection and power needs, who are not sexually obsessed, and who are amenable to family treatment. In any case, no matter what the mother's prior knowledge, Cammaert describes a useful program with mothers referred by social services in Calgary that has great promise for cost-efficient replication elsewhere.

Family systems theory, gaining in popularity as a therapy technique, has long been controversial for incest victims and their families. The fear is that blame or responsibility for the abuse will be evenly distributed within the system and the victim's needs will be overlooked in attempts to help all members of the family. Spencer Friedman (Chapter 16) developed his techniques to determine which incest families would benefit from family therapy at a special program at Children's Hospital in Denver, and he continues to use them in his private practice. He is careful to keep the responsibility with the offender and presents us with a viable therapy program.

Again turning to a successful Canadian community-based program, Lee Handy (Chapter 17) uses systems theory to describe a broad-based community model to reintegrate male sex offenders. Using a team approach, Handy describes the checks and balances needed to establish the external limits for these men in a behavioral treatment program. He, too, addresses those families who choose to stay together and tries to find compromises that allow children to heal and offenders to stop their abusive behavior. His model for interagency cooperation is one that should be viewed with interest by all communities trying to address this problem on a systems-wide basis.

The treatment of the male sex offender causes a great deal of debate among professionals. Some feel no treatment will be successful, while others claim offenders should be in a locked inpatient facility before treatment is attempted. Over the years, the Northwest Treatment Associates have assessed and treated over 2,000 male sexual abusers of children using a behavioral treatment model. Wolf, Conte, and Engel-Meinig discuss their treatment program and measures of its success in Chapter 18. They give detailed descriptions so that this chapter can serve as a model for those who want to establish similar programs. Interestingly, they do not address the controversial issue of whether or not the man needs to admit to his abusive behavior; rather, they demand a desire to change and proceed from there. Using the plethysmograph as well as other data to demonstrate the pedophile's deviant arousal pattern, these authors simply accept that the man has the potential to stop his abuse if he follows the program. Motivation, as always, influences the outcome.

Finally, Part V points us in a positive direction to change not just individuals but our social mores. There are a number of prevention programs that inoculate children against becoming victims of a sex offender because of fear of saying no to a family member or friend. Some are introduced into the schools. Others, like the SAFE self-defense program based in New York City, first began as secondary prevention for adult rape victims and then added a children's martial arts component for their primary prevention program. Self-help guides for adult survivors of child sexual abuse may be similarly adapted to a primary prevention program. Many of the educational books on the market that give permission to children to say no to adult touches that do not feel good are further examples of positive prevention approaches.

A recent attempt to engage public and private industry in a joint effort to prevent crimes against children has been formed by President Reagan's "Child Safety Partnership," administered by the Department of Justice. The Departments of Education and Health and Human Services are collaborating with the Department of Justice to encourage businesses to promote child-safety efforts. They have reported to the President their recommendations on ways to prevent victimization and promote the safety of children in this country. It is expected that legislation and new funding priorities for prevention may result from their work.

Barrie Levy, a pioneer in the area of sexual abuse prevention programs, describes in Chapter 19 a particularly interesting community mental health program designed to strengthen Hispanic children's ability to protect themselves against potential child sexual abuse. Levy discusses the principles of prevention and how they apply in this field. Children's awareness and self-defense programs, introduced in the schools, have had a consciousness-raising effect that Levy describes as both positive and negative. Until men learn to stop their abusive behavior, strengthening children's abilities to say no and to protect their bodies seems to be a necessary alternative. It has its difficulties, however, for those of us who love to be physically demonstrative to children.

In my own family, I have come up against my 5-year-old nephew's application of such self-protection learning. One day, I went to greet him with my usual hug and kiss. He turned to me and announced that he was only giving hugs and not kisses on that day. I replied that I was his aunt, and if I wanted a hug and a kiss, he should comply. No, he replied, it was his body and he had the right to say no if he wanted to! Regaining my composure after the surprise, I supported him by agreeing that indeed it was his right to make that decision. I see this as a small price for the hope that he and his agemates could stand up for their right to be respected and not harmed by others, too.

In the Epilogue, Carl Johnson, a Denver attorney, "comes out" and discloses his own incest experience. He describes its impact on him psychologically and his search for a therapy program to help him heal. His story is a reminder of the early beginnings when we were learning about women's incest experience. We do not yet know enough about boys' or men's sexual abuse to place his account into an empirical data base, as we can with girls' and women's stories, but there are remarkable similarities. He struggles through emotional highs and lows with long depressions, without understanding the connections; he depicts the early eroticization of the child, the worry about sexual identity and gender-related issues, the interference with interpersonal relationships, and the struggle to maintain emotional intimacy in a marriage—all are there. It is hoped that this chapter will sensitize clinicians to look for early sexual abuse in all clients who show a similar pattern.

Lenore E. A. Walker
August 1, 1987

Acknowledgments

The dream of writing this book began with the collaborative efforts of the Colorado Women's Bar Association (CWBA) and Colorado Women Psychologists (CWP). Much gratitude is deserved to the executive boards who had the foresight and wisdom to bring the joint committee into existence. The real thanks goes to my seven colleagues on the original committee: Shirley Asher, Ph.D. (CWP), Chris Chao, Ph.D. (CWP), Libby Commeaux, J.D. (CWBA), Ann Frick, J.D. (CWBA), Ruth Solomons, Ph.D. (CWP), Judge Orelle Weeks, J.D. (CWBA), and Jane Woodhouse, J.D. (CWBA).

Their commitment to finding better ways to help children and their mutual support of one another helped provide the energy for me to edit this book.

Lenore E. A. Walker (CWP)
August, 1987

Contributors

Shirley J. Asher, Ph.D., is a psychologist in private practice in Denver, Colorado, whose specialties include the treatment of adolescent and adult victims of sexual assault. She is also a consultant to community programs providing services to sexual assault victims. Much of her recent work has been in the primary prevention of violence against women and children.

Lucy Berliner, M.S.W., is Director of the Sexual Assault Center at Harborview Hospital in Seattle, Washington. She has received international recognition as a pioneer in the assessment and treatment of children who have been sexually abused and has trained other clinicians around the world in specialized intervention methods.

Mary Ann Bolkovatz, R.N., M.S., is an American Nurses' Association Clinical Specialist in the areas of adult, child, and adolescent psychiatric and mental health nursing. She received a master's degree in psychiatric and mental health nursing in 1982 from the University of Colorado Health Sciences Center and a bachelor's degree in 1976 in nursing from Montana State University. She has worked in both hospital settings and community mental health centers with child, adolescent, and adult victims of incest and domestic violence. She has been an associate of Dr. Lenore Walker's since 1985. She is currently pursuing doctoral studies in psychology.

Angela Browne, Ph.D., is a social psychologist specializing in the area of family violence, with particular expertise in violence by men toward their female partners, and patterns of threat and physical assault over time in couple relationships. She has extensive experience as a consultant for homicides in which women kill their abusive mates and the application of the self-defense plea to such cases and has conducted research on the precipitants of such homicides. She is currently studying women's involvement in homicide in the United States, both as perpetrators and as victims, based on comprehensive national data for 1976–1984. Dr. Browne is active in the Seacoast Task Force Against Domestic Violence and on the board of A Safe Place, a shelter for battered women in Portsmouth, New Hampshire, and works as an advocate for battered women in prison. She is a research associate with the Family Research Laboratory at the University of New Hampshire and teaches in the College of Criminal Justice at Northeastern University in Boston, MA. Dr. Browne is Editor of the interdisciplinary research journal *Violence and Victims* and author of the recently published book *When Battered Women Kill* (1987).

Lorna P. Cammaert, Ph.D., is a psychologist who currently holds the position of Associate Vice-President (Academic), University of Calgary. She received her Ph.D. in counseling and developmental psychology from the University of Oregon. Her professional interests encompass female sexuality, sexual harassment, assertiveness training, and counseling women. Dr. Cammaert is a Canadian Psychological Association fellow, currently serves as a member of the CPA Board, and chairs the Status of Women and the Education and Training Committees. She co-authored with Dr. Carolyn Larsen the book *A Woman's Choice: A Guide to Decision-Making.*

Jon R. Conte, Ph.D., is currently an Associate Professor and Associate Dean of Academic Affairs at the School of Social Service Administration at the University of Chicago. The author of numerous publications, Dr. Conte is a frequent lecturer at national and international meetings. Dr. Conte is the Principal Investigator of a study funded by the National Center on Child Abuse and Neglect on the effects of childhood sexual experiences on child and adult survivors. He is also the Principal Investigator of a research project funded by the National Institute of Mental Health on prevention education for children. He is the Editor of the *Journal of Interpersonal Violence* and President of the American Professional Society on the Abuse of Children. A clinical social worker and researcher by training, Dr. Conte maintains a private practice working with the victims of interpersonal violence and consults to treatment providers and other private and public agencies.

Christine A. Courtois, Ph.D., received her Ph.D. in 1979 from the University of Maryland. She is currently employed in private practice in Washington, D.C. and is a consultant to the Arlington County Department of Social Services Victims of Violence Program and Montgomery County Sexual Assault Services. She was previously employed by the Women's Medical Center, Washington, D.C., the U.S. General Accounting Office Counseling Center, and the University of Maryland Counseling Center. She is a member of the American Psychological Association, the American Association for Counseling and Development, and the National Organization for Victim Assistance.

Glenace E. Edwall, Ph.D., Psy.D., is assistant professor of psychology at Baylor University, Waco, Texas, where she teaches in the Psy.D. program. Dr. Edwall holds the Ph.D. in learning and cognition from the University of Minnesota and a Psy.D. in clinical psychology from the University of Denver.

Her chief research interests are in the psychological sequelae of abuse, friendship and social support, and substance abuse and eating disorders.

Mary B. Engel-Meinig, M.S.W., Family Therapist, has specialized in the treatment of children and families since 1972. She received a Masters of Social Work degree from the University of Washington in 1974. She previously worked as a residential treatment supervisor and intake coordinator at Luther Child Center. Since 1982 Ms. Engel-Meinig has worked at Northwest Treatment Associates as the Family Treatment Specialist, a position that includes treating families affected by sexual abuse, victim treatment, and the re-entry of the offender into the home. Ms. Engel-Meinig is on the faculty of the Child Sexual Abuse Treatment and Training Institute of the Sexual Assault Center in Seattle, Washington. She has provided consultation and training to other community agencies on the treatment of families affected by sexual abuse.

David Finkelhor, Ph.D., is the Associate Director of the Family Research Laboratory and the Family Violence Research Program at the University of New Hampshire. His latest publication is *Sourcebook on Child Sexual Abuse* (1986), a compilation of research on the subject of sexual abuse. He has been studying the problem of child sexual abuse since 1977 and has published two other books, *Sexually Victimized Children* and *Child Sexual Abuse: New Theory and Research* and over two dozen articles on the subject. He has been the recipient of grants from the National Institute of Mental Health and the National Center on Child Abuse and Neglect. His other research interests include elder abuse and sexual assault in marriage.

Spencer Friedman, Ph.D., received his doctorate in psychology from the University of Northern Colorado. He is licensed as a psychologist in the states of Colorado and California. He has worked in a variety of clinical settings during his 16 years as a psychologist. He was the clinical director of the Family Therapy Program at the Children's Hospital in Denver, Colorado, which was a family-oriented treatment program for incestuous families. Dr. Friedman is presently in private practice in Denver, Colorado, where he works with individuals, couples, and families. Dr. Friedman also serves as an expert witness in both civil and criminal cases.

Gail S. Goodman, Ph.D., is Associate Professor and Director, Dual Degree Program in Psychology and Law in the Psychology Department of the University of Denver. She has published widely in the areas of children's testimony, children's memory, and children's perceived credibility and has received several awards for her work in these areas. Dr. Goodman received her B.A., M.A., and Ph.D. degrees from the University of California, Los Angeles.

Lee Handy, Ph.D., received his bachelor's and master's degrees from Iowa State University and his doctorate from the University of Oregon. A Fellow of the Canadian Psychological Association, he is a University Counsellor and

Associate Professor at the University of Calgary. He is also a senior partner in Alberta Psychological Resources, Ltd., based in Calgary. Dr. Handy has worked for many years in the areas of marital and family concerns, dealing particularly with the issues of human sexuality and sexual ethics. Recent professional presentations and publications have included the topics of family dysfunction as related to the psychological impact of child sexual abuse and the development of marital and family treatment approaches primarily from a behavioral perspective.

Vicki Helgeson, Ph.D., received her bachelor's degree from Valparaiso University in 1982, with a major in psychology and journalism. In 1984 she completed her master's degree in psychology at the College of William and Mary, and in 1987, her doctorate in social psychology at the University of Denver. She is currently a postdoctoral fellow in health psychology at the University of California, Los Angeles. Dr. Helgeson has co-authored several articles with Gail S. Goodman, including an article on the credibility of child witnesses and an article in preparation on children's rights.

Norman Hoffmann, Ph.D., received his doctorate in clinical psychology from the University of Minnesota in 1976. He is currently a research associate with the Ramsey Clinic and Assistant Professor of Psychiatry at the University of Minnesota. Dr. Hoffmann is the founder and Executive Director of CATOR, a patient registry system that serves chemical dependency treatment programs throughout the United States. In addition to his work on treatment outcome, Dr. Hoffmann is also co-developer of the SUDDS, a structured diagnostic interview for documenting the diagnoses for alcohol and other drug dependencies. He directed a team of consultants who developed model criteria for admission and discharge for adult and adolescent chemical dependency treatment facilities. Dr. Hoffmann has authored and co-authored numerous articles and book chapters on chemical dependency topics. He is also a frequent presenter at national and international conferences.

Carl E. K. Johnson, J.D., is a family lawyer specializing in the representation of children and of parents in custody disputes involving child abuse and neglect and complex psychiatric and psychological issues. He is a member of the Executive Council of the Family Law section of the Colorado Bar Association, Founding Chair and current Co-chair of the Juvenile Committee of the Section, and Co-chair of the Guardian *Ad Litem* Standards Committee of the Juvenile Committee. He has published several articles in the areas of child representation and parent representation in custody and dependency and neglect proceedings.

Hannah Lerman received her Ph.D. in clinical psychology from Michigan State University in 1963. She has been a member of the clinical faculties of the Menninger School of Psychiatry and of the University of Southern California School of Medicine. She has also been Academic Dean of the California

School of Professional Psychology–Los Angeles. She has been in full time practice as a clinical psychologist and feminist therapist since 1973. A co-founder of the Feminist Therapy Institute, she has also served as the President of the Division of the Psychology of Women of the American Psychological Association. Dr. Lerman is the author of *A Mote In Freud's Eye: From Psychoanalysis to the Psychology of Women* (Springer, 1986).

Barrie Levy, L.C.S.W., is Director of Prevention at the Didi Hirsch Community Mental Health Center, Culver City, California. She is on the faculty of the School of Social Welfare at the University of California at Los Angeles and a therapist in private practice. She is the founder and former director of the Southern California Coalition for Battered Women and a founding member of the Los Angeles Commission on Assaults Against Women. Ms. Levy's extensive experience includes research, community organizing and development, prevention education, and clinical practice related to sexual assault and child sexual abuse.

Gregory F. Long, J.D., is the District Attorney for the 14th Judicial District of Colorado. He is a Past President of the Colorado District Attorney's Council and the Western Colorado Peace Officers Association and is a member of several professional committees. He has also taught other law enforcement professionals and published several articles.

Kevin B. McGovern, Ph.D., is a nationally renowned clinical psychologist, sex therapist, author, and lecturer specializing in the assessment and treatment of sexual abuse, sexual dysfunction, and social inadequacy. Dr. McGovern's clinical interests focus on preventive education programs, the false allegation of child abuse, AIDS, and other topics of foremost importance in today's society. In 1978, Dr. McGovern founded *Alternatives to Sexual Abuse,* an educational foundation dedicated to teaching other professionals about sexual abuse problems. Dr. McGovern has developed a game, *Be Safe . . . Be Aware,* and authored a book, *Alice Doesn't Babysit Anymore,* for use by professionals and the general public to increase public education about the prevention of child sexual abuse. His private practice is in Portland, Oregon, where he serves as a clinical associate professor of Psychiatry at the Oregon Health Sciences University, in addition to lecturing nationally and providing expert testimony in sexual abuse court cases. Dr. McGovern has also provided consulting services on forensic issues related to the assessment and treatment of sexual offenders for correctional and mental health agencies in Oregon, Washington, Illinois, and Hawaii. He is a frequent guest on television and radio talk shows and also co-hosted *Front Street Weekly,* a locally produced public affairs program for public television.

Margaret A. Nicholson received her M.S.W. from the University of Denver in 1973. She was formerly a child protection worker, director of national research and demonstration projects, a mental health therapist, and founder of a community treatment program for abused children. She is currently a consultant and trainer with Nicholson, Spencer & Associates, Inc. and a private psychotherapist treating retrospective incest victims, children, and families in Denver, Colorado.

James M. Peters, J.D., is a deputy prosecuting attorney in Vancouver, Washington. Over the last 10 years he has developed an expertise in the area of child sexual abuse prosecution. He teaches a class on this subject at Clark College in Vancouver and has been invited to make presentations to professional groups across the country.

Diana Russell, Ph.D., is a Professor of Sociology at Mills College, where she has taught since 1969. She is author of *The Politics of Rape* (1975), author and co-editor of *Crimes Against Women: The Proceedings of the International Tribunal* (first published in 1976, republished in 1984), and author of *Rape in Marriage* (1982), *Sexual Exploitation: Rape, Child Sexual Abuse and Workplace Harassment* (1984), and *The Secret Trauma: Incest in the Lives of Girls and Women* (1986).

Barbara R. Slater, Ph.D., is Professor of Psychology and Coordinator of School Psychology at Towson State University, Baltimore, Maryland. She holds the A.B.P.P. Diplomate in School Psychology and is a licensed psychologist and a certified school psychologist in California, Maryland, and New York. In addition, she has maintained a private practice dealing with children and women since 1969. Her research has been in issues related to children and to women, and she is the co-author of a children's test, the Boehm/Slater Cognitive Assessment Battery for Children, and of a psychodiagnostic text, Psychodiagnostic Evaluation of Children: A Casebook Approach. Currently she and her co-author are in the process of standardizing two personality tests for children, the Slater/Gallagher Sentence Completion Test for Youths and the Gallagher/Slater Theme Creation Test for Youths.

Cassie C. Spencer, M.S.W., M.P.A., received her M.S.W. from the University of Denver in 1981. She was formerly a child protection worker in Denver, Colorado. She is now a consultant and trainer with Nicholson, Spencer & Associates, Inc. and a private psychotherapist treating incest victims, retrospective incest victims, victims of domestic violence, and families in Denver.

Judith E. Sprei received her Ph.D. in 1979 from the University of Maryland. She is currently employed in private practice in Laurel, MD and is co-director of the Maryland Institute for Individual and Family Therapy, Ltd., in College Park, MD. She is also a consultant to Howard County, Anne Arundel County and Montgomery County Sexual Assault Centers. She was previously employed at the Prince George's County Hospital, Sexual Assault Center and as a part-time instructor in the Psychology Department, University of Maryland.

Steven C. Wolf, M.Ed., has specialized in the treatment of adult sexual offenders since 1976. He holds a B.A. in Education and a Master's in Educational Psychology. He has worked as a teacher for behavior-disordered students and as a counselor with a Pre-Trial Diversion program in Snohomish County, Washington. Since 1977 he has been the Co-Director of Northwest Treatment Associates-Mercer. He is on the faculty of the Child Sexual Abuse Treatment and Training Institute of Harborview Hospital's Sexual Assault Center in Seattle. He has presented at conferences in the United States, Canada, and Europe, published a number of chapters and articles, and is on the editorial board of the *Journal of Interpersonal Violence.*

PART I
Overview

1

The Effects of Childhood Sexual Abuse: A Review of the Issues and Evidence

Shirley Joseph Asher

Sexual abuse of children is an issue deserving vigorous scrutiny and formal investigation. The emergence of this issue parallels that of rape and spousal abuse. Although occasional articles on these subjects have appeared in the literature in the past 50 years, it was not until the women's liberation movement called attention to the victimization of women and children that data regarding the incidence of these phenomena were more rigorously collected and disseminated and research studies were implemented. The sexual abuse of children is currently receiving the type of attention in both the popular press and professional journals that rape, child abuse, and spouse abuse received 5 to 10 years ago. Many of the same controversies that surrounded these other issues, including the veracity of the reports, the extent of the negative effects, and who is to be held accountable for these acts, are now being debated with regard to the sexual abuse of children.

Sexual abuse of children includes many types of sexual trauma suffered by children, from single attacks by strangers to long-term incestuous relationships with parents. The definition of sexual abuse varies from study to study. In this chapter, the term *sexual abuse* will be used to denote all types of sexual victimization, whereas *incest* will be used only with respect to sexual experiences between children and adults in parental roles.

Recent findings regarding the immediate and long-term effects of sexual abuse on children will be reviewed. Trends in the literature will be examined. In addition, an overview of the issues and controversies facing researchers who study the effects of sexual abuse on children will be discussed.

3

THE SCOPE OF THE PROBLEM

Despite widespread coverage of the sexual abuse of children in the press and most recently on television, no official statistics on the incidence of such abuse currently exist (Van Buskirk & Cole, 1984). Estimates of incidence have been obtained, however, through a variety of surveys, large and small. The National Center on Child Abuse and Neglect estimates that there are 100,000 cases of child sexual abuse each year (Justice & Justice, 1979). The American Humane Association estimates that in 1985 113,000 children were found upon investigation by child protection agencies to have been sexually maltreated. These statistics are based upon official reports to child protective services and are undoubtedly a substantial underestimation of the incidence of the problem. Herman (1981), in reviewing five studies on the prevalence of sexual abuse in female children, found that one fifth to one third of the women had some sort of sexual encounter with an adult male and 4% to 12% of the women reported a sexual experience with a relative. In addition, 1% of the women reported an incestuous relationship with a father or grandfather. Russell (1983), in a random survey of 930 women living in the San Francisco area, found that 31% of the sample had at least one experience of extrafamilial sexual abuse prior to age 18, and 16% had experienced sexual abuse within the family (see also Russell, Chapter 2 of this volume). In Finkelhor's (1979) study of 796 New England college students, 19.2% of the women and 8.6% of the men reported having been sexually victimized. Of those who had been victimized, 43% of the females and 33% of the males had been abused by a family member. In each of these studies, it has been documented that 94% to 97% of the perpetrators were male and the vast majority of the victims were female.

A trend noted by Kempe and Kempe (1978) is that a number of children are being abused at increasingly younger ages. The authors stated they are seeing increasing numbers of very young children who require urgent care. Whereas children under 5 years of age used to comprise only 5% of the sexually abused who were brought in for treatment at Denver General Hospital, these very young children accounted for 25% of the total at the time of the study.

FREUD AND THE ISSUE OF FALSE ACCUSATIONS

An issue often raised with regard to the sexual abuse of children is whether these children are telling the truth. Although research indicates that false accusations of incest and other forms of sexual abuse by children are rare (see below and Goodman & Helgeson, Chapter 7 of this volume), many professionals still tend to treat such accusations with suspicion. In part, this is due to the continued influence of Freud. During the early 1890s, Freud theorized that the origin of hysterical neuroses lay in the early sexual traumas experienced by young girls. The seduction theory held that these sexual traumas, often perpetrated by the father, were real and resulted in a variety of neurotic symptoms. By 1897, however, Freud renounced the seduction theory in favor of drive theory and the Oedipal complex. The reasons for this evolution in Freud's thinking are complex (see Lerman, Chapter 3 of this volume; Malcom, 1983; Masson, 1984; Rush, 1980).

The idea that many fathers were guilty of seducing their daughters was distressing to Freud. In public writings and lectures he declined to identify fathers as perpetrators, instead naming nurses, governesses, maids, and distant relatives as the seducers. Freud became aware of hysterical symptoms in his sisters that cast suspicion on his own father. Through his self-analysis he unearthed vague incestuous fantasies regarding his own daughter and also of his early sexual feelings toward his mother and hatred toward his father. Freud then hypothesized that girls have sexual feelings toward their fathers and a concomitant hatred for their mothers. He concluded that the memories of sexual trauma were based on sexual wish-fulfillment fantasies of the child. Thus, fathers were exonerated and were no longer viewed as responsible for causing the symptoms Freud saw in his young female patients. Rather, the culprit lay within their own psyches. The seed of doubt had been planted and has taken root. Children are often brutally questioned concerning the reality of their experiences. Many psychoanalysts still interpret women's childhood experiences as fantasies arising from Oedipal conflicts.

Research does exist on the veracity of children's allegations of sexual abuse. Cantwell (1981), in reviewing 287 cases of alleged abuse in Denver in 1979, found that 26 cases could not be substantiated. In only two of these cases, however, had the child brought the allegation. A literature review of 88 psychiatric papers on incest published between 1973 and 1978 revealed not a single case report of a false accusation of incest, although there were four cases in which a false retraction of a valid incest accusation was made (Goodwin, Sahd, & Rada, 1982). Peters (1976) studied 64 children who were seen at an emergency room with complaints of sexual assault. In four cases the staff concluded that no sexual assault had occurred.

While false accusations are rare, false retractions of sexual abuse, incest in particular, are not uncommon. A girl may retract an incest allegation for a variety of reasons. She may fear being sent away and separated from the rest of her family. The father may threaten her or threaten to abuse younger siblings unless she recants the statement. Her mother may pressure her because the family will suffer financially if the father goes to jail, or she may become scared at the consequences her allegation has set in motion. It seems, then, that professionals involved with children—whether they be teachers, nurses, physicians, social workers, or mental health professionals—

should consider allegations of sexual abuse made by children to be the truth and not statements based on fantasy wishes or hostile impulses.

THE IMMEDIATE EFFECTS OF SEXUAL ABUSE ON THE CHILD

Many children are reluctant to reveal that they are being sexually abused, particularly if the abuse involves an ongoing relationship with a family member. Many victims of sexual abuse are too young to verbalize such information. Therefore, it is imperative that mental health professionals be aware of the signs and symptoms of child sexual abuse. Articles on this subject are appearing with increasing frequency in medical, psychiatric, and psychological journals. The majority of these articles focus on the impact of prolonged incestuous relationships between girl victims and men in parental roles.

Many of the signs and symptoms of sexual abuse in the preschool child are typical of other emotional disorders of childhood, whereas others are clearly indicative of sexual abuse. Physical signs and complaints include sudden weight loss or gain, abdominal pain, vomiting, and urinary tract infections (Kempe & Kempe, 1978; Pascoe & Duterte, 1981). Perineal bruises and tears, pharyngeal infections, and venereal disease are signs more clearly indicative of sexual abuse (Brant & Tisza, 1977; Sgroi, 1979). A history of physical abuse should raise the question of sexual abuse either in the identified child or in siblings (Goodwin, 1982; Pascoe & Duterte, 1981). Goodwin (1982) found that in 50% of incest cases reported to protective services, there was also evidence of physical abuse or neglect in one or more of the siblings. Behavioral symptoms in young children can include sleep disturbances, nightmares, compulsive masturbation, precocious sex play, loss of toilet training, frequent bathing, crying with no provocation, staying indoors, and regressive behavior such as finger sucking or clinging (Brant & Tisza, 1977; Burgess & Holstrom, 1975; Goodwin, 1982; Pascoe & Duterte, 1981). These behaviors are generally interpreted as manifestations of fear and anxiety. Browne and Finkelhor (1984; see also Finkelhor & Browne, Chapter 4 of this volume), in their recent review of the effects of child sexual abuse, found fear and anxiety to be the symptoms most commonly reported in clinically based studies. Burgess and Holstrom (1975) hypothesized that in cases of incest the "burden of the pressure to keep the secret is experienced psychologically as fear" (p. 88). These fears included fear of punishment if the child reveals the secret, fear of not being believed, fear of being blamed, and fear of abandonment or rejection, that is, being separated from the family.

Most of the findings described above were based on clinical impressions. Standardized instruments were not used. In a recent study, however, 156 children who had been sexually abused were tested using the Louisville

Behavior Checklist (Gomes-Schwartz, Horowitz, & Sauzier, 1985). The abused group was compared to a normal group and a standard group of children using psychiatric services. Thirty children ages 4 to 6 were included in the sample. In general, the sexually abused preschool children scored between the normal group and the psychologically disturbed group on the behavior checklist. On a scale measuring severity of pathology, 17% of the abused group were found to be significantly disturbed. Twenty percent of the children presented with symptoms of fear, anxiety, or depression. In addition, 20% showed serious deficits in intellectual, physical, and social development, and 23% were rated as being immature. The types of symptoms displayed by the abused children were generally consistent with the clinical studies cited above. One unexpected discrepancy was that only 13% of the abused sample presented with somatic complaints. Clinical studies have often mentioned headaches, vomiting, and abdominal pain as signs of possible sexual abuse.

The school-age child may exhibit many of the same symptoms as the younger child. Additional symptoms that may develop at this age include depression, insomnia, sudden school failure, truancy, or running away from home (Justice & Justice, 1979; Kempe & Kempe, 1978). Peters (1976), in a study of 64 child victims in Philadelphia, 82% of whom were black, found that 46% expressed increased fear of being on the streets, 34% had more negative feelings toward strange men, 32% had more negative feelings toward men they knew, 31% had difficulty sleeping, 20% had nightmares, and 20% reported a decrease in appetite.

Gomes-Schwartz et al. (1985), in their study of sexually victimized children, found that 40% of their sample age 7 to 13 were seriously disturbed in one or more areas of functioning. As with the preschool children, the school-age children were generally more disturbed than the normal group but less disturbed than other children receiving psychiatric treatment. The school-age children exhibited some of the same behaviors as did the preschool children, such as fear and anxiety (45%), as well as immature behavior (40%). They differed from the preschool children in that they began to exhibit some aggressive, impulsive, and antisocial behaviors (45%).

As the child approaches adolescence, more antisocial behavior such as petty crimes, drug use, promiscuity, and prostitution are seen (Pascoe & Duterte, 1981; Romney, 1982). Maisch (1972) found that 25% of his sample of 78 incest victims presented with behaviors such as lying, sexual promiscuity, truancy, and running away; deYoung (1982) noted that 28% of her sample of 80 incest victims reported they engaged in promiscuous behavior as adolescents. Adolescents may run away in order to escape their intolerable situation or as a cry for help and as a way of calling attention to their dysfunctional families. Nearly one third of Herman's (1981) sample of 40 incest victims attempted to run away from home as adolescents. When Gomes-Schwartz et al. (1985) found less psychopathology than expected among their sample of teenagers, they hypothesized that "the severity of their disturbed behavior may have caused them to run away or to be placed in mental health, corrections, or social welfare institutions" (p. 507). Thus, it was unlikely that severely disturbed teenagers would turn to a Family Crisis Program for help, which is where this study was conducted.

It is not uncommon for a runaway to turn to prostitution as a way of financially supporting herself. Silbert (1981) found that of 200 women prostitutes studied in the San Francisco area, 60% had been sexually abused prior to age 16 by an average of two people each. Other studies report similar results (see Renvoize, 1982). Although most runaway incest victims fall into prostitution as a way of supporting themselves, many find they can tolerate the situation because it is the first time they are in a position to exert power over men. In addition, during their sexual contacts with the perpetrators they have learned to dissociate from what is happening to their bodies (Brady, 1979; Gelinas, 1983; Renvoize, 1982).

Depression is a symptom more commonly noted with regard to adolescents than with younger victims of sexual abuse. Maisch (1972) reported that 28% of his sample was depressed and 4 of the 78 attempted suicide. Sixty-eight percent ($n = 54$) of deYoung's sample attempted suicide at least once, with 27 women making more than one attempt. The first attempt occurred either during the incest or within 2 years of its cessation.

When the incest-abused girl reaches her teenage years, she is increasingly at risk of the additional complication of pregnancy. In Maisch's (1972) study of 78 incest cases that came before a German court, 18% of the girls were pregnant by their fathers. Roybal and Goodwin (1982) have observed a decrease in pregnancy rates associated with incestuous relationships since Weinberg's (1955) study in which the pregnancy rate was 20%. They believe this decline is the result of the use of birth control pills (although they do not mention any studies of incest victims using the pill) and sex education in the schools. Roybal and Goodwin have observed that the pregnancy rates are higher in studies based on court referrals as opposed to those based on clinical samples. Meiselman (1978), for example, reported a pregnancy rate of only 1.7%.

Pregnancy, either by the incest perpetrator or by another male, is one way the daughter can exit the abusive relationship. In Herman's (1981) study of 40 incest victims, 45% had an adolescent pregnancy as compared with 15% of the control group. She noted that the pregnancies usually did result in ending the incestuous relationship.

The risk of revictimization is a consequence of sexual abuse that has recently been documented for both children and adults. Adams-Tucker (1981) sampled 28 children who had been assaulted by a total of 36 molesters, indicating that some of the children had been victimized more than once.

As well, deYoung (1982) found that 38% of her sample was sexually victimized by someone other than the original perpetrator either during or within 2 years of the incest. Russell's (1983) data indicate that repeated victimization occurred with girls who had been incestuously abused as well as with those assaulted by someone outside of the family. Hypothesized reasons for this vulnerability to repeated victimization include lack of proper supervision and protection by mothers, lack of sex information, lack of assertiveness, and ignorance of self-protective behaviors (deYoung, 1982).

Sexually abused children exhibit different symptoms at different age levels. Young children generally present with behavioral symptoms that are manifestations of anxiety. As children enter latency and early adolescence, aggressive and impulsive behavior begins to appear. Older children seem to be more disturbed by sexual victimization than are younger children, perhaps because of their increased awareness of the meaning of sexual behavior (Gomes-Schwartz et al., 1985). As children reach adolescence, acting out becomes more common as a way of expressing overwhelming feelings and also as a plea for help. Few sexually victimized children of any age are able to directly verbalize the distress they are experiencing.

LONG-TERM EFFECTS

Numerous theoretical papers and clinical and research studies on the long-term effects of sexual abuse have been published during the past 10 years. The research methodologies of these studies are as diverse as the findings. Such a situation is not uncommon, however, when a topic first receives a great deal of attention. Criticisms of much of the current research focuses on sampling procedures (many subjects are self-selected therapy patients), the lack of control groups, and the lack of objective outcome measures (Browne & Finkelhor, 1984; Conte, 1984). These methodological weaknesses have been used by some theoreticians to invalidate findings and to bolster arguments minimizing the negative impact of child sexual abuse (Constantine, 1981). Despite the varied research designs used to explore the long-term effects, there are a few studies using control groups and objective measures, and trends can be seen in this growing body of work.

Four studies on the long-term effects of child sexual abuse utilizing control or comparison groups include Briere (1984), Herman (1981), Meiselman (1978), and Tsai, Feldman-Summers, and Edgar (1979). Briere's and Meiselman's control groups consisted of therapy patients who were not sexually abused, whereas Herman's comparison group consisted of women who were not incest victims but whose fathers were seductive (talked with their daughters about sex, etc.). Tsai et al. used two comparison groups—one consisting of women who had been molested as children but were not in therapy, and a matched control group of women who had never been sexually as-saulted.

Sexual dysfunction, repeated victimization, suicide attempts, and depression are often the focus of studies on the effects of sexual abuse. Meiselman (1978) and Briere (1984) reported that the women who had been sexually abused had a significantly higher percentage of sexual problems than the comparison groups, although Herman (1981) found no difference between the two groups. Tsai et al. (1979) found that victims seeking therapy had significant sexual problems but the control group of victimized women not seeking therapy did not have more sexual difficulties than the nonvictimized matched control group. Sexual problems have been reported as a long-term effect in studies not utilizing comparison groups (Courtois, 1979; deYoung, 1982; Justice & Justice, 1979; Tsai & Wagner, 1978).

As noted in the section on the effects of sexual abuse on children, victims of sexual abuse are at risk of repeated victimization. In adults, the revictimization may take the form of increased risk of being raped or being involved in a battering relationship with a spouse or partner. Both Briere (1984) and Herman (1981) found that significantly more of the incest victims had been involved in battering relationships than had those in the control groups, but there were no significant differences between the two groups with regard to rape.

Briere (1984) and Herman (1981) found that more incest victims than controls had a history of suicide attempts, although in Herman's study the two groups did not differ significantly. Herman also reported that 60% of the incest victims exhibited major depressive symptomology but so did 55% of the women in the comparison group. Again, in studies not utilizing control or comparison groups, it was noted that depression and suicide attempts were problems presented by victims of childhood sexual abuse (deYoung, 1982; Justice & Justice, 1979).

A myriad of other symptoms have been mentioned as long-term effects of childhood sexual abuse. These include anxiety, phobic reactions, guilt, sub-stance abuse, difficulty trusting both men and women resulting in poor marital and interpersonal relationships, low self-esteem, extreme passivity, and episodes of dissociation or derealization. Research has not shown, however, that childhood sexual abuse is linked to specific psychiatric di-agnoses. This observation has prompted comments that such abuse therefore is not particularly harmful to the victim's psychological well-being. Yet there is no evidence in the psychiatric literature that definitively links any one life event with a specific psychiatric disorder.

Two efforts, one based on empirical findings and the other more theoreti-cal, have recently been made to examine the constellation of symptoms most commonly reported by victims of sexual abuse in an effort to define a syndrome related to the abuse. Briere (1984) has suggested that victims of sexual abuse may develop a Post-Sexual Abuse Syndrome "consisting of symptomatic behaviors which were originally coping mechanisms or conditioned reactions to a childhood characterized by victimization" (p. 12). Briere suggests that this syndrome develops in much the same way as other personality disorders, particularly the borderline personality. A child in an incestuous family develops maladaptive responses in order to cope with the dysfunctional family system. Once these responses are learned, they persist into adult life even when they are no longer necessary and may be viewed as inappropriate. Briere notes the similarity between diagnostic criteria for borderline personality disorder as defined by the Diagnostic and Statistical Manual of Mental Disorders, Third Edition (DSM-III) (American Psychiatric Association, 1980) and the constellation of problems commonly experienced by women who have been incest victims. These symptoms include many of those mentioned above, among them impulsive behaviors (substance abuse, sexual promiscuity), suicide attempts or other physically self-damaging acts, severe interpersonal difficulties, and episodes of dissociation.

Gelinas (1983), in her synthesis of the literature on the long-term effects of incest, suggests that the symptoms commonly associated with such abuse constitute a chronic traumatic neurosis. She contends that the neurosis emerges only after the incest has been disclosed and discussed to some extent. The symptoms such as intense expression of affect, cognitive impairment, overwhelming fear and anxiety, dissociative states, and hallucinations can be mistaken for a psychotic decompensation. Secondary elaborations such as substance abuse, chronic depression, guilt, low self-esteem, and suicidal ideation and suicide attempts may emerge when the neurosis goes untreated. Furthermore, it is for these symptoms that many previously abused women seek therapy.

Briere (1984) and Gelinas (1983) have examined some of the more common psychiatric sequelae of child sexual abuse and have attempted to define a post-abuse syndrome. On the other hand, not all incest victims will fit one pattern of symptom presentation. A victim's account of abuse must not be discounted simply because she presents with symptoms not commonly thought to be associated with childhood sexual abuse.

SUGGESTIONS FOR FUTURE RESEARCH

Most of the research studies on the effects of sexual abuse on children are clinical investigations of self-selected assault victims or special populations such as prostitutes, substance abusers, or college students. Such studies have been extremely helpful in providing focus and direction for other investigators, but the limitations of such designs have been acknowledged (Browne & Finkelhor, 1984; Conte, 1984). The inability to generalize results from such populations is a significant problem. Along with increasingly sophisticated research methodology, stronger conceptual bases in this area of research are needed. Gelinas' (1983) theoretical paper and Briere's (1984) empirical study on sexual abuse as a traumatic event provide one framework for viewing sexual abuse.

A major methodological problem in the research design of studies on sexual abuse victims, whether the population being studied consists of children or adults, is that data collection has taken place at only one point in time. Prospective longitudinal studies are needed to determine how children adjust to sexual assault at different stages in their development. Such studies will also provide information on what variables mediate between the occurrence of such assault and the development of various symptoms. The financial expense and time-consuming nature of longitudinal research is an obstacle with regard to its implementation.

An additional methodological problem in determining the effects of sexual abuse on children concerns the concept of adjustment or, conversely, pathology, as it has been measured in the existing research. The measure of adjustment most commonly used in recent research consists of the self-report of the subject's emotional symptoms and an assessment of the severity of problems encountered in social relationships and in their overall functioning. Standardized instruments such as the Minnesota Multiphasic Personality Inventory (MMPI) have rarely been used in this research, and when they have been used the results have been difficult to interpret (see Conte, 1984).

Although the use of these instruments often lends an air of legitimacy to empirical studies, a rationale must exist for using a particular scale. The instrument may not be measuring factors directly related to the abuse experience. In such a case, a group of assault victims could score higher on a measure of adjustment then a control group and lead a researcher to conclude incorrectly that the victimized group was not adversely affected by the assaults. The development and subsequent refinement of assessment techniques related to incest and sexual assault needs to be a high priority in studying the negative effects of sexual victimization.

Furthermore, studies on the negative effects of child sexual abuse are generally confined to examining psychiatric sequelae. Other effects, such as a higher utilization rate of medical services, vulnerability to disease, infertility problems, underachievement, or unstable work histories, should be considered in future studies. It seems that the concept of adjustment needs to be enlarged to include an assessment of functioning in a variety of roles, and multiple measures of adjustment should be incorporated into future research designs.

Despite the literature that has just been reviewed, some researchers continue to question or minimize the negative effects of child sexual abuse. The effects of abuse are discounted because it appears that not all victims are negatively affected and that not all those who are affected are diagnosed as having developed major psychiatric disorders. It can be argued, however, that not every Vietnam combat veteran develops a posttraumatic stress disorder. Not every person who experiences an ugly divorce exhibits similar symptomology. In fact, Bloom, Asher, & White (1978) documented the variety of negative sequelae that may arise following marital separation and divorce, ranging from increased psychiatric hospitalization rates to increased risk of motor vehicle accidents to increased risk of death by homicide or suicide. Sexual abuse during childhood, whether a single event or a long-term incestuous relationship, can be viewed as a stressor. People undergoing stressful life events are at increased risk of developing a variety of disorders, psychiatric illness being only one of these (Dohrenwend & Dohrenwend, 1974).

Events impact on individuals differently because of mediating factors. Browne and Finkelhor (1984), in their literature review, examined factors directly related to the abuse, such as age of onset, relationship to the perpetrator, the use of force, or whether the abuse was disclosed. They found that "several studies indicate that abuse by fathers or stepfathers has a more negative impact than abuse by other perpetrators. Results of some studies also suggest that experiences involving genital contact are more serious, and that the use of force results in more trauma for the victim" (p. 30). With regard to several other factors, however, the results were inconclusive. Tsai et al. (1979) found that negative effects were associated with being older at the time of the last molestation, stronger negative feelings associated with the molestation, and greater frequency and longer duration of molestation. The factors mitigating against negative effects were support from friends and family, and sympathetic sex partners. Mediating factors may not be variables directly related to the abuse but may include external resources or deficits (e.g., the presence or absence of a social support system, employment) or inner resources or deficits (e.g., intellectual abilities, physical health, inherited strengths and vulnerabilities) (Dohrenwend, 1979). Future research on the differential impact of child sexual abuse should more closely examine characteristics of the victims as well as factors directly related to the abuse.

The negative effect of incest is questioned by researchers who state that it is impossible to separate the impact of sexual abuse from the pathology of the family. As Meiselman (1978) notes, incest is not merely a sexual act and must be seen within the context of the family. Gelinas (1983) theorizes that although exposing a child to chronic marital estrangement and role reversal with the mother will have negative effects, it is sex with the parent that produces the traumatic neurosis. Herman (1981) has attempted to separate the effects of incest from those of the family dynamics in her study of incest victims and women whose fathers were described as seductive. Herman found that women in both groups came from patriarchal families in which the father held the power, sex roles were traditionally defined, and attitudes concerning sex and religion were very conservative. The incest families, however, were characterized by extreme male dominance. Women from both types of families exhibited similar types of emotional depression, relationship difficulties with men and women as a result of overvaluing men and devaluing women, and a confused self-image. Although the problems of the two groups were similar, the severity was greater in the incest group. The desperation of the incest group was particularly noticeable during adolescence, when many made runaway attempts, had adolescent pregnancies, and married early to escape their home situations only to be abused in their marriages.

> The similarities between incest victims and the daughters of seductive fathers once again confirm the contention that incest represents a common pattern of traditional female socialization carried to a pathological extreme. . . . Those who consider masochism, selflessness and deference to men desirable attributes of mature womanhood may be unable to recognize the harmfulness of incest, and may even consider a little bit of paternal seduction desirable for proper female development. (Herman, 1981, p. 125)

An interesting extension of Herman's research would be a study utilizing the nonabused sisters of incest victims as a comparison group. This would further aid in differentiating the effects of the sexual experience from that of the family dynamics. Obtaining subjects might be difficult, however, since in many incest families the daughters are serially abused.

As noted below, one of the most subtly pervasive effects of child sexual abuse, and of incest in particular, is that it reinforces the traditional sex roles of men and women. Although this finding is consistently described in clinical studies, there has been no empirical research on the sex role orientations of victims of sexual assault. An instrument such as the MAFERR Inventory of Feminine Values (Steinman & Fox, 1974) could be incorporated into studies on the effects of sexual abuse. Scoring of this inventory yields a family orientation score and a self-orientation score. A woman with a high family orientation would put the interests of her husband and children ahead of her own interests and aspirations, while a woman with a high self-orientation score would be characterized as achievement-oriented and self-motivated.

SOCIETAL IMPLICATIONS

Perhaps the most insidious and profound impact of child sexual abuse is the fact that it contributes to the maintenance and perpetuation of a patriarchal society—the society that provides the context in which sexual abuse can occur in the first place. Men dominate this society in terms of political power, economic power, and the control they exert over women's bodies (see Leidig, 1981). Such a male-dominated society renders many women powerless to protect themselves and their children from being sexually exploited. This social structure has been discussed as a major element contributing to the sexual victimization of women and children (Herman, 1981; Russell, 1984), but the vicious cycle operating with respect to sexual abuse must be reiterated. The effect of sexual abuse serves to increase the power of men over women and to create women who simultaneously fear men, overvalue and overidealize men because of their immense power, and are dependent on them.

The dynamics of the incestuous family have been delineated elsewhere (Butler, 1978; deYoung, 1982; Gelinas, 1983; Herman, 1981). The typical family structure in which incest occurs has been described as male-dominated and authoritarian, a replication in miniature of the patriarchal society. The fact that girls growing up in such families become passive, depressed women with poor coping skills often unable to protect themselves from further abuse or to protect their daughters from sexual victimization has been documented in many case studies. Boys learn to devalue women at an early age and begin experiencing the power they have over them. The fact that these dynamics are perpetuated from generation to generation is even acknowledged by a researcher whose intention it was to minimize the effect of incest among 18 female psychiatric patients. "The effects of the early sexual experiences of these patients are difficult to ascertain. None of the patients was overtly psychotic, and, in terms of social adjustment among the adults, most seemed to have made adequate adjustments, *usually similar to their parents* [italics added]" (Rosenfeld, 1979, p. 794).

There does seem to be some concensus that the dynamics of the family in which incest occurs are transmitted intergenerationally and that individual victims of sexual abuse suffer certain negative consequences. The idea that all women, whether they have been sexually abused as children or not, suffer negative effects of such exploitation is a more radical notion (see Brownmiller, 1975; Leidig, 1981). Sexual abuse prevention programs provide an example of how all girls are affected by sexual abuse. Children as young as three are being taught what to do when approached by strangers. Although the goal of such programs is to empower children and to teach self-protective measures, these presentations also instill fear of men and further reinforce the concept of men as powerful. In teaching children to protect themselves, it is implicitly conveyed that the children are, at least in part, responsible for their own victimization. This is a tremendous burden for children to carry—one that can lead them, girls in particular, to curtail outside activities in favor of remaining close to home. Girls will hear the message that they need protection. The victim mentality is internalized by all women because all are potential victims (MacFarlane, 1978). The only people who have the power to protect them adequately are those who also have the power to exploit them physically and sexually.

REFERENCES

Adams-Tucker, C. (1981). A socioclinical overview of 28 sex-abused children. *Child Abuse and Neglect, 5,* 361–367.

American Humane Association. (1986). *Highlights of official child neglect and abuse reporting, 1985.* Denver, CO: Author.

American Psychiatric Association. (1980). *Diagnostic and statistical manual of mental disorders* (3rd ed.). Washington, DC: Author.

Bloom, B. L., Asher, S. J., & White, S. W. (1978). Marital disruption as a stresser: A review and analysis. *Psychological Bulletin, 85,* 867–894.

Brady, K. (1979). *Father's days.* New York: Seaview Books.

Brant, R. T., & Tisza, V. B. (1977). The sexually misused child. *American Journal of Orthopsychiatry, 47,* 80–90.

Briere, J. (1984, April). *The effects of childhood sexual abuse on later psychological functioning: Defining a post-sexual-abuse syndrome.* Paper presented at the Third National Conference on Sexual Victimization of Children, Children's Hospital National Medical Center, Washington, DC.

Browne, A., & Finkelhor, D. (1984). *The impact of child sexual abuse: A review of the research.* (Available from Angela Browne, Family Violence Research Program, University of New Hampshire, Durham, NH 03824).

Brownmiller, S. (1975). *Against our will: Men, women and rape.* New York: Simon & Schuster.

Burgess, A. W., & Holstrom, L. L. (1975). Sexual trauma of children and adolescents: Pressure, sex and secrecy. *Nursing Clinics of North America, 10,* 551–563.

Butler, S. (1978). *Conspiracy of silence: The trauma of incest.* San Francisco: New Glide.

Cantwell, H. B. (1981). Sexual abuse of children in Denver, 1979: Reviewed with implications for pediatric intervention and possible prevention. *Child Abuse and Neglect, 5,* 75–85.

Constantine, L. L. (1981). The effects of early sexual experiences: A review with synthesis of research. In L. L. Constantine & F. M. Martinson (Eds.), *Children and sex: New findings, new perspectives* (pp. 217–246). Boston: Little, Brown.

Conte, J. (November, 1984). *The effects of sexual abuse on children: A critique and suggestions for future research.* Paper presented at the Third International Institute on Victimology, Lisbon, Portugal.

Courtois, C. C. (1979). The incest experience and its aftermath. *Victimology, 4,* 337–347.

deYoung, M. (1982). *The sexual victimization of children.* Jefferson, NC: McFarland.

Dohrenwend, B. P. (1979). Stressful life events and psychopathology: Some issues of theory and method. In J. E. Barrett, R. M. Rose, & G. L. Klerman, (Eds.), *Stress and mental disorder* (pp. 1–15). New York: Raven Press.

Dohrenwend, B. S., & Dohrenwend, B. P. (Eds.). (1974). *Stressful life events: Their nature and effects.* New York: Wiley.

Finkelhor, D. (1979). *Sexually victimized children.* New York: Free Press.

Gelinas, D. J. (1983). The persisting negative effects of incest. *Psychiatry, 46,* 312–332.

Gomes-Schwartz, B., Horowitz, J. M., & Sauzier, M. (1985). Severity of emotional distress among sexually abused preschool, school-age, and adolescent children. *Hospital and Community Psychiatry, 36,* 503–508.

Goodwin, J. (1982). *Sexual abuse: Incest victims and their families.* Boston: John W. Wright.

Goodwin, J., Sahd, D., & Rada, R. T. (1982). False accusations and false denials of incest: Clinical myths and clinical realities. In J. Goodwin (Ed.), *Sexual abuse: Incest victims and their families.* Boston: John W. Wright.

Herman, J. L. (1981). *Father-daughter incest.* Cambridge, MA: Harvard University Press.

Justice, B., & Justice, R. (1979). *The broken taboo: Sex in the family.* New York: Human Sciences Press.

Kempe, R. S., & Kempe, C. H. (1978). *Child abuse.* Cambridge, MA: Harvard University Press.

Leidig, M. W. (1981). Violence against women: A feminist-psychological analysis. In S. Cox (Ed.), *Female psychology: The emerging self* (pp. 190–205). New York: St. Martin's.

MacFarlane, K. (1978). Sexual abuse of children. In J. R. Chapman & M. Gates (Eds.), *The victimization of women* (pp. 81–109). Beverly Hills, CA: Sage.

Maisch, H. (1972). *Incest.* New York: Stein & Day.

Malcom, J. (1983, December 5, December 12). Annals of scholarship: Psychoanalysis (Parts I and II). *The New Yorker,* pp. 59–155, 60–119.

Masson, J. M. (1984, February). Freud and the seduction theory. *Atlantic Monthly,* pp. 33–60.

Meiselman, K. C. (1978). *Incest: A psychological study of causes and effects with treatment recommendations.* San Francisco: Jossey-Bass.

Pascoe, D., & Duterte, B. O. (1981). The medical diagnosis of sexual abuse in the pre-menarcheal child. *Pediatric Annals, 10,* 40–45.

Peters, J. J. (1976). Children who are victims of sexual assault and the psychology of offenders. *American Journal of Psychotherapy, 30,* 398–421.

Renvoize, J. (1982). *Incest: A family pattern.* London: Routledge and Kegan Paul.

Romney, M. C. (1982). Incest in adolescence. *Pediatric Annals, 11,* 813–817.

Rosenfeld, A. A. (1979). Incidents of a history of incest among 18 female psychiatric patients. *American Journal of Psychiatry, 36,* 791–795.

Roybal, L., & Goodwin, J. (1982). The incest pregnancy. In J. Goodwin (Ed.), *Sexual abuse: Incest victims and their families.* Boston: John W. Wright.

Rush, F. (1980). *The best kept secret: Sexual abuse of children.* Englewood Cliffs, NJ: Prentice-Hall.

Russell, D. E. H. (1983). The incidents and prevalence of intrafamilial and extrafamilial sexual abuse of female children. *Child Abuse and Neglect, 7,* 133–146.

Russell, D. E. H. (1984). *Sexual exploitation: Rape, child sexual abuse, and work place harassment.* Beverly Hills, CA: Sage.

Sgroi, S. M. (1979). Pediatric gonorrhea beyond infancy. *Pediatric Annals, 8,* 326–336.

Silbert, M. H. (1981). Sexual child abuse as an antecedent to prostitution. *Child Abuse and Neglect, 5,* 407–411.

Steinmann, A., & Fox, D. J. (1974). *The male dilemma.* New York: Aronson.

Tsai, M., Feldman-Summers, S., & Edgar, M. (1979). Childhood molestation: Differential impacts on psychosexual functioning. *Journal of Abnormal Psychology, 88,* 407–417.

Tsai, M., & Wagner, N. N. (1978). Therapy groups for women sexually molested as children. *Archives of Sexual Behavior, 7,* 417–426.

Van Buskirk, S., & Cole, C. F. (1984). Characteristics of eight women seeking therapy for the effects of incest. *Psychotherapy: Theory Research and Practice, 20,* 503–514.

Weinberg, S. K. (1955). *Incest behavior.* Secaucus, NJ: Citadel.

2

The Incidence and Prevalence of Intrafamilial and Extrafamilial Sexual Abuse of Female Children

Diana E. H. Russell

There is no consensus among researchers and practitioners about what sex acts constitute sexual abuse, what age defines a child, nor even whether the concept of child sexual abuse is preferable to others such as sexual victimization, sexual exploitation, sexual assault, sexual misuse, child molestation, sexual maltreatment, or child rape. Furthermore, these terms have frequently been limited to sexual behavior that occurs between adults and children (e.g., Finkelhor, 1979; Mrazek & Kempe, 1981; National Center on Child Abuse and Neglect, 1981). Consequently, cases in which children are raped or otherwise sexually abused by their peers, younger children, or children less than five years older than themselves are often discounted as instances of child sexual abuse. The terms sexual abuse and sexual victimization will be used interchangeably in this chapter; these terms should be understood to include sexual abuse by peers or other children.

The data gathering phase of the research was funded by the National Institute of Mental Health, Grant RO1 MH 18960. The analysis of the data on child sexual abuse was funded by the National Center on Child Abuse and Neglect, Department of Health and Human Services, Grant No. 90-CA-813/01.
Acknowledgment—The author would like to thank Patricia Mrazek and David Finkelhor for their useful suggestions in response to an earlier draft of this manuscript, Karen Trocki and Bill Wells for their assistance with the data analysis, and Jan Dennie for her help in the preparation of this chapter.

LITERATURE REVIEW OF INCIDENCE AND PREVALENCE

Both the incidence and prevalence of child sexual abuse, in the family and outside of it, are unknown.[1] Weinberg, in his classic study originally published in 1955, estimated that there was one case of incest per million persons in 1930 in the United States (Weinberg, 1976). Ferracuti estimated in 1972 that between one and five cases of incest per million persons occur every year throughout the world (Ferracuti, 1972). Many other estimates have been made, but none of them are based on representative samples. Meiselman attempted to list all studies of incest with samples larger than 5 published in this country (Meiselman, 1978). The highly select and nonrepresentative nature of the samples used in all 36 studies listed is very apparent. Studies of extrafamilial abuse are equally unrepresentative.

The National Incidence Study, which includes cases known to other investigatory bodies besides child protective service agencies, as well as other professionals in schools, hospitals, and major agencies, estimated a rate of 0.7 case of child sexual exploitation per 1,000 children per year, as compared with 3.4 cases of other physical assault, 2.2 cases of emotional abuse, 1.7 cases of physical neglect, 2.9 cases of educational neglect, and 1.0 case of emotional neglect per 1,000 children per year. The number of substantiated cases of sexual exploitation was 44,700 (National Center on Child Abuse and Neglect, 1981). Surprisingly, there were proportionately more serious injuries associated with sexual exploitation than with physical assault (National Center on Child Abuse and Neglect, 1981). This finding suggests that only the most serious cases of sexual abuse were seen as qualifying for inclusion. Just as so many cases of reported rapes are "unfounded" every year by the police, it appears that many legitimate cases of child sexual abuse were "unsubstantiated."

Most other estimates have focused on the prevalence of incest and/or other child sexual abuse rather than the incidence. Herman presents data from five surveys that have been undertaken on the prevalence of sexual abuse of female children since 1940. She points out that cumulatively these studies have recorded information from over 5000 women from many different regions of the United States, and primarily from the more privileged strata (Herman, 1981). According to Herman:

> The results of these five surveys were remarkably consistent. One-fifth to one-third of all women reported that they had had some sort of childhood sexual encounter with an adult male. Between four and twelve percent of all women reported a sexual experience with a relative, and one woman in one hundred reported a sexual experience with her father or stepfather. (Herman, 1981, p. 12)

---

[1]For purposes of this analysis, *incidence* will refer to cases of child sexual abuse that occurred within a specified period of time, and *prevalence* will refer to the percentage of children victimized by such an experience, whether once or many times.

However, none of these surveys were based on representative samples. A major objective of the research reported here was to obtain a more valid basis on which to arrive at estimates of both intrafamilial and extrafamilial child sexual abuse.

METHODOLOGY[2]

The Sample

A probability sample of 930 women residents of San Francisco 18 years and older was interviewed during the summer of 1978 about any experience of sexual abuse they might have had at any time throughout their lives. San Francisco was selected because, among other reasons, it was believed that women in that city would be more willing to disclose such experiences than women in many other parts of the country. The probability sample of households was drawn by Field Research Associates, a respected public opinion polling organization in San Francisco. Carefully trained women interviewers enumerated households to find out whether a woman 18 years or older resided there. If there was more than one eligible woman in a given household, a procedure was applied to randomly select the one to be interviewed. Detailed interviews, the average length of which was 1 hour and 20 minutes, were then arranged with the selected women.

The Interview

Because it appeared that many prior surveys suffered from underdisclosure of sexual assault experiences, every effort was made to discourage this from occurring in this study. The interview schedule was carefully designed to encourage good rapport with the respondent. Interviewers were selected for their sensitivity to the issue of sexual assault as well as for their interviewing skills. They received 65 hours of intensive training that included education about rape and incestuous abuse, as well as desensitization to sexual words and rigorous training in administering the interview schedule. Interviews were held in private, and whenever possible, race and ethnicity of interviewer and respondent were matched. Each respondent was paid $10 for her participation.

Refusal Rate

Nineteen percent of the women who were selected as respondents refused to participate after being informed that the crimes to be discussed were rape

[2]A more detailed account of the methodology of this study is described in Russell, D. E. H. *The Secret Trauma: Incest in the Lives of Girls and Women.* Basic Books, New York (1986) pp. 19–37.

and other sexual assault. An additional 17% of people, men as well as women, declined to give a listing of those in the household prior to being told about the topic to be studied. This amounts to a refusal rate of 36%. However, if one also takes into account all households where no one was ever at home, or where the interviewer could not gain access to the house because of locked gates, fierce watchdogs, and the like, as well as those where the women randomly selected to be interviewed simply were never available because they were out of town, or because their husbands or some other persons would not give the interviewer access to the women, or for some other reason, then the refusal rate is 50%. Although this refusal rate is higher than desired, it must be remembered that Kinsey and his colleagues (Kinsey, Pomeroy, Martin & Gebhard, 1953), Masters and Johnson (1966), as well as Hite (1976), all based their studies on volunteers because they considered a probability sample unfeasible. Even an imperfect probability sample such as ours is still unprecedented for research in the area of sex or sexual abuse.

The Definitions

For purposes of our survey *extrafamilial child sexual abuse* was defined as one or more unwanted sexual experiences with persons unrelated by blood or marriage, ranging from petting (touching of breasts or genitals or attempts at such touching) to rape, before the victim turned 14 years, and completed or attempted forcible rape experiences from the ages of 14 to 17 years (inclusive).

Since intrafamilial child sexual abuse was expected to be generally more upsetting and traumatic than extrafamilial child sexual abuse, and since the issue of whether or not the sexual contact was wanted or not is so much more complex in intimate relationships, a broader definition of what constitutes intrafamilial sexual abuse was used. More specifically, *intrafamilial child sexual abuse* was defined as any kind of exploitive sexual contact that occurred between relatives, no matter how distant the relationship, before the victim turned 18 years old. Experiences involving sexual contact with a relative that were wanted *and* with a peer were regarded as nonexploitive, for example, sex play between cousins or siblings of approximately the same ages. An age difference of less than 5 years was the criterion for a peer relationship.[3]

It should be noted that our definitions of these two forms of child sexual abuse are narrower than those used by some other researchers who include exhibitionism and/or other experiences that may involve no actual contact or attempted contact, for example, a sexual proposition that is not acted upon (e.g., Finkelhor, 1979; Gagnon, 1965; Landis, 1956).

---

[3]The 40 cases of exploitive sexual contact between relatives where the respondent was 18 years or older when it started are excluded from this analysis of child sexual abuse.

Initially, the age of 13 and younger was chosen as the criterion for child sexual abuse because California law, the state in which this research was undertaken, defined child molestation as "all sex acts upon children under age of fourteen, when the intent of sexually stimulating either party is involved" (Public Education and Research Committee of California, 1973, p. 160). Other researchers have used other ages; for example, Finkelhor defined a child as a person under 17 years of age (Finkelhor, 1979), and the National Child Abuse and Neglect publications use 18 years as their criterion (National Center on Child Abuse and Neglect, 1981). Eighteen is, of course, the age of consent in many states, and it is also the age specified in the Child Abuse and Neglect reporting statute. However, since it seems inappropriate to regard many 16- and 17-year-olds as children, both because of their physical and emotional maturity, prevalence rates will be reported for both the ages of 13 and under, and 17 and under.

The Interview Schedule

Extensive pretesting revealed that when a number of different questions are asked in a wide variety of ways, the chances of tapping memories stored under many different categories in a person's mind are greatly facilitated. The questions used to elicit memories of child sexual abuse experiences were as follows:

1. Before you turned 14, were you ever upset by anyone exposing their genitals?
2. Did anyone ever try or succeed in having any kind of sexual intercourse with you against your wishes before you turned 14?
3. In those years, did anyone ever try or succeed in getting you to touch their genitals against your wishes (besides anyone you've already mentioned)?[4]
4. Did anyone ever try or succeed in touching your breasts or genitals against your wishes before you turned 14 (besides anyone you've already mentioned)?
5. Before you turned 14, did anyone ever feel you, grab you, or kiss you in a way you felt was sexually threatening (besides anyone you've already mentioned)?
6. Before you turned 14, did you have any (other) upsetting sexual experiences that you haven't mentioned yet?

The following few questions did not stipulate an age limit, including the two questions on intrafamilial sexual abuse, but nevertheless yielded many experiences of child sexual abuse.

---

[4]The sections in parentheses were read by the interviewer only if the respondent had already mentioned a childhood sexual experience.

7. At *any* time in your life, have you ever had an unwanted sexual experience with a girl or a woman?
8. At any time in your life, have you ever been the victim of a rape or attempted rape?
9. Some people have experienced unwanted sexual advances by some-one who had authority over them, such as a doctor, teacher, employer, minister, therapist, policeman, or much older person. Did *you ever* have *any* kind of unwanted sexual experience with someone who had authority over you, at *any* time in your life?
10. People often don't think about their relatives when thinking about sexual experiences, so the next two questions are about relatives. At *any* time in your life, has an uncle, brother, father, grandfather, or female relative ever had *any kind* of sexual contact with you?
11. At any time in your life, has anyone less closely related to you such as a stepparent, stepbrother, or stepsister, in-law or first cousin had *any* kind of sexual contact with you?
12. In general, have you *narrowly missed* being sexually assaulted by someone at any time in your life (*other* than what you have already mentioned)?
13. And have you *ever* been in any situation where there was violence or threat of violence, where you were also afraid of being *sexually* assaulted—again, *other* than what you (might) have already men-tioned?
14. Can you think of any (other) unwanted sexual experiences (that you haven't mentioned yet)?

Separate questionnaires were administered for all the more serious cases of sexual abuse. Interviewers were instructed to obtain descriptions of the sexual contact(s) sufficiently detailed to insure that the level of intimacy violated could be precisely coded.

FINDINGS

Prevalence Figures

As may be seen in Table 2.1, *16% of the sample of 930 women reported at least one experience of intrafamilial sexual abuse before the age of 18 years.* These 152 women reported a total of 187 experiences with different per-petrators. *Twelve percent (108) of these women had been sexually abused by a relative before 14 years of age.* These prevalence figures exclude eight cases of intrafamilial sexual abuse where information on the age of the respondent at the time it occurred was missing, as well as two cases where it was not known whether actual sexual contact occurred between the respondent and her relative. Hence these figures err on the side of underestimation, even presuming that all respondents were willing to disclose their experiences of intrafamilial sexual abuse; this is undoubtedly a poor presumption.

Using the more stringent definition of extrafamilial sexual abuse, *31% of the sample of 930 women reported at least one experience of sexual abuse by a non-relative before the age of 18 years.* These 290 women reported a total of 461 experiences with different perpetrators. *Twenty percent (189) of these women had been sexually abused by a non-relative before 14 years of age* (see Table 2.1).

As might be expected, there is some overlap between the respondents who have experienced intrafamilial and extrafamilial child sexual abuse. When both these categories of child sexual abuse are combined, *38% (357) of the 930 women reported at least one experience of intrafamilial and/or extrafamilial sexual abuse before the age of 18 years, and 28% (258) reported at least one such experience before 14 years of age* (see Table 2.2).

While these prevalence figures for child sexual abuse are already shockingly high, it would be interesting to know how much higher they would be had broader definitions of both intrafamilial and extrafamilial child sexual abuse more comparable to some other studies been adopted. Although the two

TABLE 2.1 Different Measures of the Prevalence and Incidence of Intrafamilial and Extrafamilial Child Sexual Abuse (Separated)

	Women who had at least one experience (Prevalence) (N = 930)		Number of experiences of sexual abuse with different perpetrators* (Incidence)
	Sample Percentage	Number	Number
Intrafamilial abuse of females involving sexual contact under 18 years**	16	152	187
Intrafamilial abuse of females involving sexual contact under 14 years**	12	108	134
Extrafamilial sexual abuse of females involving petting or genital sex under 18 years	31	290	461
Extrafamilial sexual abuse of females involving petting or genital sex under 14 years	20	189	255

*Multiple attacks by the same perpetrator are only counted once; abuse involving multiple perpetrators is also counted as only one experience.
**8 cases of intrafamilial abuse are excluded because of missing data on the age of the respondent.

TABLE 2.2 Different Measures of the Prevalence of Intrafamilial and Extrafamilial Child Sexual Abuse of Females (Combined)

	Women who had at least one experience (N = 930)	
	Sample percentage	Number
Intrafamilial and/or extrafamilial sexual abuse of females under 18 years	38	357
Intrafamilial and/or extrafamilial sexual abuse of females under 14 years	28	258
Intrafamilial and/or extrafamilial sexual abuse of females under 18 years—broad definition (includes noncontact experiences, e.g., exhibitionism, sexual advances not acted upon, etc.)	54	504
Intrafamilial and/or extrafamilial sexual abuse of females under 14 years—broad definition (as above)	48	450

questions asked about intrafamilial sexual abuse specifically stipulated sexual contact as the criterion, some respondents replied by describing experiences that did not involve actual physical contact. While we can be sure that many other respondents would have told us about their non-contact experiences had they been asked about them, these inadvertently obtained data are valuable despite their incompleteness. Additional quantitative data were also obtained on other non-contact experiences in childhood, such as being upset by someone exposing their genitals. In the case of extrafamilial child sexual abuse there were additional quantitative data on unwanted kisses, hugs, and other non-genital touching that did not meet our definition of sexual abuse by nonrelatives.

When applying these broader definitions of intrafamilial and extrafamilial child sexual abuse that includes experiences with exhibitionists as well as other unwanted non-contact sexual experiences, *54% (504) of the 930 women reported at least one experience of intrafamilial and/or extrafamilial sexual abuse before they reached 18 years of age,* and *48% (450) reported at least one such experience before 14 years of age* (see Table 2.2).

The narrower definitions of intrafamilial and extrafamilial child sexual abuse will be used throughout the remainder of this article.

The Perpetrators of Intrafamilial Child Sexual Abuse

Thirty-eight percent of the perpetrators of intrafamilial child sexual abuse were members of the nuclear family in our survey (i.e., the perpetrators were parents or siblings). Forty-two women reported an incestuous relationship with their fathers before the age of 18 [including 27 biological fathers, 15 step, 1 foster, and 1 father by adoption. Since two women were sexually abused by both their biological and stepfathers, the count includes two more perpetrators (44) than victims (42).] This constitutes *4.5% of our probability sample of 930 women* (see Table 2.3).

Sexual abuse by uncles is only very slightly more prevalent than father-daughter incestuous abuse, with 4.9% of the women in the sample reporting at least one such experience before the age of 18. Just over 3% of the women surveyed reported a sexually abusive experience with a first cousin before they turned 18, all but two of whom were male. Two percent of the women reported at least one incestuous experience with a brother, 1.2% with a grandfather, 0.8% with a brother-in-law, 0.3% with a sister, 0.1% with a mother, and 1.8% with some other male or female relative, not including grandmothers or aunts, with whom not a single case of sexual abuse was reported.

Had males as well as females been interviewed, the percentage of female perpetrators would likely have been higher. Nevertheless, it is of interest that in this probability sample survey, only 10 female perpetrators of intrafamilial child sexual abuse were reported, that is, only 5% of all incest perpetrators.

TABLE 2.3 Women under 18 Years Reporting Intrafamilial Sexual Abuse by Type of Perpetrator

Perpetrator	Number of women*	Percentage of women in sample $N = 930$	Number of incidents with different perpetrators
Father (biological, step-, foster or adoptive)	42	4.5	44
Mother (biological, step-, foster or adoptive)	1	0.1	1
Grandfather (biological or step-)	11	1.2	11
Brother	19	2.0	25
Sister	3	0.3	3
Uncle	46	4.9	48
Brother-in-law	7	0.8	8
First cousin (male or female)	30	3.2	30
Other relative (male or female)	17	1.8	19

*If a woman was sexually abused by more than one category of relative, she is included in each. If she was sexually abused by more than one relative within a particular category, she is included in this category once only.

The Perpetrators of Extrafamilial Child Sexual Abuse

As may be seen in Table 2.4, only 15% of the perpetrators of extrafamilial child sexual abuse were strangers, while 42% were acquaintances, and 43% were more intimately related to their victims (friends of the respondent, friends of the family, dates, boyfriends, and lovers). Forty percent of these perpetrators were also classified as authority figures. Two thirds of them were so classified because they were much older adults, including strangers, acquaintances, friends of the family, parents' lovers, household employees, and neighbors.[5]

Those who abused female children not related to them in our survey were overwhelmingly male: as may be seen in Table 2.4. only 4% were females. This is very close to the 5% figure for female perpetrators of intrafamilial child sexual abuse.

TABLE 2.4 Perpetrators of Extrafamilial Sexual Abuse of Females under 18 Years

Perpetrator	Male perpetrators		Female perpetrators	
	Percent-age	Number	Percent-age	Number
Stranger	15	(71)	0	(0)
Acquaintance	40	(185)	2	(8)
Friend of family	14	(64)	0	(2)
Friend of respondent	9	(43)	2	(7)
Date	9	(40)	0	(0)
Boyfriend, lover, husband*	7	(33)	0	(0)
Authority figure (not classifiable)	2	(8)	0	(0)
Total	96	(444)	4	(17)

*Five women who were raped by their husbands before they turned 18 are included here, since, although they are relatives, clearly sexual abuse by husbands cannot be regarded as incestuous.

[5]Obviously, authority figures such as medical physicians, employers, and professors are almost always much older adults in the case of children, as well as having authority by virtue of their profession. The criterion for determining whether someone qualified as a "much older adult" was not strictly based on the age of the perpetrator nor the age difference between this person and the victim. Instead, an attempt was made to ascertain, from what respondents said, what had determined the perpetrators' status as an authority figure in their eyes. While this method is somewhat subjective, both on the part of the coders and for the respondents, this seemed less disadvantageous than applying age criteria that, while "objective," are arbitrary and whose meaning may be dubious.

The Perpetrators of All Child Sexual Abuse Combined

While it is becoming more widely recognized that most child sexual abuse is perpetrated by those known to the victims, our survey reveals that when all cases of intrafamilial and extrafamilial child sexual abuse are combined, the majority of the perpetrators were not relatives. More specifically, 11% were total strangers, 29% were relatives, and 60% were known to the victims but unrelated to them.

Seriousness of Intrafamilial Child Sexual Abuse

The experiences of intrafamilial sexual abuse included in our survey range from unwanted but non-forceful kissing by a cousin to forcible rape by a biological father. Eighteen different categories of sexual abuse were differentiated according to whether or not force was used as well as the degree of sexual violation involved. For purposes of simplification, this 18 category typology was collapsed into the following three categories: (1) *Very Serious Sexual Abuse,* including experiences ranging from forced penile-vaginal penetration to attempted fellatio, cunnilingus, analingus, anal intercourse—*not* by force; (2) *Serious Sexual Abuse,* including experiences ranging from forced digital penetration of the vagina to nonforceful attempted breast contact (unclothed) or simulated intercourse; and (3) *Least Serious Sexual Abuse,* including experiences ranging from forced kissing, intentional sexual touching of the respondent's buttocks, thigh, leg or other body part, including contact with clothed breasts or genitals, to attempts at any of the same acts without the use of force. The frequency with which these different degrees of intrafamilial child sexual abuse occurred in our survey is presented in Table 2.5, along with the relationship between the victim and the perpetrator and the sex of the latter.

This table reveals that 23% of all incidents of intrafamilial sexual abuse were classified as *Very Serious,* 41% as *Serious,* and 36% as *Least Serious.* When differentiating between forceful and nonforceful forms of intrafamilial child sexual abuse, 41% (77) of the cases involved force and 59% (109) involved no force. Note that force includes threat of force as well as the inability to consent due to being unconscious, drugged, asleep, or in some other way totally helpless. Only one of the ten female perpetrators, a distant female relative, used force, and none were reported to be involved in the most serious category of sexual violation.

It is apparent from the data reported in Table 2.5 that when stepfathers abuse their daughters, they are more likely than any other relative to abuse them at the most serious level.[6] In almost half the cases of sexual abuse by

---

[6]Although step-, adoptive, and foster fathers are included in the same category, experiences with only one foster father and one adoptive father were reported.

TABLE 2.5 Seriousness of Intrafamilial Child Sexual Abuse by Relationship with the Perpetrator (under 18 Years)*

	Male perpetrator								Female perpetrator**				Total
	Biological father	Step-adoptive father	Grandfather	Brother	Uncle	In-law	First cousin	Other male relative	Biological mother	Sister	First cousin	Other female relative	
1. *Very serious sexual abuse* Completed and attempted vaginal, oral, anal intercourse, cunnilingus, analingus, forced and unforced.***	7 26%	8 47%	0 —	6 24%	8 17%	2 22%	7 26%	7 32%	0 —	0 —	0 —	0 —	42 22%
2. *Serious sexual abuse* Completed and attempted genital fondling, simulated intercourse, digital penetration, forced and unforced.	9 33%	5 29%	3 27%	16 64%	14 29%	1 11%	15 56%	6 27%	1 —	3 —	1 —	3 —	76 41%
3. *Least serious sexual abuse* Completed and attempted acts of intentional sexual touching of buttocks, thigh, leg or other body part, clothed breasts or genitals, kissing, forced and unforced.	11 41%	4 24%	8 73%	3 12%	26 54%	6 67%	5 19%	9 41%	0 —	0 —	2 —	0 —	69 37%
Total	27	17	11	25	48	9	27	22	1	3	3	3	187

*8 cases of intrafamilial sexual abuse are excluded because of missing information on the age of the respondent at the time of the abuse.

**Categories of relatives where there were no incidents of sexual abuse are omitted.

***The term "force" includes physical force, threat of physical force, or inability to consent because of being unconscious, drugged, asleep, or in some other way totally physically helpless.

stepfathers (47%) *Very Serious* abuse was reported, as compared with 26% of biological fathers and a range of from 17% to 32% for other male relatives. In addition, since many more females are accessible to biological fathers than stepfathers, the fact that as many as 15 stepfathers (8% of all incestuous perpetrators) were reported by these women as compared with 27 biological fathers (15% of all incestuous perpetrators) confirms the widespread belief that stepfathers are more likely to abuse their daughters than biological fathers.

Table 2.5 also reveals that when intrafamilial sexual abuse occurs within the same generation, the *Least Serious* incidents are much less likely to be reported. Only 12% of the incidents with brothers and 19% with first cousins involved abuse at this level, as compared with 73% of the incidents with grandfathers and 54% with uncles. It may be that even relatively mild experiences will be remembered because they are more disturbing when they are cross-generational than when they are not. Or it could be that the incest taboo is weaker for brothers and cousins, so that, like stepfathers, they are more likely to engage in more seriously abusive behavior if they so desire.

Seriousness of Extrafamilial Child Sexual Abuse

When the same differentiation is made between the *Very Serious, Serious,* and *Least Serious* incidents of extrafamilial child sexual abuse, 53% (243) were classified as *Very Serious,* 27% (125) as *Serious,* and 20% (93) as *Least Serious* (see Table 2.6). When these percentages are compared with those reported for intrafamilial child sexual abuse, it is apparent that children who are sexually abused outside the family are abused in a significantly more serious manner. It may be that the incest taboo, though frequently violated, serves to restrain those who abuse their relatives. Or it may be a consequence of our methodology, since from the ages of 14 to 17 only incidents of rape and attempted rape are included for extrafamilial child sexual abuse. Also, more minor episodes of sexual contact were included for relatives.

Table 2.6 reveals that authority figures are by far the most likely perpetrators to engage in the less serious kinds of sexual abuse. Only 25% of them were involved in *Very Serious* sexual abuse as compared with 90% of dates, 88% of boyfriends/lovers, 73% of strangers, 72% of acquaintances, 70% of friends of the respondent, and 50% of friends of the family.

Reporting to the Police

Only 4 cases (2%) of intrafamilial child sexual abuse and only 26 cases (6%) of extrafamilial child sexual abuse were ever reported to the police. These extremely low figures provide powerful evidence that reported cases are only the very tip of the iceberg. This finding is all the more alarming when we see

TABLE 2.6 Seriousness of Extrafamilial Child Sexual Abuse by Relationship with the Perpetrator (under 18 Years)

	Male perpetrator							Female perpetrator*			
	Stranger	Acquaintance	Friend of family	Friend of resp.	Date	Boyfriend, lover	Authority figure	Acquaintance	Friend of resp.	Authority figure	Total
1. *Very serious sexual abuse* Completed and attempted vaginal, oral, anal intercourse, cunnilingus, forced and unforced.**	37 73%	54 72%	10 50%	30 70%	36 90%	29 88%	45 25%	0 —	2 —	0 —	243 53%
2. *Serious sexual abuse* Completed and attempted genital fondling, simulated intercourse, digital penetration, forced and unforced.	7 14%	7 9%	7 35%	7 16%	3 7%	3 9%	80 44%	1 —	4 —	6 —	125 27%
3. *Least serious sexual abuse* Completed and attempted acts of intentional sexual touching of clothed breasts or genitals, forced and unforced.	7 14%	14 19%	3 15%	6 14%	1 3%	1 3%	57 31%	3 —	1 —	0 —	93 20%
Total	51	75	20	43	40	33	182	4	7	6	461

*Categories of perpetrators where there were no incidents of sexual abuse are omitted.
**The term force includes physical force, threat of physical force, or inability to consent because of being unconscious, drugged, asleep, or in some other way totally physically helpless.

in addition that in 32% of the cases of intrafamilial child sexual abuse, the respondent reported that the perpetrator had also sexually abused one or more other relative (16% of the respondents said they did not know if this had occurred, and 53% said that another relative had *not* been sexually abused by the person who abused them).[7]

Comparisons with Other Studies

Since Finkelhor's research on the sexual abuse of children was also based on survey data—albeit a population of students who were not randomly selected—his findings regarding those who abuse their young female relatives are the most comparable with ours (1979). In terms of prevalence, Finkelhor stated that 26% of the students surveyed reported a sexual experience with a relative, as compared with only 16% who reported a childhood sexual experience with an older person. The latter experiences included both intrafamilial and extrafamilial child sexual abuse. It will be remembered that our notion of child sexual abuse was not limited to child–adult contacts. With regard to incestuous abuse, our prevalence rate of 16% for females 17 years and under is substantially lower than Finkelhor's. This difference is partially due to his not applying any age limit in cases of incest.

In general, it is apparent that far more cross-generational intrafamilial child sexual abuse was reported in our survey than in Finkelhor's. If we exclude the categories of "other" male and female relatives, since generation is not self-evident for them, then 60% of the intrafamilial child sexual abuse in our survey is cross-generational, as compared with only 14% in Finkelhor's study. More specifically, 24% of the perpetrators of intrafamilial sexual abuse in our San Francisco survey were fathers (including stepfathers, 1 adoptive, and 1 foster father) and 26% were uncles as compared with only 4% fathers and 9% uncles in Finkelhor's sample.

One striking similarity is that no aunts were reported as sexually abusive in either study, and only one mother in both studies. In general, there was a minority of female abusers in both studies. However, in our survey there were only 10 cases of female abusers (5% of all abusers) compared with 35 cases (19%) reported by Finkelhor.

One reason for the very large disparities in the findings of our survey and Finkelhor's is that his definition of what constitutes incest is much broader than ours. For example, he included "an invitation to do something sexual"; "other people showing his/her sexual organs to you"; and "you showing your sex organs to other person" (Finkelhor, 1979, p. 178). Only experiences that involved some direct physical contact or attempted contact qualified as

---

[7]These figures add to 101% because of rounding to the nearest whole number.

incestuous abuse in our study. Second, Finkelhor did not differentiate between abusive and nonabusive experiences. Experiences that do not involve
actual sexual contact are much more likely to be nonabusive, particularly
when they occur between peers. Finally, some of the differences in the
findings of these two surveys may also have occurred because women may
be less likely to disclose the more taboo experiences of father–daughter
and other cross-generational incestuous abuse on a self-administered
questionnaire completed in a classroom situation, as was required by
Finkelhor's methodology, than in a face-to-face interview with well trained
interviewers who have had an opportunity to build good rapport with
the respondent.

Another dramatic difference between the findings of our representative
survey and other non-representative surveys is that while only 11% of the
perpetrators of child sexual abuse in our sample were total strangers, this
figure is much lower than the 24% reported by Finkelhor (1979), the 58%
reported by Gagnon (1965), and the 65% reported by Landis (1956). Similarly, 60% of these perpetrators in our sample were neither total strangers
nor related, compared with 26% in Gagnon's study, and 33% in Finkelhor's.

One explanation for these differences may be that our survey tapped into
more of the types of experiences that are usually never detected or divulged,
including those not volunteered to agencies or researchers.

SUMMARY, CONCLUSION, AND IMPLICATIONS

Although we can be virtually certain that some of our probability sample of
930 women were unwilling to disclose experiences of child sexual abuse, and
although it seems reasonable to assume that there may be a significant
number of women who have repressed such experiences from their conscious memories, and despite the fact that the definitions used in our study
were narrower than those used in other major surveys, astonishingly high
rates of child sexual abuse were nevertheless disclosed. One of the reasons
for this uncommonly high disclosure is undoubtedly due to the methodology
employed, for example, the use of female interviewers only, the careful
selection of the interviewers, the inclusion of training sessions to sensitize
them to the issue of child sexual abuse, the creation of an interview schedule
that facilitated the development of effective rapport before broaching the
topic, and the multiplicity of questions asked.

Finkelhor commented on his estimate of a one percent prevalence rate of
father–daughter incest as follows:

> One percent may seem to be a small figure, but if it is an accurate estimate, it
> means that approximately three-quarters of a million women eighteen and over

in the general population have had such an experience, and that another 16,000 cases are added each year from among the group of girls aged five to seventeen. (Finkelhor, 1979, p. 88)

In fact, the rate of father–daughter incestuous abuse reported in our survey is close to 5 times higher than Finkelhor's 1% estimate. The rate of other intrafamilial and extrafamilial child sexual abuse is similarly very much higher than any prior study had led us to believe. More specifically: (1) Sixteen percent of the sample of 930 women reported at least one experience of intrafamilial sexual abuse before the age of 18 years, and 12% reported at least one such experience before the age of 14 years; (2) thirty-one percent reported at least one experience of extrafamilial sexual abuse before the age of 18 years, and 20% reported at least one such experience before the age of 14 years; (3) when both categories of sexual abuse are combined, 38% reported at least one experience before the age of 18 years, and 28% reported at least one such experience before the age of 14 years.

These alarming prevalence rates are based on the first probability sample survey ever conducted on this subject. Although the study was undertaken in the city of San Francisco, there is no reason to believe that the sexual abuse of female children would be any more prevalent there than in other cities of comparable size. Assuming that the findings are indicative of the prevalence of child sexual abuse in other areas, this means that over one-quarter of the population of female children has experienced sexual abuse before the age of 14, and well over one-third have had such an experience by the age of 18 years. Furthermore, this study confirms the fact that only a minute percentage of cases ever get reported to the police (2% of intrafamilial and 6% of extrafamilial child sexual abuse cases). It is imperative that the magnitude of this problem in the United States be addressed, and it is urgent that more effective preventive strategies be developed and implemented.

REFERENCES

Ferracuti, F. (1972). Incest between father and daughter. In H. L. P. Resnick & M. L. Wolfgang (Eds.), *Sexual behaviors* (pp. 169–183). Boston: Little, Brown.

Finkelhor, D. (1979). *Sexually victimized children.* New York: Free Press.

Gagnon, J. (1965). Female child victims of sex offenses. *Social Problems, 13,* 176–192.

Herman, J. (1981). *Father–daughter incest.* Cambridge, MA: Harvard University Press.

Hite, S. (1976). *The Hite report: A nationwide study of female sexuality.* New York: Dell.

Kinsey, A. C., Pomeroy, W. B., Martin, C. E., & Gebhard, P. H. (1953). *Sexual behavior in the human female.* Philadelphia: Saunders.

Landis, J. T. (1956). Experience of 500 children with adult's sexual deviance. *Psychiatric Quarterly Supplement, 30,* 91–109.

Masters, W. H., & Johnson, V. (1966). *Human sexual response.* Boston: Little, Brown.

Meiselman, K. C. (1978). *Incest.* San Francisco: Jossey-Bass.

Mrazek, P. B., & Kempe, C. H. (Eds.). (1981). *Sexually abused children and their families.* New York: Pergamon.

National Center on Child Abuse and Neglect. (1981). *Study findings: National study of the incidence and severity of child abuse and neglect* (DHHS Publication No. OHDS 81-30325) (pp. 4–5). Washington, DC: U.S. Government Printing Office.

Public Education and Research Committee of California. (1973). *Sex code of California: A compendium.* Sausalito, CA: Graphic Arts of Marin.

Russell, D. E. H. (1986). *The Secret Trauma: Incest in the Lives of Girls and Women.* New York: Basic Books.

Weinberg, S. K. (1976). *Incest behavior.* (Revision of 1955 ed.) Seacaucus, NJ: Citadel.

3

The Psychoanalytic Legacy: From Whence We Come

Hannah Lerman

FREUD'S STARTING POINT

Clinical workers often forget that the original theory proposed by Sigmund Freud claimed the origin of neurosis to be premature sexual exposure in childhood (Freud, 1896/1962c). We have recently been reminded of that fact by the publicity around the work of Masson (1984). The original view actually was held by Freud only for a short period before he began to indicate that such sexual activity was more likely to be fantasized by children; instead, if sexual activity did occur in childhood, Freud later said that it occurred mainly with other children and was of relatively little psychological significance (Freud, 1924/1959). Freud's inability to stay with his original theoretical position, which many are coming to view as having been more accurate, may be seen as typical of our society's general inability to accept the empirical reality of the sexual abuse of children.

After Freud abandoned his belief in the adult seduction of children, he substituted for them sexual fantasies that the child found conflictual, usually fantasies involving the parents, as the theoretical nucleus for subsequent neurosis. At an even later stage, after Freud had fully developed his theory of the psychosexual development of women, he further suggested that the fantasied first seducer of both male and female children was the mother and that the triggering stimulus for these fantasies was her cleaning of the children's genital areas (Freud, 1932/1964a; 1938/1964b). Actual sexual activities of adults toward children, especially those of adult males, had completely been eliminated from any theoretical consideration.

Studying the progression—from actual childhood sexual abuse as the theoretical cause of neuroses to the later interpretation that what Freud heard from his patients were their fantasied wishes toward their parents—would simply be an interesting historical exercise in esoterica if the change did not have continuing implications for our psychological world view today. Most clinical practice in evaluating and treating child sexual assault victims has been directly influenced by what now appears to be theoretical distortion introduced by the intrusion of Freud's own personal issues. To delete this bias from our practice, we must have a clearer understanding of how it got there.

To understand the relationship of Freudian theory to our current ideas about childhood sexual abuse, the unfolding of Freud's step-by-step progress through the development of the original hypothesis and the transition into his later theoretical position is informative. We are fortunate in now having available to us the complete letters of Freud to Wilheim Fliess, his intimate confidant during the period when these ideas were evolving (Masson, 1985). The articles Freud was publishing in the late 1890s and early 1900s presented his current and developing theory as it existed at any fixed moment without reference to his preceding thoughts, motives, or doubts. His papers were illustrated by case material, the details of which we learn (mostly from the letters to Fliess) to have been deliberately distorted. It is only in the letters that the passage from one theory to another is recorded along with the hesitations, the backtracking, and the confession of the nature of the distortions in the printed work and of their rationale.

Studies in Hysteria by Freud and Josef Breuer, which appeared in 1895 (Breuer & Freud, 1893–1895/1965), was the first large-scale presentation of the theory that the origin of hysterical neurosis was in actual sexual behavior in childhood, although Freud's 1894 paper "The Neuro-Psychoses of Defense" (Freud, 1894/1962d) had presented the theory more clearly. The very clearest statement of this early point of view about the determinants of hysteria, however, was in Freud's 1896 paper, "Heredity and the Aetiology of the Neuroses":

The event of which the subject has retained an unconscious memory is *a precocious experience of sexual relations with actual excitement of the genitals, resulting from sexual abuse committed by another person;* and *the period of life* at which this fatal event takes place is *earliest youth*—the years up to the age of eight to ten, before the child has reached sexual maturity. (Freud, 1896/1962c, p. 152)

In "The Aetiology of Hysteria," also written in 1896, Freud went further in his elaboration of the phenomenon of sexual abuse of young children:

It seems to me certain that our children are far more often exposed to sexual assaults than the few precautions taken in this connection would lead us to expect. When I first made enquiries [sic] about what was known on the subject, I learnt from colleagues that there are several publications by paediatricians [sic] which stigmatize the frequency of sexual practices by nurses and nursery maids, carried out even in infants in arms; and in the last few weeks I have come across a discussion of "Coitus in Childhood" by Dr. Stekel (1895) [Freud's reference, not this author's] in Vienna. I have not had time to collect other published evidence; but even if it were only scanty, it is expected that increased attention to the subject will very soon confirm the great frequency of sexual experiences and sexual activity in childhood. (Freud, 1896/1962a, p. 206)

When Freud described cases in his published articles, the perpetrators of the sexual activity were frequently identified, as in the above, as female servants. In "Further Remarks on the Neuro-Psychoses of Defence," Freud indicated that:

Foremost among those guilty of abuses like these, with their momentous consequences, are nursemaids, governesses and domestic servants, to whose care children are only thoughtlessly entrusted; teachers, moreover, figure with regrettable frequency. (Freud, 1896/1962b, p. 194)

In the published material, Freud, however, omitted mention of what he told Fliess in the same year:

The essential point of hysteria is that it results from *perversion* on the part of the seducer, and *more and more* that heredity is seduction by the father. (Masson, 1985, page 212)

Freud later indicated that he changed the identity of the seducer in two cases described in *Studies in Hysteria* so as not to implicate the father in the case. At the very same time, he was continuing to describe case material to Fliess in which the one involved was the father (Masson, 1985, p. 238).

In his letters to Fliess, Freud expressed his doubts about attributing the genesis of neurosis entirely to the father. Nowhere in any of the articles published during this period is such doubt even mentioned. In one significant letter, Freud described and interpreted a dream about his daughter, attributing its meaning to his theoretical concerns:

Recently I dreamed of overaffectionate feelings for Mathilde, only she was called Hella; and afterward I again saw "Hella" before me, printed in heavy type. Solution: Hella is the name of an American niece whose picture we have been sent.

Mathilde could be called Hella because she recently shed bitter tears over the defeats of the Greeks. She is enthralled by the mythology of ancient Hellas and naturally regards all Hellenes as heroes. The dream of course shows the fulfillment of my wish to catch a *Pater* as the originator of neurosis and thus puts an end to my ever-recurring doubts. (Masson, 1985, p. 249)

Very soon after this dream report about feelings toward his eldest daughter, Freud repudiated the seduction theory of the origin of neurosis. This was also in a letter to Fliess. Not until considerably later, however, did the actual shift appear in his published work. The direction of his thinking in the letter in which he discussed this raises further questions about the psychological meaning to Freud himself of this shift. He came to suggest that the actual occurrence of sexual activity could not be as frequent as it would have to be to explain the incidence of hysteria:

And now I want to confide in you immediately the great secret that has been slowly dawning on me in the last few months. I no longer believe in my *neurotica*. This is probably not intelligible without an explanation; after all, you yourself found credible what I was able to tell you. So I will begin historically [and tell you—Masson's addendum] where the reasons for disbelief came from. The continual disappointment in my efforts to bring a single analysis to a real conclusion; the running away of people who for a period of time had been most gripped; the absence of the complete successes on which I had counted; the possibility of explaining to myself the partial successes in other ways, in the usual fashion—this was the first group. Then the surprise that in all cases, the *father*, not excluding my own, had to be accused of being perverse—the realization of the unexpected frequency of hysteria, with precisely the same conditions prevailing in each, whereas surely such widespread perversions against children are not very probable. The [incidence—Masson's addendum] of perversion would have to be immeasurably more frequent than the [resulting—Masson's addendum] hysteria because the illness, after all, occurs only where there has been an accumulation of events and there is a contributory factor that weakens the defense. Then, third, the certain insight that there are no indications of reality in the unconscious, so that one cannot distinguish between truth and fiction that has been cathected with affect. (Accordingly, there would remain the solution that the sexual fantasy invariably seizes upon the theme of the parents.) Fourth, the consideration that in the most deep-reaching psychosis the unconscious memory does not break through, so that the secret of childhood experiences is not disclosed even in the most confused delirium. If one thus sees that the unconscious never overcomes the resistance of the conscious, the expectation that in treatment the opposite is bound to happen, to the point where the unconscious is completely tamed by the conscious, also diminishes.

I was so far influenced [by this—Masson's addendum] that I was ready to give up two things: the complete resolution of a neurosis and the certain knowledge of its etiology in childhood. (Masson, 1985, pp. 264–265)

The phrase "not excluding my own," which was omitted from the very first published volume of these letters (Bonaparte, Freud, & Kris, 1954), refers to neurotic symptomatology demonstrated by Freud's brother and sisters. According to Freud's theory at this time, Freud's father would have to be labeled a seducer and a pervert.

Although Freud wrote this crucial letter in 1897, it was not until 1905 that he publicly repudiated his previous theory. The complete letters to Wilheim Fliess reveal somewhat more vacillation between the two positions than has previously been public knowledge. Even after the letter quoted above, Freud is seen as being sometimes more and sometimes less accepting of the seduction hypothesis, and of its reverse, that children's fantasies are the major issue. The letters also tell us that Freud's former patient, Emma Eckstein, was practicing then as an analyst (the very first we know of after Freud himself), and was verifying the seduction hypothesis with a patient of hers while Freud was in the process of giving it up (Masson, 1985).

When Freud came to publish his altered views, he indicated that:

I have learned to explain a number of phantasies of seductions as attempts at fending off memories of the subject's *own* sexual activity [infantile masturbation]." [Freud's italics] (Freud, 1905/1953b, p. 274)

Later, in "An Autobiographical Study", in reporting on this period he revealed:

When, however, I was at last obliged to recognize that these scenes of seduction had never taken place, and that they were only phantasies which my patients had made up or which I myself had perhaps forced on them, I was for some time completely at a loss. . . . When I had pulled myself together, I was able to draw the right conclusions from my discovery: namely, that the neurotic symptoms were not related directly to actual events but to wishful phantasies, and that as far as the neurosis was concerned psychical reality was of more importance than material reality. I do not believe even now that I forced the seduction-phantasies on my patients, that I "suggested" them. I had in fact stumbled for the first time upon the *Oedipus complex,* which was later to assume such an overwhelming importance, but which I did not recognize as yet in its disguise of phantasy. Moreover, seduction during childhood retained a certain share, though a humbler one, in the aetiology of neuroses. But the seducers turned out as a rule to have been older children. [Freud's italics] (Freud, 1924/1959, p. 35)

Few today would venture to say that adults never fantasize sexual activities as having occurred with their parents when they were children. The point here is the shift from "always" to "never." It is impossible to relate Freud's switch here to any body of data. In the early days of his psychotherapeutic work, Freud sought and often obtained verification about adult patients' childhood sexual traumas from relatives and surviving servants. What happened to that verification information? Freud never dealt with that information again nor explained how he could have gotten patients' associates to verify what he was now calling fantasy and untrue.

FREUD'S MOTIVES FOR THE THEORETICAL SHIFT

Because of the impact his theories have had upon our world, exploration into the motivations of Sigmund Freud has become a prominent intellectual endeavor, both within and outside the psychoanalytic world. Everyone wants to know what influenced his ideas. Various explanations have been offered for Freud's shift from his original theoretical position to the view that the seductions reported to him were most often fantasy and that neurosis originated in psychic conflict about sexual impulses, primarily toward the parent of one's opposite sex.

The generally accepted view within psychoanalytic circles is that when Freud began his self-analysis, he discovered sexual wishes in himself toward his mother, accepted these as being universal, and felt that he had allowed himself to be misled into thinking that his patients' fantasies of sexuality with adults (usually fathers, as has been indicated) were reality.

The shift from the expectation that

increased attention to the subject will very soon confirm the great frequency of sexual experiences and sexual activity in childhood (Freud, 1896/1962a, p. 207)

to

such widespread perversions toward children are not very probable (Masson, 1985, p. 264)

had to have been made on internal bases, that is, Freud's own conceptualization of the nature of events, without any reference to any externally ascertainable information. The time between the two statements is 1 year.

Kris (1954, pp. 33–34), in his commentary on the earlier published version of the letters to Fliess in *The Origins of Psychoanalysis,* expressed the psychoanalytic consensus in attributing the shift in thought to the process of Freud's own self-analysis. Minimal interpretation of the letter that reported Freud's dream about his daughter suggests that this might well have been so, but for reasons opposite to those implied by Kris. Kris implies that it was the success of Freud's self-analysis that led him to make the change. It is just as possible to postulate the reverse, that blocks and resistances created the attitudinal change and subsequent theoretical shift. Freud obviously ignored or was unaware of the possibility of the dream's revealing any real "over-affectionate" feelings on his part toward Mathilde. This possibility should be apparent to any modern reader, especially one versed at all in psychoanalytic styles of interpretation. We also see in the letter describing his abandonment of his earlier position that he also had difficulty with the idea that his own father would be implicated by the logic of his original theoretical position. Even many knowledgeable persons may not realize that, after Freud had altered his theory and decided that conflictual sexual feelings (particularly in the Oedipal period) rather than actual sexual activity were the source of neurosis, he never again anywhere in his voluminous writings dealt with the sexuality of adult males toward children! Surely his own feelings had to have played a part in that significant gap in his psychoanalytic theory, considering that he focused so much attention on the other dyadic possibilities (Lerman, 1986). The present author is not alone in suggesting such motivations.

Florence Rush (1977, 1980) had elaborated on this very point but it was not prominent in the public eye until the work of Masson (1984) appeared. Masson expanded this view about Freud's theoretical shift and related it further to Freud's emotional relationship to Wilheim Fliess. Masson sees Freud's unwillingness to give up his idealized view of his friend in the face of clear evidence of ineptitude in an operation by Fliess upon Freud's patient, the same Emma Eckstein previously referred to, as related to Freud's abandonment of the seduction hypothesis. Masson suggests intellectual dishonesty, rather than purely internal personal emotional dishonesty and lack of moral courage, in the shift of viewpoint. He points to evidence of Freud's having been aware of the work of earlier French forensic physicians who reported the physical consequences of sexual violence toward children, information apparently gained during Freud's stay in Paris in 1885 but which was not widely known in Vienna. As another significant factor, Masson comments upon the professional isolation involved in Freud's maintaining his original position. Masson also speaks to the vested interest of later psychoanalysis in maintaining the Oedipal theory as the linchpin of psychoanalytic theory and therefore being unwilling to reconsider Freud's earlier view. As an example of this, Masson quotes Anna Freud's letter to him in which she said:

> Keeping up the seduction theory would mean to abandon the Oedipus complex, and with it the whole importance of phantasy life, conscious or unconscious phantasy. In fact, I think there would have been no psychoanalysis afterwards. (Masson, 1984, p. 113)

THE PSYCHOANALYTIC LEGACY

In his later discussions of incest (psychological, i.e., fantasied), Freud primarily focused upon the mother–son combination. He viewed the situation mainly from the son's perspective, although he occasionally also suggested the sexual significance that the boy's phallus had to the mother. When the total body of Freud's work is examined, the psychological mechanisms dealing with male parental sexual behavior stand out sharply by virtue of their absence, particularly because we know that the largest proportion of incest experiences occur between fathers or father surrogates and daughters—not between mothers and sons, a fact as true in his time as in our own.

Researchers and therapists both often find what they expect to find. This truism is now well supported empirically (Rosenthal, 1969; Rosenthal & Rubin, 1978). If we choose to look, we can find it operating in Freud's own accounts wherein, when he believed in the prevalence of childhood seduction, he found much evidence to support it, and, when he no longer believed in it, he no longer found it to exist. It is highly probable that the questions Freud asked his patients changed during these two periods and that the depth of inquiry into content that led in this direction might also have changed, all without Freud himself necessarily being aware of changes in his own process and procedures.

One of the first results of this significant theoretical shift was that Freud began to disbelieve what his patients, particularly his women patients, told him. When Freud became convinced, at the point of transition in his theory, that infantile seduction by the father was factually rare, he then easily discounted the verbal accounts of his women patients who told him that precisely this had actually occurred to them. His process of therapy came, therefore, to incorporate interpretations designed to convince these women that their memories were fantasies and that *in all cases* they were the results of their childish Oedipal longings for their fathers.

There are indications in case notes written even earlier of Freud's imposing his views upon his patients. These instances were intermixed with occasional expressions of concern about whether or not he had pushed the patients. Freud usually followed expression of such doubts by concluding that his influence was not significant in determining the direction of the patients' verbal accounts.

In 1896, he explained that memories of sexual scenes were not forced by the physician:

> Is it not very possible . . . that the physician forces such scenes upon his docile patients, alleging that they are memories, or else that the patients tell the physician things which they have deliberately invented or have imagined and that he accepts those things as true? . . . Doubts about the genuineness of the infantile sexual scenes can, however be deprived of their force here and now by more

than one argument . . . the behavior of patients while they are reproducing these infantile experiences is in every respect incompatible with the assumption that the scenes are anything else than a reality which is being felt with distress and reproduced with the greatest reluctance. Before they come for analysis the patients know nothing about these scenes. They are indignant as a rule if we warn them that such scenes are going to emerge. Only the strongest compulsion of the treatment can induce them to embark on a reproduction of them. While they are recalling these infantile experiences to consciousness, they suffer under the most violent sensations, of which they are ashamed and which they try to conceal; and, even after they have gone through them once more in such a convincing manner, they still attempt to withhold belief from them, by emphasizing the fact that, unlike what happens in the case of other forgotten material, they have no feeling of remembering the scenes. (Freud, 1896/1962a, p. 204)

Once he had changed his theory, he was equally adamant about his view of the new theoretical perspective as correct. When the patient known as Dora rejected his interpretations about her infantile love of her father, he said:

My expectations were by no means disappointed when this explanation of mine was met by Dora with a most emphatic negative. The "No" uttered by a patient after a repressed thought has been presented to his conscious perception for the first time does no more than register the existence of a repression and its severity; it acts, as it were, as a gauge of the repression's strength. If this "No," instead of being regarded as the expression of an impartial judgment (of which, indeed, the patient is incapable), is ignored, and if work is continued, the first evidence soon begins to appear that in such a case "No" signifies the desired "Yes." (Freud, 1905/1953a, p. 58)

This view of the analyst–patient relationship was consistently maintained in Freud's later writings. For example, in 1912, he wrote:

Where there is a dispute with the patient as to whether or how he has said some particular thing, the doctor is usually in the right. (Freud, 1912/1958, p. 113)

And in 1916:

Nothing takes place in a psycho-analytic treatment but an interchange of words between the patient and the analyst. The patient talks, tells of his past experiences and present impressions, complains, confesses to his wishes and his emotional impulses. The doctor listens, tries to direct the patient's processes of thought, exhorts, forces his attention in certain directions, gives him explanations and observes the reactions of understanding or rejection which he in this way provokes in him. (Freud, 1916/1963, p. 17)

In "An Autobiographical Study" in 1924, Freud returned to the question of whether he had forced the seduction fantasies on patients at the earlier period and answered it in the negative (Freud, 1924/1959). The question of the role of suggestion in Freud's therapeutic work has been a continuing sore point for psychoanalysis and continues to be debated to this day both in the psychoanalytic literature and in critiques of psychoanalysis (cf. Collins, 1980; Sadow et al., 1968). That Freud exerted psychological pressure on his patients both before and after the abandonment of the seduction hypothesis seems evident to an informed outsider. This then cannot in itself be used to invalidate the reality and effects of sexual abuse. Freud's general negative attitude toward women can be well documented, however (Lerman, 1986). His disbelief in the reports of his women patients, especially after the development of the Oedipal theory, is clear. There is no comparable evidence that Freud came to disbelieve equally the reports of his male patients about their infantile sexual experiences (Freud, 1909/1955a; 1918/1955b), although his later theoretical structure did not focus upon these experiences either.

Freud's assumption, reinforced when he shifted to the Oedipal theory, was that he knew more about the origins of the psychological distress of his patients than they themselves did. This knowledge extended so far as to include the actual contents of their early experiences. His manner of reconstructing the childhood of his patients required the introduction of still other assumptions. His concept of patient resistance came to coincide (in effect) with patients' disagreements with the assumptions and interpretations he had introduced. Although less case material is available to us from his later years due to the end of the kind of intimacy revealed in the correspondence with Fliess, the examples above nevertheless provide ample illustration from Freud's later writings of his need to coerce, persuade, and convince his patients of the rightness of his interpretations.

In 1924, describing the general social resistance to psychoanalysis, Freud made the analogy between society at large and the situation in therapy but suggested that, within the analytic relationship with patients, persuasion or its like was more likely:

> It is possible . . . by patient work to convince these latter individuals that *everything* [italics added] happened as we maintained it did; we had not invented it ourselves but had arrived at it from a study of other neurotics covering a period of twenty or thirty years. (Freud, 1924/1961, p. 221).

This passage is similar to others in illustrating Freud's perspective and his unwillingness to let his patients speak for themselves.

Understandably, the formulator of an innovative theory and approach to psychological problems can be expected to believe in his system. The fact of this belief and its impact, on his colleagues but particularly on his patients, is the significant issue. Since Freud's followers emulated the master and perpetuated his dogmatic style as well as the content of the theory and the psychotherapeutic method he propounded, his process has achieved even greater significance. The message that the analyst knows better than the patient, particularly when the patient is female, and that this knowledge includes not only what the patient is experiencing, but also the real content of the past experiences, has certainly remained within the system. This attitude consistently conveys to the female patient that she is resistive, incompetent, highly neurotic, and frequently a liar as well. It also connotes all the other negative messages Freud built into his theory itself about the nature of women (Lerman, 1986). When one's experiences are discounted, one's being itself is invalidated. This has been a major part of the psychoanalytic legacy for women who looked toward psychoanalysis as a potential mode of relief from the effects of their childhood experiences. If we ask why women accepted this message, we only have to look at the difficulty of many women even today, in a somewhat more egalitarian time, in accepting their own views as valid when faced with the opposing views of someone (usually male) whom they have been taught to view as expert. Psychoanalysts, starting with Freud, have also taught their truth about other aspects of psychological experience to women.

The idea that the achievement of vaginal orgasm was a valid measure of psychic maturity lasted until the start of the current women's movement and new research that documented the existence of clitoral orgasms. It provides another concrete example of the general point that is being made: therapists armed with psychoanalytic theory have caused women to disbelieve themselves and push themselves into what they were being told was the appropriate psychological mold. Given the acceptance of many Freudian tenets into everyday psychology, it has been very easy for therapists who were not trained psychoanalysts to follow the psychoanalysts in disbelieving what the women they treated told them. This disbelief of women's account of their psychological lives has led to many erroneous diagnoses and poor treatment (cf. Chesler, 1972) and eventually to a new psychology of women, Feminist Therapy, which begins with a prime belief in and acceptance of women's own knowledge of their own experiences (Rosewater & Walker, 1985).

Psychoanalytic theory includes many psychological implications relating to the Oedipal concept that cannot be elaborated in this paper (cf. Lerman, 1986). They include the proposition that the process of sexual identification, which is seen as a result of the resolution of Oedipal issues, is more difficult for females than for males. This has been one of the aspects of the theory that the research literature pertaining to psychoanalytic theory has been able to focus upon. Sherman (1971), for example, after reviewing the literature, concluded that there was very little evidence for the female Oedipal complex, although she also indicated that the question had not been adequately studied. More studies, instead, emphasized the significance of the mother–daughter relationship in the development of the girl child. In fact, some psychologists are extrapolating further from the mother–child bonds and sometimes suggest that men's mental health difficulties come from being *the other* in that relationship and their need to struggle to define themselves as separate.

Fisher and Greenberg (1977) found some evidence supporting Freud's ideas about identification with the same-sex parent, but also found that most of the hypotheses bearing upon Oedipally linked sex difference have not received any appreciable support. The Freudian idea that girls have an extra psychic task to perform, and hence greater difficulty, in achieving heterosexual adaptation was actually contradicted by the empirical literature that was reviewed. Fisher and Greenberg's conclusion was that the female had less rather than more difficulty than the male during the process of sex role identification. On the other hand, Kline (1981) found sufficient empirical evidence for him to conclude that there was support for the general concept of the Oedipus complex. He questioned the inclusion of some of the data that Fisher and Greenberg considered relevant and also pointed out the complexity of the concept of the Oedipus complex. He did not, however, address the question of the purported universality of the Oedipus complex nor deal specifically with hypotheses that could be derived from psychoanalytic theory about females. All three of these reviews of the psychoanalytical research literature, although they date variously from 1971 through 1981, cover quite similar research material because empirical validation of psychoanalytic hypotheses seems to have fallen out of favor as a research endeavor and very little additional such research has been done in recent years.

Despite a literature that has burgeoned over the past 15 years and that has documented the experiences Freud discarded, even today a survey of psychotherapists would probably still show greater acceptance of the Oedipal hypothesis for their women patients than acceptance of the reality of women who describe the incest experiences perpetuated upon them by fathers, stepfathers, uncles, grandfathers, brothers, and other adult males within and outside their childhood family circles. Some eyes remain closed to anything outside the very narrow circumference of the psychoanalytic literature.

Mental health workers, like the rest of the world, retain an investment in that which they have previously learned. Because of the large literature, some of which has focused upon the abuses to which psychoanalytic interpretation have been put (American Psychological Association, 1975), another large group of therapists would probably accept both the reality and the Oedipal fantasy as operative possibilities for psychological difficulty despite the research literature that finds little if any verification of the Oedipal theory as it is applied to women. They accept the new uneasily, but cannot yet discard the old.

When clinical cases are discussed in training, supervision, case conferences, and the like, Oedipus is still being evoked for women as well as for men despite the lack of research support for it as a concept viable for females.

Within the psychoanalytic literature, there has until recently been barely a reference that has even suggested the possibility that childhood seduction of children by adults who are significant in their lives does in fact occur. The major writer here is Alice Miller (1984). She is almost the first person from within the psychoanalytic camp who has proffered what is being suggested here, that Freud's Oedipal theory has supported the silence with which society has wished to surround the existence of childhood sexual abuse.

The question of the extent and frequency of parent–child (and most usually, father–daughter) incest as well as its actual psychological impact in both Freud's day and our own is open. Available statistics are far from adequate but probably reflect underestimations of the extent of this phenomena rather than the reverse, because of the problems involved in discovering the incidence—such as failure to report to authorities outside the home because of fear of disbelief and ridicule, the collusion of the mother to protect her security by ignoring what signs she may see and disbelieving and rejecting the daughter should she speak of it, among others (Karpman, 1954). There has been a growing awareness of the issue and an increased attempt to gather statistical data in recent years (Finkelhor, 1979; Russell, 1983). We also have a provocative, although preliminary, report that 50% of a group of psychiatric patients of both sexes had a childhood history of physical and/or sexual abuse (Carmen, Rieker, & Mills, 1984). This, of course, needs to be followed up by further study, but it supports the clinical impressions of many of us.

No one who has worked with individuals who are trying to move from the psychological state of having been incest victims to the more integrated psychological state of being incest survivors can ignore the traumatic impact, piled upon the original sexual trauma, of children being disbelieved by their parents or other significant adults in their lives. Not all of this can be laid at the feet of Freud and the later psychoanalysts—but much of it can.

The concept that children are sexual beings from birth has often been considered to be one of Freud's foremost contributions. Once seduction was eliminated from consideration by fiat, however, the theory dealt with sexuality only or primarily as a psychological reality for children (and *not* as a physical reality) and has totally ignored (where it did not actively contradict) any attempts to deal with the behavioral sexuality instigated by adults—the most overt aspects of sexuality that many children are likely to experience before adulthood. The current research and clinical work on childhood sexual abuse has had to push against the still prevailing viewpoint—perpetuated by the psychoanalysts but which has permeated our entire society until very recently—that Oedipal fantasies rather than childhood sexual trauma are the most likely events that cause most psychological distress amid the almost total absence of consideration of reality events over which the child had no control.

REFERENCES

American Psychological Association. (1975). Report of the task force on sex bias and sex role stereotyping in psychotherapeutic practice. *American Psychologist, 30,* 1169–1175.

Bonaparte, M., Freud, A., & Kris, E. (Eds.). (1954). (E. Mosbacher & J. Strachey, Trans.). *The origins of psycho-analysis: Letters to Wilhelm Fliess, drafts and notes: 1887– 1902 by Sigmund Freud.* New York: Basic Books.

Breuer, J., & Freud, S. (1965). Studies in hysteria. In J. Strachey (Ed. and Trans.), *The standard edition of the complete psychological works of Sigmund Freud* (Vol. 2, pp. 1–306). London: Hogarth Press. (Original work published 1893–1895.)

Carmen, E. H., Rieker, P. P., & Mills, T. (1984). Victims of violence and psychiatric illness. *American Journal of Psychiatry, 141*(3), 378–383.

Chesler, P. (1972). *Women and madness.* New York: Doubleday.

Collins, S. (1980). Freud and 'the riddle of suggestion'. *International Review of Psycho-Analysis, 7,* 429–437.

Finkelhor, D. (1979). *Sexually abused children.* New York: Free Press.

Fisher, S., & Greenberg, R. P. (1977). *The scientific credibility of Freud's theories and therapy.* New York: Basic Books.

Freud, S. (1953a). Fragment of an analysis of a case of hysteria. In J. Strachey (Ed. and Trans.), *The standard edition of the complete psychological works of Sigmund Freud* (Vol. 7, pp. 7–122). London: Hogarth Press. (Original work published 1905)

Freud, S. (1953b). My views on the part played by sexuality in the aetiology of the neuroses. In J. Strachey (Ed. and Trans.), *The standard edition of the complete psychological works of Sigmund Freud* (Vol. 7, pp. 271–279). London: Hogarth Press. (Original work published 1905)

Freud, S. (1955a). Analysis of a phobia in a five-year-old boy. In J. Strachey (Ed. and Trans.), *The standard edition of the complete psychological works of Sigmund Freud* (Vol. 10, pp. 5–149). London: Hogarth Press. (Original work published 1909)

Freud, S. (1955b). From the history of an infantile neurosis. In J. Strachey (Ed. and Trans.), *The standard edition of the complete psychological works of Sigmund Freud* (Vol. 17, pp. 7–122). London: Hogarth Press. (Original work published 1918)

Freud, S. (1958). Recommendations to physicians pratising psycho-analysis. In J. Strachey (Ed. and Trans.), *The standard edition of the complete psychological works of Sigmund Freud* (Vol. 12, pp. 111–120). London: Hogarth Press. (Original work published 1912)

Freud, S. (1959). An autobiographical study. In J. Strachey (Ed. and Trans.), *The standard edition of the complete psychological works of Sigmund Freud* (Vol. 20, pp. 7–74). London: Hogarth Press. (Original work published 1924)

Freud, S. (1961). The resistances of psycho-analysis. In J. Strachey (Ed. and Trans.), *The standard edition of the complete psychological works of Sigmund Freud* (Vol. 19, pp. 213–222). London: Hogarth Press. (Original work published 1924)

Freud, S. (1962a). The aetiology of hysteria. In J. Strachey (Ed. and Trans.), *The standard edition of the complete psychological works of Sigmund Freud* (Vol. 3, pp. 191–221). London: Hogarth Press. (Original work published 1896)

Freud, S. (1962b). Further remarks on the neuro-psychoses of defence. In J. Strachey (Ed. and Trans.), *The standard edition of the complete psychological works of Sigmund Freud* (Vol. 3, pp. 162–195). London: Hogarth Press. (Original work published 1896)

Freud, S. (1962c). Heredity and the aetiology of the neuroses. In J. Strachey (Ed. and Trans.), *The standard edition of the complete psychological works of Sigmund Freud* (Vol. 3, pp. 143–156). London: Hogarth Press. (Original work published 1896)

Freud, S. (1962d). The neuro-psychoses of defense. In J. Strachey (Ed. and Trans.), *The standard edition of the complete psychological works of Sigmund Freud* (Vol. 3, pp. 45–61). London: Hogarth Press. (Original work published 1894)

Freud, S. (1963). Introductory lectures on psycho-analysis. Parts I and II. In J. Strachey (Ed. and Trans.), *The standard edition of the complete psychological works of Sigmund Freud* (Vol. 15, pp. 15–239). London: Hogarth Press. (Original work published 1916)

Freud, S. (1964a). An outline of psycho-analysis. In J. Strachey (Ed. and Trans.), *The standard edition of the complete psychological works of Sigmund Freud* (Vol. 23, pp. 144–207). London: Hogarth Press. (Original work published 1938)

Freud, S. (1964b). New introductory lectures on psycho-analysis. In J. Strachey (Ed. and Trans.), *The standard edition of the complete psychological works of Sigmund Freud* (Vol. 22, pp. 5–182). London: Hogarth Press. (Original work published 1932)

Jones, E. (1953). *The life and work of Sigmund Freud* (Vol. 1). New York: Basic Books.

Karpman, B. (1954). *The sexual offender and his offenses: Etiology, pathology, psychodynamics and treatment.* New York: Julian Press.

Kline, P. (1981). *Fact and fantasy in Freudian theory* (2nd ed.). New York: Methuen.

Kris, E. (1954). Introduction. In M. Bonaparte, A. Freud, & E. Kris (Eds.) (Trans. by E. Mosbacher and J. Strachey), *The origins of psycho-analysis: letters to Wilheim Fliess, drafts and notes: 1887–1902 by Sigmund Freud* (pp. 3–47). New York: Basic Books.

Lerman, H. (1986). *A mote in Freud's eye: From psychoanalysis to the psychology of women.* New York: Springer Publishing Company.

Masson, J. M. (1984). *The assault on truth: Freud's suppression of the seduction theory.* New York: Farrar, Straus & Giroux.

Masson, J. M. (1985). (Ed. and Trans.). *The complete letters of Sigmund Freud to Wilheim Fliess 1887–1904.* Cambridge, MA: Belknap Press of Harvard University Press.

Miller, A. (1984). *Thou shalt not be aware: Society's betrayal of the child.* New York: Farrar, Straus & Giroux.

Rosewater, L. B., & Walker, L. (Eds.) (1985). *Handbook of feminist therapy: Women's issues in psychotherapy.* New York: Springer Publishing Company.

Rosenthal, R. (1969). Unintended effects of the clinician in clinical interaction: A taxonomy and a review of clinician expectancy effects. *Australian Journal of Psychology, 21* (1), 1–20.

Rosenthal, R., & Rubin, D. B. (1978). Interpersonal expectancy effects: The first 345 studies. *Behavioral and Brain Sciences, 1,* 377–415.

Rush, F. (1977). The Freudian cover-up: Sexual abuse of children. *Chrysalis, 1,* 31–45.

Rush, F. (1980). *The best kept secret: Sexual abuse of children.* Englewood Cliffs, NJ: Prentice-Hall.

Russell, D. E. H. (1983). The incidence and prevalence of intrafamilial and extrafamilial sexual abuse of female children. *Child Abuse and Neglect, 7,* 133–146.

Sadow, L., Gedo, J. E., Miller, J., Pollack, G., Sabshin, M., & Schlessinger, N. (1968). The process of hypothesis change in three early psychoanalytic concepts. *Journal of the American Psychoanalytic Association, 16,* 245–273.

Sherman, J. (1971). *On the psychology of women: A survey of empirical studies.* Springfield, IL: Charles C. Thomas.

PART II
Impact on the Child

4

Assessing the Long-Term Impact of Child Sexual Abuse: A Review and Conceptualization

David Finkelhor
Angela Browne

Since the problem of child sexual abuse first came to the forefront in the 1970s, clinicians have been amassing observations about the impact of this type of child abuse on its victims. However, few efforts have been made to review and organize these observations in a way to advance scientific knowledge and clinical practice. In this chapter, we review the status of empirical research findings concerning the long-term effects of child sexual abuse and suggest a framework that might be applied for future research investigation and clinical assessment.

The idea that sexual abuse in childhood can have a serious long-term impact is generally accepted by clinicians who work with the phenomenon. However, this assumption has been periodically attacked by skeptics who argue that the trauma is greatly overstated or that evidence for negative effects is meager (e.g., Constantine, 1977; Henderson, 1983; Ramey, 1979). It is true that until recently the argument for long-term impact was based primarily on less than rigorous clinical studies. However, as evidence from empirical

The authors would like to thank Linda Gott and Ruth Miller for help in preparing this manuscript. This research has been supported by grants from the National Center on Child Abuse and Neglect (1R01AG04333-01), National Institute of Mental Health (MH15161), and the Eden Hall Farm Foundation.

studies accumulates, it generally confirms the clinical impression that sexual abuse in childhood poses a serious risk to mental health, even into adulthood.

At least eight nonclinical studies have now found that women[1] in the general population with a history of child sexual abuse have identifiable mental health impairment when compared to nonvictims. Three of these studies were sophisticated random sample, community surveys that compared sexual abuse victims with nonvictims in the normal population. Bagley and Ramsay (1985), using a variety of standard epidemiological measures—including the Coopersmith Self-Esteem Inventory, the Centre for Environmental Studies Depression Scale (CES-D), and the Middlesex Hospital Health Survey—documented significant mental health impairment among women with a history of sexual abuse in a random sample in Calgary, Alberta, Canada. Russell (1986) found victimized women in a random sample in San Francisco to be significantly impaired on a number of objective and subjective measures of adjustment. And Peters (1984), surveying a random sample of women in Los Angeles, found sexual abuse victims to have significantly more problems with depression and substance abuse than did nonvictims. Five other studies, based on college student samples (Briere & Runtz, 1985; Finkelhor, 1984; Fromuth, 1983; Sedney & Brooks, 1984; Seidner & Calhoun, 1984) also found indications of impairment in victims. Only one study that looked for impairment in nonclinical samples failed to find it (Tsai, Feldman-Summers, & Edgar, 1979).

Findings of impairment in nonclinical groups challenge the objection that the problems clinicians observe in sexual abuse victims are simply a function of the clinical setting. These findings are also impressive in that the studies were looking at differences associated with an event that occurred from 5 to 25 years previously. Moreover, all of these studies used very broad definitions of sexual abuse that included single episodes, experiences where no actual penetration occurred, and experiences with nonrelatives, as well as the more "serious" kinds of abuse. In the four studies in which multivariate analysis was used (Bagley & Ramsay, 1985; Finkelhor, 1984; Fromuth, 1983; Peters, 1984), sexual abuse remained associated with mental health impairment even after a variety of other background factors had been controlled. All of this provides increasingly strong evidence that sexual abuse may have long-term deleterious effects for a substantial number of people.

Unfortunately, research evidence is much less specific about what these effects may be. The list of problems that have been associated with a history of child sexual abuse is long (see reviews by Browne & Finkelhor, 1986;

---

[1]Even though it is recognized that approximately one fifth of all child sexual abuse victims are boys, there are very few studies of its impact on them. (The exceptions are Finkelhor, 1979; Rogers & Terry, 1984; Wood & Dean, 1984.) All of the findings cited in this paper unless otherwise indicated apply solely to women.

Gelinas, 1983; Jehu & Gazan, 1983; Tufts New England Medical Center, 1984). This list includes depression and self-destructive behavior, anger and hostility, poor self-esteem, feelings of isolation and stigma, difficulty in trusting others (especially men), marital and relationship problems, and a tendency toward revictimization. Many sexual difficulties—including frigidity, vaginismus, inability to tolerate sexual arousal, and flashbacks—have been linked to the experience of child sexual abuse. In addition, childhood molestation is frequently cited as a background factor in the etiology of drug and alcohol abuse, prostitution, multiple personality disorder, and borderline disorder. However, the connections between sexual abuse and most of these factors are based, once again, primarily on clinical observations. Few of them have been confirmed in more rigorous empirical studies. In this paper, we will try to summarize which of these effects has received empirical support; that is, has been confirmed in a study either with a clinical or nonclinical sample, using some comparison group and/or formal measures of the effect in question.

One of the areas receiving the most attention in empirical literature on long-term effects is the impact of early sexual abuse on later sexual functioning. At least six studies, five utilizing some kind of comparison group, have found more sexual problems in women who have been victims of child sexual abuse than in nonvictims (Briere, 1984; Courtois, 1979; Finkelhor, 1984; Herman, 1981; Langmade, 1983; Meiselman, 1978). These studies show higher levels of specific sexual dysfunctions such as difficulty with arousal, vaginismus, and flashbacks, as well as emotional problems related to sex such as sexual guilt, sexual anxiety, and low sexual self-esteem (Finkelhor, 1984; Langmade, 1983).

However, the prevalent supposition that sexual abuse victims tend toward promiscuity has not been empirically confirmed. Two researchers (Herman, 1981; Meiselman, 1978) do report promiscuity in clinical samples. However, in conducting research with a college population, Fromuth (1983) found that, although many sexual abuse victims *described* themselves as promiscuous, the actual number of their sexual partners and sexual experiences did not differ significantly from those of their peers. This suggests the possibility that the so-called promiscuity of sexual abuse victims may be more a function of negative self-labeling, due perhaps to their low self-esteem, than a representation of actual behavior patterns.

One of the most alarming findings in regard to long-term effects concerns the apparent vulnerability of women who have been sexually abused as children to revictimization later in life. Five empirical studies found higher rates of subsequent rape among sexual abuse victims than nonvictims (deYoung, 1982; Fromuth, 1983; Herman, 1981; Miller et al., 1978; Russell, 1984), and two found higher rates of wife abuse (Briere, 1984; Russell, 1986). In Russell's (1986) community survey of 933 women, for example, child sexual abuse victims were two to four times more likely to suffer subsequent sexual assault when compared to women who were not childhood victims. One possible explanation is that those who divulge sexual abuse feel more comfortable reporting other types of abuse, and thus the finding is a methodological artifact. However, it is more likely that sexual abuse—through its impairment of self-esteem, self-protection, and trust—makes victims vulnerable to abusive individuals or unable to anticipate dangerous sexual situations.

Depression and related behavior are other hypothesized outcomes of child sexual abuse that have received empirical confirmation. In a study of sexual abuse victims in a community population, Peters (1984) found that victims of childhood molestation had experienced more episodes of depression and had been hospitalized more often for depression than nonvictims. In another community study, Bagley and Ramsay (1985) found a history of sexual abuse to be associated with current depression, psychiatric treatment for depression, suicidal ideation, and a history of deliberate suicide attempts. Similarly, Briere (1984), studying a clinic population, reported child sexual abuse victims as more depressed than the comparison group, with a more extensive pattern of suicide attempts and self-mutilation. Two controlled studies of college populations (Briere & Runtz, 1985; Sedney & Brooks, 1984) also found the victims of child sexual abuse to report more depression than their peers. At least three studies, however, were not able to confirm more depression among sexual abuse victims than among nonvictims, perhaps because depression is such a widespread psychiatric symptom and occurs across a continuum with less severe symptoms more difficult to rate (Fromuth, 1983; Herman, 1981; Meiselman, 1978).

An association between child sexual abuse and later substance abuse has also received some strong empirical support. Peters (1984) found that a higher percentage of victimized women manifested symptoms of alcohol abuse than did the comparison group. More of the victimized group abused at least one type of drug as well. Two other studies (Briere, 1984; Herman, 1981) also found a higher incidence of alcohol abuse and drug addiction among victims of child sexual abuse than among their nonvictimized counterparts.

Other clinical observations confirmed by the results of empirical studies include high levels of anxiety in victims (Bagley & Ramsay, 1985; Briere, 1984; Sedney & Brooks, 1984); feelings of isolation and stigma (Briere, 1984; Courtois, 1979; Herman, 1981); poor self-esteem (Bagley & Ramsay, 1985; Courtois, 1979; Herman, 1981); hostile feelings toward parents, particularly toward mothers (deYoung, 1982; Herman, 1981; Meiselman, 1978); and fear of others, especially men (Briere, 1984; Courtois, 1979; Meiselman, 1978). A few studies also link the experience of child sexual abuse to later prostitution (Fields, 1981; James & Meyerding, 1977; Silbert & Pines, 1981); and to particular types of pathology, such as eating disorders (Oppenheimer, Palmer, & Braden, 1984). However, without adequate comparison groups, the results of studies conducted with such specialized populations are hard to interpret.

A currently popular question is whether sexually victimized children later become abusers themselves. A number of studies have looked at this hypothesis, but almost all have serious weaknesses, one of the most important being that most of these inquiries have been conducted with male incarcerated convicts. For example, researchers at the Bridgewater, Massachusetts Treatment Center (Bard et al., 1983) found that 57% of male child molesters had been sexually molested as children, compared to 23% of the adult rapists. At least three other studies (Groth & Burgess, 1979; Langevin, Handy, Hook, Day, & Russon, 1983; Pelto, 1981) found more victimization in the background of male molesters than in some comparison groups, although the comparison groups were not always clearly appropriate. In a study conducted with women, Goodwin, McCarthy, and Divasto (1981) found that 24% of a sample of mothers from families in which there was physical child abuse reported incest experiences in their childhoods, compared to only 3% of women recruited from community organizations (again, not the best comparison group). Such studies do suggest that sexual abuse may be an important etiologic factor on the route to later abusive behavior. However, they do not tell us how many sexual abuse victims actually take this route, or what prevents others from doing so.

In general, most studies have been better at establishing the fact that sexual abuse constitutes a risk factor for later long-term effects than at ascertaining how great the risk is. This is in part because studies based on samples of individuals seeking help are likely to overstate risks. Thus, surveys of nonclinical populations give us an opportunity to check this perspective against a wider population. For example, Bagley and Ramsay (1985) found clinical signs of depression according to the CES-D in 17% of Calgary community women who said they had suffered a serious sexual assault in childhood. Five percent were acutely depressed and 16% had been in psychiatric treatment in the past year for depression. As noted earlier, Peters (1984), in the Los Angeles community survey, found alcohol and drug abuse in 22% and 31% of child sexual abuse victims, respectively. She also found a major depressive episode in the histories of 85% of the sexual abuse victims, as well as in 66% of nonvictims.

Overall, then, when measured with standard epidemiological tools, most victims of childhood molestation show up as slightly impaired or normal. Victims as a group demonstrate impairment, compared to their nonvictimized counterparts, but less than one fifth evidence serious psychopathology. This does not mean, however, that the rest are symptom-free. Standardized tests in general are not sensitive to more subtle forms of discomfort and difficulty, and are often ill suited to measure some effects associated with the experience of sexual molestation as a child. How many victims truly have no negative long-term effects is difficult to establish.

IMPACT OF DIFFERENT TYPES OF ABUSE

The knowledge that some victims of child sexual abuse suffer serious impairment whereas others do not has sparked considerable speculation about what kinds of abuse are more or less traumagenic. Groth (1978), for example, based on his clinical experience, contended that the greatest trauma occurs in sexual abuse that (1) continues for a long period of time, (2) occurs with a closely related person, (3) involves penetration, and (4) is accompanied by aggression. Increasingly, there have been studies that looked empirically at these speculations. Unfortunately, however, these studies have not always come to the same conclusions.

For example, clinical speculation has generally been that experiences with close relatives are more traumatizing than experiences outside of the family. What empirical findings suggest is that sexual abuse involving fathers and stepfathers is indeed more traumatic (Finkelhor, 1979; Russell, 1986). However, not all studies have found a clear difference between experiences with relatives versus those with nonrelatives. This may well be because the distinction of family versus nonfamily does not always reflect the closeness of the relationship between the abuser and the child. Abuse by a trusted neighbor may actually be more betraying than abuse by a distant uncle or grandfather.

Clinical observation has also suggested that sexual abuse involving intercourse is more traumatic, and this observation has received empirical support. Russell (1986) found that 59% of those victims who had suffered completed or attempted intercourse, fellatio, cunnilingus, analingus, or anal intercourse said they were extremely traumatized by the abuse. This compared to only 36% of those who suffered manual touching of the breasts or genitals, or 22% who suffered simply from unwanted kissing or touching of clothed parts of their bodies. Similarly, Bagley and Ramsay (1985), in a multivariate analysis, found penetration to be the variable most predictive of impairment on a composite of standard epidemiological measures. Other empirical studies have also shown greater trauma associated with genital contact but have not always been able to demonstrate a difference between intercourse and other types of genital touching (Fromuth, 1983; Landis, 1956; Tufts, 1984).

In assessing the empirical literature on the trauma of different kinds of abuse, one of the most prominent traumagenic factors seems to be the use of force. Five studies found strong associations between the degree of trauma and whether force occurred (Bagley & Ramsay, 1985; Finkelhor, 1979;

Fromuth, 1983; Russell, 1986; Tufts, 1984). These findings cast doubt on a commonly heard speculation that victims who are forced have an easier time coping because they are less prone to attribute blame for the abuse to themselves (e.g., MacFarlane, 1978). Apparently, the fear and powerlessness created by being forced to comply act to increase, rather than decrease, the long-term trauma.

One of the main surprises in the research on different kinds of sexual abuse concerns experiences that extend over a long period of time. Although clinical wisdom assumes that longer duration is linked to greater trauma, the case has been very difficult to prove. Out of eight studies, only three find longer lasting abuse associated with greater trauma (Friedrich, Urquiza & Beilke, 1984; Russell, 1984; Tsai et al., 1979). On the other hand, three studies find no relationship (Courtois, 1979; Finkelhor, 1979; Langmade, 1983), one finds mixed results (Seidner & Calhoun, 1984), and one even finds longer lasting abuse associated with less trauma (Courtois, 1979).

Another surprising finding concerns the effect of telling others about the abuse. Two studies have not found any relationship between whether the incident is disclosed and long-term trauma (Bagley & Ramsay, 1985; Finkelhor, 1979), and another finds that children who do not tell, or at least do not tell right away, show fewer symptoms (Tufts, 1984). It is true that in some cases silence may create isolation and suffering, but it may also spare the child from the additional traumatic effects of parental and community reactions.

Research is also very equivocal in answering the ongoing controversy about whether children are more traumatized if the abuse occurs at earlier or later ages. Two studies (Courtois, 1979; Meiselman, 1978) found more serious impact associated with abuse at a younger age. Four other studies (Bagley & Ramsay, 1985; Finkelhor, 1979; Langmade, 1983; Russell, 1986) found no significant differences of effect according to age. The effects of age have not yet been studied in a sophisticated way, however. Few have tried to partial out the effects of other aspects of the experience, such as intercourse, which tend to covary with age. In addition, not enough consideration has been given to the possibility that the relationship between age and trauma may be curvilinear, with the most serious effects occurring in preadolescence.

A small number of studies have looked at the specific traumatic impact of various other aspects of the experience. Two studies (Finkelhor, 1979; Russell, 1986) found that experiences with male perpetrators were more traumatic than those with female perpetrators. Three studies (Finkelhor, 1979; Fromuth, 1983; Russell, 1986) reported that experiences with adult perpetrators were more traumatic than experiences with adolescents. Two studies (Anderson, Bach, & Griffith, 1981; Tufts, 1984) found that negative parental reaction was associated with more severe trauma. And one study

(Tufts, 1984) found that children removed from their homes following sexual abuse exhibited more overall behavior problems, particularly aggression, than did children who remained with their families.

From this review, then, it is apparent that there is still substantial work to be done before we fully understand the effects of different types of child sexual abuse. It would appear that sexual abuse by fathers and stepfathers is consistently more traumatic, as is abuse involving force and/or intercourse. Male perpetrators and adult perpetrators (as opposed to adolescents) also are associated with more trauma. And we might tentatively conclude that when families are unsupportive of victims or victims are removed from the home, the effects are more serious. However, in other matters where there has been much controversy, no firm conclusions are available. It has not been demonstrated that abuse at any particular age is more harmful. Longlasting abuse has not been clearly demonstrated as more traumagenic. And there are contradictory findings about the effects on victims of keeping the abuse a secret.

TRAUMAGENIC DYNAMICS

One of the shortcomings of research on the effects of child sexual abuse is the absence of any underlying conceptual framework. Researchers have tended to cast a wide net in a search for effects, without attempting to formulate a model of just how the experience of childhood molestation might lead to these effects. Such a model might help to focus the search for traumagenic factors, as well as clarify the different impact of various types of abuse. The remainder of this paper is concerned with outlining such a model.

We would like to propose that the injury of child sexual abuse can be broken down into four components, which we call *traumagenic dynamics*. These components are: (1) traumatic sexualization, (2) stigmatization, (3) betrayal, and (4) powerlessness. These are generalized traumatizing phenomena that occur in other kinds of events as well, but their conjunction in one set of circumstances makes the experience of child sexual abuse somewhat unique.

The operation of these dynamics can be described in a general way: We suggest that they alter a child's cognitive and emotional orientation to the world, and thus create trauma by distorting a child's self-concept, world view, and affective capacities. For example, stigmatization might distort a child's sense of his or her own value and worth. Powerlessness distorts a sense of ability to control critical events in life. When children attempt to cope with the world through these distortions, it may result in many of the problems commonly noted in victims of sexual abuse. Let us describe in more detail some possible components of each of these dynamics.

Traumatic sexualization is the process by which a child's sexuality is shaped in developmentally inappropriate and interpersonally dysfunctional ways. This may happen in a variety of ways in the course of sexual abuse. Traumatic sexualization can occur when a child is repeatedly rewarded by an offender for sexual behavior that is inappropriate to his or her level of development. It can also occur through the exchange of affection, attention, privileges, or gifts for sexual behavior, so that a child learns sexual behavior as a strategy for manipulating others to get other developmentally appropriate needs met. It occurs when certain parts of a child's anatomy are fetishized and given distorted importance and meaning. It also occurs through the misconceptions and confusions about sexual behavior and sexual morality that are transmitted to the child from the offender. And it occurs when very frightening or painful memories and events become associated in the child's mind with sexual activity.

Sexual abuse experiences can vary dramatically in terms of the amount and kind of traumatic sexualization they provoke. Experiences in which the offender makes an effort to evoke the child's sexual response, for example, are probably more sexualizing than those in which an offender simply uses a passive child to masturbate with. Experiences where the child is enticed to participate are also likely to be more sexualizing than those where brute force is used. However, even with the use of force, a form of traumatic sexualization may occur as a result of the fear that becomes associated with sex in the aftermath of such an experience. The degree of a child's understanding may also affect the degree of sexualization. Experiences in which the child, because of young age or developmental level, understands few of the sexual implications of the activities may be less sexualizing than when a child has full awareness. Children who have been traumatically sexualized emerge from their experiences with inappropriate repertoires of sexual behavior, with confusions and misconceptions about their sexual self-concepts, and with unusual emotional associations to sexual activities.

Betrayal refers to the dynamic in which children discover that someone on whom they were vitally dependent has caused them harm. This may occur in different ways in a molestation experience. For example, in the course of abuse or its aftermath, children may come to the realization that a trusted person has manipulated them through lies about or misrepresentations of moral standards. They may also come to realize that someone whom they loved or whose affection was important to them treated them with callous disregard. Children can experience betrayal not only at the hands of offenders, but also with family members who were not abusing them. A family member whom they trusted but who was unable or unwilling to protect or believe them—or who has a changed attitude toward them after disclosure of the abuse—may also contribute to the dynamics of betrayal.

Sexual abuse experiences that are perpetrated by family members or other trusted persons obviously involve more potential for betrayal than those involving strangers. However, the degree of betrayal may also be affected by how taken in the child feels by the offender, regardless of who the offender is. A child who was suspicious of a father's activities from the beginning may feel less betrayed than one who initially experienced the contact as nurturing and loving and then is suddenly shocked to realize what is really happening. Obviously, the degree of betrayal is also related to a family's response to disclosure. Children who are disbelieved, blamed, or ostracized undoubtedly experience a greater sense of betrayal than those who are supported.

Powerlessness—or what might better be called *disempowerment,* the dynamic of rendering the victim powerless—refers to the process in which the child's will, desires, and sense of efficacy are continually contravened. Many aspects of the sexual abuse experience contribute to this dynamic. We theorize that a basic kind of powerlessness occurs in sexual abuse when a child's territory and body space are repeatedly invaded against the child's will. This is exacerbated by whatever coercion and manipulation the offender may impose as a part of the abuse process. Powerlessness is then reinforced when a child sees his or her attempts to halt the abuse frustrated. It is increased when the child feels fear, or is unable to make adults understand or believe what is happening, or feels trapped in the situation by conditions of dependency.

An authoritarian abuser who continually commands the child's participation by threatening serious harm will probably instill more of a sense of powerlessness. However, force and threat are not necessary: Any situation in which a child feels trapped, if only by the realization of the consequences of disclosure, can create a sense of powerlessness. Obviously, a situation in which a child tells and is not believed will also create a greater degree of powerlessness. On the other hand, when a child is able to bring the abuse to an end effectively, or at least exert some control over its occurrence, she or he may feel less disempowered.

Stigmatization, the final dynamic, refers to the negative connotations (e.g., badness, shame, and guilt) that are communicated to the child surrounding experiences of molestation and that then become incorporated into the child's self-image. These negative meanings are communicated in many ways. They can come directly from the abuser, who may blame the victim for the activity, denigrate the victim or, simply through furtiveness, convey a sense of shame about the behavior. When there is pressure for secrecy from the offender, this can also convey powerful messages of shame and guilt. Stigmatization is also reinforced by attitudes that the victim infers or hears from other persons in the family or community. Stigmatization may grow out of the child's prior knowledge or sense that the activity is considered deviant and taboo. It is reinforced if, after disclosure, people react with shock or hysteria or blame the child for what has transpired. The child may be additionally stigmatized by people in his or her environment who now impute other negative characteristics to the victim (loose morals, spoiled goods) as a result of the molestation.

Stigmatization occurs in various degrees in different abuse situations. Some children are treated as bad and blameworthy by offenders and some are not. Some children, in the wake of a sexual abuse experience, are told clearly that they are not at fault, whereas others are heavily shamed. Some children may be too young to have much awareness of social attitudes and thus experience little stigmatization from that source. Others may have to deal with powerful religious and cultural taboos, in addition to the usual stigma. Keeping the secret of having been a sexual abuse victim may increase the sense of stigma, since it reinforces the sense of being different. By contrast, those who find out that such experiences occur to many other children may have some of their stigma assuaged.

IMPLEMENTING THE MODEL

The potential of separate kinds of traumagenic dynamics within the experience of child sexual abuse immediately suggests some hypotheses. For example, in analyzing the differential impact of different kinds of abuse, the main question asked has been: Was it more or less traumatic? The conceptualization proposed here suggests that the question should not simply be the degree of trauma, but what kind of trauma has occurred. Different traumagenic dynamics should lead to different types of trauma. Thus we were encouraged to go back to the traumatic effects cited in the literature on child sexual abuse and see whether some might appear more likely to be associated with certain traumatic dynamics. Potential groupings are illustrated in Table 4.1. Obviously, there is no simple one-to-one correspondence, but there are some clear general clusterings.

It would be plausible to hypothesize that *traumatic sexualization* is particularly associated with impacts on sexual behavior. These effects would include sexual dysfunctions, promiscuity, sexual anxiety, and low sexual self-esteem. *Stigmatization,* we would hypothesize, might be most clearly related to such long-term effects as guilt, poor self-esteem, a sense of differentness and isolation, and secondary problems such as drug and alcohol abuse, criminal involvement, suicidal ideation, and suicide attempts. *Betrayal* would seem most plausibly associated with effects such as depression, dependency in extreme forms, impaired ability to trust and to judge the trustworthiness of others, and anger. Some of the manifestations of this might be a vulnerability to subsequent abuse and exploitation, discomfort in intimate relationships, and marital problems. Finally, *powerlessness* would seem most likely to be associated with fear and anxiety, a lowered sense of self-efficacy, perception of the self as a victim, and sometimes an identifica-

TABLE 4.1 Traumagenic Dynamics in the Impact of Child Sexual Abuse

I. TRAUMATIC SEXUALIZATION
Dynamics

Child rewarded for sexual behavior inappropriate to developmental level
Offender exchanges attention and affection for sex
Sexual parts of child fetishized
Offender transmits misconceptions about sexual behavior and sexual morality
Conditioning of sexual activity with negative emotions and memories

Psychological impact

Increased salience of sexual issues
Confusion about sexual identity
Confusion about sexual norms
Confusion of sex with love and care-getting/caregiving
Negative associations to sexual activities and arousal sensations
Aversion to sex-intimacy

Behavioral manifestations

Sexual preoccupations and compulsive sexual behaviors
Precocious sexual activity
Aggressive sexual behaviors
Promiscuity
Prostitution
Sexual dysfunctions: flashbacks, difficulty in arousal and/or orgasm
Avoidance of or phobic reactions to sexual intimacy
Inappropriate sexualization of parenting

II. STIGMATIZATION
Dynamics

Offender blames, denigrates victim
Offender and others pressure child for secrecy
Child infers attitudes of shame about activities
Others have shocked reaction to disclosure
Others blame child for events
Victim is stereotyped as damaged goods

Psychological impact

Guilt, shame
Lowered self-esteem
Sense of differentness from others

Behavioral manifestations

Isolation
Drug or alcohol abuse
Criminal involvement
Self-mutilation
Suicide

III. BETRAYAL
Dynamics

Trust and vulnerability manipulated

Violation of expectation that others will provide care and protection
Child's well-being disregarded
Lack of support and protection from parent(s)

Psychological impact

Grief, depression
Extreme dependency
Impaired ability to judge trustworthiness of others
Mistrust, particularly of men
Anger, hostility

Behavioral manifestations

Clinging
Vulnerability to subsequent abuse and exploitation
Allowing own children to be victimized
Isolation
Discomfort in intimate relationships
Marital problems
Aggressive behavior
Delinquency

IV. POWERLESSNESS

Dynamics

Body territory invaded against the child's wishes
Vulnerability to invasion continues over time
Offender uses force or trickery to involve child
Child feels unable to protect self and halt abuse
Repeated experience of fear
Child is unable to make others believe

Psychological impact

Anxiety, fear
Lowered sense of efficacy
Perception of self as victim
Need to control
Identification with the aggressor

Behavioral manifestations

Nightmares
Phobias
Somatic complaints; eating and sleeping disorders
Depression
Dissociation
Running away
School problems, truancy
Employment problems
Vulnerability to subsequent victimization
Aggressive behavior, bullying
Delinquency
Becoming an abuser

tion with the aggressor in an attempt to regain some sense of power. Manifestations here might include nightmares, somatic complaints, depression, running away, school problems, employment problems, vulnerability to subsequent victimization, aggressive behavior, delinquency, and/or becoming an abuser.

As mentioned earlier, these clusterings are not meant to suggest that there is any strict one-to-one correspondence between each traumagenic dynamic and each effect. Some effects, like depression, are undoubtedly associated with many dynamics. However, postulating associations between these general dynamics and specific effects can be useful in several ways. For instance, they suggest research hypotheses that might lead to an increase in our understanding of the effects of child sexual abuse. Instead of simply looking at sexual abuse in terms of whether abuse by fathers causes more general trauma, we might look at whether abuse involving more betrayal results in more subsequent marital and relationship problems. Likewise, instead of simply looking at whether intercourse has more negative impact than does other types of sexual abuse, we might look at whether abuse involving more sexualization (perhaps more sexual involvement on the part of the child) results in more subsequent sexual dysfunctions. Testing these more specific hypotheses will yield much useful information about just how child sexual abuse causes injury.

The notion of traumagenic dynamics can also be used as a guide for developing assessment instruments. Up until now, research on child sexual abuse has been conducted primarily with broad psychological inventories like the Child Behavior Checklist (Tufts, 1984) or the California Psychological Inventory (Seidner & Calhoun, 1984). These instruments are not geared to detect trauma specifically associated with childhood molestation. Breaking down child sexual abuse into traumagenic dynamics suggests elements that might go into an instrument specifically designed to assess the traumatic impact of such abuse.

A third use of the idea of traumagenic dynamics, even in the absence of empirical research, is in making clinical assessments of sexual abuse victims. The model of four traumagenic dynamics reminds clinicians of the various ways in which child sexual abuse may cause harm and encourages them to check for injuries in all of those areas. Thus clinicians might ask: How traumatically sexualizing was the experience; how betraying; how stigmatizing; how disempowering? This framework could then be used to guide planned interventions. If a clinician determined that one of the main traumas occurred in the area of stigmatization, for instance, this would suggest interventions designed to counteract the effects of stigma—for example, contact with other victims of child sexual abuse who could assuage the sense of differentness. If the trauma appeared to be primarily in the area of powerlessness, this would suggest therapy to restore the victim's sense of power and self-efficacy. Moreover, the framework may remind clinicians that recovery in one area may not mean automatic recovery in another. A victim may overcome the sense of stigma and still feel very powerless in the world, or may still have sexual dysfunctions stemming from traumatic sexualization.

CONCLUSION

The study of the effects of child sexual abuse is still in its infancy, but already the time has come for a change of emphasis. Early efforts have been directed at proving the seriousness, even the legitimacy, of sexual abuse as a problem of mental health and social policy. Thus we have endeavored to demonstrate that childhood molestation has long-term effects that can be identified years after the occurrence of the abuse. We have also tried to show that sexual abuse may be implicated in a host of other already recognized social and psychological problems, and research has tended to support these contentions.

What is needed now is research that gives more specification to prior findings, research that is not simply concerned with establishing that child sexual abuse can have serious consequences, but that is designed to investigate: (1) how serious these consequences are, (2) to whom, (3) in what ways, and (4) under what circumstances. It is true that policymakers still need to be persuaded that this troubling problem deserves attention and resources. But other audiences must also be addressed. For example, victims and their families need reassurance that many victims recover well from the trauma of sexual abuse and go on to live happy and productive lives. Clinicians need to know how to guide interventions for victims, based on the dynamics of the victimization and victims' life circumstances. And social scientists need to be enticed to consider how sexual abuse articulates with general principles of human development, as well as with other pathologies of childhood, and encouraged to take a more sophisticated approach to the study of this particularly important and complex problem.

REFERENCES

Anderson, S. C., Bach, C. M., & Griffith, S. (1981). *Psychosocial sequelae in intrafamilial victims of sexual assault and abuse.* Paper presented at the Third International Conference on Child Abuse and Neglect, Amsterdam, The Netherlands.

Bagley, C. & Ramsey, R. (1985). *Disrupted childhood and vulnerability to sexual assault: Long-term sequels with implications for counselling.* Paper presented at the Conference on Counselling the Sexual Abuse Survivor, Winnipeg, Canada.

Bard, L., Carter, D. Cerce, D., Knight, R., Rosenberg, R., & Schneider, B. (1983). *A descriptive study of rapists and child molesters: Developmental, clinical and criminal characteristics.* Unpublished manuscript. Bridgewater, MA: Massachusetts Treatment Center.

Briere, J. (1984, April). *The effect of childhood sexual abuse on later psychological functioning: Defining a "post-sexual-abuse syndrome".* Paper presented at the Third National Conference on Sexual Victimization of Children, Washington, DC.

Briere, J., & Runtz, M. (1985, August). *Symptomatology associated with prior sexual abuse in a non-clinical sample.* Paper presented at the annual meeting of the American Psychological Association, Los Angeles, CA.

Browne, A., & Finkelhor, D. (1986). The impact of child sexual abuse: A review of the research. *Psychological Bulletin, 99,* 66–77.

Constantine, L. (1977). *The sexual rights of children: Implications of a radical perspective.* Paper presented at the International Conference on Love and Attraction, Swansea, Wales.

Courtois, C. (1979). The incest experience and its aftermath. *Victimology: An International Journal, 4,* 337–347.

deYoung, M. (1982). *The sexual victimization of children.* Jefferson, NC: McFarland.

Fields, P. J. (1981, November). Parent-child relationships, childhood sexual abuse, and adult interpersonal behavior in female prostitutes. *Dissertation Abstracts International, 42,* 5.

Finkelhor, D. (1979). *Sexually victimized children.* New York: Free Press.

Finkelhor, D. (1984). *Child sexual abuse: New theory and research.* New York: Free Press.

Friedrich, W. N., Urquiza, A. J., & Beilke, R. (1984). *Behavioral problems in sexually abused young children.* Manuscript submitted for publication.

Fromuth, M. E. (1983, August). *The long term psychological impact of childhood sexual abuse.* Unpublished doctoral dissertation, Auburn University, Auburn, AL.

Gelinas, D. J. (1983). *The persisting negative effects of incest. Psychiatry, 46,* 312–332.

Goodwin, J., McCarthy, T., & Divasto, P. (1981). Prior incest in mothers of abused children. *Child Abuse and Neglect, 5,* 87–96.

Groth, N. (1978). Guidelines for assessment and management of the offender. In A. Burgess, N. Groth, S. Holmstrom, & S. Sgroi (Eds.), *Sexual assault of children and adolescents.* Lexington, MA: Lexington Books.

Groth, N. (1979). *Men who rape.* New York: Plenum Press.

Groth, N. A., & Burgess, A. W. (1979). Sexual trauma in the life histories of rapists and child molesters. *Victimology: An International Journal, 4,* 10–16.

Henderson, J. (1983). Is incest harmful? *Canadian Journal of Psychiatry, 28,* 34–39.

Herman, J. L. (1981). *Father-daughter incest.* Cambridge, MA: Harvard University Press.

James, J., & Meyerding, J. (1977). Early sexual experiences and prostitution. *American Journal of Psychiatry, 134,* 1381–1385.

Jehu, D., & Gazan, M. (1983). Psychosocial adjustment of women who were sexually victimized in childhood or adolescence. *Canadian Journal of Community Mental Health, 2,* 71–81.

Landis, J. (1956). Experiences of 500 children with adult sexual deviation. *Psychiatric Quarterly Supplement, 30,* 91–109.

Langevin, R., Handy, L., Hook, H., Day, D., & Russon, A. (1983). Are incestuous fathers pedophilic and aggressive? In R. Langevin (Ed.), *Erotic preference, gender identity and aggression.* New York: Erlbaum.

Langmade, C. J. (1983). The impact of pre- and postpubertal onset of incest experiences in adult women as measured by sex anxiety, sex guilt, sexual satisfaction and sexual behavior. *Dissertation Abstracts International, 44,* 917B. (University Microfilms, No. 3592)

MacFarlane, K. (1978). Sexual abuse of children. In J. R. Chapman & M. Gates (Eds)., *The victimization of women* (pp. 81–109). Beverly Hills, CA: Sage.

Meiselman, K. (1978). *Incest.* San Francisco: Jossey-Bass.

Miller, J., Moeller, D., Kaufman, A., Divasto, P., Pather, D., & Christy, J. (1978). Recidivism among sexual assault victims. *American Journal of Psychiatry, 135,* 1103–1104.

Oppenheimer, R., Palmer, R. L., & Braden, S. (1984, September). *A clinical evaluation of early sexually abusive experiences in adult anorexic and bulemic females: Implications for preventive work in childhood.* Paper presented at Fifth International Conferences on Child Abuse and Neglect, Montreal.

Pelto, V. (1981). Male incest offenders and non-offenders: A comparison of early sexual history. Doctoral dissertation, United States International University, Ann Arbor, MI. (University Microfilms #8118142)

Peters, S. D. (1984). *The relationship between childhood sexual victimization and adult depression among Afro-American and white women.* Unpublished doctoral dissertation, University of California, Los Angeles.

Prentky, R. A. (1983). Personal communication.

Ramey, J. (1979). Dealing with the last taboo. *SIECUS Report, 7,* 1–2, 6–7.

Rogers, C. M., & Terry, T. (1984). Clinical intervention with boy victims of sexual abuse. In I. Stewart & J. Greer (Eds.), *Victims of sexual aggression* (pp. 1–104). New York: Van Nostrand Reinhold.

Russell, D. (1984). *Sexual exploitation: Rape, child sexual abuse, and sexual harassment.* Beverly Hills, CA: Sage.

Russell, D. E. H. (1986). *The secret trauma: Incest in the lives of girls and women.* New York: Basic Books.

Sedney, M. S., & Brooks, B. (1984). Factors associated with a history of childhood sexual experience in a nonclinical female population. *Journal of the American Academy of Child Psychiatry, 23,* 215, 218.

Seidner, A., & Calhoun, K. S. (1984, August). *Childhood sexual abuse: Factors related to differential adult adjustment.* Paper presented at the Second National Conference for Family Violence Researchers, Durham, NH.

Silbert, M. H., & Pines, A. M. (1981). Sexual child abuse as an antecedent to prostitution. *Child Abuse and Neglect, 5,* 407–411.

Tsai, M., Feldman-Summers, S., & Edgar M. (1979). Childhood molestation: Variables related to differential impact of psychosexual functioning in adult women. *Journal of Abnormal Psychology, 88,* 407–417.

Tufts New England Medical Center, Division of Child Psychiatry. (1984). *Sexually exploited children: Service and research project.* Final report for the Office of Juvenile Justice and Delinquency Prevention, U.S. Department of Justice, Washington, DC. (Report No. 80-JN-AX-001).

Wood, S. C., & Dean, K. S. (1984). *Final report: Sexual abuse of males research project* (Report No. 90 CA/812). Washington, DC: National Center on Child Abuse and Neglect.

5

The Impact of Sexual Abuse on Children: Empirical Findings

Jon R. Conte
Lucy Berliner

Popular notions about the effects of sexual abuse on children seem to imply that victims are inevitably doomed to life as a prostitute, drug addict, or criminal. The other extreme is offered by those advocating for sex between children and adults who suggest that such contact has no adverse effects and may even have beneficial consequences for the child. Clarity regarding the nature of the effects of childhood sexual experiences is extremely important at a time when large numbers of abused children are being identified. The children, the adults who care about them, and the professionals who come in contact with them need to be able to separate the potential and probable risks of childhood sexual abuse from those that are feared but rare or unlikely.

This chapter describes a large systematic study of the effects of childhood sexual abuse. It reviews the evidence for the effects of sexual abuse and discusses variables that appear associated with more adverse effects. This chapter also offers direction for clinical work and future research on the effects of sexual abuse. We begin with a discussion of selected issues surrounding professional responses to the effects of sexual abuse of children.

THINKING ABOUT SEXUAL ABUSE IN CONTEXT

Public and professional interest in childhood sexual abuse has reached an all-time high. The topic is an increasing focus of professional meetings and publications and lay media (see, e.g., Emmerman & Crewdson, 1984-1985).

This project was supported in part by a grant from the National Center for the Prevention and Control of Rape, National Institute of Mental Health HMH37133.

We believe it is helpful for professionals to identify some issues to be kept in mind when dealing with the effects of sexual victimization on children.

Reluctance to See the Problem

Professionals have been aware of the potential negative effects of childhood sexual abuse since the late 1890s. The reasons for Freud's apparent inability to deal with the implications of his patients' reports of sexual abuse have been the subject of much debate. (See, e.g., Lerman, Chapter 3 in this book, or Masson, 1984.) Regardless of the particular reasons, it is clear that sexual abuse of children was not regarded by most professionals or the public to be a serious problem until quite recently. One of the major tasks in the early development of professional responses to child sexual abuse has been to help professionals recognize that the problem does in fact exist (Conte, 1984).

A current challenge for professionals is to recognize the full extent and nature of the experiences to which children are exposed as part of sexual victimization. As more is learned about sexual abuse, acts of sadism and cruelty more extreme than many professionals believed possible are revealed. It is important to recognize that denial, distortion, and minimization are defenses that make it possible for both professionals and sexual offenders to avoid knowing about the painful and coercive experiences that make up sexual abuse. Our task as professionals is to recognize our own psychological defenses and to be open to the increasing evidence that sexual abuse of children is even more common and varied than many of us have believed previously.

An example is beliefs about incest, often thought of as a "love relationship" where appropriate limits or boundaries are crossed. Under such a view, incest is seen as nonviolent and at most confusing. Cases in which fathers have threatened their children, sometimes even with weapons, are evidence against such a benign view of incest. Although force or threat of force appears more common in nonincestuous abuse cases, incest cases do reflect such characteristics more often than the literature suggests (see Conte & Berliner, 1981). This is not to say that all cases should be considered to contain hidden elements, but that there is no typical type of abuse situation.

When therapists allow sexually abused children to tell about their experiences without imposing a predetermined understanding about what sexual abuse consists of, many children describe events and experiences that vary from existing models. Their reactions and feelings may then be freely expressed. Children who report sexual experiences in the context of a therapy program that encourages them to talk without suggesting responses or reinforcing them for any particular content are unlikely to be led to make false statements about abuse. More importantly, therapists can help children recover from events only when they fully understand what has happened to the children and do not assume certain experiences or feelings.

Decline in Public Support for Treatment

A major issue facing professionals and members of the public concerned about sexually abused children is the availability of treatment services. The recent decline in public support for mental health and social services, expressed through decreasing funding, is occurring at the very time that increasing numbers of abused children are identified. This raises a fundamental question about what the purpose of identifying these children is. It would seem that for many, investigations of allegations of child sexual abuse and adjudication of adults who abuse children are sufficient responses to the problem.

It is extremely difficult to get a picture of what happens to most sexually abused children after abuse is uncovered because descriptive data is simply not available. It is likely that large numbers of victims never receive any treatment at all. In Cook County, Illinois, with over 1300 founded cases of child sexual abuse in 1984, less than 10% of all cases received state-financed treatment. An unknown proportion of cases received treatment provided by not-for-profit agencies or private practitioners, but the number is probably not great. Many states provide no funding at all for treatment.

Legal and ethical questions are raised about the purpose of state intervention under child protection legislation. The primary intent of such legislation is to remediate those conditions that have placed the child at risk initially and required the state to intrude into family life. Intervention, such as a child protection investigation, in the absence of any kind of service likely to alter or improve the conditions responsible for the child's sexual abuse may not be sufficient. Indeed, unless it is assumed that discovery stops abuse and that there are no residual effects, what is the purpose at all for state intervention, if the child is left as she or he was before the state intervened? It may be argued that some children are likely to suffer less trauma if they do not disclose (Finkelhor & Browne, Chapter 4 in this book). As this chapter will suggest, the effects of childhood sexual abuse are severe enough to raise serious concerns about the long-term mental health and social adjustment of sexually victimized children. For professionals and state policy makers to know the identities of abused children and to provide no service likely to prevent or lessen the risk of these effects in the future is indefensible.

As we confirm effects of abuse on children we must also seek a social policy and a professional commitment that ensures that treatment follows detection and diagnosis. There is no question that the large numbers of abused children currently being identified represent a significant impact on community resources. Major social policy decisions must be made about the provision of treatment services, who is to pay for it, and how it will be allocated. The current system permits treatment to be unevenly distributed, in all likelihood on an inequitable basis, and in insufficient quantities, so that large numbers of children receive no treatment at all.

WHAT ARE THE EFFECTS?

Previous Studies

The first professional reports on the effects of sexual abuse in childhood occurred in the late 1890s, when Freud observed that 18 of his patients with hysterical illness reported childhood sexual experiences (Miller, 1984). Since that time there have been a significant number of clinical and research reports describing the effects of sexual abuse on children (for reviews see Conte, 1985; Browne & Finkelhor, 1985; and Mrazek & Mrazek, 1981). Clinical studies of children have reported a large number of effects, including depression, guilt, learning difficulties, sexual promiscuity, runaway behavior, somatic complaints (e.g., stomach aches), and changes from normal behavior (Burgess, Groth, & McCaraline, 1981); hysterical seizures (Goodwin, Simms, & Bergman, 1979); phobias, nightmares, and compulsive rituals (Weiss, Rogers, Darwin, & Dutton, 1955); and self-destructive behaviors (Carroll, Schaffer, Spensley & Abramowitz, 1980; deYoung, 1982). Studies of adults who were sexually abused as children report problems such as drug addiction (Benward & Densen-Gerber, 1975); relationship difficulties (Meiselman, 1979); sexual dysfunction (Becker, Skinner, Abel, & Treacy, 1983); negative self-image, depression, problems in interpersonal relationships, and sexual dysfunction (Tsai & Wagner, 1978); substance abuse, suicidality, dissociative and somatic symptoms (Briere, 1987); and a sense of distance, isolation, and negative self-image (Herman & Hirschman, 1981).

Recent comparisons of nonclinical samples of abused and nonabused women show substantial differences in adult adjustment on a variety of mental health measures (Bagly & Ramsay, 1986; Briere, 1987b; Gold, 1986).

NIMH Study

Conte, Berliner, and Schuerman (1986), in a large study funded by the National Institute of Mental Health, describe the effects of sexual abuse on a sample of 369 sexually abused children. Children were assessed at or near the point of disclosure of their sexual victimization. Part of this assessment included a 38-item Symptom Checklist completed by the assigned social worker, and a 110-item Child Behavior Profile completed by a nonoffending parent. The Behavior Profile was also completed by a sample of parents of nonabused children. Children seen at the Sexual Assault Center at Harborview Medical Center in Seattle between September 1983 and May 1985 were eligible for the study. Children who had been removed from their homes and placed in psychiatric hospitals, residential or group homes, or foster homes were ineligible because one of the major measures required a nonoffending parent to describe the child's behavior. Only children for whom there was a positive finding of sexual abuse were included. Thus children likely to be the most affected by sexual abuse (i.e., those removed from their homes) were excluded from the study. Therefore it is probable that the results underestimate the effect of sexual victimization.

Children in the abused sample range in age from 4 to 17 years ($x = 9$). Seventy-six percent are female and 24% male. Eighty-two percent are white. Eighty-three percent of the assessments were conducted less than 6 months after the last incident of sexual abuse. The length of time during which the abuse occurred varied. Twenty-five percent of the children had been abused one time, 4% had been abused for a limited period of time, and 25% had been abused for a long (chronic) period of time. (In 6% of the cases duration was not clear at intake.) Children had been exposed to a variety of sexual behaviors. For example, 18% had oral sex with the offender, 19% vaginal penile intercourse, 25% digital penetration of the vagina, and 62% were fondled. The average number of types of sexual abuse children were exposed to is 3.5. Perpetrators of sexual abuse were members of the child's family in 52% of the cases, acquaintances of the child or of the family in 30% (parent's partner 5%), babysitters in 7%, and strangers in 4% (other 2%).

Symptom Checklist

Data from the Symptom Checklist completed by the social worker describe one view of the effects of sexual abuse on children. The items were derived from the literature and a survey of experienced specialized therapists. The Social Worker Score is the number of symptoms present. Table 5.1 presents the proportion of the abused sample exhibiting each of the symptoms on the Symptom Checklist. The average number of symptoms (Social Worker Score) exhibited by abused children in this sample was 3.5. There was considerable variation in number of symptoms across the sample. Twenty-seven percent had four or more, 13% three, 14% two, 17% one, and 21% no symptoms.

Child Behavior Profile

Items from the parent-completed Behavior Profile were scored with higher scores indicating more of a problem for that item. Forty items were dropped due to little variation (e.g., 84% of abused and 92% of nonabused children were described as "never" sexually active, and 97% of the abused and 100% of the nonabused children were described as "never" having tried to kill self).

TABLE 5.1 Proportion of Abused Sample Exhibiting Checklist Symptoms

Symptom	% Present
Panic/anxiety attacks	5.7
Behavioral regression	13.8
Runs away/takes off	2.7
Excessive autonomic arousal	4.6
Depression	18.7
Withdrawal from usual activity or relations	15.2
Sexually victimizes others	3.0
Generalized fear	11.7
Suicidal attempts	1.9
Body image problems	7.9
Repressed anger/hostility	19.2
Daydreaming	13.8
Major problems with police	0.3
Eating disorders	0.8
Psychotic episode	—
Overly compliant/too anxious to please	13.8
Drug/alcohol abuse	2.2
Age-inappropriate sexual behavior	7.9
Hurts self physically	1.4
Minor problems with police	3.3
Fearful of abuse stimuli	30.1
Suicidal thoughts or actions	5.7
Psychosomatic complaints	10.0
Ritualistic behavior	1.1
Indiscriminate affection-giving or receiving	6.5
Low self-esteem	32.8
Places self in dangerous situations	4.9
Violent fantasies	2.4
Emotional upset	22.8
Prostitution	0.8
Obsessional, repetitive/recurrent thoughts	5.4
Shoplifting/stealing	2.2
Nonacademic school behavior problems	9.2
Nightmares/sleep disorders	20.1
Inability to form/maintain relationships	8.7
Academic problems	15.4
Aggressive behavior	14.4
Inappropriate/destructive peer relationships	7.0

The 70 behaviors from the Behavior Profile for the abused sample were factor analyzed using principal axis factoring with varimax rotation resulting in eight factors: poor self-esteem, aggressive, fearful, conscientious, difficulty in concentration, withdrawal, acting out, and anxious to please/tries too hard. A summary score (Parent Score) was created by adding the ratings for the 70 items.

Differences between abused and comparison children on these factors are all statistically significant. Table 5.2 presents the factors, item loadings, and alpha correlations (measure of internal consistency) for each factor. As is often the case with behavior checklists, the factor analysis was somewhat disappointing. The eight factors account for 43% of the variance among the items, and the commonalities tend to be low, ranging from 0.15 to 0.67. Most of the commonalities are below 0.5.

We decided to create a series of clinical dimensions from items on the Behavioral Profile due to the relatively poor results of the factor analysis and some discomfort that in conducting the factor analysis it was necessary to delete information describing many of the problems thought to be clinically important in understanding the functioning of abused children. Characteris-

TABLE 5.2 Eight Factors from the Child Behavior Profile with Sample Items and Alpha Correlations

	Factors

Self-esteem (alpha = .80) (e.g, feels inferior, self-critical)	Withdrawal (alpha = .51) (e.g., shy or socially isolated, or withdraws from usual activities or friends)
Aggression (alpha = .74) (e.g., aggressive behavior, bullies other kids)	
	Acting out (alpha = .38) (e.g., runs away, takes off, or hangs around with a bad crowd)
Fearful (alpha = .77) (e.g., afraid of being alone, clings to parents)	
	Anxious to please/tries too hard (alpha = .46) (e.g., overly compliant, too anxious to please, or overly affectionate)
Conscientious (alpha = .64) (e.g., conscientious, able to concentrate, responds quickly to directions)	
Concentration problems (alpha = .42) (e.g., easily frustrated, unable to concentrate, or daydreams, excessive memory loss, unable to concentrate)	

tics of children from the original 110-item Behavior Profile were conceptually grouped into clusters based in part on the factor analysis, clinical judgment, and the clinical literature on child sexual abuse. This resulted in 12 dimensions of child behavior. Items were included in only one dimension, except for the last dimension (post-traumatic stress), which was made up of items in other dimensions. Differences between abused and nonabused children on the 12 clinical dimensions are all statistically significant. Table 5.3 presents the clinical dimensions, sample items from the Behavior Profile making up that dimension, and the dimension alpha coefficients.

TABLE 5.3 Clinical Dimensions of Child Behavior Profile, Sample Items, and Alpha Correlations

Concentration Problems
(alpha = .83)
(e.g., academic problems or daydreams excessively, memory loss, unable to concentrate)

Aggressive
(alpha = .84)
[e.g., aggressive behavior (e.g., yelling, hitting, breaking things) or uncontrolled, unruly, defiant]

Withdrawn
(alpha = .79)
(e.g., spends less time with friends or other children or withdraws from usual activities)

Somatic complaints
(alpha = .52)
(e.g., can't fall asleep or dizziness or faintness)

Character/personality style difficulties
(alpha = .83)
(e.g., nice or pleasant disposition or overly compliant, too anxious to please)

Antisocial
(alpha = .64)
(e.g., hangs around with bad crowd or runs away, takes off)

Nervous/emotional
(alpha = .87)
(e.g., excessive activity, restless, moods change quickly, or is able to relax)

Depression
(alpha = .32)
(e.g., has difficulty communicating or talking or depressed or very unhappy)

Behavioral regression
(alpha = .72)
(e.g., has difficulty waiting his/her turn or clings to parents)

Body image/self-esteem problems
(alpha = .70)
(e.g., overly concerned about cleanliness or does not like her/his body, feels inferior)

Fear
(alpha = .75)
[e.g., afraid of the dark or generalized fears (e.g., afraid of leaving home, riding in car)]

Posttraumatic stress
(alpha = .88)
(e.g., can't fall asleep, moods change quickly, or has panic or anxiety attacks)

Demographic Differences between Samples

Since the abused and comparison samples differed on a number of the demographic and other comparison variables (e.g., age of child, number of stressful life events experienced by child, tendency of parent to have a negative outlook on life), the differences between samples cannot be taken as evidence for the affects of sexual abuse. To explore the importance of these differences, data for the abused sample and the 10 comparative variables were entered in a series of multiple regression analyses with each of the Behavior Profile factors, clinical dimensions, and with the Behavior-Profile-based Parent Score and the Checklist-based Social Worker Score as dependent variables. The resulting regression equations indicate that a number of the comparative variables are associated with variation in the dependent measures. Most notable in this regard are the number of life stresses experienced by the child, age of child, and a tendency for the child's parent to have a negative outlook on life. Depending on measure of child functioning, the comparison variables in the final regression equations explain between 3% and 28% of the variance. Comparison variables in the final regression equations were entered as control variables in subsequent analyses.

A second set of regressions were run on the combined abused and comparison samples, entering first the control variables in the previous equations and then entering the sample dummy (i.e., whether the child was abused or not abused). The sample dummy remains in the regression equation, explaining a significant amount of the remaining variance (after controlling for demographic and other differences between samples) on all measures, except on the following factors: aggressive, withdrawal, acting out, and anxious to please/tries too hard. This indicates that for most measures of child functioning reported here, the observed differences in the functioning of the abused and nonabused children are not solely attributable to differences between samples on the control variables used in the study.

Agreement among Measures

The correlations among the various measures of child functioning vary considerably. For example, the correlations of Social Worker Score and the Behavior Profile factors vary from very low to moderately low ($r = .005$ to $.25$) and for Social Worker Score and the Behavior Profile clinical dimensions from moderate to high correlations ($r = .24$ to $.88$). The correlation of Social Worker Score and Parent Score is moderate ($r = .28$, $N = 310$, $p > .0001$).

Differential Effects

It is clear that not all children will react to the experience of being sexually abused in the same way. Consequently, there has been increasing interest in identifying factors to account for the different reactions victims have to the experience of sexual victimization. Several studies on adults victimized as children have addressed this issue, although there is substantial disagreement between studies about the importance of specific factors. Finkelhor (1979) found that the older the victim, the older the offender, the more force present in the abuse, and if abused by a male (regardless of the sex of the victim), the more negative were the effects of sexual abuse. Tsai, Feldman-Summers, and Edgar (1979) found that the older the victim was at the last sexual contact, the longer and more frequent the abuse, and that the more often sexual intercourse was attempted, the more severe was the impact of sexual abuse. Russell (1984) found that abuse of a longer duration, more frequency, and more serious sexual nature (i.e., intercourse vs. fondling) was associated with a more negative impact of victimization. Seidner and Calhoun (1984) found that particular variables were related to the particular effects of sexual abuse. For example, using a socialization factor that describes social maturity and social adjustment on an adult personality test as the measure of effects, the following variables were found to be associated with a more severe effect: abuse that was more frequent, involved more force, was committed by a male offender, involved a greater age difference between victim and offender, and in which the victim made stable attributional statements about responsibility for the victimization. On a factor that describes liberal attitudes toward sexuality (not necessarily a negative effect), the following variables were significant: abuse of a longer duration, more force, closer relationship between the offender and victim, abuse involving multiple offenders, and stable/unstable attributional beliefs.

Several recent studies have examined the relationship between abuse-related factors and the effects of sexual abuse on children as children. For example, Friedrich, Urquiza, and Beilke (1986) found that boys and girls exhibit different responses to sexual abuse. Boys are more likely to exhibit behaviors characterized as externalizing (e.g., aggression). Abuse of a longer duration, with closer relationship between offender and victim, and a longer duration since last incident was associated with more severe impact. Girls are more likely to exhibit behaviors characterized by internalizing (e.g., depression). Abuse that was more frequent, more severe, and involved a closer relationship between the offender and the victim was associated with a more severe impact. Across populations and variables no single set of variables is consistently correlated with greater impact.

The 65 variables potentially associated with variation in the effects of sexual abuse on children (see Table 5.4) were reduced to 35 on the basis (eliminated) of low zero order correlations with either Social Worker Score or Parent Score or (entered) because of clinical or theoretical interest. Two multiple regression analyses were used to identify factors associated with variation in child functioning.

Using Social Worker Score as a measure of the effects of sexual abuse, the three comparative variables previously found to be associated with variation

TABLE 5.4 Study Variables Potentially Associated with Differential Impact

Child accepts gifts and rewards in response to abuse
Child takes some part in initiating abuse
Child felt she or he would be believed if abuse was revealed
Child felt that she or he would not be believed if abuse was revealed
Child feared negative consequences to self if abuse was revealed
Child feared negative consequences to others if abuse was revealed
Nonoffending parent was supportive at time of disclosure
Child has a supportive relationship with sibling(s)
Child was coerced into abuse via threat of physical harm to self or others
Child was coerced into abuse via physical harm
During the abuse, the victim was physically restrained
During the abuse, child made effort to resist, escape, avoid abuse
Offender denies abuse took place
During the abuse, child passively submits, goes along
During the abuse, child pretends nothing happening
Child initiates report of abuse
Child was previously a victim of sexual abuse
Child believes that others in family knew about abuse and took no action to protect
Degree relationship with offender was important to child
Child perceives some responsibility in own abuse
Child has been pressured to recant abuse
Primary parent does not believe that abuse took place
Primary parent believes that abuse took place
Degree of seriousness of sexual behavior
Degree child perceives relationship with offender (other than abuse) as important
Child perceived no secondary gain from abuse
Number of family problems experienced by child's family
Frequency of abuse
Child had a supportive relationship with an adult
Degree of relationship between child and offender
Number of types of sexual abuse
Number of characteristics of a poorly functioning family

in Social Worker Score were entered as control variables at step one, and the 35 variables potentially associated with variation were entered in a backwards multiple regression. Thirteen variables are in the final equation, explaining 42% of the variance in Social Worker Score.

As can be seen in Table 5.5, a victim's having a supportive relationship with an adult or with a sibling is inversely related to Social Worker Score. Characteristics of a poorly functioning family were positively associated with Social Worker Score. The victim being exposed to more types of sexual behavior, the victim receiving some kind of reward for the abuse, and the victim being physically restrained as part of the sexual abuse were all positively associated with Social Worker Score. Two of the variables describing the victim's coping during the abuse (the victim making some effort to escape, resist, or avoid the abuse and during the abuse the victim passively submitted) are negatively associated with Social Worker Score. The victim's fearing negative consequences to self if the abuse was revealed, the offender's denying that the abuse took place, and the more important the victim perceived her(his) relationship with the offender to be were positively associated with Social Worker Score. The degree of relationship between the victim and offender was negatively associated with Social Worker Score. The negative beta results from the distribution of scores can be seen in Table 5.5. Generally, the closer the relationship, the more the victim is affected.

TABLE 5.5 Results of a Multiple Regression with Social Worker Score as the Measure of Effects (Adjusted r^2 = .42)

Variable	Beta[a]	t	Significance	Increase in r^{2b}
Amount of support available to victim and family	−.07	−1.6	.11	.004
Age of victim	.10	2.3	.02	.009
Parent tendency to give socially appropriate responses	−.09	−2.1	.03	.007
Victim has supportive relationship with an adult	−.12	−2.4	.02	.01
Victim has supportive relationship with sibling(s)	−.10	−2.1	.03	.007
Family has characteristics of poorly functioning family	.39	7.7	.001	.1
Number of types of sexual abuse	.09	1.9	.02	.006
Victim received reward for abuse	.11	2.5	.01	.01
Victim was physically restrained during abuse	.08	1.8	.07	.005
Victim made some effort to resist, escape, avoid abuse	−.13	−2.4	.02	.009
During abuse, victim passively submits	−.22	−4.0	.001	.03
Victim feared negative consequences to self if abuse revealed	.11	2.6	.009	.01
Offender denies abuse took place	.12	2.7	.006	.01
Degree to which victim perceived relationship with offender as important	.10	1.8	.07	.005
Degree of relationship between victim and offender	−.12	−2.4	.02	.01

[a]Beta in final regression equation.
[b]Part correlation squared. This figure represents the amount of variance explained by a variable controlling for all other variables in the equation. The sum of all part correlations squared is less than the total r^2 for the entire equation.

Amount of variance explained by a variable or set of variables is not a concept easily understood by many clinicians. The relative importance of these variables is more readily visualized when viewing the breakdown of number of symptoms (Social Worker Score) for selected variables in the final regression equation. Table 5.6 contains the mean number of symptoms for categories of selected variables in the regression equation in Table 5.5.

Using Parent Score as the measure of the effects of sexual abuse, three

TABLE 5.6 Mean Number of Symptoms (Social Worker Score) for Categories of Selected Variables in Final Regression Equation Presented in Table 5.5

Child was physically restrained during abuse
    absent   present
    3.3   4.2

Child accepted rewards or gifts in response to abuse
    absent   present
    3.3   5.0

Degree of relationship between child and offender

0	1	2	3	4
stranger	friend or acquaintance	parent's partner	other relative	natural parent
3.4	2.9	2.6	3.2	4.6

Child feared negative consequences to self if abuse was revealed
    absent   present
    2.7   4.0

Degree child perceived relationship with offender (other than abuse) as important

absent	not important	somewhat important	important
1.5	2.7	3.7	4.8

During the abuse, the child makes some effort to escape, avoid or resist abuse
    absent   present
    3.3   3.7

During the abuse, child passively submits, goes along
    absent   present
    4.1   2.9

Offender denies abuse took place
    absent   present
    2.9   4.4

Child has a supportive relationship with an adult
    absent   present
    7.1   2.7

Child has a supportive relationship with sibling(s)
    absent   present
    4.7   2.5

comparison variables were entered as control variables, with the 35 variables entered as a second step in a backward multiple regression. As can be seen in Table 5.7, the 3 comparison variables and 4 of the independent variables are the final equation explaining 20% of the variance in Parent Score. The victim's having a supportive relationship with an adult and the victim's being pressured to recant the story of the abuse are negatively associated with Parent Score. The number of problems in living experienced by the victim's family and the degree to which the victim sees self as responsible for the abuse are positively associated with Parent Score.

DISCUSSION

Several points should be kept in mind in thinking about the implications of the research presented above. Abused children in this sample were assessed, on the whole, relatively soon after an abuse incident, and had not been through the full investigative and intervention process. It is not clear how they will be affected by those intervening events or how many of these children will ultimately end up in treatment programs. Nevertheless, there are substantial differences between the abused and nonabused samples at the time of assessment. The data also raised a number of issues both for clinical practice and research. However, several methodological shortcomings of this research limit the utility of the findings. These matters will be briefly reviewed below.

TABLE 5.7 Results of a Multiple Regression with Parent Score as the Measure of Effects (Adjusted r^2 = .20)

Variable	Beta	t	Signifi-cance	Increase in r^2
Tendency for parent to give socially appropriate response	−.08	−1.5	.14	.008
Tendency for parent to have negative outlook on life	.24	4.5	.001	.08
Number of stressful life events victim has faced	.16	3.1	.002	.03
Victim has supportive relationship with an adult	−.20	−3.7	.001	.05
Number of problems in victim's family	.16	2.9	.004	.02
Degree victim sees self as responsible for abuse	.03	1.7	.09	.003

Methodological Limitations

Several methodological problems deserve special consideration. For example, comparative data on the Symptom Checklist for a not-abused sample would be helpful in understanding the differences between abused and nonabused children. Data from the 12-month follow-up assessment of these children on a parent version of the Symptom Checklist indicate large differences in the number of symptoms exhibited by abused and nonabused children in these samples at follow-up (198 abused children had a mean of 7.4 and 160 nonabused a mean of 2.7 symptoms). Additionally, it would be important to know the patterns of these symptoms in other groups of traumatized or stressed children to understand the differential effects of other types of trauma.

When this project was designed almost 7 years ago it was not clear what measures were likely to accurately assess the effects of abuse on children. Experience during the project pretest with standardized measures of psychopathology in children and a more general measure of child behavior raised several concerns about existing measures. Measures of psychopathology do not appear to successfully describe the behavior or functioning of many abused children. Both our pretest and the Tufts New England Medical Center Study found abused children falling between scores for nonabused children and samples of children in psychiatric care (Gomes-Schwartz, Harowitz, & Sauzier, 1985).

And yet, the measure developed for this project, The Child Behavior Profile, has many limitations as well. The statistically created factors do not appear useful in describing the differences between abused and nonabused children. While the clinical dimensions and a summary total score do reliably describe the difference, there is some question in our mind how useful these broad descriptors are either in directing clinical practice or in research efforts.

The relatively poor agreement between the social-worker-completed Symptoms Checklist and the parent-completed Behavior Profile raises a number of questions. The reliability studies (Conte, Berliner, & Schuerman, 1986) conducted as part of this research, as small as they are, seem to suggest that both social workers and parents are consistent in how they describe the child on their respective measures. Additionally, although there are a number of parent variables (e.g., social desirability response set and parent tendency to have a negative outlook on life) associated with parent report of child behavior data, even in controlling for the influences of these variables, abused and nonabused children appear to be functioning differently.

One wonders whether the low correlations between parent and social worker measures of sexually abused children might be due to the very different judgments each was called upon to make. Social workers were asked to indicate the presence of certain symptoms. Parents were asked to indicate on a five-point scale how characteristic a behavior was for their child. It may be that social workers, in part because of clinical training and in part because of the nature of the judgment they were making (presence or absence), required a higher level of the behavior than did parents who were asked to indicate the degree to which something was present. Social workers focused on anthology or disturbance while parents described a range of behaviors. Additionally, it is generally recognized that different data sources, especially parents and professionals, are likely to view events and behavior differently in part because they use different perspectives to view behavior and in part because they see the child in very different environments and under different conditions.

Sexual Abuse Does Have an Effect

The data present in this chapter, as well as in a number of other recent and current investigations, establish the fact that children who are exposed to sexual victimization are affected by the experience. The differences between abused and nonabused children are substantial on all dimensions. The study and much of the research to date has described that difference in terms of overt or observable behavior such as somatic complaints, withdrawal from usual activities, increased aggression, and sexual acting out. The costs of these behaviors to the victim and those who live with her or him have never been calculated in financial or personal terms; they are likely to be great. More importantly, to the extent that such behaviors reflect human suffering, they are likely to be beyond reasonable calculation. However, behavioral reactions to sexual abuse are only a part of the potential impact of childhood sexual experiences.

Future research and practice should discover ways to understand and measure other psychological processes that are influenced by childhood sexual experiences. These processes may be conceptualized in a number of different ways, but include such dimensions as cognitions, expectations, emotional sets, and the like. These processes are important because they serve as the link between historical events (e.g., childhood sexual abuse) and subsequent functioning (e.g., behavior in adulthood).

Psychological processes as mediating events between experience and subsequent functioning is not a new concept in mental health. However, identifying the mediating events of childhood sexual abuse or other abuse experiences is likely to be a quite important application of this approach. For example, it may help us understand how it happens that many adults victimized as children have serious relationship problems. For example, it is possible that through a childhood sexual experience in which betrayal by a trusted adult is perceived as a key dimension, the victims' capacity for or expectations about relationships are altered; the identification of these exact psychological processes, such as the ability to form relationships and expectations of relationships, can be important in directing therapy. Limiting generalizations of abuse effects while the victim is still a child should help prevent the occurrence of problems later in the victim's life.

The Effects Vary across Children

Consistent with other research, the research reported here indicates that children vary in their reaction to sexual abuse. Indeed, using Social Worker Score as the measure of the effects of sexual abuse, the finding that 21% of the children known to have been sexually abused have none (Social Worker Score = 0) of the symptoms thought to be behavioral indicators that a child has been sexually abused (e.g., behavioral regression, somatic complaints, fearfulness) should caution those who are charged with determining if a child has been abused not to place undo reliance on a child's behavior as proving what the child may or may not have experienced.

With the exception of sexual behavior or developmentally inappropriate sexual knowledge (behaviors that the Symptom Checklist does not do a good job of addressing), it is generally accepted that most of the behaviors on the Symptom Checklist simply indicate that the child is under some kind of stress. In this regard, a child whose parents are divorcing or a sexually abused child may exhibit many of same kinds of behavior (Kelly & Wallerstein, 1976). It will be important to further explore variation across types of stressful experiences in childhood to identify common elements as well as distinguishing features.

Sources of Variation Can Be Identified

Research reported here, as research preceding it, has been successful in identifying sources of variation in child functioning. The ability of this research to do so is much greater using a social-worker-completed measure than a parent-completed measure of child functioning. We speculate the reasons for this to be that the parent-completed Behavior Profile is a more general measure of child functioning and that such functioning is influenced by a large number of factors, one set of which may be abuse and abuse-related events. Abuse and abuse-related variables collected during the clinical assessments of the social workers are more likely to explain variation in problematic functioning, which is more directly assessed by the Symptom Checklist than the Behavior Profile.

Several of the variables identified in this research (e.g., during the abuse the victim passively submitted, during the abuse the victim made some effort to escape, avoid, or resist the abuse) raise interesting questions for future research. Both responses serve to reduce the impact of sexual abuse and both describe coping activities during the abuse that would appear to be incompatible. Of the 145 children described as trying to resist, avoid, or otherwise escape from the abuse while it was going on, only 21 (14%) were also described as passively submitting during the abuse. (Both coping strategies could be indicated for the same child if she or he used more than one during any incident or if she or he used different strategies during different abuse incidents.)

Perhaps these coping behaviors may actually describe a child's general coping strategy in life (e.g., an active effort to control events vs. a general acceptance of events). As such either strategy may be more "healthy" than an inability to deal with events or to fall apart in the face of certain events.

Given the popularity of programs to teach children to escape, resist, or avoid their own sexual abuse, the finding of the importance of this descriptive variable should be viewed very cautiously. It is not clear what specific resistance strategies were employed by these victims, whether the child's description of the behavior is accurate, or if it worked. Until such information is available, this finding does not necessarily support this aspect of current prevention activities.

Why Identify Sources of Variance?

There has been relatively little discussion about why identifying sources of variation in the effects of sexual abuse is an important endeavor. One reason is that such an effort could form the basis of a more rational way to distribute services to sexually abused children. Although it is not clear empirically how services are actually distributed to abused children, experience suggests that distribution is often based on which child has the most assertive worker and, perhaps, on class, race, or economic basis or because of a professional bias about the nature of the problem. For example, incest victims appear more likely to get treatment than other victims.

In a more rational system, victims would receive service depending on their need. Victims whose current functioning indicated a severe effect or victims with a number of the risk factors known to be associated with a more serious effect could be placed in more intensive intervention. Other victims might be helped in less intensive, and therefore less expensive, treatment interventions.

The danger of such a system in a scarce resource environment would be to suggest that victims less effected or with few of the risk factors for a more severe effect would receive no service at all. Such a decision is clearly not justified by the available evidence. While some victims may appear not to be effected at the time of disclosure or mental health assessment, it is currently not known which of these victims may, without treatment, exhibit problems later in life.

Research to date has tended to focus on risk factors that are relatively static (e.g., frequency of abuse, relationship between victim and offender, the victim's coping during the abuse). While these may be helpful in understanding variation in impact of abuse and in identifying victims as the greatest risk for more serious reactions to abuse, they do little to direct the actual therapy of specific victims in that they cannot be the targets of treatment themselves. Future work will likely profit by identifying risk factors associated with a more serious effect that can themselves be altered by treatment.

These risk factors might be thought of as mediators between the abuse and abuse situation and specific problems in living experienced by the victim. For example, it is generally recognized that many victims report feelings of guilt over not having told about the abuse sooner or feeling that they got something out of the abuse (e.g., attention). Should it be found that feelings of guilt are related to a more serious impact, therapeutic efforts could be directed toward the guilt feelings themselves.

Similarly, there has been much interest in where victims place responsibility (e.g., blame themselves vs. blame others) for their own victimization. Research reviewed by Conte (1985) suggests that attributions victims make of responsibility do not always operate in the way traditionally assumed by many mental health professionals. For example, blaming oneself in an uncontrollable situation may be the only means of maintaining a sense of control and is therefore associated with a less serious impact of victimization (Janoff-Bulman & Frieze, 1983) or with differential impacts (Gold, 1986). It is not currently known what attributional beliefs child victims of sexual abuse have and how these are associated with the effects of such experiences. If known and if certain attributional statements are associated with a more serious impact, then these attributions may become the target of intervention.

Support to Victim Is Important

One of the major findings of the study is the importance of support from a nonoffending parent or from a sibling in reducing the impact of sexual abuse, and that the more characteristics of negative family functioning the victim's family has, the more problems the victim will have. Consideration of the level of support and of the family environment of the victim should be part of any clinical assessment conducted with these cases.

The importance of these variables accounting for negative effects of childhood sexual victimization also suggests an area for clinical innovation. Currently, many families of victimized children receive little or no intervention, especially intervention designed to help them be supportive of their victimized child. Father or stepfather incest families may receive treatment, a part of which may focus on the family's (especially mother's) support of the victim. Many other types of cases receive little intervention beyond initial crisis management.

Therapists may well develop interventions designed to assess and increase the family's understanding of child sexual abuse, of the needs of victimized children, and of the ways that family members can be helpful to the victim in recovery. Assessment should identify families with substantial pathology where longer-term intervention is likely to be necessary, and these families could be referred directly to such intervention, bypassing the more short-term structured "support" intervention.

A special note should be made of the importance of the victim's relationship with his or her siblings. Currently, little if any therapeutic attention is directed toward the siblings of victims. The NIMH research calls attention to the importance of clinically assessing the relationship of the victim with her or his siblings, and where that relationship is poor (conflictual or unsupportive), therapy might be directed toward improving the relationship. It is likely that a number of innovative therapeutic approaches might be developed to respond to victim/sibling relationships. For example, therapy groups for nonabused siblings or sibling/victim dyads could be evaluated.

In many ways, research on the effects of sexual abuse has just begun. Greater collaboration between therapist and researcher in identifying and altering the effects of childhood sexual experiences should be encouraged.

REFERENCES

Bagley, C., & Ramsay, R. (1986). Sexual abuse in childhood: Psychosocial outcomes and implications for social work practice. *Journal of Social Work and Human Sexuality, 4,* 33–47.

Becker, J. V., Skinner, L. J., Abel, G. G., & Treacy, E. G. (1983). National disaster and technological catastrophe. *Environment and Behavior, 15,* 333–354.

Benward, J., & Densen-Gerber, J. (1975). Incest as a causative factor in antisocial behavior: An exploratory study. *Contemporary Drug Problems, 4,* 323–340.

Briere, J. (1987a). Post-sexual abuse trauma: Data and implications for practice. *Journal of Interpersonal Violence,* in press.

Briere, J. (1987b). Symptomatology associated with childhood sexual victimization in a nonclinical adult sample. *International Journal of Child Abuse and Neglect,* in press.

Briere, J., & Ruwtz, M. (1986). Adolescent "acting out" and childhood history of sexual abuse. *The Journal of Interpersonal Violence, 1*(3).

Browne, A., & Finkelhor, D. (1985). The traumatic impact of child sexual abuse: A conceptualization. Available from the Family Violence Research Program, University of New Hampshire, Durham, NH 03824.

Burgess, A. W., Groth, N., & McCaraline, M. P. (1981). Child sex initiation rings. *American Journal of Psychiatry, 51,* 110–119.

Carroll, J., Schaffer, C., Spensley, J., & Abramowitz, S. I. (1980). Family experience of self-mutilating patients. *American Journal of Psychiatry, 137,* 852–853.

Conte, J. R. (1984). Progress in treating the sexual abuse of children. *Social Work, 29,* 258–263.

Conte, J. R. (1985). The effects of sexual abuse on children: A critique and suggestions for future research. *Victimology: The International Journal, 10,* 110–130.

Conte, J. R., & Berliner, L. (1981). Sexual abuse of children: Implications for practice. *Social Casework, 62,* 601–606.

Conte, J. R., Berliner, L., & Schuerman, J. (1986). Impact of sexual abuse on children. Final Report. Available from the authors at The University of Chicago, School of Social Service Administration, 969 E. 60th Street, Chicago, IL 60637.

deYoung, M. (1982). Self-injurious behavior in incest victims. *Child Welfare, 61,* 557–584.

Emmerman, L., & Crewdson, J. (1984–1985). Child abuse. *Chicago Tribune,* May 13, 14, 15, June 24, 25, 26, September 23, 25, 26, 1984, and February 14, 1985.

Finkelhor, D. (1979). *Sexually victimized children.* New York: Free Press.

Friedrich, W., Urquiza, A., & Beilke, R. (1986). Behavior problems in sexually abused young children. *Journal of Pediatric Psychology, 11,* 47–57.

Gold, E. (1986). Long-term effects of sexual victimization in childhood: An attributional approach. *Journal of Consulting and Clinical Psychology, 54,* 471–475.

Gomes-Schwartz, B., Harowitz, J. M., & Sauzier, M. (1985). Severity of emotional distress among sexually abused preschool, school age and adolescent children. *Hospital and Community Psychiatry, 35,* 503–508.

Goodwin, J., Simms, M., & Bergman, R. (1979). Hysterical seizures: A sequel to incest. *American Journal of Orthopsychiatry, 49,* 698–703.

Herman, J., & Hirschman, L. (1981). Families at risk for father–daughter incest. *American Journal of Psychiatry, 138,* 967–970.

Janoff-Bulman, R., & Freize, I. (1983). A theoretical perspective for understanding reactions to victimization. *Journal of Social Issues, 39,* 1–17.

Kelly, J. B., & Wallerstein, J. S. (1976). The effects of parental divorce: Experiences of the child and early latency. *American Journal of Orthopsychiatry, 46,* 20–32.

Masson, J. M. (1984). *The assault on truth: Freud's suppression of the seduction theory.* New York: Farrar, Straus, and Giroux.

Meiselman, K. C. (1979). *Incest.* San Francisco: Jossey-Bass.

Miller, A. (1984). *Thou shalt not be aware.* New York: Farrar, Straus and Giroux.

Mrazek, P. B., & Mrazek, D. A. (1981). The effects of child abuse: Methodological considerations. In P. B. Mrazek & C. H. Kempe (Eds.), *Sexually abused children and their families.* New York: Pergamon Press.

Russell, D. E. H. (1984). *Sexual exploitation.* Beverly Hills, CA: Sage Press.

Seidner, A. L., & Calhoun, K. S. (1984). *Childhood sexual abuse: Factors related to differential adult adjustment.* Paper presented at Second National Conference for Family Violence Researchers, University of New Hampshire, Durham.

Tsai, M., Feldman-Summers, S., & Edgar, M. (1979). Childhood molestation: Variables related to differential functioning in adult women. *Journal of Abnormal Psychology, 88,* 407–417.

Tsai, M., & Wagner, N. (1978). Therapy groups for women sexually molested as children. *Archives of Sexual Behavior, 7,* 417–427.

Weiss, J., Rogers, E., Darwin, M., & Dutton, C. (1955). A study of girl child sex victims. *Psychiatric Quarterly, 29,* 1–27.

6

Correlates of Incest Reported by Adolescent Girls in Treatment for Substance Abuse

Glenace E. Edwall
Norman G. Hoffmann

Public and professional attention has increasingly been drawn to the issue of child sexual abuse. Estimates of incidence in specific populations and attempts to assess the relationship of sexual abuse to later patterns of psychological functioning have been reported. There have been major studies that have recently confirmed that between 1 out of 10 (Herman, 1981) to 38% of all girls (Russell, 1984) have been sexually abused, almost all (95%) by males (Berliner, 1982).

The question of psychological sequelae is certainly complicated by theoretical and political differences among authors as well as substantial methodological differences among the studies (Herman, 1981; Ward, 1985). A number of case reports in the literature purport to show no psychological harm to the child as a result of sexual contact or even incestuous involvement with an adult. These date back to Bender and Blau (1937), and are cited as extending into the current literature (Ward, 1985). Nonetheless, a picture is emerging

The authors wish to acknowledge the support of the following treatment facilities: Fountain Center/Albert Lea Adolescent Unit/Fountain Center, Albert Lea, MN; Winnebago Adolescent Treatment Center, Winnebago, MN; Frances Mahon Deaconess Adolescent Hospital, Glasgow, MT; Glenbeigh Adolescent Hospital, Cleveland, OH; Glenbeigh of Tampa, Tampa, FL; Gordon Chemical Dependency Center, Sioux City, IA; Parkview West Adolescent Treatment Center, Eden Prairie, MN; St. Francis Medical Center, La Crosse, WI; St. John's Hospital, St. Paul, MN; St. Luke's Adolescent Hospital, Cleveland, OH; Theda Clark Hospital, Neenah, WI. Appreciation is also extended to Lynda Hurt for assistance in preparation on this manuscript.

that suggests substantial clinical consequences common to sexual abuse victims (see also Finkelhor & Browne, Chapter 4 in this volume, and Conte & Berliner, Chapter 5). Critical components of the clinical findings are shame and guilt, depression and low self-esteem, difficulty with relationships, and reports of sexual problems (Herman, 1981; Kaufman et al., 1954; Meiselman, 1978; Tsai & Wagner, 1978).

One of the first systematic reports in the literature is that of Karin Meiselman (1978), who compared a group of 20 women therapy patients with a known history of incest with a matched control group of patients, none of whom reported any sexual abuse. All women in the incest group were initiating treatment at least 3 years subsequent to the cessation of the incest. The groups were compared with regard to presenting problems as well as diagnostic categories assigned after an intake interview. The most marked differences between the groups had to do with conflicts experienced by the women with heterosexual partners, and also with parents or in-laws. The incest victims also reported a higher incidence of sexual problems. The groups were similar in their presentation of symptoms of depression, anxiety, suicidal ideation, hostility, and phobias. While the differences were not statistically significant, Meiselman found that the incest group tended to have a greater number of presenting complaints and that these were judged by the intake evaluators to be of a more serious magnitude, and a larger percentage had a previous psychiatric hospitalization. There were no clear-cut differences in the diagnostic picture presented by the two groups, although there was some tendency for the incest victims to be more frequently seen as having a depressive neurosis. In particular, Meiselman found no difference in the incidence of a diagnosis of alcohol addiction in the two groups.

Herman (1981) also contrasted a group of 40 adult women incest victims who were therapy patients with a control group of women in treatment and found significant differences between them in reports of adolescent pregnancy, having been beaten concomitantly by family members, and having markedly negative self-concept. Trends were also observed for the incest victims to report more runaway attempts, more suicide attempts, and greater drug or alcohol abuse. They were, however, no more likely than the control group to report major depressive symptoms or sexual problems. Herman also obtained histories from both groups that showed a significantly greater proportion of the incest fathers to have had a history of violent behavior, although there was no difference in the report of fathers being alcoholic. Mothers of the incest daughters were significantly more likely to have had a major illness, and also to have been separated from their daughters for some period of time during childhood, most often due to depression, alcoholism, or psychosis. There were no significant differences in any of a number of demographic variables or family background characteristics, which appears consistent with Berliner's (1982) observation that while alcohol or drug abuse figured in about 20% of the Harborview cases, a full 50% of cases were characterized by having no other reported problems in the family.

Another study (Finkelhor, 1979; 1984) compared 121 sexual abuse victims with 685 nonvictims, all in a college population. Given that entire classes of students were surveyed, Finkelhor contends that his was not as highly selected a population as in other studies. Perhaps most interesting in this study was the development and use of a sexual self-esteem scale to investigate the hypothesis that abuse has particular negative impact on sexual feelings and behavior. On this six-item, 4-point Likert scale, Finkelhor found that victimized women scored six points lower than nonvictims, a statistically significant difference, and that a major locus of the difference between the groups was that victimized women reported more often finding themselves in awkward sexual situations. Finkelhor found only weak support for an associated hypothesis that child victims would be more likely to be subject to further sexual victimization as adults, although he argues (Finkelhor, 1984) that early abuse certainly has the potential to increase the risk of adolescent or adult susceptibility by forcing children out of their families at an earlier age, to escape the abuse or blame or both, and by undercutting the development of self-esteem in victims.

There appears to be some evidence in clinical reports that the longer the duration of a course of sexual abuse, the greater the psychological effects on the victim (Sgroi, 1982), a possibility confounded with the substantially greater effects found for incest as opposed to extrafamilial sexual abuse (Herman, 1981). Berliner (1982) found that the majority (73%) of reported extrafamilial abuse involved only one incident, while 29% of the family cases included incidents that had occurred during a period of from 1 to 5 years at the time of disclosure. Correspondingly, Berliner also records that report and treatment followed disclosure in significantly less time for nonfamily than for family cases. These effects were seen as early as Bender and Blau's (1937) controversial report, in that they found more serious disturbance in the two cases of father–daughter incest that they observed than in cases involving nonrelated adults.

The literature is thus suggestive that the sequelae of ongoing sexual abuse may accumulate to create particularly severe problems for the adolescent female. Giarretto (1982) observes that the reactions of these girls have been more thoroughly internalized than those of younger children, leading to deep feelings of shame and low self-esteem as well as frequently to acting-out behavior. While Meiselman (1978) disputes a previous suggestion (Sloane & Karpinsky, 1942) that incest during adolescence causes more serious disturbance than at earlier ages, there has apparently been little attempt to separate effects of age at onset from duration of the incest episodes. It may be the case that adolescent-onset incest is actually less common than adolescent revelation of longer-duration sexual abuse.

In this regard, one might begin to look for forms of psychological disturbance in the adolescent conveying a particular sense of helplessness regarding their family situations. Goodwin (1982), for example, found eight suicide attempts by adolescent girls in a sample of 201 families followed by a protective service agency for up to 33 months. All 8 were between 14 and 16 years old; three made their suicide attempts more than a year after disclosure of the incest. None of these girls had been diagnosed as depressed, but five were runaways, four were truant, three were described as promiscuous, and two had admitted to abusing drugs. Seven of the eight made their suicide attempts with a drug overdose.

Analyses in this pilot study relied primarily on contingency analysis in comparing the 31 cases reporting some intrafamilial sexual experience (possible incest cases) and the 107 cases (nonincest cases) not reporting such experiences on variables and variates from the CATOR data set. Multivariate procedures were not employed because such analyses performed on data sets with a relatively small sample size relative to the numbers of variables can result in spurious findings. That is, results may reflect chance nuances in the data rather than generalizable phenomena or relationships. Multiple comparisons also may yield some spurious relationships based on chance. Thus, the current results should be considered only as a preliminary indication of where future research might focus rather than as definitive findings.

FINDINGS

Family Variables

We began by examining the hypothesis that the possible incest might have occurred in family contexts that were significantly different than those of girls not reporting such experience. Specifically, the adolescents were asked about both physical and sexual abuse of other family members, as well as about their own physical abuse. As shown in Table 6.1, the possible incest cases reported higher rates of all of these forms of abuse than did non-incest cases. Girls acknowledging intrafamilial sexual abuse were more likely to report both physical and sexual abuse experiences of other family members. They were also more likely to report that they were physically abused by a family member.

While there is a trend toward further sexual victimization outside the family for the possible incest victims, there is not a statistically significant difference (even at $p = .05$) between incest and nonincest groups in this regard, and there is also no difference between the groups in reporting physical abuse outside the family. Thus, the focus of greater physical and sexual victimization of the possible incest group has been quite clearly within the family. The data also support the observation that both physical and

TABLE 6.1 Other Abuse in Families of Adolescent Girls in Treatment for Substance Abuse

Question	Possible incest cases (N=31)	Nonincest cases (N=107)
Adolescent beaten by family member *	65%	28%
Family member beat other family member **	74%	33%
Adolescent beaten by anyone else	29%	21%
Family member sexually abused by other family member **	52%	4%
Adolescent sexually abused by anyone else	42%	28%

$^*p < .001$
$^{**}p < .0001$

sexual abuse tend to be perpetrated against other family members. This suggests that when an incest case is found, her siblings are likely to be at risk for similar abuse.

The role abuse of alcohol and other drugs plays in intrafamilial physical and sexual abuse is not clear from the literature or this data base. The adolescent girls were asked if parents or siblings used alcohol or drugs to excess. While no statistically significant differences were observed, the trend was for girls reporting intrafamilial sexual experiences to cite more excessive alcohol use by both the fathers (46% versus 39%) and their mothers (27% versus 12%). These results would be compatible with other findings such as Herman (1981) suggesting that other female family members including the mother may be abusing chemicals, perhaps to medicate the effects of their own victimization. Further studies with clear identification of the perpetrator(s) should shed more light on this question.

It has been hypothesized that at least for some types of incest (Groth & Hobson, 1983) there is a connection between stresses in the perpetrator's life and the occurrence of incest. In this regard, the adolescents were asked about stresses in the family in the past year. The only significant difference between the groups had to do with remarriage of a parent, with a greater percentage of incest cases reporting these marriages (13% versus 2%). It is not clear whether the remarriage may be associated with previous abuse by the past partner or whether the abuse involved the current partner. As adolescents were also asked about their living arrangements in the past year, an attempt was made to analyze the data for incidence of incest as well as chemical use in this subset of reconstituted families, but the absolute number of cases was too small to allow meaningful comparisons. It should also be noted that there were trends toward larger percentages of separations and divorces among the parents of incest cases as opposed to nonincest cases, but the form of reporting employed makes it impossible to hypothesize whether these marital disruptions were related in any way to the reported incest.

In summary, this sample of incest cases differs from nonincest cases in the greater incidence of physical and sexual abuse in their families. This suggests that the incest case is likely to live in a generally abusive and exploitative environment. It further suggests that other family members of incest cases are at elevated risk for abuse. Group differences regarding substance use and stress are not nearly as striking. The issue of step-parents' use is not clear since the relative proportions of incest and nonincest cases living with step-parents, not the identity of the perpetrators, was discernable from this data base.

Substance Abuse

All subjects within this sample are known to have abused drugs or alcohol, but questions may be raised regarding differences in the patterns of use of incest and nonincest cases. A number of questions were asked regarding substance use, and results for frequency of use are reported in Table 6.2. Incest cases were found to be significantly more frequent users of alcohol and also were characterized by greater use of stimulants. There are no differences between the groups in reported use of marijuana, sedatives, or tranquilizers, nor in reporting the use of hallucinogens, synthetic analgesics, opioids, cocaine, inhalants, or other nonprescription drugs. Significantly more of the incest cases began using alcohol by age 9 (45% versus 21%; $p <$ .05), and there is a trend for earlier use of other drugs by these girls.

The significantly more frequent use of both alcohol and stimulants on the part of incest cases appears consistent with hypotheses that they have become fundamentally detached from their physical experiences and feelings in order to reduce their pain. Such persons may simultaneously attempt to sedate themselves, as with heavy alcohol use, and also to escape into the transient high afforded by stimulants, which may be the only safe and predictable way to have any experience of feeling. For this population, however, it should also be noted that the drugs of choice are very similar for the incest and nonincest groups and may chiefly reflect what is available and well advertised in the adolescent community.

Emotional Distress and Psychopathology

The adolescents were asked about a variety of psychological symptoms reflecting anxiety, depression, and dissociative phenomena, as well as suicidal ideation and attempts. Results for these questions are shown in Table 6.3.

TABLE 6.2 Drug and Alcohol Use Reported by Adolescent Females in Treatment for Substance Abuse

Question	Possible incest cases (N=31)	Nonincest cases (N=106)
Average use of alcohol: **		
< once/week	45%	38%
Weekly	29%	53%
Daily	26%	9%
Average use of marijuana		
Not used	13%	11%
< once/week	16%	33%
Weekly	26%	23%
Daily	45%	33%
Average use of sedatives:		
Not used	67%	76%
< once/week	20%	17%
Weekly	7%	5%
Daily	7%	3%
Average use of stimulants: *		
Not used	32%	45%
< once/week	26%	31%
Weekly	13%	7%
Daily	29%	9%
Average use of tranquilizers:		
Not used	83%	84%
< once/week	0%	2%
Weekly	3%	3%
Daily	3%	1%

* $p < .05$
** $p < .01$

Rates of reporting a number of indications of psychological distress were high for both incest and nonincest cases and did not distinguish between the groups. In particular, the incidence of self-reported depression was very high in this sample, occurring in 84% of the probable incest victims and 82% of nonvictims. Anxiety symptoms and vegetative symptoms of depression were also extremely common in both groups, and ratings by counselors suggest that between one third and one half of the combined sample would be described as having depressed mood.

Despite this high baseline of distress, however, there were consistent

TABLE 6.3 Depression and Suicide in Adolescent Females in Treatment for Substance Abuse

Question	Possible incest cases (N=31)	Nonincest cases (N=103)
Inpatient psychiatric hospitalization *	29%	10%
Overdose	23%	10%
Psychological symptoms		
Nervousness	77%	61%
Tension	81%	73%
Restlessness	65%	77%
Depression	84%	82%
Suicidal thoughts *	77%	51%
Sleeplessness	58%	47%
No energy	64%	68%
Sexual problems	36%	23%
Eating problems	45%	34%
Depression index		
No depression	16%	18%
Depressed mood	36%	44%
Possible depression diagnosis	48%	38%
Suicide index *		
No ideation	23%	47%
Ideation	23%	26%
Attempt	55%	27%

$* p < .05$

indications of a more serious form of distress among the incest cases or that these girls exhibited behaviors that were more likely to precipitate some intervention. These adolescents were significantly more likely to have had an inpatient psychiatric hospitalization, with 10 of the 31 victims having been hospitalized. They were also more clinically depressed, with 15 of the 31 seen by counselors as having a probable diagnosis of a depressive episode. Most importantly, however, more than 75% of the incest cases reported suicidal thoughts, and 17 of the 31 had made a suicide attempt in the past year—a rate twice as high as for the nonincest group. It thus appears that the depression that characterizes the incest cases may consist to a greater extent of perceptions of hopelessness and helplessness as opposed to nonincest cases and may thus be more likely to manifest in suicide attempts. Further research employing more precise diagnostic questions is critical to understanding the potential psychological correlates of incest and providing appropriate interventions.

Self-concept

The literature suggests that the violation of a sense of self that occurs in sexual abuse and particularly incest is erosive of self-esteem and ultimately is related to the development of a negative self-concept. The adolescent population was asked about several aspects of self-concept, including how they felt about the way they looked; whether they took care of themselves physically; and whether they were proud, ashamed, respectful, or hateful toward themselves. None of these questions differentiated between incest and nonincest cases, with roughly a quarter of each group showing markedly negative views of self.

Three further questions were asked about aspects of self-esteem that might be reflected to the adolescent by her parents; these are reported in Table 6.4. The incest cases are here quite clearly different from nonincest cases in that they are significantly less likely to feel that their parents consistently love them and significantly more likely to see their parents as ashamed of them. This finding seems particularly noteworthy in view of the abuse phenomena discussed previously. The incest cases' sense of self includes a more negative parental component that appears to reflect the repeated victimization that they are likely to face in their families. Again, further research is necessary to understand the connections made by incest cases between their experience of abuse, their sense of self, and how they perceive others' attitudes about them.

TABLE 6.4 Attribution of Parental Attitudes by Adolescent Females in Treatment for Substance Abuse

Question	Possible incest cases ($N=31$)	Nonincest cases ($N=106$)
Parents respect you		
Rarely/sometimes	71%	58%
Often/usually	30%	42%
Parents ashamed of you *		
Rarely/sometimes	58%	83%
Often/usually	42%	17%
Parents love you *		
Rarely/sometimes	20%	8%
Usually/often	80%	92%

* $p < .05$

Legal Involvement

This area of study particularly follows Finkelhor's (1984) suggestion that incest victims are forced out of their homes at earlier ages than nonincest victims, most likely without sufficient experience or resources to avoid further victimization and/or other serious trouble. Additionally, if the "hopelessness, helplessness" hypothesis about their psychological organization is correct, there may be more numbness and acceptance of potentially dangerous (physically and legally) involvements.

Incest and nonincest cases in this sample did indeed differ in regard to the former being more likely to have been arrested, and more likely in particular to have been arrested on a status offense, reflecting their greater likelihood of having run away from home. These results are shown in Table 6.5. Incest cases are also significantly more likely to have had an out-of-control petition filed by their parents and to have experienced a variety of consequences as the result of an arrest. They were also more likely to have had an out-of-home placement and to have a social worker assigned to them. Again, it is not possible in this data set to determine whether this social service involvement was prior or subsequent to the incest incident.

DISCUSSION

This investigation was begun with the observation that while there is a growing recognition of the prevalence of incest, relatively little is known about its effects on the lives of its victims (Russell, 1986). Examination of a sample of adolescent females entering chemical dependency treatment showed approximately 23% of them to acknowledge some form of intrafamilial sexual experience. Although the instrumentation of this study was not specifically designed to identify either the other family members involved or the sequelae of sexual abuse, it was nonetheless possible to find several significant differences between the probable incest group and the remainder of the sample. These differences include:

1. Probable incest cases came from families in which there were significantly greater probabilities of their also being physically abused and of other family members also being physically and/or sexually abused.
2. Probable incest cases are more frequent users of both alcohol and stimulants than are nonincest cases, and they were also significantly more likely to have begun drinking before the age of nine.
3. Both groups in this sample report numerous psychological complaints, but girls reporting incest appeared to suffer more serious forms of distress and/or behaviors likely to result in psychiatric care, as reflected

TABLE 6.5 Legal Involvement of Adolescent Females in Treatment for Substance Abuse

Question	Possible incest cases (N=31)	Nonincest cases (N=106)
Been arrested **	62%	33%
Arrested on status offense **	32%	8%
Out of control petition *	39%	17%
Put into detox center	3%	0
Informal reprimand	39%	29%
Informal hearing	39%	21%
On probation	42%	25%
Required to make restitution *	26%	9%
Put in detention center	23%	9%
In jail overnight	10%	12%
In juvenile corrections facility	19%	6%
Jail sentence	3%	2%
Waived to adult court	6%	1%
Currently on parole	23%	17%
Out-of-home placement ***	48%	10%
Currently have social worker ***	48%	15%
Current charges		
None	61%	74%
Misdemeanor	29%	22%
Felony	10%	4%

$* p < .05, ** p < .01, *** p < .001.$

in their greater incidence of psychiatric hospitalization and a very high incidence of suicide attempts.

4. The probable incest cases are more likely than nonincest cases to perceive their parents as ashamed of them, and significantly less likely to think that their parents consistently love them.

5. Girls reporting probable incest experiences have substantially greater and more serious involvement with the legal system than nonincest cases. Status offenses and out-of-home placement after an arrest were significantly more common for the incest group.

These results, taken together, begin to suggest a picture of the female adolescent incest cases placed in chemical dependency treatment as having come from families in which several members have been physically and sexually abused. One may hypothesize that they experience substantial emotional distress and evolve to frequent use of alcohol and stimulants, beginning at a very early age. A large number of these incest cases run away from home and/or make a suicide attempt. In short, in this sample, the correlates of incest appear to reflect relatively serious disturbances in social and emotional functioning.

As noted repeatedly, a large number of questions, some of them fundamental, were not addressed in this research and need to be considered in future investigations. These include obtaining more specific information about the identity of the perpetrator(s), the duration and severity of the abuse, and whether there had been disclosure and intervention. Further questions about family structure and history should be included. Following suggestions in the extant literature, we would like to ask more specific questions regarding psychological variables, particularly regarding feelings of helplessness, the presence of dissociative phenomena, and further indications of disruptions of functioning. Last, given that running away from home is very common among incest cases, we could inquire more closely regarding frequency and age at the time of these incidents, how these girls lived while on the run, and what kinds of difficulties or further experiences of victimization they may have encountered.

The present research is thus clearly preliminary but suggests several substantial problem areas whose further investigation will add to our knowledge of sexual abuse, chemical dependency, and the needs that must be addressed in both treatment planning and public policy discussions. The prevalence of probable sexual and physical abuse as reported by these girls strongly suggests that substance abuse programs should have appropriate evaluation for physical and sexual abuse with adequate procedures and mechanisms for treating or referring abuse cases. Treatment programs must also have clear policies for mandatory reporting requirements.

REFERENCES

Bender, L., & Blau, A. (1937). The reactions of children to sexual relations with adults. *American Journal of Orthopsychiatry, 7,* 500–514.

Berliner, L. (1982). Counseling and follow-up interaction for the sexually-abused child. In C. G. Warner, & G. R. Braen, (Eds.), *Management of the physically and emotionally abused.* Norwalk, CT: Appleton-Century-Crofts.

Finkelhor, D. (1979). *Sexually victimized children.* New York: Free Press.

Finkelhor, D. (1984). *Child sexual abuse: Theory and research.* New York: Free Press.

Giaretto, H. (1982). *Integrated treatment of child sexual abuse.* Palo Alto, CA: Science and Behavior Books.

Goodwin, J. (1982). Suicide attempts: A preventable complication of incest. In J. Goodwin, (Ed.), *Sexual abuse: Incest victims and their families.* Boston: John Wright.

Groth, A. N. (1982). The incest offender. In S. Sgroi, (Ed.), *Handbook of clinical intervention in child sexual abuse.* Lexington, MA: Lexington Books.

Herman, J. (1981) *Father–daughter incest.* Cambridge, MA: Harvard University Press.

Kaufman, I., Peck, A. L., & Tagiuri, C. K. (1954). The family constellation and overt incestuous relations between father and daughter. *American Journal of Orthopsychiatry, 24,* 266–279.

Meiselman, K. (1978). *Incest.* San Francisco: Jossey-Bass.

Russell, D. (1984). *Sexual exploitation: Rape, child sexual abuse and work place harassment.* Beverly Hills, CA: Sage Publications.

Russell, D. (1986). *The secret trauma: Incest in the lives of girls and women.* New York: Basic Books.

Sgroi, S. M. (Ed.). (1982). *Handbook of clinical intervention in child sexual abuse.* Lexington, MA: Lexington Books.

Sloane, P., & Karpinsky, E. (1942). Effects of incest on the participants. *American Journal of Orthopsychiatry, 12,* 666–673.

Tsai, M., & Wagner, N. (1978). Therapy groups for women sexually molested as children. *Archives of Sexual Behavior, 7,* 417–429.

Ward, E. (1985). *Father–daughter rape.* New York: Grove Press.

PART III
Forensic and Mental Health Assessment

7

Children as Witnesses:
What Do They Remember?

Gail S. Goodman
Vicki S. Helgeson

Children who are sexually assaulted often fail to tell adults about the abuse, but when they do, the results may include a legal investigation and court trial. The present chapter concerns the child as a victim/witness of sexual assault in criminal court proceedings. Much of the information may also be useful in civil actions such as juvenile court dependency and neglect proceedings, child custody and visitation determinations, and personal injury lawsuits. Because a child's memory may be of central importance if legal action is taken, this chapter largely concerns children's memory and eyewitness testimony. Because testimony occurs in a legal context, legal issues will also be considered.

Child sexual abuse was once thought to be an infrequent phenomenon, and biases existed (and still exist) against believing children (Goodman, 1984; Goodman, Golding & Haith, 1984; Masson, 1984; Rush, 1980). In the past, children's memory was depicted as so fallible and children's suggestibility so great that children's testimony could not be trusted. Children were viewed as creators of sexual fantasies, as not being able to distinguish

Sections of this chapter appeared previously as "Child Sexual Assault: Children's Memory and the Law" in J. Bulkley (Ed.), *Papers from a national policy conference on legal reforms in child sexual abuse* (1985). Washington, DC: American Bar Association. Support for writing this article was provided in part from the Developmental Psychobiology Research Group, University of Colorado Health Sciences Center, Department of Psychiatry.

imagination from reality, and as inexhaustibly suggestible (Freud, 1900/1965; Stern, 1910; Varendonck, 1911). Scientific—and not-so-scientific—evidence was brought to bear to reinforce these cultural beliefs, despite the fact that the early scientific studies were methodologically flawed and their findings were never shown to be generalizable to real-life cases of victimization (Goodman, 1984).

Examples of rare historical events, such as the Salem witch trials, have also been used to cast doubt on children's testimony. In the traditional interpretation of the trials, several adolescent girls are blamed for making false allegations of bewitchment, allegations that set off hysteria in the town and led to the death of innocent people. But historical events such as these are open to multiple interpretations. A newer interpretation, for example, is that the girls and the others in Salem were suffering from ergotism, a type of food poisoning (see Carporael, 1976; Matossian, 1982). Ergotism, chemically similar to ingestion of LSD, results in symptoms similar to those described by the Salemites (e.g., delirium). If this interpretation is accepted, it leads to the conclusion that the adolescent girls may have reported their symptoms accurately; the adults believed the children because they too soon suffered the same symptoms. Given the lack of medical knowledge at the time, bewitchment may have been as reasonable an explanation as any. But in the end, we are unlikely ever to know what actually transpired in 1692. Rather than relying on folklore, modern scientific studies of children's abilities are needed.

Modern research does not support the view of children as necessarily dangerous witnesses. Moreover, it has become clear that many children truly are sexually victimized, and not just by strangers but also by their parents, relatives, and acquaintances (Russell, 1983). To give an example of the extent of child sexual abuse, one might consider reports to child protection agencies (although such reports are likely to underestimate the true extent of the problem). In 1982, child protection agencies across the country recorded over 56,607 cases of substantiated child sexual abuse (Finkelhor, 1984).

Although more research is needed, there is currently no evidence that children frequently fantasize sexual attacks or that they can be led by parents or others to report falsely such events. False reports may occur at times (as they do for any crime and for purported victims of all ages), but it is important to keep in mind that there is currently no proof that they occur frequently for the crime of child sexual assault. Studies that have examined the extent of false reports of this crime find that the percentage of possible false reports is quite small (e.g., Jones & McGraw, 1987; see Katz & Mazur, 1979, for a review). Indeed, some have suggested that children are more likely to recant true allegations of abuse falsely than to assert them falsely in the first place (Berliner & Barbieri, 1984).

Given the reality of child sexual abuse, how can we obtain accurate and complete reports of it from victimized children? To address this question, a discussion of children's memory is necessary. Studies of children's memory and eyewitness testimony provide important insights into children's ability to recount personally significant events accurately and into the techniques adults can use to obtain accurate reports from children. After reviewing the literature on children's eyewitness testimony, the legal context in which children provide eyewitness reports of sexual assault is considered.

CHILDREN'S MEMORY

Psychologists have been studying human memory for over 100 years, and many studies have been conducted on children's memory. These studies have typically taken place in the laboratory. An advantage of laboratory research is that the experimenter has an objective record of what actually happened against which to evaluate the person's report. Without some such record, one can never know whether the person is remembering the event accurately or not. In actual child sexual assault cases, an objective record of the event will not be available. It is therefore difficult to examine memory in actual cases. Instead, we make inferences from the laboratory to real-life events.

There are disadvantages to laboratory studies of memory, however. By necessity, laboratory studies typically involve emotionally neutral events, ones that are quite different from a sexual assault. Questions therefore arise as to whether laboratory findings generalize to real-life criminal events. Fortunately, psychologists are becoming more and more aware of the need to conduct "ecologically valid" research and are beginning to conduct studies outside of the laboratory, so that children's and adults' memory for real-life events is beginning to be addressed. In addition, the realization that children do report events to police and testify in courts of law is motivating studies on children's eyewitness testimony.

Memory—regardless of a person's age—is not often entirely complete and accurate. Adults as well as children will fail to notice some features of an event, forget part of what occurred, and may misorder parts of what happened. Moreover, they may show minor alterations of report based on misinformation from a variety of sources—others' statements, their own dreams and inferences, and suggestive questioning by authorities (Loftus, 1979). As time passes, people are more likely to incorporate misinformation into memory, and minor alterations can become more serious. Because false memories can be held with great confidence (Deffenbacher, 1980), it is often difficult to distinguish a false report from a true report.

Although memory is not perfect, much of what a witness tells us is likely to be accurate. Specifically, testimony is more likely to be accurate when: the report concerns "central" information, such as salient actions (Goodman, Hepps, & Reed, 1986; Marquis, Marshall, & Oskamp, 1972; Pear & Wyatt, 1914); the event was relatively extended in time (e.g., Dent & Stephenson, 1979a; Laughery, Alexander, & Lane, 1971); the assailant was familiar (Bahrick, Bahrick, & Wittlinger, 1975), such as a known neighbor, relative, or acquaintance; the event was repeated (Fivush, 1984; Sanders & Warnick, 1981); and highly suggestive questioning did not occur (Loftus, 1979). These principles hold across a wide age range and are relevant to many child sexual assault cases.

Children's Eyewitness Reports: Accuracies

How does a child's memory compare with an adult's? We tend to think of children's memory as necessarily being worse, but this assumption is incorrect. It can be demonstrated that, under some circumstances, children's memory is actually better than that of adults (Roberts & Goodman, 1985). For example, if the child understands a particular event and is more familiar with it than the adult in question, the child may provide the more accurate report (Chi, 1978). These circumstances probably occur infrequently, however; hence, children often retain and report less than adults do.

Even so, children's errors tend to be errors of omission rather than commission. That is, though children often recall less than adults do, what they do recall may be quite accurate (Fivush, 1984; Slackman & Nelson, 1984; see Johnson & Foley, 1984, for a review). For example, laboratory studies indicate that, when asked open-ended questions, such as "What happened?", young children tend to say relatively little (Goodman & Reed, 1986; King, 1984; Marin, Holmes, Guth, & Kovac, 1979), and their reports are not always completely coherent (Sheehy, 1980), but *low* error rates indicate that their reports are seldom wrong (Goodman, Aman & Hirshman, 1987a; Goodman, Hepps, & Reed, 1986; Goodman & Reed, 1986; Marin et al., 1979).

In an attempt to obtain more detailed reports from children, it is often necessary to question them. Several studies have shown that children as young as 5 years of age can answer objective questions about simple concrete events as well as adults can (Goodman & Reed, 1986; Marin et al., 1979; but see King, 1984, for contradictory results). Questions about central actions that took place are more likely to be answered correctly than are questions about more peripheral information or about an unfamiliar culprit's description (Goodman, Hepps, & Reed, 1986; Pear & Wyatt, 1914). A child's ability to answer objective questions can be expected to vary, however, depending upon the difficulty of the question in relation to the age of the child. For example, even 8-year-olds can be expected to have difficulty answering objective questions that involve units of measurement (e.g., height, weight, and age; Goetze, 1980). Questions that require abstract inferences about such issues as people's motivations may also be difficult for children (Schultz, 1980). But children's ability to answer questions about witnessed or experienced events is better than was formerly recognized.

In addition to purely verbal questioning, toy props can be used to help children describe what happened. Price and Goodman (1984) found that children can recount much more about an event if their memory is supported by toy props than if it is not. The props did not elicit fantasy responses, even though the children in the study ranged in age from 2.5 to 5.5 years (but see Nelson & Gruendel, 1986). This research indicates that a young child who, for example, has been kidnapped and sexually assaulted might be able to say relatively little when asked "What happened?" but be able to show what happened if given a toy car, dolls, and other props. There are at least two reasons why children's memory might be particularly aided by props. One is that it saves the children from having to recount the event on a purely verbal level. The second is that children seem to need more cues than do adults to retrieve memories.

One type of prop, anatomically detailed dolls, has proven to be particularly controversial. Researchers have now explored abused and nonabused children's behavior with these special dolls (Boat & Everson, 1986; Goodman & Aman, 1987; Jampole & Weber, 1986; White, Strom, Santilli, & Halprin, 1986), as well as professionals' interpretations of children's doll use (Boat & Everson, 1986). Both White et al. (1986) and Jampole and Weber (1986) report that observers, blind to children's abuse histories, can discriminate allegedly abused and allegedly nonabused children's behavior with anatomical dolls. White et al. found that the discrimination was not perfect: The observers were more likely to err in the direction of classifying an allegedly abused child as nonabused than vice versa. Jampole and Weber (1986) report that, while 9 out of 10 abused children demonstrated sexual behaviors with the dolls, a small percentage of children with no known history of abuse also acted out sexual behaviors with the dolls.

Although studies that compare allegedly abused and nonabused children's behavior with anatomical dolls provide us with valuable information, they suffer from one inherent methodological flaw. Specifically, it is impossible to know if the allegedly nonabused children have been abused or not. Thus, when a child assigned to a "nonabused" group acts out sexual behaviors with the dolls, it is possible that the child does so as a result of undetected abuse. To avoid this problem, Goodman and Aman (1987) took a different tack than have former researchers. They videotaped 3- and 5-year-old children while the children played games with an unfamiliar, adult male confederate. All of the children had been screened in an attempt to eliminate abuse victims from the study, but in any case, the children were only interviewed about the games they played with the confederate, and it was guaranteed that no abuse occurred then. Goodman and Aman found that, despite an intentionally leading interview, the use of anatomical dolls compared to regular dolls or no dolls did not heighten the children's suggestibility.

Further research is needed on the use of props—particularly anatomically detailed dolls—in interviewing children, but preliminary studies indicate that the use of props may be a promising technique in obtaining complete and accurate reports from children.

One question that might arise in a child sexual assault investigation concerns the effects of trauma on memory. The trauma a child experiences during a sexual assault is likely to vary considerably across different cases. The child who is fondled by a well-liked family member may experience much less stress at the time of the assault than the child who is kidnapped and raped.

Psychologists have attempted to study the effects of stress on memory. It is generally believed that the Yerkes-Dodson law describes the relation between stress and performance on a number of tasks. For difficult tasks, this law predicts that, as stress increases to a moderate level, performance is enhanced. But as stress increases to very high levels, performance will decline. Easterbrook (1959) presents a mechanism for understanding the Yerkes-Dodson law by proposing that stress causes a narrowing of attention. Under moderate levels of stress, irrelevant, distracting information is excluded from attention as attentional focus becomes narrowed. A person may focus only on relevant information and therefore perform well. But as stress increases, the further narrowing of attention leads to the exclusion of some of the relevant information, and performance declines. While these ideas are supported by animal research, studies of adults' eyewitness testimony have offered only limited support for Easterbrook's proposal and for the Yerkes-Dodson law (Deffenbacher, 1983).

Studies of the effects of trauma on adults' memory are not numerous and the findings are inconclusive, but scientifically sound studies of children's memory for stressful events have, until recently, been nonexistent. This type of research is extremely difficult to conduct for obvious ethical reasons: We cannot and would not want to bring children into the laboratory and expose them to high levels of stress. We recently, however, conducted a study that overcomes this ethical problem (see also Goodman et al., 1987a; Peters,

1987). We videotaped 22 children at a walk-in clinic who were having inoculations for medical purposes. After 3 to 4 days, or 7 to 9 days, the children's memory for the event was tested. We compared these children's memory to that of a control group of children (matched in age and sex to the experimental group) who came to the clinic but had a design placed on their arm rather than an inoculation. In contrast to Easterbrook's predictions, we found that all of the children, regardless of stress level, answered more questions correctly about central information (e.g., the actions performed) than about peripheral information. Of course, we do not yet know if higher levels of stress will produce the same or different results. Many more studies like ours will be needed before we fully understand the effects of stress on children's memory.

In most child abuse investigations, the question of children's suggestibility will emerge as a major issue. As we discuss below, research findings show that young children are more suggestible than adults about some types of information. However, most studies have not examined children's suggestibility for the types of information of central concern in child sexual abuse investigations, namely, abusive actions such as being hit or kissed. Instead, the studies have focused largely on children's suggestibility for peripheral details presented in mundane stories or pictures, hardly the type of information of central importance in abuse cases. It is likely to be more difficult to lead a child witness into false affirmations concerning more central information (Goodman & Reed, 1986), a finding that applies to adults as well (Marquis et al., 1972).

In recent work, we went to the heart of the matter: We examined children's suggestibility for actions that might be associated with abuse (Goodman et al., 1987a; Goodman & Aman, 1987; Goodman, Hirschman, & Rudy, 1987c; Powders & Goodman, 1987; Smolensky & Goodman, 1987). To do so, we first videotaped children while they experienced either a fun event (playing games) or a stressful event (e.g., medical procedures). The children were questioned about such things as whether they were hit, kissed, had their clothes removed, had their private parts touched, or had anything placed in their mouths. Some of the questions were quite leading, such as "How many times did he spank you?", "He took your clothes off, didn't he?", and "He kissed you like this, didn't he?" (at which point two anatomically detailed dolls were shown kissing on the lips), none of which had actually occurred. In general, the children were surprisingly resistant to these questions. For example, 100% of the 4-year-olds could correctly resist the suggestion that their clothes had been removed. Only young 3-year-olds made a substantial number (about 33%) of false affirmations to these questions. When they did, their responses were never followed with verbal descriptions or behavioral indicators of abuse.

Children's Eyewitness Reports: Inaccuracies

While children can be accurate when answering open-ended and objective questions as well as suggestive questions about abuse, they do have difficulty remembering certain types of information. Moreover, certain aspects of children's reports, like adults', can be altered by suggestion. Defense attorneys often try to discredit a child's testimony based on these deficiencies. Below we discuss some of the areas in which children's memory can be expected to falter. It should be noted, however, that adults, to a greater or lesser degree, have the same kinds of memory problems.

One noticeable difference between adults and children is that children often say so little in response to questioning that adults may be particularly tempted to ask suggestive questions of them, and this is one way in which inaccuracies may arise. Suggestive and misleading questioning of witnesses, particularly children, can lead to inaccuracies in report (Cohen & Harnick, 1980; Dale, Loftus, & Rathbun, 1978; Dent, 1982; Goodman, Hepps, & Reed, 1986; Goodman & Reed, 1986). Questions such as "Did he have a brown or black mustache?", when the child has not indicated the presence of facial hair, and "All of the other kids in your school say he talked to your teacher; didn't he talk to her?" are suggestive. Although children are not *necessarily* more suggestible than adults (Duncan, Whitney, & Kunen, 1982; Marin et al., 1979), they *can* be, for example, when their memory is weaker or the questioner is of relatively high status (Ceci, Ross, & Toglia, 1985; Cohen & Harnick, 1980; Goodman & Reed, 1986; King, 1984).

There are no modern studies indicating that children can be led to fabricate an entire event. Although some older studies seemed to indicate that this is possible (e.g., Varendonck, 1911), more recent research counters this assertion (Powders & Goodman, 1987). Yet because of the widespread belief that children can easily be manipulated into making false reports (Goodman, Golding, & Haith, 1984; Yarmey & Jones, 1983), the use of suggestive questioning can be a dangerous practice. At least two risks are involved: One is the risk of obtaining false information; the second is the risk that, even if the child is resistant to suggestion and provides accurate testimony, his or her statements will be discounted by jurors.

Recently, MacFarlane (1985) asserted that leading questions may be necessary in child sexual assault cases in order to break a frightened or embarrassed victim's silence. Some child sexual assault victims may be threatened with, for example, death to themselves or loved ones if they tell what happened, and many others will be too embarrassed to discuss the assault freely. Thus, the interviewer faces the dilemma of either using leading questioning, in an attempt to open the way for discussion (but taking the chance of eliciting inaccuracies), or of not being able to obtain sufficient information to permit prosecution.

Two points should be made regarding this dilemma. One concerns the degree of suggestion used. Mild suggestion, such as "Did Uncle Henry touch your penis?", would be less likely to lead to criticism than strong suggestion, such as "I bet Uncle Henry touched your penis, isn't that right?", or "Let's *pretend* that Uncle Henry touched your penis. How would he have done it?" The second point is that if suggestion is used but the child is then able to give a detailed, free report of what happened in response to the question, one can probably have somewhat greater confidence that the report is correct. This is particularly true if the report contains detailed information of sexual activity that would be beyond the child's level of understanding or normal experience.

In addition to being susceptible to some types of suggestion, children, like other witnesses, may have difficulty answering questions about peripheral detail. In cross-examination by defense attorneys, child sexual assault victims are sometimes asked about peripheral information, such as what they ate for lunch the day of the assault, what color the walls of the room were, and what time it was when they awoke the next morning. Peripheral detail is not retained well by either children (Goodman, Hepps, & Reed, 1986) or adults (Wells & Leippe, 1981). In fact, a recent study has shown that adults' memory for peripheral detail is *inversely* related to memory for more central information, such as a culprit's face (Wells & Leippe, 1981). Presumably subjects who were paying attention to peripheral detail were not paying as much attention to the culprit's face. The intuition that people who can remember color well can certainly remember more important details—an intuition taken for granted by many defense attorneys—is likely to be false.

Probably, the child's ability to report the order of events is more important than his or her ability to report peripheral detail. Children can order simple, familiar events quite well (Brown, 1976; Fivush, 1984; Slackman & Nelson, 1984), but have difficulty ordering more complex, less familiar ones (Piaget, 1923; Price & Goodman, 1984). Misorderings do not, however, imply that the rest of the report is inaccurate (O'Connell & Gerard, 1985). A child, for example, may misorder the sequence of events but still correctly report that he or she was sexually assaulted. Moreover, children cannot be expected to remember the exact dates of events. Defense attorneys may try to use children's difficulty in remembering the exact order and dates of events to discredit them as witnesses. In a recent sexual assault case, an 11-year-old victim who had spent many weekends with his teacher was asked by a defense attorney to account for his activities during every weekend from August until March (more than 30 weekends), and to indicate on which weekends he was assaulted by his teacher. Obviously, most adults would fail this task, and such questioning is demoralizing for children, who have trouble understanding that the attorney wants to wear them out and discredit them.

Another factor that can be expected to interfere with the accuracy of a child's report is intimidation. Psychological research has shown that stress and intimidation can decrease a person's ability and willingness to retrieve information from memory (Dent & Stephenson, 1979a; Spielberger, Anton, & Bedell, 1976; Suggs & Sales, 1981). Consider people who suffer from test anxiety; they may know the material well, but suffer such severe anxiety at the time of the test that they freeze and cannot perform. It is possible that a similar anxiety inhibits sexual assault victims from being able to tell their stories in certain situations, such as when facing a defendant in a court of law. It is likely that children are generally more easily intimidated than adults, so it is important to try to limit as much as possible the ill effects of intimidation.

In sum, children can be accurate witnesses, especially when questioned about central aspects of meaningful, real-life events they have experienced. Children as young as 3 years of age consistently show deficits in answering objective and suggestive questions, however. But much of a young child's report can be quite accurate despite the child's inability to remember peripheral detail, the exact order of events, or whether the assault occurred on the 23rd or 24th weekend spent with the assailant. In order to optimize the chances of obtaining accurate reports from children, stress should be kept to a minimum.

Eyewitness Identification

When an unfamiliar person is seen quickly and when a relatively long delay occurs before an identification is attempted, face recognition can be quite poor (Buckhout, 1974; Shepherd, 1983). Moreover, once an incorrect identification is made, witnesses tend to stick with that identification even if the actual culprit is later included in a new line-up (Gorenstein & Ellsworth, 1980).

In most child sexual assault cases, however, the culprit will have been in view for more than a few seconds. In many cases, the culprit will be familiar. The abuse may be repeated, so that the child has many opportunities to see the person, making correct identifications more likely (Sanders & Warnick, 1981). In one study, when 10-year-old children attended to an unfamiliar man for 5 minutes, 82% of them were accurate in their identifications of him a week later (Dent & Stephenson, 1979a). In another study, 3- and 6-year-olds and adults interacted with an unfamiliar man for 5 minutes and were tested 4 to 5 days later. Although 93% of the 6-year-olds and 75% of the adults accurately identified the man in a photo line-up, only 38% of the 3-year-olds did so (Goodman & Reed, 1986). Thus, when adults and children as old as 6 attended to a person's face for 5 minutes in a nonstressful, real-life situation, developmental differences did not appear. (In our study, the 6-year-olds were actually somewhat better than the adults.)

We can speculate that young children require longer exposures to a stranger's face before they, as a group, will be as accurate as older children and adults in later recognizing that face (Werner & Perlmutter, 1979). But certainly there are times when even a young child will be accurate: A 3-year-old who was kidnapped and sexually assaulted in Denver was able to accurately identify her abductor after viewing a line-up within 24 hours of her rescue. In this case, the young victim had been with the assailant for at least half an hour and possibly an entire day, long enough to encode and retain what he looked like.

Unfortunately, younger children have a greater likelihood of making false identifications than do older children or adults (King & Yuillee, 1987; Powders & Goodman, 1987; Rudy & Goodman, 1987). To date, all of the studies that have investigated this tendency have examined children's eyewitness identifications for unfamiliar adults who were briefly seen. It is possible that children will be less likely to make false identifications of people who are better known to them. Since most child sexual abuse is committed by adults who are familiar to the child victim, this is an important question to be answered by future research. In any case, techniques to reduce young children's tendency to make false identifications are needed.

When a child is victimized, the event is likely to be stressful. Unfortunately, children's memory for faces originally viewed under such stressful conditions has only begun to be studied (Goodman et al., 1987a; Goodman, Hepps, & Reed, 1986; Peters, 1987). Therefore, we do not know whether stress increases or decreases a child's ability to recognize someone later. We do suspect, however, that if an identification is conducted under stressful circumstances, children's accuracy is likely to suffer (Dent & Stephenson, 1979a).

As this review indicates, many factors influence people's memory for events they have witnessed. Age is only one such factor and not necessarily the most important.

THE LEGAL CONTEXT

While laboratory studies attempt to simulate the interviewing techniques used by police, attorneys, and others, it is important to understand the context in which child victims actually provide their reports. Children can be accurate witnesses if handled properly, but the adversary system is often harsh in its dealings with children. Part of this harshness stems from the number of interviews the child must endure. Children may have to describe repeatedly what happened, and this repetition may become aversive (Tedesco & Schnell, 1987). Moreover, defense attorneys almost always argue that children are so suggestible that their reports cannot be believed. They try to support their contention by arguing that the child's parents, the interviewer, or the child's peers "brainwashed" the child into believing that the event occurred when in fact it did not. They sometimes argue in addition that children fantasize sexual events, are using the accusation to get back at an adult who has angered them, or just want attention. Thus, when a child reports sexual abuse, the legal context can affect the quality of the child's report, how that report will be interpreted by adults, and the child's emotional state. Inadvertently or intentionally, the legal system is not nearly as gentle with children as are psychologists in their laboratories.

In the laboratory, a child who witnesses a staged event will typically describe the event first to a trained interviewer. In an actual case, however, the child will almost always disclose what happened to a parent rather than a legal authority (Finkelhor, 1984). Parents' reactions to the disclosure vary considerably, ranging from disbelief and hostility to tremendous sympathy and concern (Herman, 1981). Regardless of initial reaction, the parent must decide whether or not to call the police or protective services. If the parent does call authorities, an investigation will take place.

Once an investigation begins, the child and family typically become embroiled in a lengthy and often stressful legal process (Goodman et al., 1987b, in press; Runyan, Everson, Edelsohn, Hunter, & Coulter, 1987). If they are lucky, the accused will confess or agree to a plea bargain, and the family's legal involvement may end relatively quickly. If the case goes to trial, however, 6 months or more may elapse before the proceedings begin, and the child may have to appear in court as a witness. Below we detail this sequence of events and discuss some of the psycholegal issues involved.

The Initial Report

Reports to Parents

Children's initial reports of sexual abuse are often made to parents. Of course, most parents are not trained in forensic interviewing of children. Unfortunately, they may use questioning techniques that later undermine the child's credibility. Specifically, the child's credibility as a witness may be attacked if it can be argued that the parent consciously or unconsciously suggested the assault to the child. The circumstances surrounding the report make such attacks more or less likely.

In the most straightforward cases—those in which the parent's questioning is least likely to come under attack—a child will make a spontaneous statement about the abuse, the parent's motives will not come under suspicion, and the child's story will be corroborated by physical or other evidence (e.g., snapshots, a confession). For example, in Denver, a 5-year-old child ran home, 45 minutes late from school, claiming she had been raped. Physical evidence supported her statement—she was bruised and bleeding, and seminal fluid was detected. She spontaneously described to her mother how a man had grabbed her when she was walking home, took her to his apartment (not far from the girl's home), tied her down with heavy tape, and repeatedly assaulted her—attempting both oral and vaginal intercourse. Finally the assailant let the little girl go, at which point she ran home. To her mother and then again to police, she was able to describe the stranger's apartment, including the bedroom where the attack occurred, the man's dog, and the color of his couch. She walked the police to the man's door. Once inside the apartment, the police found all of the items the girl described and arrested the man who lived there. In this sexual assault case, the parent's initial questioning was not an issue; she had no motive to implicate a stranger, the girl's statement was spontaneous and was made immediately after the assault occurred, and there was convincing physical evidence of attempted rape. These circumstances are not common, however.

In contrast to the above example, sometimes a parent will elicit a report from a child because the parent suspects sexual abuse. For example, in one case (*U.S. v. Nick,* 1979), a 3-year-old boy came home with his pants unzipped. The mother observed "white stuff" on the child's clothing. The mother asked the child whether Eneas (a man whom the child had just visited) had done anything to him. The child responded that "Eneas stuck his tutu in my butt." The child also claimed that the man had hurt him and made him cry. Physical evidence corroborated the child's story. Because of the physical evidence, the parent's questioning would not be expected to come under as much attack as if corroborating evidence were unavailable, but the parent might still be accused of leading the child by suggesting that the culprit was Eneas.

In many cases, however, physical evidence will be unavailable (Russell, 1983) and the child may have been questioned by the parent over relatively long periods of time. Because children often hesitate to tell adults about abuse, parents who suspect sexual abuse may use sustained questioning in order to elicit a report. In these cases, the parent's questioning is very likely to become an issue. For example, in one case an 11-year-old boy who had spent many weekends with his male teacher started to become upset whenever the teacher called. The mother sensed that something was wrong. She asked her son but he would not respond. After repeated questioning over a period of many hours, the son finally broke down and described the sexual assaults he had endured for months. In this case, the defense attorney later claimed that the mother had brainwashed the boy after putting him under heavy pressure. The boy claimed he had been too embarrassed to tell and that the teacher threatened him with suspension from school if he did.

Perhaps the most difficult and ambiguous child sexual assault cases are ones involving custody disputes. These cases may or may not result in criminal charges, but allegations of incest can affect custody determinations.

In custody disputes where sexual assault is claimed, the credibility of the parent becomes every bit as much an issue as the credibility of the child. These cases are particularly difficult because of the possible underlying motives involved. On the one hand, charging sexual assault may be a way to obtain custody; on the other hand, many parents will want to divorce their spouse if sexual abuse is uncovered or suspected. Because custody decisions are typically handled in juvenile or divorce courts, the standard of proof is not as stringent as in criminal cases, but the complaining parent's method of obtaining the report from the child is likely to come under scrutiny.

In sum, the child's first report may be made under conditions that later lead to legal difficulties. Children are not always open about sexual abuse, and considerable questioning may be needed before the child will tell what happened. However, because of the belief that children are highly suggestible, the parent's questioning may become as much of a legal issue as the child's testimony.

Police Practices

If the authorities are called, the police are likely to be the first professionals to interview child victims. Most ordinary police officers have received little if any relevant formal training in interviewing children and seem to rely largely on vague guidelines developed for interviewing adult witnesses. Specialists, such as detectives, are sent in only *after* field officers have obtained initial reports. When mental health professionals are the first to interview children—as might occur when a protective service worker obtains the first report—they may be unaware of techniques that can be used to support the accuracy of a child's report. In addition, sometimes these professionals are unaware of the legal implications of their interviewing practices.

Police wisely attempt to obtain reports from witnesses as soon as possible. Laboratory research indicates that memory will be strongest at the time of the first interview (Dent & Stephenson, 1979b: Lipton, 1977; Loftus, 1979). Unfortunately, because children do not readily report sexual molestation, days, months, or years may elapse between the events in question and a child's first interview with police. It should be noted, however, that most laboratory research concerns memory for neutral rather than traumatic events and there is a modest literature suggesting that memory for traumatic events increases over time (Kleinsmith & Kaplan, 1963). Moreover, children in research studies and child sexual assault victims do not share the same fears. The latter may be threatened not to tell, may feel embarrassed or guilty, or may at first have difficulty retrieving details of the incident. These factors may affect the completeness and accuracy of the first report as well as contribute to delayed reporting.

Once the interview actually begins, it is the officer's responsibility to obtain information relevant to the "elements" of the charge—for example, if the victim is an adult, one element of a rape charge would be that force was used, or, if the victim is a child, that sexual contact was made. The officer also tries to obtain a complete description of what happened.

Police often correctly try to obtain free reports before specific (perhaps accidentally leading) questioning is attempted (Soderman & O'Connell, 1962). Virtually all legal sources recognize the need to ask objective, nonsuggestive questions. Through such questioning, the officer's task is to obtain reports in chronological order (Amidon & Wagner, 1978; Swanson, Chamelin, & Territo, 1977). Police attempt to obtain a complete description of the offender, the time and location of the assault, the offender's car (if appropriate), and the assault itself. The officer also typically tries to determine whether force or threats were used and what the victim did after the assault (Amidon & Wagner, 1978). If the assailant is unknown to the victim, the child's assistance in developing a composite description of the assailant may be requested, despite the lack of research evidence concerning children's ability to construct accurate depictions of previously seen faces. The interview is usually recorded on audiotape, reported from notes taken at the time, or later written down by the officer from memory.

During the interview, officers attempt to assess the witness's truthfulness—a highly subjective and difficult task, particularly when child witnesses are involved. In some jurisdictions, a polygraph test may later be used to help evaluate a child's credibility (Amidon & Wagner, 1978; Groth, as cited in Melton, 1981)—again, despite the lack of scientific knowledge concerning the validity of polygraph tests on children, or adults, for that matter (Saxe, Dougherty, & Cross, 1985). Even at the initial interview, if the officer feels that the report is not truthful, he or she may decide that the charge is "unfounded," causing the case to be dropped at this point (Amidon & Wagner, 1978; Katz & Mazur, 1979; Keefe, 1978). These unfounded cases often contribute to statistics of false reports of sexual abuse, even though they may be based only on one officer's opinion.

Some fairly common problems can arise out of initial interviews, whether conducted by police or others. One is that misunderstandings may result from children's tendency to interpret words literally and concretely. A child who is asked if the man took his clothes off might answer no, but if asked if the man took his pants off might answer yes. The officer or others who read the officer's report may conclude that the child's testimony is not reliable because of these seemingly inconsistent responses. Second, perhaps because of practical and legal realities, police are not always as aggressive about obtaining corroborating evidence as they might be. Jurors are probably more willing to believe a child if corroboration is available. If a child reports that her father massages her with a vibrator, rubs her vaginal area with lotion that comes in a blue bottle, and shows her pictures of naked people in magazines, the police officer should be aggressive in trying to obtain these items so that they can be presented as corroborating evidence in court. Often the child can tell the officer exactly where the items are to be found.

Another problem arises from the fact that interviewers rarely record the interview verbatim. Rather, they usually summarize their reports. Later, attorneys may attack the interview as leading even if it was not. Unfortunately, proof of the initial method of questioning and of the child's responses is typically unavailable.

One way to obtain a verbatim record is to videotape the initial interview. There are several advantages to this procedure, but some disadvantages, too. One advantage is that if interviewers know their interviews are being recorded and will possibly be presented at trial, they will be more likely to avoid improper questioning. A second advantage is that when an interviewer writes his or her report from notes or from memory, distortions and omissions may result, whereas with videotape they cannot. A third is that videotape lends itself to fewer ambiguities in interpreting the child's responses. Because young children's reports may seem incoherent by adult standards, adults have a tendency to impose their own interpretation on the child's statements, leading to inaccuracies that may then be attributed to the child. In addition, emotional reactions are maintained on the videotape, as are nods of the head in response to questions. Finally, Chaney (1985) finds that defendants are more likely to confess after they view a videotape of the child describing the abuse (see Walker, Chapter 10 in this volume).

In contrast, MacFarlane (1985) has noted a number of problems with videotaping the first or any interview with a child sexual assault victim. One problem is that the child may at first deny that the assault took place and only gradually admit that the incident did indeed occur. Because the defense may subpoena the videotape, the child's initial denial may be used by the defense to discredit the child in court. Chaney (1985) reports, however, that the use of videotaped interviews with child victims in Texas has not led to the use of videotapes to discredit the children. Perhaps in most sexual assault cases denial is not a problem; since the child is likely to be the one who initially reports the abuse to parents, the child will already have made the abuse public. In some types of cases—notably incest, where family pressure may force a child to recant, or assaults involving threats designed to assure the child's silence—MacFarlane's warning may be an important consideration.

A second problem noted by MacFarlane concerns the confidentiality of the tapes. For example, some judges have permitted children's videotaped statements to be released to the press, in which case the children run the risk of public embarrassment by, for example, seeing themselves on the nightly news. It seems obvious that the confidentiality of such videotapes should be protected: When a child accused of violating the law appears in juvenile court, his or her name is protected; certainly child crime victims should be treated at least as kindly. But because such protection is not yet ensured, special laws or heightened sensitivity on the part of judges may be required before videotaping of interviews will become widespread.

Later Interviews

It is not uncommon for child victims of sexual assault to be interviewed numerous (e.g., 20) times during their involvement in the legal process (Whitcomb, Shapiro, & Stellwagen, 1985). It is widely believed that repeated interviewing can result in emotional trauma for children (e.g., Libai, 1980; Tedesco & Schnell, 1987). Some children may come to resent the repeated interviews and refuse to discuss the assault again. Although it may be necessary to interview a child more than once as further questions arise in a case, the interviews should be kept to a minimum. Recent attempts to collapse the number of interviews into one cooperative effort involving police officers, social service workers, and attorneys (Boerma, 1985) may be a step in the right direction, particularly if one neutral, highly trained party assumes the responsibility for interviewing while the others remain out of view.

Children and the Adversary Process

Some child sexual assault victims eventually testify in courts of law—at preliminary hearings, competence examinations, and the actual trial. A number of laws and legal practices govern a child's testimony during adversary proceedings.

Competence Examinations

Children below a certain age (e.g., 10 or 14 years) will typically be required to pass a competence examination conducted at a preliminary hearing. This examination consists of direct and cross-examination by the attorneys or of an interview by the judge. The judge has broad discretion in determining the extent and course of the competence hearing, but in general the judge is required to determine whether the child: (1) understands the difference between the truth and a lie, and the obligation to speak the truth; (2) had the capacity to accurately register the event at the time it happened; (3) has an uncoached memory of the event; and (4) can communicate her or his memory in court. Thus, age per se is not the determinant of competence; intellectual factors are.

The judge will determine whether the child passes the examination. Based on exactly the same performance, a child could conceivably be deemed competent by one judge and not by another. If a child does not pass, he or she will not be permitted to testify in the actual trial. If the case rests largely on the child's testimony—as often happens in child sexual assault prosecutions—the case may have to be dropped at this point.

Competence is determined at the time of the trial rather than at the time of the event (*American Jurisprudence: Proof of Facts,* 1960). Thus it is possible for a child to be quite young (e.g., 3 years of age) at the time of the assault but 8 years older at the time of the trial. Long delay intervals can be expected to decrease the child's memory of what happened or at least affect the amount of detail the child can report.

Competence examinations are legal relics: In common law, many witnesses had to prove their competence before they could testify. There is no consistent evidence that a competence examination accurately predicts whether or not a child will be an accurate witness. The recent trend is to drop the requirement for competence examination. In the new Federal Rules of Evidence, all witnesses regardless of age are assumed competent to testify. At last count, 23 states had passed legislation presuming children to be competent (Bulkley, 1985; Whitcomb et al., 1985). (In some states, such as Colorado, this presumption applies only to children in sexual assault cases.) In 18 states, the child, regardless of age, must be able to demonstrate that she or he understands an oath. The remaining states have designated an age below which a child must demonstrate competence. Despite the recent trend to eliminate the requirement of competence examinations, an attorney may still challenge a child witness's competence, in which case a competence examination will still ensue. But the elimination of the requirement may make judges more willing to qualify a child if a challenge does occur.

Courtroom Testimony

Once a child qualifies as a witness, he or she is treated much like an adult. The child will be sworn in, seated alone on the witness stand, and questioned by attorneys. Many children express fear at seeing the defendant again, at meeting the judge, at talking in front of an audience, and at being cross-examined (e.g., Berliner & Barbieri, 1984; Goodman et al., 1987b, in press; Pynoos & Eth, 1984; Whitcomb et al., 1985). It is also likely that being physically separated from supportive others (e.g., the child's mother) will add extra stress to the court appearance (Bowlby, 1973; Goodman et al., 1987b, in press; Shaver & Klinnert, 1982). Although there are no laws against it, permitting the child to testify while sitting with his or her parents is likely to raise defense objections on the grounds that the parent might subtly suggest things to the child. If it can be demonstrated that the child would experience undue trauma, it is possible for the judge to clear the courtroom of spectators.

The child will first undergo direct examination. Leading questions are typically forbidden on direct examination of adult witnesses, but are used more liberally during direct examination of child witnesses (*American Ju-*

risprudence: Proof of Facts, 1960). Support for the child's memory can be provided by the use of props, such as anatomically detailed dolls.

Cross-examination follows direct examination. The Sixth Amendment of the Constitution has been interpreted to indicate that the accused has the right to cross-examine all witnesses. During cross-examination, the express goal of the defense attorney is to discredit the witness. Even broader leeway is granted in the use of suggestive questioning. Attorneys may attempt to confuse the child by the use of double negatives, "big" words, and difficult sentence constructions. (Even if the attorney is not trying to confuse the child, lack of experience with children may result in confusion anyway, and this applies to prosecution and defense attorneys alike, as well as to judges.) A defense attorney's accusatory manner may intimidate the child. Furthermore, the attorney may undermine the child's confidence by asking about peripheral detail or about the specific order of events that occurred many months or years ago.

Sometimes, children undergo cross-examination for days. In the well-known McMartin case in Los Angeles, one 10-year-old was on the stand every day for over a week. Seven defense attorneys questioned him. He was only one of the many child witnesses to be called to testify. To make matters worse, the 7-day ordeal occurred during preliminary hearings. The trial had not yet begun!

If the trial is to a jury, the jury members must determine the child's credibility as a witness. In some states, special instructions are read to the jury before deliberations commence, and these instructions may contain information that is likely to bias jurors against believing children. For example, some instructions state that the jury should consider whether the witness is insane, a drug addict, or a child (*American Jurisprudence,* 1976). Others claim that children are more suggestible than adults and do not understand the importance of their testimony (Greene & Guidaboni, 1978). These instructions may reinforce adults' biases against believing children and lead to an increase in acquittals. If the verdict runs counter to the child's testimony, the child may fear retaliation, experience a decline in self-esteem, and come to doubt the effectiveness of our justice system.

Several researchers have attempted to determine whether criminal court involvement is traumatic for children. The studies, as well as clinical observation, indicate that it is stressful for many children (Defrancis, 1969: Gibbens & Prince, 1963; Goodman et al., 1987b, in press; Pynoos & Eth, 1984), though perhaps not for all (Berliner & Barbieri, 1984). (There is even some evidence now that testimony in juvenile court can be helpful for children. See Runyan et al., 1987.) In addition to the factors mentioned above, several other factors probably affect whether the experience will be highly stressful for the child. One source of stress associated with a trial is the many continuances often involved. The child will prepare emotionally to testify, come to court, and be told that he or she will not take the stand that day. After several experiences of this kind, children have been known to refuse to speak about the event in court. In addition, if the child has been threatened with death or bodily harm if she or he tells what happened or if the child is testifying against a loved one, the child might be expected to be particularly anxious. The degree of emotional support the child is receiving from his or her family is an important influence (Conte & Berliner, 1985). In fact, some have claimed that if the child is emotionally supported by family members, as well as by legal professionals, the experience may even be therapeutic for some children.

Innovative Techniques

Across the country, a number of legal innovations are currently being implemented or considered in an effort to reduce the stress presumably experienced by children in court. One innovation is to permit a videotaped interview to be shown in place of the child testifying in open court. Fear that videotaping laws may eventually be deemed unconstitutional has, however, limited the use of videotaped testimony (Whitcomb et al., 1985). Moreover, prosecutors fear that a videotape will not be as effective as the real child in eliciting the sympathy of the jury and hence in obtaining convictions.

The use of closed-circuit TV is another practice that has been proposed. When closed-circuit TV is used, the child and a support person typically sit in a room apart from the courtroom. The child is questioned by the prosecution and defense attorneys from this room. The child's image is shown in the courtroom via the TV system. At the same time, a camera in the courtroom is poised on the defendant, and his or her image is shown on a TV monitor that the child can see. Thus, face-to-face confrontation is achieved. While the status of laws permitting closed-circuit TV is still in question—face-to-face confrontation might be interpreted to require physical presence of the witness in the courtroom—a number of states have passed legislation permitting this practice.

Another innovation that can help reduce the child victim's involvement in the adversary process concerns hearsay exceptions. Traditionally, hearsay is not permitted as evidence in a court of law, except under rare circumstances. These circumstances may, however, apply to child sexual assault cases. In fact, courts have been fairly liberal in interpreting hearsay exception rules in cases involving child victims. For example, an excited utterance *(rea gesta)* exception exists. If a child is still in a state of excitation caused by an event and makes a statement to an adult about what happened (e.g., "Uncle Henry made me suck his pee wee"), the adult can testify to the child's statement in a court of law. Typically, only a few minutes can elapse between the event and the initial statement, but in child sexual assault cases, courts have granted the exception even if longer intervals were involved. In Colorado, hearsay to professionals or others is admissable if a child is declared medically unavailable, in other words, competent but it would be psychologically harmful for the child to testify (see Long, Chapter 8 in this volume). While several such exceptions to hearsay have been in place for some time (see Bulkley, 1985, for a review), several jurisdictions are currently considering a "residual" exception. This exception is much broader than the rest. It grants the judge power to decide whether a statement made to another is likely to be credible. If the judge decides that it is, the judge can permit an adult to testify about a child's statements.

Other innovations cannot be put into law because of constitutional considerations but have been adopted in individual cases when all parties agree. For example, variants on "children's courtrooms" (Parker, 1982) have been used in which the child is interviewed by a neutral party (e.g., a mental health professional) in a playroom. The defendant, defense attorney, prosecution, and judge may watch from a one-way mirror and can communicate with the interviewer through a "bug-in-the-ear device." The interview may be videotaped and become part of the court record. Or, at a deposition, a mental health worker may interview the child based on questions submitted by the defense attorney.

Research is needed on the advantages and disadvantages of the traditional methods of obtaining testimony from children as compared with these newer innovations. But it is clear that many in the legal and mental health fields have been unsatisfied with the traditional standard of treating children like any other witnesses. Cross-examination in open court by a defense attorney in the presence of the accused *may* be one way to obtain the truth from adults, but it seems unlikely to be the method of choice when trying to obtain the truth from a child.

Expert Testimony

In trials involving charges of child sexual assault, professionals are sometimes asked to serve as expert witnesses. Different states and different courts within a state vary considerably in their willingness and standards for permitting expert testimony.

Before an expert is permitted to testify, a *voir dire* will take place—sometimes outside the presence of the jury—in which the expert will be interviewed about her or his credentials and what information he or she can offer that is relevant to the case. Sometimes the expert will be the child's therapist or someone who has conducted an evaluation of the child. At other times the expert may be a specialist in child development, child sexual assault, or eyewitness testimony. In the latter case, the expert should have an advanced graduate degree in a relevant field (e.g., psychology, social work, psychiatry), have conducted research on child sexual assault or children's eyewitness testimony, and have published at least some of this work in professional peer-reviewed journals.

In determining whether the expert will be permitted to testify, the judge will typically consider whether the expert's testimony will provide information that is beyond the common knowledge of the jurors, will not invade the province of the jury, will not take up too much time, and will be in accord with generally accepted explanatory theories in a field. In addition, the probative value of the testimony should outweigh its prejudicial effect (see Loftus, 1984, for a review of these various considerations). Some courts may also be concerned that, if one side is offering an expert to counter the other side's expert, a "battle of the experts" may result. Despite these concerns, many courts have permitted professionals to testify about children's reactions to and memory for a sexual assault. When the expert has not seen the child but will rather testify about research findings, the court will typically only permit general statements about the findings and not statements that directly link the research to the specific case being tried.

On a practical level, experts must be prepared to present their testimony concisely and in terms that jurors can understand. Graphs and visual aids can be helpful. For the uninitiated, valuable examples of expert testimony can be found in several sources (Berliner, Blick, & Bulkley, 1983; Loftus, 1979), workshops are offered by various groups (e.g., Psychological Associates), and several books describe the ins and outs (e.g., Blau, 1984). But no matter how much experience a professional has had in court, it is important for experts and attorneys to work together before the trial to ensure that the expert is fully informed about the case and understands the types of questions that may be asked.

We do not know at present how expert testimony affects jurors, although a few relevant studies have been conducted (Hosch, Beck, & McIntyre, 1980; Loftus, 1980; Wells, Lindsay, & Tousignant, 1980). In general the findings indicate that jurors tend to deliberate longer when an expert has testified. None of the studies, however, examined expert testimony concerning children's testimony or child sexual assault.

CONCLUSION

In conclusion, children's ability to recount events and adults' ability to interview children can have profound effects on police investigations and subsequent trials. In the laboratory, we find that children can accurately report events if they are interviewed properly, although they do not always provide the detail one would hope for. In actual cases, the same principles would be expected to hold true. But, in actual cases, family or offender pressure and the legal context itself may place undue stress on the child and therefore affect the child's reliability. In some cases (e.g., incest) the child's family may also pressure the child to alter his or her testimony. Interviews— by parents, police, mental health workers, attorneys, or judges—may be improperly conducted, leading to less than accurate reports. Of course, in real-life cases we do not often have a record of what actually occurred, so we cannot be completely sure about accuracy. Nevertheless, it is quite likely that children are capable of accurately remembering a great deal about being sexually assaulted.

REFERENCES

American jurisprudence (2nd ed.). (1976). Rochester, NY: Lawyers Cooperative Publishing Co.

American jurisprudence: Proof of facts (Vol. 6). (1960). San Francisco: Bancroft-Whitney.

American law reports. (1962). Rochester, NY: Lawyers Cooperative Publishing Co.

Amidon, H. T., & Wagner, T. A. (1978). Successful investigation and prosecution of the crime of rape: A descriptive model. *Journal of Police Science and Administration, 6*(2), 141–156.

Bahrick, H. P., Bahrick, P. O., & Wittlinger, R. P. (1975). Fifty years of memory for names and faces: A cross-sectional approach. *Journal of Experimental Psychology: General, 104,* 54–75.

Berliner, L., & Barbieri, M. K. (1984). The testimony of the child victim of sexual assault. *Journal of Social Issues, 40*(2), 125–138.

Berliner, L., Blick, L. C., & Bulkley, J. (1983). Expert testimony on the dynamics of intra-family child sexual abuse and principles of child development. In J. Bulkley (Ed.), *Child sexual abuse and the law* (pp. 163–183). Washington, DC: American Bar Association.

Blau, T. H. (1984). *The psychologist as expert witness.* Somerset, NJ: Wiley.

Boat, B., & Everson, M. (1986). *Use of anatomically correct dolls in evaluation of child sexual abuse.* Paper presented at the Fourth National Conference on the Sexual Victimization of Children, New Orleans, LA.

Boerma, L. (1985). How to overcome barriers and to develop creative and innovative approaches in the prosecution of child sexual abuse cases. In J. Bulkley (Ed.), *Papers for a national policy conference on legal reforms in child sexual abuse cases* (pp. 31–39). Washington, DC: American Bar Association.

Bowlby, J. (1973). Separation, anxiety, and anger. *Attachment and loss* (Vol. 2). New York: Basic Books.

Brown, A. L. (1976). The construction of temporal succession by the preoperational child. In A. D. Pick (Ed.), *Minnesota symposium on child development* (Vol. 10, pp 28–83). Minneapolis, MN: University of Minnesota Press.

Buckhout, R. (1974). Eyewitness testimony. *Scientific American, 231*(6), 23–31.

Bulkley, J. (1985). Evidentiary and procedural trends in state legislation and other emerging legal issues in child sexual abuse cases. *Miami Law Review, 40.*

Carporael, L. R. (1976). Ergotism: The Satan loosed in Salem? *Science, 192,* 21–26.

Ceci, S. J., Ross, D. F., & Toglia, M. P. (1985). *Suggestibility of children's memory: Psycho-legal implications.* Unpublished abstract, Cornell University, Ithaca, NY.

Chaney, S. (1985). Videotaped interview with child abuse victims. In J. Bulkley (Ed.), *Papers for a national policy conference on legal reforms in child sexual abuse cases.* Washington, DC: American Bar Association.

Chi, M. T. H. (1978). Knowledge structures and memory development. In R. Siegler (Ed.), *Children's thinking: What develops?* (pp. 73–96). Hillsdale, NJ: Erlbaum.

Cohen, R. L., & Harnick, M. A. (1980). The susceptibility of child witnesses to suggestion. *Law and Human Behavior, 4*(3), 201–210.

Conte, J., & Berliner, L. (1985, October). *Report on the NIMH-funded research project on the effects of sexual abuse on children.* Paper presented at the National Summit Conference on Diagnosing Child Sexual Abuse, Los Angeles.

Dale, P. S., Loftus, E. F., & Rathbun, E. (1978). The influence of the form of the question on the eyewitness testimony of preschool children. *Journal of Psycholinguistics Research, 7,* 269–277.

Defrancis, V. (1969). *Protecting the child victim of sex crimes committed by adults: Final report.* Denver, CO: The American Humane Association, Children's Division.

Deffenbacher, K. H. (1980). Eyewitness accuracy and confidence: Can we infer anything about their relationship? *Law and Human Behavior, 4,* 243–260.

Deffenbacher, K. H. (1983). The influence of arousal on the reliability of testimony. In S. M. A. Lloyd-Bostock & B. R. Clifford (Eds.), *Evaluating witness evidence.* New York: Wiley.

Dent, H. R. (1982). The effects of interviewing strategies on the results of interviews with child witnesses. In A. Trankell (Ed.), *Reconstructing the past* (pp. 279–298). Deventer, The Netherlands: Kluwer.

Dent, H. R., & Stephenson, G. M. (1979a). Identification evidence: Experimental investigations of factors affecting the reliability of juvenile and adult witnesses. In D. P. Farrington, K. Hawkins, & S. M. Lloyd-Bostock (Eds.), *Psychology, law, and legal processes* (pp. 195–206). Atlantic Highlands, NJ: Humanities Press.

Dent, H. R., & Stephenson, G. M. (1979b). An experimental study of the effectiveness of different techniques of questioning child witnesses. *British Journal of Social and Clinical Psychology, 18,* 41–51.

Duncan, E. M., Whitney, P., & Kunen, S, (1982). Integration of visual and verbal information in children's memories. *Child Development, 53,* 1215–1223.

Easterbrook, J. A. (1959). The effect of emotion on the utilization and organization of behavior. *Psychological Review, 66,* 183–201.

Finkelhor, D. (1984). How widespread is child sexual abuse? *Children Today, 13,* 18–20.

Fivush, R. (1984). Learning about school: The development of kindergartners' school scripts. *Child Development, 55*(5), 1697–1709.

Freud, S. (1965). *The interpretation of dreams.* New York: Arrow Books. (Originally published 1900)

Gibbens, T. C. N., & Prince, J. (1963, October). *Child victims of sex offenses.* London, England: The Institute for the Study and Treatment of Delinquency.

Goetze, H. (1980). *The effect of age and method of interview on the accuracy and completeness of eyewitness accounts.* Unpublished doctoral dissertation, Hofstra University, New York.

Goodman, G. S. (1984). The child witness: Conclusions and future directions for research and legal practice. *Journal of Social Issues, 40*(2), 157–175.

Goodman, G. S., & Aman, C. (1987, April). Children's use of anatomically detailed dolls to report an event. In M. Steward (Chair), *Evaluation of suspected child abuse: Developmental, clinical, and legal perspectives on the use of anatomically detailed dolls.* Symposium presented at the Society for Research in Child Development Convention, Baltimore, MD.

Goodman, G. S., Aman, C., & Hirschman, J. (1987a). Child physical and sexual abuse: Children's testimony. In S. Ceci, M. Toglia, & D. Ross (Eds.), *Children's eyewitness memory* (pp. 1–23). New York: Springer-Verlag.

Goodman, G. S., Golding, J. M., & Haith, M. M. (1984). Jurors' reactions to child witnesses. *Journal of Social Issues, 40*(2), 139–156.

Goodman, G. S., Hepps, D., & Reed, R. S. (1986). The child victim's testimony. In A. Haralambie (Ed.), *New issues for child advocates.* Phoenix, AZ: Council of Attorneys for Children.

Goodman, G. S., Hirschman, J., & Rudy, L. (1987c, April). Children's testimony: Research and policy implications. In S. Ceci (Chair), *Children as witnesses: Research and social policy implications.* Symposium presented at the Society for Research in Child Development Convention, Baltimore, MD.

Goodman, G. S., Jones, D. P. H., Estrada-Prado, L., Pyle, E. Port, L., England, T., Mason, R., & Rudy, L. (1987b, August). *Children's reactions to criminal court testimony.* Paper presented at the American Psychological Association Meeting, New York, New York.

Goodman, G. S., Jones, D. P. H., Pyle, E., Estrada-Prado, L., Port, L., England, T., Mason, R., & Rudy, L. (in press). The emotional effects of criminal court testimony on child sexual assault victims: A preliminary report. In G. Davies & J. Drinkwater (Eds.), *New directions for psycholegal research and criminology.* Oxford, England: British Psychological Association.

Goodman, G. S., & Reed, R. S. (1986). Age differences in eyewitness testimony. *Law and Human Behavior, 10,* 317–332.

Gorenstein, G. W., & Ellsworth, P. C. (1980). Effect of choosing an incorrect photograph on a later identification by an eyewitness. *Journal of Applied Psychology, 65,* 616–622.

Greene, H. & Guidaboni, T. (1978). *Criminal jury instructions for the District of Columbia* (3rd ed.). Washington, DC: American Bar Association.

Herman, J. (1981). *Father–daughter incest.* Cambridge, MA: Harvard University Press.

Hosch, H. M., Beck, E. L., & McIntyre, P. (1980). Influence of expert testimony regarding eyewitness accuracy on jury decisions. *Law and Human Behavior, 4,* 287–296.

Jampole, L., & Weber, M. K. (1986, May). *An assessment of the behavior of sexually abused and non-sexually abused children with anatomically correct dolls.* Paper presented at the Fourth National Conference on the Sexual Victimization of Children, New Orleans, LA.

Johnson, M. K., & Foley, M. A. (1984). Differentiating fact from fantasy: The reliability of children's memory. *Journal of Social Issues, 40*(2), 33–50.

Jones, D. P. H., & McGraw, J. M. (1987). Reliable and fictitious accounts of child sexual abuse. *Journal of Interpersonal Violence, 2,* 27–45.

Katz, S., & Mazur, M. A. (1979). *Understanding the rape victim.* New York: Wiley.

Keefe, M. L. (1978). Police investigation in child sexual assault. In A. W. Burgess, A. N. Groth, L. L. Holmstrom, & S. M. Sgroi (Eds.), *Sexual assault of children and adolescents* (pp. 159–170). Lexington, MA: Heath.

King, M. A. (1984). *An investigation of the eyewitness abilities of children.* Unpublished doctoral dissertation, University of British Columbia.

King, M. A., & Yuille, J. C. (1987). Suggestibility and the child witness. In S. Ceci, M. Toglia, & D. Ross (Ed.), *Children's eyewitness memory* (pp. 24–35). New York: Springer-Verlag.

Kleinsmith, L. J., & Kaplan, S. (1963). Paired associated learning as a function of arousal and interpolated interval. *Journal of Experimental Psychology, 65,* 190–193.

Laughery, K. R., Alexander, J. E., & Lane, A. B. (1971). Recognition of human faces: Effects of target exposure time, target position, pose position, and type of photograph. *Journal of Applied Psychology, 55,* 477–483.

Libai, D. (1980). The protection of the child victim of a sexual offense in the criminal justice system. In L. G. Schultz (Ed.), *The sexual victimology of youth* (pp. 187–245). Springfield, IL: Charles C. Thomas.

Lipton, J. (1977). On the psychology of eyewitness testimony. *Journal of Applied Psychology, 62,* 90–93.

Loftus, E. F. (1979). *Eyewitness testimony.* Cambridge: Harvard University Press.

Loftus, E. F. (1980). Impact of expert psychological testimony on the unreliability of eyewitness identification. *Journal of Applied Psychology, 65,* 9–15.

Loftus, E. F. (1984). Expert testimony on the eyewitness. In G. L. Wells & E. F. Loftus (Eds.), *Eyewitness testimony: Psychological perspectives* (pp. 273–282). New York: Cambridge University Press.

MacFarlane, K. (1985). Diagnostic evaluations and the uses of videotapes in child sexual abuse cases. In J. Bulkley (Ed.), *Papers from a national policy conference on legal reforms in child sexual abuse cases* (pp. 119–144). Washington, DC: American Bar Association.

Marin, B. V., Holmes, D. L., Guth, M., & Kovac, P. (1979). The potential of children as eyewitnesses. *Law and Human Behavior, 3*(4), 295–306.

Marquis, K. H., Marshall, J., & Oskamp, S. (1972). Testimony validity as a function of question form, atmosphere, and item difficulty. *Journal of Applied Social Psychology, 2,* 167–186.

Masson, J. M. (1984). *The assault on truth.* New York: Farrar, Straus & Giroux.

Matossian, M. K. (1982). Ergot and the Salem witch affair. *American Scientist, 70,* 355–357.

Melton, G. (1981). Children's competency to testify. *Law and Human Behavior, 5*(1), 73–85.

Nelson, K., & Gruendel, J. (1986). Children's scripts. In K. Nelson (Ed.), *Event knowledge: Structure and function in development* (pp. 21–46). Hillsdale, N.J.: Erlbaum.

O'Connell, B. G., & Gerard, A. B. (1985). Scripts and scraps: The development of sequential understanding. *Child Development, 56,* 671–681.

Parker, J. (1982). The rights of child witnesses: Is the court a protector or a perpetrator? *New England Law Review, 17,* 643–717.

Pear, T. H., & Wyatt, S. (1914). The testimony of normal and mentally defective children. *British Journal of Psychology, 3,* 388–419.

Peters, D. (1987). The impact of naturally occurring stress on children's memory. In S. Ceci, M. Toglia, & D. Ross (Eds.), *Children's eyewitness memory* (pp. 122–154). New York: Springer-Verlag.

Piaget, J. (1923). *The language and thought of the child.* New York: Meridian.

Price, D. W. W., & Goodman, G. S. (1984, April). *The development of children's comprehension of recurring episodes.* Paper presented at the Society for Research in Child Development, Toronto, Canada.

Powders, M., & Goodman, G. S. (1987). *Fact or fantasy: Children's memory for a hypothetical event.* Unpublished manuscript.

Pynoos, R. S., & Eth, S. (1984). The child as witness to homicide. *Journal of Social Issues, 40*(2), 87–108.

Roberts, R., & Goodman, G. S. (1985, April). *Reverse development trends: Developmental as the acquisition of constraints.* Paper presented at the Society for Research in Child Development, Toronto, Canada.

Rudy, L., & Goodman, G. S. (1987). *"Did he kiss you?": Children's suggestibility and eyewitness testimony.* Unpublished manuscript.

Runyan, D. K., Everson, M. D., Edelsohn, G. A., Hunter, W. M. & Coulter, M. L. (1987, July). *Impact of legal intervention on sexually abused children.* Paper presented at the National Family Violence Research Symposium, Durham, NH.

Rush, F. (1980). *The best kept secret: Sexual abuse of children.* New York: McGraw-Hill.

Russell, D. (1983). Incidence and prevalence of intrafamilial and extrafamilial sexual abuse of female children. *Child Abuse and Neglect, 1,* 133–146.

Sanders, G. S., & Warnick, D. (1981). Some conditions maximizing eyewitness accuracy: A learning/memory model. *Journal of Criminal Justice, 9,* 136–142.

Saxe, L., Dougherty, D., & Cross, T. (1985). The validity of polygraph testimony: Scientific analysis and public controversy. *American Psychologist, 40*(3), 355–366.

Shaver, P., & Klinnert, M. (1982). Schachter's theories of affiliation and emotion: Implications of developmental research. In L. Wheeler (Ed.), *Review of Personality and Social Psychology* (pp. 37–72). Beverly Hills, CA: Sage.

Sheehy, N. (1980, December). *The child as witness.* Paper presented at the conference of the British Psychological Society, London, England.

Shepherd, J. W. (1983). Identification after long delays. In S. M. A. Lloyd-Bostock & B. R. Clifford (Eds.), *Evaluating witness evidence* (pp. 173–187). New York: Wiley.

Shultz, T. R. (1980). Development of the concept of intention. In W. A. Collins (Ed.), *Development of cognition, affect, and social relations: The Minnesota symposium on child psychology* (Vol. 13). Hillsdale, NJ: Erlbaum.

Slackman, E., & Nelson, K. (1984). Acquisition of an unfamiliar script in story form by young children. *Child Development, 55*(2), 329–340.

Smolensky, S., & Goodman, G. S. (1987). *Distinguishing the pretend from the real: Even young children can do it.* Unpublished manuscript.

Soderman, H., & O'Connell, J. J. (1962). *Modern criminal investigation.* New York: Funk & Wagnalls.

Spielberger, C. D., Anton, W. D., & Bedell, J. (1976). The nature and treatment of test anxiety. In M. Zuckerman & C. D. Spielberger (Eds.), *Emotions and anxiety* (pp. 317–346). Hillsdale, NJ: Erlbaum.

Stern, W. (1910). Abstracts of lectures on the psychology of testimony and on the study of individuality. *American Journal of Psychology, 34,* 3–30.

Suggs, D., & Sales, B. (1981). Juror self-disclosure in the voir dire: A social science analysis. *Indiana Law Journal, 56,* 245–271.

Swanson, C. R., Chamelin, N. C., & Territo, L. (1977). *Criminal investigation.* Santa Monica, CA: Goodyear Publishing Company, Inc.

Tedesco, F. J. & Schnell, S. V. (1987). Children's reactions to sex abuse investigations. *Child Abuse and Neglect, 11,* 267–272.

U.S. v. Nick, 604 F.2d 1199, 9th Cir., 1097 (1979).

Varendonck, J. (1911). Les temoignages d'enfants dans un proces retentissant. *Archives de Psychologie, 11,* 129–171.

Wells, G., & Leippe, M. R. (1981). How do triers of fact infer the accuracy of eyewitness identification?: Using memory for peripheral detail can be misleading. *Journal of Applied Psychology, 66,* 682–687.

Wells, G. L., Lindsay, R., & Tousignant, J. P. (1980). Effects of expert psychological advice on human performance in judging the validity of eyewitness testimony. *Law and Human Behavior, 4,* 275–286.

Werner, J. S., & Perlmutter, M. (1979). Development of visual memory in infants. In H. W. Reese & L. P. Lipsitt (Eds.), *Advances in child development and behavior* (Vol. 14). New York: Academic Press.

Whitcomb, D., Shapiro, E. P., & Stellwagen, C. D. (1985). *When the victim is a child: Issues for judges and prosecutors.* Washington, D. C.: National Institute of Justice.

White, S., Strom, G., Santilli, G., & Halprin, B. (1986). Interviewing young sexual abuse victims with anatomically correct dolls. *Child Abuse and Neglect, 10,* 519–529.

Yarmey, A. D., & Jones, H. P. T. (1983). Is the psychology of eyewitness identification a matter of common sense? In S. M. Lloyd & B. R. Clifford (Eds.), *Evaluating witness evidence* (pp. 13–40). New York: Wiley.

8

Legal Issues in Child Sexual Abuse: Criminal Cases and Neglect and Dependency Cases

Gregory F. Long

Prosecutors and attorneys for Departments of Social Services throughout the United States are placing increasing reliance on mental health professionals in both criminal and juvenile cases involving sexual assaults on children. This reliance extends from the investigation phase to trial with use of expert witnesses. This is particularly true in Colorado where I practice, due in part to recent developments in case law, statutes, and rules of evidence. It is important for mental health professionals to become familiar with the legal rules that impact upon the evidence they may be asked to comment on.

A sexual contact with, or assault on, a child often leads to the filing of a criminal charge or a neglect and dependency proceeding, and sometimes both. The criminal case has the primary purpose of deterrence and punishment. The neglect and dependency proceeding, often referred to as a D & N, is filed where one or both parents are either involved in the sexual activity or have neglectfully allowed it to occur. This case has the primary purpose of protecting the child. This may mean removal of the child or the abuser from the home, family counseling, individual therapy for the child and parents, and the like, depending on the facts and circumstances of the case. Although the burdens of proof and ultimate goals of the respective cases are different, the legal issues are often the same.

A criminal charge of sexual assault on a child carries with it the heaviest burden of proof known to the law, that of proof beyond a reasonable doubt. The prosecutor must establish to the satisfaction of either a judge or a jury that the defendant has committed the crime charged to the exclusion of any reasonable hypothesis of doubt. A neglect and dependency proceeding, on the other hand, is a hybrid action, governed more by the rules and burdens of proof that govern a civil case, such as when one party sues another for damages. The burden of proof in most issues in a neglect and dependency case is merely a preponderance of the evidence, which means that the scales have to tip only slightly in favor of the prevailing party. The only exception to this is that some jurisdictions require "clear and convincing" proof when the ultimate issue of termination of parental rights is addressed. Even so, the easier burden of proof in the juvenile case often influences the tactical choice the state must make when it is weighing the decision of whether to file a criminal case, a neglect and dependency case, or both. I have successfully tried a number of neglect and dependency cases wherein the court indicated it would have reached a different conclusion had a criminal charge with the higher burden of proof been the issue.

Even when the perpetrator cannot be convicted of a crime, the availability of the option to file a juvenile neglect and dependency case means that the state can control the child's well-being, which sometimes means the child can be taken from the setting where the abuse was allowed to occur and placed in a safer and more healthy environment. From a tactical standpoint, there are also procedural advantages to pursuing the juvenile case. Because the civil rules govern a neglect and dependency proceeding, the perpetrator and other adverse parties (such as the natural mother, for example, who knowingly or unknowingly allows the stepparent to engage in the abusive behavior) can actually be called as adverse witnesses by the state and cross-examined. This legal procedure forces the witness to tell what she or he knows that is relevant to the protection of the child. Even in most states where spousal immunity would allow one partner not to testify against the other, the juvenile court overrules the exemption. In a criminal proceeding, of course, a defendant is never compelled to testify at all and can never be called by the prosecutor as a witness because defendants have the right to remain silent. As a matter of strategy I have often found it beneficial to call one or both respondents in a D & N to pin them to a specific story that can be attacked with later witnesses, rather than allowing them to listen to the prosecution's case and then adjust their testimony accordingly.

ADMISSABILITY ISSUES

In both situations, attorneys bringing the action have found themselves placing increasing reliance on various health and mental health experts, ranging from clinical social workers to pediatricians and child psychologists. Because of their background and training they are more likely than law enforcement officials to conduct successful nonleading interviews of children to obtain necessary details without inducing unnecessary trauma. Their experience in detecting and analyzing behavioral symptoms that typically appear in victims of sexual abuse may also buttress a case that would otherwise be dependent only upon the child's testimony. However, sometimes the mental health care provider may have to make the decision about whether to spoil the evaluation for legal purposes, usually because of the need to ask leading questions, in order to get the child ready for treatment. See Walker (Chapter 10) for a description of appropriate assessment techniques.

Expert testimony from these professionals will generally take one of two forms:

1. *Corroboration* of the child's testimony as to sexual abuse; or
2. *Hearsay* testimony relating to statements made by the child to various individuals regarding the sexual abuse, tendered in lieu of the child's testimony.

Corroboration in the legal sense simply means that the expert can point to specific things, generally behavioral symptoms and patterns that typically appear in child victims of sexual abuse, that support the likelihood that the child is telling the truth. "Hearsay" testimony is testimony offered through someone other than the person who originally spoke the words that is offered to prove the truth of the words spoken. Unless it falls under an exception, hearsay testimony is not admissible in courts of law, because the courts have always held that a person should be able to face an accuser directly and test the reliability of his or her statements by cross-examination. When those statements are offered through a third party, the ability to effectively cross-examine the original declarant is lost.

There has been a national trend to balance the special circumstances posed by a child witness against the rights of the accused to direct confrontation given under the Sixth Amendment to the U.S. Constitution. The recent National Institute of Justice publication, *When the Victim Is a Child: Issues for Judges and Prosecutors,* which offers a detailed exploration of the issues raised in this chapter, states the dilemma succinctly:

> Theoretically, looking the defendant in the eye as one accuses him or her of a crime provides an acid test of the truth. But when the accuser is a child, the right of confrontation may offer a convenient means of intimidating the witness, resulting in serious, damaging effects on the child's testimony. (Whitcomb, Shapiro, & Stellwegen, 1985, p. 49)

The National Institute of Justice suggests that more than 90% of all child abuse cases do not go to criminal prosecution. In many of these cases, the decision is made because of concerns for the child's credibility or the adverse emotional impact testifying in open court will have on the child (Stewart, 1985). With the greater number of cases filed, what is called the *unfounded report rate* rises. This does not mean the sexual abuse did not occur but represents the legal term for saying the case could not be adjudicated, often because of the issues raised here.

The Child's Competency to Testify

The credibility of child witnesses has been legally attacked by those who question the child's competency. Rules of evidence in many states presumed competency did not occur until children reached the age of 14 years, which was the common-law rule. This is changing in most state laws, court rules of evidence, or codified rules of evidence, with only 5 states now using the 14-year-old age, 13 states presuming children over the age of 10 are competent, and 18 states requiring demonstration that the child understands the nature and obligation (and in some states the duty) of the oath to tell the truth. And in 20 states everyone is presumed competent, which is also the standard found in Federal Rule 601. Three states that normally apply the "10-year-old" standard (Colorado, Missouri, and Utah) make an exception in sexual abuse cases, allowing younger children to be presumed competent unless declared not competent by the trial court judge (Whitcomb et al., 1985, pp. 31–32). The American Bar Association Committee on Victims distributes a quarterly update of legal precedents in this area (Austern, 1986).

Generally, the legal test to measure competency is set forth in four parts:

1. The child's demonstration of an understanding of the difference between truth and lies and an appreciation for the obligation to speak the truth
2. The child's state of mind or mental capacity at the time of the incident(s) in question to observe or receive accurate impressions of the sexual assault
3. The child's memory is sufficient to have an independent recollection of the observations
4. The child's capacity to communicate that memory and to answer simple questions about the occurrence

These four areas come into the purview of the mental health specialist's assessment and therefore can be addressed in expert testimony to assist the court in determining competency should the issue arise. Recent research in the area of children's memory indicates that although children are able to retain information about as accurately as do adults, they may be less skilled in reproducing events using free recall and open-ended questions. Children are more likely to enhance their description of events when asked specific questions using props, especially with younger children (Goodman, 1984; Goodman & Helgeson, Chapter 7 of this volume).

Changing the laws to allow for the special issue posed by children's testimony has been rapid. Admissability occurs through three major processes of change. The first is a change in the actual law, which has to be voted on by members of the State Legislature. This is also called statutory change. The second is a change in the Rules of Evidence adopted by the state court system. There are also Federal Rules of Evidence for the Federal court system, which many states adopt. The third is through judicial interpretation of the laws, generally decided by appellate court decisions. Even when new laws are introduced and codified, appellate decisions are usually used as precedent guidelines by other lawyers and judges. Thus, the status of any pending case can be affected by higher court decisions should they be decided by the time the case goes to trial.

Until recent years, victims of sexual assault in general have been placed in a position of facing their accused in a courtroom without the benefit of other testimony to bolster or support theirs. Sexual assault, particularly that involving children, is by its very nature a crime involving stealth and secrecy, and the courtroom was historically a lonely and frightening place for the victim. All too rarely are there other witnesses to the act complained of, and oftentimes no physical evidence. When the victim is a young child, prosecutors often face great difficulty obtaining a successful resolution at trial from the child's testimony alone, if indeed the child is able and willing to testify at all.

Expert Witness Testimony

However, as experience has grown and data has accumulated, an increasing number of experts in the treatment field have taken the position that children subjected to sexual abuse exhibit certain behavioral signs and symptoms that are in themselves corroborative of the child's complaint. In Colorado, as in other states, trial courts are beginning to allow testimony of these behavioral observations to be admitted at trial, sometimes even in the absence of physical corroboration. This trend is starting to receive recognition and approval on the appellate level and is discussed in detail here to demonstrate the impact of legal and psychological collaboration in creating change.

In *People v. Ashley* (1984), the prosecution presented a pediatrician, Dr. Hendrika Cantwell, as an expert witness in the medical aspects of child abuse and neglect. Over objection, Dr. Cantwell was allowed to testify as to the results of both her own studies and those in medical literature regarding unfounded claims of sexual assault by children. The thrust of the doctor's testimony was that the study showed only rare cases of children's complaints that in this regard were found to be untrue, and that sexual assault "is not something that children fabricate." Cantwell was also allowed to offer her opinion that the child was telling her the truth as to the identity of the assailant.

Although the doctor's opinion dealt with one of the ultimate issues to be decided by the jury, that is, the credibility of a witness, the court found the giving of such an opinion did not invade the province of the jury. Case law in Colorado has historically allowed experts to express opinions that embraced ultimate issues. [See *People v. Martinez* (1980); also *Bridges v. Lintz* (1959).] This means that the expert can tell the jury how he or she would evaluate the evidence to determine level of guilt or innocence.

However, more recently the court has indicated that expert opinions on the child's credibility will not be allowed. The state has also recently adopted rules of evidence that essentially follow the federal rules. These rules form the basis for what evidence is allowed to be introduced at trial. Rule 704 holds that testimony in the form of an opinion or an inference from either a lay or an expert witness otherwise admissible is not objectionable because it embraces an ultimate issue to be decided by the trier of fact. Lay witnesses usually can only testify as to facts or their own direct observations. Experts can also give opinions, in some cases based in part on hearsay or other information that may in itself be excluded from evidence. Thus, using an expert witness may be an important strategy to get otherwise excluded evidence before the judge or jury.

Other recent cases have allowed testimony regarding the capacity of children to fabricate claims that they have been sexually assaulted. (See *People in the Interest of W.C.L.,* 1982.) W.C.L. was reversed by the Colorado Supreme Court on other grounds in *W.C.L. v. People* (1984). Although not directly addressing the issue, the court quoted the doctor's testimony about children not lying or fabricating without negative comment. *People v. Vollentine* (1982) allowed a victim's credibility to be supported by expert testimony rebutting efforts to depict the victim as seductive. The issue is somewhat confusing in that in *Ashley* and *W.C.L.* one division of the Colorado Court of Appeals seems to approve admission of expert testimony as to the child's truthfulness without the necessity of the child's reputation for truth and veracity having been attacked by the defense. Another division of the Court of Appeals seems to be saying that such testimony is admissible only to rebut an attack on the child's reputation for truthfulness (*Vollentine,* 1982; see also *People v. Ortega,* 1983).

The courts in Colorado have since backed away from allowing an expert to actually state that a child is telling the truth. In *Tevlin v. People* (1986) the Colorado Supreme Court disapproved an expert's opinion that went to the witnesses' truthfulness on a specific occasion where the record did not reflect that the defense had directly attacked the victim's character for truthfulness.

People v. Koon (1986) also recently held that expert testimony is to be excluded on the question of whether a witness is fantasizing or fabricating the particular facts at issue. If truthfulness is properly put at issue by the defense, testimony as to general characteristics is admissible. For example, opinion testimony as to whether children generally have the sophistication to lie about having experienced a sexual assault was held to still be admissible by the *Koon* Court.

In another recent case, *United States v. Azure* (1986), the Eighth Circuit Court of Appeals reversed Azure's conviction for child sexual abuse because the expert offered testimony on the witnesses' credibility. They stated testimony in general about a child's ability to separate fact from fiction is admissible but one witness may not comment about the testimony of another witness, as it invades the province of the jury.

WHEN THE CHILD DOES NOT TESTIFY

The second situation in which expert testimony is increasingly being tendered is when the child victim does not testify at all or is unable to give the detailed information contained in early statements to authorities, social workers, or treatment professionals. In those cases prosecutors will offer earlier statements of the child to third parties as an exception to the hearsay rule. More cases are being prosecuted as innovative trial strategies are accepted.

Historically, in Colorado as in most states, children's earlier statements could only come in if they were sufficiently contemporaneous with the event in question to qualify as a spontaneous utterance under what is called the *res gestae* exception. [See 6 J. Wigmore, Evidence Section 1747 at 195 (Cladbourn rev. 1976); McCormick, 1972.] The theory behind the admission of hearsay statements in such a circumstance is that the declaration is stimulated by the event and not by the declarant's deliberation, and is therefore made under such circumstances as to preclude fabrication.

It has been held that literal spontaneity is not required as long as the declaration is sufficiently contemporaneous with the event that it can be regarded as having been stimulated by the event. [See *McQueen V. United States, People in the Interest of O.E.P.* (1982), and *Ortega,* 1983.] Statements have been admitted in cases involving delays of several hours or even days between the event and the child's statement to another [*State v. Noble* (1977), *People v. Lovett* (1976)]. In one instance, photographs shown to a child 8 weeks after the actual event served as the exciting stimulus for the utterance (*United States v. Napier,* 1975). Psychologists working with abused children are aware that long delays in reporting, sometimes up to years, can take place when the child feels unsafe. This knowledge is slowly being acknowledged by the legal system. There is some authority to the effect that the *res gestae* rule should be applied more liberally in the case of children. However, in many jurisdictions, including Colorado, any significant delay between the stressful event and the child's statement may prevent its admission under the *res gestae* exception (*W.C.L. v. People*, 1984).

In spite of attempts by both legislatures and courts to move these cases along as speedily as possible, they necessarily face many of the same docket pressures and resultant long delays that are typical of much of the litigation in an overloaded judicial system. It is thus quite typical for a substantial period of time to pass between the reporting of the incident and the actual trial of the case. The dilemma a prosecutor faces if the child's early statements to others are not admissible is this: By the time a case gets to trial many months later, child victims often cannot or will not talk about it further. The mere mention of the act can be traumatic for them, and counterproductive to any therapy they are undergoing. The prosecutor sometimes encounters great resistance from the child, the family, and/or the therapist to the prospect of taking the stand and going through the whole set of facts again. A child can receive a message of "no one believes me" when asked to relate details again after having recounted it so many times to relatives, police, doctors, therapists, and social workers. It is not unusual in my experience for a child to be evasive and unwilling to discuss the potential subject further even in private one-on-one meetings, and this reluctance is increased by the atmosphere and numbers of people present in a courtroom setting. A reluctant child witness is less credible with juries. Thus, unless the child's initial statements to third parties are admissible as hearsay exception, the prosecutor may never be able to get the full story before the trier of fact.

Recognizing this, both courts and legislatures in recent years have searched for other ways to justify the admission of the child's statements to others at an earlier time, provided certain guarantees of trustworthiness exist. Both Washington (Wash. Rev. Code 9A. 44. 120) and Colorado (Section 13-25-129; Section 18-3-411 and Section 19-1-107, CR.S., as amended) have passed similar statutes that provide that out-of-court statements of children that would otherwise be considered hearsay are admissible if: (1) the court finds that the time, content, and circumstance of the statement provide sufficient safeguards of reliability; and (2) the child either testifies at the proceedings or is unavailable as a witness and there is corroborative evidence of the act that is the subject of the statement.

Unavailability and Corroborative Evidence

I have had occasion to tender statements made by various experts (clinical social workers, psychologists, physicians, therapists) in a number of different criminal and juvenile cases. Two issues that must be dealt with in each instance are the definitions of *unavailable* and *corroborative evidence*. Prosecutors can expect strong arguments from defense counsel in an attempt to narrow the definitions of both terms. Counsel routinely take the position that a child witness is not unavailable unless she or he is physically unavailable or is unavailable for serious medical reasons. There is, however, substantial precedent for a much broader interpretation of the term, particularly in states that have rules of evidence similar to the Federal Rules. Both Washington and Colorado, for example, have adopted such rules. Rule 804(a) defines unavailability to include situations in which the declarant, among other things: (1) refuses to testify in spite of a court order to do so; (2) testifies to a lack of memory of the subject matter; or (3) is unable to be present or to testify at the hearing because of death or then-existing mental or physical illness or infirmity. Various cases support this broader approach. In *United States v. Faison* (1982), it was held that a witness who could not testify after he suffered a heart attack was unavailable for trial. In *United States v. Allen,* (1969), the court held that previous testimony of witnesses who refused to testify at the trial of a defendant could be admitted and that they were unavailable. *United States v. Carlson* (1976) holds that where action of the defendant had led to the unwillingness of the witness to testify, previous grand jury testimony that had not been subjected to cross-examination could be used, notwithstanding the constitutional right to confrontation of witnesses. In the State of Washington, in a case specifically involving a sexual assault on a child, the court in *State v. Slider* (1984) said that a child's lack of memory to both events and her previous statements made her unavailable as a witness.

In practice, it appears that most trial judges are having little trouble in finding a child unavailable for testimony in instances where the child has blocked certain things from his or her memory and is unable to recall, or in situations where it can be established that considerable psychological trauma will ensue from being required to testify.

Having decided the question of unavailability, the court must still deal with the issue of corroborative evidence of the child's out-of-court statement. Where there are other witnesses, similar incidents, or medical evidence, this does not present a difficult hurdle. Far more difficult, however, are those cases where none of those types of evidence are available. In a case I handled last year, there were statements from the 7-year-old child regarding an ongoing sexual contact with the stepfather. Although the child's intimate areas had been stroked and touched, and the child subjected to full-body contact, no penetration had occurred. Thus, there was no corroborating physical evidence, nor were there other witnesses. During hearings on a *Motion in Limine* (which is held to try to get the judge to exclude certain evidence before the trial that may be considered prejudicial to the defendant) the People presented testimony from two separate child psychologists who had received a statement from the child. Both indicated that the child exhibited multiple behavioral symptoms of a type consistently observable in child victims of sexual abuse. They further testified that the child exhibited a knowledge of sexual matters and technique that could not have been learned from mere casual observation of others. The People argued that the multiple behavioral symptoms themselves constituted sufficient corroborative evidence of the child's statement to make it admissible. The trial court rejected that rationale, adhering to a more conservative interpretation of the corroboration requirement. The issue has apparently not been resolved on the appellate level, so it remains uncertain whether the statutory grounds for admissibility of hearsay statements will be of much assistance in cases involving sexual contact without penetration.

Interestingly enough, having denied the admissibility of the statements under the statutory basis, the trial court then found them admissible under a separate evidentiary exception to the hearsay rule, the one involving statements made for purposes of medical diagnosis or treatment.

Exceptions to the Hearsay Rule

Rule 803(4) of both the Federal and Colorado Rules of Evidence provides for the admissibility of statements made for the purpose of medical diagnosis or treatment. Ordinarily, "statements as to fault" do not qualify. (See *United States v. Iron Shell* 1984.) However, two recent Colorado and Wyoming cases have extended the exception to statements including the identity of the perpetrator. (See *Goldade v. Wyoming,* Wyoming Supreme Court; *People v. Oldson,* 1984.) The Colorado Court of Appeals in its opinion reasoned that because no effective diagnosis or treatment could take place until the child identified and was isolated from the abuser, the question of identity was "reasonably pertinent to diagnosis and treatment." The Colorado Supreme Court has since granted certiorari to review the decision of the Court of Appeals, so no final appellate posture with respect to the breadth of 803(4) is yet clear.

Meanwhile, however, yet another development has taken place to expand the possibilities for getting a child's hearsay statements before the trier of fact through both expert and nonexpert witnesses. In the 1984 case of *W.C.L. v. People,* a frustrated Colorado Supreme Court suggested the wisdom of adopting a residual hearsay exception similar to that found in The Federal Rules of Evidence 803(24) and 804(b)(5). On April 1, 1985 the Supreme Court, after full hearing, did adopt the residual hearsay exception for Colorado, tracking the exact wording of the Federal Rules. Hearsay statements of a child made to lay or expert witnesses that are not covered by other exceptions are admissible whether the child is unavailable or not if:

1. The statement is offered as evidence of a material fact;
2. the statement is more probative (the legal term for getting to prove the facts at issue) on the point for which it is offered than any other evidence that the preponent (party putting it at issue) can procure through reasonable efforts; and
3. the general purposes of the rules and the interests of justice will best be served by admission of the statement into evidence.

Oregon's Supreme Court has recently created a new exception to the hearsay rule, designated the "complaint of sexual misconduct" exception. In *Oregon v. Campbell* (1985) the court admitted into evidence the mother's testimony of the statement made to her by the child victim. The court indicated that in the future, trial courts in such cases should conduct competency hearings to determine if the child victim is capable of testifying. If they find that the child victim is not capable of testifying and the court finds "adequate indicia of reliability," the child's hearsay statement will be admissible.

As of this date it appears that 20 states have passed legislation creating special hearsay exceptions for the benefit of child victims (Arizona, Arkansas, California, Colorado, Florida, Illinois, Indiana, Iowa, Kansas, Louisiana, Maine, Minnesota, Missouri, New York, Oklahoma, South Dakota, Texas, Utah, Vermont, and Washington). It has been held by at least one court that state legislation is not a necessary predicate to permit hearsay reports of child victims (*State v. Sheppard*, 1984).

The use of hearsay is being blamed for the conviction of innocent defendants—especially the reliance on social science data that suggest that young children do not lie or fantasize about sexual abuse. A recent law review article suggests that the Florida statute (Chapter 85–84, Section 1, Laws of Florida) overlooks research that proves children do lie about sexual abuse (Case & Comment, 1986). A similar article was published in a popular journal for Colorado trial lawyers (Philippus & Koch, 1986). These criticisms have two major flaws, first, in the proof of the lie, and second, in the reliability and validity of the research cited. There is difficulty in determining when a child has lied initially and then later told the truth, or whether the truth was the initial statement that is later recanted. Some have confused the unfounded-case rate as synonymous with cases where the child lied, instead of recognizing that all cases that do not go to trial for a variety of reasons go into that category. In the Philippus and Koch article, the authors cite outdated studies, some going back to the 1920s, 1930s, and 1940s, to prove their point that children are likely to lie or fantasize about sexual abuse. Attorneys and mental health professionals need to be familiar with the newer literature that refutes such erroneous myths.

Videotaped Testimony

One of the most innovative means to protect the child has been the use of videotaped testimony. In some jurisdictions the child can be questioned in an adjacent room with her or his testimony shown simultaneously in the court-room on closed-circuit television. This helps reduce the fear element for the child, especially relative to the intimidation of the courtroom setting and to being in the same room as the defendant, who may still threaten the child even with just a look. Both the attorney and a support person can be present with the child. Critics of this method raise the confrontation issue, while proponents question if the Sixth Amendment means face-to-face confronta-tion, or if the defendant's rights are preserved by being able to watch the child testify. There is also a constitutional issue raised about the defendant's right to a public trial, but it can be argued that the courtroom itself is still open to the press and the public.

Similar issues are raised with the use of a videotape that demonstrates the child's testimony to another party at an earlier date. In some states, a videotape of the expert's evaluation can be used in lieu of the child. This, of course, presents a serious damage to the defendant's right to confrontation. However, the videotape can provide a visual record of what types of leading questions, if any, were used during the evaluation process. It also allows the defendant's expert to give an opinion without having to interview the child. In other states, such as Colorado, a videotaped deposition is admissable under the law but has not yet been tested in the appellate courts, which makes prosecutors less likely to utilize videotape if the child can withstand the actual testimony. In Colorado, both attorneys can ask the child questions, either directly or through a child psychologist, as an addition to the usual child sexual abuse evaluation. If a one-way mirror is utilized, the defendant can also witness the procedure, preserving his or her right to confrontation even if it is not face to face (cf. Walker, Chapter 10 of this volume). These new procedures are still being modified as they are being utilized. They enjoy an enthusiastic reception by judges in some jurisdictions where they are being used because of the minimization of harm to the child. However, the con-stitutional issues still have not been clarified although they are under careful study (Whitcomb, Shapiro, & Stellwegen, 1985).

Implications for the Expert Witness

Taken together, the various exceptions to the hearsay rule may give prosecu-tors a way to either bolster the child's testimony or to present expert testimony in lieu of it. Certainly, in the cases we have handled, such testimony from qualified experts has tremendously eased the burden of persuasion with the trier of fact. The various advantages of this approach include:

1. Sparing a child the trauma of the courtroom experience
2. Obtaining a more complete and descriptive statement than many children would otherwise be able to give at this juncture
3. Providing the facts through an experienced professional less susceptible to confusion or contradiction by defense counsel
4. Providing the additional benefit of an explanation of the observed behavioral symptoms that tend to corroborate the child's story

It can be a mistake to assume that the expert will be at home in the courtroom or be effective without pretrial preparation. Those who have not testified frequently will often be unnerved by cross-examination and either become petulant and argumentative or will vacillate in their opinions. Much of this can be avoided by thorough pretrial preparation in which the lawyer goes over with the expert in some detail the reason for the opinion rendered and also covers anticipated cross-examination. On the other side of the coin, some who testify frequently in a given area can tend to lose their objectivity and become more advocates than scientists. They are susceptible to the cross-examination technique of being led along subtly until they have extended their opinion to unreasonable limits. Such individuals need to be reminded that the lawyer is the advocate and that their testimony may be disbelieved if they are perceived as unfair or unreceptive to at least considering other interpretations.

Speech patterns can be a problem in the courtroom also, particularly since many professionals tend to overrely on technical jargon in the course of their testimony. This can tend to confuse as well as to destroy identity with the finder of fact, particularly a jury. The overreliance on jargon comes because the expert is insecure and feels safer hiding behind that sort of terminology. Thorough pretrial preparation can usually avoid most of this problem also, and experts should be prompted to communicate in as plain a manner as they can manage, interpreting technical terms whenever they are called upon to use them. It is also more effective to have the expert testify initially in narrative form rather than in short question-and-answer form. Numerous studies have found that this style of presentation is more credible to juries, as well as more understandable. However, it requires a good deal more pretrial preparation.

Finally, it has been my experience that many experts will be more positive and more elaborative in their personal testimony than they will in written reports. For that reason, it is also a mistake to wait until the day of trial to talk with the professional in question. Detailed pretrial preparation will pay dividends in the effectiveness and credibility of the in-court presentation.

As use of experienced professionals in this courtroom role grows and expands, it will become easier to bring the child molester to justice without putting child victims through all the rigors they have suffered in the past.

LEGAL REFERENCES

Bridges v. Lintz, 140 Colo. 582, 346 P.2d 571 (1959).

Goldade v. Wyoming, Wyoming Supreme Court (Dec. 12, 1983).

McQueen v. U.S., 104 App. D.C. 358, 262 F. 2d 455.

Oregon v. Campbell, Oregon Supreme Court No. S 30758 (decided August 20, 1985).

People v. Ashley, 687 P. 2n 473 (Colo. App. 1984).

People v. Koon (Colo. App. 84 C.A. 0583 1986).

People v. Lovett, 85 Mich. App. 534, 272 N.W. 2d 126 (1976).

People v. Martinez, 43 Colo. App. 419, 608. P. 2d 359 (1980).

People v. Oldson, 697 P.2d 787 (Colo. App. 1984).

People v. Ortega, 672 P.2d 215 at 218 (Colo. App. 1983).

People v. Vollentine, 643 P.2d 800 (Colo. App. 1982).

People In the Interest of O.E.P., 654 P.2d 312 (1982).

People In the Interest of W.C.L., 650 P.2d 1302 (Colo. App. 1982).

State v. Boodry, 96 Ariz. 59, 394 P.2d 196, *cert. denied,* 379 U.S. 949, 13, L.D. 546, 85 S.Ct. 448.

State v. Noble, 342 So. 2d 170 (La. 1977).

State v. Sheppard, 484 A. 2d 1330 (N.J., 1984).

State v. Slider, 688 P.2d 538 (Wash. 1984).

Tevlin v. People, 85 S.Ct. 236 (1986).

United States v. Allen, 409 F611 (1969).

United States v. Azure, 801, F.2d 336 (1986).

United States v. Carlson, 547 F.2d 1346 (1976).

United States v. Faison, 679 F.2d 292 (1982).

United States v. Iron Shell, 633 F.2d 77 (8th Cir. 1980), *cert. denied,* 450 United States 1001, 101 S.Ct. 170, 68 L. Ed.2d. 203 (1981).

United States v. Napier, 518 F.2d 316 (9th Cir. 1975), *cert. denied,* 423 v.s. 875, 96 s.Ct. 196, 46 L.Ed.2d 128 (1975).

W.C.L. v. People, 685P.2d 176 (Colo. 1984).

REFERENCES

Austern, D. (1986). *Legal update.* Circulated to Members, Victims Committee, American Bar Association, Section of Criminal Justice, 1800 M St, N.W. 2nd Floor, South Lobby, Washington, DC 20036-2260

Case & Comment. (1986). *Child sex abuse: The innocent accused. 91,* 6.

Goodman, G. S. (1984). Children's testimony in historical perspective. *Journal of Social Issues, 40*(12), 157–175.

McCormick, C. (1972). *Handbook of the law of evidence,* Section 297 at 704 (E. Cleary, 2nd ed.).

Philippus, M. J., & Koch, G. V. (1986, October). How to evaluate sexuality in children and to avoid using "anatomically correct dolls." *Trial Talk,* pp. 372–373.

Stewart, J. K. (1985). Foreword. In D. Whitcomb, E. R. Shapiro, & L. D. Stellwegen, *When the victim is a child: Issues for judges and prosecutors* (p. i). Washington, DC: National Institute of Justice.

Whitcomb, D., Shapiro, E. R., & Stellwegen, L. D. (1985). *When the victim is a child: Issues for judges and prosecutors.* Washington, DC: National Institute of Justice.

Wigmore, J. H. (1976). *Evidence in trials at common law* (rev. ed. by J. H. Cladbourne). Evidence Section 1747 at 195.

9

Incest Investigation
and Treatment Planning
by Child Protective Services

Cassie C. Spencer
Margaret A. Nicholson

Ruth is an intake supervisor for reports of child sexual abuse in her county. She receives an average of eight calls a day regarding child molestation. A thorough investigation of each case requires a minimum of 15 contact hours, and Ruth has two social workers to respond to reports. Of necessity, Ruth must decide which children will receive social services intervention and which will not. She has developed a triage system to investigate the more severe cases. But somewhere a child is crying who will not be seen.

Finally, the hidden secret of child sexual abuse is being revealed, and as a result, child protection agencies across the country are inundated with reports of sexual abuse. This should signify that more children are receiving help. In truth, services are not adequate to meet the demand. The major federal program for child protective services has dropped $200 million below its 1981 funding level (Children's Defense Fund, 1985). Staff is decreasing at the same time that reporting is increasing. The National Committee for Prevention of Child Abuse survey in 1983 showed only 2 states out of 50 had been able to increase their child protective services staff that year (Children's Defense Fund, 1985). Social workers in child protection are overloaded and trying to manage cases that soar far above the numbers for caseload standards. In fact, caseload standards are outdated and too high. The majority of state child welfare programs do not even have any standards.

Sexual abuse cases, particularly incest, are viewed by many child protection workers as the most difficult to manage and treat. The reasons, outlined below, are as varied and complex as the cases themselves.

Unlike physical abuse or neglect situations, social workers are confronted with their own issues of human sexuality when faced with a child victim of sexual molestation. Although time has liberated society to a certain extent, most people are still uncomfortable when discussing sexuality and often choke on the terminology. This is exacerbated when the situation also involves incest. It is not uncommon for extreme feelings of rage to emerge—particularly when confronting the perpetrator. Yet child protection workers are directed by national and state legislation to reunite the family if at all possible. It is no wonder that many are reluctant to treat such cases.

Another scar inflicted by the slashed funding is the concurrent reduction of training for social service workers. Sexual abuse cases are often handled by untrained personnel, yet these most complicated of families need highly skilled treatment. Social service workers receive little if any formal education regarding the dynamics and treatment of this social problem. Yet for effective intervention, this knowledge is a necessity.

The dynamics of incest alone make the situation extremely difficult to manage. First of all, the social worker is frequently confronted with a perpetrator who is controlling, manipulative, and one of the best "con artists" to be found. The father who has committed this act of molestation is very resistive to losing the control he has maintained over his family. Effective treatment is often an uncertain judgment because of his ability to persuade others that he has changed when in reality the abuse will continue at the first opportunity. Stories abound within social service agencies of closed cases and the reappearance of the sexual victimization months or even years later. Research studies and interviews with retrospective incest victims are horrifying in their message of the atrocities continuing after the perpetrator has been "treated" and the family reunited (Herman, 1981). It is also easy for the involved professionals to believe the pseudoreform because of the tremendous need to escape the emotional anguish that incest evokes. In addition, societal values perpetuate the patriarchal system and sanction the power of the father within the family. Any challenge of this authority is met with resistance—both internal and external. An excellent example is the difficulty in having the incest offender removed from the home instead of the child.

Sometimes the nonperpetrator spouse can present a further problem to the caseworker. In many cases, the mother is powerless, dependent, and fearful. She has everything to lose by believing her daughter's story (e.g., her husband, security, financial support). Thus the social worker and victim may be faced with not only the father's denial, but the mother's as well. This can increase the stress to the child and the frustration to the worker who is trying to intervene in the family interactions. It should be noted, however, that not all women in these situations will present themselves as helpless and dependent. Many take an active role in confronting the perpetrator, ensuring the safety of their child, and even filing divorce proceedings and/or persuading the prosecutor to file criminal charges.

If the social worker is not cautious and proactive with her or his approach, the child may become the scapegoat for the crisis. Most sexually abused children feel fearful, ashamed, guilty, and responsible for the abuse. Because of these emotions, they are easily exploited and often in danger of retracting their story due to family pressure.

Historically, psychoanalytical and legal literature has advocated that the child who reports incest or sexual abuse is lying. A classic legal textbook, which continues to be used as a source of reference, impeaches the credibility of children (Wigmore, 1934). Herman (1981) cites an example whereby Wigmore set a precedence for having children examined by psychiatrists to determine their believability. In one case, one girl, age 7, had gonorrhea, and in another, a 9-year-old girl's vagina was so inflamed and swollen the doctor could not make a physical examination. Yet Wigmore dismissed this evidence and instead discussed the cases as pathological lying in children. (See Goodman & Helgeson, Chapter 7 of this volume.) If it is determined, however, that the child is not lying and that incest did occur, the mother is often blamed and considered to be as responsible—if not more so—as the father because she failed to provide protection or she "set her child up." This nation's patriarchal system and its traditional beliefs that women and children are men's property, to do with as they please, makes it easy to divert attention from the father to other members of the family.

A final factor that encumbers the social worker's tasks to manage and treat these cases is the legal system itself. It is not uncommon to expect the case worker to gather evidence for the court, yet, in order to provide treatment to the family, the child protection worker's primary role is to establish trust and a therapeutic relationship with family members. This is often shattered when criminal charges are filed and the social worker is subpoenaed to testify. To counteract this, many child protection agencies have agreements with the district attorney's office to respect worker/client confidentiality and do not use the worker's testimony in prosecuting the perpetrator.

In summary, all of the above factors contribute to the frustration and sense of powerlessness within social service workers when faced with a case of incest. It becomes easier to: not see or acknowledge that sexual abuse is occurring; focus on the mother in assessment and treatment planning more than on the father; believe that the father has totally changed after undergoing treatment and that the abuse will not happen again; doubt the child's story;

focus the goals in treatment on problems other than the incest (e.g., alcoholism); close the case prematurely; agree to a court-approved informal adjustment; and/or view the case as hopeless. However, well trained child protection workers have a greater capacity than do any other intervening professionals to manage effectively and/or to treat incest cases and provide protection that is not detrimental to the child. Their role is vested in statute, and they often are supported in their intervention through the juvenile court and its powers.

This chapter will discuss appropriate procedures for intake assessment and treatment for the child protection worker. The discussion will cover the following topics: disclosure of abuse, interviewing (the child, the nonperpetrator spouse, and the perpetrator), assessment of credibility, assessment of danger, assessment of the mother/child relationship, and treatment planning and implementation.

THE DISCLOSURE OF ABUSE

Disclosure of incest usually comes from two sources: the child reports to the mother or other trusted adult, or a person observing physical and/or behavioral indicators reports his or her suspicions. Children report for a variety of reasons: they can no longer tolerate the abuse; the abuse becomes painful; they contract infection or disease; the abuse has led to sexual intercourse; they want to protect younger siblings from similar abuse; and, in teenagers, the perpetrator is restricting their social interactions. The interviewer will need to determine the precipitating factor for the child to make the report. One word of caution when seeking this information—be careful not to imply blame. For example, if the adult were to ask, "Why are you telling now?" the child might interpret the question to mean, "Why did you let it go on?" Instead, the question could be rephrased to, "Tell me what happened right before you decided to tell." If the report is received by another person, the interviewer will want to obtain as much information as possible regarding the reasons sexual abuse is suspected.

Response to a complaint of sexual abuse should be immediate. If the call is first received by the child protection unit, the police need to be contacted prior to any investigation. One of the unnecessary traumas these children experience is the systematic procedures they must endure once the secret has been told. It is not uncommon for victims to have to repeat their story six, seven, or more times. Not only is this emotionally stressful for the child, it may hinder legal proceedings, especially if the child's story is not entirely consistent. (See Goodman & Helgeson, Chapter 7, and Long, Chapter 8 of this volume.) For this reason, many agencies are developing investigatory policies and written procedures in conjunction with the local police department and the district attorney's office to ensure the least number of interviews possible. Social workers trained in sexual abuse intervention and in interviewing children should conduct the sessions with any others present only as nonparticipating listeners. Ideally, a one-way observation mirror with videotape facilities should be used (see also Walker, Chapter 10 of this volume). The law enforcement officer's role is to determine whether a crime has been committed and, if so, to investigate and ascertain who the alleged perpetrator is. Social workers are mandated to assess the need of a child for protection and to intervene in the child's best interests.

In addition, a medical examination of the victim and all siblings must be obtained as soon as possible. The child protection worker needs to prepare the child for this examination. It is preferable to use a pediatrician trained in conducting examinations that will not inflict secondary trauma on the child. A physician can help reduce the fear and shame by reassuring the child that he or she is going to be okay.

"Immediate response" to a complaint of incest does not mean preparation should not occur. Interviews should be carefully planned. The following section discusses some factors to consider for the child, nonperpetrator spouse, and perpetrator.

INTERVIEWING

If the child was not the one to report the abuse, the first interview should be with the reporter, to ascertain as much information as possible. If the child reported, the first interview should be with the child victim and secondly each of the victim's siblings.

The Child

Phase I

Phase I of the three phases of the initial interview with the child is to establish rapport. This is essential to enable the child to feel more at ease. In most cases, the social worker will be a stranger. Keep in mind that the abuse probably occurred over a period of time before the child had the courage to tell; it may not be easy to repeat the story in the presence of strangers. The rapport will depend on the adult's ability to convey warmth, sincerity, caring, and respect for the child.

Preferably, the interview will take place in a neutral setting. Except under extraordinary circumstances, it should not occur in the child's home. Most incest victims will be fearful of their disclosure. Many have been threatened with physical harm or the loss of parental love and support if they tell "the secret." To repeat their story to a stranger within the walls of the abusive environment and perhaps with family members nearby can increase this fear and possibly any hesitancies or second thoughts they have been harboring. Likewise, it is often frightening to a child to be interviewed at a police station. Incest victims already feel responsible and guilty, as though they have committed a crime. A law enforcement setting may reinforce the self-blame. Ideally, the location will be a school or room within the social services building especially designed for children's needs. Helpful props to have on hand include games, toys, puppets, anatomically correct dolls, drawing materials, and pillows. Even adolescents often find it easier to talk when their hands can be preoccupied with puzzles or artwork.

One difficult decision for the social worker is deciding who will be present during the interview. The interviewer does not want to overwhelm the child with too many people, yet the goal is to have the child repeat the story the least amount of times possible. Many child protection agencies are including representatives from the police department or sheriff's office and the district attorney's office in the initial interviews. Some resourceful agencies have the capacity to talk with the child behind a two-way mirror with the interviewer receiving messages and questions from onlookers through the use of microphones placed in the interviewer's ear. If the child wants, a support person may be present. This may be a teacher, a neighbor, or a school nurse. It is not a good idea to use parents, especially if the parent is the accusing party in a custody dispute. The social worker also will want to ensure that the adult ally will not show shock or in any way place judgment during the discussion with the child.

Mountain, Nicholson, Spencer, and Walker (1984) and Sgroi (1982) have identified the following information needed from the child:

- Identification of the perpetrator
- Description of the abusive acts (either verbally or through some other medium such as anatomically correct dolls, puppets, playhouse dolls, or drawings)
- Over what period of time the abuse occurred (with young children, the interviewer can identify approximate dates using significant events such as holidays or birthdays)
- How often the abuse occurred
- The secretive nature of the abuse
- Whether force was used and, if so, how much and to what extent
- Knowledge of the abuse by others (e.g., siblings)
- Emotional reaction of the child to the abuse (guilt, fear, anger, responsibility, repression, withdrawal, other behavioral symptoms)
- Child's perception of her or his relationship with the perpetrator (positives and negatives)

- Child's perception of his or her relationship with siblings
- Child's perception of her or his relationship with nonperpetrator spouse
- How the child feels the abuse and disclosure of the abuse will impact life in the future and family relationships (determine whether the child is fearful of returning home or of encountering family members)
- Child's adjustment in school and with peers
- Child's goals for self and family (look for age-appropriate responses)
- Child's willingness to be involved in a treatment program (look for age-appropriate responses)

Throughout the case investigation, planning, and treatment, but particularly in interviews with the children, the worker's nonjudgmental attitude is essential. Children are experts at detecting signs of disgust, anger, and embarrassment. The social worker needs to establish a relaxed atmosphere and, through training and supervision, should have achieved a level of comfort in discussing sexual abuse. Although it is important to gather as much information as possible, the interview should be first and foremost a therapeutic encounter. The social worker's warmth, support, and empathy will assist the incest victim through the painful descriptions of the abuse. Some adults are uncomfortable when talking with children. This will be a tremendous hindrance to the process. The one selected as the interviewer should not only have knowledge about sexual abuse but should like working with children and be skilled in interacting with them. It also is helpful if the interviewer is the same sex as the child.

To begin with, the social worker needs to introduce herself and explain her role and reason for being there. This must be done, of course, in terms that are age appropriate. Other adults who are present also should identify themselves and briefly engage with the child. Before proceeding further, show an interest in the child; ask what she or he likes or involve the child in an activity such as drawing or playing a game. If possible, get the child to begin talking about herself, her likes, dislikes, friends, and so forth. When some comfort has been established, tell the child what is expected and what will occur in the interview. It is sometimes helpful for the interviewer to relate that she or he has worked with other children in similar situations. Describe a variety of these contacts, such as children who have been sick, children who have been sad, children who have been bruised or hurt, or children who have been touched in ways they did not like. If said in one sentence, it will not prejudice the child in any way and will not single them out as someone different or strange.

Phase II

At this point, try to ascertain what happened to the child. This is the second phase of the interview. In so doing, the interviewer should clarify and use the child's terminology. One way to facilitate this may be through the use of anatomically correct dolls. Point to various body parts and ask the child to name them. Other ways would be to have the child draw pictures of the sexual abuse and label what is occurring, or to have the child point to his or her body parts that were violated and describe what happened. If the child is very young and nonverbal, the interviewer may point to body parts of the anatomically correct dolls, with the child indicating whether that was a place of abuse by nodding yes or no. It is essential not to ask leading questions. This can interfere with the court's acceptance of the interview. However, the interviewer can use response statements that enable the child to further describe what happened (Benjamin, 1981). The focus is to create spontaneous responses from the child.

The tendency will be to try to get as much information as possible in the first session. However, the interviewer must be sensitive to the child's need to go at her or his own pace—especially in dealing with this difficult topic. Several interviews may be necessary, even if they are spread throughout one day. If the child is hesitant to disclose much during the first encounter, it is well to heed the cues. Focus instead on forming a relationship and schedule another time, perhaps a half hour or an hour later. These delays may be difficult for the social worker or other authorities when protection of the child is a major concern, yet it can be damaging to the child to proceed when the interviewer is feeling impatient or frustrated and conveying anger. If the interviewer is faced with a child who is not willing to talk (often in cases with adolescents), the social worker can attempt to get a verbal court order or police custody hold for temporary placement. The capacity to do this will vary from case to case and jurisdiction to jurisdiction, but if available it may provide enough time for the interviewer to establish enough rapport for the child to discuss the abuse. During the first session, the interviewer may want to get only enough information to enable the agency to provide protection and to give emotional support and validation to the victim. Not all of the information items listed previously need to be obtained in the first meeting. However, it is vital to avoid confrontation between the child and powerful family members until the allegation is validated. Premature confrontation can endanger the child emotionally and physically and interfere with the validation process. *Interview the child exclusive of other family members.*

Phase III

Throughout the interviewing process, show a willingness to help by giving the child specific information and helping him or her deal with feelings of fear and guilt. Show a belief in the child and convey the message that she or he is not to blame for what happened. It is very important to state up front that what the child tells you cannot be kept secret but must be shared with others. The last phase of the child's interview is to give information to the child. Encourage the child to ask questions. The interviewer's responses need to be as informative as possible. Often the social worker is not clear what will occur with the perpetrator and nonperpetrator spouse and, if so, then that needs to be said. However, the social worker needs to explain what the plan is and what the next steps are for the child. This information needs to be presented in a manner that enables the child to understand. If placement is imminent, the worker needs to prepare the child and, it is hoped, whomever will be the placement person.

Children should not be left alone immediately following the interview. Professionals often need to confer after these interviews, and as a result the child is left alone in an interviewing room. This is emotionally difficult for a child, and thus a teacher, nurse, or aide should be introduced to the child and some rapport established prior to the interviewer's departure.

The Nonperpetrator Spouse

The nonperpetrator spouse in cases of incest is usually the mother. After interviewing the child victim and siblings, the social worker should talk with the mother to make further assessments of the family situation.

Most women in these circumstances will present a crisis affect to which the interviewer must be sensitive. There may be indications of shock, anger, confused thinking, immobility, inability to make decisions, and feelings of vulnerability. Some will deny that the abuse occurred; others will believe the incest report but experience a shocked disbelief that this is happening to them.

The stereotype that mothers know about the incest and willingly tolerate it seems to pervade much of the literature and attitudes of professionals. This perception is not entirely accurate and is an unfair judgment of the mother. In a research study (Lukianowicz, 1972) cited by Herman (1981), 16 out of 26 mothers did *not* know about the incest. (See Cammaert, Chapter 15 of this volume.) It is important for the social worker to confront and change personal biases and prejudices on this issue; otherwise, there is a tendency to place all the blame and focus the treatment solely on the mother. This practice can be detrimental and even damaging to the family's prognosis.

Yet there will be cases where mothers suspect or know their daughters are suffering from sexual abuse but are unable to take actions to stop it. These women often are powerless within their families. They are most likely emotionally and financially dependent on their spouses and experience tremendous fear that their marriage and livelihood will be in danger if the incest is revealed. Practical concerns such as divorce or separation, going on welfare, social ostracism, and initiation of criminal proceedings against their husbands prevent them from reporting the abuse. Some women may realistically fear retaliation—particularly if the husband is physically abusive as well. Another reality is the loss of their children through placement in foster care. Consequently, the mother may not trust the "system" nor the social worker representing it. These mothers, compared with others in nonincestuous families, marry younger, have more histories of pregnancy problems, bear more children, and have less education and work experience outside the home (Herman, 1981). This being the case, what would the mother do if she consciously recognized the abuse and reported it? The whole family would be disrupted. Her husband might be placed in jail. He would probably deny the incest charge. Who is she to believe? If the choice is between the daughter or the husband upon whom she is emotionally and economically dependent, she may see no other choice than to go along with or ignore the incest.

Regardless of whether or not the mother knew about the incest, the above practical concerns need to be addressed for all clients. In addition to collecting information, the social worker should begin immediate planning with the mother for physical and emotional needs. These may include protection from possible coercive behaviors by the perpetrator, financial support, legal aid, and shelter care.

An atmosphere of empathy, warmth, and acceptance should be created. If the mother allowed the molestation to continue even after her awareness of it, the interviewer may experience normal feelings of anger towards her. These emotions must be expressed and dealt with under supervision in order for the social worker to rely on a solid belief that every individual has strengths, to demonstrate a willingness to find strengths within the mother, and begin immediately to build on these. One of the most helpful treatment strategies in cases of incest is to augment the mother/child relationship, but this will not be accomplished without first strengthening the mother.

Below are key factors that should be assessed (Mountain et al., 1984):

- strengths
- feelings toward the perpetrator and the daughter (many mothers feel betrayed)
- ability to be empathic towards the child
- ability to meet daily needs
- immediate needs that can be met through social services assistance
- extent of the acceptance or denial of the situation
- ability to provide protection for the child
- willingness to receive help and intervention
- resources (friends, family, other support systems)
- feelings toward other children in the family
- psychiatric and personal history (e.g., history of abuse)
- drug/alcohol problem
- perceptions of her role as wife and mother
- perceptions of the marital relationship
- existence of wife abuse

Again, not all of this information can be assessed during the first interview. However, in the initial session, the social worker should begin to establish a therapeutic relationship and to examine the mother's immediate needs and how they will be met. The social worker should also assess the mother's perception of the sexual abuse and whether she will be capable of providing protection for the child—particularly if there is a plan being considered to remove the father from the home rather than the victim.

The Perpetrator

One of the reasons perpetrators engage in sexual activity with children is the need to feel powerful and in control. Once the secret is revealed, they fear losing this control over their family as well as their job, their home, and their community status. Suddenly, they face the possibility of incarceration. If discovered, offenders usually deny everything. They may present themselves as bewildered, confused, nice, and charming. They are very adept at getting others to help them out of a jam. Frequently, the father's denial is aided by relatives and neighbors who insist he is a wonderful person and could never commit such an act.

If the denial does not work, the perpetrator may minimize the abuse by saying it only happened once or that he just touched the victim. He may justify the behavior by saying it was good for the child (e.g., sex education at home rather than on the streets). He may blame the child. "She seduced me" is a common excuse used by offenders for the incest. One client claimed that if his daughter had not worn "short shorts," the molestation would never have occurred. Such accusations, of course, are ludicrous. The child is never to blame. Wives also are implicated through comments like, "She's cold and frigid," "She's never at home, and I didn't want to use a prostitute." Somehow the father feels commendations are in order if he met his sexual needs within the confines of home rather than on the street.

The perpetrator will do his best to rally his wife and others (e.g., judges, jurors, police officers, social workers) to his side. He may threaten the daughter, if given the chance, to get her to retract her report. Unfortunately, this happens all too often and is one reason why the social worker, with judicial support, should insist that all contact between the child and perpetrator be closely supervised.

In spite of any anger the interviewer may feel toward the perpetrator, the interviewer must enter the session with a nonjudgmental attitude. Any display of anger will put the client immediately on the defensive. Because of the legitimate rage many feel toward perpetrators, ongoing, supportive supervision for the social worker is essential.

Interviews should be carefully planned and coordinated with the law enforcement agencies *prior* to the initial encounter. As with the other interviews, the social worker will need to clearly identify and explain her or his role and purpose. A police officer and representative from the district attorney's office also may be present. It is their duty to protect the father's legal rights and to give the Miranda warning. The father may at this time request an attorney and refuse to respond to any questioning. This is his right; however, the social worker's role is not to implicate the offender criminally but to begin the process of establishing a relationship and treatment planning. It is hoped that the social worker can immediately engage the father in the interview. To assist with this, many district attorneys, under statutory authority, offer perpetrators deferred prosecution in exchange for the father's commitment to treatment. This agreement may encourage the perpetrator to talk. Using these strategies, the Sexual Abuse Team in Boulder County, Colorado reported a 78% acknowledgment rate of the sexual abuse in perpetrator interviews throughout one year (Carroll & Gottlieb, 1983).

When confronting the perpetrator, the interviewer should not implicate the child. In other words, avoid saying, "Your daughter told me that you did. . . ." This puts the child in a precarious, even dangerous situation when the parent and child are together again, because the parent can confront the child with, "Why did you tell? You're responsible for this mess we're in, for Daddy being arrested." Say instead, "We are concerned that you may have hurt your child. Can you tell me more about this?" Try to avoid confrontation, punitive responses, and improper use of authority in the first interview, because these only increase the anger and defensiveness. Rather, pursue information gathering and practice reflective listening as with any other client when doing the initial assessment. The perpetrator should be made aware of the procedures within the child protection agency, the law enforcement agencies, and the court.

The interviews with perpetrators need to address the factors listed below (Mountain et al., 1984):

- If the perpetrator acknowledges abuse, what are his perceptions of the severity of the abuse?
- Is there a criminal history?
- Is there a history of child molestation?
- Is there a psychiatric history?
- Family history: Was there physical and/or sexual abuse; nurturing, loving parents; and what are his perceptions of his childhood?
- Does he acknowledge the victim's story of abuse?
- Does he feel remorse?
- Does he have any empathy for the child's condition?
- Is he concerned about the victim's emotional well-being?
- What does his family mean to him? How does he perceive his role as husband and father?

- How does he perceive the marital relationship? (Is physical abuse present? What is the quality of the sexual relationship?)
- Is there a drug/alcohol problem? Has and/or will he receive help?
- What are the perpetrator's resources—friends, hobbies?
- Does he express willingness to engage in treatment?
- Does he exhibit suicidal/homicidal tendencies?

ASSESSMENT OF CREDIBILITY

Children rarely lie about sexual abuse. However, several elements that assist authorities in determining that sexual abuse has occurred have been identified in the professional literature.

First of all, the child will be able to give specific details regarding the incest. When a 5-year-old can accurately describe or demonstrate with dolls the act of fellatio, the evidence is fairly convincing that some type of sexual exploitation of the child has transpired. Particularly when eliciting details, the social worker needs to clarify the child's terminology. For example, a 3-year-old boy kept using the words "monkey" and "chocolate-covered banana" when referring to his penis. Further investigation revealed he was being sexually molested by his mother's boyfriend, including penetration of his rectum with the boyfriend's penis. When the child was asked about the words, he was able to demonstrate what happened with the anatomically correct dolls and explained that it was a "game" taught him by the boyfriend. Similarly, when obtaining information from adolescents, the interviewer cannot assume that the youth understands the youth's own terminology, and therefore the interviewer needs to request more detailed descriptions. For example, the adolescent may refer to having intercourse with her father when in reality he touched her genitals with his penis but did not penetrate. One 14-year-old said she had been "raped" by her uncle; however, with more questioning, it became clear that he had taken off her clothing but did not have intercourse. Clearly in both examples sexual abuse occurred; but accuracy is essential for treatment planning and court intervention.

A second consideration is that most sexual abuse will not be limited to one encounter, and the multiple contacts probably will be progressive. In other words, the perpetrator may begin with fondling, then move to forced masturbation, to oral-genital contact, to actual penetration. However, many cases fall short of penetration; thus, medical evidence may not be present. Sometimes penetration or intercourse can occur so gradually that signs of force are nonexistent. It is for this reason that the social worker should pay close attention to other indicators of the molestation.

Third, even if threats or violence are not used by the perpetrator, there usually will be elements of secrecy involved. The father may pressure his daughter into silence because "Mom won't understand and will be hurt" or "they might take you away" or "this is our special time and no one needs to know." Thus, many children do not report the sexual abuse. Because of their feelings of shame, their love for the parent, their trust in a caretaker not to harm them, or their dependency upon adults, it is easy for the perpetrator to command silence.

A fourth element is the array of behavioral and physical indicators of possible sexual abuse. Below is a list, but the presence of any of these problems—except for a sexually transmitted disease—*is not conclusive.* Most are typical signs of distress and may be present due to other reasons. However, if these signals are unexplained by other experiences that may be troubling the child (e.g., recent divorce, a move, a new sibling), they may indicate sexual abuse.

- A sudden reluctance to be with a specific person or go to a specific place, such as a new fear of being alone with a male teacher, a babysitter, or any particular adult
- Inappropriate displays of affection, such as attention to adult genitalia (e.g., crawling into an adult's lap and purposefully fondling breasts or genitals)
- The sudden rejection of normal physical affection, such as hugging, especially if this affection has been previously accepted
- Sudden overinterest in the child's own genitalia beyond a normal child's interest in her or his body; use of unusual vocabulary and unfamiliar names for sexual organs
- Behaviors that go beyond the normal sex play of young children, actions that suggest an understanding of adult sex, or sexually aggressive behavior
- Self-destructive behavior such as self-mutilation or suicidal feelings, and refusal to eat
- Unexplained regressive behavior (bedwetting, thumbsucking, whining)
- Personality changes—an outgoing child who suddenly becomes shy and withdrawn, or a shy child acting uncharacteristically bold
- Sudden school problems such as a drop in performance, not doing homework, classroom problems, inability to concentrate
- Sleep problems—insomnia, nightmares, restlessness, insisting on a night light, or sudden exhaustion and tiredness in school
- Arriving early at school and leaving late with few, if any, absences
- Poor peer relationships or inability to make friends
- Lack of trust, particularly with significant others
- Nonparticipation in school and social activities
- Extraordinary fear of males
- Running away from home

- Physical complaints (e.g., pain or injury in the genital area, discomfort in walking or sitting, unusual odors or itching around the genitals, or contracting a sexually transmitted disease)
- Depression
- Bloody underclothing

Finally, although witnesses often are not available, other corroborative evidence can be identified and is essential. This evidence can come from a medical examination, investigation of the place of abuse to verify descriptions and physical instruments, siblings confirmation they were not allowed in the bedroom while the father and daughter were there, the mother's absence, or other pieces of information. *Report on Scott County Investigations* (Humphrey, 1985) in Minnesota reported that in some of the sexual abuse cases no corroborative evidence was collected prior to arrests, and thus the criminal proceedings were dismissed.

ASSESSMENT OF DANGER

Although a complete investigation will not be possible in the first encounter with the family, the social worker will need to determine the danger to the child and whether the father and daughter should be separated based on the information initially collected. The following factors should be considered when assessing the level of endangerment for the child:

- The age of the victim. The younger the children, the more vulnerable they are.
- The degree, duration, and frequency of the sexual contact. A one-time situational abusive incident has a better prognosis and is usually less dangerous than abuse that has occurred frequently and over a long period of time. One-time voyeurism may be less dangerous than sexual intercourse.
- The presence of physical force and abuse.
- The child's perception of what will happen if she remains in the home.
- The child's fear of remaining in the home. If the child is frightened and does not want to face the perpetrator, the social worker should heed these cues.
- The supportiveness of the mother (refer to Assessment of Mother/Child Relationship in the following section of this chapter).
- Feelings of or lack of remorse or empathy in the perpetrator. A word of caution, however: Many perpetrators are very adept at presenting a facade of remorse and concern for the child.

If, after looking at these elements, the social worker decides the father and child should be separated, it must be determined who will leave. It is hoped that the child can remain at home and that the father will be restrained through a court order. Yet for this to occur in some jurisdictions, the father has to agree to go voluntarily. Other jurisdictions have provisions for orders of protection under new domestic violence protection acts. If the father does leave, the mother and child must be willing to report violations of restriction from the home. It is critical for the social worker to continually assess this willingness to report. Many mothers, angered by their husbands' behavior and betrayal, adamantly agree initially to these terms. However, their determination may waver after a few days of living alone as they become fearful of solving practical survival issues. Tangible evidence of support from social services and other helping agencies can be a deciding factor in these situations. Finally, the child must have an ally in the mother. The mother and siblings must not thrust blame on the child for the father's absence and must be able to provide protection if he appears. This alliance should be continually nurtured by the social worker. Long-term prognosis for healing may rest on restoring and strengthening the mother/child bond.

If the perpetrator cannot be removed, and the child must be placed, visits from *all* members of the family must be carefully supervised and monitored. Reabuse is a reality. Cases have been cited of revictimization while a social worker or other monitor was present in a separate room. In addition, pressure may be put on the child to retract her statements.

While the family is apart, the social worker will be working actively for their reunification. However, fathers should not be readmitted into their families unless five conditions have been met:

1. The father is under supervision of the court.
2. The father is actively involved in a treatment program. Treatment should deal with his inappropriate sexual arousal and behavior and his associated features of intrusiveness, possessiveness, propensity to violence, and needs for power and control. (See in this volume Friedman, Chapter 16; Handy, Chapter 17; and Wolfe, Conte, & Engle-Menig, Chapter 18.)
3. The father accepts complete responsibility for the incest and apologizes to the child in the presence of the entire family.
4. The mother is strong enough to provide protection and emotional support to the child.
5. It is in the best interests of the child.

Judith Herman, in *Father/Daughter Incest* (1981), also adds that reunification is *not* the end of treatment and that the father should remain on probation as long as the daughter remains in the home.

ASSESSMENT OF MOTHER/CHILD RELATIONSHIP

Assessment of the mother/child relationship begins with the first interviews but also will be an ongoing activity throughout the work with the family. The mother and child should be seen separately and jointly by the social worker in order to determine the following:

- What are the feelings of the mother for the child and vice versa?
- Does the mother deny the abuse or believe the child?
- Does the mother blame the child for the abuse and subsequent consequences after the disclosure?
- What is the extent of the child's anger toward the mother because of the lack of protection? Most children eventually must deal with this anger; the question is how. Once it is acknowledged, what is the mother's response?
- What was the mother's reaction to the disclosure? Remember that most women will experience normal feelings of denial, anger, and betrayal. However, the mother must be able to get past the shock/denial stage before she can emotionally support her child.
- Is the child able to talk about the abusive incidents with the mother? Does the mother listen and acknowledge the child's feelings and pain?
- Is there evidence of role reversal? This will be likely if the incest has been going on for awhile. It is not, however, an automatic indictment of the mother. A popular misconception is fostered in the following scenario: The mother actively sets up her daughter to become the pseudowife and "service" the husband upon demand. The game begins with the mother abdicating housekeeper, cook, and babysitting roles to the child; it then becomes part of the natural sequence of events for the daughter to occupy the perpetrator's bed while the wife is conveniently absent. Yet a much more realistic picture is developed by reviewing the woman's situation and emotional status. Many mothers of incest victims are absent from their families due to physical, emotional, and/or economic reasons. The problem begins when the father demands nurturance and care, and when this is not forthcoming from the wife, he automatically turns to the children—usually the oldest daughter. She then becomes responsible for a clean house, prepared meals, and supervision of siblings. Rather than ask, "Where was the mother?!" it should be equally important to ask, "Why didn't the father assume nurturing and caring roles over the children rather than demanding nurturance for himself?"
- Is the mother sensitive to and able to provide for the child's needs?

In addition to assessing the above issues, the social worker also should get a social history of the mother/child relationship:

- What did the mother feel about her pregnancy? Was the child wanted? If the child was not wanted and was even resented, there may have been no or only a faint emotional bond from the beginning.
- Has the mother been available to the child in other crises? In what way was she available? Look at times the child was ill, had problems with friends or in school, encountered developmental milestones such as the onset of puberty, experienced losses such as changing schools or moving away from friends. Assessing the mother's behavior and feelings during the child's life situations can offer the social worker a perception about the parent's capacity to provide support.
- Who does the child turn to with problems?

An accurate assessment of the mother/child relationship will indicate whether or not the child can remain safely at home and how much work needs to be accomplished in treatment to strengthen the alliance. Most mother/child relationships will be strained; one of the primary goals for the social worker is to lift the barriers of incest and release the bonds of trust and love.

TREATMENT PLANNING AND IMPLEMENTATION

If warranted by the initial assessment, the social worker should file a dependency and neglect (D & N) petition immediately. Experience has shown that cases with the best prognosis to stop the abuse are those with court involvement. This type of authority is necessary to realistically immerse the perpetrator in treatment. Without this authoritative backing, most perpetrators will not attempt to change their behavior. Because of the tremendous power the father traditionally has exercised in the family, one of the goals of the social worker is to restrict this excessive and abusive domination. Use of the court is one avenue toward this end.

The impact of processing the case in the legal arena will be neutralized if the social worker and attorneys agree to an informal adjustment. With an informal adjustment, the client agrees to treatment and the court supervises the progress, but only for a designated amount of time—usually 6 months. After that, the court has no legal jurisdiction over the client, and the initial charges cannot be re-filed. The perpetrator is free—at least in civil proceedings—to disengage entirely from social services and return to his family. Life with father continues . . . until the next complaint.

In some cases, criminal charges will be filed simultaneously with the civil dependency proceedings. As part of the team effort, the child protective services agency needs to have written agreements with the district attorney's office to clarify in which cases the social worker will not be testifying against the perpetrator. This testimony may impede any therapeutic relationship that has developed and any hope of the perpetrator and his family authentically engaging in treatment. The social service agency's role should be therapeutic and protective of the child—not punitive.

A common mistake is to focus the goals of the treatment plan on related problems rather than on the incest itself. For example, in a case where the father sexually abuses the daughter only when intoxicated, a tendency of the social worker may be to concentrate on the father's participation in an alcohol treatment program. The erroneous reasoning is that if the father gains control over his drinking, the sexual abuse will cease. Russell (1984) cites several studies showing an association between alcohol and incest; however, there is no evidence to indicate that alcohol consumption *causes* incest. The main focus of intervention for the child protection worker is *not* the alcoholism, but the sexual abuse. This is not to say that the perpetrator, if alcoholic, should not be expected to engage in an alcohol treatment program. No therapy will be effective without sobriety on the part of the perpetrator. However, the child protective services worker should focus her or his efforts and the agency's resources on dealing with the incest. Do not assume that if the father stops drinking the incest will stop. Thus, the treatment goals, plan, and contracting should be directly related to the purpose for which the case was referred to the agency—sexual abuse.

Treatment Planning for The Victim

As discussed earlier, the ideal situation is for the perpetrator to move out of the home, provided the mother can protect the child. Yet this is not often possible due to a lack of state statutes and to judges' attitudes. This means that most children will be placed. The placement of choice will be a foster home as opposed to a group home, residential, or shelter facility. The decision will depend, of course, upon the emotional stability and age of the child. Placing younger children in more restrictive settings than foster homes may increase the secondary trauma of placement. On the other hand, adolescents may benefit more from a group setting, especially if the facility encourages and organizes healthy peer support.

The federal budget reductions have necessitated the diminution of foster parent training. This is unfortunate because foster parents can contribute greatly to the treatment process and become very therapeutic for the child, provided they understand the dynamics of incest. Social service agencies have a responsibility to recruit and adequately train foster parents to enable them to appropriately respond to and interact with the victim of sexual abuse. Many victims learn behavior that is sexual in nature and use this when they relate to adults. It is the way they have learned to gain affection and love. However, unaware and untrained foster parents who encounter this behavior feel uncomfortable and even threatened by their foster child. They do not know how to respond or what to say. Many become angry and punitive because of the embarrassment and threat they feel. Foster mothers who do not understand the situation may feel jealous and try to keep the child from relating to her husband. Some foster fathers misinterpret the child's need to please as being sexually seductive, and they too commit sexual abuse!

Disruptive placements often occur due to lack of training and the foster parents' inabilities to deal with the special problems and emotional issues of these children. Social service agencies bear the responsibility for this and the increased victimization and harm done to the child when the placement fails. Everyone should be blamed because everyone is responsible for the care that is given to children in this country.

Once the case is reported, the social worker needs to make a commitment to see and talk with the child on a regular, consistent basis. The ideal is to have at least one social worker who will be with and help the child from beginning to end. The abuse often has severed the child's ability to trust. The consistency and availability of one individual can help mend this break and encourage the child to begin to trust again.

The foster parents' and social worker's continual message to the child should be that the child is not to blame and that she is not responsible for the incest *or* the consequences of the incest. Many children feel tremendous guilt for the family break-up, their father being in jail, and their siblings being placed in out-of-home care. They need reassurance from many sources that it is not their fault. Other messages to the victim should be that she is not alone and that her story is believed. Older children participate in group therapy and it seems the best way to let the child learn that there are others like her. Much healing can come from this knowledge and from the sharing that goes on among group members. While in placement, and throughout the process, the social worker needs to reinforce not only that the child's story is believed but also needs to convey an awareness that the social worker knows that pressure is sometimes put on children to "take back" their story, but that if this happens, the social worker will still have belief in the child's original story and will not abandon her. The child needs reassurance of protection.

Because of high caseloads, most child protection workers will not be able to provide in-depth counseling to the victim. However, the child should be referred to individual therapy in order to deal with the trauma she has experienced. As case manager, the social worker will make referrals, but an assessment first needs to be made of the therapist's experience and attitudes towards incest victims. If the therapist gives the message to the child—however subtly—that she was in any way responsible for the incident (e.g., she was seductive; she should never have dressed that way) or that she was lying (e.g., "Did your father *really* have intercourse with you?"), the therapy will be more detrimental to the child than *no counseling at all.* In addition, the therapist should be flexible in terms of time; sessions often need to be more than 50 minutes once a week.

Siblings also should be referred to treatment so they can deal with the family disruption, anger and fear they may feel.

At some point the child may need to appear in court to testify. This can sometimes be avoided by the court's acceptance of a videotaped interview. If not, the social worker should take the child to the courtroom prior to the hearing to familiarize her with the setting. Let her sit in the witness chair. Show her where the social worker will sit and move chairs, if possible, so the child can have the social worker in her direct line of vision. Explain the court procedure in terms the child can understand. She should meet the agency's attorney and talk with him or her so that at least the prosecutor will be an ally. The social worker should assure the child of her or his presence and protection. If possible, the agency may persuade the judge to agree to alternatives other than the traditional need for "direct confrontation of the accuser" (the child). Some jurisdictions have allowed the social worker to question the child instead of the attorney. Especially if the child is very young, this questioning may incorporate the use of anatomically correct dolls. (See Long, Chapter 8, and Walker, Chapter 10 in this volume.) In other cases, the child has been taken into the judge's chambers and questioned by the judge. Without adequate planning, preparation, and sensitivity, the legal proceedings can be emotionally damaging to the child.

RESTORING THE MOTHER/CHILD RELATIONSHIP

As indicated earlier, the restoration of the mother/child relationship may be the most crucial step in the long process toward family reunification. From the beginning, the social worker and/or therapist needs to empower both the mother and child. Issues upon which to focus for the child will be increasing her self-esteem, developing a trusting relationship, relieving her of guilt and responsibility, assuming a more age-appropriate role in the family, expressing her anger at being victimized and her feelings of betrayal, and teaching her skills in self-protection (similar to those taught in the prevention programs now being offered in some schools). For the mother, treatment issues will focus on assertiveness training, increasing her self-esteem, moving beyond the denial (in appropriate cases), expressing her anger and sense of betrayal, and supplementing her living skills (e.g., finding a job if she has never worked before). Additionally, the social worker can help the mother to understand the impact the betrayal of trust has on the child and the child's resulting anger directed at both parents. Some mothers also may need instruction on child development in order to have age-appropriate expectations of their children. Supervised visitation between the mother and child should be arranged at the outset; however, joint counseling between the two to strengthen the bond will probably be more effective after each has participated in individual therapy.

Once together, the child needs to express her anger towards the mother for the victimization. At this point, the mother—if she harbored doubts about the reality of the incest—should be able to acknowledge that it happened and be able to hear and understand the message her child is sending. Each mother/child dyad will have different content issues on which to work. For example, an adolescent may want more independence and freedom; a 5-year-old may want more of the mother's presence; the mother may feel taken advantage of by her children and family. The therapist needs to assist them in dealing with these problems, but the ultimate goal is to enhance honest, direct communication between the mother and child and to reestablish trust. In addition, each should exhibit behavior indicating they are assuming appropriate roles and behaviors in their relationship.

CONCLUSION

Incest investigation and treatment requires highly skilled intervention, close coordination among agencies, treatment resources, and community financial support to provide staff to protect children. The public agency is mandated to provide extensive services but rarely is supported to actually carry out its responsibilities. Thus, it often becomes the scapegoat for the community's outrage. If children are truly to be protected, if the community really cares, if perpetrators are to be stopped, if incest is illegal, then all professionals, lay groups, and individual citizens must bond together to create a safe, secure environment for our nation's children.

The techniques and resources described in this chapter *can* be made available to incestuous families. Whether they *will* be or not is up to all adults who work with and care about children. When a child experiences the *ultimate betrayal of trust*—to be a sexual object for the parent—then the state, courts, therapists, and community must respond to enable the child to learn to trust again.

REFERENCES

Benjamin, A. (1981). *The helping interview* (3rd ed.). Boston: Houghton Mifflin.

Carroll, C. A., & Gottlieb, B. (1983). *Sexual abuse: Therapeutic and systems considerations for the child and family.* Denver: Colorado State Department of Social Services, Division of Family and Children Services.

Children's Defense Fund (1985). *A children's defense budget: An analysis of the president's FY 1986 budget and children.* Washington, DC: Author.

Herman, J. L. (1981). *Father-daughter incest.* Cambridge, MA: Harvard University Press.

Humphrey, H. H., III. (1985). *Report on Scott County investigations.* Minnesota Attorney General's Office.

Lukianowicz, N. (1972). Incest: *British Journal of Psychiatry, 120,* 201–212.

Mountain, H., Nicholson, M. A., Spencer, C. C., & Walker, L. E. A. (1984). *Incest: Colorado State Department of Social Services revitalization training.* Denver, CO: Nicholson, Spencer & Associates.

Russell, D. (1984). *Sexual exploitation: Rape, child sexual abuse, and workplace harassment.* Beverly Hills: Sage.

S.L.A.M.—Society's League Against Molesters. Littleton, CO: Author.

Sgroi, S. M. (1982). *Handbook of clinical intervention in child sexual abuse.* Lexington, MA: Lexington Books.

Wigmore, John H. (1970). *Evidence in trials at common law* (rev. ed. by James H. Chadbourne) (Vol. IIIA, sec. 924a) (pp. 736–747).

10

New Techniques for Assessment and Evaluation of Child Sexual Abuse Victims: Using Anatomically "Correct" Dolls and Videotape Procedures

Lenore E. A. Walker

The large increase in reports of the sexual abuse of a child has created the need for many more mental health professionals and child protective service workers to become familiar with appropriate interview techniques. These techniques should provide the least intrusive means of verifying whether the child's current mental status is consistent with the allegation of sexual abuse. The major purposes of such an assessment are usually twofold: first, to provide a sufficient amount of information from which to determine the child's current emotional status so as to design a treatment plan if necessary, and second, to assess who did what to the child in order to provide future protection to the child. The latter is most often conducted in conjunction with state authorities, including but not limited to police, attorneys, child protective services, and family. It is not uncommon to find that none of these professionals assigned to the interview task has had experience in developmentally understanding or actually interviewing children. Thus, a high standard must be followed by the psychologist or other mental health professional who conducts this assessment.

A variety of ways of collecting assessment data are available to clinicians. The standard clinical interview, which is a flexible discussion between client and clinician covering certain prearranged areas, is routinely used, sometimes as a part of a more comprehensive assessment plan and sometimes by itself. Allowing the parent (guardian) and child to set the pace has benefits of establishing good supportive rapport. Its major difficulty is in setting the proper balance between too little structure, which can result in overlooking pertinent facts, and too much structure, which can result in putting words in the child's mouth. This can become critical when assessing for suggestibility in the child's testimony.

Selecting the developmentally appropriate way to ask questions of children of varying ages can also be a problem, especially for those interviewers who have had little training or experience in child psychology. Generally, a childhood history is obtained in this manner directly from the client, although factual data such as pertinent dates and developmental milestones can be gotten via questionnaire. Semistructured interviews with preselected questions are another way to glean factual information. Medical history, school history, and other significant interpersonal relationship factors need to be recorded. Much of this information can be obtained from the parent and verified by school and medical records. However, it is often useful to corroborate with information obtained directly from the child. Sometimes it can help determine how well the reporting parent knows the child's typical behavior and how the incident fits into the total picture.

Another rich source of information is an assessment of the child's current developmental status. This is especially crucial for young children under the age of eight. Affective, cognitive, and behavioral domains need to be measured to determine if the child is functioning at the expected level for his or her age. Behavioral observations of naturalistic situations, play situations, and standardized psychometric assessment all provide important data. The use of props such as flexible dolls with anatomically "correct" genitals helps the child discuss the specifics of the sexual abuse. Recording the interview using audiotape or videotape procedures as well as newer videotape depositions may save the child from having to repeat the story to others or in court. The National Institute of Justice provides specific guidelines for legal use of the evaluation (Whitcomb, Shapiro, & Stellwegen, 1985), and this is further discussed by Long in Chapter 8 of this volume.

This chapter will discuss the evaluation techniques developed at Walker & Associates, a private psychology firm providing assessment, treatment, and legal consultation. The techniques are a combination of those customarily used by child psychologists in order to sample enough of a variety of behaviors so as to assess the child's strengths and deficits in cognitive, affective, and behavioral domains. The evaluation is generally used to give attorneys some verification of how reliable and valid is the child's accusation of sexual abuse and to assess damages in personal injury lawsuits, as well as to design a therapy program for a particular youngster. Although our staff are interdisciplinary mental health professionals, this chapter will discuss assessment and evaluation from a psychologist's perspective. To date, we have provided such information for judges, prosecutors, and defense attorneys in dependency and neglect actions and in criminal cases. We have also worked with the child's attorney, usually called a *guardian-ad-litem*. In civil cases, we have been asked to evaluate a child by both the plaintiff's and the defense's attorneys. Judges have ordered us to perform an evaluation, even over the protests of attorneys. When social services departments prefer an outside expert, perhaps for additional clout in court on a particularly difficult case, they also call us in to assist. Even in cases where a parent under suspicion asks us to intervene, according to the law, we must bring in the authorities should we suspect child sexual abuse.

It is rare to work with child sexual abuse cases without some collaboration or contact with the legal system. Because normal confidentiality rules do not extend to child abuse cases, records can be subpoenaed; willful nonreport is against the law and punishable by a fine or jail sentence. Clients suspected of being perpetrators must be informed of their legal rights during any psychological investigation, and care must be taken not to promise them that the information given to the psychologist will not be shared with others. This can change the typical client-evaluator relationship and must be acknowledged in interpreting the findings. Even defining who the client is can be problematic. Does the psychologist work for the legal agency who hired her or him, for the child's parents, for the child, or for all of them? In practice, the child's needs must always come first, and so the child could be considered the primary client, although the others may be defined as clients, too. It is possible to respect everyone's rights if the situation is openly acknowledged and handled sensitively. Even verbal discussion with attorneys may not be protected if the usual privileged communication rules are suspended for them as they are for psychologists in child abuse cases, so care must be taken to protect defendants' legal rights. Only communicate the substantiated psychological findings to the attorney.

To further protect the child, the raw data from an evaluation should be zealously guarded so that it cannot be misinterpreted by nonpsychology professionals. For licensed psychologists this may mean going to court in response to a subpoena and making a record that the American Psychological Association (APA) Ethics Code and Standards for Providers of Psychological Services (APA, 1985) prevent turning over raw data to someone untrained in their use. Since the license to practice psychology is granted under administrative law, two bodies of law conflict (i.e., juvenile, civil, or criminal statutes, and administrative statutes that include the APA Ethics Code in the licensing law). The judge, then, must make the decision as to which one prevails. On occasion, it may become necessary to hire your own attorney to protect your rights.

Most of the evaluations are conducted in our playroom where there is a one-way mirror and video equipment set-up. If attorneys or the alleged perpetrator wish to observe the interview, we usually allow them to watch behind the one-way mirror. The child is introduced to the attorneys, but not to the alleged perpetrator (who rarely has attended), and is shown the one-way mirror. Children usually do not pay attention to the mirror after the interview gets under way. The child is also introduced to the video equipment and we practice taping her or him. Then we show it to the child while checking that the equipment is working, a must in today's technological world. Most children delight in seeing themselves on TV, but also learn not to pay much attention to the camera after a short while.

ASSESSMENT PROCEDURES

Initial Observations

The assessment actually begins by observing the child and his or her family in the waiting room. This provides a naturalistic setting from which to observe parent/child interactions. We provide cookies, milk, hot chocolate, soda pop, and other food in a corner of the waiting room. Observations of how the child handles food as well as the kind of help given by the parent can provide informative data. For example, does the 5-year-old child fix her own snack? Does she make sure her mother has something to eat, too? This may be evidence of caretaking behavior often seen in sexually abused children. Does the 9-year-old stuff a dozen cookies in her mouth? Does the 4-year-old smash his food on the floor? What are the child's food habits? Eating disorders are common in those with posttraumatic stress disorders. And so on. If we have pretzel nuggets on a particular day, I might ask the child to count a specific number to bring into the playroom with us to get an idea of the child's ability to count. These observations approximate a naturalistic setting and often provide a rich source of comparison data with the more planned observations.

   Once the psychologist greets the child and the family, I ask to see either the child alone or both the child and the parent in the playroom.

Establishing Rapport and Permission Giving

The child should not be kept waiting while a parent is interviewed first. If the interviewer prefers to have already received the parent's information, it should be done prior to this part of the assessment process. Although it is appropriate to touch nonabused children as they accompany the examiner to the playroom, it is not a good idea to touch those suspected or known to have been sexually abused. They have had another person intrusively touch them in unwanted ways and need to be reempowered about their body integrity and to assert their ability to say no. Therefore the rule is not to touch unless initiated or agreed upon by the child. I might hold out my hand as an invitation to hold hands as we walk together, but it is done without pressure and as unobtrusively as possible. The child learns he or she can ignore it or decide to hold hands, as he or she so chooses.

During this time, establishing rapport is begun. Children like the un-divided attention they get in the playroom. It is important to set the stage for discussion by asking the parent to give the child permission to speak to the psychologist. Because keeping a secret was initially important to the sexually abused child, openly giving the child permission to tell makes it easier for the child to comply with the examiner. On the other hand, this has to be done without actually using words about what allegedly happened in order to avoid undue suggestion. Not following this caution can cause the interview to be spoiled as well as so bias the child that any future interviews can remain tainted (see Goodman & Helgeson, Chapter 7 in this volume).

Generally a statement such as, "Remember when you told Mommy about the bad things or secrets or nasty touching Uncle Harry did to you? Well, I want you to tell this lady all about it. She is a special kind of doctor who helps children, so it's okay to talk about it with her." Using the child's own words, at first, demonstrates that the parent is willing to share information with the psychologist too. After the child agrees or at least indicates understanding, the parent tells the child he or she is going to be sitting in the waiting room (or will return at a prearranged time for older children), and the interview proceeds with just the child and the examiner. Sometimes very young chil-dren need more time with the parent in the room or need to see where the parent has gone to wait, and they then come back to the playroom to see all the toys. Even those as young as 2 years old have been able to spend some time alone with the psychologist in the playroom. Although presence of a parent could provide support for the child, it could also influence the child's reports in direct or subtle ways (cf. Spencer & Nicholson, Chapter 9 of this volume). It is better not to allow another challenge to the child's credibility using parental bias as an issue when it can be avoided (cf. Long, Chapter 8 of this volume).

Our playroom is stocked with toys and games designed to appeal to children of varying ages. Most are stored in full view on shelves which line one wall. There are many soft stuffed animals there, too. A child-sized table and chairs are placed against another wall, while a wooden stove, sink, and doll's cradle face a third side. Most of the center area in the carpeted area of the room is vacant, allowing the psychologist and child plenty of room to be comfortable on the floor rather than on furniture. This arrangement helps the child accept the focus on her or him and facilitates communication. The interview is as child-centered as possible, starting with encouraging the child to choose whatever play materials are pleasurable. With a young child, verbally naming what she or he is doing is a further trust-building tech-nique. It also informs the child that words as well as play materials will be used to convey messages about his or her experiences. And children can provide immediate feedback should the examiner not label some act properly.

Obtaining Baseline Data

The initial 10 to 20 minutes are spent establishing trust and rapport as well as in learning much about what the child can and cannot do developmentally. It is essential to learn the child's sense of time, ability to count and name colors, and concept of concrete and abstract thinking. This period is frequently marred by a lack of patience for the child's own process. It is not just a preparatory period before the real questioning about the possibly abusive event(s), but is an essential one during which baseline data are gathered about the child's functioning under less stressful circumstances. Here is where the reliability of statements, especially for those under the age of six, can be estimated. It also helps frame the kind of questions that will be needed to get at certain information that form the legal elements (cf. Patterson, 1982, for a description of behavioral observation techniques).

One such example is in gathering information about the time of the alleged abusive events. A knowledge of developmental norms is required here. It is rare that children under the age of eight reliably know the days of the week and months of the year in correct sequential order. But they should be able to provide information relative to the four seasons and by using birthdays, holidays, and other such personal markers. They may not understand the hours of the day but can know morning, afternoon, and night, or before, during, or after school. Sometimes more precision occurs with favorite television shows or other activities. Care must be taken with those under five or six to ascertain if they know how to count sequentially without concrete objects. Most can differentiate between one time and more than one time, but greater precision is not always available. One way to get at the information for those who cannot follow abstract concepts is to ask the child to use props to show another time, such as with the dolls or through drawings. It is to be expected that long-term repeated sexual experiences will not be clearly differentiated by what exactly happened each time because the details may merge or get confused by children—as they can for adult abuse victims (cf. Walker, 1987).

It is also important to know the extent of a young child's ability to name colors. Under age five, some can match colors, indicating attention is paid to using this as a category; but other children even by age six cannot use color names accurately. A box of crayons and drawing paper should be available to be used as props. Crayons can also be used to demonstrate counting ability of concrete objects and to test the child's cognitive ability to shift categories from quantity to color classification. It is common to ask for or evaluate information about ejaculation by means of children's comments about the whitish or opaque color and sticky consistency. In one case on which I consulted, a 2½-year-old child told of "blue pee." Before such information could be discarded, it was necessary to know if she knew the difference between blue, white, or yellow colors. Further information indicated she could match yellow with the color of urine and knew other colors were not the same. But she could not use color names accurately, as would be expected in most 2-year-olds. Thus, her statement of "blue pee" could more reliably be considered to be a description of semen and the use of "blue" could simply mean she knew it was not the usual color of pee. Color blindness may also need to be assessed in older children.

A frequent error in examining young children is to fail to observe their ability to properly use abstract words to denote time and place, which are needed elements for some prosecutions to be filed (cf. Long, Chapter 8 of this volume, Whitcomb et al., 1985). Yesterday, tomorrow, last week, a few hours ago, next, under, over, before, after, and other similar concepts are not expected to be mastered until after age five or six. The general rule is to use as many concrete props as possible to help the young child tell his or her story as is discussed in this book by Goodman and Helgeson (Chapter 7) and Slater (Chapter 11). Questions requiring more precise differentiation of these terms need to be carefully designed in order to really tap the child's knowledge. This is also true for pronouns. Three-year-olds frequently mix up gender so that she, he, her, his, and such are interchanged—as are the singular and plural pronouns. Under stress, children just mastering these concepts will be likely to mix them up.

A 3-year-old who has been using language accurately since age one will be more likely to have a better grasp of the English language irregularities than a child who has been speaking fluently only for the last 6 months. Such a wide variation in development is normal, especially if more than one language is spoken to the child. However, one of the effects of sexual abuse is to cause the child to regress to an earlier developmental level, to develop unevenly, or not to use speech at all. Careful attention should be paid to the child's language usage at this lower stress point in the interview, so as to compare it with how the child describes the abuse later on. Many children give their own kind of clues to tell us about their different levels of stress in describing a variety of situations. Care must be taken not to present questions eliciting just a yes or no without asking the child for descriptive detail. A child's desire to comply may distort responses to other people's words. It is also necessary to check children's responses with their developmental ability to take words at their literal and concrete meaning.

There are numerous other behavioral indicators that can be observed during this portion of the interview. Since what the child says spontaneously about abusive acts seems to be a good indicator about believability, another goal is to get the child speaking or behaving spontaneously. Questions can be asked to test the limits of the child's reliability—though there is time for that later on, too. Observations about how the child uses play materials and the ability to engage in mimicking behavior, parallel play, and play together with an adult can be helpful in making a determination. This is also a good time to check on the child's awareness of truth and fantasy, which may go to demonstrating competency when required under the law. Some bright 4-year-olds create a fantasy playmate who—they argue—is real. In such cases, this behavior does not by itself indicate incompetence. Rather, it may suggest some caution in evaluating who the child names as the offender. Sexual abuse victims frequently display their need for control, order, and predictability. An overly bossy child or one who just does not engage may be conveying information about their damage. In Chapter 11, Slater provides useful indicators to differentiate nonsexually abused emotionally disturbed children's responses from those who are also sexually abused.

Children who have been physically abused and neglected as well as sexually abused often move quickly from one activity to another in a frenetic way, usually trying to get the examiner's attention. Sometimes I think they operate under the theory that you can't hit a moving target! The quality of their actions differs from those with learning disabilities when both are faced with a highly stimulating environment. Sexually abused children especially try to engage the examiner but then drop the activity once that goal is achieved. Seductiveness and intermittent concern for the psychologist's feelings may help identify the sexually abused as well as physically abused child, but not always. In one case, a 6-year-old child slapped the examiner across the face when pushed to describe the sexual abuse after she had clearly refused to touch the dolls. In reviewing the videotape afterwards, it was clear that she had consistently refused any earlier attempts to control her by less dramatic acting-out behavior. Her mother's boyfriend, whom she had accused of sexually abusing her, was convicted and incarcerated on another charge, so it became unnecessary to put the child through any further diagnostic interviews.

Anatomically "Correct" Dolls

When the psychologist has sufficient developmental and behavioral data and rapport has been established, the anatomically "correct" dolls are brought out and the child's attention is focused on them rather than on the other play objects.

The use of props to interview children, especially those under the age of eight, is an important technique to elicit accurate recall without contaminating the interview with too many leading questions. The event-memory retention of children has been found to be about as good as that of adults, but their ability to recall the information needs the greater specificity that dolls can provide (Goodman & Helgeson, Chapter 7). For children whose language is less well developed, who freeze up verbally under stress, or who have not yet developed adequate abstract concepts but do have concrete cognitive ability, demonstrating the abusive incident(s) by using the dolls will be the best way they can communicate their abusive experiences. However, not all children will respond by using them, so refusal should not be misinterpreted as indicating a false report.

It is not clear how the use of anatomically "correct" dolls began, but references in the literature occur in MacFarlane (1978), Berliner (1983), and Sgroi (1982), among others. Actually, the dolls are not really anatomically correct (each may have its own particular distortion), but they are explicit in that they have some identifiable representation of male and female sex parts. In a recent case in which I testified as an expert, the opposing attorney asked me if the male dolls I use have "oversized" genitals, which he apparently thought would distort the child's responses. Of course, what is considered oversized would differ depending the subjective experience of the reporter! Actually, our children have mentioned the small size of our male doll's penis rather than the other way.

There are several commercial sets of four dolls (adult male, adult female, boy, and girl) that are available for purchase, usually with skin tones and sometimes features representing white, Black, Hispanic, Native American, and Asian-American racial and ethnic groups. Why the manufacturers settled on a 2-child family is unknown, though it most likely was for economic reasons. Obviously, it is inadequate for most situations, and most evaluators have two sets to allow for flexibility.

To date there is no empirical evidence suggesting that one kind of doll is better than another, but developmental studies suggest that the closer the match to the real characteristics of the offender, the more accurate will be the young child's identification and spontaneous story. For adolescents, use of dolls that are less accurate in depicting the actual abuser may facilitate a discussion of the abuse details because it permits them the emotional distance the older child sometimes needs. For young children, where fondling, digital penetration, and oral sex is more common than actual intercourse, dolls without mouth and genital openings or separate fingers and toes are less useful. In any case, it is standard procedure to use the dolls within a carefully constructed interview despite their limitations because of the rich clinical data they can elicit in many sexually abused children.

The use of these dolls has come under recent criticism by those who believe the dolls themselves are suggestible and stimulate normal children's fantasies and sex play rather than memories of abusive incidents (cf. Philippus & Koch, 1986). The studies cited by critics have dubious scientific value today. There have been few empirical data to demonstrate that sexually abused children really do use the dolls differently than do those children who have not been abused, although the criticisms have spurred such examination. Slater's (Chapter 11) research in a school setting with sexually abused and nonsexually abused children who are diagnosed as emotionally disturbed finds significant differences in how sexually abused children utilize the naked and clothed dolls in the Theme Creation Test for Youths. They are less creative and more likely to use the naked dolls to describe detailed, explicit sex acts or acts involving seduction. This is similar to clinical reports of children with the anatomically correct dolls. Another study, this time using the anatomically correct dolls, found significant congruence between the results of the doll interview with other sexual assault indicators (White, Strom, Santilli, & Halpin, 1986). Their finding that the control group of children who had not been referred for child sexual abuse did not utilize the dolls to demonstrate explicit sexual play or sexual abuse situations refutes the claims that exposure to the dolls per se will produce affirmative sexual abuse indicators. Goodman and Helgeson (Chapter 7) review several other studies with similar findings.

We keep the dolls dressed on a shelf in the playroom. Children could spontaneously take them to play with, although it rarely happens. A child who has used them in a prior assessment will frequently become observably distressed by the dolls, as if they remind him or her of the actual abusive situation. This conditioned response is similar to that of battered women or rape victims when they retell the event and reexperience its emotional impact (cf. Walker, 1984a, 1987). Examiners should acknowledge the child's emotional response by saying they understand how difficult this part of the interview is but they want to hear about what happened so they can help the child feel safe and prevent it from happening again. Psychologists have to be careful not to promise too much. In one case, the child demanded to know exactly how I was going to manage that! In another, a 6-year-old child told me she now was safe, and so she did not have to tell me anything. Understanding her need for control, I admitted that what she said was true, but I told her I wanted to hear what had happened so I could help others, not just her. Fortunately, in her case, altruism began early.

A 5-year-old child said she would tell me, but I was not to tell anyone else because she did not want to get her Dad in trouble. I had to tell her that I could not promise not to tell anyone because I was ordered to tell the judge. She accepted that explanation but did not believe it would matter. When it came to her turn to talk to the judge, she told me she intended to just cry and then the judge would not know what to do because he would feel sorry for her. When the judge saw the videotape, he was astounded at how easily that 5-year-old, who had only met him once before, had figured him out. Early sensitivity to other's responses and clever manipulative behavior are part of the victim's survival skills. Again, there are similarities with the adult rape victim and battered woman's responses (Walker, 1984a, 1987).

After introducing the dolls, I generally make some comments, telling the child that the dolls have anatomical features. Then I calmly and steadily begin undressing one, asking the child to assist. This procedure helps engage the child in a specific task that will increase compliance and use of the dolls. Sometimes I ask the child to name the dolls or to choose the first one to be undressed before I start. Other times, I began in a random order or even in a predetermined order based on what other information I have received about the possible abuse and the questions requested by the attorneys.

It is of critical importance to undress the dolls calmly, with little emotion— except perhaps for light humor displayed to help reassure an anxious child. This is to avoid any suggestibility or to avoid giving the child the subtle message that the stimulated memories are in any way bad. It may be appropriate to ask the child questions as the doll's clothes come off, but only if it helps to create joint interaction between the psychologist and child. It may be difficult to get the child to begin to use the dolls, and some coaxing is appropriate.

The child's own words used to describe all of the body parts are first established. Then the psychologist should ask the child to demonstrate what he or she remembers happened, referring back to the accompanying parent's earlier words of permission, if necessary. Always go from the general to the specific, prompting the child with neutral probers as far as possible. Younger children need more specificity in order to talk about actual incidents. However, too many direct questions can spoil the interview for legal purposes. A proper balance needs to be set.

Probing for Details

The psychologist has the ethical responsibility to decide when the probing or questioning should stop or change course in order to protect the child. Sometimes it is necessary to disregard the legal imperative in order to deal with the child's trauma. Videotapes help document those decisions to the legal authorities. More often, young children become frustrated at the lack of specificity in the questions, the repetition that tells them they have not delivered the right information yet, and the prolonged neutrality rather than their needed social approval. Victims of violence frequently misinterpret neutrality as dislike in their splitting of positive or negative thoughts, feelings, and actions (Walker, 1987). Younger children need more leading questions to be able to discuss the abuse. Without the knowledge of what probably happened to the child, it is difficult to develop an adequate intervention plan. Yet we know that the actual details may not be revealed until after months of therapy has begun.

Many children seal over the trauma memory after one or more periods of questioning. For them their therapy can deal with observations of the lasting impact but not directly with the abuse itself because the details have not yet been revealed. More information about therapy can be found in Walker and Bolkovatz (Chapter 13 of this volume).

Therefore, knowing there may not be any other chance to gather important information may cause the psychologist to abandon the more general questions approved for the legal proceedings and get on with the therapy assessment. Given the slow, deliberate process of this type of interview, it is important not to get too excited if and when the child starts talking about the abuse directly rather than just from innuendos. Some examiners cannot handle hearing the details because of their own emotions. Prior personal experiences with sexually exploitative behavior, molestation, or actual abuse can interfere, although once put in their proper perspective can enrich an examiner's sensitivity. Those very details lend authenticity and reliability to the child's report and so must be carefully recorded. Many of these abused children have lost their faith in adults' ability to provide safety or protection for them. Indicating loyalty to the child while not alienating the rest of family is helpful in getting the child ready for therapy.

If the child does use the dolls to express what has happened to her or him, the psychologist can follow up on the spontaneous disclosure to test the limits by asking questions to assure consistency and reliability. Other names being put forth by the defense can be substituted for the alleged offender who was actually named by the child. Thus, in one case a teenage stepbrother was mentioned as a suspect in lieu of the father. Such testing of the limits revealed little likelihood that the stepbrother had any part of the abusive incident; the child was clear that it was the father no matter how the question was phrased. This is the time to ask other questions proposed by the attorneys, particularly those questions that could be considered cross-examination in another type of hearing. A more gentle children's hearing, using a deposition type of approach, can be tried at this point in the interview. If there is a bug-in-the-ear device providing instant communication from the attorney in the other room to the therapist, all the examiner has to do is translate the question into a more appropriate format (cf. Whitcomb et al., 1985, for further discussion). Again, signs of distress should be watched for and this phase terminated should the psychologist find it necessary in the child's best interests.

Children who have been coached or are not sexual abuse victims can be identified by the different way in which they handle the dolls (White et al., 1986). First of all, those who have been abused usually demonstrate some observable anxiety when the dolls come out and are undressed. They may become distractable, get up and move around to avoid them, or they might throw the dolls and attempt to mutilate them. Abused children are less likely to engage in spontaneous play with the dolls initially, and actually do try to avoid them. Their lack of creativity is marked, compared with their play with other toys. Here is where the earlier established baselines become useful. When the abused child uses the dolls to tell the story, he or she can demonstrate sexually explicit acts with greater sophistication than can most children their age. They often add details that are only relevant to their own abuse experience. On the other hand, nonabused children may become fascinated with the dolls, demonstrate initial curiosity, and then often incorporate them in other play, ignoring the sex parts. The child and the examiner can put all the clothes back on the doll before they are returned to their special shelf, which may help seal off some of the displayed anxiety, although some children cannot tolerate this part. For them, the dolls can be placed out of sight when you are done and redressed after the child leaves.

Concluding the Interview

The interview is completed with another period of time spent rewarding the child for talking to the adult; it does not matter how much was actually revealed. If the child feels overwhelmed by having revealed more than he or she wanted to, which is not uncommon with adolescents, therapeutic actions need to be given more prominence (cf. Walker & Bolkovatz, Chapter 13). The child needs to feel able to cope again, after the interview is terminated, and the psychologist's next steps need to be discussed with the parent(s). These next steps may include further formalized cognitive or personality assessment, should that become appropriate. Sometimes we have also videotaped an administration of the Stanford-Binet test, done at a different time, which can provide good cognitive baseline data with which to compare the child's performance.

We rarely perform standardized psychological tests right after an interview using the dolls, except if objective measurement of anxiety and fear levels is needed. However, the videotape of the doll interview often gives dramatic examples of the child's behavior, which can be interpreted if it is used in a court proceeding.

The last 15 minutes or so of the interview should be used to observe the child's own natural ability to recover from the stress of talking about the events in question. Some children withdraw for a while, others distract themselves with activities, still others appear visibly shaken no matter what is done for them. Their level of resiliency is important in assessing damages, because recent research suggests a vulnerability to poor recovery and future victimization may occur from sexual abuse as a child (see in the volume Finkelhor & Browne, Chapter 4; Conte & Berliner, Chapter 5; Courtois & Sprei, Chapter 14). Inability to sustain concentration with a developmentally appropriate game may suggest an interruption in the child's performance of other tasks or relationships with others, especially adults. Destruction of toys may indicate an unleashing of anger and rage in an aggressive manner. Overcompliance with the examiner's suggestions could be one way of relieving fear stirred up by reexperiencing the coercive events. In some children a quick shift back and forth through a variety of emotions is an important observable reaction. Rarely can the abused child exercise assertive behaviors right after the abuse is discussed; behavior is more likely to be passive acceptance, compliance to please, passive refusal to participate, or aggressive and demanding outbursts. In some children, a pseudo-independence is seen that makes them appear more grown-up than their chronological age.

At times they try to take care of the examiner, trying to reduce their sense of shame and guilt by wanting approval. With older children and adolescents, their inability to set limits may cause them to say more than they intended. Afterwards, they may feel guilty and try to bargain or manipulate the examiner so as to avoid anticipated harm to themselves when what they said is revealed. This period of time, then, is critical to reassure the child of your acceptance of their information as a gift they have shared with you, that you respect their pain, and that you will take care to use the data judiciously to help keep them safe.

Discussing the Abuser with the Child

It is not appropriate for the examiner to say negative things about the perpetrator, no matter what the child says. Reflecting what the child actually says is permissible, as is a statement that you are sorry the child has been so hurt. It is also unwise to make excuses for the perpetrator. One child told me that the previous psychiatrist had told her that her father was sick and she should forgive him because he did not mean to harm her. She felt unheard, because in her mind he did intend to hurt her and she was not ready to forgive him. The child has a right to reach that conclusion on her own if she so desires. It is perfectly appropriate for the child to experience a variety of feelings toward the abuser, especially if he is family or a close friend. Loving experiences can occur even where there has been sexual abuse. The child's denial may cause her to focus more on the love and specialness of their relationship, sometimes fooling an untrained interviewer into believing the abuse could never have occurred. This is most frequently observed in evaluations by child custody teams who try to ignore allegations of incest against well-dressed professional men.

The important close of the emotionally stressful interview should acknowledge the child's feelings—especially her pain—but not promise her anything except that she will have emotional relief at some point in time. Some psychologists want to do something else to protect the child—forgetting how healing the cathartic method can really be.

Communicating with the Parent

It may be appropriate to allow the child to play alone in the playroom while the parent is interviewed in another office. Most children get restless after 15 to 20 minutes, so a longer interview needs to be scheduled at another time.

Because the parent is usually anxious about the findings, it can be appropriate to share a little information in a positive way. For example, I often say, "I do think your child was sexually abused but she is a strong little girl and should be able to heal." I add a short comment about a cute incident that does not break the confidentiality of the child but lets the parent know you like and know the child. For example, I have commented on a child's special dexterity or experience of pleasure with a particular play item. It is important to compliment the parent on some aspect of parenting, so that an alliance between the psychologist and parent on behalf of the child is established. I make the assumption that each parent, even those who are at times abusers, wants the best for her or his child. If the psychologist can find a way to join with the parent in the best interests of the child, then all will be able to work toward putting the child's needs ahead of the parent's or even the psychologist's.

INTEGRATION OF CORROBORATING DATA INTO FINDINGS

Family and Social History

Once the assessment is complete it is customary to analyze and interpret the data, using corroborative materials when available, to come to a diagnosis, conclusions, a treatment plan, and some sense of prognosis. In completing this phase after evaluating a child who reports sexual abuse, care must be taken to assess the credibility of the data. The kinds of data typically used for corroboration cannot be relied upon in child sexual abuse cases. Rarely are there witnesses to the assault. Mothers, who may have suspected incest, are often found less credible as witnesses because of antiwoman attitudes or other accusations of bias. Siblings and mothers in battering homes may sense their own vulnerability too much to be able to tell accurately what they know at the time of the evaluation. Preconditioning activities, which can be better identified now, are too frequently discounted. These include a variety of sexually seductive activities and secrets between the child and father. Then, if incest is later discovered, the mother's warnings might be turned against the woman, saying she gave them the idea or pushed the child into it by her outspokenness. These mothers feel as though anything they do or say is never good enough. If they ignore their suspicions, they are accused of colluding; if they report them, they are seen as vindictive in trying to keep the father away from the child (cf. Cammaert, Chapter 15 of this volume).

Family loyalties and long-term friendships are broken with great difficulty. Upon discovery, those who are closest to the child also are dealing with their own emotional crisis. For many women, their child's abuse reawakens buried memories of their own earlier abuse. In one case, a mother tearfully explained how carefully she watched her daughter but never suspected that her own father, who abused her as a child, would be abusing her son. Situational factors of opportunity, knowledge, and past abusive history, if known, must be considered with more relevance.

Physical Evidence

Physical evidence, often present to corroborate physical abuse of a child, is frequently not available for young children, especially if penile-vaginal or penile-anal penetration did not take place. Forceful intercourse, which leaves tears in the vaginal or anal walls, only occurs in a small number of cases. However, a dye that is utilized in detecting cervical cancer can detect smaller fissures if it is applied to the vaginal area within 48 hours after intercourse takes place (*The Denver Post,* 1986). Digital penetration and oral sex rarely leave physical marks. Sexual abuse that occurs over a long period of time usually includes a long, preparatory phase that slowly stretches the vagina and hymen. In some cases, pediatric child abuse examinations do reveal changes in the hymen and anal sphincter muscles, indicating penetration, but most of the time such evidence is difficult to obtain. Sometimes vaginal and urinary infections prompt the detection of sexual abuse, as can persistent irritation of the genitals. Frequent ear infections may indicate presence of a fungus that also causes vaginal discomfort. But little children learn to accept their early sexualization as a part of earning love, and for many the psychological pain outweighs any major physical distress.

Child's Credibility

Children, like adults, have their own sexual preferences, and although such disclosures usually are not revealed until well into therapy, sometimes a child will tell the psychologist. One 5-year-old girl expressed distaste for oral sex but liked digital fondling; another, at the same age, had the opposite preference. An 8-year-old boy said he liked it when his penis was stroked but did not want to touch the abuser. After discovery, these children often feel a tremendous sense of guilt for enjoying the attention and erotization. They often see themselves as accomplices, if not outright seducers, which explains why they are not angrier at victim-blaming comments. It is important not to misinterpret such children's learned seductive behavior as the cause of rather than the result of the sexual abuse. Many adult women report that they enjoyed some of the sexual behavior as children, but it prevented them from being able to enjoy sexual relations as an adult. Thus, care must be taken not to interpret the child's acceptance or enjoyment of sex as precluding evidence that damage has occurred.

The mixed feelings experienced by sexually abused children cause them confused reactions to their having told, as well as about the subsequent evaluation. It is not unusual for them to both admit and deny their stories. Recanting, or denying later what was said earlier, can be a result of this ambivalence. Children also recant because of fear. They are afraid they will be punished, and they are scared at the crisis of which they find themselves at the center. Many have compassion for their abuser and may succumb to pressures to say it really isn't so. The details of the abusive behavior must be used to help determine which version is the credible one. A 6-year-old child who is now found sexually abusing agemates is more likely to have learned the behavior from his or her own sexual abuse no matter how much he or she later denies it. Thus, characteristics of the dynamics known to be exhibited by sexually abused children and described in detail in other chapters in this book should be used to compare with what is observed during the current assessment.

Some children's credibility may seem more questionable than that of others. Those who discuss more details of the abuse along with some peculiarity that could not have been known by others are more believable. An 11-year-old girl who was molested along with two other friends in a hot tub by a neighbor giggled as she told of watching the rising bubbles she imagined as coming from his flatulence. Such attention to minor details often serves as a distraction to help the child distance from the emotion. Another 8-year-old girl told of staring at the abuser's tattoos. She also giggled when she told of the tattoo of kissing lips on his buttocks. Although the perpetrator never acknowledged abusing her, his admission that he did indeed have such a tattoo caused his lawyers to advise that he accept the plea offered by the prosecutor. Obviously, that child should not have seen the tattoo. In still another case, a 4-year-old child was unable to say more than three sentences about the abuse. No details were forthcoming, even using the dolls and other props. It was concluded that the child's story was not credible after no other evidence to support the allegation could be obtained from the child's behavior or feelings. However, the abuse could have occurred even though there was no current credible evidence to support it.

Although most professionals find it difficult to believe, it is possible to use brainwashing techniques on young children so they will give false reports of sexual abuse. These are often extremely difficult to detect by usual assessment methods, and the truth may never be known. In two cases on which I have consulted, fathers were accused of using such techniques to get the children to report sexual abuse by the mother and her new boyfriend in order for the fathers to gain custody. Both mothers had been previously battered by these men. In one case, the child's therapists denied any evidence of sexual abuse by the mother but noted the negative emotional impact of the father's derogatory comments about the mother, his need for control, and ultimate kidnapping of the child after court rulings were made that were not in his favor. The legal investigation shows that it is possible that under hypnosis this child was trained to say "Mommy bit my pee-pee" when told "to tell the truth." The child has never been able to give many more details and says it in a routinized fashion. Of course, this rigidity could also come from overexposure to questioning and from being kept away from the mother for much of the 2-year battle. Professionals hired by the father helped polarize this case by exhibiting a disrespect for other clinicians involved and supporting the father's allegations without a careful assessment of all evidence in the case. Here the child is the real loser and, after all the scrutiny and emotional upheaval, it can be expected that the true story may never be revealed.

Alleged Abuser's Statements

It is most difficult to rely upon acknowledgment by the abuser that he did indeed harm the child as evidence that an assault did occur because so few men are willing to confess. Although some men are in acute emotional distress when their behavior is exposed, and others self-righteously believe sexual activity with the child is the abuser's own choice, most abusers do not admit the truth for fear of the consequences, such as legal sanctions or the demise of their home. Those who do not feel anxiety about their sexual behavior or do not perceive that they harmed the child are able to appear nondeceptive on polygraph tests. As is indicated by McGovern and Peters in Chapter 12, and by Wolf, Conte, and Engle-Menig in Chapter 18, it can be difficult to demonstrate men's guilt or innocence through formal assessment procedures. Therefore, much weight is placed on the evaluation of the child.

In some cases, men are accused of molesting children, and they did not do it. These cases are difficult to prove because those who do molest as well as those who do not both claim to be innocent. There is also confusion between children's recanting and their lying originally. Many poorly prepared cases are taken to trial and win convictions anyhow, which places the entire system in jeopardy. Community values are changing rapidly, leaving jurors with little tolerance for child molesters (cf. Attorney General's Task Force on Family Violence, 1984). However, the current status places a greater responsibility on the psychologist to do a thorough evaluation. Greater care must be taken during child-custody evaluations to investigate thoroughly any allegations of family violence. Specific methods are suggested elsewhere (Walker & Edwall, 1987). It is not uncommon for children to disclose incest that occurred after parents separate, because they then feel safe. However, in bitter child-custody fights unsubstantiated child sexual abuse accusations can be introduced by one party as more ammunition to win.

Some psychologists spend their professional time traveling the country determined to prove fathers are unfairly denied access, unjustly accused, and should have more rights to their children (cf. Unterweggen et al., 1985). An organization called Victims of Child Abuse Laws (VOCAL) has been formed to help fathers regain access to their children. In one case in which I was one of five experts hired, one out-of-town psychologist served a lawsuit for libel and slander against another local psychologist right in the courtroom while waiting for the hearing to begin. Each claimed the other was incompetent and misinterpreted findings. The judge attempted to remove the child from the battle by placing him briefly in a foster home that had not been previously inspected, and the father kidnapped the child after the state supreme court upheld the decision for the mother to have custody. A civil lawsuit on behalf of the child has been filed against the father for denying the child access to his mother. Certainly the psychologists who defended the father's behavior should also have some ethical, if not legal, responsibility for the outcome, which obviously has not met the best interests of the child.

In another case, a poorly conducted evaluation determined that a 3-year-old child was sexually abused by her stepfather, whom she called Daddy. Upon further investigation, it became clear that she had displayed signs of child sexual abuse while previously living with her biological father, whom she also called Daddy. The evaluator and prosecutor in this case refused to consider the earlier medical evidence of vaginal infections and injuries from physical abuse, the eyewitness testimony from a 6-year-old brother, the mother's abuse, and the father's history of sexual assault on his young sister. This evidence was considered too old because it happened over a year before the child disclosed the abuse. Those knowledgeable about sexually abused children are aware that disclosures can take place at various times in their lives. The stepfather was convicted without the right to confrontation, either at trial or during a videotaped deposition. The case is on appeal.

This latter case demonstrates the necessity to present findings on two separate issues. First, was the child sexually abused? And second, does the child give clear evidence of who was the abuser? The thorough assessment suggested in this chapter can allow both questions to be answered by the psychologist.

Diagnosis and Findings

Finkelhor and Browne's (see Chapter 4) classification of four traumagenic categories (betrayal, sexualization, powerlessness, and stigmatization), with their observable behavioral and emotional concomitants, is a useful system with which to compare a particular child's behavior. Knowledge of rape-trauma syndrome symptoms is also necessary to substantiate the findings for an individual child, particularly from single abusive acts by a stranger (Walker, 1984b). Battered woman syndrome, with its emphasis on betrayal by someone who loves her as well as abuses her, is also relevant (Walker, 1984a). Since there is no separate diagnostic category for the sexually abused child in the official diagnostic manual, the *Diagnostic and Statistical Manual of Mental Disorders (DSM III)* (American Psychiatric Association, 1980), a Post Traumatic Stress Disorder diagnosis is appropriate on Axis I. An Adjustment Disorder of Childhood diagnosis is commonly given but is usually inaccurate when the child's reaction is appropriate to the trauma. Thus, the symptoms observed are expected from the trauma of sexual abuse even though they may be maladaptive for the child in other areas of development (cf. Walker, 1986).

Short-term as well as long-term prognosis is often requested by the referral source. It is important to be familiar with and to cite the literature on impact and on retrospective incest therapy to guide the prognosis (cf. other chapters in this book). Young children may seal over the trauma, only to have it reawaken at puberty when sexual feelings normally occur, or later in adolescence when dating occurs. A crisis caused by another trauma can also stimulate the negative effects again. Even when the child appears to forget the incident, an association can cause the whole emotional as well as cognitive memory to reappear.

Incest and sexual abuse may be thought of as a time bomb, just waiting to explode should the right combination occur to set it off. There is not enough experience with specific therapy for children to learn if such counseling minimizes or prevents later recurrences. Clinical evidence suggests it can be very useful to help children heal enough to move ahead developmentally (Conte & Berliner, Chapter 5; Walker & Bolkovatz, Chapter 13; Sgroi, 1982).

COMMUNICATING THE FINDINGS

It is customary to prepare a written report in addition to the videotape, which is more appropriately considered raw data like test protocols. We use the standard report format that outlines the reason for referral; procedures used and time spent; brief summary of significant history; results and findings including integration of observations, assessment data, school, medical, and other corroborating data; diagnosis; conclusions; and recommendations. Prognosis is also estimated for legal cases involving damages. Since evaluators do not always get to see the child in therapy, a treatment plan for another therapist can be prepared if requested.

Even when our evaluation is done at the request of the defendant, we believe we have an ethical obligation to put the child's needs first without breaking confidentiality or diminishing the defendant's rights. We are always careful to reach this balance when discussing our findings with other professionals. For example, we will not always re-interview a child and instead may rely on previously collected data, if we think the re-interview will be detrimental to a child and a court hearing can be averted. Providing an opinion of another interviewer's videotape certainly facilitates the second evaluation in ways that the standard audiotape cannot, although in some cases the technique does not cover sufficient areas so as to permit its use. However, our opinion can often assist the defendant's attorney in making subsequent legal decisions.

For cases that go to trial, the videotape has been ruled admissable in about one third of the states, either to support the credibility of the child or to substitute for the child's appearance (Whitcomb et al., 1985). Even in jurisdictions that do not allow the latter, the tape gives the judge or jury another view of the child, in a more child-centered setting than the courtroom. Unfortunately, the judge may get bored with watching a child play on the television monitor. I have had some cases where the judge appeared to fall asleep! If the psychologist can interject comments or interpretations as to the significance of what is being observed, better attention can be expected. In one case the judge asked for an explanation of what to look for prior to viewing the tape in his own home. Perhaps someday the technology will be sufficiently developed so that interpretations can be interspersed over the original tape, and the report will be contained on the tape ready to be played on any VCR. I believe that many more abusers will accept responsibility for their sexual misconduct when they see and hear the child's descriptions. Unfortunately, face-to-face confrontation is often too traumatic for the child. The videotape may be another way to do it.

There have been a number of high-publicity cases that have gone to trial without enough credible legal evidence to substantiate the prosecutor's claims. A preschool case in Los Angeles where hundreds of children were involved is one example. By the time the case went to trial—several years after disclosure, which itself occurred several years after the incidents in some cases—the children were unable to remember or unwilling to testify. Many of the charges had to be dismissed because of unsubstantiated evidence that could have been preserved with videotape depositions had the initial evaluations and cross-examinations been recorded. Even when there is good preservation of evidence, there is much disagreement in psychology as to validity of techniques used and their meaning. Battles of the experts are not uncommon, with advocates taking absolute stands—such as children never lie about abuse, young children's memory is faulty, or all children are susceptible to manipulation by an overzealous parent or evaluator. Each case must be carefully evaluated using as many different samples of behavior as possible to find consistency.

CONCLUSIONS

This chapter has attempted to describe the practical application of the new literature and techniques for assessing children who have been sexually abused. The use of videotape equipment and the anatomically correct dolls have been the focus, along with descriptions of how to elicit and interpret typical responses. Caution about careful use of the usual corroborating material has been discussed, in order to prevent discounting the credibility of the victim. A proper evaluation of the child is critical for legal purposes as well as for intervention to help healing occur. It is hoped that eventually the data on videotape will be compelling enough to prevent the child from having to undergo multiple interviews and court appearances.

REFERENCES

American Psychiatric Association. (1980). *Diagnostic and statistical manual of mental disorders* (3rd Ed.). Washington, DC: Author.

American Psychological Association. (1985). *Biographical directory.* Washington, DC: Author.

Attorney General's Task Force on Family Violence. (1984). *Final report.* Washington, DC: Department of Justice.

Berliner, L. (1983). *Impact of sexual assault: Therapeutic intervention.* Paper presented at seminar, Sexual Assault: Representing the Victim. Emerging legal and psychological issues. Available from Northwest Women's Law Center, 701 N.E. Northlake Way, Seattle, WA 98105.

The Denver Post. (1986, December 27). Story on new technique to identify sexually abused children with dye.

MacFarlane, K. (1978). In J. Chapman & M. Gates (Eds.), *The victimization of women* (pp 81–109). Beverly Hills, CA: Sage.

Patterson, G. R. (1982). *Coercive family processes.* Eugene, OR: Castaglia Press.

Philippus, M. J., & Koch, G. V. (1986, October). How to evaluate sexuality in children and avoid using "anatomically correct dolls." *Trial Talk* (Colorado Trial Lawyers Association), pp. 372–373.

Sgroi, S. (1982). *Handbook of clinical intervention in child sexual abuse.* Lexington, MA: Lexington Books.

Unterweggen, R., Benson, P., Cleary, G., Erickson, J., Jerde, J., Johnson, A., Legrand, R., & Wakefield, H. (1985). *Child sexual abuse.* Minneapolis, MN: Institute for Psychological Therapies.

Walker, L. E. A. (1984a). *The battered woman syndrome.* New York: Springer Publishing Company.

Walker, L. E. A. (1984b). *Women and mental health policy.* Beverly Hills, CA: Sage.

Walker, L. E. A. (1986, August). *Abuse disorders: DSM-III politics or science?* Symposium presented at the annual meeting of the American Psychological Association, Washington, DC.

Walker, L. E. A. (1987). Intervention with victims. In I. Weiner & A. Hess (Eds.). *Handbook of forensic psychology.* New York: Wiley.

Walker, L. E. A., & Edwall, G. E. (1987). Battered women and child custody and visitation determination. In D. J. Sonkin (Ed.), *Domestic violence on trial* (pp. 127–152). New York: Springer Publishing Company.

Whitcomb, D., Shapiro, E. R., & Stellwegen, L. D. (1985). *When the victim is a child: Issues for judges and prosecutors.* Washington, DC: National Institute of Justice.

White, S., Strom, G. A., Santilli, G., & Halpin, B. M. (1986). Interviewing young sexual abuse victims with anatomically correct dolls. *Child Abuse and Neglect, 10,* 519–529.

11

Assessment-Intervention Interface Using the Theme Creation Test for Youths

Barbara R. Slater

Although the sexual exploitation of children by adults has a very long and extensive documented history, it has been only recently that professionals dedicated to working with children have begun to focus on this use as abuse and to incorporate it into the framework of child abuse. Kline, Cole, and Fox (1981) pointed out that it was only after the passage of the Child Abuse, Prevention, and Treatment Act of 1974 that attention turned from the physical effects of battering to its consequences. Blain, Bergner, Lewis, and Goldstein (1981), in discussing the amount of child abuse that goes undetected, remarked that ". . . one vital area in which our knowledge has not increased appreciably is that of detection" (p. 667), and that ". . . at present we have developed little in the way of an assessment technology that would help us in this regard" (p. 667).

The picture when we look from physical to sexual abuse is even more dismal. Following the extension of child abuse laws to include sexual abuse, more attention was focused on this aspect of abuse, but much of the energy was directed toward medical issues and the abuser rather than toward emotional consequences for the child. One reason for this may have been the negative opinions voiced by some of the earlier authors. For example, Bender and Blau (1937) noted the unexpected lack of marked fear, anxiety,

The author wishes to acknowledge Towson State University for its initial support in the development of the Theme Creation Test for Youths. She also wishes to thank her co-author of that test, Mary M. Gallagher, for her assistance in scoring protocols and in preparation of this manuscript.

guilt, or psychic trauma, and the presence of charming and attractive characteristics in the 16 children they examined in a hospital setting. They stated that "these children undoubtedly do not deserve completely the cloak of innocence with which they have been endowed by moralists, social reformers and legislators" (p. 514). They felt that it was possible that such charming and attractive children might have actually been the seducers. No reference was made as to adult responsibilities to children or how these children might have developed the traits mentioned. Weiss, Rogers, Darwin, and Dutton (1955) also mentioned the seductive and charming aspects of sexually abused children evaluated by male therapists. Rascovsky and Rascovsky (1950), in discussing one case of an incestuous situation, indicated that incest might prevent the later appearance of victim overt psychosis. Even more recently, Schultz (1980), in a paper on the diagnosis and treatment of child sexual abuse victims, suggested that incest victims might have been seeking or permitting adult affectionate behavior. In what now seems to be a startling statement, Revitch and Weiss (1962) wrote, "the majority of pedophiles are harmless individuals and their victims are usually known to be aggressive and seductive children" (p. 78).

In contrast, Ferenczi (1933) stated that the child was always to be considered as the adult's innocent victim because of the overall sense of helplessness in the face of adult authority. In Ferenczi's opinion, the most critical issue was, ". . . introjection of the guilt feelings of the adult which makes hitherto harmless play appear as a punishable offense" (p. 228). Lewis and Sarrel (1969) and Katan (1973) also related various negative effects of child sexual abuse. Finkelhor (1979a,b) discussed the asymmetry of power between adults and children and stated that any possibility of free and informed consent was impossible within the imbalanced state. Becker and Skinner (1985) further discussed the effect of the authority of the adult over the child. The majority of current literature has been of the opinion that child sexual abuse produces negative results in the victim, either in childhood or in adult life. (See in this book Asher, Chapter 1; Finkelhor & Browne, Chapter 4; and Conte & Berliner, Chapter 5.)

Another possible reason for the lack of attention to the psychological consequences may have been controversy surrounding the definition of child sexual abuse. For example, while conflicting opinions have been voiced as to whether or not incest ought to be subsumed under sexual abuse, Summit and Kryso (1978) clearly reflected this author's point of view in their statement that "we are convinced that incest is a specific variant of child abuse with identifiable antecedents and predictable consequences" (p. 239). From a legal perspective, child sexual abuse has sometimes been limited to forceful penetration, with medical evidence of the act. However, this is inappropriately restrictive from the mental health perspective. Broadhurst (1979) presented a much more comprehensive view of child sexual abuse as

". . . any contact or interaction between a child and an adult in which the child is being used for the sexual stimulation of the perpetrator or another person" (p. 152). In a like manner, Brant and Tisza (1977), in an unpublished manuscript cited by Rosenfeld, Nadelson, Krieger, and Backman (1977), defined child sexual abuse as ". . . exposure of a child within a given social-cultural context to sexual stimulation inappropriate for the child's age and level of development" (page unknown). The broader concept of child sexual abuse is the one adopted by this author in light of the limited evidence connecting type or degree of abuse to degree of emotional trauma.

Currently there is a considerable body of opinion and evidence that child sexual abuse can result in short-term and long-range psychological damage (Adams-Tucker, 1982; Blain, Bergner, Lewis, & Goldstein, 1981; Brassard, Tyler, & Kehle, 1983; Browne & Finkelhor, 1986; Chandler, 1982; Christiansen, 1980; Conte, 1982; Finkelhor, 1979a, 1984; Gelinas, 1983; Kempe & Kempe, 1984; Kerns, 1981; Kline, Cole, & Fox, 1981; Lusk & Waterman, 1986; MacVicar, 1979; Mrazek & Kempe, 1981; Porter, 1984; Rosenfeld, Nadelson, Krieger, & Backman, 1977; Steele, 1983; Steele & Alexander, 1981; Summit & Kryso, 1978; and Zager, 1982). Effective means of identification most certainly are needed.

EXISTING METHODS OF IDENTIFYING CHILD SEXUAL ABUSE

Authors have referred to the informal use of projective testing in the identification and treatment of sexually abused children (Mrazek, 1981; Mrazek & Mrazek, 1981; Shamroy, 1980), but little has been done to standardize a psychometric technique specifically for identification of sexually abused children or to develop scoring and interpretive systems for currently existing techniques that would serve the same purpose. Burgess, McCausland, and Wolbert (1981) did discuss the unusual aspects of sexually abused children's figure drawings. Mrazek and Mrazek (1981) deplored this lack of techniques graphically in their statements that "few studies have utilized any standardized outcome measures of cognitive or psychological functioning" and "while some standardized, projective instruments exist, they have rarely been applied in reported case studies of the effects of sexual abuse" (p. 237).

Those involved in the identification and treatment of sexually abused children have attempted to rely on medical evidence and behavioral patterns. Because only a small portion of these children have been brutalized so as to evidence physical injury or involvement signs (Christiansen, 1980) such as bleeding, tissue damage, venereal disease, or, in older girls, pregnancy, the medical evidence approach ensures identification of only the more grossly abused children. Because at least some evidence exists that severity of abuse is not related to degree of trauma (Finkelhor, 1979a), this approach seems not to be efficient if our goal is to prevent or ameliorate the emotional damage of sexual abuse.

Our current methods of identification are useful in more blatant or extensive cases of child sexual abuse. However, in cases where medical evidence is not available, when the child does not emit classical behavioral patterns, when the child does not divulge because of an admonishment not to reveal the activity, when psychological defenses such as repression block revealing of data, or when the child lacks verbal skills to reveal information, these methods fail. Although psychologists ought to be able to develop tests to measure samples of behavior that will be more efficient means of identifying sexually abused children as early in the abuse cycle as possible, this seems not to have happened. The present chapter describes the beginning stages of an approach that combines the diagnostic and therapeutic aspects of the Theme Creation Test for Youths, the Experimental Edition (TCTY) (Gallagher & Slater, 1982) in an attempt to develop better means of identification and intervention with such children.

DIAGNOSIS WITH THE TCTY

The TCTY is a projective instrument designed for use with children. It was developed in response to literature indicating the need for a well-standardized projective technique representing a cross-section of today's multicultural/pluralistic society and standardized specifically on children. The TCTY, which is grounded in object relations theory, is currently under standardization (Gallagher, 1984). While the TCTY is of the story-telling variety, it differs from currently used tests in significant ways. It permits flexibility, allowing for better production of individual fantasies more effectively than do the more structured Thematic Apperception Test (Murray, 1943), Children's Apperception Test (Bellak & Bellak, 1949), Educational Apperceptive Test (Thompson & Sones, 1973), School Apperception Test (Solomon & Starr, 1968), or Roberts Apperception Test for Children (McArthur & Roberts, 1982) by separation of figures and backgrounds. TCTY backgrounds sample most essential environments of children (living room, bedroom, nursery, bathroom, classroom, office, playground, street, jail, and physician's office). It offers a more varied pool of moveable figures than does the Make-A-Picture Story Test (Schneidman, 1952), including human beings (infants, children, adolescents, adults, and senior citizens), fantasy figures (ghost, troll, Santa Claus, and male and female superheroes), and animals (dogs, cat, snake). The TCTY addresses itself to the multicultural aspects of society through inclusion of Anglo, Afro-American, Hispanic, Native American, and Oriental figures portrayed with positive, neutral, and negative affect. It also directly taps the youth's perception of her or his future roles in conjunction with the youth's perception of positive and negative aspects of parents.

Youths select one or more of the 76 available figures to populate each of the 10 backgrounds, and examiners note the figures selected and their placement on the background. A story is then told to each of the created pictures. Finally the youths select figures representing specific aspects of self and parent(s).

The overall scoring system examines figure selection, figure placement, affective presentation, story characteristics, and identification of figures with self and parent(s). However, in using the TCTY for identification of sexually abused children, a separate means of looking at the data is suggested, based partly upon the literature discussing behavioral characteristics of known sexually abused children.

The realization that the TCTY might be effective in the identification of sexually abused children was quite accidental. In the early standardization process, several known sexually abused children were included in the sub-sample of seriously emotionally disturbed children. The authors noted that their style of responding was markedly different from other seriously disturbed children and from nonsexually abused children in general. This awareness became stronger when Mary Gallagher used the instrument with other emotionally disturbed children in her work environment. The combination of these two experiences led to the preliminary research described in the following section.

Children Evaluated

A sample consisting of 18 seriously emotionally disturbed children with histories of sexual abuse was roughly equated on the basis of age, sex, and cultural characteristics with a sample of 18 seriously emotionally disturbed children with no known history of sexual abuse. All but two of these children, one in the experimental group and one in the control group, were in special education placement for seriously emotionally disturbed children. Ages ranged from 5 to 12 and all but the two above-mentioned children were from lower socio-economic families. The sexual abuse status was determined by social services involvement, parent statement of abuse, or the statement of abuse made by a caregiver familiar with the child and family constellation. A continuation of this study will examine a much larger sample with a broad variety of kinds and intensity of abuse. Table 11.1 presents demographic data.

In 15 out of the 18 cases, the sexual abuse consisted of direct contact, including fondling, masturbation, oral-genital contact, and/or insertion. The other three cases involved severe sexualization: repeated exposure to adult sexual behavior, repeated use of sexually explicit language, and/or repeated watching of sexually explicit videotapes. In 4 cases the abuser was father/

TABLE 11.1 Demographic Characteristics of Subjects ($N = 36$)

Characteristics	Sexually abused		Nonsexually abused	
Age	Female	Male	Female	Male
5–7	6	7	6	7
8–10	1	2	1	2
11–13	0	2	0	2
Socioeconomic status				
Low	6	11	6	11
Middle	1	0	1	0
Cultural aspects				
Anglo	3	4	3	3
Afro-American	4	7	4	8

father substitute, in 6 cases the abuser was a male outside of the family, in 7 cases the abuser was the mother, and in 1 case the abuser was another female. In comparison with the other literature on sexually abused children, this sample was slanted strongly toward boys who were abused by females. However, the sample was consistent with noted instances of sexual abuse among special education children, quite possibly because the number of boys outweighs girls in such classes. When the study is extended to clinic and private practice children, this bias will likely disappear.

Based on the literature pointing out behavioral signs of sexual abuse, it was decided that such behavioral signs would be examined in the current research. The specific signs chosen because of frequency of appearance in the literature were: severe sexualization, anxiety related to sexuality, depression, hostility, guilt, somatization, and aggression. Sexualization was measured by sexually tinged verbalizations, use of naked figures, and sexual content in stories.

Test Administration

Each child was administered the TCTY, according to the standard test instructions, by one of the two test developers. In order to avoid interpretational bias, data categorizing was done by Mary Gallagher rather than by the present author. These data are presented in Table 11.2. Because of the small number of responses in some categories, adjacent categories were collapsed for analysis. With a larger sample, it may be possible to separate out each category for individual analysis.

Looking at the number of figures selected, we see that sexually abused children selected more naked figures, used naked figures more in-

TABLE 11.2 Numbers, Means, and Significance of Response Patterns

Categories	Number	Mean	Range	t
Fantasy figures				
Sexually abused	104	5.78	0–14	ns
Nonsexually abused	121	6.37	0–26	
Naked figures				
Sexually abused	134	7.44	0–38	2.083*
Nonsexually abused	56	2.95	0–11	
Naked figures: inappropriate use				
Sexually abused	121	6.72	0–38	2.152*
Nonsexually abused	40	2.11	0–9	
Naked figures: appropriate use				
Sexually abused	13	.72	0–3	ns
Nonsexually abused	15	.79	0–2	
Direct reference to sexuality				
Sexually abused	21	1.17	0–7	2.240*
Nonsexually abused	1	.05	0–1	
Indirect reference to sexuality				
Sexually abused	15	.83	0–3	2.460**
Nonsexually abused	5	.26	0–1	
Clothed figures: sexually toned behavior				
Sexually abused	44	2.44	0–30	4.140***
Nonsexually abused	1	.15	0–1	
Naked figures: no story reference				
Sexually abused	31	1.72	0–12	ns
Nonsexually abused	30	1.58	0–8	
Rejection of naked figures				
Sexually abused	16	.89	0–5	ns
Nonsexually abused	12	.63	0–4	
Hostility				
Sexually abused	25	1.39	0–5	ns
Nonsexually abused	16	.84	0–5	
Anxiety				
Sexually abused	31	1.72	0–5	ns
Nonsexually abused	15	.79	0–5	
Depression				
Sexually abused	58	3.22	0–9	2.126*
Nonsexually abused	32	1.68	0–7	
Guilt				
Sexually abused	5	.29	0–4	ns
Nonsexually abused	2	.11	0–1	
Somatization				
Sexually abused	8	.44	0–2	ns
Nonsexually abused	9	.47	0–2	
Aggression				
Sexually abused	56	3.00	0–7	ns
Nonsexually abused	54	2.84	0–8	

*$p < .05$ **$p < .02$ ***$p < .001$

appropriately, made indirect reference and direct reference to sexuality more frequently, included clothed figures in sexually toned behavior more frequently, and demonstrated hostility, anxiety, depression, and guilt more frequently than nonsexually abused children in this sample. The use of naked figures appropriately, the use of naked figures with no story reference, the rejection of naked figures, and the demonstration of somatization and aggression were essentially equal for both groups. Nonsexually abused children tended to use slightly more fantasy figures than did sexually abused children.

While the means are quite small for each group, this is a function of the marked variability from child to child. The most appropriate measure of variability would be the standard deviation. However, in order to provide a clear picture of the kind of scatter with which we are dealing, it was decided to report the range for each category. There was a tendency for sexually abused children to be somewhat more variable than nonsexually abused children in categories related specifically to sexuality. No differentiating variability was noted on those categories not related directly to sexuality, and a reverse variability was noted on the use of fantasy figures, with nonsexually abused children demonstrating greater variability.

Results

In order to test for significance of differences between means, a series of t tests was used. It was recognized that with a small sample and considerable variability, mean differences would have to be very large to attain significance. Five of the 8 categories tied directly to sexuality attained significance as follows:

Number of naked figures selected for placement on the backgrounds ($t = 2.083, p < .05$).

Number of naked figures used inappropriately in stories, for example, a naked man directing traffic or a naked child in the classroom ($t = 2.152, p < .05$).

Number of direct references to sexuality, for example, "two people humping" or "they screwing again" ($t = 2.240, p < .05$).

Indirect reference to sexuality, for example, "she thinkin' bad thoughts about what those two been doing alone" or "them two going to get caught for something bad they doing alone" ($t = 2.460, p < .02$).

Clothed figures portrayed in sexually toned behavior, for example, two clothed figures of children in bed playing secret games or two clothed adults in the bathroom touching each other all over ($t = 4.140, p < .001$).

Of the six categories not linked directly to sexuality and derived from behavioral materials, only depression differentiated between the two groups, with *sexually abused children demonstrating significantly more signs of depression* ($t = 2.126, p < .05$). As anticipated, there was not a significant difference between the two groups in the use of fantasy figures.

In addition, an informal estimation of language level in terms of sexual sophistication was attempted, although it was not possible to score this in any formal manner. With the exception of one child in the nonsexually abused group, *only sexually abused children used actual sexual terminology.* Such terminology was common among the sexually abused children. The use of words such as *screwing, humping, fucking, sticking his dick in her, pussy, cunt,* and so forth illustrate this sophistication. A similar note of *negatively toned references to sexuality* was made rather than attempting a formal analysis. When it is noted that, of the 56 naked figures selected by nonsexually abused children, there were 15 instances of appropriate use (27%) such as bathroom, getting ready for bed, or medical examination stories, compared to 13 out of 134 instances of appropriate use (10%) by sexually abused children, we gain perspective on feelings about the open portrayal of sexuality. *At least for younger children, sexualization may become a way of life so that it is perceived as "normal," if unpleasant, behavior.* This would account for the small number of directly negative statements about sexuality noted in this sample. Older children might be expected to perceive the sexual act(s) they have been subjected to in a more negative light rather than as "normal" because of more sophisticated knowledge and thinking.

In order to determine whether or not the TCTY can identify sexually abused children, one must examine the meaning of the above data. Looking at both qualitative and quantitative data seems to be a productive approach. Because all of the children in this sample were seriously emotionally disturbed, one would expect that their ability to maintain impulse control and to think logically would be more impaired than in the typical child. Therefore, differences seen in this sample would take on more dramatic overtones if they appeared in children with fewer problems.

Discussion of Results

A pattern seems to have emerged that will be useful in identifying children who are likely to have been the victims of extreme sexualization or direct sexual abuse. It seems quite clear that sexually abused children demonstrate their history by the explicit use of sexually toned materials on a projective technique that allows for this use. The pattern includes both the selection of naked figures to populate the test backgrounds and the relating of stories that include indirect and direct reference to sexual behavior. The relating of sexually toned behavior to clothed figures seems to be of special significance. The above-mentioned test behaviors are quite atypical of nonsexually abused children. Although many of the behavioral indices of sexual abuse did not evidence themselves significantly on the TCTY with this sample, it may be that the direct expression of sexuality permitted a reduction in behavioral signs typically associated with sexually abused children on this personality measure. For children with a greater command of cognitive and emotional processes, the direct expression might well be blocked, resulting in greater evidence of the behaviorally related signs on the test. Further studies with less disturbed children will clarify this issue.

For the present time, it seems safe to assume that children who present the following pattern on this projective instrument need to be considered as likely having experienced inappropriate sexual stimulation. This author has encountered two children recently who were being evaluated for entirely different problems, who demonstrated the sexual abuse pattern, and upon further inquiry turned out to have been abused by non-family members.

The sexual abuse pattern seen on the TCTY consists of:

1. Sexually sophisticated language and knowledge.
2. Selection of naked figures to populate test backgrounds, and relating of stories in which these figures are used inappropriately, with indirect or direct reference to sexuality.
3. The use of clothed figures in sexually toned behavior.
4. Depressive stories in the presence of the above-noted factors.
5. Anxiety related to sexuality as demonstrated by clear evidence of the first three criteria with expressed anxiety.
6. In the face of the above factors, especially 1 through 3, additional signs of hostility, guilt, and overall anxiety on the projective evaluation.
7. Additional evidence of behavioral signs, particularly if associated with school-related problems, night problems, regression, and/or lowered self-esteem.

It is not suggested that the TCTY be used in exclusion of other measures to identify sexual abuse. The most appropriate use will be to include this test as part of a battery to be used in the personality assessment of all children. Signs of sexual abuse would then be followed up immediately by more traditional means of exploration.

An interesting side note has to do with the children's ability to differentiate between fantasy and reality. At the conclusion of the testing, the author made a point of asking most of the children who used fantasy figures if such figures really existed. This informal approach seemed to indicate that even emotionally disturbed children, with poor ego strength and impulse controls, are able to differentiate between reality and fantasy when given an appropriate structured question. Only two of the children experienced difficulty in making this differentiation. Certainly this area is worthy of a more formal examination in light of the difficulties in having children admitted to court for testimony regarding sexual abuse on the basis of answers to questions such as, "Do you believe in Santa Claus?"

THERAPEUTIC CONSIDERATIONS

In therapy it may be extremely difficult for the sexually abused child to work on the abusive situation, although such work is critical to the therapeutic process. Because the child may have been told very specifically that he or she is never to mention the situation and may have been subjected to strong threats of dire consequences for such revelation, therapists working with these children face a uniquely difficult task. Although many children in therapy resist dealing with major issues underlying the original referral because of guilt, anxiety, withdrawal, fear, or other such emotional factors, the direct censure against revelation seems generally limited to child sexual abuse victims. Attempts to encourage or reassure the child may well meet with an escalation of resistance. The child's verbal skills also can become a critical factor in the child's ability to work on issues related to the abuse in instances when sophisticated verbal skill is limited or when speech or language problems exist.

While nondirective or analytic techniques will allow the child to gradually approach the major issues, this may take a considerable amount of time. With clear-cut, traumatic factors contributing to or underlying the distress/psychopathology, such an initial expenditure of time may not be in the best interest of the child. An additional element comes into play when the child's parent(s) or caregiver(s) are economically disadvantaged and sufficient funds may not be available for long-term therapy. Shortcutting the often lengthy initial stages of therapy without decreasing the quality of that therapy is essential if the overall time available is limited.

Rather than engaging in lengthy entry stages or possible counterproductive resistance with a child whose ego strength may already be damaged, it is recommended that the therapist approach the actual abuse in an indirect manner that can move toward the situation relatively quickly. Having already become familiar with the TCTY materials in the psychodiagnostic setting, it is likely that the child will commence therapeutic work with them with minimal resistance or anxiety. If the child related stories linked to sexual abuse or used figures in a sexually related way quite openly during the diagnostic process, it is even more likely that sexuality expressed in a developmentally inappropriate manner will enter the TCTY play quickly. Obviously this technique will not be as necessary with a verbally competent child who is ready to deal directly with the abuse.

Therapy Using the TCTY to Tell Stories

There are a number of possible variations of therapeutic TCTY use. This author has found the following technique quite useful. Prior to introducing the materials to the child, the therapist selects a few of the backgrounds that seem most likely to produce the desired kind of interaction, dependent upon the individual child's abusive background. For example, if the child was abused by a neighborhood adolescent, it would be useful to include the playground and street scenes as well as one or two indoor scenes. If the abuser was the father, then the bedroom, living room, and bathroom would be likely selections. The number of figures also needs to be reduced to about one third of the total number. Care must be taken to represent the sociocultural background of the child and the abuse constellation. The naked, prone, handicapped, fantasy, and animal figures are always included. The therapist will also need to have a clear picture of the abuse situation, the child's ego strength, the child's cognitive ability and style, major conflicts, the child's available coping mechanisms, and the child's support system. These bits of information ought to be available in the diagnostic materials.

Early in therapy, ideally within the first two sessions, the TCTY is brought out and the child is told that she or he and the therapist will be doing some storytelling each session. The child is then encouraged to select a background, populate it, and tell a story to the completed picture. It is suggested that the therapist record the figures selected and the framework of the story so as to assess progress.

During the actual storytelling, or once the story has been completed, the therapist can move in one of two directions. For those who prefer a more analytic approach, a modified interpretive style is suggested. However, in order to avoid overwhelming the child, a stepwise interpretation will be most useful. The first step is to provide a nonthreatening, general interpretation. If the child confirms or accepts this by verbalization, nonverbal positive response, or continued production of relevant material, then a second, more specific but still indirect interpretation may be offered followed by another pause for confirmation or disconfirmation. In the early stages of therapy it is most likely that the therapist will want to stop at this point, regardless of whether the child confirms or disconfirms. If the child disconfirms at the first step, by indicating no, by disagreeing, by shifting theme or characteristics of activity, or by demonstrating discomfort, the interpretation on that point stops. In later stages of therapy, the therapist can continue interpretations following each confirmation, gradually moving closer to the direct interpretation at a pace the child can tolerate. The therapist will want to watch for negative confirmations, instances in which the child indicates that the interpretation was correct but the affectual experience is more than the child can tolerate. In such instances interpretation will cease and support will be given to the child.

An example of stepwise interpretation follows. Alex, age 5 ½, has arranged an angry-appearing boy, the small dog, and two male teenagers in the playground scene. Alex was abused over a period of several months by his adolescent uncle during babysitting situations.

ALEX: This kid and his dog was on the playground with his ball and he wishted (sic) some kids would come play with him. And these big kids come in and walks over. And he quicklike picks up the puppy. (Long pause)

THERAPIST: Sometimes things can get real scary. (General interpretation)

ALEX: Well his puppy's real little and maybe he'd try and bite if they comed (sic) near. (Confirmation)

THERAPIST: Someone like the puppy might try to protect himself if some-one tried to hurt him. (More directed but still not related to a human being)

ALEX: Ya, but he's too little bitty. (Confirmation) (Early in therapy, stop the interpretation. Later, continue)

THERAPIST: Sometimes boys and girls can't protect themselves and bad things happen. (Much more direct, but not actually aimed at Alex)

ALEX: Not me, can I do another one now? (Disconfirmation—stop)

or

ALEX: (Turns and looks directly at the therapist, wide-eyed) (Partial confirmation, the therapist can stop or continue)

THERAPIST: I think something like your story might have happened to you.

ALEX: How long before we stop? (Disconfirmation)

or

ALEX: I got to pee. (Disconfirmation)

or

ALEX: But this puppy gets keeped safe. (Partial confirmation)

Therapists who do not have experience with this technique or who do not wish to use it may achieve equally positive effects with the TCTY through application of a technique based on that developed by Richard A. Gardner (1971) and described in *Therapeutic Communication with Children: The Mutual Storytelling Technique.* Although Gardner seems not to have used his technique specifically with sexually abused children, it certainly is highly appropriate. Gardner has used the backgrounds of the Make-A-Picture Story Test (Schneidman, 1952) therapeutically to encourage the child to commence work. Because of the relatively negative nature of many of the original figures, he substitutes small plastic figures for the original figures (Gardner, 1985). Because the concept of the TCTY is similar to that of the Make-A-Picture Story Test, this adaptation of Gardner's technique seems particularly relevant. Readers who are not familiar with the Mutual Storytelling Technique may wish to review Gardner's text in order to gain a better view of how the present adaptation works.

In modified form, the therapy would proceed as follows. Following the child's completion of a TCTY story, the therapist tells the child that she or he will also tell a story to the same child-created picture. The therapist starts a story in the same manner as the child but then alters it so that the conclusion is either more favorable and illustrates a more healthful situation and/or adjustment to life, or gradually comes closer to the child's traumatic situation. Gardner has the child make up a moral for each story and then adds his own moral when he has completed the altered story, and this is certainly a viable aspect with sexually abused children using the TCTY.

As in the first technique, one must move in stepwise fashion so as not to trigger fear and resistance in the child. The therapist will keep in mind a dual goal, assisting the child in working through the abusive situation more and more directly and in developing more effective means of coping with himself/herself and with, it is hoped, a positively altered environment.

An example using the first situation follows.

ALEX: The boy and his dog was on the playground with his ball and he wishted some kids would come play with him. And then two big kids come in and walks over. And he quicklike picks up his puppy. And they grabs that puppy and put it down the slide and the kid runs up and they grab him and twists his arm and he falls down and wishted a cop would come and help him but nobody does. (Q: What happens in the end?) They gotted tired and lefted and he just cried cause he couldn't do nothin'.

THERAPIST: Tell me the moral of your story.

ALEX: Little kids and puppies get hurted real bad and nobody even cares.

THERAPIST: You are a very good storyteller; now let me try a story with your picture. This little boy was on the playground with his dog and his ball. He hoped some of his friends would come and play with him. Then he saw two teenagers come in and he knew one of them was a bad guy. He felt real scared and mad all at the same time. They came over and one of them grabbed him. (The therapist can now choose a direction in which to proceed)

1. Then one of them did something to him that hurt him and made him feel real bad. Afterwards he told his mother and she helped him understand that it wasn't his fault. She taught him what to do if anyone else tried to hurt him so that he could protect himself better. The moral is that even when kids have bad things happen to them, some adults can help them. (Assumption: a supportive mother, otherwise the conclusion would be inappropriate. This story handles both of the aspects mentioned earlier, the abusive situation and a coping strategy.)

2. And they took the puppy and he got so scared and frustrated that he just started to cry. Then he remembered what he saw on TV and he started yelling "help" as loud as he could. The guard came running and got his puppy for him and took the teenagers away. The moral is that, even when kids are scared, sometimes they can find a way to get help. (This ending avoids the direct abusive situation and stresses coping skills. In a story where the child becomes angry and hits someone, the ending might stress less harmful ventilation of anger, perhaps with a punching pillow, or a form of relaxation to dissipate the anger.)

3. Then one of them took him and did something that hurt him and made him feel real bad. Then they went away and left him. He was ever so scared and thought he was to blame so he didn't tell anyone. Then he just kept on feeling bad and letting more bad things happen to him. The moral of this story is that sometimes kids get hurt and blame themselves even when it wasn't their fault. (This conclusion places the focus on the trauma directly so it becomes less secret. It also attempts to begin the process of helping the child give up the sense of guilt. This approach would not be used unless the therapist was confident that the child was ready to handle the trauma.)

It is the therapist's responsibility to determine how many stories are to be told in a session, dependent on the child's readiness to move ahead, the length and relevance of each story, and how far a story is followed. Sometimes a single story provides such a richness of material that any further storytelling would be moving away from the therapeutically desired direction. On the other hand, a more guarded child may tell several stories before "pay dirt" is hit in the form of material that can be helpfully interpreted or altered.

Obviously, it is also the therapist's responsibility to determine how rapidly to move with the individual child. Generally, the stronger the child's ego strength is, the more rapid safe progress will be. Fragile children will need to move much more slowly, with many indirect interpretations or alterations of stories. It is also advisable to explore carefully the child's support system. The stronger the available support system, the more possible it is for the child to move quickly into conflict-laden material without being overwhelmed.

There are other techniques that can be used to help sexually abused children provide material or tell stories for interpretation in therapy (MacFarlane & Bulkley, 1982), for example, anatomically correct dolls or pictures. The TCTY technique can be integrated into the overall therapeutic framework as one useful and productive technique. Although the test itself is grounded in object relations theory, its therapeutic use would seem sufficiently flexible to fit into any number of theoretical orientations without conflict.

Because the materials are set up to permit the child to determine what figures to use and how to use them in the story, the child experiences a very real sense of sharing of overall responsibility for the success of therapy with an adult, who then becomes a safe and helpful figure. This serves an additional reparative purpose for sexually abused children, many of whom have lost their sense of control over their lives and their ability to depend upon adults. It is one more tool in the enormous task of helping these children to regain a sense of self-worth and of trust in adults who are able to demonstrate that they are worthy of such trust.

SUMMARY

It seems essential that psychologists devote energy to the development of effective means of identifying sexually abused children through psychodiagnostic evaluation. Concurrently, more effective means of assisting such children therapeutically also need further development. The purpose of this chapter has been to describe a pattern demonstrated by emotionally troubled, sexually abused children on the Theme Creation Test for Youths, the Experimental Edition (Gallagher & Slater, 1982). To provide for continuity of assessment and intervention, the therapeutic use of the TCTY with sexually abused children from either an interpretive or a modified mutual storytelling technique (Gardner, 1971) has also been described.

REFERENCES

Adams-Tucker, C. (1982). Proximate effects of sexual abuse in childhood: A report on 28 children. *American Journal of Psychiatry, 139*(10), 1252–1256.

Becker, J. V., & Skinner, L. J. (1985). Sexual abuse in childhood and adolescence. In D. Shaffer, A. E. Ehrhardt, & L. L. Greenhill (Eds.), *The clinical guide to child psychiatry*. New York: Free Press.

Bellak, L., & Bellak, S. (1949). *Children's Apperception Test (CAT)*. New York: C. P. S. Co.

Bender, L., & Blau A. (1937). The reactions of children to sexual relations with adults. *American Journal of Orthopsychiatry, 7,* 500–518.

Blain, G. H., Bergner, R. M., Lewis, M. L., & Goldstein, M. A. (1981). The use of objectively scorable House-Tree-Person indicators to establish child abuse. *Journal of Clinical Psychology, 37*(3), 667–672.

Brant, R. S. T., & Tisza, V. B. (1977). The sexually misused child. *American Journal of Orthopsychiatry, 47*(1), 80–90.

Brassard, M., Tyler, A., & Kehle, T. (1983). Sexually abused children: Identification and suggestions for intervention. *School Psychology Review, 12*(1), 93–97.

Broadhurst, D. (1979). The educator's role in the prevention and treatment of child abuse and neglect (DHEW Pub. No. OHDS 79-30172). Washington, DC: U.S. Department of Health, Education and Welfare.

Browne, A., & Finkelhor, D. (1986). Initial and long-term effects. In D. Finkelhor (Ed.), *A sourcebook on child sexual abuse.* Beverly Hills, CA: Sage.

Burgess, A. W., McCausland, M. P., & Wolbert, W. A. (1981). Children's drawings as indicators of sexual trauma. *Perspectives in Psychiatric Care, 19,* 50–58.

Chandler, S. M. (1982). Knowns and unknowns in sexual abuse of children. *Journal of Social Work and Human Sexuality, 1*(1–2), 51–68.

Christiansen, J. (1980). *Educational and psychological problems of abused children.* Palo Alto: R & E Research Associates.

Conte, J. R. (1982). Sexual abuse of children: Enduring issues for social work. *Journal of Social Work and Human Sexuality, 1*(1–2), 1–19.

Ferenczi, S. (1933). Confusion of tongues between adults and the child. *International Journal of Psychoanalysis, 30,* 225–230.

Finkelhor, D. (1979a). *Sexually victimized children.* New York: Free Press.

Finkelhor, D. (1979b). What's wrong with sex between adults and children? Ethics and the problem of sexual abuse. *American Journal of Orthopsychiatry, 49,* 692–697.

Finkelhor, D. (1984). *Child sexual abuse: New theory and research.* New York: Free Press.

Gallagher, M. M. (1984). *Exploration of selected psychometric characteristics of the Theme Creation Test for Youths.* Unpublished doctoral dissertation, California School of Professional Psychology, San Diego, CA.

Gallagher, M. M., & Slater, B. R. (1982). The Theme Creation Test for Youths, Experimental Edition. Baltimore: Authors.

Gardner, R. A. (1971). *Therapeutic communication with children: The mutual storytelling technique.* New York: Aronson.

Gardner, R. A. (1985, May). *Helping families in transition.* Address given at the Pupil Services Spring Conference, Ocean City, MD.

Gelinas, D. J. (1983). The persisting negative effects of incest. *Psychiatry, 46,* 312–332.

Katan, A. (1973). Children who were raped. *Psychoanalytic Study Child, 28,* 208–224.

Kempe, R. S., & Kempe, C. H. (1984). *The common secret: Sexual abuse of children and adolescents.* New York: Freeman.

Kerns, D. (1981). Medical assessment of child sexual abuse. In P. B. Mrazek & C. H. Kempe (Eds.), *Sexually abused children and their families* (pp. 129–140). New York: Pergamon Press.

Kline, D. F., Cole, P., & Fox, P. (1981). Child abuse and neglect: The school psychologist's role. *School Psychology Review, 10*(1), 65–71.

Lewis, M., & Sarrel, M. (1969). Some psychological aspects of seduction, incest, and rape in childhood. *Psychiatry, 8,* 609–619.

Lusk, R., & Waterman, J. (1986). Effects of sexual abuse on children. In K. MacFarlane & J. Waterman (Eds.), *Sexual abuse of young children: Evaluation and treatment.* New York: Guilford.

MacFarlane, K., & Bulkley, J. (1982). Treating child sexual abuse: An overview of current program models. In J. Conte & D. Shore (Eds.), *Social work and child abuse.* New York: Haworth.

MacVicar, K. (1979). Psychotherapeutic issues in the treatment of sexually abused girls. *American Academy of Child Psychiatry, 18*(2), 342–353.

McArthur, D. S., & Roberts, G. E. (1982). *Roberts Apperception Test for Children Manual.* Los Angeles: Western Psychological Services.

Mrazek, D. A. (1981). The child psychiatric examination of the sexually abused child. In P. B. Mrazek & C. H. Kempe (Eds.), *Sexually abused children and their families* (pp. 143–154). New York: Pergamon Press.

Mrazek, P. A., & Mrazek, D. A. (1981). The effects of child sexual abuse: Methodological considerations. In P. B. Mrazek & C. H. Kempe (Eds.), *Sexually abused children and their families* (pp. 235–245). New York: Pergamon Press.

Mrazek, P. B., & Kempe, C. H. (1981). *Sexually abused children and their families.* New York: Pergamon Press.

Murray, H. A. (1943). *Thematic Apperception Test: Manual.* Cambridge, MA: Harvard University Press.

Porter, S. (Ed.) (1984). *Child sexual abuse within the family.* London: Tavistock.

Rascovsky, M., & Rascovsky, A. (1950). On consummated incest. *Journal of Psychoanalysis, 31,* 42.

Revitch, F., & Weiss, R. (1962). The pedophiliac offender. *Diseases of the Nervous System, 23,* 73–78.

Rosenfeld, A. A., Nadelson, C. C., Krieger, M., & Backman, J. H. (1977). Incest and sexual abuse of children. *Journal of the American Academy of Child Psychiatry, 16*(2), 327–339.

Schneidman, E. S. (1952). *Manual for Make-A-Picture Story method.* Los Angeles: Projective Technique Monograph.

Schultz, L. G. (1980). Diagnosis and treatment—Introduction. In L. G. Schultz (Ed.), *The sexual victimology of youth.* Springfield, IL: Charles C. Thomas.

Shamroy, J. A. (1980). A perspective on childhood sexual abuse. *Social Work, 25,* 128–131.

Solomon, I. L., & Starr, B. (1968). *School Apperception Method (SAM).* New York: Springer Publishing Company.

Steele, B. F. (1983). The effect of abuse and neglect on psychological development. In J. D. Call, E. Galenson, & R. L. Tyson (Eds.), *Frontiers of infant psychiatry* (Vol. I). New York: Basic Books.

Steele, B. F., & Alexander, H. (1981). Long-term effects of sexual abuse in childhood. In P. B. Mrazek & C. H. Kempe (Eds.), *Sexually abused children and their families* (pp. 223–234). New York: Pergamon Press.

Summit, R., & Kryso, J. A. (1978). Sexual abuse of children: A clinical spectrum. *American Journal of Orthopsychiatry, 48*(2), 237–251.

Thompson, M. M., & Sones, R. A. (1973). *Education Apperception Test: Manual.* Los Angeles: Western Psychological Services.

Weiss, J., Rogers, E., Darwin, M., & Dutton, C. (1955). A study of girl sex victims. *Psychiatric Quarterly, 29,* 1–27.

Zager, R. P. (1982). Sexual abuse of children. *Delaware Medical Journal, 54*(11), 627.

12

Guidelines for
Assessing Sex Offenders

Kevin McGovern
James Peters

The need for adequate collaborative relationships between the legal and mental health professionals who deal with child sexual abusers has intensified as more such cases are being identified and communities demand effective resolutions. The ideal of resolving reported cases of sexual abuse using an interdisciplinary group including law enforcement officers, mental health professionals, judges, probation officers, educators, ministers, and health care providers has been difficult to achieve. Disparate reactions from these professional groups when confronted with child sexual abuse sometimes has led to chaos, confusion, and mishandling of cases. It is probable that a lack of standardized training as well as difficulty in controlling one's own emotional reactions lead to such unpredictable case resolutions. To help add stability, uniformity, and fairness to these systems, a series of practical guidelines can be used to identify and prepare appropriate dispositional plans for sexual abusers. Such guidelines have recently been developed in Portland, Oregon and in Vancouver, Washington, neighboring Northwest United States communities. The authors advocate a prosecution model; all cases in which an adult is accused of sexually abusing a child are reviewed by the elected local prosecutor for consideration of the filing of criminal charges. The guidelines presented in this chapter can be used to ensure that all relevant information has been obtained before the decision is made. Some of these data may be gathered by specially trained mental health professionals using up-to-date assessment procedures including physiological arousal measures. If guilt is established, these same guidelines can then assist both the legal and mental health professionals to contribute information to be used in deciding the appropriate dispositional plans—for example, use of desistance deference, rehabilitation, or punishment, as required in each case. It is on issues of disposition that this chapter will focus.

When a sex offender has been found guilty, one important issue for both the courts and health care providers is the ability to differentiate between the habitual sexual offender and the sexual abuser who will be able to successfully complete an inpatient and/or outpatient treatment program. Predicting acts of future sexual deviance is a difficult clinical and legal task that relates to the whole issue of prediction of dangerousness (Monahan & Klassen, 1982). Neither the clinician nor agents of the court want to take the chance that a sexual abuser will reenact these crimes, yet protection of the offender's rights is also an important issue (see for example the discussion in Whitcomb, Shapiro, & Stellwegen, 1985). Many communities have chosen to provide treatment alternatives or adjuncts to incarceration for certain "treatable" sexual abusers. Based both in the community and in various institutions such as state hospitals and prisons, these programs are designed to reduce the likelihood that these men and/or women will reoffend. Much of what is presented in this chapter has been utilized in the authors' own communities and formed the basis of training workshops nationwide.

INTRODUCTION TO ASSESSMENT

Sound theory and clinical research is crucial when evaluating sexual offenders. For example, some clinicians base their entire findings on a brief clinical interview and a review of psychological test results. This superficial assessment approach is not sufficient to make decisions regarding dangerousness, incarceration, and other related issues. Brief assessments do not usually provide enough information regarding these behavioral disorders. Although the clinical interview may provide some relevant information, most sexual abusers minimize their sexual deviance and/or past propensities to engage in inappropriate behavior. Thus, the evaluator may not learn much about the deviant behavior if only verbal self-report is used. Adding psychological inventory data provides added information but can also be misleading. In many cases, sexual abusers do not appear to be highly pathological on the Minnesota Multiphasic Personality Inventory (MMPI) profile (McGovern, 1984). A comprehensive evaluation should also include a penile plethysmography assessment and the other measures described in the suggested guidelines in Table 12.1.

Offenders typically minimize their behavioral problems, especially when they realize that their self-disclosure could lead to a long term of incarceration. In one evaluation, an offender was interviewed on six different occa-

TABLE 12.1 Guidelines for Evaluating Child Sexual Abuse Offenders

1. Review the police reports and be familiar with the official version of the offense.
2. Where appropriate, interview victim(s) and witnesses.
3. Review medical, psychiatric, and treatment history.
4. Review military, vocational, and educational history.
5. Identify what part alcohol, drugs, codefendants, pornography, social isolation, environmental issues, or other factors played in the commission of the offense(s) and to what extent these factors are still in operation.
6. Review social and marital history, including consultations with former spouse(s) and/or girlfriends and children, where applicable, to ascertain a possible prior history of sexually deviant, violent, or to her abnormal behavior.
7. Review offender's family history, including any indication of physical or sexual abuse or other relevant factors in his or her upbringing.
8. Determine prior criminal history, including arrests, convictions, and nonconviction data such as admitted criminal activity that was not abjudicated.
9. Investigate whether there have been unreported sexual offenses committed by this offender.
10. Evaluate to what extent the offender accepts responsibility for his offenses and to what degree guilt, remorse, or moral accountability is now being experienced.
11. Provide psychological testing, such as the Minnesota Multiphasic Personality Inventory (MMPI), Rorschach, Rotter Incomplete Sentence Blank, Cornell Medical Index, the Thematic Apperception Test, and the Sone Sexual History Questionnaire.
12. Make comparison of the offender's Minnesota Multiphasic Personality Inventory (MMPI) profile with that of imprisoned felons in general and with patients in sex-offender programs.
13. Complete a penile plethysmography evaluation.
14. Conduct a polygraph or voice-stress analysis regarding prior sexual offenses and current matters in dispute.
15. Make a determination of how long the deviant sexual behavior has been occurring in this person's life.
16. Record relevant clinical observations.
17. Compose a detailed treatment plan.

sions. He had been accused of sexually abusing a babysitter. Throughout the evaluation, this man continued to reiterate his innocence. His clinical evaluation consisted of several interviews, administration of an array of psychological tests including the Minnesota Multiphasic Personality Inventory (MMPI), the Rorschach, Cornell Medical Index, Rotter Incomplete Sentence Blank, the Sone Sexual History Questionnaire, and a penile plethysmograph assessment (McGovern & Jensen, 1985). During this assessment, the man continued to deny his involvement with the victim. Eventually, he pleaded guilty to a lesser charge of sexual abuse. During the dispositional planning interview, this man was asked why he had not been more direct and honest during the evaluation. He said, "Why should I tell the truth? I was trying to beat the system. What did I have to lose? I knew I was wrong."

Obviously this man, like many other sexual abusers, was trying to manipulate the system. In some states, the legal consequences are so severe that an individual convicted of sexual abuse charges will spend more time in prison than will an individual who has been convicted of aggravated assault with intent to kill or even one who has been convicted of murder. In addition, the sexual offender knows he often faces greater hardships than do other inmates in a prison environment. Prison inmates often verbally harass, physically abuse, sexually intimidate, and/or assault known sexual offenders (Groth, 1979). Thus, it is to be expected that sex offenders will be less likely to give reliable and valid self-report data. Knowing this about the abuser, we have developed specialized methods to be used both by the mental health care providers and by officers of the court that are designed to obtain reliable information. These methods are set forth in detail later in this chapter.

Unfortunately, even when conducting an interview for a sentencing report, many offenders still say they do not believe that they need treatment. They will tell their evaluator, or even their psychologist or psychiatrist, that they have been cured. Mental health professionals can be manipulated into believing that their client's sincerity and motivation can be a measure of therapeutic success. Even if this is an honest representation of the sex offender's feelings, without evidence of change in the man's deviant arousal pattern or behavior, there is a high probability of recidivism.

Because many sexual abusers minimize their deviant behavior, thorough clinical assessments can utilize the guidelines in Table 12.1 in conjunction with the *P & M Rating Scale: Risk Assessment For Sexual Abusers of Children* found in the Appendix. In Vancouver, Washington, the Prosecuting Attorney's office suggests mental health practitioners use the Evaluation Guidelines as well as this rating scale and a check on how closely the offender's story matches the facts. Sexual abusers who obtain high scores on the P & M Rating Scale are usually inappropriate candidates for outpatient therapy and most often are sent to a residential-care facility, such as a state hospital, or to prison (Saylor, 1984). On the other hand, individuals with low scores are usually adequate candidates for outpatient therapy programs that could be one condition of a strict probationary sentence. Each of the 17 guidelines is discussed in more detail in the following.

REVIEW POLICE AND SOCIAL SERVICE REPORTS (GUIDELINE 1)

The mental health professional assessing the alleged offender must review all available police, social service, and other reports of the offense and be aware of the victim's claims about what occurred (*Guideline 1*). Failing to comply with this seemingly basic requirement may cast doubt on any recommendations made by the treatment professional, as was the case with the clinician who examined Mr. SA, a schoolteacher accused of molesting children at the school where he was employed. The clinician met with SA for 1 hour in his office after the man's arrest, but before the police reports had been written. Unbeknownst to him, investigators had learned that SA had engaged in sexual contacts with virtually every minor in his classroom, had molested children from prior classes, had a history of involvement in bestiality, read child pornography, and frequently masturbated to thoughts about the children in his classroom after they had left for the day. While en route to the police station after his arrest, Mr. SA was observed removing a number of papers from his pants pocket and placing them into his jacket. The police reports indicated that these papers were, in fact, hardcore pornographic photographs depicting children engaging in various types of sexual activity with adults. On these photographs SA had written a number of names that corresponded with the names of students and other teachers at his school, which SA used to feed his sexually deviant fantasies. SA told the police that he used these photographs to fantasize while he was masturbating.

Without having seen this information, the clinician, who had been asked by SA's attorney to prepare an evaluation for the court, reported:

> I believe that SA is a good candidate for outpatient treatment. He is not dangerous now to be at large. SA recognizes his difficulties and is agreeable to various treatment suggestions. An inpatient treatment program is not, in my opinion, appropriate for SA. He has a good relationship with his wife, good employment history, and restriction of victims to a classroom setting all indicate that he is at no risk to re-offend. Following successful outpatient treatment, he will pose no danger regardless of environment, though of course he will undoubtedly not teach young children again.

A subsequent treatment professional who evaluated SA after reviewing the police reports and conducting a thorough background and psychological analysis revealed that SA had been preoccupied with sexual issues over an extended period of time, and this evaluator came to quite a different conclusion about the risk this man posed to the community:

> His interest in sexual matters included engaging a variety of animals in sexual behaviors. His behavior is chronic in that he engaged in deviant sexual acts daily. He could be considered predatory in that he selected children on the basis of their responses to him and manipulated their environment in order to gain more frequent access to them. He utilized his position as an authority and parental figure to control the children as well. He identified approximately 25 females he has fondled in the 3 years before his arrest. He has engaged in bestiality throughout his life, and fantasized and reinforced this deviant behavior through regular masturbatory activity. SA has utilized pornography involving a variety of inappropriate sexual themes, including children, over an extensive period of time.

> The sexual molestation of his students over a 3-year period indicates he is a compulsive pedophile. Test data support our belief that he lacks insight into his offending behavior and minimizes his involvement in these offenses. He has a marked unwillingness to be open about himself and we suspect there is more information regarding his deviant sexual activities than he is currently willing to admit. We consider him to be a sexual psychopath who is dangerous to be at large.

The first evaluation is an extreme but not uncommon example of work by a mental health professional, uneducated about the true extent of his client's problems, assuming the role of an advocate for the offender. This clinician's recommendations were disregarded by the sentencing court after it reviewed the latter evaluation, which presented a more thorough review of the man's true situation.

INTERVIEWING VICTIMS AND WITNESSES (GUIDELINE 2)

In many cases, it would be appropriate for the mental health professional to interview the victims and witnesses. This may be especially necessary when the investigatory reports that have been provided are vague and poorly constructed. Information obtained during the interview can help the evaluator in comparing the victim's version of the offense with that of the perpetrator. Comparisons regarding the degree of minimization and denial can then be made that help predict the potential to reoffend. During these interviews, the clinician can also seek to understand what effect the sexual abuse had on the victim, his or her feelings regarding the offender, and consider the form of restitution the abuser should make to help the victim heal.

In some cases, the evaluator will not be able to meet the victim. Some families move out of state or are unwilling to allow their child to go through another interview. It is believed that multiple interviews can have a damaging effect on the abused child. In fact, insensitive and repetitious interviews are reported as detrimental by victims when they seek therapy as adults. However, if the interview can be accompanied by reassurance to the child that what happened was not the child's fault, or even by an apology from the offender, healing might be facilitated. If the victim is not available for an interview, then the mental health care provider may want to contact the physician, social worker, school counselor, law enforcement officer, or whoever is currently working with the child. These professionals can provide valuable insights regarding the credibility of the victim's statements, emotional adjustment since the abuse was disclosed, and overall psychological characteristics, all of which may be important to the sentencing judge. There are new laws requiring a victim-impact statement to be presented at sentencing, so some idea of the child's current well-being will be available.

TREATMENT HISTORY (GUIDELINE 3)

Numerous studies have concluded that mental disorders frequently play a role in the commission of sexual offenses. Persons with psychotic, sociopathic, or other personality disorders are seen to be at higher risk for reoffense than so-called normal individuals, because they may have weak impulse control and may engage in inappropriate behavior in exchange for the most fleeting gratification, without regard for the consequences. A review of the person's medical, psychiatric, and treatment history, together with an examination of the documentation of this history, can provide the evaluator with valuable information.

Until recently many child molesters and incest offenders were not formally prosecuted by law enforcement personnel. Unfortunately, many offenses were not reported, and even when they were, legal difficulties with evidence made them difficult cases for the criminal justice system to deal with (see, for example, *Attorney General's Task Force on Family Violence Report,* 1984). Many sexual abusers were never identified as offenders by the legal authorities even when apprehended. In numerous cases, they were perceived as unstable individuals with serious emotional and family problems, but were not classified as "criminals." Instead, they were referred to mental health care clinics. The issue of criminal responsibility was never addressed. For years, they may have continued their abusive behavior but avoided further confrontations with the legal authorities. During their current arrest, many will pretend to be "first-time offenders." A conscientious mental health professional will attempt, in his or her examination, to discover and include in the written report whether the individual being evaluated has committed, been accused of, or undergone treatment for an alleged sexual offense in the past.

In some cases, the sexual abuser has been evaluated by another health care provider or has a substantial history of past mental health care problems. The sexual abuser may not want to share this information with the clinician who is completing the evaluation. Release-of-information forms should be obtained at the initial meeting with the offender. Refusal to grant permission to share information must be viewed with skepticism and concern and reported in the evaluation.

MILITARY, VOCATIONAL, AND EDUCATIONAL HISTORY (GUIDELINE 4)

A thorough evaluation of a sex offender's lifestyle will include a review of the individual's military, vocational, and educational history. This information can provide important insights into the individual's ability to satisfy long-term commitments. In many cases, the clinician is attempting to determine whether or not an offender presents an acceptable risk for outpatient treatment, which may encompass several years of regular therapy sessions. His history of completing other lengthy obligations provides a gauge for assessing his ability to complete treatment. An individual who graduated from high school, has been honorably discharged from the military, and who has a steady vocational history is usually a more reliable outpatient treatment candidate than is a sexual abuser who dropped out of school in the ninth grade, could not complete his military obligation satisfactorily because of disciplinary violations, and who has had an unstable work history. A person's prior ability or inability to complete a series of long-term tasks may serve as a predictive indicator of future behavior. The individual who has failed almost every major endeavor he has undertaken may be less likely to complete a treatment program. Conversely, sexual abusers who have been able to complete a series of tasks may prove to be dedicated treatment candidates.

THE ROLE OF CHEMICAL DEPENDENCY (GUIDELINE 5)

The evaluating mental health care professional needs to identify what part chemical dependency plays in the commission of these offenses and to what extent this factor is still in operation in the abuser's life. Unfortunately, some abusers use chemical dependency as a way to excuse their sexual deficits, whereas others minimize the effect of the chemical dependency upon their behavior. In many cases, self-report statements are unreliable indicators of the levels of drug and/or alcohol abuse. Specific details regarding the type and frequency of these abusive-substance-related patterns (i.e., how many beers, ounces of alcohol, pills, or joints were consumed) should be gathered and made part of the written report. As in addressing the individual's sexual history, and particularly the details of the offense(s), self-report of chemical usage may not be adequate. Minimization should be anticipated. These questions should be asked of both the offender and those who know him best, including the alleged victim(s). If there is a question regarding current chemical usage, the offender should be required to submit to urine or blood testing. Some studies reveal that at least 50% of all sexual offenders (primarily rapists) use alcohol prior to the commission of their offenses. Although there is no evidence proving that alcohol and/or drugs are the major cause for the commission of sexual offenses, in many cases they play an important role in allowing the person to reduce inhibitions before engaging in irresponsible behaviors. Those who are chemically dependent and/or impaired should be referred to a chemical dependency program prior to beginning treatment for the sexually offensive behavior. This may need to be an inpatient facility, depending on the degree of dependency and impairment. Since chemical abuse is a significant factor in the offense cycle of certain offenders, this deficit needs to be identified and arrested so that it neither provides an impediment to specific treatment for sexual deviancy nor places the offender in a state of mind where he is more likely to reoffend.

PORNOGRAPHY (GUIDELINE 5)

Both the investigating officers and the mental health professional should evaluate what role pornography plays in the life of the offender. Child molesters often obtain sexual gratification not only from actual physical contact with children, but also from fantasy involving the use of pictures or other erotic and/or pornographic materials. Sex offenders may collect a library of sexually explicit materials consisting of photographs, magazines, motion pictures, videotapes, books, and slides to use for their own sexual gratification. Some will also use sexually explicit materials for lowering the inhibitions of children. These erotic materials can be used for sexually stimulating the victims and themselves, and for demonstrating the desired sexual acts before, during, and after sexual activity with children. Some sexual abusers have been known to obtain and collect photographs of the children they have been or are involved with on an ongoing basis. These photos may depict children fully clothed, in various states of undress, totally nude, and/or in various sexually explicit activities. These photos are rarely if ever disposed of. They are often kept upon the pedophile's person, as was the case with Mr. SA, discussed in the previous section. Sex offenders may use such photos as a means of reliving fantasies or actual encounters. In some extreme cases, they utilize the photos as keepsakes and as a means of gaining acceptance, status, trust, and psychological support by exchanging, trading, or selling them to other sex offenders.

Pedophiles have been known to cut pictures of children out of magazines, catalogs, and newspapers and then to use them as a means of provoking erotic fantasies. They may also collect books, magazines, newspapers, and other writings on the subject of sexual activities with children, maintaining them in order to justify their own feelings toward children, and to find countenance for their illicit behavior and desire. These materials are rarely destroyed, and an offender may go to great lengths to protect them, including the rental of safe-deposit boxes or the use of other storage facilities outside the immediate residence.

Some sex offenders may also maintain diaries of their sexual encounters with children. These accounts are used as a means of reliving the encounter when the offender has no children available to molest. Such diaries might consist of a notebook, scraps of paper, calendars, or a formal diary. One offender recently prosecuted in Vancouver, Washington, maintained a color-coded indexing system cataloging his activities with the nine children he was molesting at various times in the months prior to his arrest. Depending upon the resources available to the offender, these records may be contained on audiotape or computer entries in a home computer. It is now known that a group of highly organized child molesters have their own "bulletin board," using home computers to communicate with one another on a national basis. A thorough evaluation of an alleged sex offender will inquire into his or her habits regarding the collection of pornographic material, cut-out pictures of children, diaries, and computer activity. Steps must be taken to alter these habits and patterns to assure protection of children and lower recidivism. These materials must be confiscated from the offender as a prerequisite to treatment.

SOCIAL AND FAMILY HISTORY (GUIDELINE 6)

The comprehensive evaluation will also include a review of the suspect's social and family history, including consultation with any children, former spouses, and lovers. Intimate acquaintances from the past can be a valuable source of information about the individual's history—if they are willing to talk to the evaluator. Multiple partnerships where children were involved can be of help to the evaluator. Marriages or relationships may have ended because an individual was sexually abusing his own children, stepchildren, or other minors living in the community. There may also be undetected patterns of domestic violence, which could be an important factor in assessing the offender's current safety to be at large. Additional abusive behaviors, such as marital rape and physical or psychological abuse of the spouse or children, should be explored. In many cases, such maladaptive behaviors were not reported to a social or police agency and will not be uncovered without inquiry. A conscientious mental health professional, recognizing the shroud of secrecy that obscures so many cases of domestic violence and child sexual abuse, will inquire into these taboo topics that family members may discuss only reluctantly, if at all.

In some cases, the sexual abuser will blame his spouse's "frigidity" and/or promiscuity as the major reason for his inappropriate sexual behavior with children. From his point of view, her continuous sexual rejections and/or infidelities encouraged his clandestine sexual relationships. Many of these cases are actually battering relationships in which the man is unreasonably jealous, fears abandonment, and rationalizes his own abusive behavior. A number of these abusers will become intoxicated, verbally abusive, and physically assaultive. Other offenders engage in sadomasochistic activities with their families. Obviously, information on these abusive behaviors needs to be integrated into the comprehensive evaluation as another measure of dangerousness. All too often, some evaluators devalue the offender's abusive behavior within his family as less dangerous than violence toward others. Obviously, this is inappropriate.

FAMILY HISTORY (GUIDELINE 7)

In many cases, as children, these abusive offenders were themselves severely victimized by adults. Studies of incarcerated sex offenders, those deemed by a court as too dangerous to be in the community, suggest that more than half of the offenders were themselves sexually abused as children (Freeman-Longo, 1985). With this in mind, the clinician needs to carefully examine the type and frequency of past victimization. There are major differences between incidents of sexual abuse. For example, in some cases, the abuse consisted of an older male exposing himself or encouraging his younger brother to touch his penis on two or three occasions. The traumatizing effects, if any, of such behavior may be short-lived and minimal. In other situations, the child may have been raised by an abusive, alcoholic stepfather who forced his stepchildren into acts of fellatio and anal sex. If the children objected to these activities, such men reportedly would then torture the children's favorite pet and/or beat their mother. These dehumanizing experiences can be extremely demoralizing and cause long-term psychological scars. A review of the offender's family history, including a detailed exploration of any physical or sexual abuse, can be of assistance in judging both amenability to treatment and the risk of allowing the person to remain in the community.

CRIMINAL AND SEXUAL OFFENSE HISTORY (GUIDELINES 8 AND 9)

A prior criminal record for sex crimes may be one of the best predictors of future criminal sexual behavior. With this in mind, the evaluator should obtain a copy of the criminal justice records to help determine an offender's prior criminal history. The chronic recidivists generally begin their deviant sexual behavior at an early age and may avoid detection for years. Data from the Sex Offender Treatment Program at the Oregon State Hospital shows that—beginning their history of sexual offenses in adolescence or even earlier—many sex offenders had committed sexual crimes for 15 years or longer before their first arrest and conviction (Freeman-Longo, 1985). In addition to checking official records, therefore, the patient himself, as well as his family, should be questioned about prior juvenile and adult arrests, as well as about "undetected" crimes.

The possibility that the individual may have participated in a "diversion" or "deferred prosecution" program should also be examined. In some parts of the country, certain sexual abusers, particularly exhibitionists and incest offenders, have escaped criminal prosecution by agreeing to enter into a treatment program as part of so-called diversion or deferred prosecution. There is no national or intrastate method of recordkeeping for such prosecution-avoidance programs. That means an individual could molest a child in one county and participate in a treatment program that does not involve criminal conviction, then move to the adjoining county or state and reoffend without fear that his prior acts would be discovered through the criminal justice system. Although it often seems to be a more humane method of dealing with a "mental health problem," these programs erase an offender's record of deviant sexual behavior, which is an important variable in designing a current disposition. A thorough evaluation will inquire into the possibility that the offender may have been assigned to such a program. However, patients will often minimize their past involvement and not discuss prior convictions. This information needs to be in the report to the sentencing judge.

Obviously, a long history of arrests and convictions demonstrates that a specific offender has previously engaged in similar behaviors. In some cases, a careful review will reveal an escalation in the types of sexual deviancy and the frequency with which these behaviors occur. For example, in one case a man was first detained for public indecency. The police told him the charges would be dropped if he promised to leave the community. Years later, this man was again arrested for a similar incident in a conservative east coast town. After spending several days in jail and completing a superficial clinical assessment, he was referred to a clinician for outpatient therapy. These weekly sessions lasted for 3 weeks. Several years later, he was again arrested. This time he was accused of sexually abusing his nieces on numerous occasions. A brief jail sentence and enrollment into a structured therapy program was required by the court. Several years later, this man was again arrested for disruptive sexual behavior. He was sexually abusing children at his local church where he taught Sunday school. Obviously, an outpatient program is inappropriate for this offender.

When sexual abusers provide a long history of past criminal sexual behavior, their clinical assets and deficits must be cautiously reviewed. In some of these cases, the best form of clinical intervention is residential confinement and intensive treatment. Unfortunately, some of these abusers will continue to be a significant risk to engage in antisocial activities and may never be safe if released back into the community.

RESPONSIBILITY (GUIDELINE 10)

The evaluator should identify to what extent the offender accepts responsibility for his offenses, and what degree of guilt, remorse, or moral accountability he is experiencing. Since most sex offenders are adept at manipulation and denial, the evaluating professional should look not only at the offender's words, but at his actions as well. Sex offenders diagnosed as psychopathic, or who have other personality disorders, may exhibit little remorse or guilt over their offenses and make no pretext of accepting responsibility for their actions. Others will make a grand show of remorse during the clinical interview and in front of authority figures such as the judge, their clergyman, or the district attorney; but, given the opportunity, they may continue to psychologically, if not sexually, abuse their victim and/or family. Thus, a thorough assessment requires consultation with appropriate victims, family members, and others with access to the offender and knowledge of his conduct outside of clinical and courtroom settings. A note of caution: The bias of the individual must be factored into any information obtained from a family member. Cases of intrafamily sexual abuse are especially known for divided loyalties and sometimes blind, unreasoning alliance to the offender—even when the perpetrator has admitted his or her guilt. Sometimes this is caused by fear that there is no way to control the abuser from continuing to hurt them all.

PSYCHOLOGICAL TESTING (GUIDELINES 11 AND 12)

In order to obtain an accurate picture of an abuser's assets and deficits, a thorough and comprehensive psychological evaluation should be obtained. In our opinion, superficial interviews are often plagued with error. During a psychological evaluation, a thorough analysis should include: (1) reviewing pertinent records, (2) obtaining a thorough social history, (3) administering an array of psychological tests and questionnaires, and (4) physiological examination on the penile plethysmograph. By carefully examining the abuser's past records and comments made during the clinical interviews, as well as his overall responses during the psychological testing and plethysmograph evaluation, the clinician can then determine the extent and frequency of psychological deficits and assets. Obviously, the severely and habitually impaired offender who has had extensive previous therapy may not profit from another therapeutic program. On the other hand, individuals with few psychological deficits who are extremely motivated to change may be adequate candidates for outpatient therapy.

The Cornell Medical Index

After reviewing the responses on this questionnaire, the clinician will have information to help decide if obtaining past medical records can be useful. The information obtained from state hospitals, private clinics, and/or medical facilities may provide the clinician with other valuable reports regarding the psychological assets/deficits of the sexual abuser. In one case, a sexual offender had been misdiagnosed for years as schizophrenic. Psychiatric, psychological, and neurological examinations eventually revealed the existence of brain damage and a seizure disorder. In this case, the sexual abuser was placed on a regimen of medications to reduce his seizures and aggressive tendencies. In another case, a sexual abuser had complained about chronic headaches and began to act inappropriately during a group therapy meeting. Over a short period of time, he began to act in an immature and adolescent fashion. During a neurological examination, an inoperable brain tumor was found. Six months later, this man died. These cases are unusual and care should be taken, however, not to utilize neurological symptoms as an excuse for most offenders' behavior.

In addition, while reviewing an individual's medical history, questions may arise regarding the efficacy of pharmaceutical agents such as Depo-Provera. This synthetic hormone has been utilized to extinguish obsessional thoughts and impulsive deviant sexual behaviors. Clinicians have demonstrated that some sexual abusers can absorb reasonable levels of this prescribed medication in order to control their aberrant sexual activities. Although there are opponents to this pharmacological therapy, others report that the combination of Depo-Provera and a multifaceted treatment program can be used successfully to reduce the frequency and intensity of aberrant sexual fantasies, impulses, and behaviors. Before this medication can be utilized, the clinician must thoroughly review an individual's medical history and carefully evaluate the short- and long-term side effects of this pharmaceutical approach.

Minnesota Multiphasic Personality Inventory (MMPI)

This multi-item true-and-false questionnaire was developed to identify an array of psychological assets and deficits. Since its initial use, over 5000 research studies have been conducted on this instrument. After the sexual abuser has completed this self-report questionnaire, the responses can be either scored by hand or through a computerized scoring system. The latter usually provides a profile analysis that discusses the individual's psychological strengths and deficits. This provides valuable information regarding the sexual abuser's test-taking response set. Validity scales indicate whether or not the abuser is purposely portraying himself in an overly positive and/or negative fashion. These test results also demonstrate whether or not the abuser has endorsed an overabundance of unusual or bizarre items. It can provide valuable information regarding the presence of a characterological disorder, depression, anxiety, cognitive distortions, manic disorders, antisocial personality disorders, chronic impulsivity, sexual identity conflicts, and a host of other psychological characteristics.

Rorschach Test and Thematic Apperception Test

Two projective tests, the Thematic Apperception Test and the Rorschach, may provide additional information regarding the offender's psychological abilities. These tests can be used to identify distorted thinking, psychotic thought processes, levels of intellectual functioning, depression, anxiety, impulsivity, somatic concerns, and a preoccupation with sexual themes. In some cases, sex abusers may be able to camouflage their current psychological deficits during clinical interviews and while responding to the standardized tests. However, during the administration of these less structured tests, they may reveal a number of other psychological characteristics. Others are unable to handle the ambiguity of the task and become defensive, revealing little. Both styles are unusual.

During one assessment, a sexual abuser who had been arrested for child molesting portrayed himself as a healthy individual during the clinical interviews and while completing the Cornell Medical Index and the MMPI. However, while responding to the Thematic Apperception Test, he began to decompose and a number of unhealthy themes emerged. In addition, his responses to the Rorschach portrayed him as an impulsive individual who was extremely preoccupied with sexual objects and anatomical parts. Interestingly, after responding to the projective tests, this offender revealed that he repressed many of his original responses. In a later session he provided an even higher incidence of unique responses while identifying an array of female child, prepubescent, postpubescent, and adult female genitalia on the Rorschach cards.

Rotter Incomplete Sentence Blank

This sentence blank test consists of 48 open-ended items. On this test, each offender is asked to fill in each incomplete sentence with whatever words appear to be appropriate. While reviewing the sexual abuser's responses, a number of interesting patterns may emerge. In some cases, the offender is extremely defensive, unwilling to share his psychological concerns, and cannot respond to these ambiguous materials. In other cases, the abuser will openly portray his concerns, anxieties, and fears. By examining these items, the evaluator in most cases will gain more valuable information about the offender's inner concerns, thoughts, feelings, and emotions.

Sone Sexual History Questionnaire

Since the completion of Masters' and Johnson's initial research, a series of questionnaires have been developed by clinicians to assess an individual's basic understanding of human sexual behavior and to identify specific sexual dysfunctions and concerns. The Sone Sexual History Questionnaire is a 15-page questionnaire that asks germane questions regarding the individual's sexual development, history, sexual arousal patterns, fantasies, masturbatory behaviors, heterosexual and homosexual experiences, and a host of other pertinent topics. This questionnaire was designed specifically for sexual abusers. A section is provided that asks questions about how the sexual disorder began, what environmental cues are most sexually arousing, and other general questions regarding sexual behavior and arousal.

PHYSIOLOGICAL ASSESSMENT (GUIDELINE 13)

Although the information obtained from psychological tests, questionnaires, and self-report procedures provides the clinician with valuable information, the importance of obtaining a physiological measurement of aberrant and nonaberrant arousal patterns cannot be underestimated. The data obtained from the standardized psychological tests and questionnaires rely on a person's integrity, long-term and short-term memory, and the ability to read and write. While responding to an array of questionnaires, an offender can provide an unreliable description of his personality characteristics and sexual preferences. With this in mind, physiological assessment approaches appear to be another valuable way to obtain information regarding an individual's sexual arousal responses.

Because many abusers are mandated by court to obtain evaluations and treatment, they often minimize their problems and sexual arousal patterns in order to appear as healthy as possible. During their therapeutic contacts, they often proclaim high levels of self-control. They want to believe they will never offend again. Many sexual abusers are quite convincing with their verbal comments, but they may be both inaccurate and offer a gross misrepresentation of reality.

No thorough evaluation of a sexual abuser will be complete without a physiological assessment of the suspect's arousal patterns on the penile plethysmograph. Under the supervision of a competent technician, this instrument can assess the single best index of male sexual arousal, penile erection. As with the more conventional psychological tests, however, responses to physiological testing must also be judged with some caution. The instrument measures penile tumescence, a response that can be both knowingly and unknowingly suppressed or inhibited by fatigue, masturbation, anxiety, discomfort, nervousness, aging, drugs, and alcohol. In addition, not all individuals can become sexually aroused in a contrived environment. However, many subjects will become partially or highly aroused in response to various sexual materials presented to them during this evaluation. In these situations, this assessment approach provides the clinician with another sample of behavior.

The subject, who is comfortably seated in a private room, slips a strain gauge over his penis, which is then electronically connected to the plethysmograph. The suspect is then exposed to a variety of erotic stimuli, ranging from "normal" to "deviant," and involving males, females, adults, and children. Various themes are presented, including consenting interactions, forced sexual behavior, and exploitive variations such as child molesting. The stimuli may include slides, audiotapes, films, and videotapes. The instrument monitors the subject's arousal, or lack thereof, and produces a graphic or digital readout. The resulting data demonstrate those themes that the subject does and does not find arousing. On occasion, the data indicates virtually no arousal to any stimuli. This could occur because the suspect was physically dysfunctional, anxious over the clinical context of the examination, or because he masturbated shortly before undergoing the examination in an effort to distort the results. When little or no arousal is detected, another examination under controlled conditions is indicated before the results can be considered conclusive.

What do the results of this examination mean to the criminal justice system? Obviously, the presence of high levels of arousal to "deviant" stimuli in a laboratory setting does not mean that the individual will expose himself, molest children, rape, or act out in other sexually inappropriate ways. However, high levels of arousal to deviant sexual stimuli coupled with lower arousal to nondeviant themes is highly indicative that the subject is more sexually attracted to deviant sex than to normal sex. This can be helpful if the man is continuing to deny any abusive behavior and does indicate a higher risk to reoffend because of the arousal pattern. It also is a useful means to assess treatment efficacy.

When an offender is provided with a copy of his own actual arousal patterns, he is often more willing to engage in a behavioral treatment program designed to modify his current aberrant thoughts and activities. In most cases, this is the first time that anyone has provided this individual with objective data regarding his normal and deviant arousal patterns. By reviewing the chart recordings, the offender can see which materials actually caused highest levels of arousal, and begin to understand the correlation between deviant arousal and inappropriate sexual behavior. Although it may be extremely difficult to convince an offender that he should obtain treatment because of his responses to a true-and-false questionnaire and inkblot test, a sexual offender certainly understands the need for treatment if he has become highly aroused by themes describing sexual behavior with children and adolescents and/or aggressive, sadistic behavior with adults.

Any assessment conducted without a physiological evaluation is incomplete, since the therapist must rely upon observations or self-report of the suspect regarding his arousal. Accurate self-reporting, when the suspect knows the therapist is going to report to the judge and the district attorney, may not occur. The instrument, therefore, provides the therapist with a powerful tool for confronting an individual who may be denying or minimizing his problem.

POLYGRAPH (GUIDELINE 14)

In those jurisdictions where probation and community-based treatment for certain sex offenders are available, it is customary that a prerequisite for a probationary sentence be the individual's acknowledgment of responsibility for his or her actions. That task may not be an easy one for the attorney or therapist attempting to work with a person who fears going to prison, losing his spouse, his family, his church, and his friends if he admits that he has molested a child. Yet that admission is often the key to a treatment alternative that may keep him out of prison. Sometimes the polygraph can be a useful tool in arriving at the truth.

In contrast to the penile plethysmograph, which traces arousal patterns, the polygraph instrument can record the emotion of fear: fear of being caught in a lie, or fear of detection. The polygraph records an individual's physiological responses to carefully prepared questions. It operates under the theory that when the subject answers the polygrapher's relevant question with a lie, the lie creates the fear of detection, which stimulates a variety of physiological and psychological responses within the subject's body. Those include changes in respiration, blood pressure, pulse rate, and galvanic skin response. Changes in these responses are recorded on moving chart paper by the instrument. The examiner then numerically evaluates these changes and renders an opinion that the subject is either telling the truth or being deceptive about the issue. In some cases no opinion can be rendered; thus the test results will be inconclusive. It has been our experience that a polygrapher trained to work in conjunction with the evaluating therapist can be very helpful in overcoming stubborn denial in some offenders. Lie-detection techniques may not be very helpful, however, with psychopaths and others with reduced levels of autonomic response. Men who do not believe sexual acts with children are either bad or harmful to the child may also not be detected by the polygraph examination.

ORGANIZING THE DATA

Once all available information on the offender, his offense, and his victims has been accumulated, a risk assessment using the P & M Rating Scale (see Appendix) can be undertaken. The validity of this assessment will obviously be contingent upon the thoroughness and accuracy of the compiled data. Most of the questions can be answered using the information collected from the evaluation guidelines presented. This rating scale is only intended to help organize and quantify the data so that decisions can be made. It should not be considered a psychological test.

On the P & M Rating Scale, items are assigned a numerical value from 0 through 5. Experience as well as a review of the available literature were used to choose those items that make up the scale. It identifies those activities, behaviors, and factors that suggest that an individual is more or less likely to succeed in an outpatient, community-based setting. Viewing the scale as a whole, the more the individual offender falls into categories 0, 1, and 2, the more likely he is to be successful in outpatient treatment. Generally, the more ratings in categories 3, 4 and 5, the more risk he is to be at large. This scale is meant to assist professionals in identifying various factors that should be taken into consideration in the risk-assessment phase. We have identified four major areas of importance: criminal history, the facts of the present offense, personal data about the offender, and personal data about the victim. Within these four groups are 45 subcategories touching on a wide range of variables. If each of these categories is accurately investigated and scored on the P & M Rating Scale, the clinician or other professional evaluating the offender can assume with confidence that a thorough assessment of the offender has taken place.

SUMMARY

We have discussed aspects of thorough clinical evaluations, court investigations, police interrogations, and presentence evaluations in this chapter. It is recommended that mental health care providers and agents of the court cooperate, and together work toward resolution of this complex social problem. As more reported cases of sexual abuse are reviewed by the court, there will be an even greater demand for clinical evaluations, treatment alternatives, and dispositional plans. Both the court and the community are asking mental health care providers to furnish them with guidance and assistance regarding recidivism and related concerns. Communities need sensible guidelines that will allow them to make the often difficult decisions regarding prediction of recidivism, restitution, amenability to change, and potential for family reunification.

REFERENCES

American Psychiatric Association. (1987). Diagnostic and statistical manual of mental disorders (3rd ed., rev.). Washington, DC: Author.

Attorney General's Task Force on Family Violence. (1984). Washington, DC: U.S. Department of Justice.

Freeman-Longo, R. (1985, October 23). Paper presented at sexual assault conference. Gonzaga University. October 23, 1985. Co-sponsored by Forensic Mental Health Associates and Alternatives to Sexual Abuse.

Freeman-Longo, R., & Wall, R. V., (1986, March). Changing a lifetime of sexual crime. *Psychology Today,* p. 58.

Groth, N. (1979). *Men who rape.* New York: Plenum.

McGovern, K. (1984). *The clinical assessment of sexual offenders.* Available from ASA, P.O. Box 25537, Portland, OR 97225.

McGovern, K. (in press). The assessment of sexual offenders. In Maletzky (Ed.), *The assessment and treatment of sexual abusers,* New York: Grune & Stratton.

McGovern, K., & Jensen, S. (1985). Behavioral group treatment methods for sexual disorders and dysfunctions. In Upper & Ross (Eds.), *Handbook of behavioral group therapy* (pp. 421–442).

Saylor, M. (1984). Sex offender treatment program: Treatment success and recidivism rates between 1967 and 1982. Unpublished manuscript, Western State Hospital, Sexual Psychopathy Program, Ft. Steilacoom, WA.

Whitcomb, D., Shapiro, E. R., & Stellwegen, L. D. (1985). *When the child is a victim.* Washington, DC: U.S. Department of Justice.

Appendix

THE P & M RATING SCALE: RISK ASSESSMENT FOR SEXUAL ABUSERS OF CHILDREN AND ADULTS
(Circle the appropriate number)

I. CRIMINAL HISTORY

    1. Prior sex offenses (convictions):

        (0) none

        (5) one or more

    2. Allegation or arrest for sexual offense without conviction:

        (0) none

        (1) one

        (2) two

        (3) three

        (4) four

        (5) five or more

    3. Total number of victims of sexual offenses that did not result in conviction:

        (0) none

        (1) one

        (2) two to five

        (3) six to ten

        (4) more than ten

        (5) more than twenty

    4. Years since deviant sexual fantasies or behaviors began:

        (0) less than one month

        (1) less than one year

    (2)   less than two years

    (3)   less than five years

    (4)   less than ten years

    (5)   more than ten years

5. Nonsexual criminal history (juvenile):

    (0)   no convictions

    (1)   misdemeanor convictions only

    (2)   one felony conviction

    (3)   two felony convictions

    (4)   three felony convictions

    (5)   four or more felony convictions

6. Nonsexual criminal history (adult):

    (0)   no convictions

    (1)   misdemeanor convictions only

    (2)   one felony conviction

    (3)   two felony convictions

    (4)   three felony convictions

    (5)   four or more felony convictions

7. Incarceration history:

    (0)   never incarcerated

    (1)   incarcerated in jail more than ten years ago

    (2)   incarcerated in jail within the last ten years

    (3)   incarcerated in prison more than ten years ago

    (4)   incarcerated in prison within the last ten years

    (5)   incarcerated in prison within the last five years

8. History of violence (not including present offense):

    (0)   no history of violent or assaultive behavior

    (1)   threats of violence not carried out

    (2)   assaultive, but not during sexual offenses

    (3)   assaultive during sexual offenses

    (4)   previously incarcerated for violent act

    (5)   previously incarcerated for both violent and sexual acts

Score:_____

II. PRESENT OFFENSE

    9. Nature of offense:

        (1) one isolated incident or impulsive act

        (2) fewer than five isolated instances over five years

        (3) fewer than five planned or premeditated offenses

        (4) multiple planned or premediated offenses

        (5) part of an habitual pattern or central to the individual's life, as in a hobby or addiction (Carnes, *The Sexual Addiction—Pedophile, DSM-III*-R, APA, 1987)

    10. Type of illegal or deviant behavior:

        (1) verbal communication or indecent exposure

        (2) sexual fondling or rubbing

        (3) digital or genital penetration or oral sex

        (4) multiple victims during the same episode

        (5) victim(s) forced to perform or endure degrading acts not set out above

    11. Aggressive behavior:

        (0) no force or violence used in present offense

        (1) mild verbal coercive statements

        (2) aggressive verbal threats

        (3) force or violence used, but only to the point necessary to gain victim's submission

        (4) force or violence *beyond* that needed to overcome resistance or gain control: biting of victims; shaving or bathing victims; victim kidnapped; use of weapon; bondage; ritualistic behaviors

        (5) torture, mutilation, or injury to victim

    12. Offender's degree of accountability:

        (1) complete admission, consistent with victim's account

        (2) minor to moderate minimization, or accepts only partial responsibility

        (3) gross minimization, and uses alcohol, drugs, victim's education, sex education, discipline, religion, etc., as an excuse

        (4) total denial of acts

      (5)   required victim to testify in court in face of compelling evidence of guilt

13. Defendant's current grasp of the effect the offenses had on the victim:

      (0)   fully understands effect on victim

      (1)   moderate understanding

      (2)   minimal understanding

      (3)   uncaring and ambivalent

      (4)   hostility and rationalization observed

      (5)   projection and blames the victim for his behavior

14. Number of victims—present situation:

      (1)   one

      (2)   two

      (3)   three

      (4)   four

      (5)   five or more

Score: _____

III. OFFENDER—PERSONAL DATA

15. Number of marriages:

      (0)   zero

      (1)   one

      (2)   two

      (3)   three

      (4)   four

      (5)   five or more

16. Marital stability

      (0)   stable, intact marriage with supporting spouse

      (1)   minimal marital problems

      (2)   moderate marital problems

      (3)   major marital problems

      (4)   irreconcilable marital problems

      (5)   history of chronic domestic violence

17. Status of spouse or girlfriend:

    (0)   no spouse or girlfriend

    (1)   maintaining relations with defendant, acknowledges his guilt, willing to participate in his treatment, and supports the victim(s)

    (2)   maintaining relationship with defendant, acknowledges his guilt, but not willing to participate in his treatment though acknowledges the abuse

    (3)   maintaining relationship with defendant but denying his guilt and openly hostile to treatment plan

    (4)   maintaining relationship with defendant, denying his guilt, openly hostile to both treatment plan and victim(s)

    (5)   maintaining relationship with defendant, denying his guilt, encouraging him to leave treatment

18. Substance abuse:

    (0)   no use of alcohol or illegal drugs

    (1)   very infrequent use of alcohol or drugs

    (2)   situational or social drug or alcohol involvement

    (3)   alcohol and/or drug abuser currently in remission for at least one year

    (4)   alcohol or drug abuser in remission for less than one year

    (5)   chronic and untreated drug or alcohol abuse or addiction

19. Precipitating stress factors at time of offense

    (1)   major precipitating stress factors (e.g., loss of loved ones, loss of job, etc.)

    (3)   moderate precipitating stress factors (e.g., marital disturbance, financial difficulties, etc.)

    (5)   absence of identifiable extraordinary stress

20. Offender's social relationships:

    (0)   stable social relationships with numerous peer appropriate agemates

    (1)   stable social relationships with few peer appropriate agemates

    (2)   social relationships with both children and peer appropriate agemates

(3) prefers social relationships with children but able to function socially with agemates

(4) feels uncomfortable interacting with adults, seeks interactions with children

(5) avoids functioning socially with agemates and seeks friendships with children

21. Offender's mental health status:

(0) no apparent mental health care problems

(1) minimal mental health care problems

(2) moderate mental health care problems

(3) frequent mental health care problems

(4) frequent and rarely changeable health care problems

(5) chronic and untreatable health care problems

22. History of treatment for sexual deviancy (include all programs started, whether or not they were completed):

(0) no prior treatment

(1) one treatment program

(2) two treatment programs

(3) three treatment programs

(4) four treatment programs

(5) five or more treatment programs

23. History of treatment for other mental health concerns:

(0) no prior treatment

(1) one treatment program

(2) two treatment programs

(3) three treatment programs

(4) four treatment programs

(5) five or more treatment programs

24. Offender's present motivation for treatment:

(0) highly motivated

(1) moderately motivated

(2) minimal motivation

(3) ambivalent

(4)   manipulative—looking for "easiest way out"

(5)   does not desire treatment

25. Pornographic or violent literature:

(0)   no known history of using pornographic or violent literature

(1)   has read a few erotic magazines

(2)   uses or collects pornography on a regular basis

(3)   owns a large library of pornography and/or possesses sexual paraphernalia

(4)   creates and/or sells pornography

(5)   reads, collects, or views pornographic materials depicting people in scenes of torture, rape, death, or other forms of helplessness

26. Employment:

(0)   employed in steady fulltime job plus other appropriate activities, leaving little or no discretionary time

(1)   employed in steady fulltime job, but has discretionary time

(2)   retired but has time-consuming hobby or activities

(3)   retired and without time-consuming hobby or activities

(4)   has part-time or unsteady employment, or time-consuming hobby or activities but unemployed

(5)   Unemployed and without time-consuming hobby or activities

27. Relationship to victim:

(1)   parent, grandparent, or sibling

(2)   stepparent

(3)   friend, acquaintance, or other relative

(4)   occupied position of "special trust" (i.e., teacher, coach, religious leader, youth group leader, doctor, foster parent, daycare worker, etc.)

(5)   stranger

28. Abscondence history (circle highest number applicable)

(0)   none

(1)   continuously leaving home prior to age 12

(2)   continuously leaving home prior to age 18

(3)   AWOL from military or failures to appear in court

(4) Absconded from jail, juvenile institution, work release center, mental health hospital, or other similar facility or situation

(5) Absconded from prison

29. Personal and family background:

    (0) normal childhood

    (1) mild emotional, sexual, or physical abuse as child or adolescent

    (2) moderate emotional, sexual, or physical abuse as child or adolescent

    (3) severe emotional, sexual, or physical abuse as child or adolescent

    (4) multiple foster home placements as child or adolescent

    (5) institutional placement as child or adolescent

30. History of other deviant behavior/disorders (e.g., gender identity, conflict, cross-dressing, etc.)

    (0) none

    (3) one

    (5) more than one deviation

31. Chronological range of known deviant sexual behaviors:

    (1) less than one month

    (2) less than six months

    (3) less than one year

    (4) one to five years

    (5) more than five years

32. Frequency of known deviant sexual behavior:

    (1) first offense (verified by polygraph or other corroborative evidence)

    (2) occasional offenses at random times

    (3) approximately weekly offenses

    (4) daily offenses

    (5) multiple times daily

33. Offender's educational background:

    (0) college and/or high school graduate

    (1) GED or equivalent

(2) completed 3 or more years of high school but never gradu-
     ated

(3) dropped out before finishing 11th grade

(4) completed eighth grade

(5) dropped out—did not complete grammar school

34. Offender's military history (circle highest number applicable):

    (0) no military history or received honorable discharge

    (3) subject of disciplinary proceedings in military

    (4) left military before completing tour of duty on other than
         honorable basis

    (5) dishonorable discharge

35. Aberrant arousal patterns as tested on penile plethysmograph:

    (0) none

    (1) minimal

    (3) moderate

    (5) high

36. Normal arousal patterns as tested on penile plethysmograph:

    (0) high

    (1) moderate

    (3) low

    (5) none

37. Psychological test results—cognitive abilities:

    (0) normal

    (1) mild psychological deficit

    (3) moderate psychological deficit

    (5) severe psychological deficit

38. Psychological test results—behavioral:

    (0) normal

    (1) mild psychological deficit

    (3) moderate psychological deficit

    (5) severe psychological deficit

39. Psychological test results—characterological:

    (0) normal

      (1)   mild psychological deficit

      (3)   moderate psychological deficit

      (5)   severe psychological deficit

40. Psychological test results—impulsivity:

      (0)   none apparent

      (1)   mild psychological deficit

      (3)   moderate psychological deficit

      (5)   severe psychological deficit

41. Associated paraphilia (other types of deviant behavior):

      (0)   none

      (1)   voyeurism or exposure

      (2)   public masturbation

      (3)   incest

      (4)   child molesting outside the domestic situation

      (5)   rape, bestiality, necrophilia

Score: _____

IV. VICTIM—PERSONAL DATA

42. Physical and psychosocial trauma to victim (circle highest number):

      (1)   minimal negative effects of victimization

      (2)   moderate effect—victim coping adequately

      (3)   victim physically injured or suffering serious psychological problems

      (4)   victim required hospitalization for physical or mental trauma

      (5)   pregnancy, venereal disease, or life-altering negative effect from victimization

43. Victim's attitude toward consequences (circle highest number):

      (1)   undecided

      (2)   probation, outpatient treatment, local jail

      (3)   inpatient treatment

      (4)   prison

      (5)   gross retribution desired

44. Nonoffending spouse's or victim's parents' attitude toward consequences:

(1) undecided

(2) probation, outpatient treatment, local jail

(3) inpatient treatment

(4) prison

(5) gross retribution

45. Age of victim:

(1) eighteen or over

(2) twelve to seventeen

(3) seven to eleven

(4) four to six

(5) under four

Score:_____

PART IV
Treatment Approaches

13

Play Therapy with Children Who Have Experienced Sexual Assault

Lenore E. A. Walker
Mary Ann Bolkovatz

The use of play therapy to help young children heal from the effects of sexual abuse has been modeled after its traditional use as described in Schaefer (1976) and adapted for use with victims (Conte & Berliner, 1981, and Chapter 5 of this volume; Sgroi, 1982). Play is considered the child's natural medium for rehearsing new developmental skills, mastering them, and for working through conflicts. For many children under the age of 10, verbal psychotherapy, which is dependent upon abstract symbolic thinking with language, is not a very useful way of learning new emotional responses and behavioral skills. Actually, even adults sometimes need to use elements of play to resolve emotional conflicts. Psychodrama and other Gestält therapy techniques have much similarity to play therapy. The use of play materials to either simulate presentation of, focus on, or work through certain problems has been used successfully by the authors to help heal sexually abused children.

DEVELOPMENT OF PLAY THERAPY

There are a number of different types of play therapy that appear in the literature (cf. Schaefer, 1976, for a more complete description). Child analysts such as Anna Freud (1946) and Melanie Klein (1949) were early advocates of its use with emotionally disturbed children. Anna Freud viewed the theoretical approach to play therapy as different from adult analysis in that children need a preparatory period for transference between the child and the therapist to develop. The therapist must make the therapy interesting to the child, demonstrate its usefulness in practical terms, and become the child's ally or protector for that transference relationship to facilitate healing. She also discussed the opportunity for education and remediation because of children's simultaneous developmental growth during the therapy process. There have been numerous other variations on analytic models, each discussing a particular aspect, such as more or less control over the selection of play materials used, or how much contact to have with parents. Garfield (1974) provides a brief, comprehensive review. Klein suggests using more interpretation that makes use of traditional analytical symbolism to replay the Oedipal conflict, a technique that seems to have less usefulness with sexually abused children who have experienced real—not fantasized—sexual aggression.

As the field of psychotherapy expanded beyond psychoanalysis, a variety of play therapy techniques developed. The common theme in all describes the usefulness of the child–therapist relationship, even though suggestions of how to create such a relationship differ according to the therapist's philosophy and theoretical perspective. Moustakas (1973) stated that three important attitudes must be conveyed to the child. They are faith in the child, acceptance, and respect. His existential approach utilizes encouragement of the child's creative expression as an important technique to stimulate positive growth. Cognitive development of the child can also be stimulated through the use of play. Jean Piaget and other cognitive-developmental psychologists believed that make-believe play is an intrinsic form of growth that can help organize the child's experience and promote further development (Pulaski, in Schaefer, 1976). The repetition allows for the expansion of cognitive bands using Piagetian assimilation and accommodation concepts.

Most play therapy described in the literature has been with children exhibiting serious emotional disturbance or problems that are irritating to parents or school authorities. It is a treatment usually expected to last a long time, over several years. Axline (1964) has a particularly detailed description of its use with one particular child. The only use of play therapy dealing with specific trauma is reported by Solomon (1940, cited in Garfield, 1974, p. 362). He suggests that the length of play therapy treatment could be shortened if the therapist sets up situations based on knowledge of the specific trauma. We have found that this is not appropriate when working with repeatedly sexually abused children, either from multiple abusers or incest, because working through the long-term trauma effects, especially betrayal of trust and love in a relationship, simply takes more time. However, it may be a useful variation for those who have experienced a single assault from a stranger.

More recently, MacFarlane and Waterman (1986) suggest the use of play therapy with groups of young sexually abused children, partly to facilitate the removal of stigma by exposure to others who have similar trauma experience. It does not permit the same significant therapeutic relationship with an adult as does individual therapy. Some emphasize specific types of materials to use with children. Naitove (in Sgroi, 1982) advocates the use of art therapy as a way of addressing the needs of the sexually abused child to express feelings, deal with issues symbolically, and accept and integrate the trauma, thus allowing for self-acceptance. Though she cautions that art therapy should only be used by those who are specially trained, we have found it to be useful when integrated into other play activities, even without an art therapist on our staff. Others suggest the use of a sandbox to work through different issues, including breaches in body integrity.

PHILOSOPHY AND GOALS OF PLAY THERAPY WITH THE SEXUALLY ABUSED CHILD

The major goal of play therapy in this context is to reduce the present and future negative psychological impact on the child arising from the trauma of sexual abuse. It does so by providing a place to heal from the shock of the abuse and the emotional aftermath of discovery. Emotional space is provided for the repetitive expression of the experience needed by trauma victims. Feelings, especially anger, can be freely expressed in a safe place. It provides a cognitive structure on which to relearn about one's own power and control as well as to deal with the memory of feelings without needing to use words. This provides for the development of new behavioral skills that can be rehearsed in the safety of a play situation. It is assumed that mastery over current symptoms as well as recognition of one's growing competence will prevent the developmental delays often seen in abused children and restore their emotional readiness for future growth. In addition to the new skills learned, an intense and close relationship with the play therapist is seen as one way to regain trust in loving adults who will not betray intimate feelings.

Our therapy theory presented here emphasizes repairing the disruption of personal power and loss of body integrity experienced by sexually abused children. Analysis of the child–therapist relationship in terms of the child's need to control her or his own life can provide the reempowerment needed to heal. It integrates analytic, relationship, cognitive-behavioral, and developmental theories with the feminist analysis of power and oppression in order to understand the dynamics expressed by the child to the therapist. The child is encouraged to utilize more power and control within the therapy session than she or he would ever be permitted in real-life situations. Development of mastery and competence over feelings, cognition, and behavior is shaped by social-learning theory. The need for the child to learn separation and individuation from parental figures is seen as less important than the reestablishment of the capacity to develop a close relationship with an adult who can protect the child. Repairing parent/child relationships may also be facilitated, especially in incest cases.

For children seen at the Walker & Associates offices, the modeling of a feminist consciousness is an additional benefit. The children learn to separate their own psychological issues from the reality of living in an environment that does not really protect children and that discriminates against women. Learning about what it means to be part of an oppressed class, through play and not rhetoric, helps children to move beyond being a victim and toward building a healthy self-image. Victims of nonaccidental trauma heal as they regain personal control (Walker, 1987). For those who have difficulty in getting free of both the positive and negative feelings they have for the abuser, feminist therapy provides an important activist model (Walker, 1985). It supports the strength that is evidenced in the victim's own coping skills while also encouraging development of additional survival mechanisms. A positive, growth-oriented philosophy that acknowledges the realities about situational trauma prevails in feminist therapy rather than a deterministic psychodynamic orientation. The revisionist theories of Jean Baker Miller and her colleagues at the Stone Center at Wellesley College have important application, especially to the development of a relational ego (cf. Kaplan & Surrey, 1984).

The feminist theoretical orientation also accepts that child victims, like adults, do not deserve to be hurt, no matter what they do. A child's desire for love and intimacy, expressed by learned seductive behavior or even enjoyment of some aspects of the sexual experience, does not detract from its coercive nature. Rather, those children who have been eroticized at so young an age have simply been taught prematurely to know such feelings. They do not cause their own victimization. Learning sexual intimacy before mastering emotional intimacy may prevent the development of the latter. The trauma occurs not only because of the bruises or the type of sexual acts but is also created by the impact of the offender's need to dominate, manipulate, and have power over the child. Thus, the child may develop numerous psychological techniques to help her or him cope with the emotional loss of personal power. Although these skills may be helpful to survive the experience, they can keep the child reacting as a victim, who is then more vulnerable and less resilient should other trauma be experienced. Therefore, the specific goals of play therapy with sexually abused children are to assist the child in healing from the actual experience, prevent or reverse the development of shame and stigma, support the development of emotional intimacy, provide a trust experience, and regain personal power to become a survivor.

Play Therapy Issues

There are a number of issues that need to be addressed during the course of therapy as discussed in Mountain, Nicholson, Spencer, and Walker (1984). Briefly presented here, they are:

Fear and lack of trust are almost always present in children who have been sexually abused, although they may not be directly expressed. In treatment the child may recant or deny parts of the original story as an attempt to make it go away. Or the child may refuse to discuss the trauma, needing some emotional distance from dealing with the sexual abuse issues with the therapist to first build trust by dealing with less anxiety-producing issues. The child rarely wants to play with the anatomically correct dolls in therapy after the evaluation is completed, so other props must be available. Reducing fear and building trust is a slow process, one that is quite dependent upon time. A belief in the genuineness of the relationship with the therapist facilitates its redevelopment.

Mastery and desensitization to abuse often occur in adults through the repetition of the details of what happened. Children have more difficulty in retelling the incident(s). Play therapy allows for it to be worked through using other symbols. Guided-imagery techniques, which are used in treating adult rape and assault victims, can be modified and applied to the children through the use of drama. Dissociation, the separation between mind and body to modify the experience of pain, is often experienced by children who have been abused. During a play sequence, the child will frequently admit knowing how to make her or his mind go away to another place. Expressing feelings that originated during trauma incidents when using play materials can teach the child to avoid the need to continue this emotional splitting.

Emotional pseudo-independence is frequently observed in children, especially in their nurturing and caretaking behavior toward adults. Although initially the child may seem very mature for her or his age, it is not unusual to witness regression to earlier stages as the child feels safe enough to heal. The timing for changing the adultlike behavior should be determined by the child's readiness and not imposed by the therapist. Some children are too afraid to give up the little control they have, and never regress; but still they can use the play therapy for effective healing. Others, particularly some preadolescents, try to remain a child. They may have a delayed menses. This is commonly seen in conjunction with anorexia and other eating disorders.

Precociousness and seductiveness is an important issue to address in therapy, especially if the child is easily aroused sexually, masturbates frequently, and behaves in a sexually aggressive way toward other children. Acceptance of the child's feelings, including any possible enjoyment of sexual stimulation while simultaneously teaching appropriate behavior (stressing the consequences), is a useful and practical way to handle this issue. Acknowledging that sex can feel good but is an activity reserved for grown-ups and not children needs to be done. Sometimes a direct message about negative consequences of continued acting out, such as isolation and loss of friends, is appropriate. Children of all ages may enjoy reading some of the new "good touch/bad touch" books together with the therapist. Use of stuffed animals or puppets rather than people can help a child learn his or her own boundaries, as well as those of others, indirectly.

Protection of self and others is often dealt with when the child tries to overprotect both the therapist and himself or herself. Young children want games to be fair, although they also want to win most of the time. So they may change the rules or even cheat blatantly. For a therapist to allow this to occur while verbalizing feelings for both the child and the therapist is an appropriate initial step toward a legitimate use of power by the child. Thus, the therapist may simply state, "I'll bet it feels good to win" or "Oh, no, I've lost again." Later on, the process can be more directly confronted.

The older child is particularly concerned with reliability, so therapist inconsistencies or even frequent absences are of concern. Often these children are excessive worriers, reflecting their feelings of powerlessness. They make assumptions about the therapist's needs that are never checked out, and then try to please the therapist. Initially, they need constant reassurance that they are liked by the therapist. Their guilt about anything that goes wrong can be overwhelming. Attention to these feelings can facilitate the development of the therapeutic relationship, which can then be used to model more appropriate interpersonal relationships.

Emotional distancing and a lack of genuineness is often seen in these children. They can appear to be doing all the right things but never really fully engage or commit themselves. They interact in a superficial way and may move quickly from one thought or activity to another. As they perceive their increasing personal power, they will become more genuine in their relationships. Sometimes they seem impulsive or elusive, but they usually do have some controls. Adolescents often miss developing the intense same-sex friendships that can be important to gender identity and establishment of emotionally intimate bonds with both sexes. Here, too, dissociation may be observed. Just being with the child as the pain is reexperienced can help the child work through it.

Shame and self-blame are constant themes with sexually abused children, as is discussed by Finkelhor and Browne in Chapter 4 of this volume. Denial and repression are two defenses used to push away the negative feelings. The positive regard of the therapist for the child is an important component in reversing the sense of shame. Contact with others in the same situation is also helpful. If it is possible to get the offender to admit his guilt to the child and acknowledge that the abuse was only his responsibility, it can assuage self-blame and speed the resolution of that issue. We prefer to facilitate how the child learns of this admission, for a meeting between them may be premature for a particular child, and other means of delivering the message, such as by letter or telephone, may be better. Sometimes children react by adopting the "bad kid" image and, adolescents especially, can begin sexual acting out as a way to gratify some emotional needs. Others may try desperately to "buy" friends by giving presents. It may be appropriate to interact with the child's schoolteachers, should there be problems.

Lack of assertiveness or lack of awareness of their personal rights is frequently observed in these children. They move quickly from one mood to another and may demonstrate extreme emotional lability under stress. Recognition of their rights and pointing out instances of their violation can be useful for both children and adolescents. Teenage girls may get into another abusive relationship, while boys seem more likely to become the abuser. Assertiveness training and confrontation can be useful, particularly with older children. Pointing out inconsistencies between acts, events, and thoughts can also be of use. These children may not consistently set limits for themselves or others. Thus, they can be more easily victimized by others' intrusive behaviors toward them. This is especially true when a child fears losing love and approval. One way to deal quickly with this assertiveness is around the issue of touch. We teach the child that he or she has the right to allow or deny any touching of their body. Thus, when walking from the waiting room to the playroom, we ask for permission first before even holding hands. The same is true for a hug or any other physical touch that might seem quite natural with a nonsexually abused child. Naturally, any physical play during the session also is discussed first so direct permission can be obtained.

Confrontation with anger is an area with which all violence victims have difficulties, because feelings of anger toward the abuser are usually associated with rage at having been hurt. Child sexual abuse victims are extremely sensitive, do not like to confront or take direct action, and may react by withdrawal, crying, and/or temper tantrums. It is important to work very slowly toward the expression of angry feelings so as not to be overwhelmed by them. Play with dolls, puppets, or stuffed animals can help children become desensitized to recognizing, acknowledging, and expressing anger. For young children under the age of five their feelings should be named and accepted as natural while also giving them lots of love. Love, of course, is a critical component for healing at all ages.

Lack of resiliency and vulnerability to other physical and psychological problems is frequently seen in children who have been sexually abused. They have a lowered resistance to stress and can react poorly to frequent or sudden change. Physical ailments—including vaginal and urinary tract problems, yeast infections including ear infections, and psychophysiological illnesses—are often reported. There are some new theories that the trauma causes a suppression of the immunological system, but no conclusive evidence is available, yet. Some believe in a special nutritional program along with vitamins and dietary supplements. Other than usual precautions, there is little known about prevention.

A sense of specialness, which underlies a *sense of betrayal,* is a common occurrence that feeds into the lack of trust and subsequent difficulties with interpersonal relationships. The sense of betrayal is often profound and may be a large component behind suicide threats or attempts. Adolescents may fulfill their need for feeling special by getting involved with a boyfriend who also may be exploitive. A special relationship with the therapist helps serve as a substitute, although rebuilding an alliance with the nonoffending parent in incest cases is critical. Overcoming dependence on male relationships to provide the feeling of specialness is important. The development of self-efficacy and mastery is an important component in shifting the focus from reliance on others to self-reliance. Use of spirituality is also helpful here and will be discussed later in this chapter.

Anger toward women is frequently expressed by daughters (and sometimes sons) for not protecting them better even when they have never told the mother. For girls, negative feelings about being a woman are connected with their feelings of shame and powerlessness. Many girls do not develop close girl or women friends, often reporting being more comfortable with boys—whereas the opposite is true for boys. Doll, puppet, stuffed animal, and dramatic play are useful here. Clarifying the mothers' role while accepting and acknowledging their own feelings helps move them toward final resolution of the abuse. Cognitive restructuring about previous or even currently learned sex-role stereotypes is important, too. Woman therapists provide a good role model for girls and young women.

Anger toward men is also observed, although the rage may be buried and not shown openly until the therapeutic relationship is well established. Girls are apt to feel sorry for their incest fathers and forgive them quickly, never really dealing with their own pain. They do remain vulnerable and angry with other men and may try to control those relationships through using their sexuality. Boys are likely to question their sexual identity and—like the girls—they feel anger toward being a man. This needs to be dealt with similar to other identity issues and the child assured that sexual abuse does not need to change his or her sexual orientation although it can impact on how he or she feels about all sexual relationships.

PROCESS OF PLAY THERAPY

The process of play therapy is usually best facilitated by having a playroom or at least a separate corner of the office devoted to play materials. Young preverbal children need an open space with minimal furniture. Older children may also like space in which to put on drama or utilize other symbolic materials. We have only a child-size table and chairs and cushions, as we usually sit on the carpeted floor unless the table is needed. In our playroom, we have corners with typical children's furnishings. They include a wooden sink, stove, and dishes for recreating mealtimes (often the scene of conflicts), a wall of shelves filled with stuffed animals, puppets, building materials, and board games, and another corner with various dolls and a doll bed. Some of the 2-year-olds can actually crawl in bed with the dolls. There is a blanket that can be used to create hiding spaces by using some ingenuity. We have thought of adding a sandbox. Lack of water has made the clean-up a great chore for the therapists to undertake in order to leave the room ready for the next child. However, we have replaced the carpeting with tile in one section and put in an easel to be used with washable watercolor paints and felt-tip markers, a favorite of many children.

Children in therapy vacillate between attending to the reality of their lives and using make-believe to symbolize their issues. Play therapy allows the therapist to get into the child's ideas by playing along. Often the materials are merely props with symbolic value that cannot be understood right away. Sometimes themes appear; other times it may seem like aimless play. Experience has taught us that the play is rarely totally aimless. It usually has meaning for the child even if the therapist does not understand it. The meaning may be embedded in the nature of the relationship, or it may facilitate direct resolution of the sexual abuse. It is not always necessary for the therapist to understand its meaning or provide an interpretation in order to be of therapeutic value to the child. The learning that occurs from doing is sufficient to create change.

At times intervention may be required with schools, family members, and others who have contact with the child. Helping others to understand that the child is a victim but also has lots of strengths to cope with this event(s) and is not culpable can be helpful. It is important when making any interventions with others to be aware of and not violate the trust of the child in the relationship, which could be further damaging to the child's ability to trust an adult. The child may express concern about his or her body in various ways. It is important that the therapist deal with this very charged issue with sensitivity, allowing the child to express his or her concern and to correct any distortions that may be present.

For example, early in treatment 6-year-old Ellie began to draw a hearing aid. She would cut it out, and place it over her ear so she could hear. Ellie insisted she could only hear with her hearing aid and would not do anything else in the session until it was properly in place. An examination determined that her hearing actually was okay. After several weeks, she stopped taking it home because her nonabusive stepfather did not like it. So we kept each one at the office in a special container marked with her name. She would never use the last session's hearing aid, however. Part of the process for her was the repetitive ritual of drawing, coloring, and cutting out a new one each week. Even after her grandmother found an old, nonworking hearing aid for her, Ellie still followed the ritual of making her own in each therapy session. Then one day she announced she did not need the device to hear and, as quickly as it began, the ritual was stopped.

The therapist chose to interpret her insistence on being able to hear only when she chose as a means of reestablishing power over her own life. She needed a way to enhance her own power to hear until she was able to trust that the therapist would be her ally. While the hearing aid may have had other significance to her, too, she could not articulate it. In fact, 4 years later she was again asked about any special significance and still could not provide any reason other than perceiving she could not hear very well. Allowing her the control was an important part of the treatment even without understanding its other symbolic value. The ritual is a form of mastery that helps the child to regain personal power.

The following year, Ellie began another long ritual in therapy. She created a witch/child fantasy and assigned each of us to play either one of the roles as she wished. The witch always captured the child, mutilated her, threw her into a boiling pot of water, covered her with vermin and other disgusting things, and ate her in a stew. As the weeks progressed, the child character became more clever at devising ways to escape the witch's horrible fate for her, but never could quite do it. The therapist introduced various themes on the basic plot, such as bringing in other child or adult characters to provide help and to teach the child to recognize early cues of danger. Ellie was able to incorporate many of the ideas into her fantasy, but not the characters. She at first alternately identified with being the aggressive witch and the child victim. But as the game progressed and the child character grew stronger and less willing to be a victim, Ellie delighted in being the child who could foil the witch's most clever plans. Only then could she bring other characters into the play.

Ellie's use of this play fantasy paralleled the increase in visits with her offender-father that were ordered by the court. Although she said she was eager to spend more time with him and denied any overt fears of being hurt again, this game indicated her concerns. It also demonstrated her perception that she could be either aggressor or victim and, given a choice, this child initially preferred the aggressor role. She was able to master new skills so the child character did not have to be a helpless victim, and eventually could deal with her own feelings directly rather than symbolically. The new skills did carry over into the relationship with her father, and her sexually aggressive behavior toward other children also stopped.

Another case also illustrates the benefits of play therapy even without the therapist's understanding what exactly is happening for the child during the process. Janet was 11 years old when she first joined a therapy group with five other girls her age. They were successful in helping each other heal and eventually the group disbanded, but Janet's mother wanted her to continue in individual therapy. Formerly talkative with the other girls, she refused to say anything when alone with the therapist, other than conversation called for in playing several different board games. The therapist had to choose what games were played. After several months, Janet was asked what she got out of these sessions. She did not respond. The therapist tried to reflect what might be her feelings. This included an acknowledgment that her mother could force her to come but could not make her "work" in therapy. She denied this interpretation and insisted it was she who wanted to come. It was clear Janet was struggling with issues around authority figures in her life and the therapist represented one type of powerful other. But it was also important for Janet to have a committed relationship with an adult outside of her family so she could be less anxious about her relationships at home.

At one point, Janet and the therapist got into a power struggle around the therapist's need to get Janet to assume control in the sessions. The therapist refused to choose a game or speak for Janet, saying she had to do at least that much. Janet demonstrated her power through her stubbornness. She was prepared to sit mute for the entire 50 minutes; the therapist was unable to last more than 20 minutes, and even that reportedly was torture! Once the therapist realized that indeed Janet was in control of the therapy, it could be reflected in the play. Board-game strategies were then varied to demonstrate different ways to win, broadening Janet's repertoire of skills with which to exercise power. It was obvious the treatment was generalizing into her daily life when her school phobia stopped (the original referral reason) and her teachers reported spontaneous classroom participation. Therapy was then gradually terminated.

Several years later the therapist saw Janet at a shopping mall with a group of her friends. When Janet recognized the therapist, she ran over and spontaneously said how helpful therapy had been for her. "How so?" the therapist asked her, trying to understand the answer. "I don't know," Janet replied, "But I know it helped me sort through all my confusion." Obviously, she was working hard inside her own mind at that time, even though she was unable to communicate more directly about the issues.

Other children are much more direct about their play. For example, Melissa, a 4-year-old, was clear about the sexual abuse, as is typical of many her age. She did not like it and wanted both her stepfather and mother punished. Her angry feelings came out in her play. She took the male doll and pounded on its genitals, as though she would crush them if she could. None of the stuffed animals got a kind or compassionate word from her. They could come for tea and cookies but often got sent away for misbehavior. She continued to rage and withhold affection until she seemed spent with exhaustion, and then she stopped discussing the abuse totally. However, the same themes of power, control, shame, trust, competency, and intimacy still came through when using indirect play methods.

Sean was an almost nonverbal 2-year-old when first brought for therapy by his Mom. The initial referral was to assess his spontaneous claims that his father bit his "dinky," his word for penis. Child protective services refused to take the report seriously, blaming the mother for being unreliable and hysterical. She was seen as using her child to defend against a change-of-custody lawsuit, which initially had not been contemplated and was not filed until the mother tried to protect the child by refusing to comply with visitation. The mother began to bring the child for twice-a-week play therapy. Sean demonstrated many developmental behaviors often seen in childhood schizophrenia, but he had so little language and was so obviously traumatized by the sexual abuse that such a diagnosis was deferred. After 2 years of therapy, it was hard to believe such a label was ever contemplated.

The therapist initially engaged Sean by mimicking and reflecting his behavior and by using language to name what he would do. Sean soon began to talk, putting his own labels on his actions. Getting him to go into the playroom was often a chore; he preferred to run screaming up and down the hallway. Our neighbors and other clients were not pleased, so at times he and his therapist went to the park. His masturbation and thumb-sucking behavior eventually receded, although when his Mom remarried he was found humping on top of his same-age stepsister. Interestingly, the court never did acknowledge this child's abuse history. Nor did a specially appointed child custody team who performed their evaluation after he had improved following a year of play therapy. Even without the legal validation and support, Sean responded well to the therapy and made good progress anyhow.

Understanding Children's Repetitive Play Rituals

As noted earlier, the goals of play therapy are to assist the child in healing from the actual experience, to prevent or reverse the development of shame and stigma, to support the development of emotional intimacy and other age-appropriate skills, to provide a trust experience, and to enable the child to regain personal power to become a survivor. In order to allow the child to have those experiences, the therapist must respond to the ways a child presents himself or herself and tells of his or her trauma. Each child does it in a unique way. It has been our experience that the child may work on a particular theme using a ritualized presentation in play. The therapist can use the play ritual as a guide to assess the healing progress of the child and can use the ritual in ways to facilitate healing.

The child's repetitive play ritual can be mistaken for an obsessive-compulsive behavior disorder by an unknowledgeable observer. But it is the ritual of the play that allows the child to work through the trauma of sexual abuse. As is true with victims of any type of abuse, repeating the experience along with the accompanying feelings while imposing one's own limits is a part of healing. This repetition of the experience with a child can be on a symbolic—rather than direct—level that may perplex the therapist. However, it is essential that the therapist accept the assumption that when allowed to choose activities and control the session, the child will present his or her issues through play in a way that is useful to the child. It is then the therapist's job to use the play material in an appropriate way. That is done by entering into the play story for the goal of helping the child learn to reestablish his or her own safety limits. Reflection of feelings and clarification are used, as are empathy and understanding. Later in therapy, interpretations and generalizations may be given through the use of the play symbols but, as with adult victims, if interpretations occur too early in therapy, it interferes with reestablishing a trust relationship.

An example is a 5-year-old girl, Donna, who initially always wanted the therapist to play board games with her. In the early part of her treatment she insisted on being first, on bending the rules when it was in her interest, and on dictating how the therapist would be able to move on the board. After several months of this play, she began to be able to play by the rules and not have to cheat. Later in her treatment, Donna began to build what she called her "secret place," using pillows to make a tent where she could be totally hidden from view. Using this ritual, the therapist encouraged her to write a sign that she could tape onto her secret place signed with a pseudonym, "Kathy." The rationale was to teach Donna that she could protect herself by hiding from others in a variety of ways, including using a pseudonym, instead of totally disappearing. The therapist kept the sign and Donna used it from week to week. When she felt ready for more exposure, Donna began to leave the "roof" off her tent. Then she became a bear who could both threaten and control the therapist from her safe corner. When she finally was able to be herself she gave up that particular play ritual.

Donna's behavior demonstrates her initial need to manipulate in order to feel safe and her gradual ability to tolerate her not being able to control everything in her environment. It also illustrates Donna's movement from feeling she is a helpless victim to feeling able to create her own safety. Here she was able to allow the expression of her rage in a way that was safely contained for this child. She will still need to get to the other side of her feelings before therapy will be complete.

Prevention of and/or reversal of the development of shame and stigma demands a multifaceted effort. At times just simple matter-of-fact approval is needed. For example, when an 11-year-old talked about her assuming fault for the abuse, it was gently pointed out that she was only 5 years old when the abuse began and that she was subject to the will of adults. Pointing this out to her was extremely helpful in her healing process. Other children need to learn how to develop compassion for that little 5-year-old child. With smaller children, again a simple nonblaming approach is useful. Children will sometimes say words or use symbolic or even more direct play to describe their experience. A nonjudgmental caring approach by the therapist that does not make the mistake of either blaming the child victim or feeling pity is essential.

It is also important not to communicate shock, which the child could misinterpret as a statement that he or she has done something bad or wrong. This means the therapist must have his or her own issues about sexuality in general and about child sexual abuse totally in order.

Allowing the child to express freely himself or herself and accepting what is presented in the play is useful to the development of an emotionally intimate relationship. Again, respecting the spontaneous play rituals is helpful. In order to heal and to develop emotional intimacy, the child must feel that the therapist respects and cares for the child and does not blame the child for what has happened. Being genuine and honest with a child will facilitate the development of the relationship. Allowing the child to express the range of emotion and concern about the experience is essential, and attention to and use of the play ritual can facilitate such expression. The experience of a trusting relationship in which the child is not violated is needed to heal the wounds of the abuse. This includes being honest and responsive to the child. The play ritual can be a very special experience for both the child and therapist, and it is both the enactment and analysis of ritual that serves as a major means of regaining power and personal efficacy.

ROLE OF SPIRITUALITY

It has been our experience that many parents who bring their children to our offices wish to turn to religion as a primary or adjunct means of assisting in their own and their children's healing process. We have labeled this concern as *spirituality,* by which we mean a belief in a Greater Being or order of the universe into which all individuals fit. For adults such spirituality often gives comfort because of the knowledge that there can be important learnings that may follow the experience of this tragedy. It also places the trauma into a larger context of order that makes one's own responsibility and, of course, subsequent guilt seem less overwhelming. The notion of a greater power such as God does minimize an individual's personal power, but it also fosters the belief in the stability of one's world. For children the message becomes more concrete: "If God still loves me, then I am okay." And "God, not me, can be responsible for punishing or healing my abuser," an attitude that can facilitate the child's concentration on his or her own healing process.

Religion, which is a formalized spiritual system, has sometimes been utilized to help children learn to forgive their abuser. We have found it to be potentially useful, but that is only true when the child comes to such forgiveness independently. It is inappropriate for adults to tell the child that she or he must either ask for forgiveness, or be willing to forgive—or even that God forgives—because it interferes with the healing process. As was illustrated in several of the cases presented here, expression of intense anger or even aggressive rage is critical to the resolution of the victimization experience. The child must reach a forgiveness constructed from her or his own individual experience. Once that process is begun, then the child can invoke a religious or spiritual forgiveness, too. If forgiveness is demanded too soon, the child may lose her or his belief in a just God. Some children cannot give up their anger until they know they will continue to be safe from further abuse. This part of resolution may take more time than adults realize, sometimes many years.

There is concern that some who turn to religion for healing may reinforce the notion of a "Zapping God" who wreaks terrible punishment for not being good enough. Hendricks (1984, 1985) provides an excellent discussion of the development of the Zapping God, and techniques for reversing such a God-image and developing other, more positive views of spirituality. Religious parents and pastoral counselors may inadvertently or even purposely reinforce a negative belief by using religion and prayer exclusively in trying to help the child heal. What is damaged is the child's belief in her or his own personal competence, which is a major component of self-esteem and so must be restored. Spiritual belief only provides an adjunct to that restoration by helping the child place him- or herself back into his or her proper place in a greater ordered world. It too can provide ritual that may be therapeutic, but only in conjuction with experiencing personal efficacy.

Some spiritual belief systems can speed the healing process by giving the child some ritual or spiritual companion to foster the feeling of safety. Objects such as a rabbit's foot, an amulet, a crystal, or other security symbol can be soothing at the right time. In certain cultures, the spiritual aspects can be attended to by others. We have worked with a curandera, a shaman, a Native American healer, and several psychic healers, as well as with formal organized religious leaders. Each child is unique in her or his capacity for forgiveness and, as has been the theme of our entire therapy process, we suggest allowing the child to proceed slowly, at her or his own pace.

ROLE OF FAMILY

Play therapy is usually an individual treatment modality, although it has been successful when used with groups of children (Sgroi, 1982) and integrated as part of family therapy. The original psychoanalytic conceptualization of play therapy viewed it as the child's special time with the therapist and, therefore, as little communication with parents as possible was practiced (Axline, 1964). Yet families do exert enormous influence over the child's total development. In an outclient setting where children are only seen for one or two sessions per week, family members can be trained to provide additional support needed in the healing process. Conte and Berliner's findings, presented in

Chapter 5 of this volume, demonstrate that those children who made the most therapeutic gains had the support of the nonoffending parent (in incest cases, usually the mother) and of their siblings. Therefore, we do spend time with other family members, answering questions, providing suggestions to reinforce our treatment plans at home, and teaching parent/child interaction skills, often in the playroom.

It can be therapeutic for mothers to learn how to relax and play with their children so as to stimulate positive growth experiences. Often the mother becomes so intense due to worry about the potential damage to the child that she takes everything too seriously. Those who have been scrutinized by the social service and legal systems are so scared they will do the wrong thing that they do not trust their own instincts anymore. Play can help get the child/parent interaction back to a more normal mode. For some, the exposure of sexual abuse also exposes an otherwise abnormal parent/child interactive pattern. In these cases a combination of play therapy both alone and with the parent, concentrating on the development of good parenting skills, is the preferred intervention. In some cases, we learn that the mother also experienced sexual abuse as a child and has not yet dealt with its effects on her. The child's experience can reawaken the mother's own buried memories. It is essential to refer that mother to her own therapist so as not to confuse the child's issues with her own.

It is not uncommon for the court to order one or both parents into parenting classes when a dependency and neglect action is pending. It is our experience that the didactic classes are not sufficient for parents of sexually abused children. The opportunity for modeling and immediate positive reinforcement or corrective feedback supplements the intellectual knowledge and enhances its integration into everyday child-raising practices. We have a one-way mirror that provides numerous observation opportunities for training parents and siblings, as well as graduate students. There is video equipment, which can record the session for later analysis and discussion, too. The child is always told if there is someone observing or if a play session is being videotaped. If introduced in a matter-of-fact manner, it rarely concerns the child. In the few cases where the child seemed upset by the knowledge that others were watching, we stopped the observation and proceeded with the play therapy, concentrating on rebuilding trust by repairing feelings of shame, powerlessness, and loss of control.

Visitation with Offending Incest Parent

Most states that incorporate into law the Uniform Children's Code are by statute required to address the reunification of the family in any treatment plan. Thus, for children who have been referred for therapy by the court, visitation with the offending parent (usually the father) must be addressed. No matter how heinous the abuse or how detrimental it might be for the child, practically speaking, if an incest parent acknowledges his wrongdoing, attends some counseling, pays for the child's therapy, and expresses his love and willingness to visit, the courts simply do not deny him his rights to visit with his child.

Supervised visitation may be ordered, but the shortage of trained supervisors and the artificial constraints placed on such visits make the courts willing to risk reoffense of the child after a period of observation. Judges' orders indicate they believe a man's verbal assurances; if he says he will not reoffend, he is believed capable of keeping his word. Judges also demonstrate they believe sex only happens at night by allowing daylong visits but not overnights. Given this climate of too little support from the legal system, even when the abuser is found guilty, we have begun to train the child in self-protection techniques.

Children who have been abused learn to recognize the cues of danger. Often they do not pay attention to them, or they tell a supportive adult who ignores them, or they attempt to develop their own coping skills to minimize harm, since they rarely can escape it. Therapy can help validate and support the child's own ability to recognize danger early, and it can teach effective escape strategies as well as reinforce appropriate coping skills. If the offending father is willing to participate in play therapy with the child and the child accepts it, then in-vivo training can occur with them as participants. We have several fathers in such parent-training therapy who are ordered there as one of their weekly supervised visits.

In addition to the actual sexual abuse, incest fathers also attempt to exert their power and control needs in other aspects of their relationship. They typically want to make all the decisions for the child. These men rarely have skills necessary to interpret accurately the child's feelings, wants, or needs around this issue unless the child can tell them directly. These children, of course, have difficulty standing up for their own rights or assertively telling the offender anything directly, especially if they anticipate anger or rejection. But children can acknowledge their feelings through play, and the therapist can then use the example in interpreting the child's behavior with the father. It is easier for the father to accept the representations when they come directly from the child.

Unfortunately, in our experience, many of these fathers have little ability to generalize what is learned from one specific situation to another one with similar characteristics, so therapy for them is rarely completed. But it does help the child begin to view the father as having potential to modify his oppressive and intrusive behavior. Many can then begin to be more direct about their own demands. They also see that their therapist can place limits on the father in a neutral, nonjudgmental way, which helps to keep them safe. This can help reduce some children's fear that they will be more seriously harmed after telling the secret. Some older children simply learn to recognize their fathers' limits and rebuild their relationship accordingly. Although we have not had any direct experience, it is expected that this conjoint play therapy can generalize to the child's later opposite-sex relationships. It is also valuable to be able to help the child give up the fantasized image of the perfect or the most awful father. Many are able to get on with their lives; some even file civil lawsuits to recover for their now clearly perceived damages—although this is more likely to occur when they become adults.

Nonfamily Offenders

It is rare that the child will be expected to have any continued contact with nonfamily offenders, but it sometimes occurs. For example, a 12-year-old girl who was molested by a neighbor had to stand in front of his house to catch the school bus daily. Her parents did not realize how seriously this affected her until they were told by the school that she could no longer ride the bus because of her aggressive and verbally rude behavior. At the same time, the child began pulling out her eyebrows and eyelashes, an anxiety symptom directly related to the abusive incident. Neither family could afford to move, although the abuser's home was up for sale. Finally, as a temporary solution, her parents changed her school and drove her to the new one each day. She also learned to play out of the range of sight of the abuser's home and developed support from others in the neighborhood. This was possible because several other neighborhood children were also molested. This simple environmental manipulation by itself was successful because there had been only one abusive incident and the offender was apprehended. If it had been repetitive, as is more common with neighbors who molest children, other therapeutic interventions might have been needed. Civil lawsuits asking for financial compensation for psychological damages are also helpful to the child in healing. Therapists need to be knowledgeable and supportive if a lawsuit is ongoing simultaneously with therapy. Special care must also be taken in protecting records. In Colorado, treating therapists are permitted more flexibility in keeping treatment notes confidential if a legal showing is made to persuade a judge that it is necessary to foster the child/therapist relationship (cf. *Bond vs. District Court, Colorado,* 1984).

Therapist Qualities

A note about the qualities needed in therapists who work with children using play therapy seems appropriate here. Both the understanding and enjoyment of children is needed by the therapist who engages in play therapy. Respect for the child's own healing process and ability to continue to grow in a healthy developmental way is an important ingredient in the child's relearning trust. The therapist must be able to convey to the child the sense of specialness that may be lost when a repetitive abuse situation with a loving and abusive person is terminated. A good sense of humor and tolerance for flexibility both with the child and the parent helps to maintain the therapeutic relationship. It is the therapist's responsibility to recognize potential conflicts or power struggles with parents and to utilize effective means to deescalate them immediately. Children should not be placed in a tug of war between different adults vying for the privilege or right to help them. A therapist's negative attitudes or angry feelings toward parents are quickly sensed by children and confound the treatment goals.

Adherence to time commitments is especially important to a child. Thus, in the same manner as would adult therapy time be protected, nothing should be allowed to interrupt the schedule. It is the interaction between the therapist and child that is therapeutic. Therefore, activity and responsiveness needs to be a part of the therapist's behavior. We recommend sitting on the floor rather than on adult-sized furniture because it helps to remind the therapist to engage with and not just observe the child. Children who have been abused need to learn to say no to powerful adults. The therapist's willingness to give up her or his control and let the child decide when it is all right to be touched is an important step in the therapeutic process. The therapist should expect the child's memory of exploitation to cause her or him confusion in interpreting the therapist's kind behavior, and so the therapist must behave in very direct ways to avoid any unnecessary confusion for the child. This is especially important for male therapists who may need to learn how to be playful with girls in a nonseductive manner. Many men do not recognize their own subtle behavior, which reinforces such seductive and coy behavior.

Therapists need to get in touch with their own personal issues about sexuality as well as their own feelings of anger that a child could be abused by an adult. A thorough reading of the literature such as presented in this book is invaluable when working together with these children. Care not to betray the child's confidences is of high priority. Although children may be forgiving once they know your intent is good, it is the little things that build their trust. The guidelines set down for feminist therapists are also therapeutically important and should be followed (Rosewater & Walker, 1985). This includes mutual respect, care not to misuse the power inherent in being the therapist, openness, and genuineness, among other qualities.

CONCLUSION

Play therapy has the potential to help a child heal from a sexual assault experience. Facilitating the development of personal power is important for the child to move from victim to becoming a survivor. Allowing the child to control and dictate the rituals of the play can be helpful as a beginning building block. Encouraging the child to develop his or her ways of expressing personal power in the play is useful. The example cited earlier of the child who built her own "secret place" illustrates a child's efforts to feel safe and in control. Pointing out new options to a child in play is useful. A 5-year-old girl drew a picture of herself in a hurricane. The therapist suggested she draw a house, which the child then noted was not safe from the hurricane. Adding a basement, however, provided the child with the needed sense of safety. As a child heals, he or she will present unique ways of demonstrating personal power. Recognition and support of this developing sense of reempowerment will allow the child further healing and growth to become a survivor. Facilitating the support of family and other significant others is also therapeutic. Play therapy allows the child to move at her or his own pace to develop emotional intimacy with the therapist. It helps rebuild the sense of trust and personal efficacy lost through the abuse. It can prevent developmental delays that cause secondary trauma, and it teaches the child how to positively control his or her world again.

REFERENCES

Axline, V. (1964). *Dibs: In search of self,* New York: Ballantine Books.

Bond v. District CT in and For Denver Cty, 682 p. 2d 33 (Colo. 1984).

Conte, J. R., & Berliner, L. (1981). Sexual abuse of children: Implications for practice. *Social Casework, 62,* 601–606.

Freud, A. (1946). *The psychoanalytic treatment of the child.* London: Imago Publishing.

Garfield, S. L. (1974). *Clinical psychology: The study of personality and behavior.* Chicago: Aldine.

Hendricks, M. C. (1984). In L. E. A. Walker (Ed.) *Women and mental health policy.* Beverly Hills, CA: Sage.

Hendricks, M. C. (1985). In L. B. Rosewater & L. E. A. Walker (Eds.), *Handbook on feminist therapy: Psychotherapy issues with women.* New York: Springer Publishing Company.

Kaplan, A. & Surrey, J. (1984). In L. E. A. Walker (Ed.), *Women and mental health policy.* Beverly Hills, CA: Sage.

Klein, M. L. (1949). *The psychoanalysis of children.* London: Hogarth Press.

MacFarlane, K., & Waterman, J. (1986). *Sexual abuse of young children: Evaluation & treatment.* New York: Guilford.

Mountain, H., Nicholson, M. A., Spencer, C. C., & Walker, L. E. A. (1984). *Incest: Colorado State Department of Social Services revitalization training.* Denver, CO: Nicholson, Spencer & Associates.

Moustakas, C. (1973). *Children in play therapy.* New York: Aronson.

Schaefer, C. (1976). *The therapeutic use of child's play.* New York: Aronson.

Sgroi, S. M. (1982). *Handbook of clinical intervention in child sexual abuse.* Lexington MA: Lexington Books.

Walker, L. E. A. (1985). Feminist therapy with victims of violence. In L. B. Rosewater & L. E. A. Walker (Eds.), *Handbook on feminist therapy: Psychotherapy issues with women.* New York: Springer Publishing Company.

Walker, L. E. A. (1987) Intervention with victims. In I. Weiner & A. Hess. (Eds.), *Handbook on forensic psychology.* New York: Wiley.

14

Retrospective Incest Therapy for Women

Christine A. Courtois
Judith E. Sprei

At present, therapists are reporting a substantial increase in the number of women overtly seeking help for the aftereffects of incest experiences in their childhood and adolescence. This overt presentation is attributable to the current societal acknowledgment of and attention to child sexual abuse, its circumstances and aftereffects. The incest experience and its attendant conflicts and emotions have rarely, until recently, been the focus of treatment. Instead, the aftereffects have been treated without acknowledgment or recognition that incest, at least in part and often to a large degree, accounted for their etiology. Although some of these aftereffects have been treated successfully without a focus on their origins, others have been resistant. The result for numerous women has been incomplete or unsuccessful therapy or therapy that caused further confusion or damage to them. In many cases where the woman dared to reveal the incest secret, the therapist discounted, minimized, or disbelieved it, or interpreted it as fantasy or as a wish—responses derived in large measure from Freudian Oedipal theory. As will be discussed in this chapter, responses of this sort serve to compound reactions rather than to alleviate them because these reactions serve to reinforce denial and disbelief, which are the primary dynamics associated with the occurrence of child sexual abuse.

Retrospective treatment for women incest victim/survivors is a new treat-

Although this article is written specifically to address the therapy of female victim/survivors, most of the information is applicable to males as well.

ment modality. The recent research on the impact of sexual abuse on the child (described in detail in Chapters 1, 4, and 5 of this volume) and on the adult (Briere, 1984; Browne & Finkelhor, 1984; Courtois, 1979) has underscored its potential for disruptive and destructive consequences in many aspects of the victim's life. If left untreated in childhood (as is usually the case), these effects have been observed to manifest in adulthood and may result in sporadic and/or chronic adult life disruption. Peters (1976) likened the effects to "psychological time bombs" that may go off without warning and are similar to acute stress responses seen in other types of intense trauma. In retrospective treatment, the underlying trauma, its resultant emotions, and the immediate and long-term aftereffects are treated. This chapter outlines treatment and includes a detailed examination of the dynamics associated with incest, their impact on the therapy process, conceptualizations and approaches needed for this therapy, and special issues that may arise.

INCEST VICTIM/SURVIVORS: A NEGLECTED POPULATION

The woman seeking therapy for past or ongoing incest experience is both a member of a shunned and neglected population and a victim/survivor. She brings the abuse experience to therapy, its occurrence at a time when it was not talked about or responded to and her efforts to cope with and to survive both the abuse and its context. The conceptualizations of denial/ neglect and victim/survivor are central to the retrospective treatment of incest.

Throughout history, incest has been a taboo in most cultures. Despite the taboo, evidence is available that incest and other forms of child sexual abuse have occurred regularly in many Western civilization cultures (Rush, 1980). This contradiction between what is prohibited in public and what occurs with great regularity in private led Armstrong (1978) and other feminist writers to conclude that the taboo is not as much applied to the occurrence of incest as it is to the recognition and discussion of its occurrence.

All forms of sexual abuse have secrecy and denial as hallmarks. Secrecy serves two purposes by protecting the perpetrator and allowing for repetition and continuation of the behavior (Sgroi, 1982). The child is admonished or coerced by the perpetrator to keep the secret, which typically she does. Attempts at disclosure are generally met with denial and disbelief. When reports are believed, a common reaction is for the behavior to be minimized or excused. Disclosure of incest and child sexual abuse have only recently been treated as worthy of investigation and as signifying a real rather than an imaginary event, although this type of response still constitutes the exception rather than the rule (Summit, 1983). Lack of knowledge or under-standing of incest and its dynamics, including the pressure a child faces both inside and outside the family to retract her disclosure, continue to make the investigation and validation of incest problematic in many com-munities.

Butler (1978) constructed a model of what happens to the child in the case of incest, based on interviews conducted with a number of victim/survivors. Typically, the child experiences three levels of betrayal: First, from the perpetrator, whom she should be able to trust and expect sexual distance; second, from family members and friends she tries to tell and who do not believe her and/or blame her; and third, from caregivers such as teachers and mental health professionals who she may try to tell and who disbelieve or discount her story. Faced with this wholesale denial or with help that is usually ineffectual or short-lived, the child copes by disbelieving or detaching from her own experience, thereby setting up a fourth level of betrayal, self-betrayal. The child disconnects from her own reality because she is unable to get outside validation for that reality. She learns to keep the secret and to cope as best she can. Both efforts may cost her enormous amounts of psychic and physical energy.

This societal denial and neglect serve to allow the abuse to become chronic. The usual abuse pattern is a compulsive/addictive one in which contact begins before the child reaches puberty, lasts for several years, and involves a progression of sexual activity ranging from fondling to inter-course. Denial and secrecy also serve to compound reactions to the abuse, causing a secondary victimization or second injury (Symonds, 1980). As a consequence of the abuse and the lack of response, the individual begins to believe that something is wrong with her, that she is bad and/or that she caused the abuse. The negative self-concept and sense of shame have yet another consequence: the development of secondary effects such as poor interpersonal skills and relations, sexual problems, self-abusive be-havior, and vulnerability to revictimization. Both the primary and second-ary effects are presented by the victim/survivor and should be addressed in therapy.

The term *victim/survivor* accounts for the full range of the individual's experience. Wise (1985) aptly describes victim/survivor as a paradox, which takes into account the victimization within the context of societal denial along with the behaviors the individual uses to endure and persevere. This con-ceptualization is useful to therapist and client alike and further serves to outline the course of therapy. Retrospective therapy requires an acknowl-edgment and working through of the victimization with the goal of inte-grating and surpassing survivor status to enable a life less encumbered by the past.

THE COMPLEXITY OF INCEST

The causes and circumstances of incest are complex. Although patterns have been outlined by theorists to account for most types of incest, each case is nevertheless unique, with its own set of precipitants and circumstances. A brief overview is provided as orientation for the reader before treatment issues are discussed, since a detailed examination of causes and circumstances is beyond the scope of this chapter.

The current psychiatric and psychological definitions of incest resemble the one developed by Benward and Densen-Gerber (1975) provided below. They are comprehensive in nature and recognize a range of relationships between perpetrator and victim as well as a range of sexual activity, usually occurring over quite a long period of time. Although such a comprehensive definition is useful clinically, the therapist should be aware that it may be too broad to meet the legal criteria of incest in his or her jurisdiction. The clinician is urged to become knowledgeable about the state child sexual abuse and incest laws but to adopt a broad definition that behaviors that do not meet the legal criteria for incest may still have incestuous psychological connotations and impact (Rosenfeld, 1977). Furthermore, this psychological impact can be created without direct sexual contact, but rather through a sexualized family atmosphere or through comments and gestures.

Benward and Densen-Gerber's (1975) definition is as follows:

> It (incest) refers to sexual contact with a person who would be considered an ineligible partner because of his blood and/or social ties (i.e. kin) to the subject and her family. The term encompasses, then, several categories of partners, including father, step-father, grandfather, uncles, siblings, cousins, in-laws, and what we call 'quasi-family'. This last category includes parental and family friends (e.g. mother's sexual partner). Our feeling is that the incest taboo applies in a weakened form to all these categories in that the "partner" represents someone from whom the female child should rightfully expect warmth or protection and sexual distance. Sexual behavior recorded as positive incest ranged from intercourse with consent; intercourse by force; attempted intercourse or seduction; molestation, primarily fondling of breasts and genitals, and exposure. We included other sexual behaviors as intercourse; namely, all penetration, anal, oral and vaginal, both passive and active. Cunnilingus and fellatio were not uncommon activities, nor was sodomy. (p. 326)

A wide range of factors is believed to account for the occurrence of incest. Most if not all factors involve the perpetrator seeking to satisfy such unmet need(s) as affection, dependency, authority, aggression, and sex by sexualizing his contact with a child. Children are selected precisely because of their immaturity, vulnerability, trusting natures, and accessibility. Family factors—

such as the general family atmosphere (extended as well as nuclear); the relationship between spouses and other family members; problems like alcoholism and illness; a history of past abuse; and family values, beliefs, attitudes, and interaction styles—can be critical determinants in the development of incest. A multigenerational pattern and occurrence of incest is not uncommon, nor are multiple victims and perpetrators within one family.

Until recently, a widely held belief was that peer incest (i.e., between siblings and between cousins) was the most frequent and the least harmful type due to the fact that it involved mutual exploratory behavior. Recent research (Courtois, 1979; Finkelhor, 1984; Russell, 1983) suggests that intergenerational contact, especially father–daughter and stepfather–daughter, is the most prevalent and that peer contact may be nonmutual, exploitive, and quite damaging.

As with the variability of incest circumstances, aftereffects and responses have also been found to vary. The available empirical and clinical data (see Chapters 1, 4, and 5 of this volume) indicate broad typical patterns of response. These data also show that the net effects of incest experience on growth and development are negative rather than positive (Finkelhor, 1984). Yet the clinician cannot begin treatment assuming that all incest is negative and devastating for the victim and that all victims respond to incest the same way. A number of writers have indicated that an individual's response is multidetermined (Browne & Finkelhor, 1984) by the variables of the particular case, that response is idiosyncratic (Courtois, 1979), and that the therapist must expect the aftereffects in various life spheres to run the gamut from negative to positive. In addition, other types of childhood trauma may result in similar coping mechanisms and response. If more than one type of trauma has been experienced in childhood—as is often the case in incestuous families because parental alcoholism, violence, and family isolation are characteristic of many of these families—it may be difficult to disentangle the exact sources of effects. This difficulty was discussed by Browne and Finkelhor (1986) and found by Courtois (1979) and other researchers who asked victims to discuss the aftereffects of incest in different areas of their lives. Many researchers indicated an inability to say whether a particular effect was the sole result of the incest or was due instead to a confluence of problems.

Many ambivalent and conflicted emotions and aftereffects are common due to the inherent conflictual characteristics of incest, especially its occurrence within the family and within existing relationships. The therapist should try to keep in mind the common response patterns and the typical dynamics of incest but should not predetermine responses. The most common presenting concerns and therapy issues will be discussed in this chapter, with an emphasis on aspects of the more severe case and its management. It is not warranted to overgeneralize that all cases are totally devastating for the victim nor is it warranted to deny or discount the serious symptomatology often resulting from incest.

TREATMENT: PRESENTING CONCERNS AND DIAGNOSIS

Presenting Concerns

According to studies that place prevalence rates at 30% to 44% (Briere, 1984; Rosenfeld, 1979; Spencer, 1978), incest survivors are well represented among therapy outpatients. These rates, of course, reflect those cases where the incest is disclosed to the therapist. More women are now entering therapy specifically to deal with the effects of child sexual abuse, but many continue to make a disguised or undisclosed presentation. Briere (1984) found that only 39% of the female outpatients in his sexual abuse sample had reported their abuse experience during intake and assessment. Incest is not disclosed or discussed as a presenting concern for many reasons. The most common reasons include lack of recognition or acknowledgment that certain behavior was abusive; fear due to coercion and intimidation on the part of the perpetrator or others, or due to previous negative experiences with disclosure; shame and guilt about the behavior and its taboo status in society, with related fear of betraying or shaming the family; and survival/defense mechanisms such as repression, denial, dissociation, and suppression.

Many victims of childhood abuse genuinely have no knowledge that certain behavior constitutes abuse. This often occurs when it is embedded within patterns of "normal" family behavior or when it is strongly masked or denied. For example, in some families abusive behavior may be seen as positive or as not causing distress for anyone. Additionally, the behavior may not be associated in any way with presenting therapy concerns and therefore may not receive mention.

Many incest victims were coerced to keep the sexual activity secret. They may have been warned that others would blame them or not believe them, or that they would cause the breakup of the family, or that Daddy would have to go to jail. Some were threatened with violence, with other types of severe punishment, or with rejection or abandonment. Some victims did disclose despite the admonishments only to find that their abusers were telling the truth: They were castigated, rejected, and blamed, or their stories were not believed, or nothing was done to assist them. And for some, the abuse escalated after their disclosure, due to the abuser's increased rage or because the abuser was emboldened by learning that nothing would be done to put a stop to the behavior.

As discussed earlier, the societal taboo on incest has resulted in strong feelings of shame, guilt, and differentness on the part of many incest survivors. In fact, according to Browne and Finkelhor (1984), the stigmatization associated with incest is one of its major sources of trauma. It is not un-common for the child to grow up feeling isolated and different from others, especially as she realizes that she is more sexually experienced than they are and that her peers have not had sexual experiences with family members. These realizations often affect the child's view of herself, resulting in the development of low self-esteem and acute feelings of badness, shame, and guilt. These feelings may also be reinforced by the perpetrator who tells the child that she seduced him or that he is punishing her because she is so bad or disgusting. Similarly, responses of denial, disgust, blame, and rejection that often follow attempts at disclosure also reinforce a negative sense of self.

A role reversal takes place in many incest families where the child is given the role of parent or family protector. In the most common pattern, she becomes the mother's mother or protector and the father's wife and con-fidant. The child is given the overt or covert message that the family relies on her to keep the family unit together and functioning. Thus, she learns to take care of others at her own expense as her own needs go unmet, a pattern of relating that may be very difficult for her to either recognize or break. Talking about the abuse may come to represent a betrayal of those she worked so hard to protect. She may, therefore, continue to cling to both her "special role" and her secret.

Finally, some women do not present their incest history at intake because its memory is not consciously available to them—due to repression or because it is denied, dissociated, or suppressed. Many children survived episodes of abuse by pushing awareness of it from their conscious minds and/or by dissociating. These disconnections may continue into adulthood. Therapy and certain life events may trigger the recall of memories or of memory fragments. Typical precipitating life events include the death of the abuser, the nonoffending parent, or some other significant person; other life crises or transitions such as marriage, divorce, or the birth of a child; episodes of revictimization such as spouse abuse or the physical or sexual abuse of the victim/survivor's own child; the disclosure or discovery of other sexual abuse in the family, particularly of younger siblings whom the woman may have tried to protect by being silent about her own victimization; and a safe relationship where the individual feels secure and protected, such as a love relationship or a therapeutic alliance. The recent pervasive publicity regarding child sexual abuse has similarly caused sudden recall for many women. The abrupt onset of memories, emotions, and symptoms may, in itself, create a crisis and result in a crisis presentation in therapy.

The therapist must be aware of symptoms that suggest a history of incest due to the regularity of disguised presentation. The characteristics described below should be seen as cues or guidelines—but not as definitive proof in assuming the existence of child sexual abuse. Generally, several symptoms will be present. The therapist should rely on such patterns rather than attempting to make a determination of incest based on one symptom alone. One symptom, however, may be enough to alert the therapist to probe for others.

The Disguised Presentation

Gelinas (1983) described the disguised presentation, which is comprised of the secondary elaborations of the untreated negative effects of incest. According to Gelinas, the client presents with "a characterological depression with complications and atypical impulsive and dissociative elements" (p. 326). A recent study by Briere and Runtz (1985), as well as a study by Briere (1984), give empirical validation to Gelinas' clinical observations. Briere and Runtz found that sexual abuse victims scored higher than nonabuse subjects on Somatization, Anxiety, Depression, and Dissociation. According to Gelinas, the depression may be complicated by substance abuse, eating disorders, poor relationships, sexual dysfunction, and self-destructive behavior. Low self-esteem, passivity, guilt, isolation, and mistrust are also in evidence. Impulsive elements include a history of running away, juvenile delinquency, impulsive spending, eating, or sexual activity, alcohol or drug abuse, and self-mutilating and other self-destructive behaviors or gestures. Dissociative features include recurrent nightmares, selective amnesia, and episodes of depersonalization, such as seeing oneself as from a distance or self-perceptions of being in a fog or a shell or behind a wall. Symptoms of anxiety such as phobias, panic attacks, and hyperventilation are also common.

Gelinas also described another type of disguised presentation, that of the "parentified" client. Women who have been raised in the role-reversal situation described above are very responsible individuals who are usually socially and professionally successful and present as competent, confident, and mature. Probing by the therapist will reveal that the success and achievement are genuine but mask other concerns and difficulties. These women have not received adequate attention and nurturing and, as a result, they often feel like little girls and have extremely high unmet dependency needs, low self-esteem, and feelings of worthlessness and badness.

Lees (1981) provided a listing of cues to identifying women with incest histories that overlap with those provided by Gelinas but have some differences as well. These include (1) a history of alcohol/drug abuse, repeated victimizations (especially sexual), self-inflicted injury, and suicide attempts; (2) physical and emotional symptoms such as flashbacks to frightening scenes, nightmares, and sleeplessness; (3) high anxiety levels, especially fear of people, of being trapped or attacked, or of someone coming into the room; (4) feelings of grief and anger; (5) vomiting, gagging, nausea, stomach pain, anorexia; (6) loss of memory about large parts of childhood; (7) chronic feelings or symptoms of illness that defy medical diagnosis; and (8) polarized patterns of behavior and thought that alternate between the two extremes. The survivor's presentation may include polarities of behavior and thought, such as: feeling bad about herself/feeling superior or better than anyone else; being totally distrustful of others/naively trusting everyone; selflessly taking care of others/totally selfish and self-oriented behavior with no concern for others; total desperation/depression about everything/feeling that everything is fine/euphoria; extreme isolation/extreme social behavior; sexual abstinence/compulsive sexual behavior and promiscuity; and feeling very different from others/feeling overly normal or average.

Feelings about the Self and Relations with Others

Courtois and Watts (1982) divided presenting problems into the categories of feelings about the self and relations with others. They wrote:

> Concerns pertaining to self . . . fit into four main areas: identity, self-esteem, physical functioning, and sexual functioning. . . . Many of these women have a very negative self-image, have a sense of being different and distant from 'ordinary' people, have a sense of being powerful in a malignant way, express self-hatred, and are depressed and anxious. They may also be self-destructive and suicidal. Physical complaints include feelings of dissociation, migraine headaches, severe backaches, gastrointestinal and genitourinary problems, inability to concentrate, lethargy, anxiety, phobic behavior, and substance abuse. . . . Sexual identity conflicts and impairment in sexual functioning are also presenting complaints. Sexual problems ranged from an inability to function sexually at all to promiscuity and masochistic behavior. A range of sexual dysfunction, such as inability to relax, vaginismus, inability to orgasm, and so on, occurs between these two extremes.
>
> Concerns pertaining to relationships also have four main areas of manifestation: relationships in general, marital relations, and parental relations with both their own parents or their in-laws and their children. Relationships in general are often described as empty, superficial, conflictual, or sexualized. The inability to trust is pronounced. Good or pleasurable relationships often increase guilt and shame because they are viewed as undeserved or impossible. Conflict is most apparent in marriage or other intimate relations with men. Many of these women have very negative feelings toward men but at the same time overvalue men and search for a protector. Paradoxically yet predictably, these women very often end up with men who, like themselves, have been abused. These men are often abusive to or neglectful of them, so this type of relationship serves to recapitulate early experience and reinforce a negative sense of self-worth. (p. 276)

Personality and Trauma-Specific Symptoms

Still other common presenting concerns have been noted. Hysterical seizures usually diagnosed as psychogenic epilepsy have been associated with incest (Goodwin, Simms, & Bergman, 1979), as have sudden personality changes, "sliding personality," and multiple personality (Brickman, 1984). Unexplained damage to the rectal, vaginal, or mouth areas, including the long-term effects of sexually transmitted disease (which may flare up in adulthood), and pelvic, back, neck, hip, leg, or feet injury may be indicative. Some symptoms may be trauma-specific. For example, clients with temporomandibular jaw (TMJ) and gagging/swallowing/respiratory distress may have been forced to perform oral sex or may have been choked during the abuse. Sexual difficulties and aversions may relate very specifically to the particular activity and locus of the assault. Clients may also show conversion reactions at various times during the therapy. As an example, one client experienced unexplained soreness in her finger for a period of time during therapy before recalling that her father forced her to stick the same finger in his anus when he was abusing her.

Borderline-Type Symptoms

Borderline-type symptomatology, including volatile emotions, unstable relationships, and anger, may be manifest. Some female incest victims themselves become victimizers, although in far smaller numbers than do male victims. A history of neglecting or abusing children either sexually or physically, of not being able to protect them from other sources of abuse, or of strong denial in the face of abuse evidence may be indicative. Unmastered or unresolved childhood trauma may be repeated in a family. Some mothers are unable to offer protection to their daughters due to their own powerlessness, strong denial, or the destructive effects of their own abuse and its secondary elaborations. For some, the abuse of their child may symbolize an attempt to master the original situation by allowing for its recreation.

Symptoms as Coping Mechanisms

Many of these symptoms served as coping mechanisms during the abuse and may have been very functional at the time. Summit (1983) described these mechanisms: "The healthy, normal, emotionally resilient child will learn to accommodate to the reality of continuing sexual abuse. . . . Much of what is eventually labelled as adolescent or adult psychopathology can be traced to the natural reactions of a healthy child to a profoundly unnatural and unhealthy parental environment." Furthermore, "The child faced with continuing helpless victimization must learn to somehow achieve a sense of power and control. The child cannot safely conceptualize that a parent might be ruthless and self-serving; such a conclusion is tantamount to abandonment and annihilation. The only acceptable alternative for the child is to believe that she has provoked the painful encounters and to hope that by learning to be good she can earn love and acceptance. . . . The child will have profound rage that she will either contain and express later in life or will express actively at the time in self-hateful behavior" (p. 188). Summit also wrote that the therapist must take care to avoid reinforcing a sense of badness, inadequacy, or craziness by condemning or stigmatizing the symptoms. Rather, the therapist should strive to understand them within the context of the abuse as mechanisms of accommodation and survival.

The therapist should ask all clients about childhood sexual experiences with related or unrelated adults as part of the routine intake and history-taking. Doing so gives the client permission to discuss such experiences and indicates a willingness on the part of the therapist to hear about episodes of abuse. The recommended approach is to ask, either verbally or in writing in a straightforward, matter-of-fact manner, about sexual experiences with adults in childhood or adolescence. The words "abuse" or "victim" or other words with the same connotations should not be used, since many women do not see themselves as victims or what occurred as victimization. Still others may be very fearful to admit to behavior that is so labeled. Should the client deny knowledge of abuse in the face of indications to the contrary, the therapist can continue to probe and can verbalize suspicions about past abuse to the client. The therapist in such a circumstance must continue to "sift evidence" and may come to the conclusion that abuse occurred even without conscious validation or memory on the part of the client.

As mentioned above, some memories return gradually over time, and some recur quite suddenly and intensively, as in the case of flashbacks. The remembering process may be very difficult. The inability to remember either childhood or its details can be very frustrating. Some women maintain selective amnesia for certain aspects of the abuse, usually those that are the most traumatic or conflictual. The emergence of repressed memories, especially those that counter the client's previously held memories or wishes of what childhood or certain relationships were like, or when extremely violent or sadistic memories surface, may cause the woman to doubt her reality or sanity, or to be sorry that the memories ever emerged. The recapturing of memories may be extremely stressful and anxiety-provoking. For some survivors, it may symbolize losing control due to losing that which allowed her to function. This feeling, in turn, might feel life-threatening and lead to a self-destructive/self-mutilating gesture. For other women, it may symbolize betrayal of the family and of the secret. This meaning may also lead to a need for self-punishment. All current relationships, especially those with family members, may be called into question when memories surface. The client may have to confront previously denied realities such as lack of response or denial on the part of significant others. Confrontation and disclosure will become therapy issues and their management will be outlined later in the chapter.

At whatever point a client discloses a history of incest, the therapist should proceed cautiously in asking about it. The therapist should attempt to discern the meaning of disclosure and should discuss childhood messages and beliefs about giving up the secret in order to be able to anticipate possible reactions. The most important consideration for the therapist is to make explicit and clear that the client's story will be believed. In cases of selective amnesia or conflictual aspects of the presentation, the therapist should indicate a willingness to work with the client to explore the material and its significance. The victim/survivor needs the assurance that her experiences, whatever they are, will receive validation and not further suppression.

Several authors have devised assessment instruments to assist in identification of incest history. The reader is referred to Gelinas (1983), Mayer (1983), and Renshaw (1982). In addition, Courtois (1979) found that her research questionnaire was useful in gathering details of the incest circumstance.

Diagnosis

Several terms have been suggested to describe the psychological effects of incest, including traumatic neurosis (Gelinas, 1983), stress-response syndrome (Horowitz, 1976), post-sexual abuse syndrome (Briere, 1984), and child sexual abuse accommodation syndrome (Summit, 1983). Since none of these is available as a diagnostic category in the *Diagnostic and Statistical Manual* (3rd ed. rev.) (American Psychiatric Association, 1987), a diagnostic determination will need to be made from other categories. It is recommended that the posttraumatic stress disorder (PTSD) category be given consideration in combination with other appropriate diagnoses based on the client's personality style, emotional state, and level of functioning. Adults with an incest history often exhibit both a chronic and a delayed posttraumatic stress disorder with the duration of symptoms lasting 6 months or more (chronic) and the onset of symptoms beginning at least 6 months after the trauma (delayed). The criteria for this diagnosis include the existence of a recognizable stressor, which in the case of incest is the actual sexual contact and the way it was perpetrated, its context, its disclosure (if any), and its aftermath. Common reactions such as intrusive thoughts and nightmares, recurrent dreams of the event, sudden acting or feeling as if the event were recurring, numbing of responsiveness to or involvement in the external world, feelings of detachment from others, constricted affect, startle responses, sleep disturbances, survivor guilt, difficulty concentrating, memory impairment, and avoidance all conform to the criteria included under the heading posttraumatic stress disorder.

The diagnosis of PTSD can be helpful to both client and therapist. For the client, it may assist the process of normalizing her responses. Many incest survivors are fearful that they are crazy and view their symptoms and behavior as proof. The PTSD diagnosis offers a different perspective and may actually provide the first step in a reinterpretation of events and aftereffects. In a similar way, the PTSD diagnosis helps the therapist to conceptualize the treatment process. A dual diagnosis ensures that related personality disorders and other diagnoses also receive attention. The treatment plan can then be based on all of these diagnoses and their determined severity. It should be noted that some diagnoses will take precedence over the immediate treatment of the incest. For example, alcoholism, acute anorexia, acute depression, self-mutilating and suicidal behavior, and other crisis circumstances may need to be stabilized before other treatment is introduced. Some of these symptoms may not respond to treatment if the underlying issues such as low self-esteem, shame, guilt, self-hatred, and self-punishment are unexamined. Simultaneous treatment of the incest and other disorders will be warranted in many cases.

With the increased investigation of and publicity about the aftereffects of child sexual abuse, clinicians and researchers have noted a similarity between features of the typical response such as the impulsive and dissociative elements of the depression as described by Gelinas (1983) and criteria used to make the diagnosis of Borderline Personality Disorder. Briere has discussed this issue in detail in his 1984 paper. In it, he presents the effects of childhood sexual abuse on later psychological functioning by reporting on differences found between a sample of sexually abused individuals and a comparison nonabuse sample. He terms the typical constellation of aftereffects the Post-Sexual Abuse Syndrome and examines the ways in which the aftereffects resemble the criteria for the borderline diagnosis. His thesis is that the aftereffects and the criteria overlap in significant ways that have previously gone unrecognized in the mental health community. The lack of recognition of child sexual abuse as etiologic to behaviors that constitute the borderline diagnosis has serious implications for treatment. He states:

> To the extent that a significant proportion of "borderline" diagnoses involve symptomatology arising from sexual abuse, an absence of training and interest in sexual abuse trauma among mental health professionals becomes a major concern. This is somewhat exacerbated by the fact that current treatment approaches to borderline personality disorder stress theoretical formulations which are relatively devoid of reference to sexual victimization (e.g., Object Relations theory). The absence of traditional treatment approaches to chronic sexual abuse trauma (whether designated 'PSAS' or 'Borderline') which address childhood victimization may partially explain the traditional wisdom that such cases 'rarely get better'. Although the outcome data is [sic] incomplete in this area, it is quite probable that treatment approaches which directly deal with the abuse, somewhat in the way that Rape Trauma Syndrome is treated by 'working through' the assault (Burgess and Holmstrom, 1979), will be more successful with such clients. (Herman, 1981, p. 14)

TREATMENT: CONCEPTUALIZATIONS, APPROACHES, AND ISSUES

Philosophical Underpinnings

Strategies and techniques from a variety of theoretical orientations can prove therapeutic for this client population; however, the philosophical underpinnings of some theories, especially as concern the psychology of women and power dynamics, may be detrimental. Brickman (1984), Herman (1981), and Chapter 13 of this volume argue that a feminist perspective and therapy model are necessary for incest therapy, whether the therapist is working with the entire family following the disclosure of current incest or is doing retrospective work. The reader is referred to these works and to Finkelhor (1984) for a more comprehensive discussion than is presented in this chapter.

In general, therapists must be aware of the biases regarding sex-role stereotypes and incest that are contained within their theoretical orientation. At the most extreme are those theories that hold that incest is not real but rather constitutes Oedipal wishes on the part of the child. Closely related but distinct is the tradition that incest does occur (although rarely) due to the girl's desire for her father: She is the seductive party who gains pleasure, gratification, and power. The incest is not considered necessarily harmful to her. Some writers have commented upon the seductive and pleasing personalities of these youngsters, implying that they were the ones responsible for the sexual contact (Bender & Blau, 1937). In this tradition, the authority and power of the involved adult goes unrecognized. The perpetrator is instead usually viewed as "the victim of dominant mothers, ill-tempered wives, or seductive daughters" (Brickman, 1984, p. 56) who do not properly fill his needs. Therapy is geared toward the adjustment of unbalanced, traditional family roles. The incest itself goes untreated.

Other theories accept the reality of incest but ignore or minimize gender aspects of the problem and the issues of responsibility as discussed by Brickman and by Finkelhor (1984). The prevalence of the problem is downplayed with females viewed as contributing equally to the victimization. This latter point contradicts research findings that male perpetrators constitute a majority of about 95% (Finkelhor, 1984). Family therapy is the treatment of choice in ongoing incest. All family members are seen as victims and each is urged to change behavior and take responsibility. Almost all family problems are viewed as contributing to the occurrence of incest. The therapy goal is the reconstitution of the family if at all feasible.

The feminist orientation focuses on the experience of the victim and views sexual violence as a logical consequence of women's less powerful status in society. The perpetrator is held responsible for his actions irrespective of the behavior of other family members. The goal in cases of ongoing incest is not necessarily family reconstitution but rather the safety and protection of the child. The experience and emotions of the child or adult are given foremost consideration with the goal of providing safety and relief.

Retrospective incest therapy draws heavily from the feminist perspective, which stresses belief in and support of the surivor and her experience. The use of this perspective should not be taken to imply that family dynamics, including the possible roles played by family members in the occurence, ought to be ignored or dismissed; rather, they should not constitute the only focus of the therapy and therapeutic interventions. It is generally of crucial importance that the survivor obtain some understanding of events and dynamics in her family and of characteristics of the perpetrator that contributed to the incest. Such understanding will in turn lead to a greater understanding of her own responses and behavior.

Therapy Stance and Assumptions

The therapist's philosophical orientation contributes directly to the attitudes, values, and assumptions and stance brought to treatment. We have found the following approaches and assumptions, derived in part from the feminist orientation, to be the most useful with this population. Of course, each therapist should adapt them to his or her own unique style and philosophy.

The basic therapy stance should be nurturing and reality-based versus abstinent and aloof. Some caveats apply, however. Initially, a neutral position is best because many survivors have difficulty with positive regard and caring. Westerlund (1983) has noted that one-to-one contact in a private setting with an authority figure may be very threatening and that positive regard may be viewed as undeserved and/or unsafe. The relationship should be allowed to develop slowly with understanding on the part of the therapist that trust is difficult for many survivors. As the relationship develops, the therapist should be nurturing but not indulgent.

The therapist must often be quite active in this therapy due to the denial, shame, stigma, and repression that many survivors experience. It may be necessary for the therapist to continuously ask and indicate a willingness to hear about the abuse. In many ways, the therapist will function as a witness to the past who attests to and validates it with the survivor. The therapist must guard against being intrusive or voyeuristic, particularly concerning details of the sexual activity. Although it is often necessary for the client to tell about and for the therapist to hear about the sexual behavior, its discussion should be approached with sensitivity and an appreciation for the client's privacy. In a similar vein, the therapist must guard against talking only about the incest to the exclusion of other issues or aspects of the client.

At times, the therapist will have to function as an alter ego to the survivor, reacting for her when she is emotionally blocked. The therapist may need to provide education about and modeling of appropriate emotions and their expression. Understandably, negative emotions are often the most difficult. The survivor may fear losing control if, for example, she expresses anger or outrage. She may also fear that she will become just like the abuser, that she will abuse others, or that she will go crazy if she allows expression.

The release of intense emotion is sometimes accompanied by extreme anxiety reactions such as dissociative responses, hyperventilation, dizziness, fainting, and shortness of breath. Breaking through defense/survival mechanisms and experiencing intense emotions can be overwhelming and feel life-threatening for some women. The therapist should be cautious in encouraging expression, should help the client from becoming overwhelmed, and should explain the anxiety that results. Underlying feelings of guilt and shame should also be addressed.

Finally, the therapist must indicate a willingness to hear about and be open to all feelings about the incest and not just the negative. As Sommers and Marcus (1982) remarked, many survivors have held a second secret, that they had sexual responses or feelings or that there were some positive aspects to the incest for them. In addition, strong loyalty to the family will be expressed by many survivors. The therapist should support this loyalty and not scapegoat the family while holding the perpetrator responsible. Loyalty to the family differs from protection of the family. The therapist must avoid a condemnatory stance and instead strive to assist the survivor in exploring all of her reactions and her resultant feelings. Only by doing so will she be able to work through the situation.

The recommended assumptions for the therapist to hold relate to the information presented in the beginning of this chapter, specifically, that the client is a victim/survivor and a member of a neglected population, that the neglect resulted in secondary victimization and compounded reactions, that incest is complex as are the reactions to its occurrence, that treatment must take into account the uniqueness of response without predetermination, and that the child is never responsible no matter what the circumstance.

The Therapy Process and Goals

Retrospective incest therapy can be conceptualized in a variety of ways. It will vary greatly in terms of the needs of the survivor and in intensity and duration. At its least intense, reassurance, information, and/or short-term counseling may be sufficient. At its most intense for those women suffering the most serious effects, long-term reconstructive treatment is needed. Incest therapy generally involves breaking the secret, catharsis, and a reevaluation of the incest, its circumstances, and its effects. Family rules and patterns are explored and clarified. Conceptualizations of the self are probed and reevaluated with the intent of developing a stronger and more healthy self-concept and healthier modes of behavior. Defenses are gradually dismantled as their utility is explained and understood in the context of the past and as the need for them diminishes.

A number of authors have recently offered conceptualizations of the therapy process and goals. Butler (1985) suggested that, at its most basic, incest therapy is the encouragement of expression rather than repression and suppression. Wise (1985) labeled therapy as a remembering process with the central therapeutic issues being family rules, self-destructive behaviors as survival strategies, and shame and internalized guilt. Summit (1983) discussed the necessity for therapy to help the survivor understand the accommodation behaviors that a child typically devises to foster a change in negative self-concept and self-defeating patterns of behavior. Similarly, Wooley and Vigilanti (1984) conceptualized childhood incest as a double-bind situation that the child survived at great personal expense. Teaching the survivor ways of breaking the double bind and fostering separation and individuation from the family and its patterns are critical tasks according to these authors. Silver, Boon, and Stones (1983) discuss the therapeutic benefit involved in finding meaning in the incest experience, including an understanding of causes, circumstances, and aftereffects, although they also caution that for some situations no explanation and meaning can be found.

In the authors' experience, the therapy process can also be conceptualized as reparenting and as a time during which the survivor can reexperience and rework developmental tasks with the goal being a more positive and healthy resolution. The process also resembles a grief or mourning process (Kubler-Ross, 1969). The survivor must achieve acceptance of past events and losses after moving through stages of denial and isolation, anger, bargaining, and depression. It is crucial that compassion and empathy are maintained throughout the process; however, in and of themselves, they are not sufficient. They form the support base from which the client is challenged and confronted to face the abuse and to modify dysfunctional cognitions and behavior.

A general set of goals to alleviate the negative effects of incest is described below. A determination with the client will need to be made regarding the focus of treatment and goals set accordingly. Some clients may seek therapy for the alleviation of specific problems (e.g., sexual aversions, marital distress, substance abuse), whereas others wish to address more global and less specific issues (e.g., to feel better, to feel less depressed, to deal with the incest). At times, it will be necessary to explain to the survivor that specific problem areas will likely resist improvement if underlying psychological issues are not treated. For example, Nadelson (1982) and Sprei and Courtois (in press) have found that, for some women, behavioral sex therapy alone is unsuccessful in treating sexual dysfunctions arising from sexual assault. A more in-depth approach that addresses salient psychological concerns is needed before symptom relief is achieved.

Brickman (1984) wrote that "These [goals in retrospective incest therapy] are long-term goals, rarely accomplished in anything less than two or three years, and certainly not assumed by the mere cessation of abuse. In severe cases, it is a question as to what extent they can be accomplished at all" (p. 63). The authors support these sentiments, having found this type of therapy to be long term due to its reparative nature. With those survivors who have suffered the most serious repercussions, the therapist can assume that the therapy is going to take years. Interventions and interpretations should be paced, with constant attention paid to the intense affect involved and the likely reactions to the material being worked on.

The survivor herself is likely to be discouraged or enraged by the length of treatment, its slow pace, and the confusion that is necessary for her to undergo as old beliefs and patterns of behavior are discarded for new. Some women will understandably see therapy as extending the amount of "life time" that the incest has taken. For obvious reasons, the outrage and dis-couragement are important to support. Explanations of the course of therapy and reasons for its likely duration can help put the process in some perspective and thus can be reassuring.

The following are the general goals for retrospective incest therapy:

Establishment of a Therapeutic Alliance

Because much of the damage of incest is in the realm of interpersonal functioning, the establishment of a relationship in therapy is central to the healing process. The alliance may be difficult to develop due to the client's impaired ability to trust or to allow closeness with anyone. The relationship is essential to support the hard work and emotional stress the survivor will likely experience in dealing with the abuse. It will also serve as a model of a healthy and growth-promoting interaction.

Acknowledgment and Acceptance of the Occurrence of the Abuse

Acknowledgment involves breaking old patterns of secrecy and silence. The defenses involved in the maintenance of silence will need to be dismantled during the therapy so the survivor can directly acknowledge what happened and work through the emotional aftermath. Acknowledgment and acceptance take time and may alternate with periods of denial and suppression before they are allowed without equivocation.

Exploration of Issues of Responsibility and Complicity

The survivor will need to explore and determine issues of responsibility and complicity that result in feelings of guilt and shame. In particular, the responsibility and authority of the involved adult(s) must be assessed. Family dynamics and any other factors that may have contributed to the incest also need to be determined.

Breakdown of Feelings of Isolation

Some of the more persistent effects of incest such as the sense of being different from other people, the need to maintain secrecy, the lack of trust, and the fear of intimacy result in isolation. Isolation in cyclical fashion fosters these same effects while contributing to lowered self-esteem and intense loneliness. The client/therapist relationship may be the first step in breaking down the isolation. Group treatment, self-help networks, and bibliotherapy can also assist with this goal.

Recognition, Labeling and Expression of Feelings

Denial and numbing result in detachment from and lack of recognition of one's emotions. As a survivor learns to recognize and label her feelings, she will be better able to explore and express them. She will achieve a different kind of self-control and a greater understanding of herself as her split-off feelings are identified and reintegrated.

Catharsis and Grieving

The recognition and expression of long-contained emotion coupled with divulgence of her story allow catharsis of the experience. A strong therapeutic alliance and improved self-concept may be prerequisites to catharsis because the expression of emotions may be very threatening or terrifying. Ventilation takes time and may alternate with periods of denial, silence, and fear of reprisal. During and after catharsis, the survivor will typically assess and mourn losses resulting from the abuse, the most typical including lost childhood, lost innocence, and lost potential.

Cognitive Restructuring of Faulty Beliefs

As a child, the survivor may have internalized many negative or faulty beliefs about herself, either as a result of childhood messages from parents or others or as a means of interpreting and understanding her own experience. These beliefs have a profound effect on self-esteem. The recognition that they are beliefs rather than facts allows for a reexamination and a determination of which ones continue to be applicable and which can be discarded. The restructuring is difficult because childhood messages are deeply entrenched and resistant to change.

Insight and Behavioral Change

Acknowledging the abuse and re-owning repressed emotions are major components of the therapeutic process, yet they do not constitute the entire therapy. As Forward and Buck (1978) point out: "People sometimes find so much relief in that initial revelation of incest . . . that they leave therapy prematurely, thinking they are 'cured.' This is known as a 'flight into health'— a short flight. When the initial euphoria wears off the patient is still struggling with unresolved conflicts" (p. 166). Insight into family and abuse dynamics provides the understanding necessary to challenge self-destructive cognitions and behaviors. These, in turn, allow for positive behavioral change and an increased sense of self-esteem and self-control.

Education and Information-Giving

Incest survivors, similar to other abused children, frequently grow up with a lack of information or are misinformed in various areas of functioning, for example, sexuality, parenting, conflict-resolution, etc. The therapist may function as both a parent surrogate and educator in teaching basic life skills and information. Specific reading and skills-building courses and/or exercises may be very beneficial.

Separation and Individuation

Wooley and Vigilanti (1984) describe the final therapeutic task, which is not necessarily completed during therapy, as the process of forming a self-identity that is differentiated from that of the parents.

> This process includes the ability to practice new ways of relating and behaving, including being able to experiment with adult behaviors rather than relying on parent/child interactions, dependency and manipulation. In essence, it is gaining and unfolding a differentiated personality. . . . The woman who is undergoing separation/individuation is in the process of resolving the anger/love/fear conflict and sees herself as better able to cope with ambivalence in relationships, including marital relationships, as well as more readily expressing appropriate emotions without the threat of loss of the relationship. In other words, she is able to behave more as an adult with the opportunity for continued individuation and independence. (p. 351)

Therapy termination issues need to be carefully and thoroughly explored as part of the separation/individuation work.

DYNAMICS OF INCEST AS THEY AFFECT
THE TREATMENT PROCESS
AND THE THERAPEUTIC RELATIONSHIP

The therapist must understand the likely transference and countertransference reactions and their impact in order to analyze, interpret, and control them successfully. The dynamics of incest and resultant transference reactions are discussed and are then followed by a discussion of the most common countertransference effects. Case examples are included where appropriate. Common transference issues include trust/betrayal; negative self-concept; shame and stigmatization; guilt and complicity; loss and mourning; control and power; conflicted and ambivalent feelings; and defenses and survivor skills. These issues may influence the therapy in a variety of ways.

Incest survivors have had their trust in others severely jeopardized. Betrayal is inherent in incest and may have reocurred at different junctures of the survivor's experience. Besides having experienced one or more of the four levels of betrayal (perpetrator(s), family members/significant others, professionals, self) (Butler, 1978), the woman may have experienced other betrayals in adulthood. Increasingly, it is recognized that survivors are at high risk for abusive relationships and marriages, as well as for additional types of assault such as rape, harassment, and molestation. Trust/mistrust is the earliest developmental task according to Erickson (1963). The irresolution of this task affects subsequent stages of development by impairing the victim's ability to form healthy and mutual relationships.

The victim will bring this lack of trust to therapy, making the development of a therapeutic alliance a slow and difficult task. The client may fear the therapist, seeing him/her as an authority or parental figure and thus as abusive, unprotective, and/or rejecting. Or the therapist may be seen as simply another person who is untrustworthy. This will be true if the woman has had negative experiences with other therapists, especially any experiences involving sexual interaction or sexual abuse.

The therapeutic alliance plays a major role in the recovery process. The therapist must be patient and reassuring and should not take trust for granted, even with a dependent or compliant client who professes to trust the therapist, or even after a certain level of trust has been developed. As the woman delves more deeply into the abuse issues, especially those having to do with betrayal and coercion, she may suffer crises in trust. She may engage in behavior to test the therapist's trustworthiness or to reinforce her belief that no one can be trusted.

A related issue is negative self-concept and low self-esteem derived from guilt, shame, and a sense of badness. Herman (1981) found that a common self-perception was as a witch, bitch, or whore. In addition to difficulties in trusting others, the survivor may feel that she is unlovable and may be unable to accept positive regard of any sort from others, including the therapist. Feelings of badness and being malignant may be projected onto relationships. Many of these women believe that, on one hand, people who cared about them or tried to help them were themselves hurt, destroyed, or taken away from them, or, on the other hand, if no one helped, it was due to the victim's inherent badness, which was apparent to others.

Loneliness, isolation, and feeling different from others are hallmarks of many incest survivors, making them extremely needy of affection, nurturance, and attention. Thus, the therapist will be faced with the challenge of a woman who does not trust or feel she deserves a relationship and who may attempt to sabotage the relationship as it develops, and yet who is extremely needy of exactly those things she fears or feels undeserving of. The therapist must constantly monitor the relationship and offer interpretations about the process.

Complicating the dynamic further is the fact that a substantial number of these women possess an overdeveloped awareness of the reactions and feelings of others, originally developed as a survival mechanism. Minor mood or behavioral changes are discerned, often unconsciously, so that the survivor can change her own behavior in response. Further, changes in others that in reality have nothing to do with her may be attributed to some fault or badness on her part. The therapist may be surprised to learn how often the client misattributes others' behavior to herself. As part of the therapy, she will have to learn first to become aware of her perceptions and conclusions; second, to test their accuracy; and third, to change her perceptions if they are inaccurate. She will also need to learn that she does not constantly need to respond to the mood state or needs of others.

Case Example: Ms. A thought that her therapist was upset. Without checking her perceptions, she automatically assumed that she had done something to displease and upset her. It was several sessions later that she mentioned her beliefs to the therapist because she was so discomforted by the situation and wanted to "make things better" between them.

Negative self-esteem and self-hatred may result in self-defeating, self-mutilating, or self-destructive behavior expressed through self-sabotage, substance abuse, suicide gestures and attempts, and abusive relationships. Feelings of guilt and complicity for the incest along with the stigmatization associated with it usually underlie self-hatred. Many survivors do not realize the degree to which they have made themselves the guilty party (and usually the only guilty party). To let go of the guilt and to transfer responsibility to the perpetrator may be very difficult and may have to be accomplished in stages. Women who have ambivalent feelings regarding their own responsibility, as is often found with close-in-age sibling contact or with those who felt some sexual pleasure or personal power in the incest, seem to have the most difficulty in assessing responsibility. Another complicating factor is that many survivors have both love and hate feelings toward the abuser, especially if he provided some nurturance and affection either through the sexual activity or in other ways. In this situation, the therapist must take care not to place too much blame on the perpetrator or do so before the client is ready. Some survivors will flee therapy in order to protect their relationship with the abuser if issues of guilt and responsibility are handled prematurely.

> *Case Example:* Ms. B sought therapy with the expressed purpose of working on the effects of incest experience with her father and on the pattern she had of developing intimate relationships with unsavory men. She maintained a close relationship with both parents and, although she did not live at home, she visited them frequently and relied quite heavily on them for support. Early in treatment, the therapist suggested she needed to confront her father's sexual fondling of her, which still occasionally occurred when she was alone with him. She professed great fear of doing anything that would upset the status quo with her parents and fled therapy instead. She was clearly not ready for such a large step.

The woman's protectiveness of the perpetrator may also be due to the role reversal or "parentification" she experienced. The parentified client will have difficulty in differentiating between caring about and taking care of others. She will almost automatically take care of others, at her own expense if need be. It is usual for her to attract dependent individuals who want someone to take care of them. Therefore, she may feel she cannot develop different types of relationships. The therapist must work against being trapped by the overly considerate client and must constantly point out when she places the needs of others, including those of the therapist, before her own. Any passive-aggressive or manipulative motivation should also be analyzed.

> *Case Example:* Ms. C was very depressed and suicidal one night. She had a difficult time controlling her self-destructive impulses and would have liked to have called her therapist. She waited until the next morning to call because she did not want to disturb the therapist's sleep, nor did she feel she had the right to bother her.

It is likely that the survivor wants the therapist to take care of her but does not know how to ask for this directly or may be prevented from asking by past experiences of having been abandoned or punished. She may become furious with the therapist if she feels the therapist is withholding or if she feels the therapist ought to be able to "read her mind" and know her needs as she is able to do with others. Self-defeating or mutilating behavior may be exhibited as self-punishment for wanting to be cared for and to express anger toward the therapist while testing her or his response. As noted above, this behavior must be processed and new beliefs and behaviors introduced to replace the old.

When the client becomes aware of her own needs and her caretaking pattern with others, she may feel overwhelmed or frightened by her neediness and by her anger at past neglect. Anger is a natural consequence of victimization, yet many victims, especially females, seem devoid of this emotion. Women's socialization typically does not emphasize the expression of anger or aggression. As a consequence, females frequently feel they have no right to anger, which becomes repressed and expressed in disguised forms such as passive-aggressive behavior, depression, manipulativeness, anxiety, and somatic complaints. The victimized female may further express her anger through self-blame, self-contempt, and self-defeating and self-abusive behaviors. A further effect of repressed, unexpressed anger is the development of rage of a frightening intensity. As the survivor becomes more aware of her anger through therapy, it will be necessary to introduce anger-management techniques and activities. She can learn to express her anger in ways that are modulated and not self-destructive but rather allow for appropriate emoting.

The survivor's caretaking style may have resulted in one-sided relationships. Attempts to equalize them may be met with resistance and rejection. The therapist can assist in analyzing past and current relationships and in determining which seem amenable to change. Some (and often many) of these relationships will no longer be satisfactory, leaving the survivor feeling alone and unsupported when a support system is most needed. She will likely be very dependent on therapy during this time, and will be until she is able to develop mutually satisfying relationships. Supportive friends and family members should be mobilized. A therapy group or self-help group may be useful in providing another source of support during this difficult transition period.

During therapy, it is necessary for the survivor to confront what was lost through the abuse experience. The most common losses include lost childhood; lost innocence and trust; lost self-identity (i.e., I am not the same person I might have been); lost potential (familial, interpersonal, and occupational); lost good family and good parenting; and many other lost opportunities. Mourning these and other losses is a necessary therapy component that will cause increased feelings of sadness, depression, and anger. Therapy or self-help groups may assist the mourning process. The woman may first be able to identify and empathize with the losses suffered by others before acknowledging and accepting her own. Having other group members support her and empathize with her can be a very powerful and healing experience.

The reality of past losses may transfer to the present. The survivor will often fear losing current relationships, especially the relationship with the therapist once it is fairly well established. Because of this, special attention must be paid to the relationship, particularly in preparing clients for any changes in therapy, such as absences, separations, and termination. The client's tendency to blame herself, to project negative self-esteem, and to find proof of untrustworthiness on the part of others have already been discussed. These will be activated during changes and will interact with fear of abandonment/rejection. Separations for events such as professional time, vacations, or childbirth should be announced and prepared for well in advance. The therapist must explore reactions and attributions of the client in order to correct faulty assumptions. Very often the client will intellectually understand the need for a separation but feel quite discomforted by it. She may even castigate herself for her feelings (i.e., for feeling like a baby for being so dependent, for being ridiculous), or she may use familiar defenses and behaviors and deny any emotions or behave in ways to take care of the therapist (i.e., to show no emotions so as not to cause problems for the therapist).

Support is needed for the client's right to her emotions and for their ventilation. Sometimes it will be appropriate for the therapist to share his or her own emotions regarding leaving and to offer reassurance that being physically absent does not mean a cessation of caring—nor is separation due to dislike of the client. Some clients will also express concern for the therapist's safety and will need reassurance for that as well. Adequate backup coverage should be planned for each separation even if the client scoffs at it or indicates she will never use it or be comfortable seeing anyone else. It nevertheless communicates appropriate caretaking and responsibility. Finally, the therapist may find it useful or necessary to devise particular strategies for individual clients. The authors have in some cases written a letter or shared a possession with a client prior to separation to encourage object constancy, or sent a note or postcard or made phone contact during separations. The therapist must avoid overly solicitous behavior and should choose strategies based upon the needs of the client at the time. On occasion, separations will be so stressful that hospitalization should be considered or implemented to assure the woman's safety.

Premature Termination

In a similar vein, termination should be carefully handled and prepared for. It will be most difficult when the therapeutic work is incomplete, as in the case of an intern leaving a placement or the therapist moving to another agency or town when the client has not yet worked through the issues of separation and individuation and is in a state of dependency. The therapist must plan for and assess the impact of abuse dynamics and determine appropriate strategies according to the individual case. The authors have found that overlapping or joint sessions with old and new therapist can be beneficial in providing the support needed for the transition. Likewise, formal termination of therapy may need extra attention and preparation with this population. Separation, individuation, and independence ought to be stated goals of treatment that are referred to periodically throughout to clearly prepare the survivor for their eventuality.

Control/Power Issues

Several other central dynamics and transference reactions will enter the therapy. The issues of control and power may be evident throughout as a consequence of the lack of either during the incest. Survivors usually felt both powerless and powerful during the abuse. On the one hand, they could not prevent or stop it; on the other, they may have been told or believed they had the power to destroy their family or to protect younger siblings. Intense self-control was a common learned coping mechanism. Many victim/survivors trained themselves to "play possum" (Summit, 1983) in order to detach themselves from their bodies, to numb all responses, and/or to build walls around themselves during the abuse. Defenses may be very strong and rigid. As a result, dismantling or lessening them may feel overwhelming and lead to strong fear or anxiety reactions such as trance states, dissociation, and hyperventilation that reenact the defenses. Power issues will be evident in therapy with many survivors needing to exert control in some way. Lateness for appointments, missed sessions, nonpayment or late payment of fees, silence, or extreme verbosity during sessions may be attempts to exert control and demonstrate power although they may have other motivations as well. Some survivors will be extremely rageful and spiteful, as a means of maintaining control and sometimes to dare anyone to try to like them. They may additionally be very resentful at being in therapy because of past unsuccessful therapy attempts or because they had received family messages that they were crazy.

Powerlessness may be manifest through extreme compliance and solicitousness about the needs of the therapist or through typical victims' nonassertive and helpless behavior. Some survivors have given up hope, resigned to being misunderstood and not helped by anyone. It may be difficult for the therapist to avoid becoming ensnared in the hopelessness and helplessness; however, the feelings must be supported and understood before progress will be made in changing them.

Due to power/control issues and to faulty learning and parenting, limit-setting and maintenance of boundaries in therapy are essential. The survivor will probably test the therapist's boundaries. The therapist needs to model being a good parent by taking responsibility to set and maintain limits. A particularly important distinction to make is that between sex and affection.

Incest survivors may have difficulty distinguishing between them because these boundaries were breached. Some survivors have learned to "lead with their sexuality" and may try to sexualize the therapy relationship. A number of motivations may be at play: Being sexual may allow her to express affection, to gain a sense of control, to reinforce her belief that anyone who cares about her must want to be sexual, or to give the only worthwhile thing she has to offer. Further, it may be a way of expressing self-hatred or a way to prove the therapist's venality. To engage in sex with a client is always unethical and unprofessional no matter what the circumstance. It is a further betrayal and a re-creation of the incest. It is the therapist's responsibility to set appropriate boundaries, to not act on sexual feelings, to interpret and help the client work them through, and to seek supervision or other means to work through the therapist's own feelings.

Defenses

Finally, defenses such as denial, repression, minimization, projection, splitting, and dissociation are common and are certain to enter the therapy process. As discussed by Summit (1983), it is crucial that the therapist conceptualize and understand these defenses as coping/surviving skills and present them as such within the therapy. To do so will enable understanding about the accommodations needed to survive the abuse and raise the possibility of gradually dropping them. Many of these same defenses will need to be managed in therapy: Denial and minimization will need to be countered repeatedly, repression lifted through exploration over time (using a variety of techniques), projection and splitting analyzed, and the need for dissociation lessened.

Countertransference Reactions

Several countertransference reactions commonly enter the process. The therapist may adapt defenses similar to those of the survivor in order to counter the pain experienced upon hearing about the abuse. The incest may be avoided or minimized by encouraging the survivor to not discuss it, by changing the subject when it is brought up, by overgeneralizing the extent to which "we are all victim/survivors," by muting language (i.e., avoiding words like incest, rape, abuse, violation), and by maintaining an overly professional, abstinent position. The therapist may feel very overwhelmed by hearing about multigenerational abuse and multiple victimizations of one child or of many within one family, or about violent, sadistic abuse.

Another reaction is the tendency to treat the client as damaged goods or as overly fragile, without an appreciation of her strength. This may result in overprotection, with the therapist functioning as rescuer. The client may be treated as overly special as the therapist makes many special efforts to accommodate her. Even the tendency to sexualize the relationship may be due to a rescuing fantasy on the therapist's part, since such behavior is frequently rationalized as providing a "corrective emotional experience."

Privileged voyeurism is a form of countertransference that leads to an excessive interest in sexual details without adequate attention to other needs and issues. The therapist may be so fascinated or shocked by the sexual behavior as to focus on it almost exclusively. Such overinterest has left many survivors feeling as though they had been on a witness stand and forced to divulge their most embarrassing memories. It is generally necessary for some details about how the abuse occurred to be disclosed, but it is not necessary to know all or to have graphic detail presented repeatedly. Therapist rage can cause problems if expressed prematurely or too intensively. It can be of great benefit for the survivor to have someone be angry about what happened to her; however, overly strong or mistimed reactions can be overwhelming or negative. Therapy will similarly be impeded if the therapist's anger blocks the client from being able to express her ambivalent feelings or any tender or loving feelings she may have for the perpetrator or other family members.

Although other dynamics will certainly be played out in the therapy process according to the experiences of the individual, the therapist, and their unique relationship, those presented above seem to be the most common.

THERAPY STRATEGIES AND TECHNIQUES

Numerous strategies and techniques from many theoretical orientations can be used to achieve the goals of retrospective incest therapy. Those presented below include many familiar to the mental health professional as well as several that have been tailored to this population by the authors or by other practitioners. The latter are presented in more detail than the former. At the present time, most clinical interventions with this population and with other populations of victims have been applied without empirical testing of their effectiveness (Report of the Task Force, 1984). Because of this, new strategies and interventions should be cross-validated with the available theoretical literature. The strategies described below should not be used in "cookbook" fashion but rather should be applied selectively. They are both a means of achieving and a supplement to the intensive exploration of core issues and the therapist/client relationship. Giarretto's (1976) comments on strategies and theoretical orientation in incest treatment remain pertinent. He wrote: "A particular psychological school or discipline is not rigidly adhered to. . . . A variety of techniques is employed in implementing the therapeutic model. None is used for its own sake. Instead, I try to tune into the client and the situation and try to apply a fitting technique" (p. 154).

As mentioned briefly in the section on diagnosis, treatment of other disorders may need to take precedence over or require simultaneous treatment with the incest. A minority of clients, moreover, will need psychiatric evaluation, the use of psychotropic drugs, and hospitalization. Concerning the involvement of medical personnel, the practitioner is advised that many survivors have had extremely negative past and present experiences with medical professionals resulting in their being highly anxious, hostile, and/or paranoid about them. Careful attention to feelings about medical staff and practices with careful preparation for contact is necessary, as is selection and collaboration with hospitals and doctors. It is useful to develop a roster of doctors and facilities selected for their knowledge of, sensitivity about, and openness to working with this population. When hospitalization is required, it is likewise useful to choose a facility that allows the therapist access to and continued treatment responsibility for the client.

The following therapeutic techniques and strategies have been used and found to be effective:

Gestalt exercises such as open chair, role reversal, and body awareness encourage identification of feeling, body state, unfinished business, spontaneous expression, the reconciliation of splits, and the reclamation of disowned parts.

Psychodrama techniques are used to rehearse or substitute for confrontations, to explore family patterns and relationships, to identify and reclaim disowned or unacknowledged feelings.

Psychoanalytic/psychodynamic approaches such as free association, dream analysis and interpretation, and analysis of transference/countertransference are used to bypass defenses and allow the emergence of underlying feelings, thoughts, and memories. Once conscious, the material becomes accessible for analysis and intervention.

Cognitive approaches that are used may include the articulation and modification of faulty or destructive belief systems, such as attributions, self-blame, and family rules. Childhood messages and family rules are often deeply entrenched because of strong reinforcement while the client was young and impressionable. These will usually be modified with repeated challenge and replacement with alternative beliefs and messages.

Social learning formulations such as Seligman's (1975) learned-helplessness theory are useful to conceptualize replacement of maladaptive behavior and belief through repeated exposure to alternatives.

Transactional analysis theory and techniques can also assist in the exploration and modification of parent–child–adult messages.

Humanistic psychology techniques and their applicability have been described by Giarretto (1976), including self-assessment and confrontation-assimilation in a supportive, compassionate treatment milieu. Self-awareness and self-management techniques drawn from psychosynthesis are also therapeutic.

Behavioral approaches and strategies teach skills and the modification of behavior. Training and role play in such areas as assertiveness, stress and anger management, and relaxation are often pertinent, as is social skills training.

Hypnosis, guided imagery, and the use of metaphor can be quite powerful. For clients who are able to visualize, imagery can assist in learning relaxation, breaking down defenses, allowing memories to emerge, and gaining control. Many incest clients describe and visualize themselves as being behind a protective wall, in a box or closet, or under the bed, images that can be used in assisting them to lower defenses. Metaphor can similarly be useful.

Hypnosis can be beneficial if undertaken with caution. Therapist-induced regressive hypnosis can assist in the recapturing of lost memories. Memories need to be brought back slowly with much time given to processing them so that the client is not flooded. Even within an established therapeutic relationship, regressive hypnosis is best used only at the client's request and when contraindications are not strong or numerous. Self-hypnosis can be beneficial because it can increase the client's sense of self-control and can be used to develop relaxation responses and control over dissociative responses.

Expressive therapies such as art, movement, music, and journal therapy provide a nonverbal symbolic mode of communication. Expressive therapies surface unconscious material and can also circumvent inhibitions arising from defense mechanisms and injunctions to secrecy.

Education about sexuality and exercises and *techniques of sex therapy* can be applied when a determination is made that the client is ready. The reader is referred to Becker and Skinner (1984), Nadelson (1982), and Sprei and Courtois (in press) for a comprehensive discussion of approaches, techniques, and contraindications.

Bibliotherapy and education and training about incest and its patterns of occurrence can offer information or can correct misinformation. First-person accounts of incest experience as found in *Daddy's Girl* (Allen, 1982), *Father's Days* (Brady, 1979), *I Never Told Anyone* (Bass & Thornton, 1983), *Voices in the Night* (McNaron & Morgan, 1982); overview books such as *Betrayal of Innocence* (Forward & Buck, 1978), *Conspiracy of Silence* (Butler, 1978), and *Kiss Daddy Goodnight* (Armstrong, 1978); selected articles; material from self-help groups such as Incest Resources, Incest Survivors Anonymous (ISA), and Victims of Incest Can Emerge Survivors (VOICES), can be used to explicitly increase information about intrafamilial sexual abuse. Other books on child abuse and other family problems, such as *Adult Children of Alcoholics* (Woititz, 1983), *Childhood Comes First* (Helfer, 1978), and *Outgrowing the Pain* (Gil, 1984) offer information on these topics. Participation in self-help and skill-building groups also fosters insight while introducing and reinforcing new behaviors.

Techniques and strategies the authors have found especially useful include the following:

A *detailed individual and family history:* Some survivors may have full recall of the past, while for others significant portions are blocked. A history, including the notation of what time periods are repressed, can offer much pertinent information. The survivor's recollections may be supplemented by those of other family members when available. Family photographs can also be used to gain information and, at times, to jog the client's memory. Compilation of family history is optimally done in a sequential series of sessions. This may be impossible for numerous survivors, making it necessary for the therapist to keep track of the history and to fit pieces together. It is not unusual for the survivor to reforget material once it has been remembered.

Writing and drawing: Through these means, the survivor may express emotions and thoughts she cannot do otherwise. Nonverbal expression may be the beginning method of telling the story, especially for those women who were strictly forbidden from ever telling and who were threatened with very dire consequences if they talked. In particular, autobiographies, journals, letter writing, and creative writing such as poetry and healing stories (Butler, 1985) are powerful means of ventilation. Keeping a list of things to express to family members and writing letters can prepare the survivor for family disclosure and confrontation. The decision to actually mail a letter will depend on the survivor's goals and readiness.

Anger-management techniques: Physical exercise and expression of anger should be encouraged as a means of "letting off steam." Keeping a "mad list" or a daily stressor list can be an eye-opener to the client who tends to minimize or discount her reactions. They provide a sequential and cumulative listing of irritants. Anger management is geared toward positive, healthy expression and is used to discourage stockpiling of anger and resultant explosive expression. It also assists the survivor to feel more in control of and less frightened by her anger.

Involvement of and treatment of family members and friends: At times, it is useful to involve family members or friends in treatment for a number of reasons—to enlist their support and assistance, to explain the course of therapy, and to prepare them for or reassure them about intense client reactions. Additionally, a partner or family member may be jealous of the therapist–client relationship, especially when strong dependency develops. Involving them can counter resistance and jealousy while offering inclusion and reassurance.

Self-nurturing exercises: The therapist can encourage self-nurturing by suggesting that the survivor get in touch with the little girl inside of herself that is scared and hurting. Even well-defended clients seem to respond to this suggestion with tears and sadness. The client can be encouraged to be kind to this little girl, to nurture and care for her, to allow her to play and to rest. Childhood pictures can be utilized to help the client focus on herself as a child. The grieving process may be triggered through the client's childhood memories.

Many survivors hate or feel detached from their bodies. They may feel that their bodies betrayed them, especially if being touched during the abuse resulted in pleasure and/or orgasm. Education regarding the normalcy of responding to touch and differentiating between good and bad touch are first steps in acceptance of her body. Exercises are available in *Childhood Comes First* (Helfer, 1978) to expand awareness of the senses.

As discussed earlier, many survivors were given the role of parent in their families and learned to take care of others when they themselves were neglected. They can now be encouraged to give themselves care and nurturance and to ask for it from others. They may initially feel selfish and guilty, so encouragement, reassurance, and follow-up are needed.

Building a support network: Clients may lack the skills and experience to form friendships due to past isolation. Group therapy and self-help activities allow for the development of support systems. The woman can be encouraged to join a consciousness-raising group, a women's organization, a hobby club, a religious activity, or a professional organization. In order to separate and individuate from her family of origin, she may need to first develop a new family, a family of friends. In particular, a close relationship with an available female role model should be encouraged, if one is available.

Self-help groups, training courses, and other adjunctive activities: Involvement should be orchestrated so the therapy relationship and work are not split or impeded. These types of activities can reinforce learning in therapy and can provide additional means of information and support.

Management of self-mutilation: Self-mutilation is designed to hurt rather than to destroy the self, although it can result in suicide. Episodes of self-mutilation can be frightening for both client and therapist as well as to friends and family. Potential for self-destruction should be first assessed and managed. Then the function of the self-hurtful behavior must be explored. It may be a way to feel something, a way to end stress, a punishment, an externalization of pain, a distraction of pain from other places, or a way to terminate a dissociative episode. Replacement of self-mutilating behaviors with behaviors that are less self-hurtful can be achieved as the therapy progresses and as motivations are worked through.

Physical contact: When consistent with the therapist's style and comfort level, touching and holding the client can be therapeutic as a part of healthy reparenting. It is crucial to explore the meaning of physical contact with the client and to ask her permission before any physical contact is made. Touching should be solely for the benefit of the client, with clear limitations discussed that the touching will not be sexual.

Public disclosure and advocacy: For some survivors, public acknowledgment and advocacy are to be encouraged. Although disclosure and advocacy are, strictly speaking, not strategies, they should be understood by professionals as a valid means for some victims to work through and transcend the victimization (Consensus Statement, 1985).

GROUP TREATMENT

The professional literature describing group therapy for survivors has been sparse up until recently, although Herman and Schatzow (1984) point out there is a strong oral tradition in supporting its use and efficacy. The combination of individual and group therapy either simultaneously or consecutively may be the most effective and complete method in treating incest survivors. Each modality allows for different issues to be addressed, transferences to arise, and types and levels of interventions to be made.

An incest survivors' group can instill a sense of identification among members by breaking their sense of isolation and differentness. The group allows for greater resolution of issues of secrecy, shame, and guilt, as well as serving as a catalyst for breaking denial and exploring feelings, beliefs, family dynamics, survivor skills, and interpersonal relationships. The group functions in a consciousness-raising capacity with members gaining new perspectives on their experiences. Recognizing commonalities, they can learn to externalize responsibility for the abuse and understand it as the cause rather than as the result of personal characteristics and problems.

A group can serve as a new family for participants, allowing for sibling as well as parental transferences to occur and be explored. Unlike the family of origin, the group models a family where conflicts can be openly discussed and worked through without the individual being rejected, discounted, or abused. In a group, the healthy expression of emotions and conflicts is modeled and social skills are practiced.

The group modality is not appropriate for all survivors, nor should the client be placed in a group without consideration of her status, needs, and motivation for such an experience. For some, a group is too threatening due to shame, secrecy, denial, and mistrust. Once some of these issues are addressed in individual work, group therapy may present a more acceptable option as a means of working on the very same issues. Other survivors may feel that group is less threatening than is individual treatment. The intimacy, focused attention, intense transference, mistrust of authority figures, and past disappointments with individual therapy, coupled with a strong desire to be with others like herself, may make group therapy a more appropriate option. Individual therapy can be undertaken later if warranted. Still other survivors are too afraid of losing control or going crazy to be in a group. They may project their own feelings of helplessness and self-hatred onto others and may be unable to conceptualize receiving help from other victim/survivors. They too may need to engage in individual treatment prior to any group involvement.

Several contraindications to group participation are mentioned in the literature, including: active psychosis, active paranoia, extreme dependency, active drug or alcohol addiction, an inability to control strong impulsive and/or aggressive tendencies, an inability to discuss her own incest experience without dissociating, and the client experiencing a current crisis. Group membership should be carefully balanced so that no one member is different from others in terms of race, sexual orientation, age, and type of abuse experience. Such differentness will reinforce feelings of isolation and uniqueness. Due to the dynamics brought to bear on the group process, small group size and the use of cotherapists are advisable.

SPECIAL ISSUES

This section addresses briefly several issues that arise quite regularly in retrospective incest work and require special consideration, including therapist gender; disclosure and confrontation; reporting laws, confidentiality, and privacy; and legal recourse.

Therapist Gender

As mentioned previously, therapist gender can impact and complicate therapy with incest survivors. Some authorities believe that male therapists should not work with this population due to their likely inability to fully understand and empathize with the victim and her experience and their likely ability to identify with the perpetrator. The authors support the perspective articulated by Herman (1981) and others that while incest therapy is likely to be more difficult for the male therapist, he should not automatically be assumed to be incompetent to do this work. He will, in all likelihood, have to work harder than his female counterpart to understand the victimization and, in addition, will need to carefully monitor countertransference reactions, especially those having to do with sexual arousal. An opposite-sex supervisor should be considered to assist in exploring and catching problematic gender-related countertransference reactions.

Some survivors can only tolerate a therapist of the same gender as that of the individual who is perceived as having been the least abusive or the most nurturing to them in the past. The survivor should be in control of this choice and should be encouraged to discuss her reasons for her preference.

Therapists of either gender have as goals the empowerment of the survivor and should use the working relationship as a model of an appropriate, caring, growth-promoting, nonexploitive relationship. Reparenting, including appropriate distance coupled with warmth and affection, is a critical element.

Disclosure and Confrontation

In retrospective work, disclosure to family and friends and confrontation of family members are often significant issues. These may be necessitated in cases where evidence suggests that a minor child in the family is being abused or is at risk. Little published material is available concerning clinical intervention with abusive families or perpetrators long after the abuse has ceased. MacFarlane and Korbin (1983) offer the most comprehensive guidelines, which include:

1. Whether to intervene. Many survivors have as their goal intervention/ disclosure/confrontation. Each of these should be explored in detail, the assumption being that it is not a good strategy for all and should not be pursued in all cases. It has the potential for positive outcome in many cases; however, it can have tragic and negative outcomes as well, such as violent or assaultive behavior and suicide. In exploring whether to make an intervention, the following points of assessment are critical: (1) assessment of the motivations of all concerned; (2) assessment of what is in the best interest of the client; (3) assessment of what the client would like to get out of such an intervention; (4) assessment of the potential for violence; and (5) determination of whether abuse of youngsters in the family is occurring currently.

2. Goals for intervention. If intervention is a feasible option, realistic goals need to be established. The client must be prepared for the types of response that are likely so that she can understand them and determine how to respond. She should be urged to disclose or confront only when she is emotionally ready and well prepared. Optimally, she should not look to the confrontation/disclosure for validation that the incest occurred, nor should she expect automatic support on the part of the family. In most cases, disclosure will bring pain and crisis for other family members. She needs to understand that it is not she who is the source of the pain. Specific strategies can be devised according to the needs and best interests of the client. Backup therapeutic and social resources may be needed.

When face-to-face confrontation is not an option or is not the option of choice, writing a letter to the abuser or to the entire family (which may or may not be mailed) and techniques such as the empty chair should be considered.

Reporting

The legal mandate to report suspected or known cases of ongoing child sexual abuse, of necessity, disturbs client privacy and the privilege of confidentiality. The limits of confidentiality should be carefully explained to the survivor during intake and assessment or very early in the treatment. Some survivors are all too happy to have someone report ongoing family abuse and will not be disturbed about losing the privilege of their communications. For others, issues of family protection, guilt, betrayal, and mistrust of the therapist will be salient. Even a report made anonymously can result in an extremely volatile situation with unanticipated consequences for all concerned. The therapist can confer with local child protection services before reporting, to become familiarized with the procedures that will be set in motion once a report is made. These can then be discussed in detail with the client to prepare her for their implementation and to anticipate likely family reactions. Additional support of the client will be needed when a report is made and a family investigated.

Legal Initiatives

A final issue currently receiving increased attention on both the national and local levels is retrospective litigation of incestuous abuse. Both criminal and civil charges are on the increase, the option determined by the statutes of each jurisdiction.

Similar to legal procedures for other types of criminal victimizations, especially rape, the victim/survivor will become the "star witness" and the sexual trauma will be recounted and cross-examined in open court. A further complication is involved because the accused is a family member and the family at large may be thrust into crisis and exhibit divided loyalty and hostility. In some situations, some family members will side with the survivor and others will side with the accused. Detailed preparation and intensive support for the client will again be called for. For a period of time during or after the legal proceedings, particularly if the perpetrator is found not guilty, the therapist should expect the remanifestation of symptoms.

SUMMARY

Retrospective incest therapy is complex and demanding work for both the victim/survivor and for the therapist. It calls upon the strength and fortitude of the survivor and upon the strength, ingenuity, and skills of the therapist. The survivor reaps the growth and development benefits of a healthy relationship, the therapist the satisfaction that comes from the reparative reparenting function of the treatment and the resultant changes in the client.

The victim becomes a survivor in the truest sense of the word when she has disengaged from the past and developed herself and her life according to her needs and preferences.

REFERENCES

Allen, V. (1982). *Daddy's girl.* New York: Berkley.

American Psychiatric Association. (1987). *Diagnostic and statistical manual of mental disorders* (3rd ed., rev.). Washington, DC: Author.

Armstrong, L. (1978) *Kiss daddy good-night: A speak-out on incest.* New York: Hawthorne Books.

Bass, E., & Thornton, L., (Eds.). (1983). *I never told anyone: Writing by women survivors of child sexual abuse.* New York: Harper & Row.

Becker, J. V., & Skinner, L. J. (1984). Behavioral treatment of sexual dysfunctions in sexual assault survivors. In J. R. Stuart & Joanne E. Greer (Eds.), *Victims of sexual aggression. Treatment of children, women and men.* New York: Van Nostrand Reinhold.

Bender, L., & Blau, A. (1937). The reaction of children to sexual relations with adults. *American Journal of Orthopsychiatry, 7,* 500–518.

Benward, J., & Densen-Gerber, J. (1975). Incest as a causative factor in anti-social behavior: An exploratory study. *Contemporary Drug Problems, 4*(3), 323–340.

Brady, K. (1979). *Father's days.* New York: Dell.

Briere, J. (1984, April). *The effects of childhood sexual abuse on later psychological functioning: Defining a post-sexual abuse syndrome.* Paper presented at the Third National Conference on Sexual Victimization of Children, Children's Hospital National Medical Center, Washington, DC.

Briere, J., & Runtz, M. (1985). *Symptomatology associated with prior sexual abuse in a non-clinical sample.* Unpublished paper, Winnipeg, Canada.

Brickman, J. (1984). Feminist, nonsexist, and traditional models of therapy: Implications for working with incest. *Women and Therapy, 3,* 49–67.

Browne, A., & Finkelhor, D. (1986). Impact of child sexual abuse: A review of the research. *Psychological Bulletin, 99,* 66–77.

Burgess, A. W., & Holmstrom, L. H. (1979). *Rape: Crisis and Recovery.* New York: Prentice-Hall.

Butler, S. (1978). *Conspiracy of silence: The trauma of incest.* New York: Bantam.

Butler, S. (1985, February). *Counseling issues and techniques for working with abuse survivors.* Workshop presented at Counselling the Sexual Abuse Survivor: A Conference in Clinical and Social Issues, Winnipeg, Canada.

Consensus Statement. (1985). *The aftermath of crime: A mental health crisis.* A Services, Research and Evaluation Colloquium. Co-sponsored by the National Organization for Victim Assistance and the Office of State and Community Liaison of the National Institute of Mental Health of the U.S. Department of Health and Human Services.

Courtois, C. A. (1979). *Characteristics of a volunteer sample of adult women who experienced incest in childhood and adolescence.* Unpublished doctoral dissertation, University of Maryland.

Courtois, C. A., & Watts, D. (1982). Counseling adult women who experienced incest in childhood or adolescence. *Personnel and Guidance Journal, 60*(2), 275–279.

Erikson, E. H. (1963). *Children and society.* New York: W. W. Norton.

Finklehor, D. (1984). *Child sexual abuse: New theory and research.* New York: Free Press.

Forward, S., & Buck, C. (1978). *Betrayal of innocence: Incest and its devastation.* Los Angeles: J. P. Tarcher.

Gelinas, D. J. (1983). The persisting negative effects of incest, *Psychiatry, 46,* 313–332.

Giarretto, H. (1976). The treatment of father–daughter incest: A psycho-social approach. *Children Today, 34,* 2–5.

Gil, E. (1984). *Outgrowing the pain.* Palo Alto: Consulting Psychologist Press.

Goodwin, J., Simms, M., & Bergman, R. (1979). Hysterical seizures: A sequel to incest. *American Journal of Orthopsychiatry, 49,* 698–703.

Helfer, R. E. (1978). *Childhood comes first: A crash course in childhood for adults.* East Lansing, MI: Author.

Herman, J. (1981). *Father–daughter incest.* Cambridge, MA: Harvard University Press.

Herman, J., & Shatzow, E. (1984). Time-limited group therapy for women with a history of incest. *International Journal of Group Psychotherapy, 34,* 605–616.

Horowitz, M. (1976). *Stress response syndrome.* New York: Aronson.

Kubler-Ross, E. (1969). *On death and dying.* New York: Macmillan.

Lees, S. (1981). *Cues to identifying women with histories of incest.* Cambridge, MA: Incest Resources.

Mayer, A. (1983). *Incest: A treatment manual for therapy with victims, spouses and offenders.* Holmes Beach, FL: Learning Publications.

McFarlane, K., & Korbin, J. (1983). Confronting the incest secret long after the fact: A family study of multiple victimization with strategies for intervention. *Child Abuse and Neglect, 7,* 227–240.

McNaron, T. A. H., & Morgan, Y. (Eds.). (1982). *Voices in the night: Women speaking about incest.* Minneapolis, MI: Cleis Press.

Nadelson, C. C. (1982). Incest and rape: Repercussions in sexual behavior. In L. Greenspoon, (Ed.), *The annual review of psychiatry* (pp. 56–66). Washington, DC: American Psychiatric Press.

Peters, J. J. (1976). Children who are victims of sexual assault and the psychology of offenders. *American Journal of Psychotherapy, 30,* 398–421.

Renshaw, D. (1982). *Incest: Understanding and treatment.* Boston: Little, Brown.

Report of the Task Force on Victims of Crime and Violence. (1984). Washington, DC: American Psychological Association.

Rosenfeld, A. A. (1977). Sexual misuse and the family. *Victimology: An International Journal, 2,* 226–235.

Rosenfeld, A. A. (1979). Endogamous incest and the victim-perpetrator model. *American Journal of Disturbed Children, 133,* 406–410.

Rush, F. (1980). *The best kept secret: Sexual abuse of children.* Englewood Cliffs, NJ: Prentice-Hall.

Russell, D. E. H. (1983). The incidence and prevalence of intrafamilial and extrafamilial sexual abuse of female children. *Child Abuse and Neglect, 7,* 133–146.

Seligman, M. E. P. (1975). *Helplessness: On depression, development, and death.* San Francisco: Freeman.

Sgroi, S. M., (Ed.). (1982). *Handbook of clinical intervention in child sexual abuse.* Lexington, MA: Lexington Books.

Silver, R. L., Boon, C., & Stones, M. H. (1983). Searching for meaning in misfortune: Making sense of incest. *Journal of Social Issues, 39,* 81–102.

Sommers, R. M., & Marcus, G. (1982). *The therapist's role in treating incestuous families.* Pittsburgh, PA: Pittsburgh Action Against Rape.

Spencer, J. (1978). Father–daughter incest. *Child Welfare, 57,* 581–589.

Sprei, J., & Courtois, C. (in press). The treatment of women's sexual dysfunctions arising from sexual assault. In J. R. Field & R. A. Brown (Eds.), *Advances in the understanding and treatment of sexual problems: A compendium for the individual and marital therapist.* New York: Spectrum.

Summit, R. (1983). The child sexual abuse accommodation syndrome. *Child Abuse and Neglect, 7,* 177–193.

Symonds, M. (1980). The "second injury" to victims. *Evaluation and Change,* Minneapolis, Minn.: Program Evaluation Resource Center.

Westerlund, E. (1983). Counseling women with histories of incest. *Women and Therapy, 2,* 17–30.

Wise, M. L. (1985, April). *Incest victim/survivor paradox: Therapeutic strategies and issues.* Presentation made at the Annual Convention of the American Association for Counseling and Development, New York.

Woititz, J. G. (1983). *Adult children of alcoholics.* Hollywood, Fla.: Health Communications, Inc.

Wooley, M. J. & Vigilanti, M. A. (1984). Psychological separation and the sexual abuse victim. *Psychotherapy: Theory, Research and Practice, 21,* 347–352.

15

Nonoffending Mothers:
A New Conceptualization

Lorna P. Cammaert

The literature on child sexual abuse relies heavily on clinical impressions and most often designates the mother "as the most culpable individual either through default or through direct involvement" (McIntyre, 1981, p. 462). This article will review the clinical literature and contrast it with the growing assessment data that are available. Following this, an alternate conceptualization of the mother's position is described that emphasizes the strengths needed by a mother, not only to survive in an incestuous family but also to protect her children.

CLINICAL LITERATURE

In the clinical literature, mother's actions or inactions are explained by four ideas. First, the family is seen to be disturbed or pathological and "mother is the cornerstone of a pathological family system" (Machotka, Pittman, & Flomenhaft, 1967, p. 100). Lustig, Dresser, Spellman, and Murray (1966), utilizing a transactional analysis framework, see father–daughter incest as symptomatic of family dysfunction and describe the incest as serving a tension-reducing function important to the continuing existence of the family. From a psychodynamic viewpoint, Guthiel and Avery (1977) see incest as expressing the collective psychopathology of all family members.

Second, mother is seen to have a disturbed personality and to greatly lack social skills. A description that has often been quoted is from the article by Kaufman, Peck, and Tagiuri (1954), whose impressions are based on eleven families:

When first seen the mothers were hard, careless in dress, infantile, extremely dependent, intellectually dull, poor housekeepers, panicky in the face of responsibility, and satisfied to live in disorder and poverty. (p. 269)

They go on to add observations and conclusions such as "the mothers went to any lengths to satisfy their need for affection, attention, and support and to deny their feelings of worthlessness" (p. 270), and "they chose masochistic methods in their attempts to fulfill their needs. At least half attempted to fill these needs by promiscuity and the others neglected their health or deliberately got into situations where they could be injured physically" (p. 270). In addition, Sgroi and Dana (1982) observed that impaired communication between family members was characteristic and stated that mothers were largely responsible because they "served as noncommunicative role models in their interactions with husbands that were observed by the children" (p. 194).

Third, the mothers are seen as neglectful in their roles as wife and mother. The mothers are judged to be derelict in the sexual role, thus forcing their husbands to find sexual satisfaction with their daughter or son. A typical observation is found in the article by Cormier, Kennedy, and Sangowicz (1962): "Certain of the wives were not only frigid, but hostile and unloving women. Some never denied their husbands and were described by them as good wives, but the relationship was ungratifying because of the wives' inability to respond" (p. 207). Thus the women are seen as sexually unresponsive and denying their husbands access to sexual release; although they may be sexually available and compliant, they remain at fault because they have failed to make sex gratifying for their husbands. Her sexual gratification does not seem to be considered. Of the many articles where the marital sexual relationship is cited as a rationale for child sexual abuse, the question of the husband's responsibility as a thoughtful, respectful, fully functioning, equal sex partner is never raised.

Another issue is that of role reversal between mother and daughter. For a number of reasons, the oldest daughter may be asked to take on more of the household maintenance; these tasks gradually become generalized until the daughter is meeting all of her father's needs, including the sexual ones. The child becomes the "household and sexual surrogate for mother" (Boekelheide, 1978, p. 88, cited in Jones, 1979). Some authors also raise the issue about mother leaving home to do paid or volunteer work and judge this as an abdication of her responsibility as a wife and mother (Kaufman, Peck, & Tagiuri, 1954; Sgroi & Dana, 1982). In some families where both parents work outside the home, they attempt to arrange disparate schedules to ensure that one parent is at home to care for the children while the other is working (Meiselman, 1978). Once again, mother is blamed as the one who irresponsibly left her children unprotected with their father or surrogate. Sgroi and

Dana (1982) state strongly that mothers "escape the frustration, unpleasantness, and boredom of their roles by seeking companionship, distraction, or employment outside the home. . . . Whatever the justification for physical absence, however, the effect is the same with respect to the incestuous relationship: mother manages to avoid setting limits for others and fails to fulfill her own role responsibilities by being elsewhere" (p. 193). Thus in an age when it is often necessary for both parents to work in order to support the family, some clinicians unfairly judge a mother's absence as a deliberate dereliction of her duty and responsibility to her children.

The fourth idea views the mother as a conscious or unconscious colluder of incest. A number of authors strongly state that the mother has knowledge of the father–daughter incest and denies it to herself and others (Guthiel & Avery, 1977; Jones, 1979; Luckianowicz, 1972; Lustig et. al. 1966; Matchotka, Pittman, & Flomenhaft, 1967; Meiselman, 1978; Sgroi, 1982). Jones (1979) states that "mother . . . seems to play a pivotal role in establishing the father–daughter incestuous tie" (p. 287), and Meiselman (1978) writes of the mother who "sets up father and daughter for the incestuous relationship" (p. 172). Luckianowicz (1972) suggests that in 6 of 26 cases, the mother's tolerance of her husband's incest can be viewed as an exchange "as long as their husbands did not object to their promiscuous behavior" (p. 306). Sgroi and Dana (1982) see mothers investing "enormous amounts of energy in submerging conscious awareness of the incest relationship" (p. 198).

Thus the nonoffending mother is seen as a primary cause and/or facilitator of incest because of four ideas held by many clinicians: (1) she is the cornerstone of a pathological family; (2) she is psychologically disturbed herself; (3) she does not fulfill her roles as a wife and mother because she is a poor sexual partner; she reverses roles with her daughter, and deliberately leaves or escapes home through work; and (4) she is collusive in providing opportunities for the incest to occur, pushing both husband and daughter into it, and then turning a blind eye. Of these traditional clinical impressions, Luckianowicz (1972) is one of the few who, while subscribing to most of these ideas, describes mothers somewhat more sympathetically: "most of the mothers appeared to be normal, hard-working, and much suffering women, usually with large families, and with either a habitually unemployed, inefficient, 'good for nothing' husband or an aggressive and demanding husband" (p. 305).

ASSESSMENT DATA

Some studies have been done recently to ascertain which of the clinical impressions can be upheld with assessment data. In a survey of 102 cases conducted by Julian and Mohr (1980), 93.1% of the incestuous households were comprised of a mother, father, and several children. In comparison to the general population where 6.3% have four or more children, incestuous families were larger, with 36.3% having four or more children. Julian and Mohr also found an extremely high level of discord in 65.7% of the families. They cited as well 32.4% alcohol dependence, 31.4% mental health problems, and 25.5% spousal abuse.

Herman and Hirshman (1981) attempted to identify families at risk for father–daughter incest by comparing family histories of 40 women who had had incestuous relationships with their fathers during childhood with 20 women whose fathers had been seductive but not openly incestuous. The only characteristic that distinguished the fathers was the greater amount of violence exhibited by incestuous fathers. Violence was used to dominate the family in an attempt to consolidate the father's power and isolate his wife and children from the outside world (Herman, 1981). Several significant differences were found between the mothers. First, 55% of the mothers in incestuous families (compared to only 15% of the comparison groups) were ill, disabled, or absent for some period of time. The mothers in incestuous families were pregnant more often than the comparison mothers and consequently had more children for which to care (mean number of children: 3.6; comparison group mean: 2.85; national mean: 2.2). These mothers were more often battered by their husbands than were those in the comparison group.

Thus, the data relating to the incestuous family is limited in scope but clearly indicates these families were experiencing stress caused by larger than average family size, high family discord, alcoholism, wife battering, and mental health problems. With the increase in reporting of child sexual abuse and a greater research focus on the issue, the high rate of child sexual abuse indicates this type of family is becoming statistically defined as normal.

Because mothers have been clinically seen as instigators, facilitators, or colluders in child sexual abuse, research has often focused on personality assessments of them. The predominant features that emerge are that the mothers have low self-esteem (Bennett, 1980; Sahd, 1980; Sgroi & Dana, 1982) and are passive and helpless (Herman & Hirshman, 1981; Knudson, 1982; Meiselman, 1978; Sahd, 1980; Sgroi & Dana, 1982). In addition, other studies have found that the mothers use an intropunitive style of anger (Bennett, 1980); have an overall elevation on the MMPI (Fredrickson, 1981); experience psychosis (Herman & Hirshman, 1981); are depressed (Harrer, 1981; Herman & Hirshman, 1981); have tendencies toward worrying and being suspicious (Fredrickson, 1981; Sahd, 1980); resort to alcohol abuse (Herman & Hirshman, 1981—15%; Julian & Mohr, 1980—32.4%); and often have been involved in incest when they were children themselves (Goodwin, McCarthy, & DiVasto, 1981—24%). Goodwin (1981) found that 5 of 11 mothers in her study had attempted suicide, but describes 3 of these as having borderline personalities and drug abuse problems along with the situations involving atypical sexual abuse.

In a national survey of intrafamilial sexual abuse treatment centers, Forseth and Brown (1981) found that within the treatment modes of individual and group therapy, "the most frequently treated persons were the sexually abused child and the nonoffending spouse" (p. 184). When calculations were made for time spent in group therapy, nonoffending spouses spent twice as much time in therapy as did perpetrators. It is necessary to question whether this is due to the need for more therapy, to more compliance or availability for therapy, and/or to therapist bias.

The identified difficulties supply only slight support for the strongly pejorative clinical descriptions about mothers. It is not clear whether the negative personal and functioning aspects (e.g., low self-esteem, passivity, depression, and alcoholism) are part of the cause of incest or whether they are the result of living in an environment of male violence. Many of these aspects are typically demonstrated in the behavior of other victims of male violence (e.g., rape, physical and psychological abuse, and children who have been sexually abused).

Data do appear to support the fact that sexual functioning is an important issue in incestuous families. Bander, Fein, and Bishop (1982), in their report on the Connecticut Sexual Trauma Treatment Program, found that 17 (or 57%) of the families in their sample reported experiencing adult sexual problems. In Harrer's study (1981) of 28 women, the women reported a low degree of comfort in expressing sexual needs to their partner. Also, as was previously stated, there are more than the national average number of pregnancies and children in these families. The data do not appear to support the idea that the sexual dysfunctioning of the couple is necessarily the woman's responsibility. Certainly the literature on sexual dysfunction therapy does not ascribe blame or fault so clearly (Handy, Valentich, Gripton, & Cammaert, 1985), nor to the extent that the clinical literature on sexual abuse does. If there are sexual difficulties, it seems reasonable to assume they are, at the very least, a couple responsibility, if not to be attributed to the male's poor technique rather than the female's poor responses. Careful interviewing of male incest offenders reveals that "even in the most disturbed marriages, the father is usually able to command sex from his wife. No father is driven to incest for lack of sexual access to his spouse" (Herman, 1981, p. 43). This statement is corroborated by Groth and Birnbaum (1979) in their work with male offenders: "There was no one for whom no other opportunity for sexual gratification existed" (p. 149). Also, data from the study by Abel, Blanchard, Barlow, and Mavissakalian (1975) suggest that male offenders' sexual arousal, measured physiologically, is stimulated by young children, not adult women.

Therefore, the hypothesis that the mothers' failure to be sexually available has driven their husbands to seek sexual gratification from their daughters is definitely not supported in the research.

The mother–daughter role reversal is upheld by the assessment data. In Herman's study (1981), 45% of the 40 women studied had been pressed into service as "little mothers" by the age of 10. It must be remembered that in 55% of these families, the mother was ill, disabled, or absent for some period of time during which the father did not take up the maternal role. This then fell to the oldest daughter. The daughters were expected to mediate parental quarrels, placate father, be father's confidant, and were responsible for holding the family together.

Mother's absence due to volunteer or paid work has not yet been assessed and reported in the literature on child sexual abuse. This hypothesis was questioned earlier in this paper, because in these economic times it is often necessary for both parents to be employed to support the family. Research on women does indicate that activities outside the home, especially paid employment, are important to a woman's sense of well-being and counteract depression and low self-worth (e.g., Baruch, Barnett, & Rivers, 1983). Such activities may help the mothers to be more effective in childrearing, especially in becoming assertive enough to protect their daughters from the typical domineering father figure found in families reporting child sexual abuse. The hypothesis that temporary escape from an extremely negative family situation may strengthen the mother and her protective abilities with her children appears to have more credence than does the negative interpretation supplied by other authors.

The issue of the mother's direct or indirect collusion in incest is brought into question by statistics that report that approximately 25% of mothers take steps to protect their daughters once they are aware of the incest (Knudson, 1982; Meiselman, 1978). When asked whether they had revealed the incest to their mothers, 58% of Herman's sample (1981) reported that they never told their mothers, although they longed for their mothers to rescue them. Of those who indicated they had told, it was clear they had indicated it quite indirectly. However, Herman reports that of the mothers who knew of the incest, most were "unwilling or unable to defend their daughter" (p. 88). A picture emerges of daughters wanting mothers to know, perhaps dropping hints, but rarely telling mother in any direct manner. When told, mother may or may not take action, but it is unclear whether inaction is due to denial, inability to act effectively, or collusion. Summit (1983) uncategorically refuted the collusion myth:

> Marriage demands considerable blind trust and denial for survival. A woman does not commit her life and security to a man she believes capable of mo-

lesting his own children. The "obvious" clues to sexual abuse are usually only obvious in retrospect. Our assumption that the mother "must have known" merely parallels the demand of the child that the mother must be in touch intuitively with invisible and even deliberately concealed family discomfort. (p. 187)

To believe the child is to accept the breakdown of the family, which the mother has striven to hold together. To believe and act on the child's confession means reporting it outside the family, risking external judgment of her as a poor mother, risking removal of all the children or the husband from the home, court appearances, and possible loss of the major, if not only, breadwinner. Given the possibility of these high costs in combination with the family's operating as described earlier with a dominant father and an ineffectual mother, the explanations based on the mechanism of denial appear more credible than those of deliberate conscious collusion.

In summary, the assessment data indicate incestuous families are stressed and are violent, although not necessarily as pathological as so vividly described in the earlier clinical literature. The data upholds the fact that mothers are experiencing some personality difficulties: low self-esteem, passivity, depression, and alcoholism—but it is not clear whether this is cause or effect in an incestuous family. Concerns about poor sexual functioning are reported by both men and women in incestuous families, but the sexual dysfunction literature deliberately does not attribute blame to either partner. Data clearly refute the notion that fathers must resort to their children for sexual release, because they do have regular access to an adult sexual partner. The mother–daughter role reversal is confirmed by the data but must be viewed in light of the fact that in many incestuous families mothers are ill, disabled, or absent for an extended period of time. The effect of mother's absence due to volunteer or paid employment appears not to have been assessed. The support for collusion appears weak and is strongly refuted by Summit (1983). Rather, mothers, because of their low self-esteem, passivity, and dependence, may have great difficulty acting effectively to protect their children because it entails acting against their husbands.

NEW CONCEPTUALIZATION OF NONOFFENDING MOTHERS

Combining the clinical literature assessment data available on nonoffending mothers with the literature on psychologically healthy and unhealthy women, two major overbearing factors emerge to provide possible explanations for the behavior of nonoffending mothers. The two factors that bear on this are the status of the women and the status of the marital relationship.

Status of Women

Many authors report that nonoffending mothers hold extremely traditional views about marriage (Groth, 1982; Herman, 1983; Stern & Meyer, 1980). They perceive the husband as the head of the household and consider him dominant and powerful (Groth, 1982). Because of this value, the husband is regarded as the authority over his wife and children, and violent behavior on his part is regarded as acceptable because it is only used to achieve discipline and hold the family together. It is his prerogative to supervise and restrict the activities of the female family members, which often results in isolating them from the outside world (Herman, 1981, 1983).

The women view themselves as being responsible for the success of the marriage and see keeping the marriage together as best for the children. In order to achieve these preeminent goals, they feel it is necessary for them to fill a role subordinate to their husbands and usually choose to be passive in either a passive-dependent or aggressive-passive relationship (Groth, 1982, pp. 218–226). Passivity and dependence of women are also mentioned as typical in couples of incestuous families by Stern and Meyer (1980). As part of being passive and submissive, the woman is sexually compliant as well, resulting in repeated pregnancies. In Herman's (1981) study, the daughters reported their mothers suffered physically from multiple pregnancies and were overwhelmed with the burden of caring for many small children. This is also confirmed in statistics provided by Julian and Mohr (1980) that 36.3% of sexually abusing families have more than 4 children as compared to the national average of 2.2 children. Herman (1981) summarizes the situation succinctly:

> No matter how badly they were treated, most simply saw no option other than submission to their husbands. They conveyed to their daughters the belief that a woman is defenseless against a man, that marriage must be preserved at all costs, and that a wife's duty is to serve and endure. (p. 78)

The women in Herman's study occasionally described their mothers as strong, but only in relation to the observation that there was no limit to their capacity for suffering.

As a result of being submissive, isolated, and sometimes beaten, it is logical that these women have low self-esteem, are depressed, and may even be suspicious or paranoid. Seeking relief through alcohol is understandable. A syndrome is created similar to that presented by the battered woman when she finally appears for help (Walker, 1984). Rosewater (1985) urges that care be taken because it is quite easy to misdiagnose women as having serious mental illness if precautions are not taken to account for the influence of having to cope with battering. These precautions can logically be extended to women who are coping in a family where sexual abuse occurs or is likely to occur. Escape is not an option, given the strong value to hold the family together; it is also mitigated against by the restricted job opportunities for women in our society, the low wages available to most women, and these women's poor preparation for the job market (Finkelhor, 1984, p. 32). Herman (1981) again summarizes the woman's situation well:

> Even by patriarchal standards, the mother in the incestuous family is unusually oppressed. More than the average wife and mother, she is extremely dependent upon and subservient to her husband. . . . Rather than provoke her husband's anger or risk his desertion, she will capitulate. (p. 49)

Status of Relationships

The marital relationship that results from this strong traditional valuing of marriage and the family and the lack of skills to achieve such a relationship results in incongruent role expectations. The man is supposed to be powerful and dominant but his weaknesses are readily apparent. The woman is supposed to be passive and submissive but must have some strengths to hold the family together. As well, Server and Janzen (1982) describe the marital relationship in families of sexual abuse as having a minimal expression of affection, faulty communication, fighting that approaches violence (offset at times by mutual withdrawal), disturbance in the sexual area, and large fears expressed by both parties over loss of the relationship. Julian and Mohr (1980) report a high level of severe discord in these families. Reposa and Zuelzer (1983) attribute the couple's inability to develop a strong, clearly defined marital coalition to the overwhelming needs of the two adults for nurturance, contact, and worth.

One obvious factor that is readily observed in these families is the extreme inequality in the power balance. Finkelhor (1981, cited in Russell, 1984) points out that abuse tends to gravitate to those relationships having the greatest power differential, so that child sexual abuse represents unequal sexual power and unequal generational power. As well, there is an extreme power differential between the husband and wife, which, although it falls into the category of unequal sexual power, also has overtones of unequal generational power because the woman is so often treated like a child (Handy & Cammaert, 1985; Herman 1981; Reposa & Zuelzer, 1983; Rush, 1980, Server & Janzen, 1982). In Finkelhor's (1979) survey of students in six New England colleges and universities, the mothers of the students were reported as often ill and poorly educated—both variables that would contribute to an unequal power balance. Tormes (1968) adds that "by brutality and by superior initiative, her husband has nullified her roles of wife and mother" (pp. 34–35).

What emerges from a review of these two major factors is a picture of a woman who values a traditional role for herself within a marital relationship with some of the unexpected but logical consequences that have been identified as having high personal costs for women (Bernard, 1975). She is extremely dependent psychologically and economically on her husband. The husband has absolute control and power over the home. The woman is often physically and mentally abused by the man, who uses violence to maintain his control over the family and to enforce isolation of the family from the rest of society. The woman has low self-esteem, little or no sense of agency, is isolated, and is depressed. Clinically the woman is often described as withdrawn and psychologically absent (Sgroi, 1982). Given the situation in which she lives, it is difficult for her to see what other options she may have.

Because of her own situation, the mother may find it extremely difficult to effectively protect her children from becoming victims of child sexual abuse (Finkelhor, 1979; Herman, 1981; Walker, 1984). Even "if the price of maintaining the marriage includes the sexual sacrifice of her daughter, she will raise no effective objections. Her first loyalty is to her husband regardless of his behavior. . . . Maternal collusion in incest when it occurs, is a measure of maternal powerlessness" (Herman, 1981, p. 49).

Build from Strengths

However, rather than viewing the mother as a second victim of child sexual abuse, it is important to conceptualize that she has strengths. Many of the aspects just described provide the mother with survival skills, a label coined by Walker (1979) in describing battered women. In spite of their poor personal and marital situations, the nonoffending mothers in a family where child sexual abuse occurs are, in fact, holding the family together: the children are fed, clothed, and disciplined. Part of the package of survival skills includes a need to be compliant and to please the powerful male in order to avoid any confrontation. Nevertheless, children may be protected from factors that their mothers hated in their own childhoods. Although some mothers may not have enough resources left to relate emotionally to anyone— after attending to the basic survival needs of the family—others may push their daughters away emotionally to ensure they are tough and able to cope in the outside world.

From their own experiences, some mothers are aware that incest in a family is a possibility. A mother may protect her daughter from her grandfather who molested his daughter, but is not aware that the current father may be exhibiting similar behavior. Or a mother watches and protects the daughter as much as possible without the awareness that the incestuous behavior can occur with sons.

In treatment of the nonoffending mother, it is important to build on her survival skills and to enlarge her skill repertoire to include the ability to provide more effective protection for her daughter, more behaviors conducive to increased self-worth and independence for herself, and skills to heal the mother/daughter split that may have occurred. Through individual and/or group therapy, the nonoffending mother can begin to understand the dynamics of child sexual abuse, can assume appropriate responsibility for her actions that may have contributed to these dynamics, can assign appropriate responsibility to the offender, can see her daughter's role as an innocent victim rather than as a seductive rival, can begin resuming an emotional relationship as mother to her daughter, and can become strong enough to assume a protective role for herself and her daughter.

Group Treatment

Review of the literature revealed only two descriptions of group therapy for nonoffending mothers. Giarretto (1982) described the formation of a Parents United group, which started with mothers but now involves men and women. With an average attendance of 200 members at weekly meetings, they are broken into smaller groups, one of which is a women's group. These smaller groups run for eight sessions, but the specific program content is not described. In general, the Parents United women's group is classified as a self-help group in which members can "compare their view of reality with that of their peers" (p. 266); the group also meets many of "the urgent emotional and practical needs of its members" (p. 267). The members often remain attached to Parents United after their own successful completion of treatment in order to help other new members. Giarretto reports approximately 130 chapters of Parents United in the United States (p. 267).

A second description of a group for nonoffending mothers is provided by Sgroi and Dana (1982). They attempted to have women join a group at a time close to the crisis point but found it difficult to engage the mothers in anything but individual therapy.

> Mothers almost uniformly resisted participation in other treatment modalities. . . . We speculate that their low self-esteem, lack of trust, isolation, and fear of developing new relationships were powerful factors mitigating against their participation in anything other than a one-on-one relationship. (p. 191)

For this reason they started an ongoing group with three members, which gradually grew to six. The group met for 1½ hours per week with two therapists for the purposes of meeting other people in child sexual abuse situations, increasing social skills, decreasing isolation, and providing a supportive network. Sgroi and Dana outline 12 treatment issues that were dealt with during the group sessions: establishing trust, sharing of past history of own abuse, dealing with denial, identifying unreasonable expectations, practicing limit-setting, dealing with anger, improving communication, assertiveness training, improving social skills, assistance with concrete services, improving body awareness, and providing support through the legal system. The therapists reported that the women felt the group was a positive and helpful experience.

At Alberta Psychological Resources, a private counseling firm, the author offered a 2-hours-a-week, seven-session group counseling program for nonoffending mothers. The majority of the families were court-mandated to have treatment and were involved in family therapy with three other therapists. Attendance at the group sessions was voluntary and nine mothers decided to participate. All families were past the crisis point of discovery; three husbands were incarcerated as a result of charges of incest, four were charged and had court cases in process, one admitted the offense but was not charged, and one denied the offense, was not charged, and was currently involved in a custody battle for the child. The incestuous behavior mostly involved female children from 4 to 16 years of age and one male child of 13 years. The women ranged in age from 30 to 40 years and had been involved in a marital relationship with the offenders ranging from 2 to 20 years. The majority of the offenders were fathers, with two of the nine cases involving stepfathers.

The group led by the author was designed to offer peer support, to provide constructive information, to help participants deal with their feelings, and to make constructive decisions about themselves and their families. The model used emphasized building current skills rather than focusing on deficiencies.

In the first session, an introductory structure to facilitate establishment of trust was used. Each woman was asked to write down answers to three questions: What is one thing I like about myself? Why am I here? and What do I hope to get out of coming to the group? The women were asked to introduce themselves to the group using their answers to the questions. Each woman freely described the incestuous situation that had occurred in her family. Strengths of the women started to emerge immediately, as they reported being survivors. All but one woman had acted strongly and immediately to protect her children when she became aware of or was made aware of the incest. Several had reported the incest to the authorities. They talked about the feelings of divided loyalties, the hurt, anger, and confusion, and their slowly growing pride in their ability to cope with a very complex and difficult situation. Because they had felt so lonely and strange, the women reported being pleased and reassured to talk with others in similar situations. Each woman could now realize on an emotional as well as a cognitive level that she was not the only mother to be involved in an incestuous family.

The second session involved a review of how the mothers had coped that week. One participant was very upset because her daughter had revealed another instance of sexual abuse, this time by a family friend. The group provided a sympathetic ear and support for her, but the woman later withdrew from the group to deal with other difficult problems with her daughters. Two other women were not able to continue in the group because of full-time employment. To help the remaining participants get to know each other as individuals, to have fun, and to build the group, each woman constructed a bag collage and shared it with the group. At their request and with their permission, a list of participants, first names only, and phone numbers was distributed.

Feelings of disappointment, frustration, anger, and guilt were the focus of the third session. Discussion of their feelings helped to normalize what the participants had experienced and laid the groundwork for discussion of other feelings they might experience as they continued through the process of counseling, court, and possible reconciliation. The women had begun to help each other with phone calls and support outside the group.

As the fourth session occurred just prior to Christmas, feelings and coping with logistics were of immediate importance. Several women had to cope with the first Christmas without "Dad," and others were faced with deciding whether their spouse would or would not be released to come home for Christmas. Discussions began over reconciliation, who decides whether this will occur, and feelings of fear, hurt, longing, and love toward their husbands.

After Christmas, the fifth session started with a review of how well their coping strategies had worked over the holiday time. Most were pleased with their ability to cope well, and growing strengths were emphasized. A presentation on characteristics of offenders and family dynamics provided information that participants felt increased their understanding of the situation. The women were not entirely comfortable with the role they had played within the family, which might have contributed to the occurrence of sexual abuse. Most were concerned that they had been too passive and were now working on becoming more assertive. A few agreed they were too passive but felt frightened of becoming assertive; they explored other possible coping mechanisms for dealing with extremely dominant, sometimes physically violent husbands who were expected to return home in the near future.

A paradigm of four preconditions for child sexual abuse (Finkelhor, 1984) was discussed in the sixth session along with reconstruction of the mother/daughter relationship. The women reported feeling closer to their daughters, no longer blaming them for the sexual abuse, and were relieved to feel they could actively protect their daughters. Their strengths and growth as individuals were emphasized by them and the group therapist.

The final session was spent in reviewing the week and then the course. Participants were asked to share their responses to three questions: Did you achieve the things you hoped in the group? Where are you going from here? and How can other group members help you? Each woman also completed the 16PF personality test.

The women reported they had a better understanding of child sexual abuse; they could see past behaviors that they were actively changing to become more independent, happier, and better able to protect their daughters; they had a better, closer relationship with their daughters; and they were able to make well-considered decisions about reconciliation with their spouses. The supportive network appeared to be active for four of six women.

Data on the 16PF are available for only five women, and results from such a small sample must be cautiously interpreted. Utilizing the four second-order factors (Karson & O'Dell, 1976; Krug, 1981), it would be expected from the ideas in the current literature that nonoffending mothers would score low on extraversion and independence and high on anxiety and tough poise. The five women all scored positively on extraversion, which indicated warmth, some optimism, little depression, some risk-taking ability, self-sufficiency, and resourcefulness. All five women also scored contrary to expectations on independence, which indicated they were confident, somewhat radical, and self-sufficient. Four of the five women scored as expected on anxiety, indicating low energy levels; low risk-taking behavior; being somewhat paranoid, resentful, and hostile; apprehensiveness; and self-reproach, with some role confusion. On the fourth factor, tough poise, all five women scored as expected, indicating some flattened affect, tough-mindedness rather than sensitivity and dependence, coupled with practicality.

Although conclusions and generalizability of the findings are limited due to the small sample, the results indicate that these women score differently on the 16PF than would be predicted from the literature review. They appear to be more optimistic, able to take risks, and are resourceful in becoming self-sufficient with resulting self-confidence. It could be argued that the phase in which these women currently are operating has thrust these aspects onto them. However, another interpretation is that these strengths have been there all along and needed only to be utilized in a better way. Perhaps as a result of their experiences, the women demonstrated some flattened affect, became less sensitive, were no longer dependent, and were concerned with practical aspects. Considering the situation, these aspects appear positive for their coping. The flattened affect could be a slight concern if it interfered with the development of a closer mother/daughter tie. The more negative feelings of paranoia, resentment, hostility, apprehension, and self-reproachment found in positive levels of anxiety seem appropriate for women in this situation. More therapy may be needed to help them resolve these feelings.

CONCLUSION

The clinical observations of mother and her role in child sexual abuse, as reported in the literature, have been extremely pejorative. Assessment data is beginning to reveal that these clinical observations do not reveal a complete picture of the families and especially of the mothers. The assessment data itself is also difficult to interpret because it is unclear whether the personality characteristics reported of mothers are a cause of child sexual abuse or are a result of living in an excessively patriarchal home. The whole role of mother in a sexual abuse family must be reconceptualized within a broader framework.

Women involved in incestuous families uphold an extremely traditional view of women's role in marriage, believing they should be passive, submissive, dependent, and compliant. This attitude results in the woman's having low self-esteem, depression, many pregnancies, and much incapacitating illness, often induced by the continuing stressful situation in which she lives. Her husband-enforced isolation and battering may cause her to become suspicious and paranoid. As well, the power imbalance in the relationship completely nullifies any effective interventions attempted by the woman.

Therapists working with nonoffending mothers must reconceptualize the role of the mother with an emphasis on the survival strengths that have enabled her and her children to survive within the father-dominated family. Utilizing these strengths and building on them will help the therapist to empower the woman. Preliminary data indicate this model can be effective and is preferable to the predominant mother-blaming that has occurred. The latter can increase the mother/daughter distance so that daughters may ultimately forgive offending fathers but are not able to forgive nonoffending mothers. With this feeling, the daughter may never learn to love her own femininity, which leads to her low self-esteem and a possible repetition of the whole cycle. Emphasis on the strengths and thus empowerment of the nonoffending mother can result in a woman who can function better both physically and mentally, a woman who can mother her daughter, a woman who can become a role model for her daughter, and a woman who can be an effective protective agent for her children.

REFERENCES

Abel, G. G., Blanchard, E. B., Barlow, D. H., & Mavissakalian, M. (1975). Identifying specific erotic cues in sexual deviation by audiotaped descriptions. *Journal of Applied Behavior Analysis, 8,* 247–260.

Bander, K. W., Fein, E., & Bishop, G. (1982). Evaluation of child sexual abuse programs. In S. M. Sgroi (Ed.), *Handbook of clinical intervention in child sexual abuse* (pp. 345–376). Lexington, MA: Lexington Books.

Baruch, G. K., Barnett, R., & Rivers, C. (1983). *Lifeprints: New patterns of life and work for today's women.* Toronto: McGraw-Hill.

Bennett, M. H. (1980). Father–daughter incest: A psychological study of the mother from an attachment theory perspective. *Dissertation Abstracts International, 41,* 6B. (University Microfilms No. 80-27412, 187).

Bernard, J. (1975). *Women, wives, mothers.* Chicago: Aldine.

Cormier, B. M., Kennedy, M., & Sangowicz, J. (1962). Psychodynamics of father daughter incest. *Canadian Psychiatric Association Journal, 7,* 203–217.

Finkelhor, D. (1979). *Sexually victimized children.* New York: Free Press.

Finkelhor, D. (1984). *Child sexual abuse: New theory and research.* New York: Free Press.

Forseth, L. B., & Brown, A. (1981). A survey of intrafamial sexual abuse treatment centers: Implications for intervention. *Child Abuse and Neglect, 5,* 177–186.

Fredrickson, R. M. (1981). Incest: Family sexual abuse and its relationship to pathology, sex role orientation, attitudes toward women, and authoritarianism. *Dissertation Abstracts International, 42,* 201.

Giarretto, H. (1982). A comprehensive child sexual abuse treatment program. *Child Abuse and Neglect, 6,* 263–278.

Goodwin, J. (1981). Suicide attempts in sexual abuse victims and their mothers. *Child Abuse and Neglect, 5,* 217–221.

Goodwin, J., McCarthy, T., & DiVasto, P. (1981). Prior incest in mothers of abused children. *Child Abuse and Neglect, 5,* 87–95.

Groth, N. A., (1982). The incest offender. In S. M. Sgroi (Ed.), *Handbook of clinical intervention in child sexual abuse* (pp. 215–240). Lexington, MA: Lexington Books.

Groth, N. A., & Birnbaum, H. G. (1979). *Men who rape: Psychology of the offender.* New York: Plenum.

Guthiel, T. G., & Avery, N. C. (1977). Multiple overt incest as family defense against loss. *Family Process, 16,* 105–116.

Handy, L. C., & Cammaert, L. P. (1985, June). Power: A major construct of child sexual abuse. Paper presented at the meeting of the Canadian Psychological Association, Halifax, Nova Scotia.

Handy, L. C., Valentich, M., Gripton, J. M., & Cammaert, L. P. (1985). Feminist issues in sex therapy. *Journal of Human Sexuality and Social Work, 3,* 2/3.

Harrer, M. N. (1981). Father–daughter incest: A study of the mother. *Dissertation Abstracts International, 41,* 12B, 4665.

Herman, J. L. (1981). *Father–daughter incest.* Boston: Harvard University Press.

Herman, J. (1983). Recognition and treatment of incestuous families. *International Journal of Family Therapy, 5*(2), 81–91.

Herman, J., & Hirshman, L. (1981). Families at risk for father–daughter incest. *American Journal of Psychiatry, 138,* 967–970.

Jones, P. S. (1979). Treating sexually abused children. *Child Abuse and Neglect, 3,* 285–290.

Julian, V., & Mohr, C. (1980). Father–daughter incest: Profile of the offender. *Victimology: An International Journal, 4,* 348–360.

Karson, S., & O'Dell, J. W. (1976). *A guide to the clinical use of the 16PF.* Champaign, IL: Institute for Personality and Ability Testing.

Kaufman, I., Peck, A., & Tagiuri, C. (1954). The family constellation and overt incestuous relations between father and daughter. *American Journal of Orthopsychiatry, 24,* 266–279.

Knudson, D. G. (1982). Interpersonal dynamics and mothers' involvement in father–daughter incest in Puerto Rico. *Dissertation Abstracts International, 42,* 7A, 3305.

Krug, S. E. (1981). *Interpreting 16PF profile patterns.* Champaign, IL: Institute for Personality and Ability Testing.

Luckianowicz, N. (1972). Incest. *British Journal of Psychiatry, 120,* 301–313.

Lustig, N., Dresser, J. W., Spellman, S. W., & Murray, T. B. (1966). Incest: A family group survival pattern. *Archives of General Psychiatry, 14,* 31–40.

Machotka, P., Pittman, F. S., & Flomenhaft, K. (1967). Incest as a family affair. *Family Process, 6,* 98–116.

McIntyre, K. (1981). Role of mothers in father–daughter incest: A feminist analysis. *Social Work, 26,* 462–466.

Meiselman, K. (1978). *Incest: A psychological study of causes and effects with treatment recommendations.* San Francisco: Jossey-Bass.

Reposa, R. E., & Zuelzer, M. B. (1983). Family therapy with incest. *International Journal of Family Therapy, 5*(2), 111–126.

Rosewater, L. B. (1985). Schizophrenic or battered? In L. B. Rosewater & L. E. Walker (Eds.), *The handbook of feminist therapy: Psychotherapy with women.* New York: Springer Publishing Company.

Rush, F. (1980). *The best kept secret: Sexual abuse of children.* Englewood Cliffs, NJ: Prentice-Hall.

Russell, D. E. H. (1984). *Sexual exploitation: Rape, child sexual abuse, and workplace harrassment.* Beverly Hills, CA: Sage.

Sahd, D. (1980). Psychological assessment of sexually abusing families and treatment implications. In W. Holder (Ed.), *Sexual abuse of children: Implications for treatment* (pp. 71–86). Denver, CO: American Humane Association.

Server, J. C., & Janzen, C. C. (1982). Contraindications to reconstitution of sexually abusive families. *Child Welfare, 61,* 279–288.

Sgroi, S. (1982). *Handbook of clinical interventions in child sexual abuse.* Lexington, MA: Lexington Books.

Sgroi, S. M., & Dana, N. T. (1982). Individual and group treatment of mothers of incest victims. In S. M. Sgroi (Ed.), *Handbook of clinical interventions in child sexual abuse* (pp. 191–214). Lexington, MA: Lexington Books.

Stern, M., & Meyer, L. (1980). Family and couple interactional patterns in cases of father/daughter incest. *Sexual abuse of children: Selected readings* (pp. 83–86). Washington, DC: National Center on Child Abuse and Neglect.

Summit, R. C. (1983). The child sexual abuse accommodation syndrome. *Child Abuse and Neglect, 7,* 177–193.

Tormes, Y. (1968). *Child victims of incest.* Denver, CO: American Humane Association.

Walker, L. E. (1979). *The battered woman.* New York: Harper & Row.

Walker, L. E. (1984). *The battered woman syndrome.* New York: Springer.

16

A Family Systems Approach to Treatment

Spencer Friedman

BACKGROUND: TREATMENT PERSPECTIVES

Because of the strong social taboo associated with incest, the occurrence of sexual contact between a child and parent appears to have impacted dramatically upon the sanctity of the family. Although the family has often been considered to be a positive resource for managing the pressures and stresses created by one's external environment, the problem of incest raises serious questions regarding the family's abilities to withstand the complex changes created by a highly technical and rapidly changing society. Families are presently required to respond to changing values that impact upon the roles its individual members play. Families must also constantly accommodate to and adapt somewhat spontaneously to an endless series of life crises that impact upon its individual members as well as the entire family unit. Understanding the reciprocal nature of family interactions and the general principles and concepts of systems theory helps explain how individual stresses impact dramatically upon the overall functioning of the family unit.

Related to the psychological impact created by the discovery of an incestuous relationship, mental health professionals have been placed in a position of having to address the issue of rehabilitation of both the victim and perpetrator. Psychotherapists have observed the long-term residual effects of an incestuous relationship upon the victim through retrospective treatment of adult women. Correspondingly, psychotherapists have attempted to treat

Many of the clinical and theoretical conceptualizations emerged from the Family Therapy Program, The Children's Hospital, Denver, Colorado.

the perpetrators of incest by identifying the precipitating factors that contributed to the aberrant behavior. For the most part, these investigations and interventions have occurred within an individual rather than a systemic context. However, with the increasing recognition and development of family therapy and the growing recognition that an individual's behavior may be more thoroughly understood within the context of their primary living environment, which is often their family, there has been a gradual broadening perspective for understanding human behavior. While not attempting to minimize the individual's particular developmental history and learning experiences that help shape their present behavior, a systems-based approach to both assessment and intervention has allowed for a broader conceptualization for understanding the precipitants for current behavior. Such a conceptual system not only addresses the historical antecedents of behavior but also allows for a clearer determination of the current life circumstances within the family system that contribute to the problematic behavior.

While the problem of incest is frequently conceptualized as a family problem that significantly impacts upon the functioning of all of its members, treatment interventions have historically focused upon the idiosyncratic personality characteristics of the adult perpetrator. Only relatively recently have there been efforts to speak to the problem of incest from a family systems perspective (Alexander, 1985; Justice & Justice, 1979). Within this context the problem of incest has been perceived as an outgrowth of a dysfunctional family unit in which confused roles, poorly defined intergenerational boundaries, and a problematic spousal relationship are primary contributing variables to the problem behavior. Conceptualizing the problem of incest in such a manner has contributed to a growing understanding and acceptance of the problem as being at least in part family-based. Subsequent interventions have therefore attempted to implement change from an interactional perspective rather than from solely an intrapsychic viewpoint. Intervention goals have correspondingly included efforts to resolve not only the individual problems with which the perpetrator presents, but also the organizational and interactional aspects of the family system that both prompted and maintained the incestuous interaction.

Other authors have similarly attempted to identify incest as a symptom of a disturbed or pathological family system, in which the overt symptom of incest is an outcome of the problematic interactions occurring between family members (Eist, 1968; Guthiel & Avery, 1977; Lustig, Dresser, Spellman, & Murray, 1966; Machotka, Pittman, & Flomenhaft, 1967; Will, 1983). While these particular authors have attempted to address the contextual aspects of the problem of incest, their formulations suggest differences with regard to the importance individual family members play in contributing to the identified problem and the function the incestuous relationship has within the family system, as well as the importance placed upon the individual psychopathology of the family members.

Review of the clinical literature has indicated that during the past 20 years family therapists have attempted to utilize a family-systems-oriented approach to resolve a variety of family and personally based problems (Bowen, 1978; Haley & Hoffman, 1967; Minuchin, 1974; Whitaker, 1982). Within these varying frameworks the deviant behavior has been conceptualized as an overt symptom of a dysfunctional family unit. Intervention has been directed toward changing the dysfunctional components of the larger family system rather than attending to the symbolic or personal variables operative in maintaining the symptomatic behavior. However, only recently have therapists attempted to address the problem of incest in a similar manner.

Clinical investigation into the problem of incest has historically occurred on an individual-case basis. Clinical case studies have attempted to provide a theoretical basis for explaining causation and have suggested considerations for intervention. Efforts have been made to identify the personality characteristics of both the incestuous perpetrator as well as those of the victim (Justice & Justice, 1979). This work attempted to develop a personality profile of the adult perpetrator and child victim as a means of assisting in the identification of an incestuous relationship as well as to provide suggestions regarding treatment. More recent studies have suggested similarities between the heterosexual incestuous perpetrator and the heterosexual pedophile with regard to their sexual preferences and high sexual arousal to young children (Abel, Becker, Murphy, & Flanagan, 1981). Implications for treatment, therefore, indicate the reduction of the perpetrator's sexual preference for young children. These various investigations tend to reflect both the diversity of treatment approaches as well as the variance in attempting to explain the causative variables of the problem behavior.

A matter of ongoing controversy and rather diverse professional opinion continues to center around the advisability and clinical wisdom of treating incestuous families as a system or unit versus initially providing individual treatment to the family's various members and then proceeding to a more systems-based level of intervention. The latter has been a widely adopted method of intervention that had its origination in San Jose, California (Giaretto, 1980). This particular model of intervention has utilized a group treatment format in which family members initially participated on an individual basis in their respective groups as determined by their particular role within the family system. Marital and/or family treatment then occurred either following or simultaneous with their participation in their respective groups. This particular model of intervention, which conceptualized incest as a family-based problem, tended initially to focus upon the individual personality variables considered to be problematic, and then proceeded to address the interactional and systemic aspects of the problem.

Though at a theoretical level the problem of incest for the most part has been recognized as a family-based problem, the process of intervention appears to have been significantly varied and more likely reflective of the particular therapist's training and specific belief system regarding the origination of the problem behavior. Clinical case studies provided the initial suggestions regarding etiology and intervention strategies. Gradually, broader-based treatment programs have evolved, each utilizing individually based and family-oriented treatment to varying degrees. However, the literature regarding a systems-based approach to assessment and intervention has only recently evolved.

CONCEPTUAL FRAMEWORK FOR A FAMILY SYSTEMS INTERVENTION MODEL

The suggested conceptual framework for the treatment of incest in this chapter will utilize a family systems model. Within this conceptual plan attention is also given to the developmental issues and specific learning experiences of the adult perpetrator that are considered to be significant in contributing to the problem behavior. From this particular conceptual framework evolves a model for intervention that primarily views the problem of incest as a symptom of a dysfunctional family system.

In considering the problem of incest from a family systems perspective, the concept of responsibility belonging to the perpetrator is neither ignored or minimized. The ultimate decision to act out in a sexual manner with a child is still that of the perpetrator regardless of the preempting variables and factors. A systems perspective of the problem essentially allows for a broader method of assessment and intervention. Within this specific model there is neither an attempt nor desire to lay blame or responsibility on the nonoffending parent or upon the child victim.

In viewing the problem of incest from this particular perspective, both assessment and intervention require a language other than that traditionally utilized for diagnostic purposes. The treating therapist is required to understand a series of complicated family interactions that set the stage for the incestuous relationship. The therapist must further determine the conditions of the family members' relationships with one another and the particular family rules and patterns of interaction that determine the family's psychological structure and allow for the maintenance of the incestuous behavior. Finally, the therapist is asked to utilize this information to design an intervention plan that will assist in terminating the perpetrator's desire to be sexually involved with the child and will facilitate changes in the patterns of the family's interactions that both contributed to and maintained the problem behavior.

Utilization of this conceptual model requires that the therapist view the problem of incest in other than a simple cause–effect manner. To adopt such an approach would tend to inappropriately dismiss a multitude of family systems variables that were contributory to the problem behavior. In addition to possibly oversimplifying the causal aspects of the problem, such an approach might also tend to lend itself to an overemphasis upon the behavior itself and to an analysis of the individual perpetrator to the exclusion of the contextual variables operative in the problem. The family systems approach to assessment and treatment tends to utilize the information available, regarding the perpetrator as important to how such variables influence behavior within the context of the broader system of the family. Identification of the personality and behavioral characteristics of individual family members is utilized as one particular source of information. While such information is oftentimes useful as a means of possibly identifying when an incestuous relationship exists, clinically it may provide little information as to a recommended treatment course. Additionally, a broader-based conceptual approach can tend to assist in deemphasizing the specific sexual aspects of the problem, thus allowing for the therapist to address more readily other relevant aspects of the problem, which are often found in the complicated personal and familial interaction patterns that combine in a contributory manner to creating the problem behavior.

Addressing the specific aspects of the sexual behavior is most appropriately and particularly relevant when perpetrators assume responsibility for their behavior. In so doing, the adult perpetrator not only assists the child in resolving the sense of guilt and responsibility they almost always experience, but by making such statements the perpetrator begins to reestablish a more clearly defined parent/child relationship in which the adult is responsible for his own behavior. Thus the parent perpetrator's assumption of responsibility becomes a therapeutic intervention that ultimately has implications for the reorganization of the family system.

Conceptualizing incest as a family systems problem not only requires that the treating therapist complete a broad-based assessment of the family system and the rules that govern how its members function with one another, but also requires that the therapist understand the function that the incestuous relationship has for that or any particular family. In any given family, the incestuous relationship may serve an entirely different function and purpose.

CONCEPTUAL FRAMEWORK

The particular systems concepts utilized will borrow heavily from those proposed in general systems theory (Bertalanffy, 1975). Clinical conceptualizations will tend to reflect a structural family therapy approach

(Minuchin, 1974). Without providing specific elaboration in this chapter, concepts such as boundaries, homeostasis, enmeshment, disengagement, rules, and roles will be inherent in the discussion of assessment and intervention.

Assessment of the incestuous family system includes identification of specific problems existing in each of the following subsystems:

1. *Individual.* Assessment of the adult/parent individual learning experiences as such have impacted upon their perception of themselves as independent adults. Further assessment of the adults' functioning is made regarding such areas as sexuality, intimacy, self-esteem, and assertiveness. Careful assessment needs to be made of the perpetrator's belief system regarding children, childrearing, and his or her rationalization system, which contributed to the maintenance of the incestuous behavior. Within this particular area of assessment a determination of the perpetrator's sexual arousal to children may also be made, as well as of the use of violence to control the child victim. It will also be important to determine whether there are victims outside of their own family.

2. *Spousal subsystem.* The spousal subsystem refers to marital partners or any male–female relationship based upon sexual liaison, mutual support, or decision making. Assessment of this particular subsystem attempts to address such issues as their abilities to meet one another's needs for intimacy and closeness, problem-solving and decision-making processes, abilities to function independently while involved in a primary relationship, their communication style, and their abilities to respond to life crises in an adaptive manner. If assessment of the perpetrator's functioning reveals a high level of sexual arousal to children, spousal subsystem problems are equally likely to be evident. Determination that the perpetrator experiences heightened sexual arousal to children does not suggest that problem resolution can be found solely through treating that particular problem area. Heterosexually based conflicts may be a contributing variable to that particular arousal pattern, which suggests that ultimately spousal relationship conflicts will need to be resolved.

3. *Parental subsystem.* The parental subsystem consists of the same members of the spousal subsystem but addresses the manner in which they engage in the role of parenting. Clinical assessment will need to determine their individual and collective parenting styles, their abilities to meet the needs of their child(ren) for nurturance and stability, their management and disciplinary strategies, and their ability to maintain appropriate expectations for behavior.

4. *Sibling subsystem.* The sibling subsystem includes the total number of siblings/stepsiblings within the family unit. Assessment of this particular subsystem focuses upon identification of coalitions and alliances among

siblings, the roles children play in adult and spousal conflicts, and the manner in which sibling behavior with one another and with their parents is created by parental messages and expectations.

5. *Extended family subsystem.* This subsystem includes relatives who participate in a significant way in the nuclear family system. Problem assessment includes a determination of the extent to which extended family members either overtly or covertly play in the decision-making process of the nuclear family. Assessment is also made regarding the particular roles extended family members may play in the operation and functioning of the nuclear family.

6. *Significant other subsystem.* This particular subsystem includes unrelated individuals who have long-term relationships or a high impact on the nuclear family's functioning. Assessment will include a determination as to the extent that the nuclear family collectively or individually utilizes outside support systems, and generally how well the family is integrated into their external environment. Such assessment will also include a determination as to the extent the nuclear family assimilates information from its environment. This concept as it applies to incestuous families has been previously investigated (Alexander, 1985). The general concept as it applies to families has also been suggested in previous literature (Pondy & Mitroff, 1979).

The conceptual scheme outlined above allows for the treating therapist to make a comprehensive assessment of both the individual and familial variables contributory to the incestuous behavior. Such a framework also allows for the therapist to understand the family's response pattern to the problem more comprehensively and to observe how the family reorganizes itself following disclosure. Rather than focusing exclusively upon the incestuous dyad or even triad, a problem-location concept that utilizes a family assessment framework provides a broader context within which to understand and determine both the precipitating and maintaining variables that are operative within the incestuous family system. This particular framework, while emphasizing contextual variables to the problem behavior, continues to emphasize that the ultimate responsibility for initiating the incestuous relationship rests with the adult perpetrator.

CHARACTERISTICS OF THE INCESTUOUS FAMILY

Attempting to define specific characteristics of an individual perpetrator or a particular family system is an extremely difficult task, given the multiplicity of family interaction patterns and the complex nature of family relationships. Resultantly it would be conceptually and clinically limiting to assume that all incestuous families fit the characteristics described below. However, the patterns of behaviors described below and suggested problems noted are oftentimes observed in the incestuous family system but not necessarily observed in all cases. The particular characteristics described below utilize the problem-location concepts previously described and inherently suggest a plan for therapeutic intervention.

1. The individual adult perpetrator often presents with personal problems associated with a low rate of assertiveness, low self-esteem, depression, problems with independent decision making, and difficulties creating intimacy other than through sexual means. The personal familial backgrounds of adult perpetrators are often characterized by marital or family conflict, physical abuse, alcoholism, and possible sexual abuse. These variables suggest the importance of early life experiences in shaping their orientation to relationships and possibly to their sexual interest in children. Perpetrators often present with unrealistic expectations regarding their children and seem to have an elaborate cognitive belief system in which there is a tendency to interpret children's behavior in an overly sexualized manner. Incest perpetrators often interpret behavior of children in such a manner so as to mistake their requests for closeness and intimacy as requests for sexual contact. Such individuals may also present with problems including excessive alcohol usage and may engage in physically violent behavior with either their children and/or spouses. Such behaviors may be associated with their depression and subsequent need to control events in their external environment.

2. Oftentimes an incestuous family system will be characterized by a multiproblem spousal relationship, which may be both contributory to and reactive to the identified problem. Conflicts regarding intimacy, assertiveness, problem-solving difficulties, physical violence, and communication difficulties are frequently noted. As suggested by other therapists, the spouses involved in an incestuous family system engage in marriage without having established a stable individual identity and, therefore, they experience difficulty functioning as independent adults (Justice & Justice, 1979). Oftentimes observed in spousal relationships where there is evidence of physical abuse, a partner's identity and self-respect is eroded from the violence. Their expectations of one another are generally unrealistic, as each expects to be taken care of by the other, thus creating an excessive demand upon one another. In their conflict to meet one another's needs and expectations, the relationship undergoes significant stress and conflict, which leaves them feeling emotionally apart and psychologically disengaged. Lacking appropriate skills and resources to resolve conflict, they remain emotionally disengaged—or the woman may disengage to protect herself from further violence.

3. Related to the spousal unit's inability to maintain a sense of emotional unity, the child who ultimately becomes the victim of the incestuous relation-

ship becomes triangulated in spousal conflicts. It is this particular child who assumes a spousal function and role within the family system. Oftentimes this child will also play a spousal role in nonsexual ways as well. Gradually the child may become the parent's emotional partner, oftentimes receiving information that is more appropriately reserved for the spousal relationship. Ultimately the needs for closeness and intimacy which are often not being met through the spousal relationship get expressed through the sexual abuse of the child. When this occurs, it appears as though the adult perpetrator feels more comfortable sustaining a sense of intimacy in a relationship with a significant power differential in contrast to maintaining intimacy in a more equal relationship.

4. Related to the child's distorted position within the family system and hierarchy, this child will often appear pseudo-mature and interact in an inappropriately adult manner. This child will often feel responsible for the incestuous relationship and may even feel overly responsible for the well-being of the entire family system. Oftentimes this child will experience considerable guilt over family-related problems that he or she perceives he or she should have some influence and control over.

5. Similar to the child's distorted position within the family system, this child may also function in an inappropriate parental role. In this regard the child may not only engage in parenting behavior with other siblings but with a parent as well. This role-reversal pattern is similar to that observed in family systems where physical abuse has occurred.

6. A general characteristic of the incestuous family system is the absence of clearly defined intergenerational boundaries. This is most clearly evidenced by the child victim of incest who may function in both an inappropriately spousal and/or parental role.

7. The incestuous family system appears to maintain a pathological dependence upon one another, which appears to be perpetuated by excessive concerns regarding fears of loss, separation, and abandonment. A primary psychological component to this organizational system appears to originate within the spousal relationship, in which the individual adults become excessively dependent upon one another because of their inability to establish clearly defined individual identities. Oftentimes the incestuous family system's antagonistic and resistant response to outside intervention reflects the concerns and fears of loss and separation. Rather than interpreting this response as a form of resistance in a more traditional manner, the response may be better understood in the context of a homeostatic function to outside intervention, therefore reflecting the family's inability to accommodate to the expectations of their external environment.

8. Paralleling the above pattern, the incestuous family system might also be considered significantly enmeshed. The incestuous family system creates a rigid psychological boundary between itself and its external environment.

The family functions in such a manner that suggests that it has psychologically insulated itself from input coming from outside its own system. The rigidity of this system sometimes makes it difficult to act out problems outside of the family unit. Subsequently the perpetrator of the incestuous behavior will often have a greater tendency to become involved sexually with a family member who possesses little risk to him of rejection and who is likely to be more responsive to his requests for control—such as a child—rather than to seek out extramarital relationships. Social-skill deficits may also interfere with the perpetrator's willingness to risk rejection in an adult relationship. Additionally, the intended impact or payoff for the perpetrator to act out within the family system through another family member may be greater with respect to the functioning and structure of that unit.

Another characteristic of the incestuous family system and the manner in which the enmeshed family structure impacts upon the functioning of its members is observed in the frequency of reports involving runaway adolescents who have been victims of incest. Because of the distorted role incestuous children are asked to play, either overtly or covertly, their participation in the maintenance and functioning of the family system becomes inordinately significant. Subsequently, their growing need to emancipate and for increased independence from the family system becomes an event upsetting to the homeostasis of the family and in particular for the adult perpetrator, who is often particularly threatened by the eventual loss. As a result, the adolescent victim is unable to participate in behaviors and relationships that represent efforts at increased independence. Unable to emancipate gradually, the adolescent has little option but to remove herself dramatically from the family system and the role she has been asked to play. She often does so by running away.

9. The incestuous family system is generally a closed system, oftentimes socially and psychologically isolated from its surrounding environment. The family system is generally distrusting of others and, therefore, tends to rely upon its own resources for information and problem resolution. The family system as a unit and its individual members are generally without extended support systems to assist them with problem solving. Subsequently, the family is left with its own ineffectual resources for resolving conflict.

10. The child victim of incest will experience a multitude of feelings and reactions related to the incestuous relationship. Oftentimes their responses will reflect anger, distrust, depression, betrayal, confusion regarding intimacy, a loss of power or control over their lives, a generalized sense of helplessness (which manifests itself in excessive attempts to control their environment), and a sense of guilt. Familial expectations that they function in an adult manner oftentimes interferes with their abilities to form effective, sharing interpersonal relationships with peers. Similarly, they are often unable to clearly differentiate situations for which they experience a true sense

of responsibility. Because of the adultlike role child victims assume, they have problems in not assuming responsibility for all situations they are involved in.

TREATMENT CONSIDERATIONS AND INTERVENTIONS

The focus of a family-systems-based intervention is on both the individual variables that contributed to the incestuous behavior and the particular psychological impact the behavior has had for the child victim—but it is as important to resolve the family-related factors that both precipitated and maintained the dysfunctional behavior. Utilizing the previously cited characteristics of the incestuous family as a conceptual basis, therapeutic interventions are designed to reach problem resolution to those particular patterns of relationship behavior that contributed to the incestuous relationship.

1. Resolution of the individual problem precipitants reflected in the perpetrator's belief system regarding intimacy, sexuality, self-esteem, independence, and children. Particular attention is given to the manner in which the perpetrator maintains sexual arousal for children. As part of this particular intervention strategy, resolution of the perpetrator's tendency to perceive children's behavior with a sexual intent is essential. Accompanying treatment issues may include developing greater self-control behavior associated with alcohol usage and violent behavior.

2. Resolution of the psychological trauma to the child(ren) created by the incestuous behavior. Specific psychological issues are likely to include those of guilt, responsibility, and betrayal of trust and safety. Additional psychological issues will include those feelings of depression and anger that accompany a generalized sense of loss of control associated with being a victim. The child victim of an incestuous relationship will need to develop nonsexual avenues for creating intimacy, and the child will need to develop a perception of herself based upon factors other than her sexuality.

3. Developing a more stable spousal relationship, which will be characterized by increased assertiveness, more clearly defined and realistic role expectations, resolution of conflicts associated with intimacy, developing more effective means of reaching problem resolution, and developing a sense of marital stability that will foster one another's independent functioning. Stabilization of the spousal subsystem is an essential ingredient in developing a more functional family system. A more clearly defined spousal unit creates an appropriate differentiation and intergenerational boundary between the spousal subsystem and child or sibling subsystems. Development of an effectively functioning spousal unit minimizes the probability that

a child will become triangulated in spousal-related conflicts. Variables that might suggest a poor prognosis for resolution of the marital conflicts might include: physical violence directed at either the victim or other family members; long-term alcohol and/or drug usage; multiple victims, which include individuals outside of the family system; and evidence of long-term problems functioning adaptively in society. Evidence of antisocial-related behaviors and/or frequent episodes of physical violence collectively suggests that family members may be at far more risk for repeated abuse than if a perpetrator has generally demonstrated an appropriate social adjustment and can respond to the expectations of social conformity.

4. Related to the development of a more adequate and functional spousal subsystem, intervention will also attempt to assist the adults in becoming more adequate parents. Stabilization of the parental subsystem helps create a more clearly defined boundary between the parental subsystem and child or sibling subsystems. This process of differentiation maintains the child(ren) in an appropriate role within the family system.

5. To facilitate the independent functioning of the various family members, intervention should be designed to assist the adult members of the family unit to develop healthier individual identities. In this process spouses will develop more realistic, appropriate, and clearly defined expectations of one another in an attempt to meet one another's emotional–psychological needs. Similarly, intervention will attempt to assist the adult member of the family to develop skills that will facilitate constructive interaction with their external environments. Intervention is designed to assist the spousal subsystem to develop a more integrated and stable marriage by more clearly defining spousal needs and simultaneously assisting the adults to develop healthy personal support systems outside of their relationship.

6. In an effort to assist the incestuous family in becoming less enmeshed, therapeutic intervention should be designed to assist the family in developing support systems in their external environment. This involvement would allow for new information to filter into the family system with the hope that such input could be effectively utilized in developing a more effective problem-solving process. Developing outside support systems might also allow for the enmeshed and psychologically isolated family to more effectively defuse emotionally charged issues that immobilize the system's functioning. Utilization of external support systems may assist the family from becoming overwhelmed because of their limited resources for resolving conflict. Effective utilization of these support systems may be significant in averting a crisis that might ultimately serve as a precipitant to further incestuous behavior.

7. The child victim of incest will need to reestablish trust in both of her parents. She will need to establish a sense of trust with the perpetrator that her efforts to seek out intimacy and closeness will not be responded to in a sexual manner. She will also need to establish a sense of trust with the other

parent and believe that person can protect her from further abuse. Related to the inappropriate sense of power that may be created by being placed into an adult role within the family system, the child may have to learn to relinquish that position and sense of control. Relatedly she will also need to resolve the sense of excessive responsibility that the position has created.

TREATMENT PROCESS

A family systems basis for understanding and treating the problem of incest attempts to take into consideration the multitude of variables that created the problematic behavior. Within this framework, treatment strategies are designed to assist the adult perpetrator in reaching problem resolution of the individual factors that contributed to the behavior, to assist the child victim in resolving the psychological trauma created by the behavior, and to assist in the restructuring of the family unit. These particular treatment goals allow for the therapist to utilize individual, marital, and family sessions as deemed clinically appropriate to help create the desired therapeutic outcome.

Utilization of a family systems orientation to treatment presumes that the ultimate protection of the child might be best assured by considering the multitude of factors that contributed to the incestuous behavior. While initially appearing contrary to a victim-advocacy position, family intervention is based upon the assumption that problem resolution ultimately ensures protection of the child from further abuse.

Within this particular framework for intervention, the therapist has maximum flexibility to include in treatment various configurations of the family system, which will include the opportunity for seeing the child individually to ensure that her particular therapeutic needs are being met adequately. This particular method of intervention also attempts to prevent blaming of the victim for the incestuous behavior and scapegoating of the nonoffending parent, while emphasizing that ultimate responsibility for control of the abusive behavior continues to reside with the perpetrator. Thus, although family intervention takes into consideration the contextual aspects of the family, it does not distract from the concept that the perpetrator is responsible for the abusive behavior.

A significant factor in treating the incestuous family is the ability to begin therapeutic intervention while the family is in crisis, which generally corresponds to the disclosure of the incestuous behavior. During this time, the enmeshed family system is most permeable to outside therapeutic intervention, because the reporting of the behavior represents a significant disruption of the rules and structure of the family. During this period of maximum crisis, the family's fears regarding loss and separation are heightened. Because the family is usually without appropriate resources to manage this crisis, rapid and frequent intervention is most effective. During this initial phase of treatment, frequent therapeutic contact helps the therapist to join the family as an ally to assist them in resolution of their crisis.

The initial phase of treatment with the incestuous family includes such therapeutic tasks as creating therapeutic alliances with all family members, labeling the problem in such a manner that addresses the systems variables that are operative, conducting a careful assessment of the family unit with regard to problem identification, and gaining an understanding of the precipitating and maintaining variables involved in the problem behavior. In a similar manner, efforts will also be made to determine the function and purpose of the incestuous relationship. Oftentimes during the initial phase of treatment the therapist may have to participate in decision making regarding removal or return of the child to the home. In a broader context the treating therapist will have to define his or her own relationship with both the family as well as with the broader social service and legal systems. This will have to be done in such a manner so that there is a clear definition and differentiation of roles and responsibilities.

During the initial phase of treatment the primary modality of treatment will be family-based. Involvement of all family members in treatment allows for identification with each family member, provides a clearer and more accurate basis for problem assessment, and reemphasizes that the problem is family-oriented. Utilizing family treatment as the initial intervention strategy also allows for the family to quickly begin developing more appropriate problem-solving strategies for managing conflict and crisis. Meeting with the family as a unit also tends to reduce their initial fears regarding the possibility that the family may not remain together as a unit, which oftentimes is a significant fear for the incestuous family. Meeting with individual family members or meeting with some family members to the exclusion of others may inadvertently reinforce the family's fear that they may not be able to remain together as a family unit. When working with families in which members present with differing opinions regarding their investment and desire to remain together as a family unit, the treatment forum may be utilized to help in reaching problem resolution. In such situations, a variety of treatment modalities such as individual and marital therapy might need to be used in addition to family treatment.

In essence the therapist utilizes the crisis associated with problem disclosure as the initial opportunity to begin assisting the family to develop more effective means of resolving the problematic patterns of behavior that have existed. In situations where it is very clear that maintenance of the family unit is not an intended treatment goal or when the victim's anger is such that it interferes with her ability to relate in any manner to the perpetrator or the nonoffending parent, more individualized treatment or family treatment without the perpetrator and victim present together may be utilized more effectively during the initial treatment phase. When the entire family system is available and willing to participate in treatment, family treatment may be supplemented with individual and/or marital therapy. However, as the primary intent is beginning to introduce problem resolution, family intervention will be the primary method through which information is obtained.

The second phase of treatment is initiated when there appears to be clear problem assessment. This phase of treatment is designed to specifically address the problem areas previously cited. During this particular phase of treatment, the therapist utilizes individual, marital, and family treatment modalities. Decisions regarding whom to include in a particular treatment session and the subsequent sequence of treatment sessions will generally be determined by the progression of treatment and the intended outcome or desired therapeutic result from that intervention.

During the second phase of intervention, the therapist will provide treatment associated with the incestuous relationship with specific focus on the victim's response to the behavior as well as with the individual problem variables that prompted the perpetrator's behavior. Therapeutic intervention with the spousal unit will focus upon resolution of the problematic aspects of the marriage, which were contributory variables to the incestuous behavior. Family therapy will focus on restructuring the family-interaction patterns, establishing more clearly defined intergenerational boundaries, developing a more functional family hierarchy, and teaching the family system more adaptive problem-solving strategies.

Individual treatment with the adult perpetrator will attempt to resolve those individual problem variables that prompted the perception of children in a sexual manner. Companion treatment issues will possibly include resolution of alcohol usage problems and problems with physical violence. During this time the child victim may be seen individually and/or with either the abusive parent or both. Treatment issues for the child victim will include those cited earlier. Involving the adult perpetrator in treatment sessions with the child victim to take responsibility for the incestuous behavior facilitates the child's resolution of her feelings of guilt and responsibility. In family situations where there happens to be multiple victims, individual treatment of all children may be suggested. In such instances family treatment may be utilized as well.

The final phase of treatment occurs at such a time when there is demonstrated resolution of the primary problem precipitants. Determination of treatment gains is evaluated and assessed in a broader context than termination of the incestuous behavior. Working from a systemic perspective, determination of treatment goals is made based upon changes observed on an individual, marital, and family basis. The adult perpetrator will need to demonstrate problem resolution in such areas of personal functioning that include his arousal to children, increased assertiveness, improved self-esteem, development of intimacy through other means than those that are sexual, and termination of excessive alcohol usage and violent behavior when such was present and observed within the context of the family. Measuring the victim's response to treatment can be determined by her ability to resolve issues of guilt and responsibility, establishing a sense of control over her life, establishing a healthy level of heterosexual functioning in which intimacy is established through means other than sexual, making a determination as to the extent the victim has been able to develop a sense of trust in adults and/or significant others in the environment, and determining the ability to respond to her or his own particular needs rather than placing the needs of others before them. Changes within the marital relationship should include an improvement in communication skills, developing more realistic expectations of one another, the ability to develop a variety of ways of establishing and maintaining intimacy, developing means to enhance one another's independent functioning, and learning how to utilize one another in emotionally supportive ways. A more clearly defined spousal relationship increases the likelihood that a child will no longer need to function in a spousal role to meet the needs of a particular spouse. Family-based measures of change might include the development of a more clearly defined parental subsystem, determining how well the parental unit assumes responsibility for the organization of the family unit, assessing the adolescent victim's ability to achieve independence through appropriate means, determining the extent to which the victim is engaged in age-appropriate tasks, and determining the extent to which the family has been able to develop external support systems or individuals.

While assessment of change and treatment gains focuses upon both the perpetrator and victim, the primary means of determining change within the family system is the family's ability to develop more clearly defined intergenerational boundaries and their ability to establish a more clearly defined hierarchy regarding the definition of family roles and responsibilities. Collectively such changes tend to minimize the risk that a child member of the family will function in an inappropriate role, which may eventually be a significant variable in setting the stage for an incestuous relationship.

SPECIAL TREATMENT CONSIDERATIONS

Single-parent Families

Oftentimes upon the disclosure of an incestuous relationship a family will decide not to remain together as a unit. Under these circumstances and conditions the focus of family intervention is with the family unit exclusive of the perpetrator. While the most apparent concern, protection of the child from further abuse, is temporarily resolved by these circumstances, family intervention continues to be a significant form of therapeutic intervention. Initially, by virtue of the incestuous relationship, there is clear suggestion of severe family disruption and disorganization. The perpetrator's absence does not mean resolution of the precipitating problem conditions. Secondly, though there may be a decision to terminate the spousal relationship in the midst of the crisis associated with disclosure, once the stress and fear associated with this crisis has subsided there may be a reevaluation of that decision and at some time in the future the marital unit may be reestablished. If such occurs, the likely probability is that the family unit will reconstitute itself in a similar manner as before, with the same dysfunctional patterns of interaction. Under these circumstances there is a high probability that the incestuous behavior would recur. Successful therapeutic intervention would mean that if the family unit were to reunite, such would occur under different conditions, thus interfering with the past maladaptive patterns of interaction that contributed to the incestuous relationship.

Treatment issues specifically addressing the concerns created by the incestuous relationship are several. Beyond those specific residual emotional issues that the child victims must resolve as a result of the behavior, they are likely to need to resolve their guilt associated with the possibility that their disclosures may have directly or indirectly contributed to the parents' separation. An issue closely allied with this factor is the possibility that the nonabusing parent may attempt to scapegoat the child victim as being the cause and source of the family's problems as a projection of anger and sense of loss associated with the spouse's leaving. This may be particularly true if there was any ambivalence associated with the decision to terminate the marriage. Another source of conflict may be associated with the child victim's anger at the remaining parent, who in spite of the fact that she or he may not have been abusive or aware of the abusive behavior may be perceived by the child as being nonprotecting. This conflict issue is significantly intensified if the nonabusing parent was aware of the incestuous behavior and did not take protective action.

Because of the confused hierarchy and roles evidenced in incestuous family systems and the child's tendency to be inappropriately adultlike within this system, the same role confusion and reversal may continue to occur in spite of the perpetrator's absence. What can result is the child's experiencing a sense of responsibility in taking care of her mother now that the spouse has left; or out of a position of guilt the child may attempt to become overly parental and assume the entire responsibility for meeting all of the family members' emotional needs, including those of her siblings. What may result is a related battle for control and a struggle for the executive or parental position within the family. Because child victims of incest often assume an inappropriate position of control and power within the family unit, they may have considerable difficulty moving back to a more appropriate position of less control and power. In either instance the goal of intervention is to restore an appropriate parent/child relationship and a more clearly defined intergenerational boundary, with the parent assuming the executive position in the family's hierarchy. In this role the parent would more appropriately be meeting the child's need rather than the reverse.

Related to the pathological nature of the spousal relationship, the loss of a partner becomes a significant crisis. Because of the enmeshed quality of the relationship and the excessive dependence upon one another, the remaining partner may tend to feel overwhelmed by the dual responsibility of being a parent and having to function as an independent adult. Therapeutic intervention is therefore designed with the goals of developing independence, enhancing self-esteem, utilizing natural and more varied support systems, and learning how to develop healthier relationships. Intervention would also assist in resolving parenting conflicts, which will ideally facilitate more appropriate parenting behavior, thus enhancing the development of a more clearly defined parent/child relationship. By reaching resolution of the above-cited problems and by subsequent restructuring of the family system, such changes would make it very difficult for the old spousal relationship to be reestablished in the same pathological manner in which it had existed in the past. Resultantly the relationship would either have to redevelop in a healthier manner or dissolve. In either instance, intervention will have minimized the risk for recreating the same conditions that were precipitants in creating the incestuous relationship.

Single-parent family issues are also observed in family constellations where a particular parent has been absent for a long period of time and a child from the relationship assumes a spousal role in the absence. When this constellation involves a father and daughter, the incestuous relationship is often symptomatic of a relationship that is more spousal in many respects than it is parent/child. Intervention in family systems such as these is often very difficult, related to the child's perception that he or she is an integral part of their parent's life, reinforced by the absence of the marital partner. Therefore they respond to intervention with the fear that change will negatively impact their relationship with their parent. Oftentimes in family systems such as these, the child has considerable difficulty relinquishing the role of feeling as though it is his or her responsibility to care for the parent. Similarly, the parent or adult in this relationship will often experience difficulty changing his or her perception of their child from that of spouse to child.

Given the rigid and enmeshed quality of this relationship, intervention should be both individual and family based. While the primary treatment focus is the development of a more clearly defined parent/child relationship, to achieve such a therapeutic outcome the adult member of the relationship will need to develop a level of competence and independence so that the child will no longer feel it her responsibility to meet the parent's needs for closeness and intimacy. The individual treatment needs of the child will be those cited earlier for a child who has been involved in an incestuous relationship. As the adult member of the relationship is able to achieve a more stable and satisfying level of independent functioning, the child may then begin to experience the freedom to develop an identity in which to engage in more appropriate age-level tasks. Another significant treatment issue will include helping the child feel as though she is not betraying her parent by developing an identity that does not include taking care of the adult. Because of the enmeshed nature of the child/parent relationship, the child may tend to confuse independence and emancipation with betrayal of the parent. Intervention will also need to help the child learn to interact with peers in other than a caretaking manner, because there may be a tendency to assume a similar role as the one she had played with the parent.

Sibling Incest

The problem of sibling incest is often overlooked as a family treatment problem. Oftentimes sibling incest is easily dismissed or inaccurately diagnosed as sexual experimentation or innocent child's play. Certainly people do not respond with the same emotional revulsion to disclosure of sexual context between siblings as they do to parent/child sexual contact. While oftentimes sexual contact between siblings does not have the same exploitive quality as is evident in parent/child sexual contact, closer assessment into the context of the sibling and family relationships is important to understand the precipitating factors to the behavior.

An important consideration in making a determination regarding the possible psychological factors operative in a sibling incest relationship is the age differential between the siblings. A significant age discrepancy, such as that between a latency-age or adolescent child and a very young child, may represent for the older of the children adjustment problems that have a family basis. Rather than act out such conflicts in the external environment, the child may choose to act out within the family system. While such behavior may reflect problems with one's heterosexual adjustment, particularly with an adolescent perpetrator, close evaluation needs to be made of family factors that may be contributing to the problematic adjustment.

An additional variable to consider is the extent to which parents are or have been aware of the behavior. In family systems where parents have been not only knowledgeable but condoning of the behavior, more serious family psychopathology is suggested and may reflect or be indicative of other incestuous interactions within the family system. In family systems where the parents have been knowledgeable of the behavior and have been unsuccessful in their efforts to introduce effective controls, closer assessment of their parenting skills and strategies needs to be made. In such situations serious parenting conflicts may be discovered, as well as evidence of spousal abuse and other violence in one partner. Information regarding the manner in which there was attempted resolution may be diagnostic of the family's decision-making and problem-solving processes. Such conflicts may represent problems in other areas of the family's organization and role definitions.

Oftentimes sibling incest may represent an attempt on the siblings' parts to join together in response to a perception that their parents are unable to respond to their needs for intimacy, closeness, and nurturing. In these instances, the significance of the behavior is not in its sexuality but in what the behavior represents structurally. Such a relationship between siblings might not only be indicative of significant parenting-subsystem problems but may also be diagnostic and revealing regarding problems associated with closeness and intimacy.

Careful examination of the circumstances contributing to and determination of the variables operative in maintaining a sibling incestuous relationship needs to occur in order to make a determination as to the extent to which such behavior is symptomatic of a broader family problem. In these situations intervention needs to not only assist the victim(s) in reaching resolution of the specific feelings associated with the incestuous behavior, but, as importantly, to reach problem resolution of the structural aspects of the family's functioning.

If the disclosure of the incestuous relationship is made within the family system rather than to an individual outside of the family network, the family may choose to attempt problem resolution on its own. Oftentimes in situations such as these and when the incestuous relationship involves a parent and child, the family's conflicts become clearly evident through the manner in which they attempt problem resolution. Frequently observed is the pattern that an older sibling is asked to assume somewhat of an executive or parental role and to closely monitor the relationship between the parent and victim. In this particular role the child is in essence asked to assume responsibility for preventing the incentuous behavior from recurring. This specific attempt at problem resolution characterizes the dysfunctional nature of the spousal relationship and typifies the frantic and ineffective means the family employs to reach resolution to problems. In doing intervention in family systems such as these, an essential ingredient to successful intervention, particularly when the behavior has recurred, is assisting the executive child in resolving personal feelings of guilt and failure associated with not having been successful in the task that was given to him or her. In instances where the problem has continued, oftentimes these particular children will appear more depressed and guiltridden than the victim.

Mother–Son Incest

In comparison to reports of father–daughter incest the incidence of mother–son incest is significantly less. However, two variables must be taken into consideration as possibly being biasing factors that contribute to an underreporting of such behavior.

Initially, the problem of incest has historically been perceived as a problem involving a father and his daughter. This perception has tended to reinforce the belief that it is generally a female child who has been victimized. The recent attention given to the problems of battering and spouse abuse, problems in which the victim is again generally a female, has collectively reinforced the perception that victims of aggressive action are generally female. While increased attention to the problems of incest and spouse abuse has been important, the perceptions created by the reporting of these events has contributed to a belief that has inadvertently set the stage for making it more difficult to perceive a male child as being a victim.

Secondly, there appears to be a biased perception that portrays men as sexual predators, subsequently contributing to a tendency to be more easily suspicious of their intentions and motivations than those of women. As a result there has been a greater tendency to scrutinize more closely the intimate aspects of a father's relationship with his daughter than those of a mother and her son. There appears to be an initial inclination to be suspicious of a father's intention with his daughter, but such is often not the case in evaluating the relationship between a mother and her son. While both lay people and professionals appear to be highly sensitized to suggestions of inappropriate intimacy in a father–daughter relationship, there appears to be less suspiciousness of the intimacy involved in a mother–son relationship. Whereas a father's overinvolvement with his daughter is often interpreted as having possible sexual connotations, such overinvolvement on a mother's part is often interpreted as being overly protective or controlling, but generally without sexual associations. Thus it appears that there is likely an inherent bias and tendency to make assumptions regarding behavior from a gender-specific perspective that ultimately may contribute to an underreporting of mother–son incest.

Therapeutic intervention from a family systems perspective in cases of mother–son incest would follow a similar pattern as that described in cases of father–daughter incest. Individual, marital, and family systems variables would be assessed in order to make a determination of the contributing factors of the incestuous relationship. Intervention would similarly employ the same strategies as suggested earlier, and the psychological conflicts created by the incestuous relationship would be resolved in a similar manner.

Father–Son Incest

A significant absence of literature regarding father–son incest seems to reflect the low frequency of reporting. Individual case studies (Berry, 1975; Langsley, 1968) have been the primary source of data gathering. The absence of a large body of clinical data has contributed to a lack of clarity in determining a viable means of problem assessment and intervention from a family systems perspective. The low rate of reporting of father–son incest may in part reflect a similar form of biasing as is suggested in the reporting of mother–son incest. The tendency to perceive sexual abuse in a heterosexually based framework might tend to influence clinicians' diagnostic approach to problem assessment and therefore to misidentify homosexual or father–son incest.

Based upon the experiences of other authors as well as of this clinician, a significant ingredient in determining the contributing variables to the identified problem behavior is to assess the father's homosexual orientation and involvement. Such assessment will allow the clinician to determine the most appropriate form of therapeutic intervention. If the perpetrator presents with a predominantly homosexual orientation, his sexual interest with his son might represent an extension of the manner in which he engages in intimacy and reflect what might be considered a longstanding preference for sexual intimacy with males. Under such circumstances, it would nevertheless remain important for the clinician to make a determination as to the extent family-related variables are operative in creating the incestuous relationship. The primary focus of intervention, though, will need to be on the perpetrator's sexual arousal and interest in children.

If such a pattern of adjustment is not evidenced in the perpetrator's background, a more thorough assessment of the family systems will need to be made to determine the contextual or interactional aspects of the problem. The process of problem identification would occur as previously described utilizing a family systems model.

The long-term psychological and related adjustment issues for the child who is involved in an incestuous relationship with his father are not well documented. Individual case histories suggest that in adolescence the male might experience concerns regarding his own sexuality as well as related heterosexual conflicts. There may be related conflicts associated with low self-esteem and excessive concerns that he might also be inclined to engage in other homosexual relationships.

Multiply Incestuous Families

A multiply incestuous family would be defined as a family system in which there is more than one dyad involved in a sexual relationship with one another that violates intergenerational boundaries. Clinical assessment of such a family system would reveal significant family problems of such a nature that there would be a pervasive absence of intergenerational boundaries and the absence of clearly defined roles that differentiate family roles within the system.

In instances where there are multiple incestuous relationships, an additionally significant treatment issue pertains to the absence of any form of protection for the children within the family system. In situations when both parents are involved in an incestuous relationship with either the same or different children, the absence of a protective parent will generally necessitate that the children be removed from the home.

Inherent within this family system will be those problems observed in other family systems where incest has been a problem. Assessment and intervention will proceed along the basis of a systems model as defined earlier. Assessment of individual problems, marital conflicts, and family-system troubles will be conducted from a similar conceptual framework as noted earlier. Intervention will also follow from an individual, marital, and family-related perspective.

REFERENCES

Abel, G. G., Becker, J. V., Murphy, W. D., & Flanagan, B. (1981). Identifying dangerous child molesters. *Violent behavior: Social learning approaches to prediction, management, and treatment.* New York: Brunner/Mazel.

Alexander, P. (1985). A systems conceptualization of incest. *Family Process, 24,* 79–88.

Berry, G. W. (1975). Incest: Some clinical variations as a classical theme. *Journal of the American Academy of Psychoanalysis, 3,* 151–161.

Bertalanffy, L. V. (1975). *General systems theory.* In B. D. Ruben & J. Y. Kim (Eds.), *General systems theory and human communication.* Rochelle Park, NJ: Hayden Press.

Bowen, M. (1978). *Family therapy in clinical practice.* New York: Aronson.

Brown, A. (1978). A family systems approach to incest victims and their families. *The Family, 6*(1), 9–11.

Eist, H. I., & Mandel, A. U. (1968). The treatment of ongoing incest behavior. *Family Process, 7,* 216–232.

Giarretto, H. (1980). Humanistic treatment of father–daughter incest. In L. G. Schultz (Ed.). *The sexual victimology of youth* (140–162). Springfield, IL: Charles C. Thomas.

Guthiel, T. G., & Avery, N. C. (1977). Multiple overt incest as family defense against loss. *Family Process, 16,* 105–116.

Haley, J., & Hoffman, L. (1967). *Techniques of family therapy*. New York: Basic Books.

Justice, B., & Justice, R. (1979). *The broken taboo: Sex in the family*. New York: Human Sciences Press.

Langsley, D. G., Schwartz, M. N., & Fairbairn, R. H. (1968). Father–son incest. *Comprehensive Psychiatry, 9,* 218–226.

Lustig, N., Dresser, J. W., Spellman, S. W., & Murray, J. B. (1966). Incest, a family group survival pattern. *Archives of General Psychiatry, 14,* 31–40.

Machotka, P., Pittman, F. S., & Flomenhaft, K. (1967). Incest as a family affair. *Family Process, 6,* 98–116.

Meiselman, K. C. (1979). *Incest*. San Francisco: Jossey-Bass.

Minuchin, S. (1974). *Families and family therapy*. Cambridge, MA: Harvard University Press.

Pondy, L. R., & Mitroff, I. I. (1979). Beyond open system models of organization. *Research Organizational Behavior, 1,* 3–39.

Whitaker, C. (1982). *From psyche to system*. New York: Guilford.

Will, D. (1983). Approaching the incestuous and sexually abusive family. *Journal of Adolescence, 6,* 229–246.

17

A Developing Behavioral Treatment Model: One Therapist's Perspective Within a Community's Evolving Response

Lee C. Handy

This chapter will address two main areas: first, a brief and selective overview of the developing response of the community of Calgary, Alberta, Canada to the concern of child sexual abuse; and second, a developing, behaviorally oriented approach to treatment. Specific issues will include the value of a community-based response, concerns of responsibility and blame, family involvement, selected sequelae and therapeutic response, and redistribution of power within the family as a major focus. Behavioral treatment models by definition call for directive intervention by the therapist. If the treatment appears to disrupt some community norms while encouraging others, there can frequently be a negative community reaction. In the case of child sexual abuse, particularly incest, facilitating the removal of the father as the controlling head of household and equalizing the power held by each family member can maintain the new behaviors taught and serve as relapse prevention to provide safety for the actual and potential victims. However, it is this author's belief that without first educating the community, an outpatient behavioral intervention program will not be as successful.

A COMMUNITY RESPONSE

By May of 1980 there were enough individuals and agencies in Calgary concerned about child sexual abuse that a conference was held, both to bring in experts to further educate the community and to increase the efficacy of the community's response through better communication and focusing of effort. The organizers of the conference succeeded. The Calgary Child Sexual Abuse Committee was formed and energies were focused through a number of working subcommittees. As an outgrowth there have been a number of accomplishments. Public and professional education has increased dramatically. The original committee is now incorporated as the Calgary Society for the Prevention of Child Sexual Abuse and continues its valuable catalytic and coordinating work in policy, education, and treatment areas.

Service delivery has improved both in quality and available resources. The treatment program, described later, probably would not be as effective without the community support. Unfortunately, the need for such services still greatly exceeds those available. The suspected cases arising from the Calgary Sexual Assault Centre's "Who Do You Tell?" program for the schools could itself tax current treatment facilities. Obviously there was much work, frustration, and many ups and downs along the way. Perhaps other communities can learn from our experience.

Needs, Resources, and Planning

From my perspective as a therapist and a committee member, the undertaking of the original committee was the formation of a Needs, Resources and Planning Study Subcommittee. Cooperation among different professions and relevant institutions was an a priori goal of this subcommittee and has remained a central objective within our therapeutic community. The subcommittee was comprised of people representing medicine, social work, law, and psychology. It involved major support from the broad-based Child Sexual Abuse Committee with invaluable support and cooperation from Alberta Social Services and Community Health (who provided funding), the University of Calgary Faculty of Medicine's Department of Community Health Sciences, and the university's Office of Trust Accounting. This subcommittee undertook four tasks: (1) a literature review; (2) a local needs and resources assessment survey of professionals; (3) site visits to existing programs; and (4) a report of the subcommittee's activities, culminating in specific recommendations for further action. The *Child Sexual Abuse: Needs, Resources and Planning Project* Report both summarizes and details the activities of this subcommittee (Kovitz et al., 1982).

In addition to its specific content this project was profitable as a process that greatly heightened professional conscientiousness within the community. It became a frame of reference for competing viewpoints; facilitated a distillation of ideas; built bridges among service delivery, research, and government personnel and agencies; and led to some basic working values that in turn resulted in a recommended model for a community-based multidisciplinary core team. The eight specific recommendations are as follows and are provided to give a flavor of our resulting goals (Kovitz et al., 1982, pp. 2–7).

> Child sexual abuse is almost universally recognized as contexual, i.e., a family or living environment concern, requiring a coordinated multidisciplinary response which entails a provision for long term treatment. This statement is the most basic overall summary of the information gathered. Further, child sexual abuse is indeed a pressing concern and its incidence and psychosocial impact are grossly underestimated. Current professional resources to deal with the problem locally are quite inadequate.

Recommendation 1

Establish a specialized multidisciplinary *core team* to deal comprehensively with child sexual abuse in Calgary.

1. The *mandate* given to the core team should encompass: (a) service to clients—both indirect consultation and referral and direct assessment and treatment; (b) education—both public and professional; and (c) evaluation and research.
2. The *professions represented* on the core team should be social work, medicine, psychology, and community health nursing.
3. Develop a close and formal *working relationship* with other community resources, in particular legal (including police) and child protection services, but also others that may be required as experience would dictate.
4. Set "*team building*" as the first priority for the core team, set the acquisition of specific *training* in child sexual abuse management as the second priority.
5. Establish clear *policies and procedures* to be used by the core team in managing child sexual abuse, giving particular attention to the desirability of removing the offender from the family rather than habitually removing the child, as well as the provision for long-term continuity of care.
6. Establish a child sexual abuse program in a *setting* such as the Health Sciences Centre adjoining Foothills Hospital or the Alberta Children's Hospital, which reflects a nontraditional patient-care philosophy.

Recommendation 2

Establish an *Advisory Committee* that is advisory to the core team and to the team's governing structure.

Recommendation 3

Provide a *mechanism for coordination* and liaison of community resources in Calgary for dealing with child sexual abuse.

Recommendation 4

Professional education:

1. Provide *training* in dealing with cases of child sexual abuse for professionals currently working in the Calgary area.
2. Provide the opportunity for training as a joint effort by professionals, individuals, associations, and agencies.

Recommendation 5

Public education:

1. Raise community awareness of sexual abuse through the media to create a *receptive climate* for programs dealing with child sexual abuse.
2. Provide public education for *prevention* (e.g., risk factors).
3. Provide information to the public about existing resources for *treatment.*

Recommendation 6

Develop strong support for clinical, epidemiological, and evaluative *research.*

Recommendation 7

Support self-help programs that entail professional leadership and/or consultation, building where possible upon existing projects and services.

Recommendation 8

As a matter of course, use the juvenile court as the most appropriate judicial arena for child sexual abuse, provided that mechanisms are specifically available for placing consequences on the offender's behavior and mandating therapy. The use of the juvenile court does not exclude the addition of criminal proceedings.

Clearly this information is not unique for our community. The conclusions might come from a variety of places, and in fact are largely consistent with information available elsewhere. However, the fact that the needs and resources assessment had been carried out in the community for which action was proposed had numerous advantages as noted above. This is not to say there was not disharmony in the process—there was and still is. In the very broadest sense such disagreements might have been categorized as a problem of unbelievers and of true believers. The unbelievers ("it's not much of a problem in *our* community") presented a problem in the realm of education. Both formal (e.g., the survey as well as numerous professional meetings and workshops) and informal (e.g., media coverage and professional social contact) activities have largely eliminated the unbelievers. The true believers ("there is only *one* right way to view and respond to child sexual abuse") presented a problem of communication and cooperation. A growing appreciation of the diversity of circumstances surrounding the occurrence of and therapeutic response to child sexual abuse has been gained. This has been fostered by the necessity of information exchange by a variety of personnel working from different perspectives in various settings, all working within the Calgary Child Sexual Abuse Committee. The result has been a more positive evolution of diverse community resources, which begins to match the diversity of need.

Current Status of Recommendations

What has happened to the recommendations? They have spurred much debate, a great deal of action, and they have not been adopted as presented. However, goals of many of the recommendations have been approached in a variety of ways. A core team has not been established, but personnel has increased and there is now an emphasis within Alberta's provincial Social Services and Community Health that allows a higher degree of coordination by their social workers. While all concerned are involved to some degree in case management tasks, it is primarily the provincial social workers who function as the case coordinators—and given the diverse arenas, amount of pressure, and high caseloads overall, they do a remarkable job. Special liaison personnel have been designated to facilitate and monitor several major service providers under yearly contracts.

The current Calgary Society for the Prevention of Child Sexual Abuse is representative of the individuals, agencies, and professionals interested in child sexual abuse. It meets regularly and in a very broad sense serves an advisory as well as stimulating function for further progress. Much of the professional and public education in our community is an indirect or direct outgrowth of the society and/or its members.

The University of Calgary has provided major impetus for research and training in child sexual abuse with at least six departments having major involvement. The Child Abuse Team of Alberta Children's Hospital is notable for their efforts both in clinical and demographic research and multidisciplinary service delivery.

One of our major resources is a program with a major self-help component (Anderson & Mayes, 1982). This program is a local adaptation of Giarretto's (1982) program and is currently one of the contracted service providers for families dealing with child sexual abuse.

Special law-enforcement personnel have been carefully selected and specially trained by the Calgary police force and regularly participate in the Society's meetings. The judicial branch has been actively represented as well. It is rare that a complaint is made against our police officers in spite of the inherent intrusiveness and disruptiveness of their task. In the judicial arena in general, function is leading form. Although the laws have not changed regarding child sexual abuse, direct experience indicates a discernible increase in the understanding of child sexual abuse in courtroom proceedings. Old stereotypes and myths are less in evidence. The increased degree to which judges seek information beyond that directly elicited by the lawyers, coupled with an increased acceptance that the role of mental health professionals is one of providing information to be considered, has led to more cooperative efforts—to the betterment of all concerned. This is not to say we are not also faced with such issues as the ubiquitous dilemma of what is acceptable evidence and how to prove a child sexual abuse case, issues also reported elsewhere in the United States (see Long, Chapter 8 of this volume). But we do manage to get many acknowledged or adjudicated offenders ordered into treatment. New treatment programs have been developed. One such program is based on a community treatment model. It probably could not have developed without the community first having been educated and organized as just described.

A DEVELOPING BEHAVIORALLY ORIENTED APPROACH TO TREATMENT

Therapist Orientation

Acknowledging that a therapist working with sexually abused children may, and probably will be, called upon to function in a variety of roles, it is important to focus on the therapeutic function. This is not to negate the importance of such activities as case management, assessment, investigation, and expert testimony. In fact, most cases require a greater or lesser degree of involvement in all of these areas.

Before looking at some specific examples of treatment, some background is in order. There are two prevalent theoretical positions regarding child sexual abuse: the "child protection" or family-based viewpoint, which stresses the pathology in the entire family, and the "feminist" or victim-advocacy orientation, which stresses the offender's sole responsibility and the damage to the victim (cf. Finkelhor, 1984, for a discussion of each model). I rest uncomfortably if forced into either viewpoint to the exclusion of the other. The two main issues for each position are the importance of family dynamics and the question of responsibility. There is no disagreement concerning the primary need to protect the child. With regard to the issue of family dynamics, I believe it is seldom therapeutically useful to view the occurrence of child sexual abuse as the result of family pathology to which all family members usually contribute, such has been suggested by some (deYoung, 1982). The fact that certain dysfunctional family characteristics have been found to be associated with child sexual abuse (Stern & Meyer, 1980; Will, 1983) does not diminish the importance of individual responsibility on the part of the person who has chosen to act inappropriately, even if it may help understand how the choice might have become available.

From the literature and our experience at Alberta Psychological Resources, we find essentially all of these families either have a characteristic of being significantly unbalanced or of having very unclear power structures. It has been suggested that power is the dimension that runs through the data related to the occurrence of child sexual abuse (Handy & Cammaert, 1985). However, at the same time, the family response to the occurrence of child sexual abuse is of great importance. If one is willing to view family dynamics as a major mitigator and not always as a facilitating factor in child sexual abuse, while one is also willing to tackle the issue of individual responsibility, then both theoretical points of view have important contributions (Pelletier & Handy, 1986). Such a combined strategy will be illustrated below.

Behavioral Principles

Since many of the issues faced in dealing with child sexual abuse stem from socialization, therapeutic responses arising from behavioral or social learning theory approaches are appealing. Many of the sequelae of abuse are concerns for which behavioral interventions have been found effective.

It is well known that the discovery of child sexual abuse causes stress and depression, which exacerbates existing marital and family difficulties. Substantial behavioral literature addresses these areas (e.g., Alexander, Barton, Waldron, & Mas, 1983; Goldfried, 1977; Jacobson & Margolin, 1979; Leiberman, Wheeler, deVisser, Kuehnel, & Kuehnel, 1980; Rosenthal & Rosenthal, 1983; Rush, 1982). Work in the areas of sexual dysfunction and aggression (Heiman, Lo Piccolo, & Lo Piccolo, 1981; Jehu, 1979; Marshall, Earls, Segal, & Darke, 1983), impulse control and self-management (Rachman, 1983; Stuart, 1977; Watson & Tharp, 1981), and substance abuse (Cooney, Baker, & Pomerleau, 1983; Sobell & Sobell, 1983) also has direct relevance for many of the therapeutic target behaviors encountered when dealing with child sexual abuse.

Several important areas include application and modification of established procedures for contracting (DeRisi & Butz, 1975), assertiveness (Bower, Amatea, & Anderson, 1976; Lange & Jakubowski, 1976; Palmer, 1977), and sleep disturbances (Bootzin, 1977; Weil, 1975). Although these examples are presented in an isolated fashion for the purpose of illustration, such interventions usually take place within a much broader and more complex therapeutic relationship. Becker, Skinner, and Abel (1982) have reported a case study whose process is similar to our efforts and those of Alexander et al. (1983); and Jacobson's (1983) comments regarding more comprehensive integrated approaches to such complex concerns provide a level of functioning to which we aspire.

The following working assumptions underlie our therapeutic approach to child sexual abuse, and any deviations are situational exceptions to the rule. These guidelines are made known to all involved, especially to the offender. They include: (1) the welfare of the victim and siblings is paramount; (2) if possible, the offender, not the victim, is removed from the home; (3) the victim is assumed to be truthful unless there is compelling evidence to the contrary (this issue is routinely explored in a nonconfrontational, nonthreatening manner with emphasis on support for the victim); (4) proper authorities have been notified; (5) someone is coordinating the various persons and agencies involved, that is, functioning as case manager (in our situation it is routinely a provincial social services and community health caseworker); (6) that it is clear to all clients that certain information may have to be shared with social services and/or the legal system; (7) within the parameters of the above, the therapist is willing to work with all persons involved; and (8) although the reunification of the family is seen as a possible goal, it is not assumed to be a predetermined goal.

Process of a Case

In a typical case the sequencing runs roughly as follows. When feasible the victim, mother, each sibling, and father are each seen individually. Father will be used throughout synonymously with perpetrator, acknowledging that fathers are the most frequent but not the only offenders (Russell, 1984). The perpetrator might in fact be another relative, acquaintance, or fatherlike person. Fathers do seem to predominate in our caseload, which is supported by recent research (Conte & Berliner, Chapter 5 of this volume; Russell, 1984). Then mother and victim are seen; fostering a positive interaction is a very high priority at this time. Mother and all the children are next seen, followed by a meeting with both mother and father. When contact between father and children is likely, parents and victim are seen together. If not, the victim and offender do not meet. Finally, the entire family may or may not meet. On occasions, when appropriate and agreed upon, other relatives and friends are also seen, in which case the objective may be their inclusion as an integral part of the therapy. In other instances, the purpose is largely informational, so that they can increase their positive support of the familiy's rehabilitative goals. This sequence, while not entirely rigid, is more likely to be followed at the onset with situational factors such as practical logistics having greater influence later in the process.

A period of catharsis is frequently required before it is possible to establish specific treatment plans. This may be legitimately viewed as a venting and sorting-out process that not only aids in decreasing the "noise" or competing stimuli from the system, but also allows the clients to make judgments regarding the degree to which they will trust and be willing to work with the therapist. Often during this cathartic/exploration period, validation of the sexual abuse is obtained, particularly if not previously acknowledged by the perpetrator. A network or mosaic of behaviors begins to be constructed as possible targets of behavior change.

The clear acknowledgment of the perpetrator's ownership of responsibility is crucial in at least two ways. It mitigates against the victim's feelings of guilt related to both the occurrence and to the disruption of the family, and his explicit acceptance of blame increases the probability of mother's being able to support her daughter without automatically having to reject the father. It creates a supportive atmosphere in the early stages, which is the time when the victim needs to perceive such support, quickly, to avoid secondary trauma. Such an attribution of personal responsibility does not require that other variables—such as destructive socialization, early traumatic events, or other predetermining factors leading to the decision to molest—be ignored, but it does presume that a person who has greater power is sexually exploiting one with lesser power and is therefore culpable. This is similar to the feminist position relative to the offender.

Contracting with Offenders

In light of the above, a modification of contracting is used with child sexual abuse offenders, similar to that which deals with other types of broken commitments within intimate relationships (Handy, 1984). This is most often a two-phase contract. The first phase is one in which the perpetrator specifically (in writing) acknowledges his personal responsibility ("I am to blame") for the inappropriate behavior (often explicitly spelled out with no qualifiers) and that it is appropriate for all other family members to expect that such behavior will not occur again. In his statement he encourages them individually or in groups to take whatever action is needed to negate such behavior. To this end he agrees to continue treatment until such time as the family, therapist, and he agree to terminate. Thus, he specifically acknowledges his new one-down position within the family, a reduction in his power (which was misused). He will have to earn acceptance in some very important areas, which leads to the second phase of the contract. The explicit adaptation of an "I owe us" stance provides all involved with a concrete frame of reference around which to rebuild a functional level of trust.

Specific behaviors for the perpetrator to engage in are often negotiated with the entire family in order to provide a tangible means of measuring his change in perspective and behavior. Behaviors that are specifically out of character for the offender are chosen and related to the power issues. For example, some negotiable behaviors previously utilized include the father taking on laundry or other unusual housework duties, or a relinquishment of a duty—such as permitting other members of the family to plan weekend activities. This is seen as retribution and must be determined carefully. Its form should be determined jointly by all involved, but most importantly it must have special relevance for the victim, mother, and also for siblings. It must obviously be something the perpetrator is willing to do, and if this contracted retribution is explicit, behavioral, and has time limits (with clause for renegotiation), the chance of compliance is very high. Accepting a one-down position and retribution as appropriate punishment does not require the offender or others to negate the offender's positive qualities, but it clearly acknowledges the importance of the transgression.

It has been said that if blame is allowed to enter the therapeutic process the client will be alienated and it may thus negate the chances for positive outcome. On the contrary, this procedure is one part of the behavioral mosaic that concretely provides a manner of rebuilding a pattern of trust.

Assertiveness Training for Family Members

Unwarranted trust could be worse than none. To this end a series of assertiveness-training exercises are used with two, possibly three, major objectives. Improvement of assertiveness and other social skills is a very desirable goal in and of itself. The acquisition of such skills can facilitate better decision making regarding possible reunification of the family, and if such a decision is made, such skills increase the functional availability of both internal and external resources that mitigate against the occurrence/ recurrence of child sexual abuse. Finklehor (1984) suggests four preconditions necessary for such abuse to occur. Behavioral skill training is seen as a way of avoiding the preconditions from occurring. Typically, individual behavior rehearsal, where new skills are practiced, is first utilized. It is then followed by joint behavior rehearsals with the victim and mother, and then with the inclusion of other siblings. Initially, practical everyday types of requests and responses are generally used as examples. There is a heavy emphasis on rewarding the exchange of positive interactions with each other, because abusive families have been found to exhibit a higher ratio of negative to positive behaviors. Then rehearsal of responses to verbal or nonverbal requests for inappropriate sexual touching behavior is introduced. Even if it is clear the perpetrator will not be having any more contact with the victim, these sessions are used as a general educational and preventive strategy. If contact is possible or probable at some time in the future, then specific reference to the perpetrator is utilized. Again, this is usually done in sequential steps: first with the victim, then teaching mother to be the coach, and then training siblings to be both supporters for the victim and participants for themselves. This training allows even very young siblings to model and develop their own repertoire of appropriate assertive responses.

Learning to Monitor Father's Behavior

When father is ready to return home or is allowed to have contact with the family, other family members are taught to monitor his behavior. Often father's participation in this aspect of therapy has been explicitly written in the second phase of the previously described contract. Behavior rehearsals teach him to tolerate the rest of the family's right to question certain of his actions by demonstrating an appropriate response. During these individual sessions, father is encouraged to actually initiate sexually inappropriate behavior so the therapist can teach the family how to respond. The entire family then rehearses their responses to father's sexually explicit requests. These are usually very active and noisy sessions, during which the seriousness of the issue is both emphasized and leavened with humor, generally through exaggeration. The therapist is careful not to let the victim be scapegoated and carefully monitors her feelings. There are at least two such therapy sessions, which take place a minimum of a week apart. In between, the entire family is told to hold at least one similar session at home, which is frequently recorded on tape. The at-home session is debriefed and discussed at the beginning of the next therapy session. The rationale of requiring an at-home session is to facilitate generalization of these changing, complex family interactions into the setting where the sexually abusive behaviors previously occurred.

These sessions dramatically remove sexually explicit activity from the realm of secrecy and clearly establish such behavior as unacceptable in view of all. Father often winds up feeling sheepish and more apologetic. At this point, the family norms are in the process of change. The rest of the family, including the actual victim, usually become more active, supportive of one another, and more comfortable interacting with father. Early concerns regarding the actual victim's possible negative reactions to this procedure have not yet materialized. Ethically it has not been possible to make comparisons, because it could be too dangerous to reunite the father without the earlier shaping steps performed in the behavioral rehearsal described above. Concerns regarding father's willingness to participate in and his reactions to such a procedure have also proved largely unfounded, particularly when they are combined with the contracting procedure described previously.

It is obvious that the therapist in the above intervention is clearly imposing certain values upon the participants. This is done with open acknowledgment. Because redistribution of power is perceived as central to the well-being of incest families, the therapist's facilitation of more egalitarian family relationships, even when not requested, can be justified on mental health grounds irrespective of other moral or political factors that may also have relevance. For a discussion of the issue of therapists' influencing "desired marital relationships," see Jacobson (1983). Greater community support for more egalitarian family relationships has been established through the original interdisciplinary committee, which included representation of the more traditional clergy.

Sleep-Disturbance Intervention

The frequency with which we have found sleep disturbances to be a major concern for victims and their aware siblings (especially those approximately 6 through 13 years of age) has stimulated development of what appears to be a promising treatment approach. Insomnia with or without nightmares or nightmares alone are the most common complaints. Behavioral techniques to treat insomnia, described by Bootzin (1977), have proved most promising when combined with a specific focus on nightmares.

First, the client is asked to describe in detail what of the nightmare can be recalled. Most can recall details that bear a striking resemblance to the current vogue of horror-rock-video productions! Second, the client is taught a short program of deep muscle relaxation, which is then interspersed with descriptions of various segments of the nightmare(s). The third phase occurs while the client, relaxed and with eyes closed, rehearses the nightmare scene out loud, often with enthusiastic therapist prompting. They become their own rock video directors, controlling the dream. In this phase there is encouragement first to include major aspects of the nightmares, and then to gradually make significant changes that make them feel better. Visual imagery is encouraged. For some, actually writing scripts has proven beneficial. Data gathered indicate reduction in the number of nightmares and a lower degree of being upset, which has been encouraging. Corroborating data are often gathered from parent(s), but the main data emphasized are provided by the client in question. This activity emphasizes control by the client and facilitates the experience of reempowerment, a necessary ingredient for a victim to become a survivor.

Family Recordkeeping and Goal Setting

In many of the behaviors tracked within the family (including such diverse activities as parental drinking and the mutual display of affection between parents), both parents and children are asked to keep records. This sharpens everyone's observational skills and facilitates early recognition of patterns to be reinforced or changed. The new behaviors are monitored in what is labeled as a relapse-prevention model, typically found in treatment of other behaviors targeted for change. Over and above improving the data base, such activity also is presented as a way of increasing shared activity, which then promotes family welfare. The therapist may also automatically contract to train parents to demonstrate positive encouragement toward their children. As in previously described behavior training, encouragement skills are first taught, then rehearsed, then practiced in a therapy session with formal feedback being accepted from the children; then these skills are rehearsed at home and again demonstrated in a session with the therapist. Some will need more than these in-vivo rehearsals to get the new behavior established in their personal repertoire.

The goal for the family members is to learn to be actors as well as reactors, to function toward common goals when feasible, and to support individual goals when possible within an environment where the balance of power is such that no one is placed in position of high vulnerability to exploitation. This is a major shift in the traditional view of the family; it gives the children and the mother strong tools with which to modify the incestuous father's inappropriate behavior.

SUMMARY

The value of our community's efforts in dealing with child sexual abuse through the development of the Calgary Child Sexual Abuse Committee was not only in terms of new information and coordination, but also in increased understanding and appreciation of the diversity of abuse situations and legitimate therapeutic responses. Such a perspective allows an increased ability to approach policy makers and funding sources with one voice while not becoming tunnel-visioned. While recognizing that we still have far to go, it is important to acknowledge the gains that have already been made.

Treatment procedures such as those described above are based on the belief that at a time of extreme family disruption, externally imposed structure can be therapeutically sound for both the family system and for the individuals involved. Offenses (transgressions) are explicitly labeled, owned by the offender, and, when appropriate, punishment is coupled with concrete procedures for improving the family interactions. Specific behavioral responses to the victim's emotional sequelae appear to assist greatly in increasing a desired sense of self-esteem. No one is left in a position of saying either "What happened wasn't really so bad" or "Our future is ruined." The viewpoint expressed is, "It was bad but we can be better!"

REFERENCES

Alexander, J. F., Barton, C., Waldron, H., & Mas, C. H. (1983). Beyond the technology of family therapy: The anatomy of intervention model. In K. D. Craig & R. H. McMahon (Eds.), *Advances in clinical behavior therapy* (pp. 48–73). New York: Brunner/Mazel.

Anderson, C., & Mayes, P. (1982). Treating family sexual abuse: The humanistic approach. *Journal of Child Care, 2,* 31–47.

Becker, J. V., Skinner, L. J., & Abel, G. G. (1982). Treatment of a four-year-old victim of incest. *The American Journal of Family Therapy, 10,* 41–46.

Bootzin, R. R. (1977). Effects of self-control procedures for insomnia. In R. B. Stuart (Ed.), *Behavioral self-management: Strategies, techniques, and outcome* (pp. 176–195). New York: Brunner/Mazel.

Bower, S. A., Amatea, E., & Anderson, R. (1976). Assertiveness training with children. *Elementary School Guidance and Counseling, 10*(4), 236–245.

Cooney, N. L., Baker, L. H., & Pomerleau, O. F. (1983). Cue exposure for relapse prevention in alcohol treatment. In K. D. Craig & R. J. McMahon (Eds.), *Advances in clinical behavior therapy* (pp. 194–210). New York: Brunner/Mazel.

DeRisi, W. J., & Butz, G. (1975). *Writing behavioral contracts: A case simulation practice manual.* Champaign, IL: Research Press.

deYoung, M. (1982). *The sexual victimization of children.* Jefferson, NC: McFarland.

Finklehor, D. (1984). *Child sexual abuse.* New York: Free Press.

Giarreto, H. (1982). A comprehensive child sexual abuse treatment program. *Child Abuse and Neglect, 6,* 263–278.

Goldfried, M. R. (1977). The use of relaxation and cognitive relabeling as coping skills. In R. B. Stuart (Ed.), *Behavioral self-management: Strategies, techniques, and outcome* (pp. 82–116). New York: Brunner/Mazel.

Handy, L. C. (1984, October). *Sin, shame, blame, & retribution: Therapeutic concerns regarding commitments within intimate relationships.* Paper presented at the meeting of the National Council on Family Relations, San Francisco.

Handy, L. C., & Cammaert, L. P. (1985, June). *Power: A major construct of child sexual abuse.* Paper presented at the meeting of the Canadian Psychological Association, Halifax, Nova Scotia.

Heiman, J. R., LoPiccolo, L., & LoPiccolo, J. (1981). The treatment of sexual dysfunction. In A. S. Gurman & D. P. Kniskern (Eds.), *Handbook of family therapy* (pp. 592–627). New York: Brunner/Mazel.

Jacobson, N. S. (1983). Clinical innovations in behavioral marital therapy. In K. D. Craig & R. J. MacMahon (Eds.), *Advances in clinical behavior therapy* (pp. 74–98). New York: Brunner/Mazel.

Jacobson, N. W., & Margolin, G. (1979). *Marital therapy: Strategies based on social learning and behavior exchange principles.* New York: Brunner/Mazel.

Jehu, D. (1979). *Sexual dysfunction: A behavioral approach to causation, assessment, and treatment.* Chichester, England, and New York: Wiley.

Kovitz, K., Barr, D., Brummitt, J., Handy, L. C., Leveque, P., Plowman, B., & Riese, R. (1982). *Child sexual assault: Needs, resources and planning project* (Report). Calgary, Alberta: Alberta Department of Social Services and Community Health.

Lange, A. J., & Jakubowski, P. (1976). *Responsible assertive behavior: Cognitive/ behavioral procedures for trainers.* Champaign, IL: Research Press.

Leiberman, R. P., Wheeler, E. G., deVisser, L. A. J. M., Kuehnel, J., & Kuehnel, T. (1980). *Handbook of marital therapy: A positive approach to helping troubled relationships.* New York: Plenum.

Marshall, W. L., Earls, C. M., Segal, Z., & Darke, J. (1983). A behavioral program for the assessment and treatment of sexual aggressors. In K. D. Craig & R. J. MacMahon (Eds.), *Advances in clinical behavior therapy* (pp. 148–174). New York: Brunner/ Mazel.

Palmer, P. (1977). *The mouse, the monster, and me: Assertiveness for young people.* San Luis Obispo, CA: Impact.

Pelletier, G., & Handy, L. C. (1986). Family dysfunction and the psychological impact of child sexual abuse. *Canadian Journal of Psychiatry, 31,* 407–412.

Rachman, S. J. (1983). The modifications of obsessions and compulsions. In K. D. Craig & R. J. MacMahon (Eds.) *Advances in clinical behavior therapy* (pp. 127–147). New York: Brunner/Mazel.

Rosenthal, T. L., & Rosenthal, R. H. (1983). Stress: causes, measurement, and management. In K. D. Craig & R. J. MacMahon (Eds.), *Advances in clinical behavior therapy* (pp. 3–26). New York: Brunner/Mazel.

Rush, A. J. (Ed.), (1982). *Short-term psychotherapies for depression.* New York: Guilford.

Russell, D. E. H. (1984). *Sexual exploitation: Rape, child sexual abuse, and workplace harassment.* Beverly Hills, CA: Sage.

Sobell, L. C., & Sobell, M. B. (1983). Behavioral research and therapy: Its impact on the alcohol field. In K. D. Craig & R. J. MacMahon (Eds.), *Advances in clinical behavior therapy* (pp. 175–193). New York: Brunner/Mazel.

Stern, M. J., & Meyer, L. C. (1980). Family and couple interactional patterns in cases of father/daughter incest. In B. M. Jones, L. L. Jenstrom, & K. McFarlane (Eds.), *Sexual abuse of children: Selected readings* (pp. 83–86) (*DHHS* Publication No. OHDS 78-30161). Washington, DC: U.S. Government Printing Office.

Stuart, R. B. (Ed.). (1977). *Behavioral self-management: Strategies, techniques, and outcome.* New York: Brunner/Mazel.

Watson, D. L., & Tharp, R. G. (1981). *Self-directed behavior: Self-modification for personal adjustment* (3rd ed.). Monterey, CA: Brooks/Cole.

Weil, G. (1975). *Treatment of insomnia in a eleven-year old child through self-relaxation.* In A. M. Graziano (Ed.), *Behavior therapy with children: Vol. II.* Chicago: Aldine.

Will, D. (1983). Approaching the incestuous and sexually abusive family. *Journal of Adolescence, 6,* 229–246.

18

Assessment and Treatment of Sex Offenders in a Community Setting

Steven C. Wolf
Jon R. Conte
Mary Engel-Meinig

The dramatic increase in the reported number of child victims of sexual abuse by adults has increased public and professional interest in how these adults should be handled. Public sentiment supporting strong criminal justice sanctions and the decline of rehabilitation as a social value serve to devalue treatment of adults who sexually abuse children. Incarceration of adult sex offenders, especially in the numbers that they are currently being identified throughout the United States, is an extremely expensive alternative to other approaches to handling this problem. Additionally, unless such incarceration is for life, the adult who is sexually interested in children will someday be returned to the community. In the absence of some treatment for the problem, such an adult is likely to represent a continued risk of harm to children.

This chapter describes an alternative to incarceration, which is community-based treatment for sexually aggressive adults. This approach has been developed over the last 7 years with over 4,000 clients at Northwest Treatment Associates in Seattle, Washington. Multitheoretical in nature, the treatment approach is based on a growing literature describing the development of adult sexual interest in children. (See, e.g., Abel, 1978; Abel, Becker, & Cunningham-Rathner, 1984; Abel, Becker, Murphy, & Flanagan, 1981; Abel, Becker, & Skinner, 1980; Abel, Rouleau, & Cunningham-Rathner,

1984; Langevin, Handy, Russon, & Day, 1985; Quinsey, 1984; Quinsey & Bergersen, 1976.) Community-based treatment for sexually aggressive clients is not the treatment of choice for every client. This chapter describes the clients served in this community program, the rationale for community-based treatment, and the therapeutic evaluation that determines whether an individual client is, in fact, appropriate for community-based service. Altering complex patterns of clients' deviant behaviors that select, manipulate, and sexually use children requires a multimodal approach to intervention. This chapter is intended to serve as a general introduction to the Northwest Model of community-based treatment of adults who sexually use children.

CLIENT CHARACTERISTICS

Clients are referred to Northwest from a variety of law enforcement, social service, and mental health agencies as well as from private attorneys and clergy. Client populations change over time, so it is important to keep in mind that descriptions of clients generated at one point in time may vary some from clients seen at other points in time. The description that follows is based on a data collection effort carried out by the authors on a sample of cases ($N = 60$) from August to December, 1984. This is a sample skewed in the direction of less serious levels of deviance. The selection criteria required subjects to have been in treatment for at least 6 months and to have passed a clinical polygraph on their histories of deviant behavior.

Table 18.1 presents descriptive data on this client sample seen at Northwest. The data paint a picture of a relatively stable sample (e.g., 60% of the men had the same job for at least 5 years) that were higher educated (46% having 1 to 4 years of college) and were otherwise a noncriminal population (67% having no arrest record prior to the charge bringing them to Northwest). Seventy-four percent of the men use pornography as a regular part of their sexual behavior; 16% are judged to be excessively involved in the use of pornographic materials (i.e., use pornography as a major component of their sexual behavior). Data on the age of onset for sexual interest in children confirm the increasing suspicion that many adult sexual offenders began their careers in their own adolescence. The average age of first overt act of sexual aggression in this clinic sample is 16.2 years; 30% of the sample experienced an onset before their 11th birthday. For men in this sample report, the average age of their first sexual experience (in which they may or may not have been the initiator) is 10.2 years of age. Sixty-three percent of these experiences are defined by the men as mutual (i.e., noncoercive), and 46% took place with a peer.

TABLE 18.1 Client Characteristics

Male = 97%	
Average age = 37.3	
Age range from 18 to 65	
White = 93%	
Education:	
11 years or less	8%
12 years	33%
13 to 16 years (college)	46%
17 to 19 years (postgraduate)	13%
No more than one job in last 5 years	60%
Current marital status:	
Married/living with someone	54%
Not married/not living with someone	23%
Never married/never lived with someone	12%
Previous arrest record:	
None	67%
Sex crimes	15%
DWI	8%
Other	10%
Pornography:	
Use	74%
Abuse	16%
Average age at onset of sexual deviancy	16.2
Average age at first sexual experience:	10.3

EVALUATION

The first and one of the most important decisions the community therapist has to make is whether the offender is "safe" enough to be treated in the community. Making the wrong judgment can result in harm to children and seriously threaten the credibility of the therapist. In this case, safety means the offenders are able, on their own, to stop sexually abusing others for at least several months.

An evaluation of a sex offender requires an assessment of his development and functioning as well as his history and level of deviance. In general, the offender appropriate for community treatment is the individual who has an overall prosocial lifestyle; one who has demonstrated the capacity to follow through on tasks; who has relationships in the community; and who has no history of pronounced physical violence. The purpose of evaluation, in part, is to determine how "dangerous" the offender is. (For material on "dangerousness," see Quinsey, 1984; and Abel, Becker, Murphy, & Flanagan, 1981.)

Dangerousness cannot be exclusively defined by the nature of the problem for which the offender has been referred. For example, incest offenders have traditionally been thought of as the least dangerous of all offenders because of the limited scope of their deviance. However, incest offenders frequently have victims outside of their own families. Abel, Mittleman, Becker, Cunningham-Rathner, and Lucas (1983) report that 44% of men identified as incest offenders also had female victims outside their own homes. Our clinical experience confirms that many offenders have histories that include other types of offenses and victims. We also find that some incest offenders use considerable violence in the abuse and control of their own children. Force and threat may be more frequently found in nonfamily cases, but still present in family abuse cases (Conte & Berliner, 1981).

An evaluation of an alleged sex offender is not intended to prove innocence or guilt. At best it is a procedure that describes the dimensions of a known problem. It is the basis for treatment planning, and while its style will vary among evaluators, it should contain several components.

The first task in the evaluation process is to define the evaluator's relationship with the offender/client. Experience at Northwest indicates that most offenders will not be completely honest with the evaluator. They will try to present themselves in the most favorable light possible. They tend to minimize, deny, and distort their motivation and behavior. Part of this distortion will be conscious and part of it will be a function of distortions in perceptions, values, attitudes, and beliefs that support sexual use of children. (For discussions, see Conte, 1985.) This situation makes reliance on the offender's self-report problematic. It necessitates corroborative contacts with other sources, such as siblings, other relatives, friends, or others who have extensive knowledge of him. This creates special problems with confidentiality.

Therapists often debate the role of confidentiality in treatment of sexually aggressive clients. Northwest has developed special client confidentiality procedures that differ from the traditional view. Clients are told that we will be obtaining information from other community agencies (e.g., the victim's therapist) and that the sharing of information may take place during evaluation and throughout treatment. Northwest assumes that the more information available to the therapist about a sex offender's behavior in the community, the better directed the treatment can be to help the offender control his behavior.

Client Information

The comprehensive evaluation consists of two parts: client-derived and community-derived data. Client-derived data are gathered from the offender/client directly through the clinical interview and psychophysiological assessment. Community-derived data are gathered through contacts with the client's family, friends, police reports, and victim, and from witness statements and reports of other victim and offender specialists.

Sexual offenders almost never come to treatment on a self-referral basis. Most Northwest clients who seek evaluation and treatment do so because of a criminal justice system mandate. The evaluator and the client should be clear as to the reason for the referral. Often the client will have only a general understanding of what an evaluation can accomplish. For example, the client may believe therapy will be short-term and consist of "talking about things." The evaluator may have to contact the offender's attorney or other referring source to clarify the purpose of the referral. The evaluator must be sure that the purpose of the evaluation is consistent with agency philosophy and is feasible. For example, often clients and their attorneys want the evaluator to state that the client is innocent or guilty. Clinical evaluations may describe factors consistent or inconsistent with sexual deviancy. Absolute statements about events that may or may not have taken place are not possible.

The clinical evaluation interview consists of several hours of client contact, usually over a period of a week, to gather information and to observe the client's behavior. The evaluator looks for a pattern of attitudes, values, or behaviors that is associated with deviant sexual preferences (Conte, 1985).

A fundamentally important component of the evaluation is a psychophysiological assessment of the client's pattern of sexual arousal and tenacity of self-report. (For description, see Abel, 1978, or Laws & Osborn, 1983.) Psychophysiological assessment of sexual arousal via the penile plethysmograph and verification of the client's self-report information using the polygraph are useful sources of data. While these measures can provide information not found elsewhere and give the clinician other areas to explore, care must be taken to not overinterpret information obtained from these measures. Some clients do not respond to any stimuli in the lab. Others have learned ways to "beat" the machine. While a lack of response to deviant stimuli cannot be used to determine innocence, a response to deviant stimuli does indicate that some level of deviant arousal does exist. (See Abel & Blanchard, 1976; Alford, Wedding, & Jones, 1983; Laws & Rubin, 1962; and Quinsey & Bergensen, 1976.)

To gather community-generated data, contacts are made with the offender's spouse or partner, as well as with parents, siblings, other relatives, and friends. These contacts are used to verify the offender's description of his childhood development, socialization, school, work, military, and deviant history. For example, what were the values of the offender's family of origin regarding physical abuse, sex roles, and the roles of adults versus children? In addition, in an incest case, it can be helpful to speak with prior wives or other relatives who may either have known or suspected that the offender had a problem or who may know of other relatives who are also deviant. The search here is for the presence of factors potentially associated with the development of the adult sexual use of children (Conte, 1985). Contacts are also made with the referral source, the offender's attorney, children's protective services, victim therapists, sexual assault workers, the investigating officer, and other sex offender therapists who may have seen the client. In each case, information is compared with information gathered from the offender. The result can be an in-depth picture of the offender, including the development of his deviance.

To be useful, the evaluation must ultimately answer several primary questions: What is the nature of the offender's sexual problem? How chronic/compulsive/addicted is he? How quickly does he recover from the shame and guilt of offending? How integrated into his personality or life-style is his deviancy?

The nature of the offender's sexual problem is evaluated by exploring the range of sexual objects in his arousal pattern. Is the male offender, referred for being sexual with a 12-year-old boy, also actively homosexual with adults? Is he also aroused by female children? Is he sexually functional with his partner without recourse to deviant fantasies? Has he been sexual with animals, prostitutes, relatives, or others? What kinds of autoerotic behaviors has he tried? Additionally, does he act out in nonsexual deviant ways (e.g., theft or physical abuse)?

The compulsivity/addiction level is measured by the client's frequency of deviant behavior. The frequency of an individual's deviant acting out is perhaps the best measure of the strength of the offender's deviancy. The time between deviant episodes represents how rapidly the offender can get over the unpleasant feelings (e.g., guilt and remorse) that often accompany the offense, and reexperience the attraction to deviance, rationalize objections to the deviance, find or set up his target victim, and act out deviantly again. The shorter the time between deviant acts, the stronger the level of deviant attraction.

It should be kept in mind that newly discovered offenders are frightened and, as a result, feel guilty about what they have done. How this is expressed can be clinically important. For example, do they focus guilt on the victim or on being caught? How quickly does the guilt dissipate and the offender feel victimized? Expressions that deal only with the impact of disclosure on the offender himself and not the victim indicate that clinical attention will need to be directed toward helping the offender see the impact of this deviant behavior on others.

In terms of making treatment recommendations, the evaluator has four choices: (1) prison, (2) inpatient placement, (3) community treatment, and (4) no treatment with monitoring.

The first option, prison, is the placement of choice for the offender who feels no guilt or other discomfort around his deviance. These offenders believe that their behavior is appropriate. They are the clients who will tell you that they do not understand why everyone is so upset about their sexual behavior. They are generally not amenable to treatment and will not live within social limits, setting few socially approved limits for themselves. They have little motivation to change and as such represent the highest level of risk to the community and must be controlled.

The second option, inpatient treatment, is appropriate for the individual who recognizes the "hurtfulness" of his or her deviant behavior but is unable to control it. This person's value system has more prosocial elements than the offender appropriate for prison. This individual is usually regularly employed, is more socially functional, and has a prosocial support system. This person may be amenable to and motivated for treatment, but needs the limits and controls that the 24-hour-a-day environment of the hospital can provide.

Community treatment is appropriate for the offender who clearly recognizes the hurtfulness of his or her behavior, who has tried to control the deviance (e.g. by avoiding deviant situations), and is willing to take responsibility for this behavior (e.g., acknowledging that he acted out because he wanted to, not because he was seduced). He is willing and able to live within the limits placed on him by the system. He is curious about himself and willing to explore his deviance. He is able to empathize with others and wants to live without deviance. His value system and social support system are prosocial. He is willing and able to reach out to family and friends for support and monitoring. His friends are individuals who also recognize the hurtfulness of the deviance and will demand that he take responsibility for it.

The final option, no treatment with monitoring, is the least desirable. This option is used with the client whose presenting deviant behavior is minimal and who, as far as is known, has no prior history. This client will often have molested his own child several years before, and the child is only now reporting it. Because of the limited history, the lack of reoffending, and his otherwise functional relationship with the family, no mandate for treatment will exist. Even if charges are brought they will often be at a misdemeanor level. In such situations, the potential for a positive treatment outcome is minimal. The most workable option here is to monitor the offender for the maximum period of time possible.

Planning

Treatment planning can be broken down into three parts: (1) control, (2) treatment, and (3) transition out of treatment. The first part, control, establishes limits and rules that help the offender control his behavior. It is important to recognize that most offenders will test and break the rules set for them. This testing is natural, and how the therapist responds is a key issue in further progress. The first level of control comes from the legal mandate under which the majority of cases are referred. This is in the form of a probation contract between the court and the offender. This contract specifies what the offender will and will not do. It brings with it the force of law and is the mandate that empowers the initial stages of treatment. The point of contact at this level is the probation officer whose responsibility it is to monitor the client's behavior for the court. He will need periodic updates on the offender's progress for the court and is the individual who will enforce the conditions of the offender's probation.

The second level of control comes from the offender's family. At most, an offender is in treatment in the community 2 or 3 hours per week. If the family is not supportive of treatment, failure is likely. The family contact is usually the offender's spouse or partner, who should be included in treatment planning if she or he is going to support it. The partner is encouraged to become involved in a support group where others are coping with a similar experience. These groups provide modeling and education to assist the partner in dealing with the stresses and limitations of living with the offender. The group supports the partner in setting limits on the offender and enforcing them. The partner also has a standing invitation to sit in on the offender's individual treatment.

The third level of control comes through restructuring the offender's life-style to help prevent access to children or the occurrence of events that in the past have supported this deviancy. For example, the incest offender must move out of the family home. This is difficult, because the individual usually thinks of the house and the people in it as "his." This move provides protection for the child by directly isolating the offender from the victim. Also, it provides protection from manipulation, threats, or promises the offender may use to get the child to change his or her story. It also allows the family to learn to function as a family before the offender returns. Additionally, the offender must give up drugs and alcohol and any other behaviors that fit into the pattern of deviance (e.g., the use of pornography, attending peep shows, or picking up teenage hitchhikers). This list of aspects of life to be restructured includes any activity that played a part in the offender's grooming of or abuse of a victim.

Once the appropriate controls have been put in place, and with the offender's agreement, a monitoring system must be implemented. This system uses the family, friends, or others to help monitor behavior by watching for warning signs that in the past were associated with the offender's sexual deviancy, for example, social withdrawal or an increase in sexual preoccupation.

Rules for living are structured to help the offender avoid situations associated with sexual acting out in the past. For example, an offender who visited topless bars while abusing his daughter would be forbidden to go to topless bars. If the abuse took place at night when everyone else was asleep, he would have to stay in his bedroom until others in the house were awake.

TREATMENT

With controls and a monitoring system in place, treatment can begin. The Northwest treatment model is comprehensive in that it addresses the problem of deviance on several different levels. Historical/characterological patterns that facilitated the development of the deviant sexuality, as well as the sexual arousal patterns that maintain it, are targets for intervention. Additionally, the environmental context that increases the potential for reoffense (e.g., family dysfunction) is also targeted. The two principal treatment modes used by Northwest are a specialized sex offender group and individual cognitive–behavioral therapy. Also available is a support group for the offenders' partners, as well as therapy for support victims, couples, and families, either at Northwest or at other public and private agencies within the community.

Group

Each offender/client enters treatment as a candidate in one of the specialized sex offender groups. In the group, they are confronted with the minimizations, denials, and other cognitive distortions that support abuse. They learn their idiosyncratic cycle of offense, how they groom the victim for sexual contact, how they push away negative feelings about their behavior (e.g., by distorting the memory of it so it becomes sex education), and the kinds of behaviors and feelings that precede offending. The ethical management of their lives is stressed. Facing the damage they have done and the chronicity of their problem is a major target. Group members who have been in the groups longer model successful management and control of sexual deviance for newer members.

The treatment group is specialized in the sense that all issues (e.g., depression) dealt with are related back to the deviancy. The group is structured in this manner to intervene in the offender's tendency to avoid dealing with his sexual aggression. The group provides a safe environment within which to change—a place were the offender learns alternatives to avoidance of problematic feelings, conflict resolution, assertiveness skills, and sex education.

The group also offers the first level of therapeutic decision making. It is the forum to which the offender brings problems and requests modification of rules. It assists the offender in developing appropriate responses to problems or shows him why his response is inappropriate in a specific situation. It helps him prepare for changes in his life-style and supports him in following through on decisions. The group also recognizes and points out to the offender when he is starting to move into a pattern that led to abuse in the past. It recognizes the warning signs and confronts the offender with them. Once placed in a group, the offender remains there until termination of treatment by graduation or termination. An artifact, by design, of this long-term involvement is the group's role as an external conscience for the offender. It is intended that the offender will continue to ask himself, "What would the group think about this?" long after he leaves the program.

The group is directed by the group therapist, who oversees all of the group decisions. The therapist is there to provide specialized information or to limit and direct the group's actions when needed. The therapist establishes the group's culture, directs its behavior, limits its actions when appropriate, and keeps its focus on deviance.

Individual Therapy

Once the offender has begun to integrate into his treatment group, as evidenced by a softening of his defenses and denials, he is assigned an individual therapist. The focus of this treatment mode is case management and therapy directed toward the idiosyncratic aspects of the individual offender's situation. Counterconditioning therapies are used to reduce attraction to deviance. These include covert sensitization, masturbatory satiation, and modified aversive behavioral rehearsal. Appropriate sexual arousal patterns are strengthened. Cognitive restructuring techniques are used with habitual, self-defeating ideation and deviance-serving defense mechanisms. Covert sensitization pairs up deviant fantasy with aversive consequences. (See, e.g., Marshall, 1973; Quinsey, 1977; Wolf, 1984.) Case management for the offender involves coordinating treatment with probation and victim/family treatment.

Individual therapy begins with having the offender define his problem, explain why it is "deviant," and define what deviance means in practical terms. (For example, recognizing that behaviors are illegal because they are deviant, not deviant because they are illegal.) This includes having the offender look at issues of consent between sexual partners and between adults and children.

Once the problem is satisfactorily defined, the structure of its pattern is identified and analyzed. The structure is the focus of the counterconditioning therapies that follow. These behavioral techniques serve two purposes. One, they act as counterconditioning therapies, and two, they help the offender confront the reality of his behavior in a nonaroused state. It is important to realize that one of the most often overlooked qualities of deviant sexual behaviors is that when they are occurring, the offender is preoccupied, tends to distort, and is driven by fantasies and urges. The result is that the offender can convince himself that his victim wants to be sexual with him. After the cessation of arousal (postejaculation for the male offender), reality returns. At this point (refractory stage of arousal), sexual needs sated, the offender sees clearly what he has done and recognizes that he is in jeopardy. When discovered in the deviance, offenders often experience the same release. They often experience guilt and will sometimes even voice relief at being caught. Caught or not, subsequent to ejaculation, offenders will promise to "never do it again."

It appears that sexual fantasy acts as a conditioning medium for acquiring sexual behaviors (Abel & Blanchard, 1976). It allows for the rehearsal in safety before approaching them in the real world. Rather like rehearsing a speech, it serves to desensitize the individual to the behavior while intensifying the focus of the behavior through reinforcement (in this example, through masturbation).

In masturbatory satiation, the offender creates an appropriate sexual fantasy and masturbates, using it, to ejaculation. Then, in refractory state, he focuses on and repeats his deviant sexual behaviors and fantasies for a preset period of time. This is recorded by the offender on a 90-minute cassette tape to ensure compliance and quality control (side A being appropriate fantasy with masturbation, side B being a 45-minute recitation of deviant fantasy and behavior without masturbation). The tape is then reviewed with his therapist and discussed. The offender, in a nonaroused state, hears himself talking, acting out his deviant behavior. Conflict between his deviant (aroused) values and his nondeviant (nonaroused) values creates a forced-choice situation. This process helps the offender begin to recognize the hurtfulness of his deviant behaviors, find them increasingly aversive, and choose his appropriate values over his deviant values (Vandeventer & Laws, 1978).

Once the offender has begun to choose nondeviant sexual values consistently, covert sensitization is used to alter his conditioned patterns of sexual responding. This technique counterconditions the offender's deviant behavior by pairing up his specific deviant stimuli with aversive consequences. This weakens the response pattern of his deviance by replacing the expectation of pleasure/reward with the expectation of punishment/aversion. (See, e.g., Cautela, 1966.)

After these two therapies, the offender is then ready for Modified Aversive Behavioral Rehearsal (MABR). This involves the offender in a videotaped role-play of his deviant acting-out in which he uses mannequins to reenact his preferred sexual behavior. During this process on camera, he will describe his behavior, number of victims, and other dimensions of his behavior. He will describe the cognitive distortions that he used to justify his behavior. He will then act out his deviance on the mannequin. This process will be replayed for him in the presence of his therapist, and his feelings about the experience are explored. The tape may also be played for the offender's significant other. This serves two purposes. It gives the other person a clear idea of the reality of the offender's behavior and threat to others. Also, it removes one more layer of secrecy from the offender. This strengthens the monitoring network within which the offender lives. [Contrary to expectations, the significant other seldom abandons the offender as a result of viewing these tapes (Smith & Wolfe, 1985).]

In addition to these therapies, the individual therapist also provides couples counseling and, when appropriate, coordinates the beginning of family therapy.

Family Therapy

The last phase of treatment consists of the reintegration of the offender into the family. This phase can last from 6 months to a year and a half. To date, this phase has been carried out with family cases in which the father or stepfather is the abuser. However, many of the therapeutic goals and tasks of work with incest cases may also be applicable to cases in which the adult has abused children he is not related to. The essential working concept of this phase is that the family must be restructured to help the offender control his sexual interests, to help family members maintain control so that he cannot abuse his power and thereby abuse other family members, and to maintain the increased personal competence of the nonoffending family members. Family therapy is never started until therapeutic gains have been achieved in the individual therapies of the offender, nonoffending mother, and victim. Additionally, family therapy would be undertaken only after family sessions with the father absent have been conducted to review the family's decision to reunite.

Evaluation prior to beginning family group intervention of each of the family members who will be participating in the group is undertaken to determine if sufficient therapeutic gains have been accomplished to make reentry of the offender possible. Although the nature of the gains that individual family members need to make before they are ready for reentry through family group therapy varies by specific case, general goals can be described for each of the family members. These include:

Mothers need to be able to verbalize an understanding that the offender is responsible for the sexual abuse and no longer blame the victim for the abuse or disruptions resulting from disclosure of the abuse. They also need to no longer be blaming themselves or feeling minimal guilt that the abuse took place. Mothers who are particularly dependent need to have shown some indication of increasing independence from the offender. For example, they need to have demonstrated a capacity to make decisions, handle home finances, or feel somewhat comfortable with the idea of not having a man in their lives. These accomplishments, or at least movement toward them, are seen as indicating that the mother has the capacity to protect her children in the future.

Victims need also to give an indication that individual or victim group therapy has been successful (at least to a degree) in reducing the likelihood that she will again be a victim (e.g., increased assertiveness). The victim needs to voice a desire to have the offender return home. This needs to be based on her own desires about the kind of family life she wants in the future and not on what she thinks her mother or siblings want. She needs to feel not responsible for the abuse and the disruptions that disclosure usually causes in family life. There needs to be some indication that her feelings about men have been or are likely to be resolved, that there is a good likelihood that she will tell her mother if the offender tries to reabuse her, and that she is functioning within acceptable limits elsewhere in her life.

Most often, prior to beginning family therapy the victim and her mother have been seen conjointly and given an opportunity to deal with the anger that they typically feel for each other and have made significant progress toward repairing their relationship. The Northwest treatment model regards a strong relationship between the victim and her mother to be an important ingredient in ensuring that the victim and her mother will work together to protect the victim from reabuse. In Northwest's experience, victims often have superficial relationships with their mothers. Developing a sense of connection with each other in which trust and mutual concern are developed has to take place before family therapy is started.

Siblings are often an ignored aspect of therapy in these cases. Typically, the siblings have not received any treatment prior to the time the offender is to be reintegrated into the family. They often lack information about the abuse and the rationale behind why certain initial intervention steps were taken (e.g., why the offender left the house). Initial assessment with siblings should determine what they understand about the abuse and events transpiring since disclosure and how they feel about the victim and the offender. Sibling reactions to their sister's abuse vary. In some cases, siblings feel guilty for taking no action to protect their sister. In other cases, they are angry that she revealed the abuse and caused so much disruption in their lives. Some siblings indicate that they would not have let the offender do to them what he did to their sister. This can be a dangerous attitude since it tends to ignore the real danger they may have of being abused. It is also important to get information about the functioning of the siblings in school and community to identify any indications of problems they may be having.

A clinical assessment in any of these areas may indicate that it is premature to begin trying to reintegrate the offender into the family. When this is the case, additional clinical work needs to be directed toward establishing gains in that part of the family where growth is necessary prior to beginning family therapy. Additionally, the offender's individual therapist and the offender's group therapy group need to indicate that the offender is ready for reentry.

Reentry

Reentry of the father/stepfather into the family is a gradual process intended to ensure that individual family members are successful in maintaining their own therapeutic growth, that the family learns new ways of interacting, and especially that the family develops family rules and procedures that work against reabuse of children. The process follows a general sequence of tasks, but at any time, individual or didactic therapy may be necessary. For example, during family group therapy, a victim may begin again to express feelings of responsibility for her own abuse, or a mother may indicate that she is now thinking of divorce. In cases such as these, family group therapy would cease and individual or marital therapy would begin.

The general tasks of reentry are outlined below. It is important to bear in mind that these tasks vary considerably by the particular family being treated.

1. Family identifies desired changes

When it appears that individual family members have made sufficient changes for reentry to begin, the family members, without the offender being present, begin meeting as a group to identify things about their family they would like to be different when the offender returns. The specific changes identified by the family vary considerably. Clinical experience suggests that there are some common themes in the families seen at Northwest to date. These include:

- Decreasing the amount of time that Dad has the entire family working around the house.
- Decreasing the arguing and fighting.
- Allowing individual family members to make decisions according to their developmental level. This is an especially important issue for mothers, whose increasing power in the family is an essential ingredient in protecting the children.

The father/stepfather will also add to the list of desired changes, but this usually does not take place until somewhat later in family therapy when other family members have developed the capacity for problem solving and negotiating for behavioral changes.

2. Offender joins or is included in family group therapy

When the family has identified desired changes and reached some consensus on the priorities for changes in the family, the offender joins the family group. At first, the family members bring each other up on what has transpired in their lives over the last few months. The offender answers questions about his therapy. The children tell him about their activities in school and at home. One of the key tasks at this phase is for the offender to demonstrate to the other family members that he has changed (e.g., that he knows how to listen to what others say and no longer needs to dominate the discussion or control how people feel about things).

3. Initial visitation

As the sharing of information and interpersonal testing of the previous phases proceeds, family members begin to talk about visitation. The first visitation of the offender with his family outside of therapy takes place in a neutral environment (e.g., a restaurant or park). Prior to the visitation, the offender identifies a set of rules that will help him control his behavior and interact with his family in new (i.e., noncoercive) ways. These rules are approved by his therapy group prior to the visitation. Typical rules are:

- Offender and rest of family go to visitation in separate cars.
- Kids are never left alone with the offender.
- Offender cannot sit next to kids or comment on how they look.
- The offender cannot discipline the kids or comment on Mom's discipline of the kids.

The remainder of the family also has special rules. For example, the victim and her siblings work out a signal with Mom that will tell her that they are uncomfortable with the visitation and Mom will terminate the visitation. Additionally, if the offender gets angry or breaks any of his rules, Mom will also terminate the visitation. After the first visitation, the family meets without Dad to discuss how the visitation went. The family often comments on things that seem different about him (e.g., "He really listened to us," or a victim might say, "He didn't look at me that way anymore"). This first visitation usually goes well.

4. Increased contact

Gradually, as the individual family members are ready to handle it, the length of the visitations increases. Both the frequency and duration of contacts may increase. However, all contact continues to be away from the family's home. This is intended to help the family develop ways of having fun with each other and to let them test each other's new behaviors in "public" before trying them out in the privacy of their own home. Over the course of these visits, problems will develop. Depending on the specific problems, the entire family group will deal with the problems or smaller subgroups will meet. The therapeutic emphasis continues to be on teaching the family problem-solving, communication, and self-protection skills. Mom's new role as the disciplinarian and her increased sense of control and personal efficacy are maintained.

5. Home visits

Visitations during the previous phase may work up to 6 hours of out-of-home contact. As these visits begin to go more and more smoothly, the family therapist begins talking with the children and mother about trying a home visit. If they indicate that they are ready to try this, the offender and his therapy group add to his rules to meet some of the problems encountered as he returns home. These include his leaving if the victim feels uncomfortable (e.g., has flashbacks of the abuse), or if he feels sexually aroused to children in some situation at home. The family also has new rules, such as the kids cannot run around the house without clothes and Mom continues to have major responsibility for disciplining the kids. The therapist also establishes rules for the offender's time at home:

- The offender is never alone with the kids.
- The family has to do something together that is "fun."
- Dad does not exercise control or discipline over children's behavior.

This phase is typically quite difficult for the offender. He begins to understand fully how much individual family members have changed and how much the old family he ruled is gone. Considerable time in the offender's individual therapy and group therapy is spent helping the offender deal with these changes. Family group time is often divided in half, with one half devoted to the children and mother talking about how the visit went and the other half spent with the offender, problem solving or negotiating. During this phase, the family therapist helps the offender learn how to express his opinion without trying to control other family members.

6. Overnights

When the family appears ready, the offender begins overnight visits. Several new family rules are established to meet the new situation of the offender sleeping overnight in the home:

- The children must have locks on their doors, even if they choose not to use them.
- The offender does not leave his bedroom, unless his wife is also up.
- If Mom works, Dad has to leave the house while she is away from the house.

Home visits are gradually extended by adding one overnight every 2 weeks or so. During family group therapy, family members talk about the time together, identify problems, and discuss solutions. If any member of the family feels that things are moving too quickly, the reintegration process will be slowed. During this final reintegration phase, increasing attention is often directed toward marital therapy. The marital dyad is spending more and more time together, and frequently the wife's new independence and personal efficacy become an issue in the marriage. Some offenders will also begin to exhibit signs of resistance or slipping back into old patterns of behavior. For example, the offender may begin to try to control all the family's money or begin to try to dominate the other family members. Some families will cease to have their out-of-home "fun" experience. These then become the topics of therapy.

7. Termination

Termination is gradual and usually involves gradually increasing the interval between appointments. Many families will periodically call for advice or request an appointment for help in handling some new crisis that has arisen. In several cases, siblings have reached the age at which the victim was first victimized and have become frightened that they may also be abused. In other cases, a change in family status (e.g., a change in job or a family discussion of moving) have caused the family some stress and they have requested an appointment to discuss this change with their therapist.

CONCLUSION

The Northwest model of community-based treatment for adults who sexually abuse children appears to address important aspects of the clinical problem represented by sexual abuse of children. It gives every appearance of being helpful to many adult sexual offenders in controlling their behavior and remaining in the community. Clearly, it is not effective with every client in every situation. Until research is available documenting the effects of the interventions making up the Northwest approach and those clients best suited for it, the model should be replicated with the care and attention to evaluation inherent in any experimental treatment. However, clinical experience generated with over 4000 sexual offenders and the results of research carried out in behavioral clinics elsewhere in the United States and Canada indicate that the techniques and approach to treatment described under the Northwest model deserve careful consideration for use in other communities.

REFERENCES

Abel, G. G. (1978). Assessment of sexual deviation in the male. In M. Hersch & A. S. Bellack (Eds.), *Behavioral assessment: A practical handbook* (pp. 437–457). New York: Pergamon Press.

Abel, G. G., Becker, J. V., & Cunningham-Rathner, J. (1984). Complications, consent, and cognitions in sex between children and adults. *International Journal of Law and Psychiatry, 7,* 89–103.

Abel, G. G., Becker, J. V., Murphy, W. D., & Flanagan, B. (1981). Identifying dangerous child molesters. In R. B. Stuart (Ed.), *Violent behavior: Social learning approach to prediction, management and treatment* (pp. 116–137). New York: Brunner/ Mazel.

Abel, G. G., Becker, J. V., & Skinner, L. J. (1980). Aggressive behavior and sex. *Psychiatric Clinics of North America, 3,* 133–151.

Abel, G. G., & Blanchard, E. B. (1976). The measurement and generation of sexual arousal in male sexual deviates. In R. M. Mittersen, R. M. Fisher, & T. M. Miller (Eds.), *Progress in behavior modification Vol. 2* (pp. 99–133). New York: Academic Press.

Abel, G. G., Mittelman, M. S., Becker, J. V., Cunningham-Rathner, J., & Lucas, L. (1983, December). The characteristics of men who molest young children. Paper presented at the World Congress of Behavior Therapy, Washington, DC.

Abel, G. G., Rouleau, J., & Cunningham-Rathner, J. (1984). Sexually aggressive behavior. In W. Curan, A. L. McGarry, & S. A. Shah (Eds.), *Modern legal psychiatry and psychology.* Philadelphia: Davis.

Alford, G. S., Wedding, D., & Jones, S. (1983). The effects of competitory covert imagery on penile tumescence responses to diverse extrinsic sexual stimulus materials: Faking "turn-ons" and "turn-offs." *Behavior Modification, 7,* 112–125.

Cautela, J. R. (1966). Treatment of compulsive behaviors by covert sensitization. *Psychological Research, 16,* 33–41.

Conte, J. R. (1985). Clinical dimensions of adult sexual abuse of children. *Law and Psychiatry, 3,* 341–354.

Conte, J. R., & Berliner, L. (1981). Prosecution of the offender in cases of sexual assault against children. *Victimology: An International Journal, 6,* 102–109.

Langevin, R., Handy, L., Russon, A. E., & Day, D. (1985). Are incestuous fathers pedophilic, aggressive, and alcoholic? In R. Langevin (Ed.), *Erotic preference, gender identity, and aggression in men: New research studies* (pp. 137–150). Hillsdale, NJ: Erlbaum.

Laws, D. R., & Osborne, C. A. (1983). How to build and operate a behavioral laboratory to evaluate and treat sexual deviance. In J. G. Greer & I. R. Stuart (Eds.), *The sexual aggressor: Current perspectives on treatment* (pp. 293–335). Toronto: Van Nostrand Reinhold.

Laws, D. R., & Rubin, H. B. (1962). Instructional control of an autonomic sexual response. *Journal of Applied Behavioral Analysis, 2,* 95–99.

Marshall, W. L. (1973). The modification of sexual fantasies: A combined treatment approach to the reduction of deviant sexual behavior. *Behavioral Research and Therapy, 11,* 557–564.

Quinsey, V. L. (1977). The assessment and treatment of child molesters: A review. *Canadian Psychological Review, 18,* 204–220.

Quinsey, V. L. (1984). Sexual aggression: Studies of offenders against women. In D. Weisstub (Ed.), *Law and mental health: International perspectives* (Vol. 1) (pp. 84–121). New York: Pergamon Press.

Quinsey, V. L., & Bergersen, S. G. (1976). Instructional control of penile circumference in assessment of sexual preference. *Behavior Therapy, 7,* 489–493.

Smith, T. S., & Wolfe, R. W. (1985, March). Modified aversive rehearsal. Paper presented at Next Steps in Research on the Assessment and Treatment of Sexually Aggressive Persons, St. Louis, MO.

Vandeventer, A. D., & Laws, D. R. (1978). Orgasmic reconditioning to reflect arousal in pedophiles. *Behavior Therapy, 9,* 748–765.

Wolf, S. C. (1984). *Evaluation and treatment of the sexual offender.* Manuscript prepared as part of manual developed by Sexual Assault Center, Harborview Medical Center, 325 Ninth Avenue, Seattle, WA 98104.

Part V
Prevention

19

"Taking Care of Me": Preventing Child Sexual Abuse in the Hispanic Community

Barrie Levy

PREVENTIVE MENTAL HEALTH CONCEPTS

Primary prevention is as old as the existance of shamans, native witch doctors, curanderas, and other healers in different societies. Stories abound about customs and rituals, such as wearing amulets with objects said to give the bearer special protective powers. Prevention strategies that have emerged to prevent mental illness and the effects of social problems have been as creative and innovative as individual communities allow. Recently, various prevention strategies have emerged to protect children from sexual abuse. Legislation has required longer and harsher sentences for convicted offenders. Criminal justice system handling of victims and offenders has been revised. Standards for hiring people who work with children have been examined. Mandated child abuse reporting laws have been established and enforced. Educational programs for parents and children have been implemented in schools.

Child sexual abuse prevention programs have been developed from the theoretical framework of Gerald Caplan. He defines three types of prevention, calling them primary, secondary, and tertiary levels. Primary prevention programs have as their goal the reduction of the incidence of mental disorders of all types in a community (Caplan, 1964).

I am grateful to Emma Guerrero-Pavich, M.S.W., and to Vivian Brown, Ph.D., of the Didi Hirsch Community Mental Health Center for their assistance with this chapter and for their wonderful work in child sexual assault prevention.

Secondary prevention programs attempt to reduce the impact (for example, the duration) of those disorders that are identified. Assessment, early identification, and crisis intervention constitute secondary prevention activities. The goals of tertiary prevention programs are to reduce the level of impairment from identified disorders by means of rehabilitation or treatment.

Primary prevention programs generally have the "long-term goal of assuring continually adequate physical, psychosocial and sociocultural supplies . . . This enables the individual to avoid stress and increases the individual's capacity to withstand future stress" (Kessler & Albee, 1977, p. 353). Roberts (1970) describes three strategies for primary prevention activities. They are removal of the source of the problem or the noxious agent (people who abuse children, in this case), strengthening the host (making the child stronger), and increasing resistance to the noxious agent or, if possible, actually preventing contact between the agent and host (in this case resistance to or no contact with the abuser).

Primary Prevention Programs

The target of primary prevention activities is anyone who might potentially be affected by the disorder. Primary prevention programs have targeted key social systems such as the family, work settings, schools, and other components of communities. Children and youth have been a major focus, and schools have been seen as having a major role in prevention and early identification of disorders, as well as in the promotion of competence. Competence as an important ingredient of self-esteem is defined by White (1979, p. 9) as "feeling confident you can do the things that matter most, that in these ways you can affect your environment and thus influence the course of your own life."

Educational programs that provide information and develop skills for children, teachers, and parents are an example of a primary prevention strategy that strengthens children and the systems in which they function so that they can resist sexual abuse. The vulnerability of potential victims is reduced by teaching skills in assertiveness and awareness that increase their competence, and by teaching parents and educators how to integrate important skills development into childrearing and teaching. As a primary prevention strategy, educational programs also reach potential offenders with information that defines coercive and nonconsensual sex as abusive, and clearly defines intrusive touching of children as unacceptable. Coping information (how to get help if such a problem arises) provides resources for early intervention.

There are a number of prevention programs that inoculate children against becoming victims of a sex offender because of fear of saying no to a family member or friend. Some are introduced into the schools, such as the Tacoma program described by Olson (1985). Others, like the SAFE self-defense program created by Colao and Hosansky (1987) and based in New York City, first began as secondary prevention for adult rape victims and then added a children's martial arts component for their primary prevention program. There is potential for the Bass and Davis (in press) self-help guide for adult survivors of child sexual abuse to be similarly adapted to a primary prevention program. Many of the educational books on the market that give permission to children to say no to adult touches that do not feel good are further examples of positive prevention approaches (cf. McGovern, 1986).

Another aim of prevention education is to influence attitudes of the general public to make sexual abuse a less hidden and unrecognized problem and to correct contradictory cultural beliefs about sexual abuse. The need to change public attitudes about sexual abuse has been recognized as the problem has been discovered to be so widespread. How could so many children be sexually abused and so few adults know about it? Efforts to break the silence were met with resistance, and it was clear that although the incest taboo made abuse difficult to acknowledge and discuss openly, it certainly had not kept it from occurring. Adults who had been molested as children told stories of repeated attempts to tell parents, relatives, teachers, ministers, or therapists that were met with disbelief, denial, and blame.

The contradictory values held about children in our society are responsible for the silence about sexual abuse. Children are treasured and protected but are also powerless and invisible. The patriarchal family structure gives the father (or any male in that role) power and control but not resources for parenting or relating to children. Herman (1981), in her work on father–daughter incest, identifies the structure of the family as the focus of the problem:

> As long as fathers rule but do not nurture, as long as mothers nurture but do not rule, the conditions favoring the development of father–daughter incest will prevail. Only a basic change in the power relations of mothers and fathers can prevent the sexual exploitation of children. (p. 206)

Ethnic Minority Cultures and Primary Prevention Programs

Individuals and groups who have limited access to resources and limited control over their own environments are especially vulnerable to exploitation and victimization. Ethnic minority families therefore are doubly vulnerable and their children at particularly high risk. Racist assumptions among "community helpers" such as teachers, police, psychologists, and social workers can cause minority children to avoid seeking help. Racist assumptions lead the general public to believe that child abusers have particular characteristics, such as being from a particular ethnic group. This can cause denial and lack of protection from the real assailants in children's lives.

Preventive education can play a key role in developing confidence for minority families. Powerlessness and lack of resources affect most people's sense of competence and control. Minority families are more likely to be challenged regarding their abilities to parent and to provide for their children, especially if they are poor. Belle reports on her research with poor minority women:

> When my colleagues and I began our interviews with low income women we began to hear from many women about the dangers involved in revealing one's vulnerability to anyone in a position of authority. We found a pervasive fear that children would be taken away. (p. 145)

Minority men are more likely to be arrested and convicted for sexual abuse, which may contribute to a minority community's conflicts about protecting "their own" from the criminal justice system versus protecting their children. Social services and other systems expect greater incidence of abuse in ethnic minority families. In reality, this is probably not true. Research on the incidence of family violence suggests that minority families do not have any greater amounts of family violence (Straus, Gelles, & Steinmetz, 1980). Another recent comprehensive study indicates that the Hispanics interviewed considered child mistreatment in general and sexual abuse specifically as more serious than do Anglos (Giovannoni & Bercera, 1979).

A primary prevention program must take into consideration the need for changing attitudes regarding sexism and racism as well as the needs for providing information and skills. The remainder of this chapter describes an example of a primary prevention program that targeted ethnic minority children that was designed and implemented by a community mental health center and a rape crisis center in Los Angeles.*

"TAKING CARE OF ME" PROGRAM

The Hispanic community involved with this program consisted primarily of working-class and middle-class Mexican-American families who had been in the United States for various lengths of time. It was assumed that many were undocumented, but the question was not directly asked. Many of the parents spoke no English, but most of the children were bilingual. Presentations in the program were offered in Spanish—even to bilingual parents and chil-

---

*The two agencies are the Didi Hirsch Community Mental Health Center, Culver City, California and the Los Angeles Commission on Assaults Against Women, Los Angeles, California.

dren—because of their greater ease in discussing these issues in Spanish. Educational presentations to these families were given at public and parochial schools, youth groups, churches, and scout troops.

Program Development

The development of this prevention approach was based on a need-assessment procedure, which involved interviewing victims, family members, and clinicians who have dealt with child molestation. Children in elementary school classrooms were interviewed regarding prevention information that was familiar to them. The major patterns identified were similar to those reported in other research (see chapters in this book for examples).

- Children were more often molested by family members or acquaintances than by strangers.
- Children often had difficulty deciding if an abusive situation was dangerous if the situation did not involve clearly violent threats.
- Children were reluctant to report the sexual assault experience to anyone, and many never told anyone until they were adults.
- Children who had been sexually abused tended to feel responsible or to blame themselves for the abuse. This was especially intense in incest situations. These feelings often lasted well into adulthood.
- Parents sometimes disbelieved or denied that a child had been molested, or did not notice early signs of their child's stress.
- Parents sometimes felt so angry or upset that the molestation had taken place that the child was frightened by the parent's reaction.
- Children who received protection and support from parents or from significant adults after an assault recovered with less long-term disturbance.

Other patterns were observed that were specific to child sexual abuse when it occurred in the Hispanic community:

- Economically poor Mexican-American women and children were especially vulnerable to sexual assault because of the frequency of poor living and working conditions and because they often rely on others for survival.
- Family issues regarding sexuality and male and female roles were areas of conflict as families become assimilated into American culture. Protecting female family members from nonmarital sexual activity as well as sexual assault—and then coping with it when it was disclosed—were conflict-ridden areas for Mexican-American families.
- Sexual issues were often considered to be too intimate to discuss with

anyone, even within the family. Thus children were reluctant to talk to or ask questions of parents.

- Women who were victims or mothers of victims often claimed that they had "no right to complain" because of the expectation that women "suffer in silence."
- Attitudes and responses to sexual abuse varied according to the degree of assimilation of Hispanic families into the dominant culture.
- Children had generally felt unable to be assertive with adults because of the cultural value of silence and respect that surrounds their relationship to adults.
- The religious and cultural value that young women marry as virgins resulted in punitive consequences and shame for young victims.

Hispanic Community Attitudes

These observations indicated that traditional prevention programs were not sufficient to deal with child sexual abuse in general and were especially inadequate to meet the needs of this particular community. Safety and crime-prevention programs for children have generally emphasized the "rules" children must follow to be safe. These rules generally pertain to strangers (e.g., "don't take rides or candy from strangers") or to unsafe locations (e.g., "don't walk in alleys" or "keep the doors and windows locked when you are home alone"). There is generally no explanation of what might happen if these rules are disobeyed, but there is clearly a threat of danger. These vague dangers that are the threatened consequence of not following these rules are often very frightening, especially to young children, and they do not know from what they are trying to protect themselves. Children who have had an assault experience often assume that it was a result of their misbehavior, even though it might have been totally beyond their control. These rules are helpful for children as guidelines for their safety, but additional information is needed to prepare children to deal with the more common exploitive or assaultive situations that take place with people known to them.

The family is very important in the Hispanic community, and communication between generations with differing levels of acculturation is often difficult. A prevention approach is needed that offers parents information about how to deal with the subject of sexual abuse with their children so that discussion from educational presentations could be continued at home. Preventive education for families should suggest techniques for using daily experiences in their lives to teach children ways to take care of themselves.

The needs assessment and observations led to the development of a program using concepts intended to meet those needs, and was then presented in a manner most effective to reach the Hispanic community. The prevention approach was designed to address the attitudes and lack of information that have been seen as obstacles in other adult and child clients who were seen in the community mental health center. With adequate preventive information, it was believed many of these difficulties could be avoided or anticipated and handled better. The preventive approach was thus designed to (1) strengthen the ability of parents and children to reduce the risk of child molestation and (2) to cope with it should it occur. The conceptual framework included four areas that were covered in every presentation: susceptibility (who is affected and how); severity (the problem is serious); prevention (ways to lower risk or deal with threatening situations); and coping (what to do if it happens).

Program Presentation

The underlying assumption of this program was that any prevention approach must strengthen the capability of the Hispanic family to deal with the stresses and social conflicts encountered. It was therefore essential that this program have a family focus and that differing levels of acculturation be taken into consideration.

Presentations for parents were scheduled to take place either before or simultaneously with presentations for children. Presentations contained three sections: (1) information about the problem of child sexual assault, (2) a description of presentations children were to receive, and (3) information regarding discussion of sexual assault prevention with children at home.

Implementation

Audiences of parents were usually mixed (male and female). They learned about the program from bilingual announcements sent home with children from school or through notices sent from churches. Often a few parents who were especially interested in the program helped to encourage their neighbors and friends to attend. Fathers often attended because their wives would not or were not allowed to go out by themselves. Presenters were aware that this prevention approach confronted traditional roles for many of these families. Traditional roles were not denied, but rather were supported. Presenters acknowledged the difficulties families face as they assimilate and must integrate new information such as this. Parents are constantly dealing with new information and conflicting values as their children assimilate culturally. Fathers were asked to participate in the discussion regarding their concerns for their children's safety and ways they feel able to protect their children. Assimilated parents were often leaders in the discussion. Feelings of vulnerability were often expressed, and parents often indicated that they felt reassured by having techniques to use to talk to their children.

It was often commented that "the parents who need it are not here." Yet it was not the intention of the program to select known families with problems. Like any prevention activity, it assumed that any audience contained undisclosed families already involved with the problem or with the potential for it. It was also assumed that a ripple effect caused by people in a community talking to one another and becoming more alert to warning signs would affect families who did not participate.

A good needs assessment before each presentation was valuable. Prior to the presentation and at its beginning, presenters found out why parents were interested in such a program and what their specific needs and expectations were. Often, an assaultive incident preceded the request or something had taken place to raise parents' anxiety about their children's safety. In these instances, the parents' reaction to the event or incident was an important subject for discussion. Community resources that are available to Hispanic families were suggested. Often the bilingual presenter became a familiar resource person to be called later.

Parents' Component

The main points of the presentations to parents reflect an emphasis on clear and open communication between parents and children, and on helping children to develop good decision-making skills.

Susceptibility

Sexual abuse can happen to anyone, and in fact the problem is widespread and underreported. Sexual abuse is defined as any forced, coercive, or exploitive sexual activity with a young person under 18. There are many myths about the nature of sexual abuse.

The child molester is most often someone the child knows, so prevention discussions with children must include what to do if "someone you know or someone in your family or a family friend (as well as a stranger) touches you when you do not want to be touched." Due to the special vulnerabilities of Mexican-American women and children, the ability to be assertive is especially important. Children can learn they have a right to do something to stop or prevent an exploitive or assaultive situation. This can help to reduce their vulnerability.

Severity

Sexual abuse is serious and traumatic for the whole family. Prevention of sexual assault is a *safety* issue, not a *sexual* issue. Discussion of sexual assault prevention can be brought up in connection with other safety issues, events in the news, or in their lives. At the same time parents discuss with children how to handle a fire or burglar, parents can discuss how to handle someone who touches them against their will.

Prevention

Assertiveness and awareness of risk are most important in protection against sexual assault. Individuals have a choice about how and when to be assertive, and must decide what is best to do in each situation. This includes weighing all the risks. It is important to let children see how parents make these decisions and to talk about difficult decisions in vulnerable situations. Children can be taught from birth that they have a right to determine whether or not they are touched and how to trust their feelings and say no when they are uncomfortable with someone touching them. These skills can be learned from any daily experiences, if the child's right to say no is respected by the family in innocuous daily contacts. The aim of this approach is to strengthen children's abilities to make decisions, to trust themselves, and to take care of themselves. There are things people can do to minimize risks, but there are no rules of behavior that will eliminate the possibility of sexual assault.

Coping

It is important for children to have family members, friends, and community people (e.g., teachers) that they can talk to if they are upset or hurt. The cultural value that women and children have no right to complain makes it difficult to speak up. It is difficult for children not to keep silent because they are ashamed and afraid they have done something wrong. However, parents must do as much as they can to encourage children to talk openly about these things when they happen. In addition, there are warning signs of stress to look for as signals that a child has been molested and is not telling anyone.

Children's Component

The needs assessment referred to earlier indicated that Hispanic children needed help to be assertive with adults and to obtain help if they had been in a sexually abusive situation. They also seemed to need varying degrees of help to deal with the conflicts created by the transition from Mexican to North American cultures. The main points covered in discussions with children were carefully not presented as "rules" or as the one way to be safe.

Susceptibility

It is often impossible to decide if someone intends to hurt someone else. One can only decide if they are bothered by or dislike what the other person is doing. It is often someone known and trusted who bothers or hurts someone, whether intended or not. It is not acceptable for bigger people to push younger people into undressing or into touching that frightens or distresses them. If it must be kept a secret then it is not okay.

Severity

It is upsetting to be touched at times and on parts of one's body against one's will. (The seriousness or severity of sexual abuse was omitted from presentations to children under 12 years of age due to the importance of not frightening them.)

Prevention

Children have a right to protect themselves. It is important for children to use their strength (for example, to kick, yell, run, say "stop it") to protect themselves. It is most important to think quickly, and to have an attitude that says, "I take care of myself." Children can practice making decisions about what to do in assaultive situations so that they feel strong. It is not disrespectful to say or do something to protect oneself from others, whether they are adults or other children. It is helpful to discuss with parents (before anything happens) what to do if something upsetting, harassing, or assaultive happens, and to ask questions about things that are confusing.

Coping

It is important for children to tell someone if they have been frightened, bothered, or hurt by someone. Children can think in advance about the adults in their lives they can talk to, such as parents, older siblings, teachers, school nurses, or scout leaders. Sometimes parents and other adults have trouble believing or helping a child deal with frightening situations. This makes it important for children to keep trying to find someone to help. It is not because a child has done something wrong that he or she becomes frightened or hurt.

It was anticipated that children, like adults, would find these concepts in conflict with traditional norms and values of their families. This was dealt with directly by the presenters. Children were encouraged to discuss the differences and disagreements among the various things they have learned about taking care of themselves. The program was designed to strengthen the confidence children have in their ability to take care of themselves, and so the discussion emphasized that they think quickly, assess any situation, and talk about it with an adult—using any approach that worked well for them, whether learned from presenters, teachers, parents, or brothers and sisters. Discussion focused on the difficulties they faced in making decisions in threatening situations and the difficult consequences they often expected. They discussed ways in which they could take care of themselves when people close to them think they are being disrespectful or that they have misbehaved.

Design of Children's Component

The format of the children's presentations was designed to reinforce the main points. This involved open-ended discussion stimulated by brief scenarios. The scenarios were deliberately ambiguous so that children were encouraged to debate the various actions and decisions of the story characters. This reinforced a key concept: Children must be prepared to make their own decisions about how to respond to a threatening situation, based on whatever information or possible action is available to them. The scenarios depicted situations with which Hispanic children could identify. Prevention and coping strategies were based on familiarity with resources and attitudes of Hispanic audiences. For example, in first through third grade the following story was told:

> Eight-year-old Maria is walking to school. She stops by her friend Therese's house so they can walk together. Therese's father invites Maria to wait on the sofa because Therese is not ready yet. He sits down next to her, and strokes her hair and back, telling her she is so pretty. Maria becomes very uncomfortable, and stands up and tells him, "Please don't do that. It scares me!" Maria says, "I have to go now," and runs to school. When Therese catches up to her, Maria is upset but doesn't say anything about what happened.

Various audiovisual aids were utilized with different presentations. Hand puppets were employed by the presenters in kindergarten through third grade. Flannel boards with magazine cutouts to illustrate the same points were planned for the youngest children, as was a drawing exercise about "a time you had to take care of yourself."

After the story was presented, the presenter checked to be sure the children had understood what happened in the story. Some questions were then asked, such as "Why was Maria upset?", "Did she do anything wrong?", "Did you think that Therese's father would hurt her?", "Would you tell anybody what happened if you were Maria?", "Why or why not?", and "Who would you tell?". The story and questions were designed to reinforce the main points discussed above.

Discussion leaders integrated discussion of rules into presentations without emphasizing them. They emphasized the child's own ability to assess a situation (even though the situation might be confusing), to use the safety rules as guidelines, and to take action appropriate to the situation. The leaders suggested that there was not usually a clear right or wrong course of action to follow, but that everyone can (1) think about what to do by assessing the situation and (2) do the best possible to take care of oneself.

Children often told stories of experiences they had had. Interestingly, the stories were not usually of sexual assault experiences, but of otherwise threatening situations. Leaders limited the numbers of such stories and always reiterated the program's main points as illustrated by the child's story. For example, the 10-year-old who told a story of being harassed by a couple of 12-year-olds in the park was questioned by the leader.

LEADER: What did you do to handle this situation?

CHILD: I told them to leave me alone and told the coach.

LEADER: Did that work?

CHILD: No, the coach made them leave the park, but they came back the next day.

LEADER: It didn't work because they came back. But you did a good job of taking care of yourself. First, you told them to stop, and then you got an adult to help you. That was good thinking.

Thus the children's stories became miniscenarios and discussion continued to reinforce the key concepts.

Results

This program was presented during a period of a year and a half to 3,935 parents, teachers, and children ranging in age from 6 to 18 years. Evaluation procedures involved administration of a postprogram questionnaire for teachers, pre- and posttests for students grade seven and above, and preprogram and postprogram or only postprogram measures for parents.

The teacher-evaluation questionnaires showed that 80% of the teachers in whose classrooms the programs were held felt the materials covered in the presentation were appropriate for the grade level of their students.

Reactions of parents were very positive. Attitude items showed positive changes except where pretest scores were already high. Parents indicated that programs were informative and made them think, and made open-ended comments to the effect that they would now be more open with their children and stress to them that they have a right not to be touched.

ISSUES RAISED ABOUT PRIMARY PREVENTION PROGRAMS

Several issues related to child sexual assault prevention education have emerged. They first became recognized as parents and community members raised questions in response to the program and by the staff who implement it. Parents and teachers have been concerned that such programs have the ability to frighten children. Staff provide reassurance that this approach does not frighten children, but rather strengthens them because neither horror stories nor absolutes such as "never do . . ." are presented. By encouraging children's active thinking and participation, the approach actually strengthens their sense of competence. Even more difficult has been the need to reassure parents and teachers that children are not learning that all touching is bad or that they cannot trust anyone. The increasing alarm in local communities about the high incidence of child sexual abuse has led to oversuspiciousness about adults touching children in any way. Teachers are afraid to touch children at all, and some parents are uncertain about how to define the acceptable "lines" that should not be crossed—for themselves and for others.

Parents and teachers are given reassurance with the understanding that the emphasis of this approach is on the individual's right to control his or her own body—to determine who touches him or her, how, when, and so forth. This should ultimately *increase* children's ability to trust (when they are adults as well) because they are being encouraged to learn whom to trust and to assert themselves when it does not feel safe. This is considered to be far healthier than the kind of blind trust of all adults that makes children so vulnerable. It is also considered to be healthier for children to feel free to choose to touch and be touched affectionately because they feel free to stop it as well.

Empowerment versus Rules

As child sexual abuse prevention education programs are being developed under various auspices, a second issue has arisen regarding hidden messages that are conveyed to children along with the safety information. The traditional safety presentations that gave children rules with no explanations or skills for decision making or assertiveness were seen as inadequate 10 years ago. Approaches such as the one presented in this chapter have been adopted by many educators, law enforcement agencies, and social service and mental health practitioners. Unfortunately, the goal of empowering children is too often lost. The important concepts that are being taught are contradicted by a manner and educational environment that continue to convey to children that there are certain "right" ways (and therefore wrong ways) to be safe, and that if they do not act correctly, they will be victimized and it will be their fault. It is important to acknowledge the reality that children are often victimized in situations in which they are absolutely powerless and can do nothing to prevent it. Here it is important to teach children to do the best they can to take care of themselves under the circumstances.

A third issue has arisen because this program model and others similar to it are being implemented in programs that educate massive numbers of children—entire schools and school districts at a time—in 1-hour or 2-hour presentations. California recently passed legislation requiring child abuse prevention education programs in every school in the state (preschool through high school). This mass education approach is valuable because of the magnitude of attitude change it influences. This is one very important goal of primary prevention of child sexual abuse. However, the other important goals involve teaching children skills so that they are less vulnerable and less likely to be victimized. These skills cannot be taught in 1 or 2 hours. They can be introduced, and if these concepts fit with what children have already learned, they can be reinforced. To the extent that they are new skills for children, the strategies that will be the most effective will target teachers and parents. Changes in childrearing practices are more likely to result in children who demonstrate assertion and decision-making skills. Teaching parents, potential parents, and teachers how to integrate these major concepts into daily interactions with children—in addition to providing an introductory education for children—is more likely to result in the children's development of skills.

CONCLUSION

Primary prevention efforts addressing child sexual abuse have created many different program models. One such program, which was described in detail, had a positive approach that supported and encouraged belief in one's ability to take care of oneself, without negating one's cultural and ethnic values. It was found that it was possible to sensitively explore realities that conflicted with one's cultural values. Perhaps the most significant value of this program was that it took a very positive stance for child advocacy by introducing the idea that children have a right to protect themselves from adults. This was presented to children as their right not to be bothered or harassed by anyone, and to parents as their child's right to be respected by adults as well as their child's responsibility to respect adults.

The presentations were given in Spanish in a nonconfrontive and nonthreatening manner. The aim was to strengthen parents' and children's self- and cultural images. All were encouraged to use the skills they already possessed in identifying, coping with, and preventing sexual assaults. Parents were encouraged to teach their children at an early age to rely on their own judgment and to make their own decisions. They were given age-appropriate ways to encourage and develop these characteristics in their children. The importance of open communication involving listening to and believing children was stressed. The culture conflicts in their lives and their vulnerabilities because of this conflict were acknowledged. Essentially this program left Hispanic parents with an improved level of self-confidence and integrity in dealing with this sensitive issue, and with some reassurance that there are ways for them to increase their level of comfort in dealing with it. Further study would be required to determine if these attitude changes are generally sustained over a long period of time.

The implications for improved coping with sexual assault within the Hispanic communities were evident. The exposure to this material tended to have a ripple effect. Some youths sought help to deal with sexual assault experiences as a result of the presentation. Possibly others who did not speak up but who had been assaulted also subsequently sought help of some sort. Parents and teachers with increased awareness and knowledge of resources more frequently identified and sought help for sexually abused children. Principals and school nurses improved school procedures for dealing with the Hispanic family in suspected or identified abuse situations. Thus a preventive program that emphasized coping strategies had the potential for improving an entire community's means of coping with child sexual abuse.

REFERENCES

Bass, E., & Davis, L. (in press). *The courage to heal: A guide for women survivors of child sexual abuse.* New York: Harper & Row.

Belle, D. (1984). Inequality and mental health, low income and minority women. In L. E. A. Walker (Ed.), *Women and mental health policy* (pp 135–150). Beverly Hills, CA: Sage.

Caplan, G. (1964). *Principles of primary prevention* (p. 17). New York: Basic Books.

Colao, F., & Hosansky, T. (1987). *Your children should know.* New York: Harper & Row.

Giovannoni, J., & Becerra, R. (1979). *Defining child abuse.* New York: Free Press.

Herman, J. (1981). *Father/daughter incest.* Cambridge, MA: Harvard University Press.

Kessler, M., & Albee, G. (1977). An overview of the literature of primary prevention. In G. Albee & J. Joffe (Eds.), *The issues: An overview of primary prevention.* Hanover, NH: University Press of New England. (p. 353)

McGovern, K. (1986). *Alice doesn't babysit anymore.* Portland, OR: Alternatives to Sexual Abuse.

Olson, M. (1985). A collaborative approach to prevention of child sexual abuse. *Victimology: An International Journal, 10* (1–4), 131–139.

Roberts, C. A. (1970). Psychiatric and mental health consultation. *Canadian Journal of Public Health, 51.*

Straus, M. A., Gelles, R. J., & Steinmetz, S. K. (1980). *Behind closed doors: Violence in the American family.* New York: Anchor-Doubleday.

White, R. (1979). Competence as an aspect of personal growth. In M. W. Kent & J. Rolf (Eds.), *Social competence in children* (p. 9). Hanover, NH: University Press of New England.

Epilogue

Retrospective Incest for Men: A Personal History

Carl E. K. Johnson

On a muggy, overcast June afternoon in 1979, the rifles of a military honor guard resounded in the gray sky over the flag-draped casket of Karl Gustav Johnson at Fort Logan Cemetery south of Denver. The small funeral party bunched close together under the burial canopy as the guard members meticulously folded the flag and handed it to their commander, who presented it to me as a symbol of America's gratitude for my uncle's service as a private in an artillery division in France during World War I.

I watched as the group of predominantly elderly mourners closed their eyes as the stolid Lutheran pastor intoned the final prayer for their friend who 3 months earlier had concluded his 89th year. Known by his friends as an upstanding citizen, I once again experienced the acute realization that I was quite likely the only one in my uncle's life who had really known him at the deepest levels of his personality. When I was about 4 years old I became the object of his sexual desire and expression and remained so until around the age of nine.

My uncle was born to a large family of poor farmers in the province of Smaland (Little Land) in Sweden, a rocky area in the southern part of the country. He emigrated to the United States in 1912 in order to avoid military conscription. Arriving in Denver, he quickly obtained employment as a laborer on the estate of a prominent family near the city. Choosing to be called "Gust," he soon changed his surname from "Jonsson" to "Johnson." In an ironic twist of fate, he was drafted into the United States Army in 1913.

Returning from the war, he assumed the first of several positions as a gardener, handyman, and chauffeur for a variety of affluent families in the Denver area, which he held over the next forty years. In 1939, my uncle's younger brother by ten years, Fridolf Edvin Jonsson, came to join him at the elder brother's urging. He began immediate employment as a maintenance worker on another large estate prearranged by my uncle. He soon adopted "Fred" as a first name, and like Gust, changed his last name to Johnson.

In the spring of 1939, Anna Kristina Nashland, a tall, slender woman with silken black hair and luminous blue eyes, came to her older brother's farm in Weld County, north of Denver. She followed her elder sibling from the northern Swedish province of Angermanland, a land of towering mountains, thick green forests, and wide rolling rivers.

Anna worked on her brother's farm for several months, but was attracted to the urban excitement of Denver. Swedish domestic servants were in great demand at the time and she soon secured employment as a combination governess, upstairs maid, kitchen helper, and meal server.

The local chapter of Vasa Lodge, a long established Swedish-American fraternal organization, was the most popular gathering place for recent immigrants. It was here that Fred and Anna met in 1940 at one of the lodge's weekly dances.

In January of 1941 they were married. After the excitement of the wedding, Fred returned to a new position he had recently taken as a chauffeur and gardener.

Like other newlyweds, Fred and Anna yearned for their own home, but lacked the money to purchase one. From his savings, Gust, who had never married, loaned them five thousand dollars. This sum constituted the full price of a small attractive home in a pleasant neighborhood. In return for the loan, Gust received basement lodgings and meals without charge. Soon it became apparent that he also expected laundry service.

At the outset, it appeared that the newlyweds had made a highly advantageous bargain. Little did they realize that they had not even begun to pay the heavy consideration in anguish that Gust would exact for his assistance over the next fifteen years.

Within a few months after the wedding, Anna became pregnant with the couple's only child. After a difficult labor, I entered the world by cesarean section in the spring of 1942.

To survive financially, it was necessary for both my parents to work. Sometimes my mother would take a steady position as a domestic servant. At other times, she would work for a popular high society caterer.

Frequently my parents' work hours overlapped, requiring them to make child care arrangements. Until I was about four, my most frequent caretaker was a patient elderly woman.

As the years passed my uncle began to complain of stomach ailments, and to spend most of his time—both day and evening—at home. Shortly thereafter he retired. Soon, Gust became virtually my only caretaker in my parents' absence.

Physically, Gust displayed a full head of slightly wavy black hair. His eyes were flinty blue and conveyed a sense of unpredictable explosiveness. His long thin narrow face was chiseled sharply, albeit delicately, reminiscent of the handiwork of an expert Scandinavian woodcarver. A layer of thin pale skin covered his high-planed forehead and stretched tautly downward to silhouette a sharp-beaked nose, prominently etched cheekbones, and thin tightly pursed lips before tucking sharply under a pointed chin to join his thin small neck. His thin-boned body rose like a reed to a height somewhat over five and a half feet. His voice, which, when he was calm, was pitched in the middle register, assumed a rapidly escalating thin strident quality as he became excited or argumentative. His disposition was intense and, when faced with opposition to his desires, abrasive.

He lived austerely in a large, drab, sparsely furnished and poorly lighted room in the basement. His quarters could be reached only by descending the back stairs and walking through a long narrow corridor that served as the laundry room.

Gust would climb the back stairs three times daily to take his meals. Occasionally, he would sit in the living room. However, most of his time was spent in his subterranean milieu. Living below ground was a lifelong habit of his.

Allowing my uncle to become my caretaker seemed to be a very good idea for several reasons. After all, he was part of the family. No special transportation arrangements were necessary. He did not require payment.

Whether either parent was aware of the sexual agenda that Gust held with respect to his role as my caretaker is still a matter of perplexity for me as an adult. On the one hand, I do not recall ever observing my parents give any indication that they had any suspicion regarding his conduct. However, I repressed explicit conscious awareness of our relationship until I was well into my thirties.

Even today I resist believing that they may have known on some level.

However, my experience in therapy has led to the examination of the possibility that at some point in time my father may himself have been sexually abused by his brother. This is consistent with the fear and abject servility which my father nearly always exhibited toward Gust. Hardly a mealtime went by without my uncle challenging the validity of some statement by my father. Stung by his brother's criticism, my father would tentatively defend his position, then abruptly abdicate in the face of Gust's relentless sarcasm.

As a lawyer representing both children and parents in child abuse cases, I am also aware of the research in the field that has found that in many, if not most, cases of incest, all of the adult family members have an awareness of what is going on at some level. This research finding has been confirmed in many cases in my own professional experience.

However, the question of my parents' knowledge will remain forever unresolved because both my mother and my father died long before I was able to allow myself to be consciously aware of my own calamitous experiences after years of psychotherapy.

Regardless of the season of the year my uncle invariably kept himself completely covered with at least two heavy layers of clothing. Even in the hottest weather, a single-piece union suit invariably constituted his foundation garment.

The pretext that my uncle used to initiate intimate contact with me was always discipline. I had done something wrong and "needed a good licking." Sometimes I made too much noise. Other times I tracked dirt into the house. On other occasions I failed to come home quickly enough from playing with friends when he called. On other occasions he contended that I had sassed him. He could interpret virtually any conduct in which I was engaged in a manner that justified his taking drastic physical measures to bring me into line.

His body tensed with excitement and his face flushed with color, transforming his usually pallid skin into a florid red hue, as he confronted me with my offending conduct. (On one terrible occasion he accosted me while I was standing with a group of friends.) He would then righteously announce that once again I needed to be taught a lesson, grab me, and pull me toward the back stairwell. As we descended the stairs (my uncle taking long forceful strides and I pedaling in short frenetic steps to keep from being pulled into the air), the tempo of his excitement rapidly escalated. His breathing became audible, beating an increasingly rapid panting cadence. The latent storm in his eyes exploded. A powerful surge of the blood streaming through his body could be felt as he squeezed my hand tightly.

Once we reached the basement he would abruptly stop, shake me, and announce that once again my conduct had far exceeded the bounds of decency and the limits of his patience. Sometimes he would then drag me to his room before completely fulfilling his desires; other times he would complete his deeds in the laundry room corridor. The late afternoon sun filtering through the tiny windows reflecting against the varied fixtures of the laundry room cast eerie shadows on the ritual that was in progress. After completing his exhortation, my uncle, whose violent frenzy continued to escalate, would forcefully disrobe me, bend over my shoulders or else pull my exposed body across his trembling lap and, now fully possessed, begin striking my buttocks repeatedly with his stiffened hands, as the cadence of his breathing made a rapid crescendo.

After a period of time that probably only lasted a few minutes, but seemed to me to last forever, the fury of the beating would suddenly abate in the same manner as the end of a violent summer afternoon mountain thunderstorm.

Gust would stop hitting me and his body would relax. Slowly, his breathing would calm. He would then gently help me to pull my underpants and pants back on. At last he would pull me close to his still rapidly beating heart, embrace me tightly, dab at the tears in my eyes with his crumpled, often soiled handkerchief, and gently stroke my tousled blond hair. He would then place his hands on my small rounded shoulders, look intently into my dark brown eyes, and quietly state that he hoped that I understood that I had been punished for my own good and that as a result my conduct would change so that it would not be necessary to repeat the process in the future. Even as he spoke, I sensed the falsity of his words and perceived his eager anticipation of a new encounter within a matter of days.

At the beginning, my uncle's touching consisted simply of corporal punishment and the conciliatory caresses with which each episode concluded. On the surface, what I regularly experienced at the hands of my uncle appeared to be similar to the spankings that most of my friends and acquaintances in the neighborhood frequently received from their parents. Yet, though I would not be able to consciously identify the nature of the difference until over two decades later, I intuitively knew there was something unusual about the discipline my uncle administered.

Whenever I witnessed another child being spanked, a terrible feeling of dread would come over me. Supplanting that feeling, however, came a tremendous sense of power and an identification with the angry, punishing parent, not the tearful frightened child. Most unsettling, however, would be the hot tingling sensations that engulfed my entire body at such moments. They were not remotely comparable to anything I had previously experienced.

As the months passed, Gust gradually expanded the scope and nature of his acts. He began to alternate the fondling of my tiny genitals with the blows. Later, he would unzip his pants and direct one of my hands to touch his covered groin area. The feel of warm moist pulsation triggered anew the strange bodily sensations within me and sent a shiver of terror cascading from my throat deep into my stomach. As our relationship continued, my uncle began to regularly touch my buttocks, anus, and genitalia with his hands, mouth, and tongue. Finally, he began to unbutton his long underwear at the crotch and force my mouth into contact with his hard throbbing member.

As we embarked upon these new activities my uncle experienced unprecedented levels of ecstasy. Strangely, however, the conclusion to our interactions changed markedly. Instead of closing our encounters with a lecture, Gust would address me in dark, halting, apologetic terms. The anxiety he felt hung heavily in the air. His blushing downturned face and darting eyes conveyed a sense of unspeakable shame. My stomach felt like a frozen stone.

At this point I knew that I had entered upon a rite of such power, mystery, and shame that I could never reveal it to anyone—not my mother, not my father, not anyone. In fact, I could not even allow myself a conscious awareness of it.

As the years progressed, my circle of friends widened and the variety and intensity of my schedule increased. My life became a whirlwind of school, athletic, and musical activity. Frequently, I would invite a handful of my closest friends to spend time at home with me. Perhaps because his opportunities to encounter me alone decreased or possibly because he believed that I was more likely to report him as I gained more maturity, my uncle's predations gradually diminished and finally stopped entirely.

In June of 1985, a feature article appeared in one of Denver's major daily newspapers focusing on my experience as an incest victim. In response, a close childhood friend who today operates an insurance agency told me that he now understood certain aspects of my childhood circumstances that were puzzling and disturbing to him at the time. Over lunch, he conveyed his recollection that my parents were rarely home in the late afternoons when we played together, but that my uncle was always present. He recounted the horrendous fear of my uncle that he observed in my eyes and remembered the extreme alacrity with which I would respond to his commands. He recalled that Gust seemed to resent the presence of my friends in our home and, in particular, recollected that my uncle made the basement area off-limits to them.

Since coming to terms with my childhood sexual experience, I have often asked myself why I so totally repressed the details of my relationship with my uncle. Why I didn't tell my mother. My father. The school principal. My music teacher. The police detective who was a close friend of my family and a childhood idol.

Child abuse studies indicate that it is not uncommon for a victim to fail to disclose his predicament. This frequently results from fear. Fear that the perpetrator will harm the child if he discloses the relationship. Fear that he will not be believed or, worse, will be thought crazy. Fear that he, not the perpetrator, will be blamed for the situation.

In my case, I cannot point to such clear-cut reasons for keeping my uncle's conduct a secret. I do not recall his making any explicit threats of harm if I told. Although it might have been difficult to find someone who would believe me, there were many adults in whom I could have confided. It is probable that at least one of them would have taken my account seriously enough to at least undertake a further investigation.

There is no rational reason why I so thoroughly repressed an awareness of my relationship with my uncle both from myself and others. The power of the experience on my mind and body was beyond rational understanding. It was simply self-evident to me that it could never be revealed.

The relationship between my uncle and me took place in a family context of extreme modesty. My parents never spoke about sex and always took great pains to make sure they were fully clothed in my presence. One Sunday afternoon I came in from playing outdoors to ask them a question and, entering their bedroom without knocking, interrupted their lovemaking. I can still recall the look of unspoken terror in their eyes that caused me to beat a hasty retreat.

During my elementary school years there was no sex education given in school. I received none at home. Although I recognized that the disturbing new bodily sensations to which I had been introduced by my uncle were unusual, I did not identify them as sexual during most of those years. Although I was a good student, my sexual knowledge was miniscule. For instance, until my early adolescence I believed that intercourse, conception, and childbirth took place in the cleavage between a woman's breasts.

In my early teenage years, I once requested my father to explain sex to me. Like the time that I had interrupted my parents in their bedroom, he recoiled from the subject in horror, managing only to mumble something about the gravity of the topic.

In addition to dominating me, Gust tyrannized the household. He insisted that my mother fix our meals to his liking, wash his clothes daily, and starch and iron his white shirts. He would govern the dinner table conversation. His ideas and proposed solutions to problems were always the only right ones. Gust would treat my parents as feebleminded children. Any ideas or plans that they advanced would be cavalierly dismissed as proof of their inexperience in American life. Neither of my parents was ever able to effectively confront him in any discussion.

Racial and ethnic problems were a frequent topic of his monologues. During the course of these declamations, Gust would adamantly vent his hatred of virtually all minorities. He repeatedly made statements such as "the niggers are getting out of hand and need to be stopped," "the Jews deserved what they got from Hitler," and "the Mexicans are filthy, lazy bums." During these venomous outbursts, the intensity of his affect and expression would resemble that which he exhibited during the course of our sexual interactions.

Outside of our household, Gust was socially ineffectual. In contrast to my parents' large circle of friends, Gust's close friends numbered a few reclusive bachelors like himself. Although he ultimately became a life member of Vasa, which was the only organization to which he belonged, he never played an active role in the lodge.

From an early age, my emotional life resembled a roller coaster. On the one hand, I was highly motivated to take a positive attitude toward life. I desperately wanted to succeed in school, sports, and music, and especially in my social relationships with my peers. Most of all I wanted to be considered "neat," "cool"—a true American kid. Even more I wanted to feel "normal."

Frequently, however, I would become extremely depressed for several hours at a time, particularly on weekends. During these periods, I would retreat to my room and avoid contact with anyone. Although I never actually attempted to harm myself, I often fantasized suicide. Sometimes when I was alone at home I would go to the basement, look at the pipes suspended from the ceiling, and think about tying some kind of noose to one of them from which to hang myself.

This habit of suicidal ideation continued through my adolescence and young adulthood. In fact, I did not completely give it up until after I had completed a number of years of therapy.

As a child and adolescent, I never felt comfortable talking about my feelings of despair with anyone. Part of me would condemn my feelings as inexcusable self-pity. As I grew older, I rationalized that these feelings were a normal part of life to be borne with serenity. From an early age I was intellectually and spiritually precocious—always seeking the ultimate Truth of existence. When I entered my adolescence, I studied the philosophy of Stoicism and solemnly resolved that I would always bear my pain privately. I vowed to never express any negative feeling in public or even to my parents or friends.

My emotional isolationism was consistent with the strict code of privacy observed by our family, which itself was an outgrowth of a broader Swedish-American cultural trait. Under the unwritten and unspoken mandate of the code, it was the duty of each person to bear his own feelings in silence. It was unseemly to burden anyone else with them.

Thus, until the onset of my mother's fatal illness when I was 14, I do not recall any significant sharing of feelings of sadness, grief, or, outside of my uncle's mealtime ripostes, anger within our family. However, the realization of her mortal predicament caused my mother to drop any pretense of observing the code as she struck out in vehement denunciation of my uncle and his despotic household behavior. Even more horrifying were her sharp attacks on my father for having permitted Gust to continue residing in the house through the years despite her numerous prior requests (of which I was totally unaware) of him to ask his brother to leave. This time she was not to be denied. A short time later Gust made his departure, returning for visits only when Anna was not home.

My father's own adherence to the code also began to falter as my mother's condition worsened. Late in the evening after my mother was asleep, at intervals of a week or 10 days, he would consume shot after shot of straight vodka. As the drinking progressed his pent-up emotional energy would explode. Alternating between periods of heavy sobbing and outbursts of vitriolic, slurred oaths, he deeply grieved the tragic plight of his wife. He raged furiously against my uncle whom, like my mother, he now held primarily responsible for the family's awful fate.

This sudden outpouring of long-suppressed emotions was not only surprising to me but unsettling as well. Although I felt a great deal of empathy toward my parents, I was also critical of the fact that they had broken down and breached the code. I renewed my vow to adhere to it with even greater determination and resolved not to be broken by the trauma I saw unfolding around me.

At the age of seven my interest in policemen and, secondarily, in music led me to join the Denver Junior Police Band, a prominent youth organization of the era. Attracted from the first to the trombone as my instrument of choice, I was initially foreclosed from being a trombonist because my short arms could barely extend to the fifth of its seven positions. Instead I was steered to the baritone horn, a three-valve instrument reminiscent of a small tuba.

After a rocky start during which I experienced difficulty in drawing more than a single tone from the yards of unyielding metal tubing, my musical proficiency rapidly soared. In addition to the youth band, I began participating in the school instrumental program. As the years went by, the self-validation I would inevitably receive through the recognition of my musical abilities proved to be a powerful stabilizer of my often fragile ego and precarious self-esteem. I would always rank among the top performers in any ensemble in which I performed. On numerous occasions from childhood into adult life, a successful performance could move me temporarily out of episodes of depression. As a result, my musical ability has served as a significant anchor of my emotional life.

My experience with my uncle caused me to view all adults with a mixture of awe and trepidation. To me, an adult was a totally independent, competent person equal to any kind of challenge. Because of his knowledge and ability, an adult could be tremendously helpful to a child in lending his experience to assist him in confronting the growing challenges of life. Adults could also supply nurturance, love, and protection.

On the other hand, I perceived adults as totally unpredictable. In an instant, the kind, helpful father, mother, uncle, aunt, teacher, or coach could be transformed into a raging monster—screaming at the child in his charge or striking out physically at him, sometimes with understandable provocation but at other times with little or no apparent reason. Parents and other primary custodians in particular appeared to have limitless power over their youngsters. They had a license to humiliate their children at any time either privately or publicly.

Along with my playmates, I accepted our powerless position without question. It never entered our minds that we had any rights other than those that our parents and teachers specifically gave to us.

Our teachers would continually tell us how lucky we were to be Americans because we enjoyed individual rights of liberty and property. However, the strong, albeit unspoken, assumption underlying these pronouncements was that the rights would be something that we would enjoy as adults, not something to which we were presently entitled.

Consequently, I looked forward with great anticipation to the day when I too would become an adult and achieve the competency, power, dignity, freedom, privileges, rights, and respect that I somehow believed all adults uniformly enjoyed. I projected an image of perfect competency and freedom upon adults while persistent feelings of insecurity bubbled internally. I experienced a nagging fear that somehow I would never measure up to the requirements of adulthood and would remain always a child.

As a primary means of adaptation to my childhood circumstances, I became the model "good boy." I kept close control of my spontaneous impulses toward fun, frivolity, and mischief, expressing them only in situations where I felt certain that no adult was present who might possibly take offense and either punish me for my behavior himself or inform my parents.

My adaptation to what I perceived to be the whims, demands, desires, and needs of the adults in my environment appeared, certainly to most adults with whom I had significant contact, to be successful. I also believed it to be successful. Many years later, as I sought to cope with the challenges of adult life, I would discover that I had gravely deluded myself. Accommodation to the adult world had been bought at the price of my own integrity as a child. I had largely suppressed my childhood nature and its spontaneity of feeling and action. Seemingly dormant for years, the desperate cry of the repressed inner child was felt with cataclysmic force during my fourth decade of life.

As the result of the two modes of adaptation to adults that I used—always striving to be the ultimate "good boy" and acting as much as an adult myself as possible—I largely succeeded in avoiding adverse encounters with adults who exercised authority over me. Nonetheless, as described, I was acutely aware of the powerlessness of the position of myself and my contemporaries as children per se in our relationship to the adult world. However, whenever I witnessed the physical chastisement of a child by an adult, my inner identification, as mentioned, would invariably switch from the child to the punishing adult.

To assuage my feelings of powerlessness, I relished those opportunities when I could exercise power over the younger children on the block. For instance, whenever we played house I would choose the role of father as often as possible, thereby gaining a pretext to verbally and physically abuse my hapless friends who were left to play the role of children.

In contrast to those cravings for power, beginning early in elementary school I began to experience sensations of tender emotional attraction to girls. Throughout my public school career, and in college, I would often engage in fantasies of love and tenderness regarding those members of the opposite sex to whom I was attracted. I frequently envisioned myself married and overwhelmingly in love, living an idyllic life with handsome vivacious children in a large tree-shrouded house surrounded by spacious gardens and lawns on a quiet residential city street.

During my school years, I would inevitably pick those girls whom I—and usually the rest of the school—viewed as most desirable to be the objects of my fantasization. Rarely, however, did I successfully progress from the level of fantasy to the point of actually establishing a successful relationship with any of the girls I desired. Instead, beginning in grade school and continuing well into my adult life, I would almost inevitably meet rejection whenever I sought to establish an intimate relationship with any member of the opposite sex.

Running parallel with my loving fantasies and dreams and with a comparable degree of frequency were those of a sadistic nature. I delighted in envisioning the girls and women about whom I had earlier experienced such tender feelings being rudely disrobed, beaten, and humiliated by such figures as a parent, teacher, principal, or minister. Even more so I enjoyed picturing myself as the punishing adult in these fantasies.

I noticed a distinct difference between the bodily sensations I would experience during the course of the tender fantasies and those that I would experience in connection with the punitive ones. When I envisioned scenes of tenderness and love, I would feel a sense of breathlessness and be acutely aware of the pounding of my heart. In the course of the sadistic fantasies, it would feel as if a warm fluid were simultaneously speeding at breakneck pace to my head, my extremities, and every other part of my body. The former sensations were certainly powerful and extremely pleasurable, but the latter were absolutely overwhelming—like nothing else I had experienced. Simultaneously, they filled me with a sense of awe and deep fear.

My sadistic fantasies were disturbing in another respect because their objects would on occasion not only be girls but boys as well. Like those involving females, those involving males would feature the boys in my circle of friends and acquaintances whom I felt to be most physically attractive.

The first real informational education in sex that I received came from listening to conversations between several of the boys in my circle of friends during the last year of grade school. They would huddle in small groups on the playground, in gym, or in neighborhood alleys to excitedly exchange observations and experiences relating to their physical maturation. Occasionally, a boy would physically display the progress of his sexual growth. These street seminars would also feature an exchange of accounts—again by the handful of the most physically developed boys—of their most recent wet dreams and other purported sexual experiences.

Gradually, the discussions expanded to include dissertations on bizarre aspects of sexuality by the most curious and outspoken of the boys, generally derived from information imparted by their fathers, older brothers, or uncles. Their revelations regarding homosexuality, during which strange new terms like "queers" and "fags" spit like venom from their mouths, were particularly disturbing.

After finishing their own accounts, the leaders would inevitably turn to the two or three boys in the group, including myself, who had remained silent during the course of the storytelling and ask us individually about our sexual development and experience. Nervously, I would mumble something about "having had a wet dream a few nights ago" or experiencing a "stiffy," the slang used for erection by the boys, whenever I saw some particularly attractive girl at school.

In reality, the truth was far different. I had yet to detect any perceptible sign of sexual maturation. Although I was attracted to the discussions both because of my interest in the subject matter and in order to maintain my standing as one of "the cool kids," I lived in perpetual dread that on some occasion I would be required to verify my accounts of sexual growth by physical demonstration leading to the humiliating exposure of the falsity of my claims.

Although I always pretended to take the sexual revelations in a blasé manner, they actually disturbed me a great deal. I compared the descriptions of the orgasmic experiences described by my peers to the intense bodily sensations that I experienced in connection with my sadistic fantasies, dreams, and impulses. Reluctantly I concluded that the latter were indeed sexual in nature. Yet the visualizations that aroused sexual excitement in me were so different from those described by my friends, reinforcing my perception of myself as perverse. I renewed my determination that none of my contemporaries would ever learn of the inner workings of my emotional life.

An even more terrifying realization was the prospect that, considering my fantasied physical attraction toward boys as well as girls, I might well be a despised queer. Trepidation regarding this issue caused me to disclose these fears to my long-time pediatrician. Although he dismissed my fears out of hand saying "Carl, you're as normal as any kid I've seen," the persistence of my concern led him to refer me for a consultation with a psychiatrist colleague. Taking a grandfatherly approach, this veteran physician calmly assured me that my fears of being a homosexual (the word sounded far less threatening than *queer*) were simply unjustified since I displayed none of the physical or behavioral characteristics that he indicated to always be the earmark of the condition.

Leaving his office I felt reassured that I was not the dread pariah I had thought, but I still felt a great sense of anxiety regarding my sexual identity. Over two decades would pass before I would be able to feel comfortable about my sexuality.

What I viewed as the enigmas of my sexuality contributed greatly to the formation in my mind of a monumental neurotic edifice that I had already begun to construct and would bring to completion in my adolescent and adult years. Yet, my urgent desire to maintain an appearance of normalcy in interactions with the world caused me to persistently refuse to face the precarious state of my emotional life. As I advanced in adolescence, it swung from deep depression (everyone feels bad now and then, I would rationalize at such times) to feelings of great euphoria during which I would experience exaggerated feelings of competency and popularity. Returning to the dark side of the pendulum, the very recollection of the positive feelings I had earlier experienced would be felt as a bitterly ironic reproach to myself. At such times, I condemned the positive competent image that I presented to the world as fraudulent.

However, the first point at which I reluctantly acknowledged the possibility that I required professional mental health assistance occurred in the aftermath of my first serious romantic involvement, when I was twenty-one. My relationship with a winsome dancer whom I had met during the course of a musical in which she was featured and for which I was part of the pit orchestra ended disastrously with her abrupt departure for Canada.

Within days of her leaving, severe depression engulfed me. Living at home with my father while pursuing my undergraduate career at the University of Denver a few miles away, I attempted to assuage my despondency by frequenting a popular Italian restaurant located in our neighborhood that offered an unlimited amount of homemade spaghetti for a fixed price. I would eat a minimum of three plates of the delicious pasta and more often five, six, or even seven plates virtually every evening. Within weeks my weight skyrocketed from 145 pounds to 210 pounds, leaving permanent stretch marks encircling my abdomen when my weight began to revert to normal several months later. Most disturbingly, I began experiencing episodes of enuresis (to the best of my recollection, for the first time in my life) two or three times a week. This horror strengthened the mocking silent inner voice of condemnation that now proclaimed: "You're nothing but a little boy! You, a man? What a farce!"

Reluctantly acknowledging that I had encountered a dilemma that I could not resolve without professional assistance, I made discreet inquiries as to what affordable mental health resources existed in the community and was referred to the outpatient clinic of a public institution, affiliated with the University of Colorado Medical School, which at that time was ominously named the Colorado Psychopathic Hospital. The outpatient program there offered an initial diagnostic interview conducted by a medical student doing his psychiatric rotation or a psychiatric intern or resident, after which a determination was made in consultation with a supervising psychiatrist as to whether the prospective patient required psychotherapy. If so, he would then be scheduled for either individual or group therapy on a sliding-fee scale depending upon availability of openings.

My interview was conducted by an intense young medical student. During the course of the 2-hour interview he amassed a vast amount of personal information and I haltingly conveyed to him the reason for seeking help. At the conclusion of our meeting, the student physician expressed his personal opinion that I was an apt candidate for psychotherapy.

About 2 weeks later I received a call from the hospital indicating that I had been placed on its waiting list for inclusion in a therapy group when an appropriate place became available. Several months then passed without word from the clinic. When at last I was informed in the fall of 1964 that a place had opened for me in a group, the university's jazz band had just been notified that it had been selected by the State Department to make a 3-month tour of several countries, including Japan, Australia, and New Zealand, which would commence shortly after Christmas. To forego this incredible travel opportunity was not an acceptable alternative and I declined to enter therapy, a decision that turned out to be a 9-year postponement of this desperately needed step.

After the tour, I embarked on a ocean journey with my widowed father to visit the many relatives on both my mother's and father's side in Sweden. In the fall of 1965, I enrolled for a year's course of graduate studies at the University of Stockholm. As the months progressed, my interest in the multiplicity of inexpensive travel opportunities for students exceeded my scholarly zeal and eventually my courseload diminished to only advanced Swedish. To support myself, I taught English to adults and began performing as a professional musician.

Although the variety of activities in my life were stimulating and I coped well, the cyclical pattern of depression continued, intensified at times by the perpetually gray Swedish sky. However, my weight had stabilized at 170 pounds and the disturbing bedwetting problem had spontaneously stopped several months earlier during the course of the jazz band tour. Once again I convinced myself that my emotional fluctuations were normal and that my periods of depression constituted nothing more than the "blues."

In the fall of 1966 I returned to Denver to enter the University of Denver College of Law and resumed my residency with my father. The cyclical pattern of depression continued and the feelings of hopelessness and self-abasement that I experienced during these episodes intensified. Still, my academic performance generally ranged from above average to excellent. On occasion, however, I would skip a class because I felt too depressed to go. Severe anxiety attacks during which I would experience a generalized fear of virtually everything also became an increasingly frequent part of my panorama of emotions. Although I would generally manage to continue the normal routine of my life despite these attacks, I would feel extremely uncomfortable in any social situation, whether a coffee break chat with friends or in the classroom. Blessedly, the flexibility of student life allowed me to make up any assignments I had failed to complete during a period of inner emotional incapacity at those times when, at the top of my emotional cycle, I would feel energetic and productive.

During my second year in law school, I met the person who would eventually become my first wife, a short vivacious woman with exotic dark eyes and flowing brown hair who had been born in Rumania and lived in Israel before emigrating to the United States as a teenager. Of a loving nature, her approach to life was predominantly emotional rather than rational. After a few months we began to live together and were married during my last year of school.

Living with her, I could no longer remain detached from my emotions. She would share her feelings with me and encourage me to do the same. Although I continued to strive to keep a lid on my emotional life, inwardly I felt like a surging volcano and found myself frequently erupting at home in spontaneous outbursts of tears for which I could ascribe no reason. Overall, however, her acceptance of me and the tremendous love that we felt toward one another gave me a sense of well-being and often euphoria, which I had never before experienced. I interpreted the fact that I had at last found acceptance in a romantic relationship and was now married as proof that, after all, I was normal despite my deep chronic doubts. Thus, once again I rationalized that I did not require psychotherapy.

The crisis that convinced me that I had no choice, from the standpoint of ensuring my personal and professional survival, but to enter therapy began after I embarked upon the practice of law at the age of 28. Upon licensure, I began work as an associate for a small suburban firm for which I had worked as a law clerk during law school. The firm conducted a general practice of a highly diversified nature, including traffic violations, divorce, personal injury, small business representation, and bankruptcy. The firm's senior partner, whose confidence I had gained during the course of my clerkship, began at once to entrust me with a large number and variety of important tasks in all areas of the practice. On the one hand this was a marvelous professional experience because it allowed me to become acquainted with many fields of law. On the other hand, it was terrifying because, inexperienced as I was, I felt sorely inadequate to the tasks which were assigned to me.

Over the next 2 years the downstrokes of my emotional life became increasingly devastating, and, for the first time, seriously disabling. Some days I would lie petrified and depressed in bed for the entire day, frightened by such innocuous sounds as the mailman's approaching footsteps on the front walk. After varying intervals—a few hours, a day, or at most, a couple of days—the attacks of depression or anxiety would dissipate and I would once again feel competent, productive, and energetic. Pervading these periods of emotional stability, however, was a new sense of urgency regarding the compensatory measures I felt compelled to undertake to keep my colleagues from discovering my emotional instability. At times, I experienced a sense of desperation as I struggled to complete the tasks that had gone undone during a period of dysfunction as quickly as possible so that my delay in completing the work would not become obvious. At other times, I felt a near manic sense of super competency that caused me to volunteer to perform tasks additional to the many I had been assigned. I felt compelled to somehow demonstrate that I was as good as or perhaps even superior to the other lawyers in the office.

When enveloped by the next episode of depression and anxiety, however, my bravado would haunt me and my sense of panic would escalate to new heights of terror. On days when my emotional state would keep me prisoner in my home, I would hide my disability by phoning the office receptionist and cryptically announcing that I would be out of the office doing research on that day. When I was faced with the prospect of a client interview, or a firm conference, I would, whenever possible, arrange to excuse myself using the pretext of a physical illness or some family emergency. Whenever this strategy was not feasible, I would muster what often seemed to me to be the last ounces of my emotional strength to fulfill the particular commitment, and then retreat into isolation.

Unlike the flexibility of student life, which allowed me to manipulate my activity schedule to accommodate the changes in my emotional state, the practice of law, even in the unregimented atmosphere in which I worked, demanded a consistent output of productive energy. Although it had been possible to skip class in undergraduate school and even in law school on an occasional or sometimes even frequent basis without serious consequence, court appearances could not be skipped. Further, the very economics of legal practice mandated such consistency. At firm meetings the principle that each attorney should produce at least six billable hours of work product each day was continually espoused.

In law school, my favorite area was that of criminal law and procedure, in which I was recognized as one of the superior students in my class. In the last year and a half of study, I immersed myself in the school's trial practice program, taking every opportunity to represent indigent defendants in misdemeanor and traffic cases in metropolitan area courts. My dream was to become a skilled trial lawyer. Upon graduation, my classmates of a similar bent flocked to district attorney offices or to employment with the state public defender. This was the logical place for an aspiring trial lawyer to begin because of the intensive daily trial experience such a position afforded. Following this course would have constituted an optimal career beginning for me as well, but I reluctantly concluded that, in view of the unpredictability of my emotional life, I could not withstand the rigors of daily trial practice. Thus, I accepted the offer from the suburban firm because I believed that it might be possible for me to handle its demands despite my emotional infirmity.

Increasingly, however, it became apparent to me that my attempts to juggle my professional responsibilities to accommodate the fluctuations in my emotional life would ultimately prove to be futile even in the comparatively low-key environment I had selected. I lived in almost perpetual dread that my emotional instability would be found out. I envisioned myself being contemptuously dismissed from my employment and ignominiously subjected to disbarment proceedings. The very contemplation of performing even routine legal tasks began to fill me with terror. In particular I recall the feelings of dread I experienced whenever I would be required to handle a matter before the austere chief district court judge of the state judicial district in which our office was located. The prospect of even applying for a default judgment before this jurist would loom in my consciousness as a horrifying ordeal. Later, in therapy, I would come to realize that this judicial officer of stern visage and irascible temperament caused a direct evocation of my uncle in my consciousness.

On my 30th birthday, I realized that I was in urgent need of psychiatric or psychological assistance that could no longer be postponed. In selecting a therapist, I chose a psychiatrist who had performed some effective forensic services for our firm in some personal injury and criminal matters. As a psychotherapist, however, he was not satisfactory to me. Uninitiated as I was to the rationale behind his nondirective method, I found his curt, aloof manner perplexing and terminated work with him after only a few sessions.

My next psychotherapist was a jovial, bearded psychiatrist whose speech hinted of a southern accent derived from his New Orleans upbringing. Recommended by a close family friend who was a social worker colleague of his, this clinician maintained his office on the top floor of a centrally located mansion he had converted into an office building for mental health professionals. Plainly furnished, the centerpiece consisted of a large dark wooden desk on one side of which sat the doctor, and on the other side, his patients.

To improve my ability to function on a consistent basis, he immediately prescribed Sinequan for the first few months I saw him. In our weekly sessions, my new therapist, whose manner was relaxed, conversational, and unpretentious, began to focus my attention on my recollections of childhood.

At this time, I decided to leave my original firm to avoid what I believed to be the inevitable point when my emotional instability would become evident to my colleagues. I then opened an office as a sole practitioner in a downtown building. Realizing that the resolution of my emotional problems necessarily constituted my primary task for the indefinite future, I carefully modulated my professional career so as to avoid undertaking responsibilities that were, either in number, complexity, or gravity of responsibility, beyond what I felt I could comfortably handle. I resolved to practice in a modest, yet competent manner, so as to avoid calling the attention of my clients, other lawyers, or judges to my plight. I would share my predicament only with my closest friends. I was determined to complete my therapy on a strictly outpatient basis. In that manner, I believed that I would be able to avoid what I perceived to be among the worst of professional stigmas—that of being classified a mental patient.

I pursued this strategy for several years until I felt certain that I was emotionally stable enough to broaden the scope of my practice. Although this course of action was successful in achieving its goal of keeping my problems from affecting my professional standing, my earnings were correspondingly meager. Fortunately, my musical talents once again served me well, both in terms of bolstering my fragile self-esteem and in providing additional income. Still, the financial demands of therapy (I enjoyed insurance coverage—and then just on a partial basis—only for the first year) overwhelmed my ability to meet my routine professional and family obligations. To survive economically, I began juggling bills and creditors, paying those that were most pressing, deferring others as long as I could. A few of my therapists would extend substantial credit to me; most, however, expected to be paid either on a cash or monthly basis. Recognizing their importance, I always made certain that my therapists were paid as requested regardless of my status with other creditors.

Although I felt far safer and more comfortable after I moved into my own practice, I still experienced myself as being under siege during the first several years of therapy. I felt that I was literally fighting for my life as a viable human being.

As the months progressed, understanding of my childhood experience deepened as my therapist and I conversed across his desk once and sometimes twice a week. The doctor frequently opined as to how my parents' extreme passivity in their approach to life had stunted my development of the ego strength necessary to lead an assertive life, particularly in my chosen profession. I came to realize that I felt a large volume of unresolved grief and anger inside of me relating to such aspects of my experience as my mother's illness, her death, and the overall household domination by my uncle.

During the course of this therapy I became adept at talking about my feelings, yet still could not express them. This was partly attributable to the structure of the therapy itself, which was primarily analytic, rather than emotive or expressive in nature. To a significant extent, however, it resulted from the fact that I was still unwilling to give up my stoical posture toward life.

During this period, my wife became involved with various forms of psychotherapy both to deal with issues in her own life and to attempt to find ways of helping me, since she was becoming increasingly frustrated by the effect that the dark side of my personality was having on our relationship. In addition, intellectually I had become a student of alternative psychotherapies, reading an average of one book on psychology a week. Thus, with the information provided by my wife, as well as my own reading, I became aware of the existence of therapies that stressed emotive, rather than analytic, methods and techniques, such as Gestalt and primal therapy. Yet, at this stage, I looked at those who utilized such methods with condescension. "I don't need to pound any pillows or make an ass out of myself in order to solve my problems," I remarked pompously to my psychiatrist one day, in response to which a brief smile crossed his face.

Still, despite my increasing intellectual understanding of my emotional dynamics and psychological principles in general, I continued to be gripped by depression and anxiety on a frequent basis. My therapist commented fatalistically that I would never be totally cured of these maladies and the best I could expect would be to learn to accommodate myself to my impaired condition as well as possible. I am not certain whether this commentary constituted a therapeutic stratagem on his part or simply expressed his honest opinion. At any rate it served as a spur to action for me since I refused to accept this pessimistic judgment. Most of my friends and associates were free of crippling depression. I wanted the same state of well-being and was determined to achieve it.

Shortly afterwards, I informed my psychiatrist that I would be terminating our two-year therapeutic relationship and entering Gestalt therapy. Commenting that it might do me some good, he wished me well.

My first evening in Gestalt therapy group was a shocking experience. As I began to tell "my story" in a hesitant, rambling manner, I was repeatedly interrupted by the impatient shouts of the co-therapists: "Stop mind-fucking! Don't talk about your feelings! Feel your feelings! How do you feel? Go ahead—cry, scream—do what you feel!" Over the next two years, gallons of rage, grief, and, on occasion, even delirious happiness poured forth from my lungs, eyes, arms, legs, and fists as I immersed myself in this new therapeutic modality, doing considerable work on my own to supplement the individual and group sessions in which I participated at least once and often two or three times a week. I hugged pillows as surrogate representations of my mother and, for the first time, fully grieved her illness and death. Consumed by a volcanic rage, I twisted and stomped numerous other pillows to "kill" my uncle for tyrannizing our family and abusing my mother. I hopped between pillows to personify the conflicting drives, beliefs, feelings, and impulses I experienced internally as I conducted extensive dialogues with myself.

My experience in Gestalt therapy constituted the first major break in the dam that held back my feelings. As a result, I felt a marked sense of relief and a renewed optimism that I would eventually conquer my emotional problems. Still, a significant amount of depression remained and the experience of my childhood sexual abuse remained buried. Although the Gestalt experience opened me emotionally, I perceived that I was becoming an "emotional junkie," wallowing ecstatically in my feelings but without reaching any point of resolution. As a result, I continued to feel a sense of severe incapacity in dealing with the demands of my professional life. I felt stuck and began to look for a new approach to my problems.

A lawyer who had been a close friend of mine since law school reported great satisfaction with his involvement in transactional analysis with a therapist who was an exponent of the reparenting mode of this method pioneered by Jacqueline Schiff. Impressed, I began an intensive 2-year period of individual and group work with his therapist.

Unique among my therapy groups, her groups would bring together persons of widely differing ages from adolescence to advanced adulthood encountering a wide variety of problems from serious disorders with psychotic manifestations to life transition problems. The group sessions would feature lively dialogue utilizing as a framework the body of concepts and theories developed by the system, including the parent, child, and adult ego state classification and the significance of game-playing and life scripts in human development and interactions. At the beginning of every session, each group member could request to become the focus of the therapist's and group's attention during its course to the extent needed in light of his or her current emotional status. Those who had arranged to participate in the reparenting aspect of the therapy also had the option to contract with the therapist to do regressive work. In this phase, the client would return on an emotional level to experience himself at some stage of his childhood development that had not been successfully negotiated at the time. The therapist would function as a new, ideal psychological parent to provide the appropriate parental response or action that had been lacking in the person's actual childhood experience.

Thus, while most of the members participated in the group dialogue, one or two others might be engaged in crawling around one side of the room, emitting babylike noises while engaged in intense exploratory activity, another might be acting out his "terrible twos" in another area of the spacious therapy room (leading inevitably to the therapist's command to "go stand in the corner"), and another client might lie sprawled face up across the therapist's lap, his head cradled in her arms, receiving a bottle. By special arrangement, a client could also participate in a catharsis of anger called a rage reduction, in which the other members of the group would work in tandem to keep the participant from harming himself, others, or property, while allowing him the maximum freedom possible to physically express his feelings of anger and hostility.

Participating in all phases of the therapy program, I found that the theoretical system of transactional analysis provided me with a practical way of understanding my own emotional dynamics as well as those of others. Even more significantly, my regressive work gradually brought to the surface some of my long-buried memories of my relationship with my uncle. Yet, it was not I but a teenage girl in the group who first clearly identified the sexual nature of the transactions with my uncle when one evening during the course of my revelations to the group she suddenly exclaimed: "Jesus! That's incest!"

Even though the lock on the memories of my childhood victimization had been broken and they began flowing to awareness, I found it difficult to believe that they were valid—that they represented real events in my past. I felt that my mind must be playing perverse tricks on me or that I really was insane.

I might have remained suspended indefinitely in a state of self-debilitating skepticism except for a fortuitous occurrence that validated the new revelations of my consciousness. After the death of my father, I had continued to maintain a close relationship with my uncle based on a well-developed sense of family loyalty that had been inculcated in me as a child. After dissolving a disastrous 2-year marriage at the age of 70, Gust had purchased a residence a few miles northwest of the old neighborhood. There he allowed a series of married couples or single ladies to occupy the upstairs in exchange for providing him with meals and laundering his clothes, and, true to his history, ensconced himself in the basement quarters.

One Saturday afternoon I took my oldest daughter, who was then five, with me to visit Gust. We found him sitting in a rocking chair in his basement living quarters, which consisted of a large room very similar to the one in which he had resided in my childhood home. Recalling that I had forgotten some item that I intended to deliver to my uncle in the car, I went outside to retrieve it, leaving my daughter alone with him. When I returned a few minutes later, I observed Gust attempting to entice my daughter into a punishment game with him. Although he was well into his eighties, his eyes were alive with desire as he leered lustfully at her.

Shocked, I quickly distracted my uncle and removed my daughter from the situation, vowing never to allow her to remain alone with him again. Reflecting on the event later that day, however, I realized that what I had witnessed gave credence to the memories of abuse that were now surfacing. No longer would I distrust them.

Although my involvement with transactional analysis had contributed greatly to the achievement of increased emotional stability, I still experienced a deep feeling of inner pain that I did not seem to be able to reach. Although my daily functioning had improved markedly, I still experienced periods of disablement. Also, my emotional upheavals had taken their toll on the relationship with my wife, leading to our separation and eventual divorce many months later. Again, I felt stuck and with my therapist's blessing, decided once again to move in a new direction. After a complete respite from therapy for a few months, I entered dream analysis with a female therapist of Jungian persuasion in order to deal with the continuing sense of malaise I felt.

Jungian psychology was extremely attractive to me both intellectually and experientially. The system possessed an artistic elegance, spiritual depth, and sense of mystery that was compelling. I was fascinated by its basic concepts such as animus, anima, persona, self, and, in particular, shadow. Still, as stimulating as the experience was, the most valuable service my therapist performed for me was to recognize early that, as a result of my childhood sexual victimization, I badly needed body therapy and to introduce me to one of the most skilled practitioners of this art in the Denver area.

A master of his profession, my body worker had absorbed principles and techniques developed by a number of theoreticians in the field, including Reich, Feldenkreis, and Rolf. Varying the strength and the nature of his touch and the accent of his voice, he pulled long-repressed emotional energy from every portion of my body, which in turn brought vivid new recollections of my childhood relationship with my uncle to consciousness. It felt as if he were rolling back a large boulder from the subterranean cavern in which the deep sense of pain I continued to experience was trapped, thereby allowing the ancient memories and feelings that fueled it to rise to the surface and eventually dissipate in the air. Intellectually, I was amazed by the discovery of the close connection between physiological, emotional, and intellectual processes. Experientially, for the first time I fully experienced my body as a vital part of my being, not as a mere appendage.

Open to other approaches to the resolution of deep-seated psychological trauma, he encouraged me in my desire to utilize hypnosis. Thus, as I continued my body work, I also began work with a talented and innovative hypnotherapist. Additional memories of my childhood victimization emerged from my subconscious through her facilitation, with an attendant release of repressed painful emotion.

Ten years after I began my psychotherapeutic journey I felt that I had achieved my primary goal of emotional stabilization, and gradually I began to turn my attention from grappling with my own internal processes toward increasingly greater engagement with the world, particularly through my professional activities. During the past few years, I have experienced moments of darkness, when the apparent progress I had made appeared to be a total illusion. However, these periods have been brief and no longer am I subject to immobilization by disabling depression or anxiety.

In the course of my therapy, I have worked on a number of significant issues unrelated to my sexual victimization but which contributed substantially to my neurotic condition. However, there is no doubt that the effects of my sexual degradation contributed the most to the debilitating emotional state in which I found myself as I struggled to meet the demands of adulthood. Only when I was able to resolve this dilemma was I able to achieve the capacity to function fully as an adult.

Although I have traced the most decisive steps along my journey in this chapter, there were a number of other psychological theories, systems, and techniques which, absorbed either through work with other therapists or through my independent study and experimentation, assisted me greatly. These include such therapeutic modalities as primal, bio-energetic, reality, and behaviorist and the writings of such prominent psychologists as Leon Janov, Alexander Lowen, and William Glasser. Sydney Jourard's views on the importance of self-disclosure to the process of growth toward authentic personhood has also influenced me greatly.

My experience of childhood victimization has vividly demonstrated for me the extraordinarily powerful effect that childhood experience has on an individual's ability to progress as an adult. At this point, my future is alive with possibilities that in the past appeared to be futile dreams. Whatever else I may do with the remainder of my life, however, my experience has led me to a commitment to do all in my power to improve the quality of childhood for children of the present and the future and to assist those persons who have been damaged by childhood trauma to once again achieve wholeness.

Index

Abdominal pain as sign of sexual abuse, 6, 7, 277
Abel, G. G., 313, 328, 365, 367, 368, 369, 375
Abstract thinking in children, 180–181, 183
Acknowledgment of abuse
 in retrospective incest therapy, 287–288
 see also Responsibility assumption
Acquaintances as abusers, 28–29, 30, 32, 76
Acting out behavior as effect of child sexual abuse, 8–9, 78, 79, 96, 253
Adams-Tucker, C., 8, 200
Adjustment Disorder of Childhood diagnosis, 194
Adolescence, sexual abuse during
 anatomically correct dolls, use of, 183
 emotional distress and psychopathology, 99–101
 family variables, 97–99
 impact of, 96, 254, 255, 335
 legal involvement of victims, 67, 68, 103, 104, 105
 reactions to disclosure, 187–188
 self-concept, 102
 sibling incest, 344–346
 signs and symptoms of, 7–8, 254
 substance abuse and, correlation between, xiv–xv, 93–105
 see also Delinquency as effect of sexual abuse
Adolescent sexual abusers, impact of, 62
Adult abusers, impact of relationship with, 61–62
 see also Male sexual abusers
"Aetiology of Hysteria, The" (Freud), 39
Age of abused children
 impact of, 61, 81, 84, 96, 166
 patterns in, 4
 see also Adolescence, sexual abuse during; Children
Age of abuser
 impact of, 61, 81
 in sibling incest, 344

Age of consent, child sexual abuse prevalence and, 23
Aggressive behavior as effect of child sexual abuse, 66, 67, 68, 77, 78, 79, 203, 204, 253, 258, 263, 303
Alberta Psychological Resources, 320–322, 356
Alcohol abuse
 among adolescent incest victims, 99, 100
 as effect of child sexual abuse, 57, 58, 59, 65, 66, 75, 95, 282, 303
 in incestuous families, 312, 315
 among sexual abusers, 95, 98, 170, 223–224, 274, 312, 333, 337, 340–341, 372
Alexander, J. F., 357
Alexander, P., 332
Amidon, H. T., 123
Amnesia, selective, in sexual abuse, 277, 280, 281
Anatomically correct dolls, use of, xii, xvi, 113–114, 115, 157, 158–159, 164, 172, 176, 182–185, 186–187, 195, 212
Anderson, C., 355
Anger of interviewer
 against nonperpetrator parent, 160
 against perpetrator, 162, 267
Anger-management techniques in retrospective incest therapy, 300
Anger of nonoffending mother, 320–321, 377
Anger of victim
 against abuser, 65, 67, 77, 81, 187, 251, 255, 256, 259, 262–263, 277, 292, 293, 335, 336, 339
 against men, 256; *see also* against abuser, *above*
 against nonoffending mother, xviii, 168, 172–173, 256, 339, 377
 play therapy and, 255, 256
 retrospective incest therapy and, xvii, 279, 293
 against self, 293; *see also* Guilt feelings of victim
 against women, 256; *see also* against nonoffending mother, *above*
Anorexia, *see* Eating disorders

Anxiety
in adolescent substance abuse/incest
victims, 9, 99–101
as sign of child sexual abuse, 6–9,
10, 58, 65, 67, 78, 95, 99, 100,
198–199, 204–208, 266, 277
APA Ethics Code and Standards for Providers of Psychological Services,
177
Armstrong, L., 271
Art therapy for victims, 251
Assertiveness training
for children, 172, 255, 336, 359–360,
388–389, 397, 399
for Hispanic families, 395, 396, 397
for nonperpetrator mothers, 319–320,
359–360
Assessment instruments, xii
traumagenic dynamics and development of, 68
see also Anatomically correct dolls;
Interview; Theme Creation Test
for Youths; Treatment; Videotaping; Chapters 7–12
Aunts as sexual abusers, 33
Austern, D., 140
Authoritarian sexual abuser, 64, 65,
67
Authority figures as abusers, 28, 32,
199, 259
"Autobiographical Study, An" (Freud),
41, 45–46
Axline, V., 250, 263

Babysitters as abusers, 76
Bagley, C., 56, 58, 59, 60, 76
Bander, K. W., 313
Bard, L., 59
Battered woman syndrome, xiii, 10,
184, 189, 193–194, 312, 316–317,
318, 346
see also Spouse abuse
Becker, J. V., 75, 199, 357
Behavioral approaches in retrospective
incest therapy, 299
see also Desensitization to abuse,
play therapy and; Guided imagery; Male sexual abusers,
counterconditioning therapies
for
Behavioral change in retrospective incest therapy, 289

Behavioral manifestations
of betrayal, 67
of child sexual abuse and incest, 146,
165–166, 181–182, 200–201, 278–
281
of powerlessness, 67
of traumatic sexualization, 66
Behavioral treatment model, 350–363
and community response, 350–355
family recordkeeping and goal setting, 362
monitoring father's behavior, 360–
361
power redistribution in family, 350
principles, 356–357
process of case, 357–360
sleep-disturbance intervention, 361
therapist orientation, 355–356
Bellak, L., 201
Belle, D., 390
Bender, L., 93, 96, 198, 283
Benjamin, A., 159
Benward, J., 75, 273
Berliner, L., 93, 96, 110, 126, 127, 130,
183
Bernard, J., 318
Berry, G. W., 347
Betrayal dynamic in sexual abuse, xiv,
62, 63–64, 65, 66, 67, 172, 193–
194, 250, 255–256, 272, 280, 335,
336
play therapy and, 255–256
Bibliotherapy in retrospective incest
therapy, 299–300
Blain, G. H., 198, 200
Blame attribution for victimization,
xviii, 15–16, 81, 90, 168, 171, 261,
294, 334, 350, 358, 376
see also Responsibility assumption
Bloom, B. L., 13
Boerma, L., 125
Bootzin, R. R., 361
Borderline Personality Disorder, 11, 57,
282
Borderline-type symptoms of incest,
279
Brady, K., 8
Brainwashing of children, 191–192
Brant, R. S. T., 200
Brickman, J., 279, 283, 287
Briere, J., 9–10, 11, 12, 55, 57, 58, 75,
271, 275, 277, 281, 282

Broadhurst, D., 199
Brother as sexual abuser, 27, 30
    see also Sibling incest
Browne, A., 6, 9, 10, 200, 271, 274, 275–276
Bug-in-the-ear devices, 186
Bulkley, J., 126, 129
Burden of proof, 137–138
    see also Legal issues in child sexual abuse
Burgess, A. W., 200
Butler, S., 272, 286, 290

Calgary Society for the Prevention of Child Sexual Abuse, 350–363
Cantwell, H., 5, 141–142
Caplan, G., 387
Carmen, E. H., 49
Carroll, C. A., 163
Carroll, J., 75
Catharsis in retrospective incest therapy, 288
Centre for Environmental Studies Depression Scale (CES-D), 56, 59
Chaney, S., 124
Child abuse, extension of laws to sexual abuse, 198–199
Child Abuse, Prevention, and Treatment Act of 1974, 23, 198; *see also* Child protection legislation
Child Behavior Profile (NIMH study), 75, 76–79, 78 (tab.), 79 (tab.), 80, 86–87
Child-centered interview techniques, 179–180
Child protection legislation, xii, 73–74, 130, 198–199, 273, 387, 399
Child protective agencies, x, xv–xvi, xvii
    adequacy of services, 152–153
    assessment of credibility, 164–166
    assessment of danger, 166–167
    assessment of mother/child relationship, 168–169
    incest investigation and treatment planning by, 152–173
    interviewing the child, 156–160, 221
    interviewing the nonperpetrator spouse, 160–162
    interviewing the perpetrator, 162–164
    restoring the mother/child relationship, 172–173

training of personnel, 153, 216
treatment planning and implementation, 169–172
Child Safety Partnership, xix
Child sexual abuse accommodation syndrome, 281
Child sexual abuse, definition of, 3, 19, 199–200, 394
Child Sexual Abuse: Needs, Resources and Planning Project report, 351
Childhood history in victim assessment, 176
    see also Family history
Children
    ability to count, 180–182
    assertiveness training for, 172, 255, 336, 359–360, 388–389, 397, 399
    color recognition by, 180–181
    concrete/abstract thinking in, 180–181, 183
    developmental assessment, 176
    discussing abusers with, 188
    interviewing, *see* Interview of victim
    language abilities of, 180–183
    not testifying in court, 143–149
    primary prevention programs for, 388–398
    reporting abuse of, *see* Reporting child sexual abuse
    role reversal among abused, 13–14, 168, 172, 276, 277, 292, 310–311, 314, 334, 342–343
    seductive behavior in, 171, 182, 190, 199, 252, 283
    sense of time among, 117–118, 123, 180–182
    separating from abuser, xiv, 137, 166–167, 170–172, 264–266, 341–344, 357
    sleep-disturbance intervention, 361
    suggestibility of, 110, 114, 115, 116–117, 118, 119–120, 127, 183–184, 185
    visitation with parent/abuser, 167, 258, 264–266, 379–381
    see also Dynamics, of incestuous family
Children as witnesses, xii, xv, 109–131
    assessment of credibility, xv, 127, 140–142, 164–166, 190–192, 195

Children as witnesses (*continued*)
  competence examinations of, 125–
    126, 140–141, 182
  courtroom cross-examination of, 127,
    129, 149, 160, 305; *see also* Con-
    frontation
  courtroom testimony by, xv, 126–128,
    172
  eyewitness report accuracy by, 112–
    115
  eyewitness report inaccuracy by,
    116–118
  interviewing, xvi, 112–119, 122–123,
    125–129, 156–160, 221; *see also*
    Interview of victim
  memory of, xv, 109–110, 111–119;
    see also Memory in children
  suggestibility of, 110, 114, 115, 116–
    117, 118, 119–120, 127, 183–184,
    185
Children's Apperception Test, 201
"Children's courtrooms," 129
Children's Defense Fund, 152
Christiansen, J., 200
Chronic traumatic neurosis as long-
  term effect of sexual abuse, 11
Civil actions on child sexual abuse,
  109, 137–138, 169–170, 177
  see also Neglect and dependency
    cases
Clinical assessment
  of abuser, 231–233, 369–371
  and traumagenic dynamics, 68–69
  of victim, 6–7, 175–189; *see also*
    Physical manifestations of sexual
    abuse
Closed-circuit TV in court, 128
Cognitive approaches in retrospective
  incest therapy, 298
Cognitive restructuring
  in retrospective incest therapy, 288–
    289
  techniques for abuser, 374–375
Cohen, R. L., 116
Colao, F., 389
Collusion in child sexual abuse, xi–xii,
  160–161, 189, 309–311, 312, 314–
  315
Color recognition by children, 180–181
Colorado prosecution of child sexual
  abuse, 137–149
Common law, 126

Community-based reintegration of offender, xviii–xix, 373–381
Community involvement, need for,
  xi
Competence development in treatment,
  251, 388; *see also* Assertiveness
  training
Competence examinations of children,
  125–126, 140–141, 182
Concentration problems as effect of
  child sexual abuse, 78, 79
Concrete thinking in children, 180–181,
  183
Confidentiality in sexual abuse cases,
  124–125, 154, 177, 184, 194, 266,
  267, 305, 368
Confrontation
  and assertiveness training, 255
  in court, 139–140, 141, 172
  in retrospective incest therapy, 304
Consciousness-raising group therapy,
  302
Constantine, L., 55
Conte, J., 11, 12, 73, 75, 90, 128, 200,
  249, 368, 369
Conversion reactions in victims, 279
Coopersmith Self-Esteem Inventory,
  56
Coping mechanisms in incest, 279–281
Coping skills, play therapy and, 251,
  252
Coppersmith Self-Esteem Inventory,
  56
Cormier, B. M., 310
Cornell Medical Index, 218, 229, 230
Corroborative evidence of sexual
  abuse, xii, 120–121, 123, 139, 141–
  142, 144–146, 166, 189, 190
Counterconditioning therapies for abus-
  er, 374–375
Countertransference in retrospective in-
  cest therapy, 296–297
Court proceedings, children as wit-
  nesses, 109–131
  see also Children as witnesses
Courtois, C. C., 10, 57, 58, 61, 271, 274,
  278, 281
Courtroom testimony by children, xv,
  126–128, 172
Cousins as sexual abusers, 27, 30
Covert sensitization techniques for
  abuser, 374, 375

Credibility of victim, assessment of, xv, 127, 140–142, 164–166, 190–192, 195
   and Freudian legacy, 4–6
   see also Competence *and entries under* False
Criminal cases, 137–149, 154, 169–170, 353
   admissability issues, 138–143
   burden of proof, 137–138
   children as witnesses in, 109–131; *see also* Children as witnesses
   courtroom testimony by children, xv, 126–128, 172
   trauma to children in court, 127–128
Criminal involvement, *see* Legal involvement
Criminal record of sexual offender, 218, 219–221, 226–227, 366, 367
Crisis intervention in family systems approach, 338–339
Cross-examination of victim in court, 127, 129, 149, 186, 305
   see also Confrontation
Custody disputes, 109, 120–122, 191, 192

Danger assessment
   by child protective agencies, 166–167
   in community treatment for offender, 367–368
   in prevention programs, 392–393
   of revictimization by victims, 265
Deferred prosecution agreements, 163, 169–170, 227, 369
Deffenbacher, K. H., 111, 112, 114
Delinquency as effect of sexual abuse, 67, 68, 103, 104, 105
   see also Legal involvement
Demographic differences in child sexual abuse samples, 80, 95
Denial of sexual abuse
   by abuser, 73, 83, 84, 154, 162, 192, 217–219, 221, 223, 228, 231, 233, 272, 276, 296, 368, 373, 374
   by victim, 254, 271, 276, 280, 284, 287–288, 296
   see also Amnesia; Dissociation; Retrospective incest therapy

Dent, H. R., 118, 119, 122
Dependency
   in incestuous family, 334–335; *see also* Dynamics, of incestuous family
   in therapy, 293
Depo-Provara, 229
Depression
   in adolescent substance abuse/incest victims, 99–101
   in nonoffending mothers, 312, 315, 316, 318
   in sexual abuser, 333
   as sign of sexual abuse, 8, 10, 11, 57, 58, 59, 67, 68, 75, 77, 79, 81, 95, 96, 97, 100, 166, 203–208, 282, 335
Derealization as effect of sexual abuse, 10; *see also* Dissociation
Desensitization to abuse, play therapy and, 253; *see also* Behavioral approaches in retrospective incest therapy
deYoung, M., 8, 9, 10, 57, 58, 75, 356
Disclosure, *see* Reporting child sexual abuse
Disempowerment dynamic in sexual abuse, 64, 65, 67
   see also Powerlessness dynamic in sexual abuse
Disguised presentation of incest, 277–278
Dissociation as effect of sexual abuse, 10, 99, 105, 253, 254, 276, 285, 296, 303
Divorce, impact of, 99
D & N cases, *see* Neglect and dependency cases
Dohrenwend, B. P., 13
Dohrenwend, B. S., 13
Dolls, *see* Anatomically correct dolls
Drug abuse
   among adolescent incest victims, xiv–xv, 93–105
   as effect of child sexual abuse, 10, 57, 58, 59, 65, 72, 75, 77, 95, 97, 277, 303
   by sexual offenders, 95, 98, 170, 223–224, 333, 337, 356, 372
DSM-III, 11, 193–194, 281
Duncan, E. M., 116

Duration of sexual abuse, impact of, 60, 61, 76, 81, 90, 96, 157, 164, 166, 180, 202
Dynamics
    of incestuous family, 13–15, 83–85, 98–99, 153–155, 189–190, 225–226, 272–275, 290–297, 309–318, 326–328, 332–336, 355–356; *see also* Family systems approach
    of powerlessness, xiv, 61, 62, 64, 65, 67, 193–194, 254, 279, 295–296, 390, 411–415
    of stigmatization, xiv, 57, 64, 65, 66, 193–194, 261, 272, 275–276, 280, 284, 290–291
    traumagenic, *see* Traumagenic dynamics
    of traumatic sexualization, xiii–xiv, 62–63, 65, 66, 193–194

Easterbrook, J. A., 114
Eating disorders as effect of sexual abuse, 58–59, 77, 101, 178, 253, 277, 282
Economic costs of child sexual abuse, x–xi
Education
    in behavioral treatment model, 353
    level of abuser, 222–223, 366–367
    in primary prevention programs, 289, 387–398
    in retrospective incest therapy, 289, 299
Educational Apperceptive Test, 201
Effects of sexual abuse on child, 72–91, 199, 200, 270
    differential effects, 80–85, 88–90, 274
    immediate, 6–9, 200, 274
    impact of different types of abuse, 60–62
    long-term, 9–11, 55–69, 200, 270–271, 274, 326–327, 410–427; *see also* Long-term impact; Retrospective incest therapy
    minimization of, 12–14, 55–56, 73–74, 89–90, 270–272, 283, 296; *see also* Minimization
Emotional distancing, play therapy and, 254
Emotional pseudoindependence, play therapy and, 253
Employment history of abuser, 222–223

Epilepsy, psychogenic, as effect of sexual abuse, 278–279
Erikson, E. H., 290
Ethnic minority cultures
    Hispanic child sexual abuse, 390–398
    primary prevention programs and, 389–390
Expert testimony in child sexual abuse cases, xv, 129–130, 137, 138, 139, 141–149
    jargon in, 149
    pretrial preparation, 148–149
Expressive therapies in retrospective incest therapy, 299
Extended family subsystem assessment, 332
Extrafamilial child sexual abuse
    definition of, 22–23
    perpetrators of, 28
    prevalence of, 24–26, 28
    reporting to police, 31, 33
    seriousness of, 31, 32 (tab.)
Eyewitness report by children
    accuracy, 112–115
    identification, 118–119
    inaccuracy, 116–118

Fabrication by children, 116, 142
Face recognition ability of children, 118–119, 123
False accusations/reports, 4–6, 110, 112, 116, 123, 154, 191–192
    see also Credibility of victim, assessment of
False identifications by children, 118–119, 191–192, 193
False retractions, 5–6, 191, 192
Family, play therapy and, 263–267
Family history
    of adolescent substance abuse/incest victims, 97–99
    closed system in incestuous families, 335
    dynamics of incest, 13–15, 153–155, 189–190, 225–226, 273–275, 285, 309–318, 326–328, 332–336
    enmeshment pattern in incestuous families, 334–335, 337, 355–356
    of nonperpetrator spouse, 309–318
    pregnancy frequency, 312, 316
    in retrospective incest therapy, 300
    of sexual offender, 218, 225–226

size of incestuous families, 312, 316
of victim, assessing, 189–190
violence, xiii, 3, 10, 184, 189, 193–
194, 225, 312–313, 315, 316–317,
318, 333, 337, 346
see also Marital relations
Family pathology, *see* Family history
Family systems approach, xviii, 326–348
to abuser, 328, 329, 331, 333, 336–
337, 338, 340–341, 342, 347
characteristics of incestuous family,
332–336; *see also* Dynamics
conceptual framework, 329–332
crisis intervention, 337–338
family subsystems assessment, 331–
332
father–son incest, 347
vs. individual treatment, 328–329
mother–son incest, 346–347
multiply incestuous families, 348
sibling incest, 344–346
single-parent families, 341–344
special treatment considerations,
341–348
treatment considerations and interventions, 336–338
treatment process, 338–341
Family therapy
for community-setting treatment,
376–378
for incest, 283, 340; *see also* Family
systems approach
for nonoffending mother, 376–377
Fantasies vs. reality differentiation in
sexually abused children, 203–207
Fathers
as abusers, *see* Incest; Male sexual
abusers
seduction theory, 5
Father–son incest, family systems
approach to, 347
Fear
as effect of child sexual abuse, 58,
61, 65, 77, 78, 79, 83, 159–160,
165, 166, 208, 253, 265
play therapy and, 253
as sign of sexual abuse, 6, 7, 198–
199
Federal Rules of Evidence, 126, 141,
145, 146
Feelings, expression of, in retrospective
incest therapy, 288

Female child victims, *see* Children
Female sexual abusers
impact of experience with, 61–62
mother–son incest, 346–347
prevalence of, 27, 28, 30, 32, 33
Feminist perspective on sexual abuse,
355, 358
in play therapy, 252
in retrospective incest therapy, 283–
284
Ferenczi, S., 199
Ferracuti, F., 20
Finkelhor, D., 4, 22, 23, 33–35, 49, 55,
60, 61, 81, 96, 98, 110, 120, 199,
200, 274, 283, 317, 318, 319, 355,
359
Fisher, S., 48
Flashbacks as signs of sexual abuse, 57,
277, 280
Fliess, W., 38–39, 41, 42
Force in child sexual abuse, 60–61, 73,
81, 83, 84, 164, 166, 190, 199, 405–
412
Forensic issues, *see* Legal issues in
child sexual abuse
Forseth, L. B., 313
Forward, S., 289
Foster parenting for sexual abuse vic-
tims, 170–171
Frederickson, R. M., 312
Freeman-Longo, R., 226
Frenetic behavior as sign of sexual
abuse, 182
Freud, A., xiii, 43, 73, 249–250
Freud, S.
Oedipal theory, xiii, 42–49, 270, 283
psychoanalytic legacy of, 44–49
seduction theory, xiii, 4–6, 37–42, 73
Friedrich, W., 81
Fromuth, M. E., 56, 57, 60

Gagging/swallowing/respiratory distress
in victims, 279
Gagnon, J., 34
Gallagher, M. M., 201, 213
Gardner, R. A., 210, 213
Garfield, S. L., 250
Gelinas, D. J., 8, 11, 12, 13, 57, 277,
281, 282
General systems theory, 330–331
see also Family systems approach
Genuineness, lack of, in victims, 254

Gestalt exercises in retrospective incest
therapy, 298, 423–424
Giarretto, H., 96, 297, 319, 328, 355
Giovannoni, J., 390
Gold, E., 90
Gomez-Schwartz, B., 7–8, 86
Goodman, G. S., 109, 110, 112, 113,
114, 115, 116, 117, 118, 119, 120,
126, 127, 141
Goodwin, J., 5, 6, 59, 75, 97, 278, 312
Gorenstein, G. W., 118
Grandfather as sexual abuser, 27, 30
Greene, H., 127
Grieving in retrospective incest therapy, 288
Groth, N., 60, 219, 313, 316
Group treatment
for nonperpetrator spouse, 319–322
for offenders, 373–374, 378–379
in retrospective incest therapy, 302–
303
for victim, 171, 263–264
Guided imagery
in play therapy, 253
in retrospective incest therapy, 299
see also Behavioral approaches in
retrospective incest therapy
Guilt feelings of victim, 75, 90, 95, 165,
171, 172, 188, 190, 203–205, 208,
254, 276, 277, 282, 286, 290–292,
302, 335, 336, 342, 358
see also Traumagenic dynamics
Guthiel, T. G., 309

Handy, L. C., 313, 317, 336, 358
Harrer, M. N., 313
Headaches as sign of sexual abuse, 6, 7
Hearsay testimony, xv, 139, 143, 146–
147
exceptions to, 128, 146–147, 148–149
Helplessness feelings of victim, 88–89,
90, 97, 105, 199
see also Powerlessness dynamic in
sexual abuse
Hendricks, M. C., 263
Herman, J. L., 4, 7, 8, 9–10, 13, 14, 20,
57, 75, 93, 94, 96, 98, 120, 154,
160, 161, 167, 282, 283, 290, 303,
312, 314, 316, 317, 318, 389
Hispanic community, prevention of
child sexual abuse in, xix–xx, 390–
398

Hite, S., 22
Homosexual sexual abuse, xx, 4, 203,
260, 347, 370, 405–410, 415–416
Horowitz, M., 281
Hospitalization for victims, 298
Hostile feelings as sign of child sexual
abuse, 58, 95, 203–205; see also
Anger of victim
Humanistic psychology techniques in
retrospective incest therapy, 298–
299
Humphrey, H. H., III, 166
Hypnosis in retrospective incest ther-
apy, 299, 426
Hysterical neurosis theory (Freud), 38–
41
Hysterical seizures as effect of sexual
abuse, 278–279

Identification by children, 118–119, 157
see also entries under False
Impact of sexual abuse, see Effects of
sexual abuse on child
Incest
definition of, 3, 22–23, 33–34, 273
disguised presentation of, 277–278
dynamics of, 13–15, 83–85, 98–99,
153–155, 189–190, 225–226, 272–
275, 290–297, 309–318, 326–328,
332–336; see also Family history;
Family systems approach
economic cost of, x–xi
false accusations, 4–6; see also False
accusations/reports
father–daughter, see Male sexual
abusers
homosexual, see Father–son incest;
Homosexual sexual abuse
impact of, 60–62, 73–74
investigation and treatment planning
by child protective agencies,
152–173
minimization of impact of, see
Minimization
mother–son, 346–347
multiple in family, 348
peer, 274
perpetrators of, 26–27; see also Male
sexual abusers
prevalence of, xiii, 20, 24–27, 273–
274, 275; see also Prevalence of
child sexual abuse

reluctance to see as problem, 12–14,
73–74, 272; *see also* Denial;
Minimization
reporting, *see* Reporting child sexual
abuse
seriousness of, 29–31, 30 (tab.), 73–
74
sibling, 344–346
and substance abuse, among adolescent girls, 93–105
taboo on, 271, 275
trauma of, *see* Traumagenic dynamics
Incestuous fantasies (Freud), 5,
37–42
Incidence of child sexual abuse, xiii, 4,
20–35, 93, 110, 175
interview schedule, 23–24
methodology of research on, 21–24
reporting and, 4, 23, 110
Individual responses to sexual abuse,
80–85, 88–89, 274
mediating factors and, 13, 274
Individual therapy
for abuser, 374–376
for victim, 171–172
Individual treatment vs. family systems
approach, 328–329
Informal adjustment with male sexual
abusers, 163, 169–170, 227, 369
Information-giving in retrospective incest therapy, 289
Insight in retrospective incest therapy,
289
Intercourse
evidence of, 145, 164, 190, 199, 202;
see also Corroborative evidence;
Physical evidence
impact of, 60–62, 76, 81
Interdisciplinary approach to child sexual abuse, 216, 351–352
Interpersonal relationships, poor, as
effect of sexual abuse, 10–11, 57,
75, 95, 277
Interview
of nonperpetrator parent/spouse,
160–162, 188–189, 357–358, 369–
370
of perpetrator, 162–164, 192–193
in prevalence assessment of child
sexual abuse, 21, 23–24
Interview of victim, xvi, 111–119, 122–
123, 125–129, 156–160, 221

assessment procedures, 175–176,
178–189, 357–358, 391
baseline data, obtaining, 180–182
by child protective agencies, 156–160
clinical, 6–7, 175–189; *see also*
Physical manifestations of child
sexual abuse
concluding, 187–188
discussing perpetrator with child,
188
information needed from child, 156–
160
initial observations, 178
probing for details, 185–187
rapport and permission giving, 178–
180
witnesses to, 157
Intimidation in questioning children,
118
Intrafamilial child sexual abuse, *see* Incest
Investigation of incest
by child protective services, 152–169
see also Child protective services;
Legal issues in child sexual
abuse; Reporting child sexual
abuse
Isolation, breakdown of, in retrospective incest therapy, 288, 291, 302
Isolation feelings as signs of sexual
abuse, 57, 75, 255–256, 276, 290–
291

Jacobson, N. W., 357, 361
Jampole, L., 113
Janoff-Bulman, R., 90
Jones, P. S., 311
Julian, V., 311–312, 316, 317
Jungian analysis, 426
Jury trials, children and, 127, 130; *see
also under* Court; Legal issues in
child sexual abuse
Justice, B., 4, 7, 10, 328, 333
Juvenile courts, 353

Karpman, B., 49
Katan, 199
Kaufman, I., 95, 309–310
Kempe, R. S., 4, 6, 7
Kessler, M., 388
Kinsey, A. C., 22
Klein, M., 249

Kleinsmith, L. J., 122
Kline, D. F., 198, 200
Kline, P., 48
Kovitz, K., 351–352
Kris, E., 42–43

Landis, J. T., 34
Langsley, D. G., 347
Language abilities of children, 180–183
Leading questions to children, 116–117, 126–127, 138–139, 182, 185
see also Suggestibility of children
Lees, S., 277
Legal context for child witnesses, 119–130
Legal expenses in court cases, x
Legal involvement
    among adolescent incest victims, 103, 104, 105
    as effect of sexual abuse, 66, 72, 77
Legal issues in child sexual abuse, xv–xvi, xvii, 216, 355
    admissability issues, 138–143
    burden of proof, 137–138
    child not testifying, 143–149
    children as witnesses, *see* Children as witnesses
    corroborative evidence, xii, 120–121, 123, 139, 141–142, 144–146, 166, 189, 190
    criminal cases and neglect and dependency cases, 137–149, 177
    and retrospective incest therapy, 305
Legislation, child protection, xii, 23, 73–74, 198–199, 273, 387, 399
Lerman, H., 46, 47
Lewis, M., 199
Lipton, J., 122
Loftus, E. F., 111, 112, 122, 130
Long-term impact of child sexual abuse, xiii–xiv, 9–11, 55–69, 200, 274, 326–327, 356, 405–427
    acknowledgment of, 55–56, 410–427
    of different types of abuse, 60–62
    future research needs, 11–14
    mediating factors, 13–14, 80–85, 274
    societal implications of, 14–16
    traumagenic dynamics, xiii–xiv, 62–69, 193, 199, 252
    see also Effects of sexual abuse on child; Retrospective incest therapy

Longitudinal studies, need for, on effects of sexual abuse, 12
Louisville Behavior Checklist, 6–7
Luckianowicz, N., 311
Lustig, N., 309

MacFarlane, K., 116, 124, 183, 212, 250–251, 304
Machotka, P., 309
MAFERR Inventory of Feminine Values, 14
Maisch, H., 8
Make-A-Picture Story Test, 201, 210
Male domination
    in incestuous family dynamics, 13–15; *see also under* Power
    sexual abuse condoned by, xi, xii–xiii, 14–15, 154, 389
Male sexual abusers
    abused as children, 59, 226, 279, 366, 367
    age of, impact of, 61–62, 367
    alcohol/chemical dependency of, 95, 98, 170, 218, 223–224, 333, 337, 340–341, 372
    assessment in community setting, xviii, 365–372; *see also* Chapters 12 and 16
    assessment guidelines, xvi–xvii, xviii, 216–246
    clinical evaluation interview, 231–233, 369–371
    contracting with, in behavioral treatment, 358–359
    and costs of incest, xi
    counterconditioning therapies for, 374–375; *see also* Behavioral approaches in retrospective incest therapy
    criminal responsibility of, 222, 390
    criminal and sexual offense history of, 218, 219–221, 226–227, 366, 367
    denial and minimization by, 73, 83, 84, 154, 162, 192, 217–219, 221, 223, 228, 231, 233, 272, 276, 296, 368, 373, 374
    diary-keeping on abuses by, 224–225
    discussing with child, 188
    educational history of, 222–223, 366, 367
    employment history of, 222–223

in extrafamilial child sexual abuse, 28
family systems approach to, 328, 329, 331, 333, 336–337, 338, 340–341, 342, 347
group treatment for, 373–374, 378–379
habitual (recidivism), 217, 226–227, 370
impact of experiences with, 61–62, 81
incarceration for, 365, 370–371
incidence/prevalence of, 4, 24–34, 283; *see also* Incidence; Prevalence
individual therapy for, 374–376
informal adjustment with, 163, 169–170, 227, 369
inpatient placement for, 370–371
interviewing, 162–164, 192–193
interviewing victims of and witnesses to, 221
in intrafamilial child sexual abuse, 26–27; *see also* Incest
legal rights of, 163, 217
marital relations of, 218, 225–226, 274, 310, 315, 317–318, 331, 333–337, 341, 356, 366, 367
military history of, 222–223
monitoring behavior on reintegration with family, 360–361
no treatment with monitoring for, 371
nonprosecution of, tradition of, 222
Northwest Treatment Associates program for, 365–381
physiological assessment of, 231–233
P & M Rating Scale, 219, 236–246 (Appendix)
police and social reports on, 219–221
polygraph testing of, 192, 218, 233–234, 369
pornography use by, 220, 224–225, 366, 367, 372
preventing access to children, in treatment, 372
pseudoreform by, 153
psychological testing of, 217, 218, 228–231
reintegration into family, 167, 258, 264–266, 357, 376–381

responsibility acceptance by, 166, 195, 217–219, 228, 329, 331, 338, 340, 355, 358–359
separation from child, xiv, 137, 166–167, 170–172, 264–266, 341–344, 357
social and family history of, 218, 225–226
treatment of, *see* Treatment of perpetrator
treatment history of, 222
visitation with victim, 167, 258, 264–266, 379–381
see also Incest *and specific relationships, e.g.,* Stepfathers; Strangers
Male therapists in sexual abuse cases, 303–304
Male victims of sexual abuse, xx, 4, 203, 256, 260, 279, 346–347, 370, 405–410, 415–416
differential effects, 81
Manipulation as self-defense in victim, 261
Marijuana use by victims of sexual abuse, 100
see also Drug abuse
Marin, B. V., 112
Marital difficulties as sign of child sexual abuse, 57, 67
Marital rape, *see* Battered woman syndrome; Spouse abuse
Marital relations
in sexual abuse families, 218, 225–226, 274, 310–313, 315, 317–318, 328, 331, 333–337, 341, 356, 366, 367; *see also* Family history
traditionalist view of, 315–318, 391–393
Marquis, K. H., 115
Masson, J. M., 37, 38, 39–40, 41, 43, 109
Masters, W. H., 22
Masturbation as sign of sexual abuse, 6, 7, 253
Masturbatory satiation therapy, 374, 375
McArthur, D. S., 201
McGovern, K., 217, 218, 389
McIntyre, K., 309
Mediating factors and individual responses to sexual abuse, 13–14, 80–85, 274
see also Effects of sexual abuse

Medical examination for sexual abuse,
156, 176, 199, 200
see also Corroborative evidence;
Physical manifestations
Medical history in victim assessment,
176
Meiselman, K. C., 9–10, 13, 20, 57, 58,
61, 75, 95, 96, 310, 311, 312, 314
Memory in children, xv, 109–110, 111–
119
and competence examinations, 126,
140–141
laboratory studies of, 111, 112, 119–
120, 122
trauma and, 114–115, 119, 122, 185
Mental health effects of child sexual
abuse, *see* Effects of sexual abuse
on children
Metaphor, use of, in retrospective incest therapy, 299
Middlesex Hospital Health Survey, 56
Military history of abuser, 222–223
Miller, A., 49
Miller, J. B., 252
Minimization
of effects of abuse, 12–14, 55–56, 73–
74, 89–90, 270–272, 283, 296
by perpetrator, 73, 83, 84, 154, 162–
163, 192, 217–219, 221, 223, 228,
231, 233, 272, 276, 296, 368,
373, 374
by victim, *see* Denial of sexual abuse,
by victim
Minnesota Multiphasic Personality Inventory (MMPI), 12, 217–218, 229–
230, 312
Minority communities, child sexual
abuse in, 389–401
Minuchin, S., 328, 331
Modified Aversive Behavioral Rehearsal
(MABR), 374, 375–376
Monahan, J., 217
Mother, nonoffending, xi–xii, xviii, 309–
323, 331, 333
absence from home, 314–315
abused as child, 59, 312
anger at perpetrator, 167
assessment data, 311–315
assessment of relationship with child,
168–169
blaming, *see* collusion by; knowledge
of abuse, *below*

child's reporting abuse to, 120–122,
155–156, 314
clinical literature on, 309–311
collusion by, xi–xii, 160–161, 189,
309–311, 312, 314–315
and family systems approach, 336–
341
family therapy for, 376–377
fear of retaliation, 160–161
group treatment for, 319–322
at interview of victim, 179
interviewing, 160–162, 188–189, 357–
358, 369–370
investigation impediment by, 153–
154, 160–161
knowledge of abuse, 160–161, 309–
311
new conceptualization of, 315–322
role reversal with, 13–14, 168, 172,
276, 277, 292, 310–311, 314, 334,
342–343
self-help groups for, 319
status of marital relationship, 218,
225–226, 274, 310–313, 315,
317–318
status of women and, 316–317
strengths of, 161, 318–319
substance abuse by, 98, 312, 313,
356
survival skills of, 318–319
traditionalist view of family, 315–318,
391–393
see also Dynamics, of incestuous
family
Mother as sexual abuser, 27, 30, 346–
347; *see also* Female sexual abusers
Mother/child relationship
assessment by child protective agencies, 168–169
restoring, 172–173, 251, 321
Mother–daughter role reversal, 13–14,
168, 172, 227, 276, 292, 310–311,
314, 334, 342–343
Mother–son incest, family systems
approach to, 346–347
Mountain, H., 157, 161, 163–164, 252–
253
Mourning process in therapy, 286, 290,
293
Moustakas, C., 250
Mrazek, D. A., 200

Multidisciplinary approach to child sexual abuse, 216, 351–352
Multiple personality disorder, 57, 279
Multiply incestuous families, family systems approach to, 348
Murray, H. A., 201

Nadelson, C. C., 287
National Center on Child Abuse and Neglect, 20, 23
National Committee for Prevention of Child Abuse, 152–153
National Incidence Study, 20
National Institute of Justice, 139, 139–140, 176
National Institute of Mental Health (NIMH) study (1986) on effects of child sexual abuse, 75–91
Neglect and dependency (D & N) cases, 109, 137–149, 169
  admissability issues, 138–143
  burden of proof, 138
Nightmares as sign of sexual abuse, 6, 7, 67, 68, 75, 77, 277, 281
Northwest Treatment Associates, Seattle, program, xix, 365–381
  client characteristics, 366, 367 (tab.)
  evaluation of clients, 367–372
  family therapy, 376–377
  group therapy, 373–374
  individual therapy, 374–376
  reentry of offender into family, 378–381
  treatment, 373–381

Obsessive-compulsive behavior, play ritual vs., 260
O'Connell, B. G., 117
Oedipal theory (Freud), xiii, 42–49, 270, 283
Olson, M., xix, 389
One-way mirrors, use of, 177–178
Order of events, children's understanding of, 117–118, 123
Oregon v. Campbell, 147

Parental subsystem assessment, 331, 341; *see also* Family systems approach
Parenting classes for parents of victims, 264
Parents United, 319; *see also* Giaretto

Parker, J., 129
Pascoe, D., 6
Passivity as effect of sexual abuse, 10, 15, 188, 277
Patriarchal system and child sexual abuse, xi, xii–xiii, 14–15, 154, 389
Peer incest, 274
Penile plethysmography, 217, 218, 231–233, 369
People v. Ashley, 141–142
People v. Koon, 143
People v. Vollentine, 142
Perineal bruises as sign of sexual abuse, 6, 7
Peripheral detail memory of children, 117–118
Perpetrator, *see* Male sexual abusers
Personality disorders in pedophiles, 222
Peters, J. J., 5, 7, 271
Peters, S. D., 56, 58, 59
Pharyngeal infections as sign of sexual abuse, 6, 7
Philippus, M. J., 147
Phobias as effect of sexual abuse, 75, 77, 95
Physical abuse correlated with sexual abuse, 6, 7, 198, 225
Physical manifestations of child sexual abuse, xii, 120–121, 165–166, 190, 199–201, 255, 279
  see also Corroborative evidence
Physiological assessment of abuser, 231–233
Piaget, J., 250
Play rituals, children's repetitive, 260–262
Play therapy for victims, xvii, 249–268
  anger toward men, 256
  anger toward women, 256
  confrontation with anger, 255
  development of, 249–251
  emotional distancing and lack of genuineness, 254
  emotional pseudo-independence, 253
  fear and lack of trust, 253
  issues, 252–256
  lack of assertiveness, 255
  lack of resiliency and vulnerability, 255
  mastery and desensitization to abuse, 253

Play therapy for victims (*continued*)
    nonfamily offenders, 266
    philosophy and goals of, 251–256
    precociousness and seductiveness,
        253–254
    process of, 256–262
    protection of self and others, 254
    role of family, 263–267
    role of spirituality, 262–263
    sense of betrayal, 255–256
    sense of specialness, 255–256
    shame and self-blame, 254–255
    therapist qualities, 266–267
    understanding children's repetitive
        play rituals, 260–262
    visitation with offending incest par-
        ent, 264–266
*P & M Rating Scale: Risk Assessment for
    Sexual Abusers of Children,* 219,
    234, 236–246 (Appendix)
Police
    at interview of perpetrator, 162–163
    at interview of victim, 155–156, 157
    reporting abuse to, 31, 33, 122–125,
        155–156, 355, 357
    training in abuse cases, 355
Police record of sexual offender, 218,
    219–221, 226–227, 366, 367
Polygraph testing
    of abuser, 192, 218, 233–234, 369
    of victim, 123
Pondy, L. R., 332
Pornography, use of, by sexual offend-
    ers, 220, 224–225, 366, 367, 372
Post-Sexual Abuse Syndrome, 10–11,
    281, 282
Posttraumatic stress disorder (PTSD),
    79, 178, 194, 281–282
Powders, M., 115, 116
Power abuse in sexual abuse, xii, 265;
    see also Powerlessness dynamic
Power balance in incestuous family,
    316–318
Power redistribution in families, 359,
    361
Powerlessness dynamic in sexual abuse,
    xiv, 61, 62, 64, 65, 67, 193–194,
    254, 279, 295–296, 390, 411–415
Precocious sex play as sign of sexual
    abuse, 6, 7, 66, 165
Precociousness, play therapy and, 253–
    254

Pregnancy as sign of sexual abuse, 8,
    14, 95, 200
Preschool children, signs and symp-
    toms of abuse in, 6–7
Presenting concerns of incest, 275–277
Prevalence of child sexual abuse, xiii,
    4, 20, 24–26, 93, 110, 175, 273–
    274, 275
    interview process, 21, 23–24
    see also Incidence of child sexual
        abuse
Prevention programs, xix, 15–16, 387–
    401
    see also Primary prevention pro-
        grams
Preventive mental health concepts,
    387–390
Price, D. W. W., 113
Primary prevention programs, xix, 388–
    389
    ethnic minority cultures and, 389–
        390
    in Hispanic community, xix–xx, 390–
        398
    issues raised about, 398–400
Privileged communication, *see* Con-
    fidentiality
Promiscuity, *see* Sexual promiscuity as
    sign of sexual abuse
Prostitution as effect of sexual abuse,
    7–8, 57, 58, 66, 72, 77
Pseudo-independence, emotional, play
    therapy and, 253
Psychiatric intervention for victims, 298
Psychoanalytic approaches in retrospec-
    tive incest therapy, 298
Psychoanalytic theory
    and child sexual abuse, xiii, 37–42,
        249–250
    see also Freud
Psychodrama techniques in retrospec-
    tive incest therapy, 298
Psychological evidence of abuse, xii,
    93, 199–200
    see also Effects of sexual abuse on
        child
Psychological impact
    of powerlessness, 67
    of sexual abuse, *see* Effects of sexual
        abuse on child
    of stigmatization, 66; *see also*
        Stigmatization dynamic

of traumatic sexualization, 66; *see also* Traumatic sexualization
Psychological testing
of abuser, 228–231
of victim, 187
Psychotic pedophiles, 222
Public interest in child sexual abuse, 72–75
Pulaski, D. K., 250

Questioning of child witnesses, 112–119, 125–129
see also under Court *and* Interview of victim

Rape trauma syndrome, 193–194
Rapport establishment in interviewing victim, 178–180
Rascovsky, M., 199
Reality vs. fantasy differentiation in sexually abused children, 203–207
Regressive behavior as sign of sexual abuse, 6, 7, 77, 165, 181, 207, 253
Reintegration of abuser into family, 167, 258, 264–266, 357, 376–381
Relationship between offender and victim, degree of, impact of, 60–61, 76, 82–83, 84, 85
Remarriage, impact of, 98–99
Renvoize, J., 8
Reparenting in therapy, 286
Reporting child sexual abuse, xv–xvi, 23, 73, 155–156, 194–195, 387
by child to parent, 120–122, 155–156, 314
to child service agencies, 152–153, 155–156
delays in, 143–144
impact of, 61, 73, 83, 84
and impact of experience, 61
and incidence statistics, 4, 23, 110
medical examination, 156
to police, 31, 33, 122–125, 155–156, 355, 357
and retrospective incest therapy, 304–305
Reposa, R. E., 317
Repression, *see* Denial
Res gestae exceptions, 128–129, 143–144
Research needs on effects of sexual abuse, 11–14, 87–88

Resiliency, lack of, play therapy and, 255
Resistance to sexual abuse, impact of, 83–84, 88–89
Responsibility assumption
in behavioral treatment model, 350, 358–359
in retrospective incest therapy, 288
by sexual abuser, 166, 195, 217–219, 228, 329, 331, 338, 340, 355, 358–359
by victim, xviii, 15–16, 81, 90, 168, 171, 261, 294, 334, 336
Retractions by victim, 5–6, 191
Retrospective incest therapy for men, xx, 405–427
Retrospective incest therapy for women, xiii, xvii–xviii, 270–306
acknowledgment of abuse, 287
anger-management techniques, 300
behavioral approaches, 299
bibliotherapy, 299–300
borderline-type symptoms, 279
catharsis and grieving, 288
cognitive approaches, 298
cognitive restructuring of faulty beliefs, 288–289
complexity of incest, 273–275
control/power issues, 295–296
countertransference reactions, 296–297
defenses, 296
diagnosis, 281–282
disclosure and confrontation, 304
disguised presentation, 277–278
dynamics of incest and, 290–297
education and information-giving, 289
expression of feelings, 288
expressive therapies, 299
feelings about self and relations with others, 278
Gestalt exercises, 298
group treatment, 302–303
guided imagery, 299
humanistic psychology techniques, 298–299
hypnosis, 299
individual and family history, 300
insight and behavioral change, 289
involvement and treatment of family members, 300

Retrospective incest therapy for women
(*continued*)
isolation feelings, 288
legal initiatives, 305
metaphor use, 299
personality and trauma-specific symptoms, 278–279
philosophical underpinnings of therapy, 283–284
physical contact, 301–302
premature termination, 294–295
presenting concerns, 275–277
psychoanalytical approaches, 298
psychodrama techniques, 298
public disclosure and advocacy, 302
reporting mandate, 305
responsibility and complicity issues, 288
self-help groups, 301
self-mutilation management, 301
self-nurturing exercises, 300–301
separation and individuation, 289
sex therapy techniques, 299
social learning formulations, 298
strategies and techniques, 297–302
support network building, 301
survivors as neglected population, 271–272
symptoms as coping mechanisms, 279–281
therapeutic alliance, 287
therapist gender, 303–304
therapy process and goals, 285–289
therapy stance and assumptions, 284–285
transactional analysis theory, 298
treatment, 283–289
Revictimization in sexual abuse, 8–9, 10, 57–58, 68, 96, 97, 187, 276, 277
Revitch, F., 199
Rewarding
child in interview, 187
of victim by abuser, impact of, 63, 66, 83, 84
Ritualistic behavior
and play therapy, 258, 260–262
as sign of sexual abuse, 77, 257–258
Roberts Apperception Test for Children, 201
Roberts, C. A., 388
Roberts, R., 112

Role reversal in sexual abuse, 13–14, 168, 172, 276, 277, 292, 310–311, 314, 334, 342–343
Rorschach test, 218, 230
Rosenfeld, A. A., 200, 273, 275
Rosenthal, R., 44
Rosewater, L. B., 47, 316
Rotter Incomplete Sentence Blank, 218, 230–231
Roybal, L., 8
Rules of evidence, 126, 141, 145, 146
Running away as sign of sexual abuse, 6–8, 14, 335
Runyan, D. K., 127
Rush, F., 43, 109
Russell, D. E. H., 4, 56, 57, 60, 61, 81, 98, 110, 121, 170, 274, 357

Sadism, child sexual abuse and, 405–409, 415
see also Force in child sexual abuse
SAFE, xix
Salem witch trials, 110
Sanders, G. S., 118
Saxe, L., 123
Schneidman, E. S., 201, 210
School intervention for victims, 257
School problems as sign of sexual abuse, 67, 68, 75, 165, 207
School-age children, signs and symptoms of sexual abuse, 7
see also Children
Schultz, L. G., 199
Sedative use by victims of sexual abuse, 100
Sedney, M. S., 57, 58
Seduction theory (Freud), xiii, 4–6, 37–42, 73, 283
repudiation of, 40–43
Seductive behavior in children, 171, 182, 190, 199, 252, 283
play therapy and, 253–254
Seidner, A., 56, 68, 81
Self-blame
play therapy and, 254–255, 261
see also Blame attribution for victimization; Guilt feelings of victim
Self-destructive behavior as sign of sexual abuse, 57, 75, 77, 165, 277, 280, 286, 291
Self-esteem/concept, poor
of nonoffending mothers, 312, 313, 315, 316, 318, 343

of sexual abuser, 333
as sign of child sexual abuse, xiv, 10, 11, 57, 58, 64, 65, 77, 78, 79, 95, 102, 276, 277, 282, 286, 288–289, 290–291, 294
Self-help groups, xix, 293, 319, 353
in retrospective incest therapy, 299, 301
Self-image of victim
play therapy to restore, 252
stigmatization, xv, 14, 57, 64, 65, 66, 95, 193–194, 261, 272, 275–276
see also Self-esteem/concept
Self-mastery, development of, in play therapy, 251, 253, 258
Self-mutilation among incest victims, 58, 66, 280, 282, 292–293
management of, in retrospective incest therapy, 301
Self-nurturing exercises in retrospective incest therapy, 300–301
Self-protection
play therapy and, 254
see also Danger assessment
Seligman, M. E. P., 298
Separation of abuser and victim, xiv, 137, 166–167, 170–172, 264–266, 341–344, 357
Separation and individuation in retrospective incest therapy, 289
Separations (marital), impact of, 99
Sex Offender Treatment Program, Oregon State Hospital, 226
Sex-role stereotypes, incest and, 283, 315–318, 391–393
Sex therapy
for abusers, xviii–xix, 373–381
in retrospective incest therapy, 299
Sexual abuse
context of, 72–75
definition of, 3, 19, 56, 199–200
impact of different types of, 60–62, 83
Sexual abusers, see Male sexual abusers
Sexual Assault Center, Harborview Medical Center, Seattle, 75–76
Sexual dysfunction
in incestuous family, 218, 225–226, 274, 310–314, 315, 317–318, 331, 333–334, 336, 356
as long-term effect of sexual abuse, 10, 57–58, 66, 75, 95, 190, 277

Sexual fantasies
and acquired sexual behavior, 375
in children, 109–110, 120, 147
Sexual offense history of abuser, 218, 226–227
Sexual penetration
evidence of, 145, 164, 190, 199, 202; see also Corroborative evidence; Intercourse; Physical manifestations
impact of, 60–62, 76, 81
Sexual promiscuity as sign/effect of sexual abuse, 7–8, 11, 57, 58, 65, 75, 97, 278
see also Prostitution
Sexual taboos
incest taboo, 271, 275
stigmatization and, 65
Sexual victimization, 19
see also Sexual abuse
Sexualization
severe, as effect of sexual abuse, 202–208, 258; see also Traumatic sexualization
of therapeutic relationship, 296
Sgroi, S. M., 96, 157, 183, 249, 251, 263, 271, 310–311, 312, 318, 319
Shame
play therapy and, 254, 261
see also Guilt feelings of victim; Self-blame
Sherman, J., 47
Sibling incest, family systems approach to, 344–346
Sibling involvement in therapy, 264, 377
Sibling relationships, importance of, to victims, 82–85, 90–91, 264
Sibling subsystem assessment, 331–332
see also Family systems approach
Siblings at risk to sexual abuse, 98
Significant others subsystem assessment, 332
Signs and symptoms of sexual abuse, xiv, xvi, 6–9, 190, 165–166, 200–201, 276, 278–281
see also Corroborative evidence; Physical manifestations *and* specific signs and symptoms
Silbert, M. H., 8
Silver, R. L., 286
Sister as sexual abuser, 27, 30

16PF personality test, 321, 322
Sixth Amendment, 127, 139, 148; *see also* Confrontation
Sleep-disturbance intervention, 361
Sleeping disorders as sign of sexual abuse, 6, 7, 8, 101, 165
see also Nightmares
Sloane, P., 96
Smith, T. S., 376
Smolensky, S., 115
Social history
    of abuser, assessing, 218, 225–226
    of victim, assessing, 189–190
Social learning approaches in retrospective incest therapy, 298
Social policy on child sexual abuse, 74–75
Social service report on sexual offender, 219–221
Social workers, *see* Child protective agencies
Social worker Symptom Checklist (NIMH), 75, 76, 77 (tab.), 80–88
Societal implications of child sexual abuse, 14–16
Society's League Against Molestation (SLAM), Colorado, xii
Sociopathic pedophiles, 222
Soderman, H., 123
Solomon, I. L., 201
Somatic complaints as effect of child sexual abuse, 67, 68, 75, 79, 203, 204, 255, 257
Sommers, R. M., 285
Sone Sexual History Questionnaire, 218, 231
Specialness, sense of, in victim, 255–256, 291
see also Betrayal
Spencer, J., 275
Spirituality, play therapy and, 256, 262–263
Spousal immunity rule, 138
Spousal subsystem assessment, 331, 336–337
see also Family systems approach
Spouse, nonperpetrator, *see* Mother, nonoffending
Spouse abuse, xiii, 3, 10, 184, 189, 193–194, 225, 312–313, 316–317, 318, 333, 337, 346

see also Battered woman syndrome
Stanford-Binet test, 187
State v. Sheppard, 147
State v. Slider, 145
Steinmann, A., 14
Stepfathers as abusers, 27, 29–31, 62, 193
see also Incest; Male sexual abusers
Stern, M., 316, 336
Stigmatization dynamic in sexual abuse, xiv, 57, 62, 64, 65, 66, 193–194, 261, 272, 275–276, 280, 284, 290–291
Stimulant use by victims of sexual abuse, 100
see also Drug abuse
Stone Center, Wellesley College, 252
Strangers as abusers, 28–29, 30, 32, 34, 64, 76
see also Extrafamilial child sexual abuse
Straus, M. A., 390
Stress-response syndrome, 281
Studies in Hysteria (Freud), 38–41
Substance abuse
    as effect of child sexual abuse, 10, 57, 58, 59, 65, 72, 75, 77, 85, 97, 277, 303
    and incest, among adolescent girls, xiv–xv, 93–105
    among nonoffending mothers, 98, 312, 313, 356
    by sexual offenders, 95, 98, 170, 223–224, 333, 337, 356, 372; *see also* Alcohol abuse
Suggestibility of children, 110, 114, 115, 116–117, 118, 119–120, 127, 183–184, 185
Suicidal ideation
    among adolescent substance abuse/incest victims, xiv, 99–101
    as long-term consequence of sexual abuse, 10, 11, 58, 65, 66, 75, 76, 77, 95, 96, 97, 99, 277, 282, 291, 412
    among nonoffending mothers, 313
Summit, R., 199, 272, 279–280, 281, 286, 295, 296, 314–315
Support network
    for nonperpetrator mothers, 319–320, 337, 341, 343, 358
    in retrospective incest therapy, 301

Supportive relationships for victim, importance of, 82–85, 90–91, 166, 167, 169, 264, 294, 301, 337, 341, 358
Swanson, C. R., 123
Symonds, M., 272
Symptom Checklist (social worker) (NIMH), 75, 76, 77 (tab.), 80–88

"Taking care of me" program, 390–398
Tedesco, F. J., 119
Temporomandibular jaw (TMJ) in victims, 279
Tevlin v. People, 142
Thematic Apperception Test, 201, 218, 230
Theme Creation Test for Youths (TCTY), xvi, 184, 201–213
  administration of, 203–204
  advantages of, 201–202
  demographics in use of, 203 (tab.)
  description of, 201–202
  diagnosis with, 201–207
  results, 205–207
  scoring system, 202
  sexual abuse pattern defined by, 207
  significance of response patterns, 204 (tab.)
  therapy and, 208–212
Therapeutic alliance
  in family systems approach, 339
  in retrospective incest therapy, 287, 290
  see also Play therapy for victims; Rapport establishment in interviewing victims
Therapist gender, 303–304
Therapist orientation in behavioral approach, 355–356
Therapist qualities in play therapy, 266–267
Therapy, *see* Treatment
Thompson, M. M., 201
Time sense in children, 117–118, 123, 180–182
Tormes, Y., 317
Touching victim of sexual abuse, guidelines for, 178–179, 255
Tranquilizer use by victims of sexual abuse, 100
  see also Drug abuse

Transactional analysis theory in retrospective incest therapy, 298, 424–425
Transference reactions in therapy, 290, 295, 296–297
Trauma
  memory and, 114–115, 119, 122, 185
  and severity of abuse, 200–201
  to victim in court trial, 127–128, 138–139
  to victim from interviews, 125
Traumagenic dynamics, xiii–xiv, 193, 199, 252
  and assessment instrument development, 68
  in clinical assessment of victims, 68–69
  in impact of child sexual abuse, 62–69, 66–67 (tab.), 193–194
  impact of different types of abuse, 60–62
  research needs, 69
Traumatic neurosis, 281
Traumatic sexualization, xiii–xiv, 62–63, 65, 66, 193–194
Treatment of perpetrator, xviii–xix, 153, 154–155
  decline in public support for, 74–75
  deferred prosecution vs., 163
  family systems approach, 326–348; *see also* Family systems approach
  group, 373–374
  individual therapy, 374–376
  Northwest Treatment Associates program, xiv, 373–381
  planning and implementation, 169–172
  previous treatment history, 222
  reintegration into family, 378–381
Treatment of victims, 170–171
  decline in public support for, 74–75
  family systems approach, 326–348; *see also* Family systems approach
  individual therapy, 171–172
  play therapy, 249–268; *see also* Play therapy for victims
  Theme Creation Test for Youths and, 208–212
  see also Retrospective incest therapy

Trials, children and jury, 127
  see also under Court
Truancy as sign of sexual abuse, 6, 7,
    7–8
  see also School problems
Trust, lack of
  family systems therapy and, 337–338
  play therapy and, 253
  retrospective incest therapy and, 172,
    290
  as sign of sexual abuse, 57, 63–64,
    65, 66, 67, 165, 291, 335, 337–
    338; see also Betrayal
Tsai, M., 9–10, 13, 55, 75, 81, 95
Tufts New England Medical Center, 61,
    62, 68, 86
Types of sexual abuse, impact of differ-
    ent, 60–62

Unavailability of child witness, 144–146
Uncles as abusers, 27, 30, 410–412
  see also Incest; Male sexual abusers
Uniform Children's Code, 264–265
United States v. Allen, 145
United States v. Azure, 143
United States v. Carlson, 145
United States v. Faison, 145
Urinary tract infections as sign of sex-
    ual abuse, 6, 7
U.S. v. Nick, 121

Van Buskirk, S., 4
Vandeventer, A. D., 375
Venereal disease as sign of sexual
    abuse, 6, 7, 200, 279
Veracity of abuse reports, 3–6
  see also Credibility of victim and
    entries under False
Verbatim records of sexual abuse re-
    ports, 124
  see also Videotaping
Victim-impact statement requirements,
  . 221
Victim support, importance of, 82–85,
    90–91, 166, 167, 169, 264, 294,
    301, 341, 358
Victim/survivor, use of term, 272
Victims of Child Abuse Laws (VOCAL),
    192–193
Victims of child sexual abuse
  as sexual abusers, 59, 226, 279
  see also Children
Videotaping

of court proceedings, 128–129
  in play therapy, 264
  of sexual abuse reports, 123, 124–
    125, 176, 184, 185, 194, 195
  testimony, 148, 172
Violent families, see Family history
Visitation rights, 109
  between abuser and incest victim,
    167, 258, 264–266, 379–381; see
    also Reintegration
Vomiting as sign of sexual abuse, 6, 7,
    277
Voyeurism, privileged, in therapy, 297
Vulnerability
  play therapy and, 255
  to revictimization, 8–9, 10; see also
    Revictimization

Walker & Associates, 252
  see also Play therapy; Chapter 10
Walker, L. E. A., 184, 192, 193, 194, 252,
    316, 318
Ward, E., 93
W.C.L. v. People, 142, 146
Weight loss/gain as sign of sexual
    abuse, 6
Weinberg, S. K., 8, 20
Weiss, 75
Weiss, J., 199
Wells, G. L., 117
Werner, J. S., 119
Westerlund, E., 284
When the Victim Is a Child (National
    Institute of Justice), 139
Whitcomb, D., 125, 126, 128, 140, 148,
    176, 195, 217
White, R., 388
White, S., 113, 184
Wigmore, J. H., 154
Wise, M. L., 272, 286
Withdrawn behavior as effect of child
    sexual abuse, 78, 79, 208
Witnesses, children as, see Children as
    witnesses
Women, devaluation of, and sexual
    abuse, 13–16
  see also Male domination; Patriarchal
    system
Women as sexual abusers, see Female
    sexual abusers
Wooley, M. J., 286, 289

Yarmey, A. D., 116
Yerkes-Dodson law, 114